New Vernacular Architecture

New Vernacular Architecture

Vicky Richardson

Watson-Guptill Publications / New York

Acknowledgements

My thanks to everyone at Laurence King Publishing, especially Simon
Cowell, Jennifer Hudson, Philip Cooper, Susan Lawson, Helen McFarland,
Laura Willis and Kerstin Peter. I am also grateful to Margaret and Tony
Richardson, Sally Goble, Dave Cowlard, James Heartfield, Volker Welter,
Penny Lewis, Claire Fox and the Institute of Ideas for their inspiration.

This book is dedicated to Adrian and Agnes.

Designed by hdr design (Hans Dieter Reichert and Peter Black)

First published in the United States in 2001 by
Watson-Guptill Publications, a division of BPI Communications, Inc.
770 Broadway, New York, NY 10003
www.watsonguptill.com

Library of Congress Card Number: 20-010867

ISBN 0-8230-3199-3

First published in the United Kingdom in 2001 by
Laurence King Publishing
an imprint of Calmann & King Ltd
71 Great Russell Street
London WC1B 3BP
www.laurence-king.com

Printed in Hong Kong

1 2 3 4 5 6 / 06 05 04 03 02 01

Contents

Vernacular architecture is surely a contradiction in terms, said many of the architects who were invited to take part in this book. Strictly speaking, they are right. The vernacular is the unconscious work of craftsmen based on knowledge accumulated over generations – the very opposite of architecture, which involves a premeditated design process with a conscious appeal to the intellect. Yet, the term is a convenient shorthand to describe an approach that adopts the spirit of the vernacular, if not its actual forms. It is not intended to indicate a new style – in fact, many of the architects featured here reject the concept of style. It instead describes their intention to reflect by 'analogous inspiration' the characteristics of local buildings, their scale in particular, whether they have chosen to concentrate on the use of materials, the landscape, the local culture or even no more than the idea of continuity with the past.

In his introduction to *An Outline of European Architecture,* Nikolaus Pevsner presented the distinction between building and architecture as simple.[1] It was the difference between a bicycle shed and Lincoln Cathedral, he said. 'Nearly everything that encloses space on a scale sufficient for a human being to move in is a building; the term architecture applies only to buildings designed with a view to aesthetic appeal.' But his definition does not reflect the occasional ambivalence felt by architects about their role in providing 'aesthetic appeal' or as conscious planners of the environment. Ever since the English architect A W N Pugin rejected imported historical styles in favour of a more crafted Gothic in the 1840s, architects have tried to blur the distinction between architecture and craft.

During the 20th century the interest in building as a craft never went away entirely, despite the tremendous impact of manufacturing and construction technology. But in recent years there has been a revival of the vernacular that echoes the English Arts and Crafts movement, which was at its height just over a century ago. In 1997 the first international survey of vernacular buildings appeared in print in three large volumes. Edited by Paul Oliver, *The Encyclopedia of Vernacular Architecture of the World* involved the work of some 250 researchers drawn from 80 countries.[2] Oliver was motivated to produce this epic work by a concern for the survival of native indigenous buildings in the face of the 'relentless drive of modernisation'. More importantly, however, as he argues in the introduction, there is still much to be learned from such structures. Vernacular architecture, for Oliver, can be understood as 'the dwellings and all other buildings of the people. Related to their environmental contexts and available resources, they are customarily owner – or community – built, utilizing traditional technologies. All forms of vernacular architecture are built to meet specific needs, accommodating the values, economies and ways of living of the cultures that produce them.'

In some ways, Oliver's concern echoes the ideas of the Arts and Crafts architects who in the 1860s began to document the local buildings of the English counties of Kent, Surrey and Sussex, in sketch books, and later in photographs, fearful that industrialization would sweep them away. Of course, Oliver's study is of a quite different scale and order of complexity and is international in its scope. It has something in common with the work of Western pressure groups seeking to protect indigenous cultures of the developing world. Oliver wants to preserve the vernacular because he believes that it is still the best solution to the shortage of housing. 'Traditional wisdom and lore in building, using renewable resources and indigenous skills, may still offer wisely managed, economically effective and culturally appropriate solutions to the world's increasing housing needs.' Unlike the Arts and Crafts architects – and the architects featured in this book – who borrow certain ideas from the vernacular and reinterpret them, Oliver argues in favour of the wholesale reproduction of traditional local buildings.

A precursor to the work of Paul Oliver was a ground-breaking exhibition, 'Architecture without Architects' at the Metropolitan Museum of Art in New York in 1964. For the first time, the shelters built by people for themselves, particularly in the Third World, were presented as beautiful and functional works of 'architecture'. In the book that followed the exhibition, the curator, anthropologist Bernhard Rudofsky, wrote, 'In a way he [prehistoric man] had more practical wisdom than modern man, for what we call his "primitive" dwellings were dwellings governed by ecological factors.'[3] Rudofsky saw the vernacular as architecture's equivalent to alternative medicine – in harmony with nature, in contrast with the artificiality of Modernism, which, he thought, created more problems than it solved. His work coincided with the end of the confident outlook of the post-war boom and the start of a profound sense of unease about human impact on the natural world.

During the 1970s an anti-utopian, conservationist outlook began to take hold against the backdrop of a world recession and the beginnings of the green movement. In Britain there was a shift from new build to rehabilitating old buildings, and the fashion started for converting barns into country cottages. In 1975 the conservation movement was initiated with the creation of Save Britain's Heritage, set up to protect English country houses. Architectural historians began to take a greater interest in the evolution of Modernism, discovering its roots in the 19th century. It was not until 1979 that Hermann Muthesius's influential book *Das englische Haus*, first published in Berlin in 1905, which had transported Arts and Crafts ideas to northern Europe, came out in English for the first time.

There are strong parallels between today's new vernacular architects and the Arts and Crafts architects of the late 19th century. A predecessor of this movement of artists, designers and architects was the Gothic revivalist Augustus Welby Northmore Pugin (1812–52). Although Pugin's religious beliefs dominated his work, what lay behind it was a belief in the vernacular of Gothic. He saw Gothic as the only true English style, as opposed to the imported foreign styles that architects picked up on their travels around Europe on the Grand Tour. Like many of the architects in this book, he went against current style – in his case, the pervading classicism and 'paper' Gothic of his day – by trying to use local materials and traditions. St Augustine's church at Ramsgate in Kent, for example, was built between 1845 and 1852 from local knapped black flints with bands of brown Whitby stone that had traditionally been brought to Kent by sea.

Pugin also put forward a functional approach to architecture that was to be a great influence on the Arts and Crafts architects. In his book *The True Principles of Pointed or Christian Architecture*, Pugin describes the two great rules for design as '1st, that there should be no features about a building which are not necessary for convenience, construction or propriety; 2nd, that all ornament should consist of the essential construction of the building'.[4] His ideas were part and parcel of a romantic reaction to the brutalizing effects of industrialization, and he idealized medieval community life. His opposition to industrialization included a call for the revival of traditional building skills incorporating ironwork, stained glass and ceramics. Pugin's aim was to achieve the effect of 14th-century churches which, he believed, were the product of craftsmen working together and creating their own details rather than following the designs of an architect. But this gave rise to a paradox which, to a great extent, is the

Shelters built by people for themselves, such as this straw-and-timber house in Africa, were acknowledged as beautiful for the first time in the 1964 'Architecture without Architects' exhibition in New York.

paradox of 'vernacular architecture' referred to above: in order to achieve the effect of crafted buildings, he had to design everything down to the most minute detail.

On the continent of Europe, a similar anti-international movement was taking shape under the influence of the French architect and theorist Eugène-Emmanuel Viollet-le-Duc (1814–79), who advocated a return to regional building traditions. Even though Viollet-le-Duc's views represented a conservative reaction against the Enlightenment, he offered a way forward for the avant-garde of the late 19th century and had a great effect on architects such as the Catalan Antonio Gaudi (1852–1926), the Belgian Victor Horta (1861–1947) and the Dutch Hendrik Petrus Berlage (1856–1934), all of whom became interested in developing a form of national architecture.

In England the architectural critic John Ruskin (1819–1900) put a moral emphasis on the adoption of Gothic and the vernacular. He believed that classical architecture was the architecture of slavery because its clean lines and defined rules could be produced only by turning men into machines. Conversely, the imperfection or 'savageness' of craft-based work was truly human and humane. He related this to Gothic naturalism, whose works were not only formed by the human hand but expressed the imperfection of the natural subject. Another aspect of the Gothic that appealed to Ruskin – and, in a different form, was to influence later generations of architects – was that of 'changefulness'. By this he meant architecture's capacity to be adapted to suit its purpose. Gothic builders, thought Ruskin, never allowed ideas of formal symmetry and consistency to interfere with what they did.[5] 'If they wanted a window, they opened one; a room, they added one; a buttress, they built one; utterly regardless of any established conventionalities of external appearance, knowing...that such daring interruptions of the formal plan would rather give additional interest to its symmetry than injure it.'

In 1877 the designer William Morris (1834–96) founded the Society for the Preservation of Ancient Buildings (SPAB), which came to popularize the doctrine of honest repair rather than wholesale restoration to a state of perfection. SPAB fought for utilitarian buildings in the countryside as well as for churches and cathedrals. One of its celebrated causes was the preservation of Great Coxwell Barn in Gloucestershire, which Morris thought was 'as beautiful as a cathedral'. Later, SPAB became a kind of school of traditional building construction. Architects such as William Eden Nesfield (1835–88) and Richard Norman Shaw (1831–1912) had already recognized the unpretentious beauty of vernacular buildings in the 1860s when they went on trips to sketch cottages and shops in Kent and Sussex. Their designs for country houses, although not fully vernacular, were moving away from using foreign styles towards 'Old English', a mixture of half-timbered or tile-hung upper storeys and brick or stone ground floors.

The Arts and Crafts architects were a diverse group who never wrote a manifesto or constituted a 'school' in the way that later modern movements tried to define themselves. In fact, such an approach was alien to their

view of architecture, which many of them were even reluctant to describe as 'architecture'. They preferred terms such as 'building' and 'doing', and thought of architecture more as a craft than as a profession. The Arts and Crafts architects were similarly opposed to the training of architects in schools, which they thought would lead to students simply learning a series of styles. In the 1890s, when the Royal Institute of British Architects tried to bring in a standardized education system, they opposed it on the grounds that trainee architects should learn from older craftsmen and by getting their hands dirty on site.

The term 'Arts and Crafts' was not of the architects' own invention but came from the Arts and Crafts Exhibition Society, which held its first show in 1888. The society believed that the decline in art and design was the result of an overemphasis on academic training, and of the separation of design and production, and was also effected by impersonal artists or craftsmen trying to produce work for an impersonal public. The Arts and Crafts architects involved did not follow one single line but picked up on different aspects of the vernacular, including the use of local materials, the expression of a building's function in the plans and elevations, working in harmony with the landscape and adopting the form of simple utilitarian structures. Often the common strands of their work were most apparent in the things they said, rather than in what they built.

The adherents of the Arts and Crafts movement never referred to their work as adopting a 'vernacular style' but preferred to talk of 'local ways'. Their models were small,

Opposite
St Augustine's Church in Ramsgate, Kent, UK (1845–52): Pugin used local materials and vernacular methods as a statement against the internationalism of the day. The spire and bell tower pictured here were never actually built.

Above left
The 13th-century tithe barn at Great Coxwell in Gloucestershire, UK, was much admired by William Morris for its utilitarian detailing.

Left
A sketch design for the Hut at Munstead Wood (1892) by Edwin Lutyens, for Gertrude Jekyll, with details inspired by the Surrey vernacular.

COTTAGE FOR C F A VOYSEY ARCHITECT
¼ SCALE

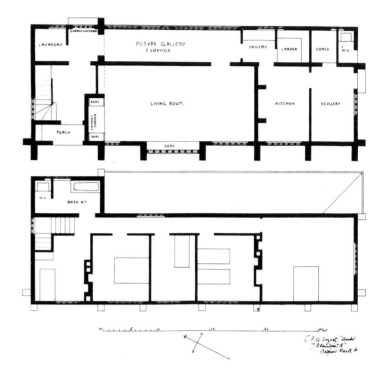

Above
William Richard Lethaby's first house, Avon Tyrrell, in Hampshire, UK (1891) used local materials such as red brick, flint and wall-hung tiles, and incorporated forms taken from small cottages.

Above right
C F A Voysey's design for a cottage for himself (published in *The Architect*, XL, in 1888) shows a simple sequence of rooms arranged in a long plan. The elevation was asymmetrical and the lower storey recessed to emphasize the building's horizontality.

Opposite
The Leys in Hertfordshire, UK (1901) by George Walton was featured in Hermann Muthesius's book *Das englische Haus* and became an important influence for the work of the German architect Peter Behrens.

unpretentious structures – particularly rural cottages and barns – as opposed to the monumental classical buildings of Italy or the great churches of France and Spain. During the 1880s many of these architects became experts on local buildings and began to base their details on what they saw around them, rather than on pattern books from libraries. Their works expressed the fear that local traditions would be swept away by standardization, and there was an emphasis on documenting rural buildings such as inns and cottages and traditional farming equipment. Believing that cottage life was disappearing, the gardener Gertrude Jekyll, for example, built up a collection of objects such as traditional furniture and domestic artefacts. She believed that 'the local tradition in building is the crystallization of local need, material and ingenuity'.[6]

Despite the movement's focus on the simple, functional nature of things, the buildings that resulted tended to be fairly lavish houses for the upper-middle classes. One of the leaders of the movement, William Richard Lethaby (1857–1931), wanted to get back to the practices of the Middle Ages when, he said, 'Art was so intimately bound up with production that their divisibility was never considered: everything was made in the customary way, just as a cook makes pies; there was no separate designer art of making pies.'[7] This reflected a view widely held by Arts and Crafts architects that drawings hampered the work of craftsmen, who should be the real authors of the details. Ironically, like Pugin, Lethaby had to pay ever closer attention to the details in order to create the

impression that his buildings were 'undesigned'. For his first house, Avon Tyrrell in Hampshire, which was completed in 1891, he produced some 229 drawings. Here he used local materials such as red brick and flint, and also wall-hung tiles, and incorporated forms taken from small cottages – for example, gables that were projected from the south elevation. Achieving the local crafted look was expensive, and the grandeur of the finished buildings had little in common – beyond fine craftsmanship – with the buildings that had inspired them. Lethaby himself was somewhat out of touch with reality and had little actual knowledge of the process of the vernacular – he even recalled admiring a Devonshire farm wagon and asking the craftsman if he had made a drawing before building it.

Such middle-class romanticism should not obscure the fact that the Arts and Crafts movement brought about a fundamental change in domestic architecture. For the first time, architects used terms like 'living room' instead of 'drawing room', and the regularization of the building plan, which implied a more utilitarian way of life, formed the basis of 1920s functionalism. The movement also showed that conservative ideas about technology and society do not necessarily translate into conservative architecture. Even if it was quite unintentional, architects such as C F A Voysey (1857–1941), who stressed the glory of nature and the simplicity of life, helped to lay the foundation for Modernism. Looking back at Voysey's work in 1936, Nikolaus Pevsner decided to include him in his book *Pioneers of Modern Design*, although the architect would almost certainly have been horrified to be linked with

Above
The Finnish Pavilion at the Paris Exhibition of 1900 by Gesellius, Lindgren and Saarinen combined elements of the Finnish vernacular in an outpouring of National Romanticism.

Right
With its ornate towers, Östberg's Town Hall in Stockholm, Sweden, mixed aspects of Swedish vernacular with more ornate Byzantine and Gothic details.

Far right
At the Amsterdam Stock Exchange, Netherlands, Berlage used traditional Dutch brick, but internally the structure was highly innovative, with metal trusses supporting a glazed roof.

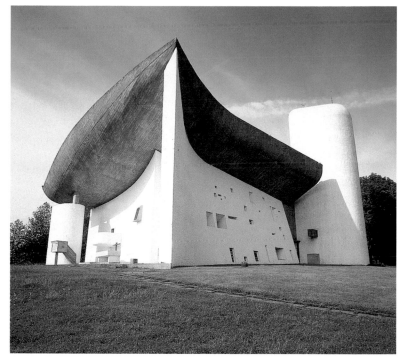

Right
The Chapel at Notre
Dame du Haut at
Ronchamp, France
(1954), with its free
use of concrete,
demonstrated the
disillusionment that
Le Corbusier felt with
the machine age.

Right
The Chapel at Notre
Dame du Haut at
Ronchamp, France
(1954), with its free
use of concrete,
demonstrated the
disillusionment that
Le Corbusier felt with
the machine age.

Below right
Le Corbusier's
Monastery of Sainte-
Marie-de-la-Tourette
at Eveux-sur-Arbresle,
near Lyon, France
(1960), was inspired
by 12th-century
monasteries and used
bare concrete to
express a sense of
primitivism.

Modernist ideas such as standardization and the use of glass.

While many of the Arts and Crafts architects turned to classicism after 1905, their ideas survived in England in the new towns and in the form of suburban building, and were translated into the half-timbered gables, hipped roofs and tile-hung walls of semi-detached houses built between the First and Second World Wars. Close links between England and Germany at the start of the 20th century enabled their ideas to travel further afield. As mentioned above, one of the most comprehensive accounts of the period – *Das englische Haus* – was published in 1905. It was produced by Hermann Muthesius, a German architect who lived in London. In it Muthesius urged Germany to 'face our own conditions squarely and as honestly as the English face theirs today, to adhere to our own artistic tradition as faithfully, to embody our customs and habits in the house as lovingly'.[8]

Germany had its own conservative reaction to the forces of urbanization and industrialization: the *Bund für Heimatschutz*, founded by the architect Paul Schultze-Naumberg (1869–1949) in 1904, opposed the culture of large cities and advocated building with local materials to preserve traditional ways of life. 30 years later it proved a convenient basis for the *völkisch* architecture of the Nazis, which provided mass housing based on the vernacular buildings of rural Germany.

There were further parallels elsewhere in northern Europe with the Arts and Crafts movement, although the movement's influence was often not acknowledged because of the contradiction inherent in the idea of a new vernacular being inspired by theories from abroad. In the 1870s the Finnish Antiquarian Society ran expeditions of student architects and scholars to document Finland's oldest buildings. Finnish nationalism had been stirring since the 1820s, although the country remained under Russian rule from 1809 to 1917. But, led by the composer Jean Sibelius, a dynamic National Romantic Movement emerged and gained strength from English Arts and Crafts as well as from versions of the movement in France, Belgium and Vienna. In architecture, Finnish National Romanticism was best represented by the work of Herman Gesellius (1874–1916), Armas Lindgren (1874–1929) and Eliel Saarinen (1873–1950), who designed the Finnish pavilion for the Paris Exhibition of 1900.

In Sweden, the town hall in Stockholm (1909–1923) by Ragnar Östberg (1866–1945) was a reinterpretation of Swedish myth and tradition merged with a modern understanding of materials. Similarly, the Amsterdam Stock Exchange (1898–1908) by Berlage was a conscious rejection of classicism and an attempt to return to the roots of Dutch brick techniques.

The very internationalism that craft architects reacted against allowed their ideas to travel abroad and influence architects with similar ideas around the world. In the United States the mass production of buildings had taken hold in the 1830s with the invention of a new form of timber construction, the balloon frame. This involved using thin timber plates and studs held together by nails, as opposed to the older timber technique of mortised and tenoned

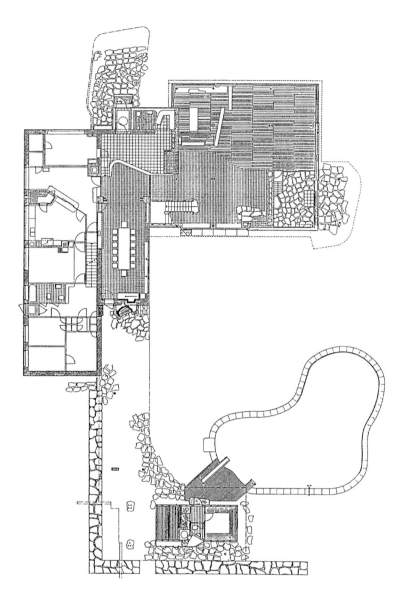

joints. The balloon frame responded to unique set of circumstances in the United States – a plentiful supply of materials coupled with a shortage of skilled labour – and its widespread adoption was made possible by improvements in sawmill machinery and the mass production of nails. By the 1850s, 60 to 80 per cent of houses were built using this technique, and a popular style of architecture emerged that combined colonial influences with the structural logic of the balloon frame.

The Chicago-based Prairie School was strongly influenced by the Arts and Crafts movement. In 1900 the English Arts and Crafts architect Charles Robert Ashbee (1863–1942) delivered a series of lectures in the city and became friends with Frank Lloyd Wright (1867–1959), who was building private houses in a Chicago suburb called Oak Park. Other English influences on the emerging Prairie School were magazines such as *The International Studio* and *House Beautiful*, which illustrated the work of architects such as Voysey. After the turn of the century the Prairie School developed its own dynamic with a series of houses built by Wright, including the Robie House in 1906. Common features were the impression of horizontality or lowness, the height of the rooms implying domestic intimacy; inglenooks and fireplaces at the centre of the plan, as if to recall the traditional hunting lodge; and asymmetrical elevations. But there were key differences between Wright's work and that of the English craft architects. While the latter rejected modern materials and romanticized past eras, Wright wanted to find an architectural language that was appropriate to his time and enthusiastically embraced modern technology.

After Wright's departure from Oak Park in 1909, the Prairie School began to slip into classicism and other historical styles under pressure from clients wanting respectability or who simply could not afford the craft details. This paralleled the decline of the Arts and Crafts movement in England, although Wright continued to adapt many of his ideas for his larger commercial and public projects.

In England, the Arts and Crafts movement was not a viable or appropriate vehicle for large civic buildings, although its pragmatism in structure and detailing was a major influence on the emergence of early 20th-century building. In Scandinavia vernacular ideas continued to be adapted for public buildings as part of the National Romantic style. But, apart from a brief period in the 1920s when the machine-age was celebrated in functionalism, for most of the 20th century a tension continued to exist between two currents within architecture – the regional and the international, whether in the form of classicism early in the century or, later on, in Modernism. The architectural critic William Curtis has pointed out that the explanation of modern architecture as a unique break from the past is a myth. Equally it is a myth that Modernists have been uninterested in respecting a regional context. 'The concept of International style tends to obscure the richness and regional diversity of modernism between the wars,' writes Curtis.[9]

Architectural historian Sigfried Giedion argued in *Space, Time and Architecture* that early Modernism emerged from primitive traditions. The usual means of expression of early 20th-century masters – for example, abstraction and transparency – were close to primeval art, he said. This represented the 'urge to probe the elemental, the irrational and the sources of symbolic expression, and was borne of a desire to counteract the damage of mechanisation'.[10] Disillusionment with the machine age had set in as early as 1930 for Le Corbusier (1887–1969), much of whose work between 1930 and 1960 relied heavily on primitive methods, natural materials and interpretations of the past – for example, Sainte-Marie-de-la-Tourette at Eveux-sur-Arbresle, near Lyon, which was completed in 1960 and inspired by French monasteries of the 12th century. His domestic architecture of this period also drew on aspects of the Mediterranean vernacular, using the juxtaposition of 'raw' materials as a means of expression. In his late works between 1945 and 1965 *beton brut*, or bare concrete, portrayed a sense of crude primitivism. The chapel at Ronchamp, completed in 1954, was roundly condemned by architectural critics such as Pevsner as 'irrational'.

Opposite top
The ground floor plan of the Villa Mairea, Noormarkku, Finland (1937–39), shows the direct influence of the Finnish landscape of forests and lakes on Alvar Aalto's work, particularly in the shape of the pool and the pattern and texture of floor surfaces.

Opposite bottom
The staircase at the Villa Mairea is reminiscent of trees growing in nature, yet the smooth finish of the timber relies on modern fabrication techniques.

Above
Glenn Murcutt's work – for example this house at Glenorie in Sydney, Australia – evokes agricultural structures through the way in which it responds to objective circumstances – the same way vernacular builders do.

Giedion pointed out the danger of architects taking inspiration from the vernacular.[11] 'The approach to the past only becomes creative when the architect is able to enter into its inner meaning and content. It degenerates into a dangerous pastime when one merely hunts for forms: playboy architecture.' For him, the best contemporary architecture was generated by the 'respect it has for the eternal cosmic and terrestrial conditions of a particular region'.

Possibly the most important 20th-century architect to have translated the characteristics of place into modern architecture was Alvar Aalto (1898–1976). Aalto's work, which became well known in the 1930s, showed that the conflict between universal ideas of Modernism and the specific characteristics of place could be resolved through architecture. While his buildings were directly inspired by the curved contours of Finnish lakes and drew on local materials, they also appealed to modern internationalist sensibilities and embraced standardization.

Aalto's work, characterized as 'new regionalism' by Giedion, showed that architecture could adopt the spirit of the vernacular without resorting to mimicking its forms. This approach was advocated by the architectural critic Kenneth Frampton in an influential essay of 1982, although he favoured the term 'critical regionalism'.[12] Frampton was responding to the problem facing Western architects of finding an appropriate form of architecture for countries in the Third World. He was also acknowledging a relativized view of Western civilization that was becoming popular in American universities. The dilemma was expressed by the philosopher Paul Ricoeur: 'In order to take part in modern civilisation, it is necessary at the same time to take part in scientific, technical, and political rationality, something which very often requires the pure and simple abandon of a whole cultural past.'[13]

Critical regionalism was also a means of defending Modernism against post-Modernism, which by the early 1980s was well established. By reconnecting Modernism with the sense of place, Frampton hoped to find a way forward. He used the word 'critical' in order to distance his view from the regressive nostalgia of post-Modernists, who would adopt vernacular and other familiar historical forms as a gesture of populism.

But, as the architect Alan Colquhoun writes with some scepticism, the idea of critical regionalism still contained within it an 'essentialist model'.[14] 'According to this model, all societies contain a core or essence, which must be discovered or preserved. One aspect of this essence lies in local geography, climate and customs, involving the use and transformation of local, "natural" materials.' While rejecting the mimicking of vernacular forms, regionalism believes in a causal relationship between the environment and architectural forms. Australian architect Glenn Murcutt, whose buildings have striking similarities with wool sheds, explains the resemblance as being a result of 'analogous inspiration' – meaning that he has simply responded to the same objective circumstances as the farmers who built them. However, as Colquhoun points out, 'The concept of regionality depends on it being possible to correlate cultural codes with geographical regions. It is based on

a traditional system of communication in which climate, geography, craft traditions and religions are absolutely determining.'[15] In a world that is becoming rapidly more global and urban, regionalism – whether critical or not – looks increasingly inappropriate. In fact, the more removed the vernacular is from the urban experience, the more it becomes an idealized vehicle for expressing a sense of dislocation.

If Frampton was concerned about global modernization undermining traditional culture in the 1980s, by the end of the 1990s globalization had become a fully-fledged demon. The term vernacular began to be associated not with nostalgia but with resistance to the homogenizing force of global capitalism, sometimes known as 'global-blanding'. In architectural terms, the forces of globalization continue to be represented by the ubiquitous air-conditioned office building, typically designed on a computer in New York and e-mailed to site in Eastern Europe or Asia. Such insensitive practice is becoming increasingly unacceptable for Western firms – even McDonald's has a multicultural policy for its global chain of restaurants.

In the mid-1990s the term 'glocal' and the expression 'act global – think local' seemed to sum up the approach of governments and multinational businesses, which were beginning to recognize that it was no longer acceptable to impose a Western agenda without consideration of cultural differences. In 1997 British Airways presented a new 'glocal' image by commissioning artists around the world to come up with indigenous images for the tail fins of its planes. Around the same time, Renzo Piano built the

Tjibaou Cultural Centre on the South Pacific island of New Caledonia, which captured perfectly the desire to use contemporary global architecture to express local culture.

Despite the popular protests against the World Bank and the International Monetary Fund at Seattle, USA, in December 1999 and Prague in the Czech Republic in 2000, the idea that a global-blanding of architecture is taking place is questionable. With the collapse of clear-cut ideologies and firmly held views about design philosophy, architecture is perhaps more diverse than ever before. In addition, commercial architectural firms such as Zeidler Roberts or HOK have put sustainability and localism at the forefront of their concerns (even though the result may be conventional corporate architecture with vernacular details added on, creating a pastiche). As an echo of the fears of small businesses, some architects have expressed concern that the large commercial firms are saturating the market and blanketing cities with high-tech edifices. But the reality is that the commercial architects are increasingly bereft of new ideas and clients are looking more and more to small, creative firms to produce them. The result is a more exotic array of buildings than ever before.

Late 20th-century unease about globalization has certain parallels with the utopianism of William Morris and John Ruskin a hundred years earlier. Yet today's 'new vernacular' is no straight rerun of the Arts and Crafts movement. One clear difference is that in 1892, when Morris published his utopian novel *News from Nowhere*, his was a voice in the wilderness – condemned as backward-looking by the new capitalists, who were striding confidently towards what they saw as a better future. Now, in contrast, the elites who control society share the cautious outlook of many of the new vernacular architects. The attitude of the latter is unequivocally expressed by the Italian architect Vittorio Magnano Lampugnani in his essay 'What Remains of the Project of the Modern?':[16] 'The dream of the new man has been shattered by the nightmare of so-called "ethnic-cleansing", which reached the apex of systematic extermination of peoples in the Nazi concentration camps. Mass society has contributed everywhere to the uniformity and destruction of territory and culture.' When the 20th century is remembered for its failed social experiments, it is not surprising that some architects are ambivalent about their role and prefer to adopt the 'unconsciousness' of the vernacular.

Another explanation for the renewed interest in traditional and local influences is that architects find themselves without an ideological framework in which to operate. Since the end of the Cold War and the collapse of an alternative to capitalism, there has been an ever-growing pluralism of ideas and values. This could have been liberating, except that it coincided with a profound crisis of confidence and lack of faith in progress. The result is that, in the absence of a philosophical framework, architecture is reduced to the status of fashion, where new materials and styles come and go as fast as the latest skirt length.

The buildings discussed here attempt in various ways to introduce a more stable, grounded basis for architecture. The term 'universal' is often used by the new vernacular architects to link their work with a tradition that cuts across architectural fashion. It implies that returning to a more particular, primitive way of building manifests the common aspects of humanity. There are problems with the idea that the vernacular is timeless and universal, however. First, it relies on being able to define a region's authentic building tradition, which is not always straightforward – migration over thousands of years has produced a movement of ideas. Second, the search for the particular aspects of building traditions often leads to parochialism rather than to the universal appeal desired by architects.

This echoes the long-running debate about language which counterposes utterance and speech. Folk-revivalists argue that the vernacular language is closer to the people because it is more immediate and authentic, whereas an abstract, structured form of language is thought to be remote. Another view is that the abstract version is in reality more democratic because it is the result of social interaction, whereas the authentic language is the preserve of an exclusive minority. These issues are likely to become even more pertinent as architecture is once again used to express the essence of identity – for example, in Eastern Europe, where National Romanticism seems to be alive and well.

If the new vernacular architects express ambivalence about the Modernist notion of progress in society and see universal ideas only in the most primitive building forms, it is because their views reflect the reality of contemporary society. Vernacular architecture, or architecture in denial, is perhaps the most appropriate mode of expression for an era that lacks a sense of transformative historic change. The architects in this book tend to put a greater emphasis on architectural history and research, which is unusual in an era where greater value is generally attached to new technology and forms. As the work of English Arts and Crafts architects has proved, learning from the past does not preclude the invention of challenging ideas.

Opposite left
The Marriott hotel in Central Warsaw, Poland, is an example of how the city's skyline has been transformed over the past ten years by bland glass towers.

Opposite right
In 1997 British Airways attempted to present a new multicultural identity by painting the tail fins of its planes with indigenous images.

Below
The Sheraton Timika in Irian Jaya, Indonesia, by HOK (1994) shows that global architects are aware of the need to acknowledge local cultures, even if the result is Western architecture with vernacular details 'pasted on'.

Walter Gropius chose to omit architectural history from his curriculum for the School of Design at Harvard in the late 1930s. He was so optimistic about the future that he felt examples from the past were irrelevant and might even distract his students from focusing on the present. These days, architectural history is taught in architecture schools but it is rarely referred to by architects after they start to practice. It is as if architects have adopted Gropius's stance on history but without his progressive ideas.

Contemporary architects have an uneasy relationship with the past. The historical eclecticism of post-Modernism, which littered building façades with classical and vernacular elements, has made architects wary of using historical references, for fear that they might be labelled revivalist or conservative. There is also an increasing appreciation of contemporary architecture by the general public, as modern buildings become fashionable settings for 'loft' apartments, restaurants and even car advertisements. As one British architectural journal put it, 'The shock of the new is just a mild surprise.'[1]

The architects featured in this first chapter are unusual because they have a sense of history. They are not particularly interested in finding new architectural forms or using the latest technology, yet their buildings are often more challenging than supposedly avant-garde examples of architecture. The ubiquitous emphasis on modernity and newness is not confined to contemporary architecture. London-based architectural writer Helen Castle says, 'The zest for innovation [in the UK] has been encapsulated by the Labour government's determination to modernize

institutions and legislation. Since the 1997 British general election, "modernization" has become an all too common soundbite.'[2] Now that the old ideologies of the left and right stand discredited, the only safe territory for politicians is the present.

At the same time, conventional notions of progress are being questioned. As Adam Caruso, a partner in Caruso St John, which designed the New Art Gallery in Walsall (see page 38), points out, 'Design plays an ever more important role. As substantial progress becomes increasingly difficult to achieve, formal novelty becomes a new focus.'[3] Caruso's argument is that architecture and design are becoming commodified products subject to the tyrannical force of the market as it continually develops new areas. From another perspective, modern architecture and design provide a technological gloss that masks the lack of dynamism and real progress in society.

Today's version of Modernism is hollow. It fails to offer anything new because, unlike the early Modern Movement, it is not based on social and economic developments. Robbed of its social agenda, Modernism has become what architect Stephen Bates of Sergison Bates (see page 20) describes as a 'catalogue of forms'.[4]

The buildings in this chapter show that we have moved beyond the familiar battle between Modernism and post-Modernism. Caruso St John describes itself as 'post-Modern' while rejecting conservatism: 'We don't see our buildings as authentic inheritors of architectural tradition,' says Peter St John.[5] The practice's New Art Gallery presents an entirely new interpretation of its context and could only have been built in today's post-industrial age.

Sergison Bates's prototype house in Stevenage started with a traditional form, the semi-detached house, because it was 'a good housing type for absorbing change', not because of a desire to hark back to a better past. The house is simultaneously familiar and new, and, almost by virtue of its familiarity, the new and different aspects of the house – for example, its splaying plan and inwardly tilted façade – are more striking.

Both Caruso St John and Sergison Bates question the Modernist idea of 'honesty of materials', which, they argue, has become an orthodoxy in contemporary architecture. In this they have been influenced by the early work and writing of the American architect Robert Venturi, in particular his book *Complexity and Contradiction*, which was one of the first written works questioning the tenets of Modernism.[6]

Architecture does not have to mimic the vernacular to be inspired by it. The Walsall Art Gallery is influenced by the approach of the vernacular without taking its literal forms. Unlike Sergison Bates, which uses a recognizable form as a means of communication ('a house-like house'), Caruso St John is less interested in the gallery as a symbol and the references are more mediated. 'The vernacular,' explains Caruso, 'is not about appearance but about presence. It is a physical artefact which contains within itself the continuously evolving social and technological situation in which it was built.'[7]

The Zachary House by Stephen Atkinson (see page 32) evokes memories of American individualism and of the frontier spirit in its construction techniques, reproducing the function of a regional housing type rather than its visual appearance. The building is an extremely cerebral construction in which, Atkinson says, 'every piece of the puzzle is there for a purpose'.[8] No detail is superfluous – in fact, there are few details to speak of. But, he says, the house is 'not so much minimal as reductive'. This distinguishes the work from the minimal, decontextualized style of architecture that has been described by Dutch theorists as 'super-Modernism'.[9] It is an approach shared by Hawkins Brown in its gallery for the Henry Moore Foundation (see page 44). The practice is more pragmatic than the others mentioned here, describing its method as 'responsive architecture'. Hawkins Brown says that the way it responds to the client, the site, the climate and the brief is 'similar to the vernacular and has more in common with tradition than fashion'.[10]

None of the architects discussed here makes claims to have invented a new language. They are more concerned with what Caruso describes as 'critically engaging with an existing situation'. But, despite the radical claims of high-tech architects and other self-proclaimed innovators, it might be that the architects included in this chapter are the true nonconformists at a time when being avant-garde has become a form of social conformity.

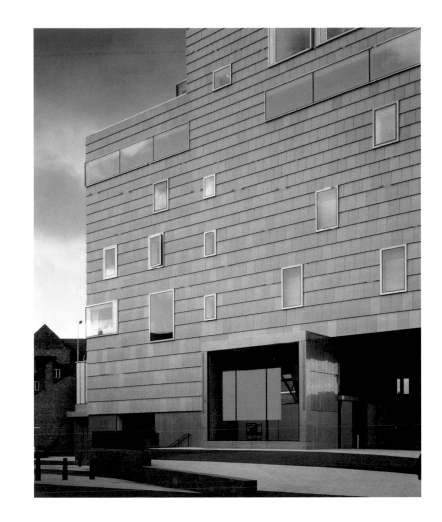

Opposite
Sheep Field Barn, designed by Hawkins Brown. The architects say that the way they respond to the client, the site, the climate and to the brief is 'similar to the vernacular and has more in common with tradition than fashion'.

Left
Stephen Atkinson was inspired by local grain silos and 'shot-gun' houses in his design for a simple weekend home in Louisiana, USA.

Above
The New Art Gallery in Walsall, England, by Caruso St John does not draw directly on vernacular forms, but interprets its former industrial context in new ways.

Year of completion
2000

Location
Stevenage, England

Architect
Sergison Bates
Architects

Think of the English semi-detached house and you think of home. That was the proposition of London-based practice Sergison Bates when it entered the architectural competition 'Innovation from Tradition' with a brief to reinvent Britain's most familiar housing type, the suburban 'semi'. Instead of leaving behind the traditional form, as many other entrants did, Sergison Bates studied it and decided that the semi had, as they put it, 'been given a meaningful value in our cultural memory'.[1]

The house that they completed for the William Sutton Housing Trust in 2000 is located on the north-east edge of Stevenage in Hertfordshire. The site chosen for the house did the architects no favours: all around are examples of bland, standard brick houses, and to the north is a distributor road that will eventually serve 2000 more new homes. But the prototype design had to be capable of adaption to many different locations. A new town dating from 1952, Stevenage itself is no stranger to experimental housing.[2] More recently, new houses have gone up in the area at an incredible pace, with developers and housing associations churning out designs that look as if they were taken from a manual.

For Sergison Bates, retaining the typology of the semi was more than just an exercise in sign-making or making a 'house-like house'.[3] It was an attempt to study the essence of the form and work out the secret of its success in corresponding to the way people live. Research into the social and built context is a common feature of the work of Sergison Bates and the practice sees itself as part of a cycle of history, working with the conditions it finds rather than starting with a clean slate.

Above
The typical suburban 'semi', which became popular in Britain between the First and Second World Wars, was inspired by Arts and Crafts Movement houses.

Right
Section showing the living spaces, which are separated by circulation routes and staircases that are placed along the party wall.

Opposite
The double pitch of Sergison Bates's prototype reflects its dual occupancy. The traditional semi-detached house is generally enclosed by one roof.

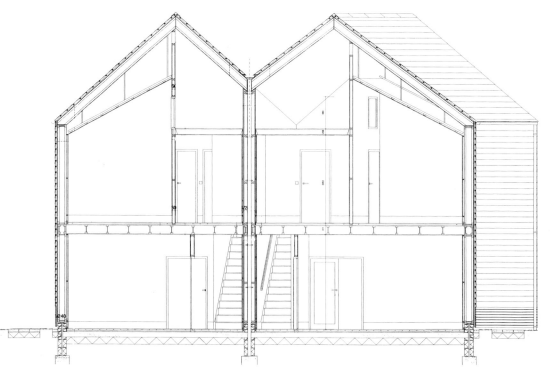

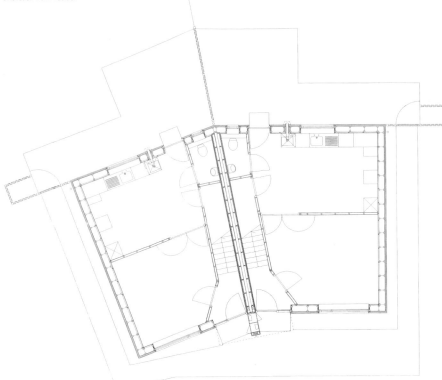

Left and below
Plans (ground floor, left; first floor, below) are angled to create two distinct faces to the house: the front is intimate, with the front doors sharing a single porch, while the rear is more expansive and provides the gardens with greater privacy.

Bottom
Drawings showing how the architect envisaged the house being replicated to form neighbourhoods. Repeating the process would also bring down the cost of each by up to 30 per cent.

Opposite
Brick panels form a protective 'skirt' around the base of the house and extend to the first floor on the rear façade.

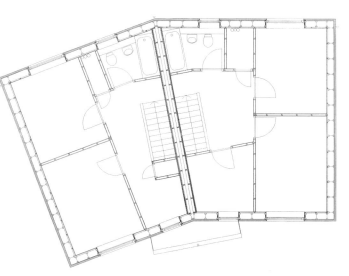

Around 60 per cent of the British population live in the suburbs – a large proportion of them in semi-detached houses built between the First and Second World Wars. The beauty of the semi, and part of the reason for its long-standing popularity, is that it combines privacy with a degree of communality: two families living side by side but with the privacy of separate front and back gardens – close enough have a chat over the garden fence but secluded enough to sustain a belief in the old saying 'An Englishman's home is his castle'.

The double pitch of the Sergison Bates house – a change from the traditional semi with one large roof – emphasizes the individuality of the occupiers, while the tilt of the façades towards each other and the shared front porch brings them together. Splaying outwards towards the rear, the plan creates extra space inside and at the back produces two façades, which face away from each other, heightening the feeling of privacy.

The misalignment of windows at the front hints at something different going on inside. By angling the sides walls but retaining right angles at the outer corners, the architect creates two very individual houses, one with three bedrooms and the other with two. While the houses retain the traditional configuration of a front living room and kitchen opening onto back garden, with bedrooms upstairs, certain elements break with the familiar pattern.

To many people, the house would simply be a normal semi built with strange materials. It sits on a brick base – nothing unusual in that – but eight courses up the brick stops and the walls, constructed from prefabricated timber panels, are clad with earth-coloured tiles, forming a rainscreen. The same

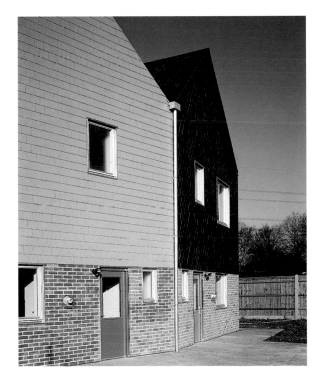

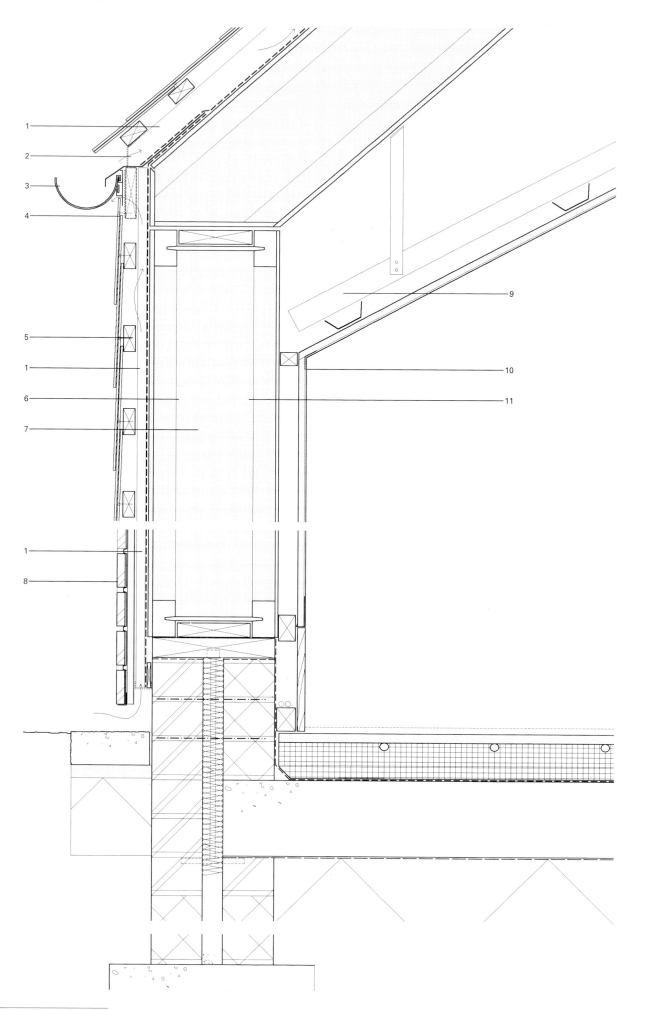

Left
Detailed section through the roof and wall showing the structure of prefabricated timber panels that were manufactured in a factory and assembled on site. High levels of insulation produce a highly energy-efficient envelope.

1 Counter battens
2 Ventilation gap with insect mesh
3 Aluminium gutter
4 Slate tile cladding
5 Battens
6 Composite timber beam
7 Cellulose insulation
8 Brick slip cladding system
9 Metal suspended ceiling system
10 Plasterboard
11 Prefabricated timber panel

Opposite left
Large-scale windows are configured on the façade according to the internal arrangement of rooms, emphasizing the individuality of each dwelling.

Opposite top
In the tradition of English tile-hung houses, both the roof and walls are clad with industrially produced slate tiles, with a minimum of detailing at the junctions.

Opposite bottom
On the first floor the bedrooms open onto a large, irregular-shaped hall, which reflects the angled plan.

tiles seamlessly continue on to the roof and the detailing between is minimal, following the Sergison Bates belief that 'quality should be apportioned with modesty'. With low-cost housing, the architects say, 'There is a lowly equivalence of all components, which is further compromised by the presumption that junctions should be elaborated.'

The structure incorporates the latest techniques in prefabrication, being assembled on site in ten days from timber panels containing a layer of cellulose insulation made from recycled newspaper. This forms a 'breathing' envelope, which dispenses with the routinely used vapour barrier and allows moisture to move through the walls and roof. Inside, the use of underfloor heating creates a sense of luxury not normally associated with social housing.

It is not clear whether this prototype will have the longevity and cost-effectiveness of the traditional semi. The architect estimates that replication of the house should bring cost savings of around 25 to 30 per cent (on an initial cost of £199,000), but the house's structural complexity, which abandons the simplicity of the semi, could work against it.

Year of completion
1995
Location
Sarzeau, France
Architect
Eric Gouesnard

In this house traditional forms and materials are parodied to such an extent that it seems as if Eric Gouesnard is playing an architectural game with the conservative planners. French planning regulations stipulated a sloping slate roof. Gouesnard did more than take them at their word by extending or 'slipping' the roof material down the walls to create two monolithic forms, which, from a distance, look like solid blocks of stone.

The site is a somewhat bleak spot at the mouth of the River Pernef on the south coast of Brittany, France. Surrounded by what Gouesnard describes as a 'strong spiny moor', the house responds not to the landscape but to the contrasting expectations of the client and the planners. The former wanted a radical house and the latter something a bit more conventional. Superficially, the construction is absolutely standard: the two linked buildings that make up the house have conventional proportions; they are constructed from cement bricks lined with plasterboard and topped with double-sloping slate roofs. But by hiding the details and structure beneath a crisp outer layer of slate tiles screwed onto a metal frame at each corner, the proportions and house-like profile become a parody of a traditional dwelling.

Gouesnard also played a game of geometry, positioning the two volumes at right angles to each other and placing them in a perfect circle of sand. Timber bridges connect the house with the scrubby landscape around it, symbolically separating the house from the landscape and emphasizing the intimacy and privacy of the occupants. From the north approach, the elevation of slate tiles is unbroken, except by small circular apertures that provide glimpses of light coming from windows on the south side of the building. Entry is through a

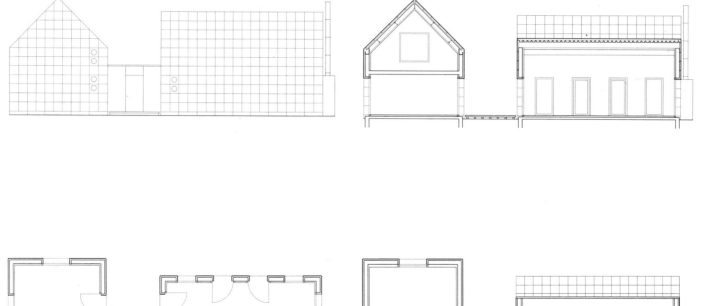

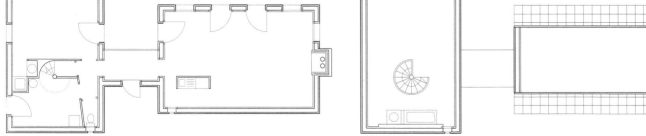

Opposite top
Elevations, left, and
sections, right, show
the geometric
precision of the
house, based on the
50 square centimetre
(6 square inch) slate
tiles covering the
walls and roof.

Opposite bottom
The simple plans
show a double-height
living room in one
building connected to
bedrooms on the
ground and first
floors of the other.

Below
Diagrammatic plan
showing the position
of the house within a
circle of sand con-
nected to the sur-
rounding landscape
by bridges.

Right
An uneven timber
path leads from
the open south-
east façade to the
nearby river.

Next page
The house is entered
through a doorway
in a passageway that
connects the two
slate volumes.

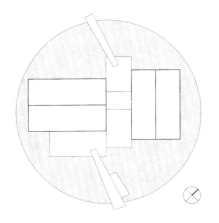

Opposite
In contrast to the austere exterior, the living room is flooded with light and coloured with warm tones.

Right
The only room partitions are at ground level in the smaller building, which is divided into a bedroom and a utility room.

Below right
Detailed section through the wall and roof.

1 Slate roof tile
2 Support for roof tile
3 Aluminium plate
4 Cross beam
5 Substrate
6 Gutter
7 Slate jamb

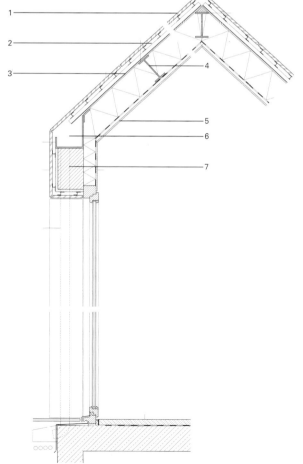

doorway in a corrugated-iron and glass tunnel connecting the two volumes. On the south side the house opens up, with views of the river through glass doorways spaced at regular intervals along the wall.

The whole composition is based on a 50 x 50 centimetre (20 x 20 inch) grid set up by the dimension of the slate tiles. This module determines, and is determined by, the angle of the roof, the size of the openings and the floor-to-ceiling height. Nothing is allowed to interfere with the clarity of the grid – water from the roof runs between the tiles on to an aluminium plate and drains into a gutter hidden behind the slate skin. The absence of details that normally determine the character of a building, such as window frames and drainpipes, heightens the sense of materiality of the slate. The tiles themselves are screwed on slightly unevenly, with the flamed texture running in different directions, and deeply set, frameless openings again create the illusion of a monolithic block of stone.

Inside, the feeling is very different. The taller volume accommodates two floors of bedrooms and a storage room, while the other volume, which is lower by precisely two modules or 1 metre (3 feet 3 inches), has an open-plan living room and kitchen. In contrast to the austere, dark exterior, the interior walls are finished in shades of bright orange and violet.

Zachary House

Year of completion
1999

Location
Zachary, Louisiana,
USA

Architect
Stephen Atkinson

Shaded by pecan trees and cooled by cross breezes, the house that Stephen Atkinson designed for his parents provides perfect shelter from Louisiana's subtropical summers. 25 kilometres (15 miles) north of Baton Rouge and 150 kilometres (95 miles) north of New Orleans, the town of Zachary is located in the northernmost zone of the Mississippi delta, not far from where the landscape changes into rolling hills farther upriver.

Atkinson's recently retired parents wanted a simple house that they could build themselves and that would allow them to spend weekends in closer contact with nature. The 18 hectare (44 acre) site, consisting of open pastures and dense woods, had been owned by the family for many years, and provides a contrasting lifestyle with that of the city, around half an hour's drive away.

Constructing their own house was more than just a financial necessity for the Atkinsons (the budget was $45,000); it also allowed them to connect with the American notions of self-reliance and individualism. In the 19th century, the construction of the railroads and mass production of lumber and nails shifted housebuilding techniques from timber framing to stick framing, conventionally using 2 by 4 members – a technique that could be mastered by anyone.

With its pitched roof and overhanging eaves, it is an archetypal house that attempts to create what Atkinson describes as a link with 'universal notions of domesticity', particularly when closed up like a box during the week.[1] The flip side of this universal appeal is the specific reference the house makes to Southern building types and traditions. It recalls what is known in the South as a 'dog-trot'; in a traditional vernacular house, this is an exte-

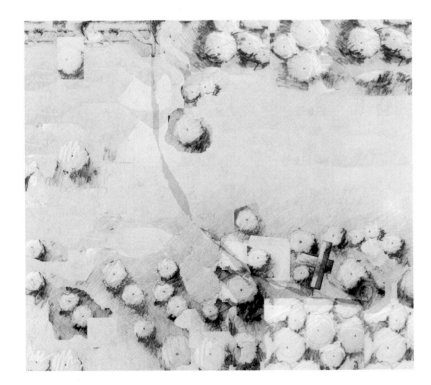

Left
Site plan showing the weekend house that Stephen Atkinson designed for his parents on a plot of land made up of open pastures and densely growing pecan trees.

Opposite top
Indoor and outdoor spaces overlap with a covered timber deck cutting across the house, allowing the occupants to feel close to nature.

Opposite bottom
Section of the house showing the timber structure raised slightly from the ground, echoing traditional 'shot-gun' houses.

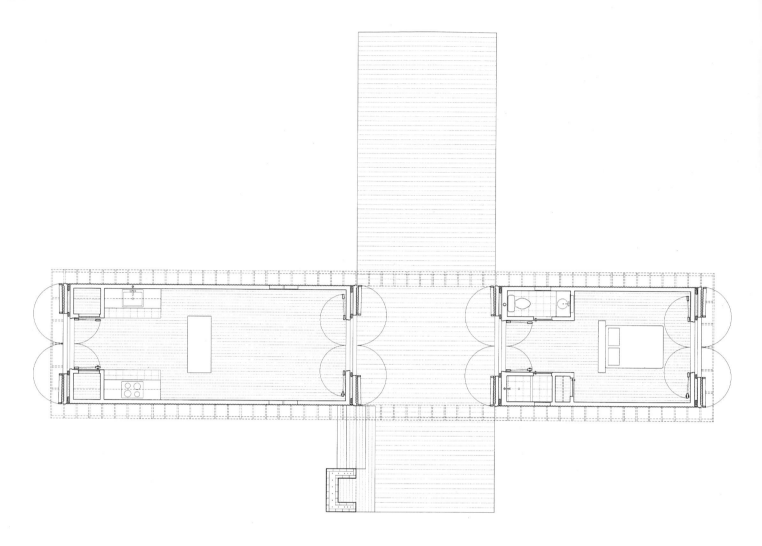

rior passageway that cools the rooms inside by removing warm air by convection. In Atkinson's version of the dog-trot, the passageway cuts the house in two and the pitched roof sails over the gap in what he describes as 'a poetic expression of the dispersion of heat'. The flow of air through the house is symbolically reflected on the ground by a raised timber deck – the modern version of a southern veranda where family life is conducted in semi-public. Since the deck has to be crossed to move between the two main rooms, the living room and the bedroom, life really does take place in the open air.

The overlap between internal and external space is reflected in the use of materials. Timber-framed glass doors are enigmatically covered with shutters made from the exterior material, corrugated steel, while the roof soffit above the breezeway is plasterboard, a continuation of the plasterboard on the ceiling inside.

Another suggestion that life takes place outside is provided by the brick chimney that stands to one side of the house, adjoining the timber deck. This echoes the Southern tradition whereby stone- or brick-built kitchens are separated from timber living spaces (mainly for safety reasons) and act as a formal device to soften the rigid symmetry of the house plan. It also forms a point of entry, with four steps leading up to the deck. On a practical level, it provides an open fire for warmth on cool evenings and continues the blurring of the division between inside and outside.

In its detailing and use of materials the house has the simplicity and rawness of local agricultural buildings. But, rather than replicating the visual

Below
The house is inspired by a nearby 1940s 'shot-gun' house, a southern house type that was long and thin in order to encourage cross-ventilation.

Opposite top
Corrugated steel covers the walls and roof, and forms shutters to close the house up during the week. The hearth is connected to the living spaces by a large timber deck.

Opposite bottom
Grain drying silos a few miles from the site are built from a similar corrugated steel as the house, an iconic material commonly used for barns and sheds.

imagery of these buildings, the house adopts their abstract qualities, what Atkinson calls their 'modesty, timelessness and direct expression of purpose'.

Like the local sheds, the structure is extremely simple – 5 x 10 centimetre (2 x 4 inch) framing clad with the most humble and cheap galvanized corrugated steel on both walls and roof. Detailing is reductive (the house had to be capable of being built by Atkinson's parents themselves), mimicking the 'method of thinking' of the vernacular. Atkinson goes as far as to say that designing the house was an exercise in 'reverse engineering' and in suppressing the hand of the architect. Ironically, this proved to be more difficult and cerebral than the traditional design process because the elements of the house had to be consciously reduced to their bare essentials. The result, he hopes, is a resonant, deep and powerful connection with the past.

New Art Gallery

Year of completion
2000

Location
Walsall, England

Architect
Caruso St John
Architects

Walsall's New Art Gallery is carefully positioned where the modern town meets the old industrial landscape of canals, warehouses and factories. The site was once a depressing reminder of a more dynamic, prosperous industrial era, but now, with the advent of the gallery – the first public building in Walsall for nearly a hundred years – there is a new optimism about life in the town.

Funding came from the proceeds of the UK's National Lottery and was awarded partly because it was hoped that such a project could play a regenerative role. But the gallery also has a genuine function, which is to house a fine collection of works of art, bequeathed to Walsall by Kathleen Garman, wife of the sculptor Jacob Epstein.

After winning the architectural competition in 1995, the young London-based practice Caruso St John assigned its entire office to the design. The gallery was inspired as much by the industrial warehouses and factories to the south and east as by Walsall's Victorian town hall, and is described by Caruso St John as a 'new, open interpretation of context'.[1] Looking much as it did when it opened in 1902, the town hall has a grandeur and solidity that the architects wanted to echo in the art gallery – which, they hope, will stand for at least a hundred years while most things around it change. The long-term view gives Caruso St John a relaxed attitude to the crude, developer-led shops that have been built alongside the gallery.

By achieving a balance between muted colour and awe-inspiring mass, the gallery has become a focus for everything around it, allowing the random collection of shops, 1960s offices and a multi-storey car park to feel like a

Left
Although located in the centre of Walsall, the gallery is clearly separate from the town, both in terms of its dominant position and colour contrast.

Opposite top
Site plan showing the building in a new public space, 'Gallery Square', which was landscaped with tarmac stripes by Lynne Kinnear and Richard Wentworth.

Opposite left
While the gallery was under construction a crude developer-led shopping centre was built on the site next door, although the two buildings have little in common.

Opposite right
The striped landscaping links Gallery Square with the towpath, and the building overlooks the canal basin like a Victorian rail terminus.

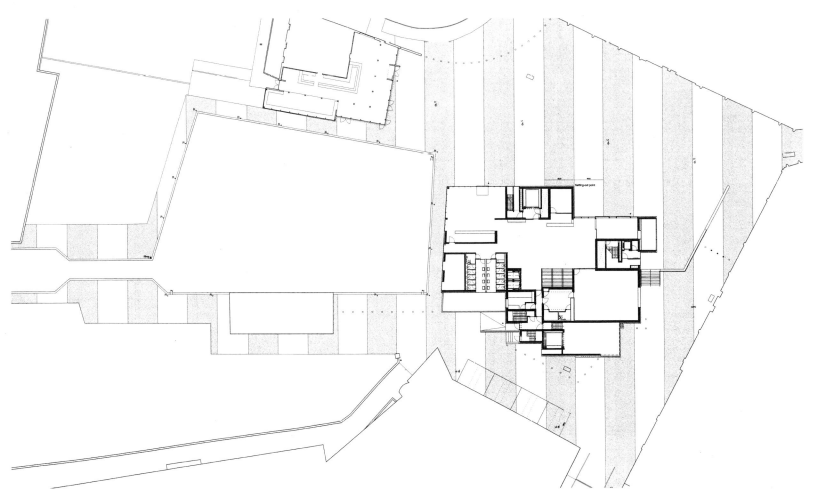

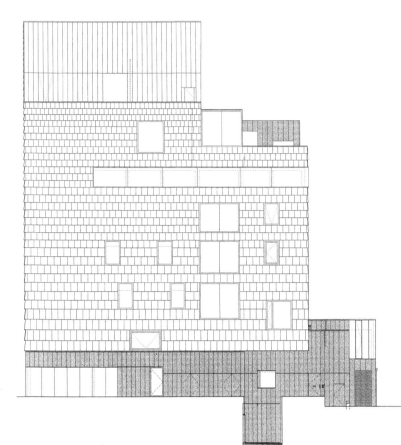

coherent group. As the town's tallest structure, the tower of the gallery refers to the tower of St Matthew's church and forms an axis with it, but it also picks up on features of the lower warehouses and factories to the south. 'They don't aim for elegance,' says Peter St John, 'but have a kind of quiet strength that we were aiming for.'

Clad in terracotta tiles and with windows whose position appears to follow no particular pattern, the building gives little away about what goes on inside. 'We wanted a simple volume but a highly charged surface,' says St John. The vitreous tiles are intended to last for years without discolouring. The natural sand colour is deliberately muted and the smooth, almost reflective surface refers to the quality of the regional brick stock.

While it might look like a simple volume, the building is structurally complex. In order to achieve an asymmetrical, intuitive composition, the tower was located directly above the cantilevered entrance, with both elements addressing a pedestrian route from the town centre. This creates a composition that steps up, with cut-away corners – which presented quite a challenge to the structural engineer. But, unlike many architects of their generation, Caruso St John is not interested in daring structures for their own sake. Rather, it embraces Adolf Loos's argument that an architect should be interested in what a building feels like on the inside and what it looks like on the outside, and not in what goes on in between.

Inside, Caruso St John draws an analogy with a house, with its range of scale and feelings, from the intimacy of the bedroom to the grandeur of living spaces. In particular, the architects took inspiration from a favourite building, Hardwick Hall in Derbyshire, England, by Robert Smythson (1590–97), which, says St John, 'deliberately tries to confound you with its awkward volumetric arrangement'. Similarly, the gallery is spatially complex, and unlike conventional 'white box' exhibition spaces, displays the permanent collection in rooms designed on a domestic scale, whose warm feeling is enhanced by Douglas fir panelling. Windows, also unusual for an art gallery, provide framed views of the townscape, creating a strange juxtaposition between the subtleties of the works of art and the gaudy neon signage of the shops outside.

Entering through two heavy sliding doors, the visitor arrives in the largest open space of the building. The floors are linked by lifts, but there are also rambling, almost secretive staircases for a more relaxed visit. Above the intimately sized galleries for the permanent collection, the floor-to-ceiling height opens up and a more conventional double-height white space houses temporary exhibitions. On the uppermost floor, contained within the tower, is a café with views through large plate-glass windows over the rooftops of Walsall's town centre. While the view is not conventionally spectacular like, say, that from London's Tate Modern, which overlooks the River Thames, it nonetheless reveals fascinating aspects of Walsall.

Above
Elevation with the location of windows determined by the arrangement of spaces inside.

Opposite
Walls are clad with sand-coloured terracotta tiles, which diminish in size towards the upper storeys to create an illusion of greater height.

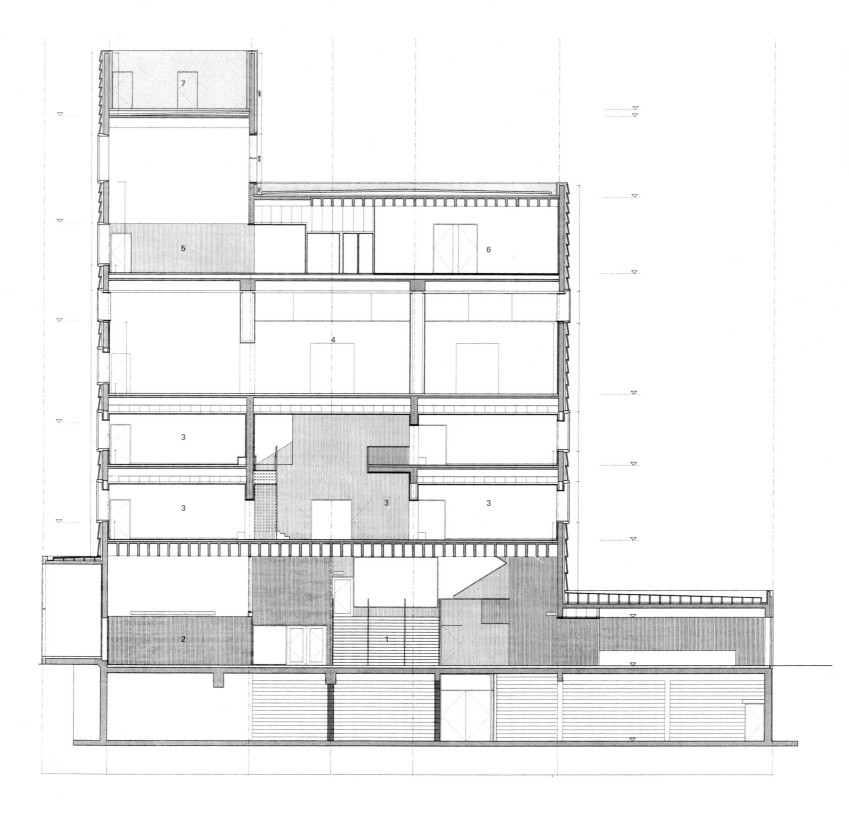

Opposite
Section revealing a double-height space at the heart of the building, onto which the domestic-scaled galleries of the Garman Ryan Collection open. On the third floor the ceiling height opens up for the more neutral temporary exhibition space.

1 Foyer
2 Lobby
3 Garman Ryan Gallery
4 Temporary exhibition space
5 Restaurant
6 Conference room
7 Plant

Right
A wide staircase leads from the entrance foyer to a mezzanine level. Walls are lined with Douglas fir timber, while the bare concrete surfaces record the timber shuttering.

Below
A double height hall provides a central focus for the rooms housing the Garman Ryan Collection, which are arranged around the perimeter of the building.

Below right
Paintings from the permanent collection are hung alongside windows which frame views of Walsall.

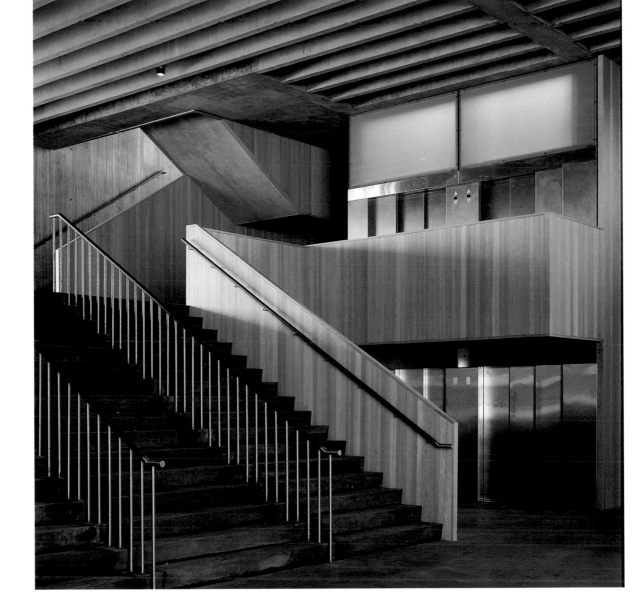

Sheep Field Barn

Year of completion
1999

Location
Perry Green, England

Architect
Hawkins Brown

For 50 years the sculptor Henry Moore lived and worked in the quiet seclusion of Perry Green, a small village in Hertfordshire, England, after his house and studio in London had been destroyed in the Blitz. Moore's estate, which consists of his house and an eclectic collection of sheds, is now open to the public and attracts around 10,000 visitors a year. One of the largest buildings on the site is a barn where for many years he worked and stored fodder for his sheep. Sheep Field Barn started life as an off-the-peg portal-frame shed, clad in asbestos, which was bought and sited in the grounds in 1977. It has now been transformed into a fully-serviced gallery for exhibiting Moore's medium-sized sculptures.

The London-based firm Hawkins Brown became involved in the scheme after a larger project by Dixon Jones had failed to win approval from the planners. Hawkins Brown suggested that a more modest approach would suit the site, location and the memory of Henry Moore, who, despite his cutting-edge work, liked to surround himself with familiar domestic objects and had a particular liking for vernacular barns and sheds.

In contrast to many recent cultural projects, the architecture of the barn was not intended to be an attraction in its own right; it was agreed that it should not dominate the works of art within. Moore liked his work to be seen on a typically English wet or overcast day. Hawkins Brown tried to capture this sense of ordinariness in its design for the refurbishment of the barn.

In fact, to meet the demanding requirements of the Museums and Galleries Commission, the muted colours and simple detailing conceal highly sophisticated servicing and security devices. The gallery also meets high standards of energy efficiency, with thermal mass being provided by 20 centimetre (8 inch) concrete blocks and 15 centimetres (6 inches) of insulation sandwiched between white plaster walls on the inside and timber panelling on the outside. The servicing strategy is passive, in keeping with the building's location in the middle of a field. In warm weather, mechanical vents installed under the eaves let in cool air during the night; and on cold days the vents stay shut and the building is heated by hot pipes set into a concrete floor.

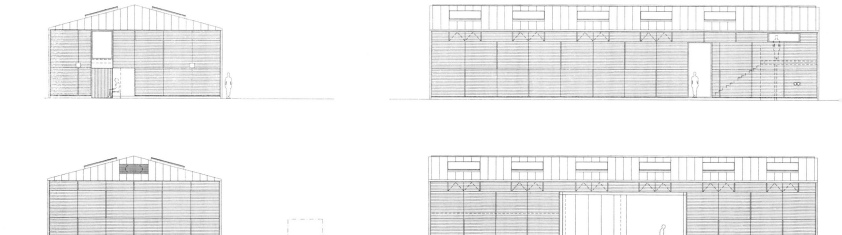

Above
The barn-turned-art-gallery is situated at the edge of a field where Henry Moore's sheep once grazed.

Opposite
Elevation. The walls of the structure are clad in black stained timber as a reminder of local shiplap timber barns.

45

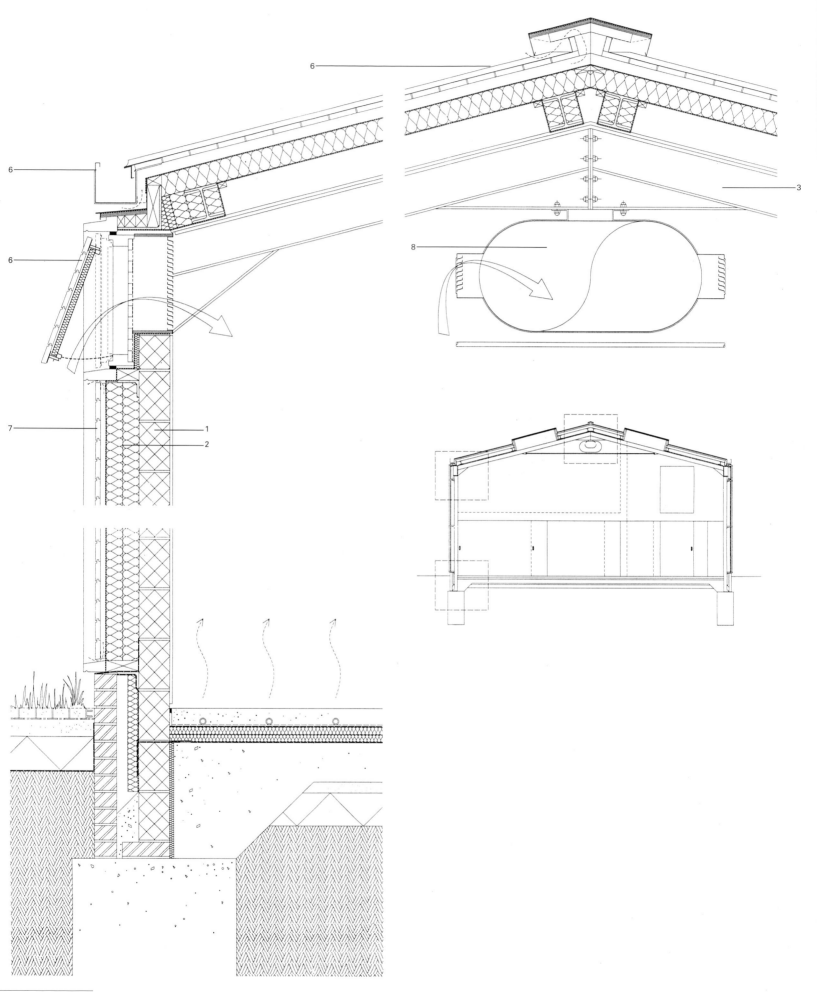

Inside is a neutral white space intended to surprise the visitor, who perhaps might expect to find hay bales and sheep. But, with its smooth white walls, polished concrete floor and exposed air-handling unit, the only reminder of the agricultural shed is the portal frame, revealed at the roof level. In Moore's day, one-third of the building was used for storing sheep fodder and the sculptor used to sit in his studio and feed the animals through the window. This memory is preserved by the internal arrangement of spaces: two-thirds is full-height gallery, while the remaining third is divided into two floors containing smaller galleries for displaying drawings and maquettes.

Having stripped back Moore's barn to its frame, Hawkins Brown reclad it using black-stained weatherboarding, a choice of material inspired by local agricultural buildings, and in particular a black shiplap timber barn nearby. The arrangement of timber panels on each façade was a nod to the timber packing cases used to transport Moore's work.

The shallow-pitched roof is covered in sheets of zinc, and rainwater is drained into square-section downpipes at the 'negative corners' of the building.[1] Hawkins Brown took great interest in the everyday function of the building, reflecting what Roger Hawkins describes as the practice's 'obsessive interest in detailing. This is a pragmatic interest in buildability. Being inspired by Mies is not something we'd mention,' he says. Getting the details right is also the way to overcome 'folksyism' and form a natural connection between old and new.

An appealing characteristic of Sheep Field Barn is that it appears simple where there has been most intervention. This is also true of the landscaping, which creates the impression of a barn located randomly on the edge of a field. The field appears to be linked seamlessly with the visitor centre, although animals are separated from visitors by means of a sheep grid installed close to the entrance of the barn. As in Moore's day, sheep graze right up to the building and leave muddy traces on the large white door as they brush past.

Opposite
Detailed cross-section through the wall and roof showing the mechanical eaves vents, which open to admit cool night air. On cold days, underfloor heating is turned on and the vents stay shut.

1   Dense concrete blockwork
2   Mineral fibre insulation
3   Original portal frame structure
4   Zinc roof with standing seams
5   Zinc gutter mounted on brackets
6   Motorized vent
7   Horizontal stained weatherboarding
8   Extract duct

Right
On the south-east elevation, a tall window provides a view of a sculpture garden and brings light onto the staircase.

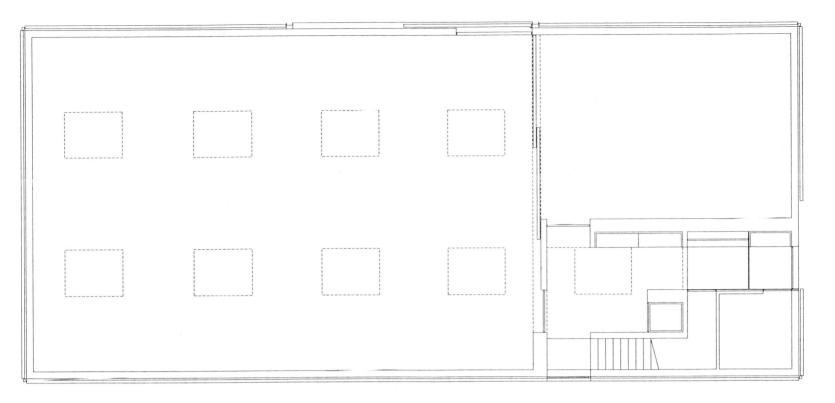

Opposite top
The design of the external weather-boarding was inspired by the wooden packing crates used to transport Moore's work.

Opposite bottom
The main gallery houses Moore's medium-sized sculpture, while two smaller rooms provide intimate spaces for his maquettes and drawings.

Above
Ground floor plan showing a third divided off from the main space as a reminder of the barn's past life when one-third was used to store sheep fodder.

Left
A row of somewhat undistinguished but listed sheds standing alongside the barn were used by Moore to store and display his work.

Flawil House

Year of completion
2000

Location
Flawil, Switzerland

Architect
Markus Wespi and
Jerome de Meuron

Without windows to give it scale, this three-storey house looks almost like a small woodshed at the side of the road – as was the intention of Caviano-based architects Markus Wespi and Jerome de Meuron. 'We wanted it to have a self-evident appearance, so that everybody understands it. It should look as if it has always been there,' says de Meuron.[1] But there is a certain amount of deception going on, for behind the crafted timber exterior is a sophisticated modern interior specially designed for the client, a teacher and his musician wife.

The reduced, simple form of the house conceals a very different history. When the client bought the house, located in an agricultural area just outside the Swiss town of Flawil (with the intention of converting it to suit their needs), it was a typical 1950s, chalet-style, suburban house with neat shuttered windows and an overhanging pantiled roof. At first, the architects thought the main structure was brick-covered with a thick layer of paint. But, beneath the rough surface, it was revealed to be timber, making it probably an early prefabricated wooden construction.

The client wanted to create a larger floor plan, but extending the house was going to cause problems: the site boundary ran close to the north side of the house and beyond the trees was an industrial estate. The south (front) side of the house seemed to be just as problematic, with a road running just a few metres away. Local planning restrictions presented another challenge, preventing the architect from expanding the house by more than a third of the existing footprint.

Wespi and de Meuron's solution was, appropriately enough, inspired by the vernacular agricultural buildings of the area, which use slatted-timber screen walls to allow air to circulate for drying grass. Having stripped the building back to its frame, they built up the walls with layers of larch, leaving a hole at the south end, which became a fully glazed extension. Extending the house by 1.5 metres (5 feet) towards the road, the all-glass façade was veiled with a slatted-timber screen for privacy. This was a continuation of the timber cladding that envelops the whole house, but uses only every third length of wood. The screen symbolically wraps around the new section of the

Left
A glass box added to the south end of the house is shaded by timber slats to evoke the construction of local vernacular barns.

Opposite top
The house sits close to the road but the timber screen shields the interior from prying eyes and sunlight, while a wood-pile wall and white concrete bike shed protect the garden.

Opposite
Sections showing the open hearth with its chimney rising as a distinct element through the bedroom above.

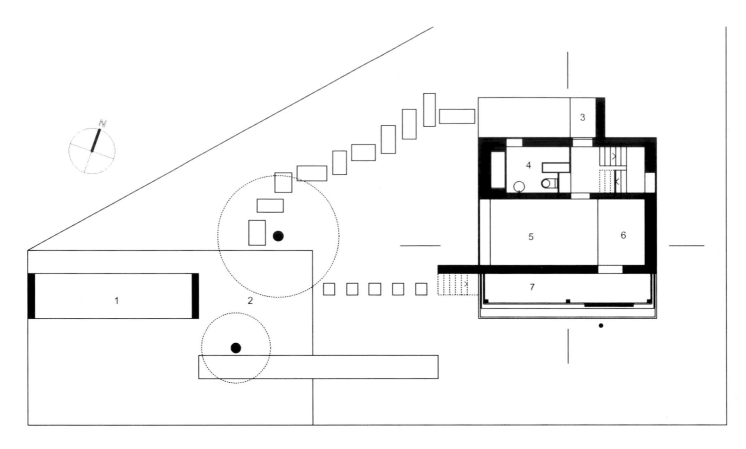

Right
A back door is flanked by
a white concrete wall,
and strip windows frame
selective views from the
kitchen and study.

Above
Basement plan

Opposite top
Ground floor plan

Opposite bottom
Top floor plan

Key
1   Bicycle shelter
2   Garden
3   Entrance
4   Bathroom/Toilet
5   Guest room
6   Storage room
7   Utility room
8   Kitchen
9   Living room
10 Fireplace
11 Study
12 Bedroom
13 Balcony

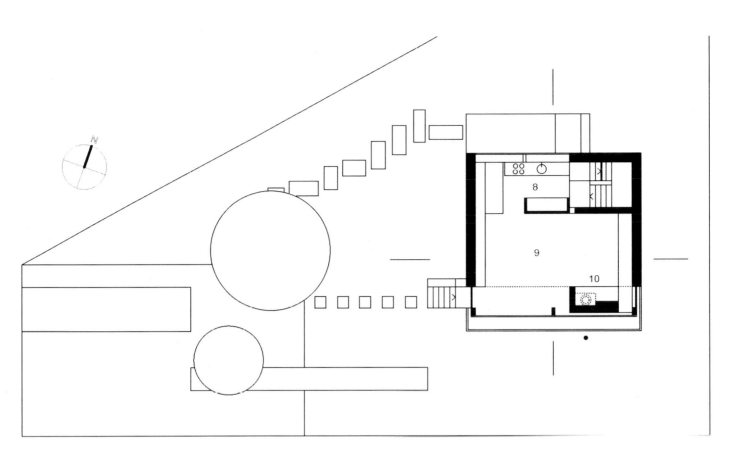

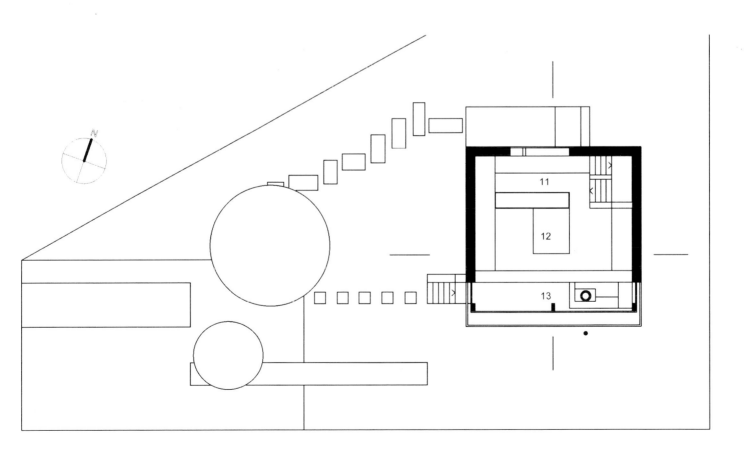

house, preventing passers-by from looking directly into the living room, and providing shade in summer, while allowing the sun's rays to enter in winter.

The remaining walls are windowless apart from two strips of glazing on the north façade, which give framed views from the kitchen and the study above. The overhanging roof of the original house has been trimmed back to emphasize the geometric, barn-like form. Terracotta pantiles have been replaced with zinc sheeting, which has rails formed from steel pipes to prevent snow slides. Gutters are dispensed with and rainwater runs straight off the roof into a gravel drain around the base of the house. A steel chimney and a single slender vent pipe from a gas boiler in the basement complement the zinc roof.

Inside, a lighter-toned softwood lines the walls, floors and ceilings, providing a sound-absorbent box with perfect acoustics for the client's piano practice. In the tradition of Swiss domestic architecture, the kitchen is tucked away at the back of the house, away from the open, light expanse of the living room. An open hearth in the living room has a chimney that passes through the bedroom above, bringing heat with it.

The basement of the original house was left intact, but two new white concrete walls were built to mark the front and rear entrances. Concrete slabs cantilevered from one wall lead up to the front porch – a galvanized-steel frame that protrudes through the timber screen and gives the doorway a degree of shelter. The concrete provides a visual link with the bicycle shelter, a simple planar structure located a few metres from the house. A low wall dividing the garden from the road, made from leftover timber from the house, recalls the precision of Swiss wood stacks.

Above left
In winter, the low sun enters through gaps in the timber screen, while the stronger summer sun is kept out.

Left
Timber linings create a sound-absorbent box and excellent acoustics for the client's piano practice.

Opposite top
The second floor has a bedroom in the roof on one side and a study and staircase on the other.

Opposite bottom
A kitchen with built-in timber furniture is tucked at the back of the house behind the main living space.

Year of completion
1999

Location
Malmö, Sweden

Architect
Thomas Sandell and
Anders Landström

The idea for the Vistet house originated in 1995, when a replica of a traditional 19th-century log house was constructed for the Swedish National Museum in the region of Halsingland. The word *vistet* roughly translates in English as 'homestead'. When visitors started saying that the house was their ideal home, the local council spotted an opportunity to create a new local industry using wood crafts to build prefabricated holiday cottages. Recognizing the need to create a modern version of the house without nostalgia, the project leader approached Thomas Sandell, a young Swedish architect known for designing both contemporary furniture and public buildings, and Anders Landström, a professor of architecture specializing in the art of timber, for their combined expertise.

The concept was based on the belief that people have an intimate relationship with wood. 'We relate to wood in a special way probably inherited over thousands of years,' writes the Vistet project leader, Bertil Harstrom, in the promotional leaflet.

Sandell and Landström started work on the prototype, aiming to create a modern, compact version of the log house. The first sketch design they came up with had a flat roof and was rejected as too modern and unmarketable in several regions of Sweden that have planning regulations specifying traditional pitched roofs.

In 1998 the Vistet house was presented at an exhibition in Stockholm. Incorporating traditional aspects of the Swedish family house, it used the horizontal-timber technique in a new way and added contemporary features such as the doors and windows. In recognition of a gap in the market for a smaller, more compact house, the prototype for the Vistet Fritid house (meaning 'holiday homestead') quickly followed in 1999; it was erected for the first time at H99, a design show in Malmö. This smaller version is now in production, with the intention that it will be sold in Europe for around £60,000 as a series of prefabricated elements that can be quickly erected on the site of one's choice.

The commercial side of Vistet Fritid was developed with the World Wildlife Fund, and the house is the first in Europe to be certified by the

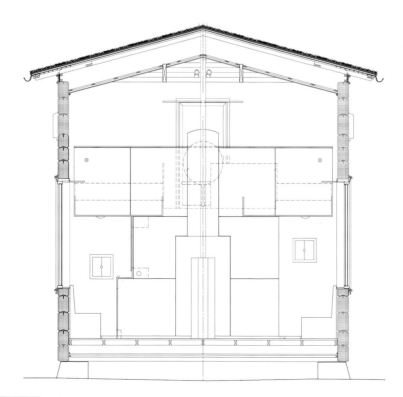

Left
Section through the house, which is a cube of 5.5 metre (18 foot) dimensions, derived from the measurements used in production by the Swedish logging industry.

Opposite
The house was built originally as a prototype for H99, a design show in Malmö, Sweden.

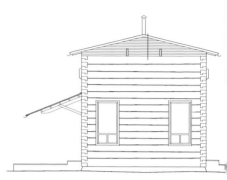

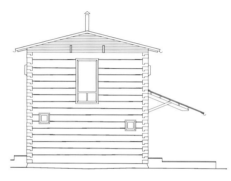

Forest Stewardship Council, which means that the pine forests from which the timber is farmed are protected and monitored to promote responsible forestry.

Vistet Fritid is a compact kit house that is meant to function like a caravan or boat. It can be erected and dismantled easily, so that people can take it with them when they move house, or move it from site to site. Basically a 5.5 metre (18 foot) cube, the house uses the functional measurements of the Swedish logging industry, which produces logs of 5–6 metres (16–21 feet) in length. In traditional fashion, the logs are laid on top of each other and sealed with a V-shaped joint filled with insulation. Wooden nails knit the logs together and can easily be removed and reused should the house need to be dismantled.

For the corners, Landström and Sandell came up with a contemporary detail of interlocking wedge-shaped joints which, according to Sandell, provides a 'more modern straight corner'. This allows the house to be read more clearly as a simple geometric form, in contrast with traditional log houses where the logs protrude at the corners. By exposing the cross-grain of the wood at the end of each log, the detail also allows moisture to drain away without causing distortion of the timber.

Vistet Fritid's dimensions provide just enough space for two simple internal spaces. Inspired by the plan principle of the *gillestuga* (the Swedish domestic kitchen or eating place), traditionally the social heart of the house, the ground floor has one open-plan room, which functions as a living and dining room and kitchen. The bathroom, a small volume at the centre of the plan, provides wall space for the kitchen and wood-burning stove, which becomes

Opposite left
Traditionally Swedish
log houses were
painted red, but here
the architects chose a
more modern shade
of grey.

Opposite right
Elevations show a
shaded timber deck,
which provides an
extra outdoor room
for the summer
months.

Left
Small portholes in
the front door
increase the sense of
scale of the house
and allow views out
while minimizing
heat loss.

the natural focus for the room. Above the bathroom a sleeping balcony provides space for two beds and overlooks the dining and living space below, benefiting from the rising warmth from the log furnace.

Another deviation from tradition was Sandell and Landström's decision to paint the house pale grey as opposed to the more conventional shade of 'Falu red', a term which derives from the copper mines of Falu where the red pigment of Swedish dwellings originates from. Large windows are located in key positions to maximize the internal light. As in typical log houses, the number and size of windows is minimal to prevent heat loss.

Opposite
In the living room, built-in furniture provides storage and makes the most of available space.

Right
A specially designed corner construction of interlocking wedge-shaped joints exposes the cross-grain of the timber, allowing moisture to evaporate.

Far right
The open sleeping deck benefits from heat rising from the living room.

Below
Floor plans show the furnace, kitchen and bathroom grouped around the staircase and a mezzanine sleeping deck above.

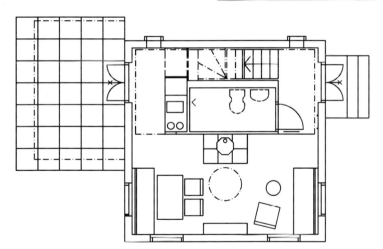

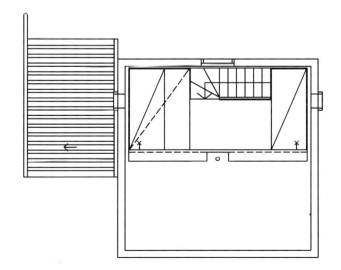

Techniques and Materials

The American architect Robert Venturi saw architectural meaning in the surface of buildings. In his book *Learning from Las Vegas*, he famously coined the term 'decorated shed'.[1] The buildings in this chapter celebrate the opposite of surface – the very substance and materiality of the 'shed'. The architects discussed here are interested in structure, techniques and materials not for their own sake but for the ideas that they convey about place, light and the building process itself.

The vast majority of buildings erected today have not been designed by architects. Although architecture without architects might be seen as the essence of the vernacular, today's 'un-designed' buildings lack craft skills and are more often than not mere assemblages of systems and building products.

Prefabrication – following the experience of 1960s system-built housing – is becoming fashionable again. Many designers are arguing that architecture should be more like the car industry and the trend (particularly in housing) is to eliminate the risk of building on site and the vagaries of skilled labour by constructing buildings in factories. The perception of many is that this will further undermine the role of the architect, who is relegated to membership of a large team, rather than being master of the whole process.

But is this really the case and do new technology and prefabrication necessarily lead to insensitive and site-unspecific architecture? For many of the architects in this chapter, architecture can be as creative and intuitive, whether buildings are crafted on site or in a factory many

hundreds of miles away. American Will Bruder (see Teton County Library, page 64) is an example of an architect who takes ordinary 'off-the-peg' products and creates extraordinary, highly contextual buildings. Bruder combines a prolific career, represented by more than 300 built works, with a truly hands-on approach, often spending days on site, working alongside the builders. He is scathing of architects who excuse the deficiencies of their buildings by blaming lack of traditional skills, small budgets or client ignorance. The skill of the architect is to rise above apparent obstacles and make something from the situation he/she finds him/herself in.

Making do with available technology and materials is part and parcel of sensitivity to the context of a building. This does not necessarily mean accepting a dogma of local materials, of the sort put forward by Charles, Prince of Wales, in his architectural interventions of the late 1980s, and implemented at Poundbury village in the English county of Dorset.[2] The global economy means that there is not necessarily a logic for using only local materials. The house built by Anthony Hoete for his father's retirement on a remote New Zealand island (see page 70) was made from both materials found to hand and products shipped from the other side of the globe. Described as a 'blurry cocktail between the pragmatic and symbolic', the house merges New Zealand's agricultural vernacular of barns and sheds with the local tradition of self-build – a practice that relies on imports of cheap, mass-produced materials.

David Chipperfield adopts the Spartan aesthetic of the vernacular at the River and Rowing Museum (see page 98), taking the form of the riverside boathouse and elongating it to create two elegant halls for displaying rivercraft. Chipperfield uses a traditional material – untreated green oak – but reinvents it as an innovative rainscreen, fixed to the structure by a system of stainless steel bolts.

Patkau Architects' Strawberry Vale School (see page 74) deals with the relationship between the man-made and the natural – neither taking a stance on which is superior nor attempting to mimic nature, but accentuating the difference between the two. It is reminiscent of the art of the wood-butchers (the owner-crafted houses of California), rejecting the conventional building vocabulary of structure with applied finishes.

The use of construction and materials to define the richness of the space is what architecture critic Kenneth Frampton would describe as 'tectonic'. As a continuation of his work on critical regionalism, Frampton argues against what he describes as the 'tendency for architecture to be reduced to scenography'.[3] He puts the case for looking at the Greek origins of the word 'architect', comprising *archi*, meaning a person of authority, and *tekton*, a craftsman or builder. While acknowledging that the meaning of the term has evolved since its first English usage in 1563, Frampton upholds a case for architecture as an astylistic craft. In this scenario the vernacular takes on particular importance because it does not represent anything outside of itself and fits into his definition of building as 'ontological rather than representational' or 'presence rather than something standing for an absence'.

By contrast, Michael Graves's Miramar Hotel by the Red Sea (see page 92) emerges from a strand of American post-Modernism and is designed to give Western tourists a supposedly authentic Egyptian experience. Working with two disciples of the late Egyptian architect Hassan Fathy, Graves used the traditional techniques of brick domes to produce a strange mix of scenography and vernacular building.

A project more akin to the philosophy of Fathy, although neither structurally nor visually similar to his work, is the orphanage at Chhebetar in Nepal (see page 80), where the building was intended to benefit local employment. Few architecture students expect their design projects ever to become reality. However, Norwegian students Sixten Rahlff and Hans Olav Hesseberg decided to take a year out of their architecture studies to travel to a remote Himalayan village to help implement their design. For six months the pair worked from a small house, drawing up the scheme and helping the villagers build it on site. The design evolved as they went along according to the needs of the orphanage and the availability of materials. Key to the success of the project was discovering how their skills could enhance certain aspects of the village's way of life, while respecting important traditions. Like Bruder, they altered the design as the building progressed.

This merging of the conventionally distinct processes of design and construction, common to several projects discussed here, runs counter to the contemporary notion of architecture as premeditated and conscious and – for better or worse – begins to resemble the intuitive, evolutionary approach of the vernacular builders.

Opposite
Two Norwegian architecture students designed an orphanage in Nepal and spent a year on site helping local people to build it.

Above
The Miramar hotel by Michael Graves draws on the Red Sea vernacular of brick domes and offers tourists an 'authentic' Egyptian experience.

Left
Anthony Hoete built a house for his father on a remote New Zealand island from a combination of cheap, locally available materials and some he shipped in from Europe.

Teton County Library

Year of completion
1997

Location
Jackson, Wyoming,
USA

Architect
Will Bruder

Jackson, Wyoming, is little more than an intersection of roads, with no industry or railroad. Three million cars pass through each year, but only 7,000 people live there. Until recently, the public library that served this community was an old log cabin with a worn shag carpet and no parking spaces. Nevertheless, local people were fond of it and were reluctant to give it up for a new building designed by an eccentric architect from Arizona.

Described as an architecture junky, Will Bruder started out as a sculptor and later trained himself as an architect, working for a time as an apprentice to the visionary architect Paolo Soleri. Since 1974 he has worked from a desert studio in New River, Arizona, and has completed more than 300 buildings. But, despite such a prolific career, he manages to maintain a remarkably hands-on approach, designing many of the details on site rather than on the drawing board.

A group of three buildings in Jackson, including the library, were Bruder's first commissions outside the desert. 'After spending the majority of my working life in the same place, I've really had to dig deep to understand Jackson,' he says.[1] When Teton County decided to replace its outdated rustic library in 1992, Bruder was working on Phoenix Central Library, which is more than ten times larger. The two buildings could not be more different, although they both demonstrate Bruder's view that 'you should look at everything around you and ask some serious questions of a place', rather than bringing a preconceived idea.

Phoenix Central Library is influenced by Arizona's agricultural vernacular of sheds and silos and its dynamic landscape of desert and jagged rocks. It was built to serve a city that is now America's fifth largest with over a million inhabitants. By contrast, Teton County Library has a more intimate connection with the community and is influenced by the romantic, rustic tradition of the American West. As Bruder explains, he was inspired by the 'landscape, the barns, the Old Faithful Inn at Yellowstone Park, by hayracks and long mystical lines of barbed-wire fences'.[2]

Situated next to a trailer park with a broken-down wooden fence, the library is basically a 2,300 square metre (25,000 square foot) shed. Built on a modest budget and with an extraordinary use of ordinary materials, it perfectly sums up Bruder's definition of architecture as 'a balance between poetry and pragmatism'.[3] The building uses primarily local materials such as rough logs and resawn board and batten wood siding. But in form it is more unexpected, subverting the orthogonal plan with a long diagonal wall, which creates strange reflections in the window panes. The effect is a building 'filled with memories of the place, but that is also undeniably a product of the early 21st century'.[4]

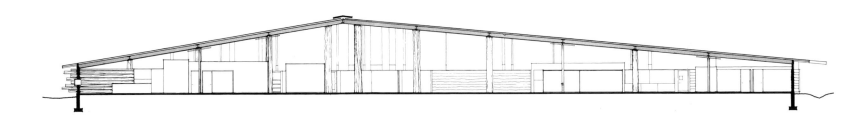

Opposite top
The original library
was built in 1947
in the style of a
log cabin.

Opposite bottom
Section showing
the gentle slope of
the roof that helps
to hide the building
in the landscape.

Below
With its timber siding
and overhanging
roof Teton County
Library celebrates
the rustic tradition
of the American West.

Right
The steel canopy of
the main entrance
contrasts with the
library's log walls.

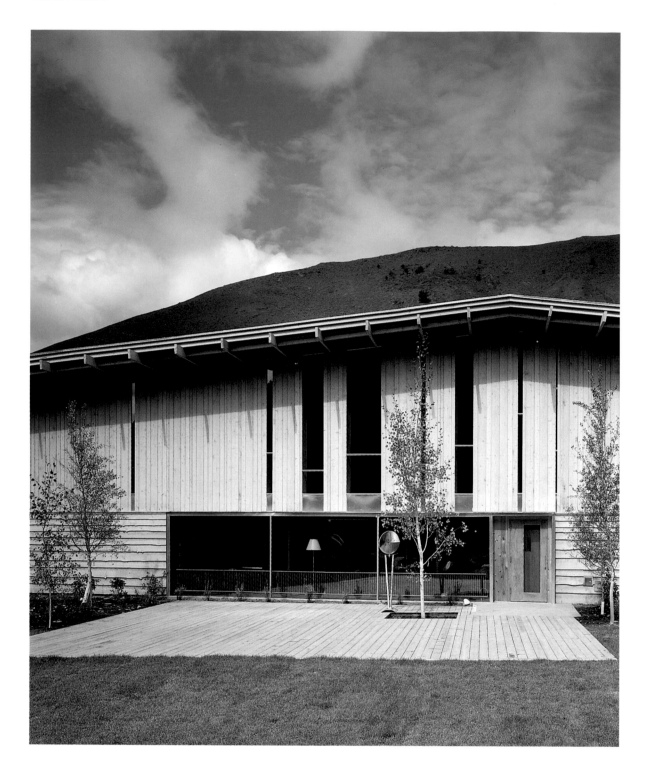

Left
Detail of the south elevation showing the deck area and planting in the community garden

Opposite
A long diagonal wall breaks the orthogonal plan. The main functions of the library are brought together in one large space.

The roof height is low, just 8 metres (25 feet), creating a long, 'lazy' slope from east to west and recalling Wyoming's gabled mountain ranches. The visitor crosses a landscaped plaza and passes beneath an overhang from the roof into a gallery-like foyer, which serves as an ante-chamber to an auditorium, meeting room and what Bruder describes as the 'great library living room'. This space, the largest such space in Jackson, contains the nuts and bolts of the library: a reception desk, a children's collection, a computer centre, a Western Americana room, the general collection and periodicals.

Gathering all these functions together in one space was intended to make the library non-institutional and flexible. The informality is reinforced by Bruder's humorous use of external features on the inside. For example, access to the main room is through a sliding barn door and the columns supporting the roof are 'unpeeled' logs arranged randomly as if they were growing out of the floor. With characteristic attention to detail, Bruder insisted that the tree trunks were positioned so that the lichen on the bark faced north, as it does in nature.

The space has a cosiness and warmth that suits Jackson's laid-back way of life. Furnishings are cherry, oak and leather, with 13 different styles of chair and 23 different fabrics, so that everyone can find a chair that suits them. The essence of place-making lies not just in materials, says Bruder. 'Light defines place more than any physical material.'⁵ He is talking primarily about natural light, although artificial light can characterize a place too; and as a reminder of the time when Wyoming's log cabins were first electrified, in the early 20th century, Bruder has invented pendant lamps from fibreglass, which hang low in the main reading room, radiating a warm, comforting glow.

Opposite
The main room has functional flexibility and removes the need for institutional corridors.

Below
Details such as unpeeled log columns and pendant lamp shades root the building in the region's history.

Below right
Rustic materials such as resawn board and batten natural wood siding are used on the inside as well as the outside.

Right
One source of inspiration was the Old Faithful Inn at Yellowstone Park, designed by Robert Reamer in 1902.

Year of completion
1998

Location
Motiti Island,
New Zealand

Architect
Anthony Hoete

The greatest influence on the design of his father's house on Motiti Island, New Zealand, says Anthony Hoete, was the 'absence of architecture'.[1] In New Zealand, using an architect is considered an unnecessary luxury. Instead, families tend to bang together house extensions over the weekend, erect impromptu beach huts, and even take their homes with them on the back of a truck when they (literally) move house. The architectural profession is also relatively young and has always struggled with the fact that there are few examples of traditional New Zealand architecture to draw on.

Motiti is separated from New Zealand's North Island by a 30 kilometre (19 mile) stretch of water, which marks a clear divide between urban and rural life. While the mainland is undergoing a tourist boom, with skyscrapers appearing fast along the coast, Motiti has no electricity, no infrastructure for sewerage and no cars.

The island is Maori land. There are 30 inhabitants who are considered *whanau* (family) and remain highly conscious of their descent from the Mataatua canoe, one of seven tribes that emigrated in around AD 1000 from Hawaiiki in the Hawaiian Islands.

On Motiti, land titles are non-existent and land cannot be bought or sold, only bequeathed. Hoete chose his site on the basis of where it was possible to land a plane. Most of the island is covered by wild grasses, and other areas are fenced off for grazing. The only approach is by sea or air, and since the airstrip and the jetty are on opposite sides of the island, the house is oriented so that there is an outside door facing towards each. 'Two doors but no front door,' explains Hoete.

The house was Hoete's final project at the Bartlett School of Architecture in London. Having grown up on Motiti island and studied architecture in Auckland, he moved to Britain in the early 1990s and worked for a number of practices before going back to college for a master's degree. Describing himself as a Maori who works for a British firm in the Netherlands, he is understandably wary of being tied to any particular identity. His diverse career means that the Motiti house is not a product solely of Maori culture. It reflects, for example, the influence of contemporary Dutch architecture with its box-like rooms and stick-thin columns. What is inseparable from the context of Motiti is the 'do-it-yourself' method of construction and the simple way of life implied by its design.

After working on the mainland for many years, Hoete's father wanted to return to a simpler existence on the island, with power supplied by the sun and wind; he was hopeful that information technology would not reach him there. The house has only two main rooms, which do not touch each other and are clearly expressed from the outside. The separation of the two rooms

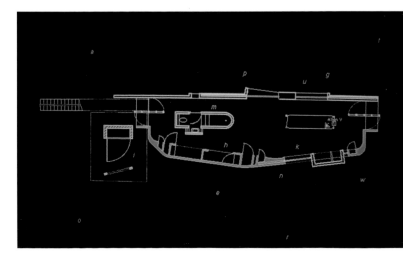

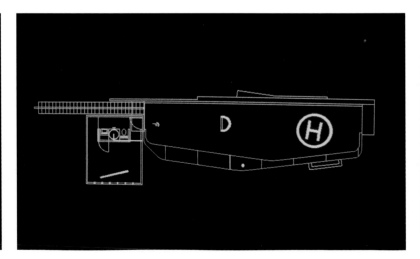

Right
The house on Motiti
island, New Zealand,
is surrounded by a
rugged landscape of
toi toi grass.

Above
Motiti island, which
is 30 kilometres
(19 miles) from the
mainland, is roughly
the size of Venice
but has a population
of only 30.

Opposite top
Materials to build
the house were
transported from
the mainland by
cattle barge.

Opposite bottom
Ground and roof/first
floor plans showing
the main living
space, which has a
pod for a WC and
shower and, on the
first floor, a separate
guest room and a
helicopter pad on
the roof.

is not just socially inspired, the 10 centimetre (4 inch) gap between them accommodates the structures' different harmonic frequencies and takes into account possible tectonic movement, since Motiti lies near the faultline that created New Zealand's mountains, lakes, geysers and craters.

The main space is described by Hoete as a 'wharehouse', a *whare* being a traditional Maori dwelling. The second space, perched above on a concrete-block staircase and stilts, is a 'motel room' for guests. Inside the 'wharehouse' are a freestanding in-situ concrete bathroom and tank for collecting water from the roof, and a 4 metre (13 foot) long table made from a plank of cedar that was shipped to Motiti from London as a piece of 'cultural flotsam'. The plank is suspended from the ceiling by a steel beam and has set within it a sink, three gas rings and drawers.

The 'wharehouse' is enclosed on one side by a bent-plywood wall to the south and a wall clad with profiled aluminium to the north. Like the cheap corrugated metal used for barns and agricultural buildings, this material does not look out of place in the New Zealand landscape. Cut into the north façade are windows framing views over Motiti's rugged terrain dotted with clumps of wild fennel and grasses, and a periscope-like window pops up above the roof to scoop up the sun and prevailing wind and direct them into the middle of the house.

In the New Zealand domestic tradition, Hoete and his father enlisted the help of a couple of relatives to build the house. Between them they dug sand and stone from the beach to make the concrete bathroom. The rest of the materials were shipped to the site on a cattle barge (island cows created havoc during construction by eating the building materials, says Hoete). As limited funds were available to build the house, and the cost of flights to and from the mainland had to be included in the budget, in typical Motiti style Hoete struck a deal with the local air club: he did the drawings for its new hangar in return for flying lessons and use of its plane.

Right
Detail of the ends of the metal-capped roof joists.

Far right
A steel stair leads up to the guest room, which is supported by a blockwork wall and two thin steel columns.

Opposite top
The north side of the house is clad with profiled aluminium, reminiscent of the agricultural buildings that litter the New Zealand landscape.

Opposite middle
A periscope on the roof scoops light and air into the small bathroom below.

Opposite bottom
A large timber-framed window captures the dramatic view of the landscape.

Strawberry Vale School

Year of completion
1995

Location
Victoria, British
Columbia, Canada

Architect
Patkau Architects

The first step for Patkau Architects is always to look for what it describes as the 'found potential' of the site: aspects of the place, climate and local culture that might provide clues as to how to approach the design. The practice's aim is to produce buildings that go beyond the concerns of modernism and classicism, to embrace the way that vernacular architecture evolves through 'subtle environmental adjustment'.

Strawberry Vale School is located in a suburb north-west of Victoria on Vancouver Island, Canada. The new building is situated at the southern end of a sequence of older school buildings. The sequence begins with a 1893 single-room schoolhouse, now used as a pre-school, continues through the column-and-beam remains of a 1950 school building and culminates with the entrance to the new building.

The architects wanted Strawberry Vale to have a strong relationship with the natural world, so they maximized the use of natural light and rainfall, and emphasized the visual connection between the interior spaces and the outside. A wood of rare Garry oaks – a species unique to the southern tip of Victoria island and rapidly becoming endangered – just south of the site was another reason to avoid disrupting the school's natural environment.

Rather than cutting into the landscape, concrete foundations and floors precisely follow the topography of the site, producing an 2.4 metre (8 foot) slope from east to west. Landscaping around the building also mitigates the environmental impact. Rainwater collected from the south side of the school in trenches beneath the roof overhangs is piped to the lower, north side of the school, where it is discharged into an area of marshy ground planted with rough grass.

Patkau Architects have been described as 'rain-coast structuralists'. John Patkau believes that the choice of materials should relate directly to the significance of different parts of the building. 'The richness of the space is developed directly out of an expression of how the space is constructed,' he says. While the school takes into account North American building conventions, using straightforward steel columns and beams for the primary structure, the craftsmanlike use of timber – the principle construction material – is reminiscent of the woodbutcher's art.

Right
The school sits close to a wood of rare Garry oaks, which are unique to the southern tip of Vancouver Island.

Opposite
Timber, which is the most accessible and renewable material on the north Pacific coast, was used to frame and clad the walls, although the column beam members are steel.

Below
Section revealing a tall 'street' that connects the various classrooms and other spaces such as the library, gym and offices. Roof slopes are kept shallow to minimize the building volume.

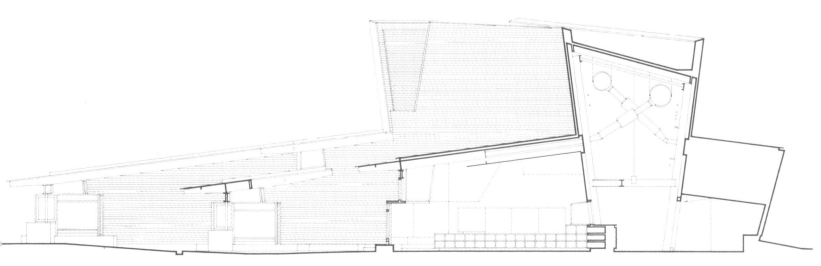

The school provides 16 classrooms for 300 students and was one of the last in a series of site-specific schools to be commissioned by the state of British Colombia. The classrooms are arranged in groups of four around a central circulation spine – the antithesis of a traditional school corridor – with each classroom 'pod' facing south and opening onto the landscape at ground level. This makes maximum use of the southern light and allows the students a window on to the rare Garry oakland.

Although the spine acts as a 'street' running from east to west and implying lateral movement, the entrance to the building is from the north, so that, spatially, the building is multi-directional. In plan, the circulation spine shifts its position to accommodate interstices such as a gym, offices and a storytelling area. In section, it ramps up 2.4 metres (8 feet), following the topography of the site.

The tallest space inside the school circulation spine is where steel columns lean outwards, creating a 10.5 metre (35 foot) high volume that widens towards the roof. Although wood was preferred as the most readily accessible and renewable material, steel was used for the primary structure because the size of timbers required would have meant using 'first-growth' wood.

As far as possible, the embodied energy of materials has been taken into account. Timber was chosen because it is the most readily available and renewable north Pacific coast material. Unnecessary cladding has been avoided, leaving the primary structure of steel, concrete and timber exposed. Following the west coast vernacular, small-scale timber construction using vented cedar makes up the walls. The roof slopes are finished in different materials to reflect the assembly beneath – insulated spaces are expressed with profiled metal and overhangs are thinner and clad with smooth steel.

In line with the desire for minimal intervention, natural forces have been harnessed for heating, cooling and lighting the school. The shallow slope of the roof minimizes the building volume, and overhangs and louvres control the amount of sunlight entering. Skylights, clerestories and reflective surfaces maximize the use of daylight and create the closest possible relationship between the inside and outside environments.

Opposite
Ground floor plan showing pods of four classrooms with in-between spaces, which are for informal use by individuals and small groups.

1 Entrance
2 Gymnasium
3 Storage
4 Multi-purpose
5 Special education
6 Classroom
7 Reception
8 Principal
9 Storage
10 Vice-principal
11 Health
12 Staff
13 Technical centre
14 Library
15 Computer
16 Storytelling
17 Recycling

Above
The classrooms, which are all oriented to the south to maximize natural light, look out onto a neighbouring park.

Left
Overhanging eaves prevent the summer sun from entering, but admit sunlight when the angle is low. Sheltered spaces between classroom pods create a strong connection between inside and out.

Below
Horizontal section
showing how different
materials were used to
represent the change
from the insulated
building envelope
to an uninsulated
overhanging roof.

Opposite top
The detailing expresses
how the construction
and cladding has been
kept to a minimum
to leave the primary
structure exposed.

Opposite middle
Service ducts run
along the spine of the
building, and the floor
level changes following
the topography of the
site.

Opposite bottom
Reflective interior
surfaces bounce light
into the classrooms
from carefully placed
clerestory windows
and skylights.

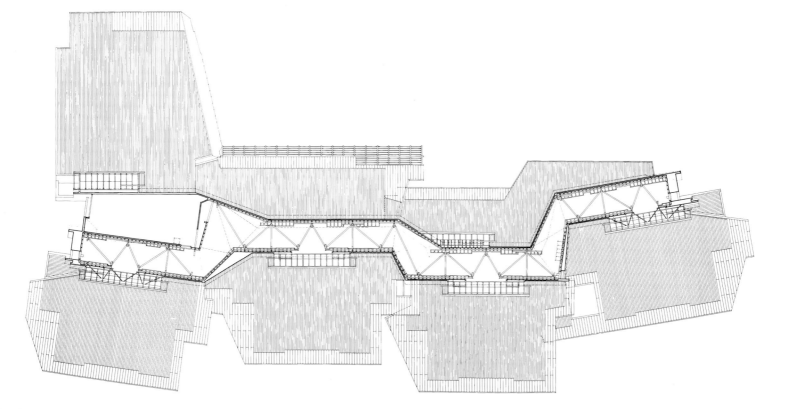

Orphanage

Year of completion
1996

Location
Chhebetar, Nepal

Architects
Hans Olav Hesseberg
and Sixten Rahlff

When the board of trustees of a Nepalese charity asked Bergen School of Architecture to run a student project to design an orphanage, two students took the idea very seriously. In 1994 Hans Olav Hesseberg and Sixten Rahlff travelled to Nepal and spent two weeks in the village of Chhebetar researching the project, which, at that stage, was purely hypothetical. The site, a sloping piece of land above the village fields, had already been allocated, and a design had been completed by a large Indian engineering firm, which planned to build a concrete box containing all the functions of the orphanage under one roof and giving little consideration to the needs of the villagers or the spectacular site.

Back at college in Bergen, the young architects drew up a preliminary scheme, but there was a limit to what they could do from so far away. The following year, with the approval of the charity and the backing of private donors, Hesseberg and Rahlff took a year out of architecture school to go back to Nepal and build the scheme.

Rahlff stresses that they did not arrive in Chhebetar with finished drawings. The building was mostly designed and drawn up from a small house that the students rented in the village. 'It wasn't like building in Europe,' he says. 'We could change a lot of things during the process.'¹ Having studied the way people lived in the village, local building techniques and the availability of materials, Hesseberg and Rahlff came up with a design that treated the orphanage almost as a settlement in itself: a series of smaller buildings grouped around communal spaces.

Phase one – which is roughly half the scheme, consisting of the director's house, dormitories and toilets – was completed in 1996. Eventually the orphanage will have some five other buildings with sheltered spaces in between forming a playground, garden and private court. The site is arranged with toilets at the top of the slope, so that grey water can be treated and used to water crops in the fields below during the dry season. There is also a biogas tank, which produces methane from human waste for cooking, since timber, the usual domestic fuel, is expensive and its use is causing deforestation, which in turn is leading to land erosion.

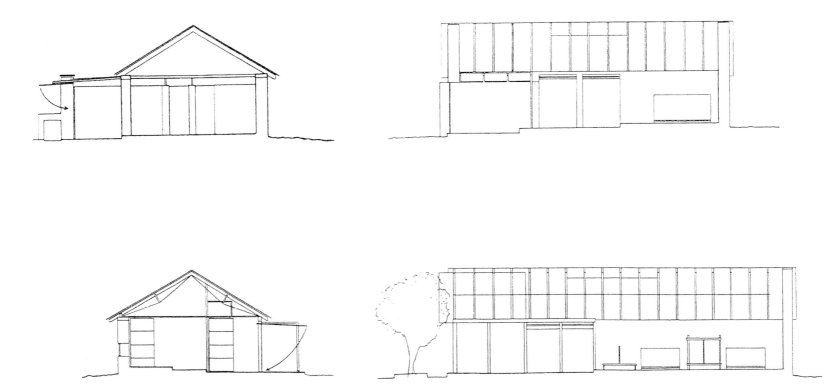

Right
The orphanage
nestles into the
hillside at Chhebetar,
a small Nepalese
village 500 metres
(1,640 feet) above
sea level.

Opposite
Long and cross-
sections through the
main building, which
accommodates
dormitories, show
the simple structure
of stone blocks and
a timber roof.

At 500 metres (1,640 feet) above sea level, Chhebetar has a subtropical climate of hot summers and mild winters. Following the tradition of using thermal mass for cooling during the day and for warmth at night, the primary material chosen was stone, built into thick walls on the south and west façades as a block to the sun. During the night and early morning, the walls radiate warmth to the interior. Stone was the most plentiful local material and large rocks were taken from the river banks and hewn into rough blocks by the villagers. Different-sized boulders were used to form contrasting textures and arranged, as in the lavatory block, in an abstract composition of surfaces. It was not necessarily the easiest or cheapest method of construction. Rahlff points out that it would have been cheaper to bring in bricks from India. But, conscious of their position as outsiders, the students were keen to root the building in its local context.

By mixing stone with modern materials such as plastic sheeting and sliding doors, they were able to solve some of the problems inherent in Chhebetar's traditional dwellings. The idea was to get as much light and air into the building as possible to help prevent the eye diseases caused by people living in houses without windows and cooking on open fires without ventilation. The north and east façades have large openings, covered with sliding doors (the metal wheels were taken from motorcycle engines) and tilting panels of transparent plastic that provide striking views of the distant Himalayan peaks and allow breezes to enter. The transparent wall panels have a double function: they allow light to enter indirectly when they are down, and they fold up to form awnings during the day. Other apertures in the walls are covered with timber flaps, which fold down during the day to make benches.

Timber, in short supply, was used sparingly for window and door frames and part of the roof structure. Posts and rafters were hand-sawn and planed using timber from a nearby wood and, to reduce the use of sections, rafters were trussed with steel wire.

Inside, the floors – which have symbolic significance in Nepal in that they are seen to connect humans to the earth – change levels to allow the occupants their own space and to mark out different areas of the room for different uses. The warm red of terracotta tiles symbolizes the earth, while the blue-grey of the roof slates above echoes the colour of the sky.

With half the orphanage built, Hesseberg and Rahlff returned to Bergen to complete their diplomas. At the time of writing, five years later, Rahlff was planning a trip back to Chhebetar to see how well the building had survived. 'I'm hoping they may have built some more when I get back,' he says.

Opposite top
Modern Western materials such as corrugated plastic were used for roof lights and awnings to allow light into the building.

Opposite bottom
The lavatory was made from concrete and local stone.

Above
Timber was in short supply and was used sparingly for window and door frames.

Below
Phase one of the
orphanage was built
by local people using
traditional skills.

Opposite top
Transparent doors lift
up during the day to
provide awnings.

Opposite bottom
Solid stone walls
provide thermal
mass for daytime
cooling and warmth
at night.

Sibelius Hall

Year of completion
2000

Location
Lahti, Finland

Architects
Hannu Tikka and
Kimmo Lintula

In Finland the design competition is practically an art form in itself, being expertly organized, inclusive and usually international in its scope. Announced in 1997, the competition for the Sibelius Hall in the southern Finnish city of Lahti added another dimension to these features: the requirement for the building to find new ways of using timber. With funding from the European Union's 'timber in construction' programme, the Sibelius Hall was the centrepiece of a five-year government plan to promote Finland's principal natural resource.

With the choice of materials already decided, another major influence on the design was the site, a former industrial area called Ankkuri next to Lake Vesijarvi about a kilometre (two-thirds of a mile) outside the city centre. Good transport connections via the lake, a canal and a railway had combined to make this a focal point of the timber industry.

One of the biggest challenges was to renovate and incorporate an old carpenters' factory into the scheme. This brick building was in a serious state of dilapidation after being used by the Finnish army for urban manoeuvres, and then standing empty for many years. A decision by the National Board of Antiquities and Historical Monuments to place the factory under protection further complicated the scheme.

The winning design team, Hannu Tikka and Kimmo Lintula, broke down the complex brief into distinct parts to provide the multi-purpose building asked for by the client, the city of Lahti. The main space of the complex is a concert and congress hall for 1,100 people; in addition there are artists' spaces, rehearsal and conference rooms and 1,600 square metres (17,200 square feet) of exhibition space, which Tikka and Lintula placed in the old factory.

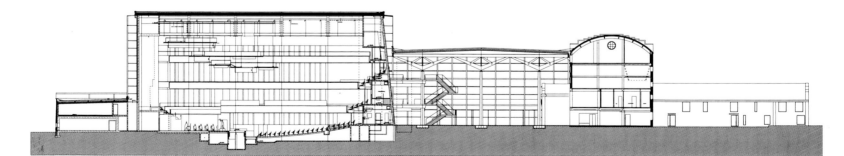

Above
Located in a former industrial area next to Lake Vesijarvi, the Sibelius Hall incorporates an old brick factory.

Opposite
Section expressing the building's three main functions: a concert hall, a public foyer and, in the renovated factory, exhibition space and conference rooms.

Left
The public foyer is a large-scale space with the roof supported by a 'forest' of columns; the construction of the concert hall is a timber box with an outer layer of glass.

Below
Plan showing how
the public foyer links
the concert hall and
the conference
rooms, which adjoin
other smaller spaces
housed in the old
brick factory.

Bottom
Timber columns with
the water beyond
are intended to be
reminiscent of the
Finnish landscape
of dense forests
opening on to lakes.

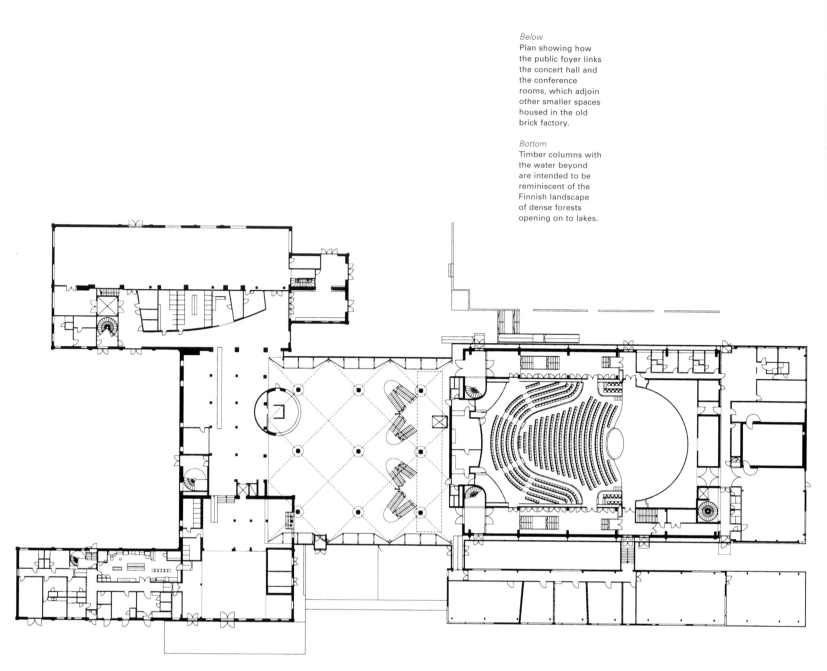

Above
The concert hall, which seats 1,100 people, is enclosed in a layered timber box with tilted walls for sound insulation.

Right
The floors and stage are finished with oiled, heat-treated birch, and the canopy and balcony fronts are made from high quality Finnish birch plywood.

As a showcase for timber construction the Finnish department of trade could not have bettered the Sibelius Hall. The building displays practically every construction technique from rough industrial prefabricated elements to beautifully textured surfaces. The public foyer, which the architects describe as a 'forest hall', is the hub of the complex, connecting the old building with the new concert hall. This double-height space provides a clear view to the lake – a fine example of the Finnish landscape of densely packed trees opening out onto large areas of water. Nine massive pillars made from glue-laminated (glu-lam) spruce support a complex space frame or 'foliage', on which sit light layers of roofing material. Large timber bow trusses – which are somewhat crude and a poor relation of the more delicate steel trusses (commonly used for this type of structure) – support a curtain wall of glass, which provides the visual connection with the lake. The massive scale of the square sections of timber used for the trusses gives the hall the rugged, peasant-like atmosphere aimed at by the architects.

Timber is used in a quite different way in the concert hall, where tilted plywood walls act as a reminder of the upturned boats in Lahti's docks. The construction of the wall is the Sibelius Hall's best example of technical innovation based on the logic of the vernacular. Taking the traditional Finnish technique of placing sand in the floors to prevent the sound of footsteps spreading, Tikka and Lintula developed an acoustic wall made of two wooden plates with sand in between, providing a metaphorical link with the lakeside. Vibrating outer walls absorb noise from the outside, while the inner core is not allowed to vibrate and reflects sound back into the hall. A further acoustic barrier is a glass skin supported by hanging horizontal kerto-beams, which protects the inner timber layer from the weather as well as providing acoustic insulation. At night the effect is of a wooden box glowing warmly from behind the glass.

Inside the concert hall, the floors and stage are finished with oiled, heat-treated birch, while the canopy and balcony fronts are made out of birch plywood. The finishing touch is acoustic doors, made from three layers of heavy plywood panels varnished to look like a precious old violin.

In Finland, says Lintula, old wooden buildings are rather thin on the ground, although there is a long history of using wood. The Sibelius Hall subverts the traditional 'cottage-like' use of timber by using it on a large scale and by inventing new methods of jointing and detailing. 'By using traditional treatments converted into the modern, we tried to link the building to the historical junction of industry, the railway and the harbour and still create the feeling of a public building,' says Lintula.[1]

Above
The multi-layered façade of the concert hall prevents sound transfer. First there is a sandwich of timber panels, then an empty reverberation chamber and finally an outer glass skin.

Opposite top
At night the inner timber walls of the concert hall glow warmly from behind the glass envelope.

Opposite middle
The 'forest hall' or public foyer has a tall roof supported by nine massive timber columns made from glu-lam spruce.

Opposite bottom
The pillars support a 'foliage' of timber beams on which the roof is laid.

Year of completion
1997

Location
El Gouna, Egypt

Architect
Michael Graves with
Rami El Dahan and
Soheir Farid

In the late 1990s the Egyptian coastline of the Red Sea went through a process of transformation after a government decision to sell off 300 kilometres (186 miles) of sites to private investors. The building boom that followed resulted in a string of bland commercial hotels offering characterless holiday accommodation to Western tourists.

After the initial flood of holidaymakers, and as the competition between resorts grew, investors had to make a little more effort. Samih Sawiris, president of one of Egypt's largest construction companies, had in mind a vision of Disneyworld's Dolphin and Swan hotels when he approached American architect Michael Graves about designing a hotel for the new tourist village of El Gouna, 22 kilometres (14 miles) north of Hurghada. But, on his first visit to the site, Graves was drawn to a new development of houses and shops that were under construction at the nearby village of Kafr El Gouna using traditional peasant techniques. He subsequently persuaded Sawiris that an Egyptian 'experience' could be just as appealing to Western tourists as a Disney-style approach, and might be more appropriate.

The buildings at Kafr El Gouna could not be more different from the concrete towers that were beginning to dominate the Red Sea coastline. The architects, Rami El Dahan and Soheir Farid, were two former students of the late Egyptian architect Hassan Fathy and had adopted the craft building techniques that he had revived in the mid-20th century. Graves saw that the techniques, which included using kiln-baked bricks to build the walls, domes and vaults, would be perfect in terms of the speed of construction they offered and the availability of labour and materials. But, being more familiar with reinforced concrete, Graves decided to appoint El Dahan and Farid as associate architects to produce the construction drawings.

Situated on land that was once desert, the Miramar Hotel forms the centrepiece of El Gouna. In plan, the building shows another departure from Graves's monumental hotels in Florida because of a height restriction introduced by planners. In order to accommodate more than 400 rooms, the Miramar had to spread out along the ground, taking up a massive 20,000 square metres (215,000 square feet). In between the buildings, a complex

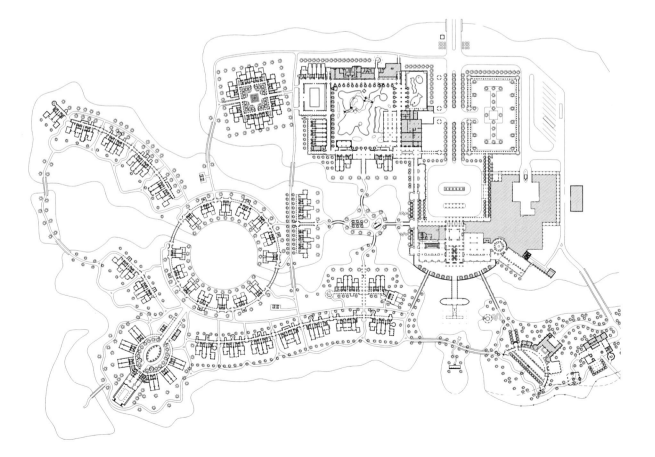

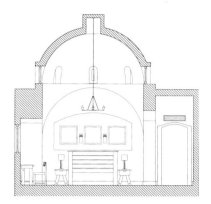

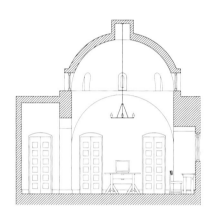

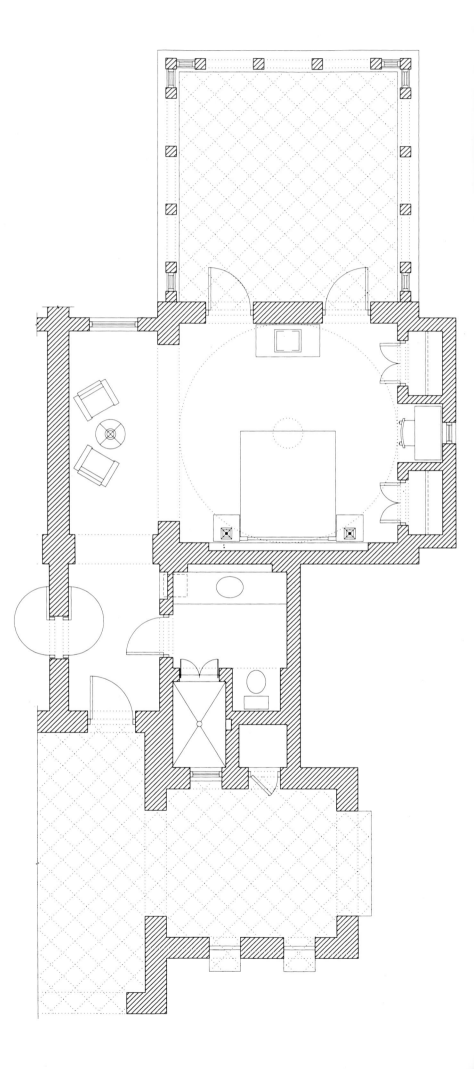

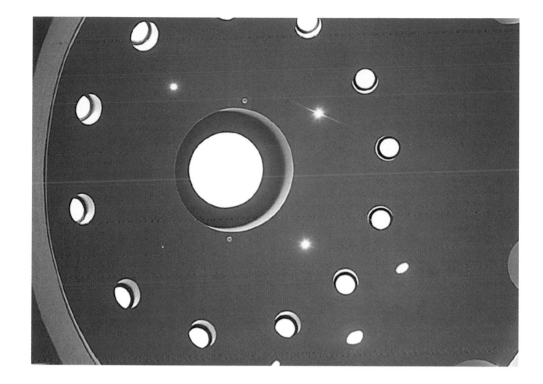

series of man-made lagoons and interconnecting canals ensures that each room has a waterside view and gives the hotel a total water frontage of half a kilometre (a third of a mile).

The Egyptian experience begins at the reception, from where guests are taken by boat to their bedrooms. The rooms are arranged in one-, two- and three-storey clusters following the curve of the lagoons or grouped around small plazas. Single-storey and top-floor rooms and porches are roofed by domes or barrel vaults built without formwork, as is traditional, by leaning courses of brick against each other. Inside, the raw bricks are left exposed.

The colourful exterior façades are more characteristic of the Graves approach – a dazzling display of coloured cones, domes and curves that one journalist likened to Alessi salt and pepper pots.

While the hotel makes use of vernacular Red Sea techniques, it is a world away from the primitive simplicity of Hassan Fathy. Although Fathy might have been relieved that El Gouna was spared a Graves Dolphin, it is unlikely that he would have had much sympathy for the Miramar's opulent use of colour and decoration, not to mention the luxurious facilities – and he would certainly be surprised to see his philosophy being applied to a resort hotel.

Architectural principles aside, the hotel is a wonderful display of imaginative detailing. Virtually everything was designed by Graves with an eclectic mix of references, from colourful folk rugs to glass lanterns that he spotted in a local market. With its high blue dome, the hotel's reception area strays farthest from the vernacular, being built from rendered reinforced concrete. Here giant columns and thick walls make Disneyesque references to Pharaonic halls, and the stripy blue vaults of the restaurant were inspired by Bedouin tents.

The furniture – also designed by Graves – was made locally and, although it is not based on authentic Egyptian designs, has a crude rustic feel. Graves's magpie instinct for borrowing forms, colours and patterns makes this a rich experience – even if life in the hotel bears no relation to life in traditional Egypt.

Opposite
The hotel is designed
to resemble a village,
each room having its
own recognizable
identity.

Below
Bedrooms tend to
be simpler in their
use of decoration,
with brick domes
left exposed.

Below right
Graves was inspired
by local vernacular
architecture to create
shading devices to
filter the sunlight.

Right
The grand reception
area, with its huge
concrete columns,
strays furthest from
the vernacular.

River and Rowing Museum

Year of completion
1996

Location
Henley-on-Thames,
England

Architect
David Chipperfield
Architects

Rowing is said to be Britain's oldest team sport and for many years was the preserve of Eton College boys and Oxford and Cambridge undergraduates. But in the last decade it has enjoyed a phenomenal revival, buoyed up by the gold medal success of the British rower Steve Redgrave at five consecutive Olympic Games. After Redgrave won his first gold in 1984, a group of enthusiasts and a wealthy donor decided to create a museum dedicated to the sport.

Such a museum could only be located at Henley-on-Thames, the home of British rowing, where the Royal Regatta has taken place annually since the mid-19th century. But, by virtue of its history and popularity with the English upper classes, Henley is also a sensitive location in which to build: a museum celebrating such a historic tradition could easily have turned into a pastiche of the vernacular.

Modernist David Chipperfield was not the most obvious architect for such a project, and at the time of the commission, in 1989, he was best known for designing elegant interiors for fashion stores.

Bearing in mind English planners' reputation for baulking at modern architecture, Chipperfield adopted an approach that made reference to the traditions and characteristics of the place, while still pursuing his interest in abstract form, texture and light. In form, the museum is immediately recognizable as a boathouse, and refers to the small, self-built timber sheds that line the banks of the Thames near the site. At the same time it can be read as a reference to Oxfordshire barns and even to the shape of the stripy canvas tents that are temporarily erected each year for the regatta.

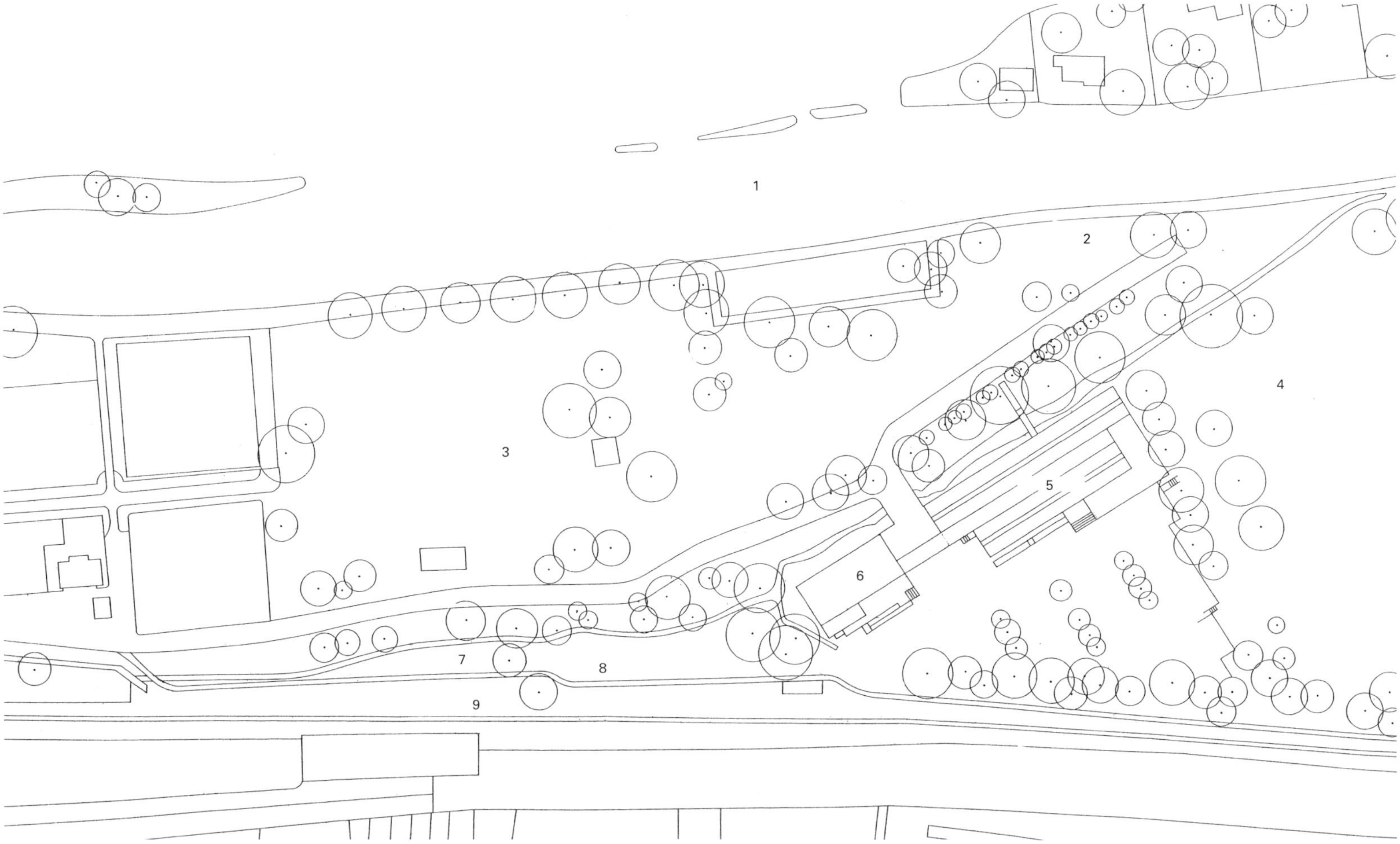

1

2

3

4

5

6

7

8

9

Opposite top
The museum's form was inspired by the shape of tents that are erected close by once a year for the regatta.

Opposite bottom
Site plan showing the position of the museum on Henley River meadows to the south of the River Thames.

1 River Thames
2 Footpath
3 Mill Meadows
4 Marsh Meadows
5 Phase one
6 Phase two
7 Stream
8 Footpath
9 Railway

Right
The museum looks like a boathouse on stilts, with the platform protecting the building when the river floods.

Below
Phase two, on the left, accommodates a caretaker's flat and extra gallery space, and is connected to the earlier building by a bridge.

**OARS, OARLOCKS
AND OUTRIGGERS**

*Two wings beat together, a whoosh through
the water. As they emerge for another
immense stroke, it becomes clear:
these are no wings. They are oars.*

– Craig Lambert, *Mind Over Water*, 1998

Oars are levers that move a boat past water, rather than
pushing water past the boat. All levers have three parts:
effort, load and a fulcrum.

- The effort on an oar is the pull given by the rower.
- The load is the boat and crew.
- The fulcrum is the blade in the water.

The load is attached to the oar by the oarlock. The catch
or lock of the blade in the water at the start of a stroke
is vital because it gives the rower a stable fulcrum to
work the lever.

In Chipperfield's own words, 'The architectural strategy could best be described as one of adopting a traditional form in principle and re-describing this form in detail'[1].

From the meadows which surround the building on the river side, the museum is barely glimpsed through the trees. The oak panelling has weathered to pale grey and the steel nuts and bolts that fix each plank catch the sunlight. Visitors approach the museum across a footbridge and enter one of two parallel elongated halls. Cars use a separate entrance, passing beneath an enclosed bridge, which links the halls to a second phase of the project – a more abstract flat-roofed building that houses a caretaker's flat.

As the museum occupies the Thames flood plain, the entire building is raised 1.5 metres (5 feet) above ground level on concrete columns, and a timber deck provides places to sit outside, as well as being a reminder of the jetties along the river. Chipperfield has also described the platform as resembling those found in Japanese temples. The floor surface continues inside on the same plane, changing to concrete in public areas such as the shop, offices and restaurant. The ground floor is fully glazed, while the first floor, which accommodates gallery space, is predominantly opaque, creating two contrasting open and closed forms.

In the galleries upstairs – fitted out by a separate design firm – the museum houses examples of rowing boats and other historic rivercraft in top-lit halls. The upper space is divided into two full-length galleries, with a third, smaller gallery between the two. The space is mostly lit from above, although it opens up with a strip of windows at the east end of the north hall, revealing the concrete columns behind the glass.

While the apparently traditional form of the building was accepted by the planners, there is no concession to conservatism. The museum is essentially modernist in its use of light and in its form and simplicity of materials. The unseasoned oak that forms a continuous rainscreen around the building is used in its 'raw' state, giving the same impression of materiality as Chipperfield's trademark material, in-situ concrete, which is used most famously in his shop interiors.

Opposite
The exhibition was created by specialist interpretative design group Land. It fills the roof space with examples of historic rivercraft.

Below
Ground floor plan showing the entrance from the north via a footbridge, a shop, restaurant, library and meeting room.

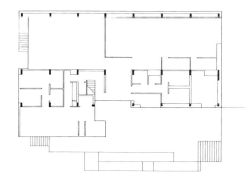

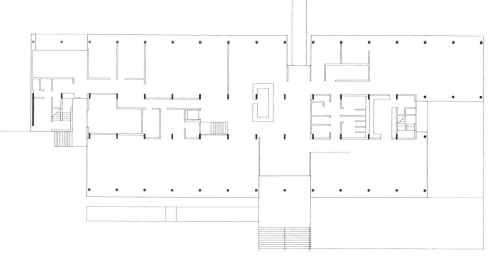

Oak, an indigenous English hardwood, was chosen for its longevity and subtle colouring – after around 25 years it becomes as hard as iron and weathers to a shade of silver grey. With the help of timber experts, Chipperfield designed an innovative rainscreen cladding system, which makes the best use of the material and has specially developed details such as stainless-steel fixings that are resistant to the corrosive tannin present in oak. The fixings, which cover the entire area of timber and continue on the horizontal plane on the deck, modify the ruggedness of the timber and provide a sense of scale.

Chipperfield's treatment of the building's pitched roofs could have easily shifted the emphasis from modernist to revivalist. But, instead of the conventional covering of slates, smooth sheets of terned stainless steel keep it strictly modern.

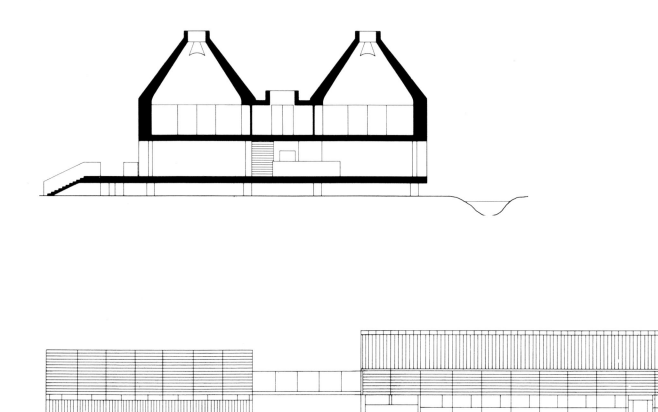

Opposite top
Cross-section showing the two boathouse-like forms side by side with services running down the middle.

Opposite bottom
The first floor is largely a solid timber box while the ground floor is mainly glass, emphasizing a strong contrast between the two.

Right
A strip window at the east end is the only glazing on the first floor while the ground floor is almost transparent.

Below
The walls constitute a timber rainscreen of untreated green oak boards fixed with stainless steel nuts and bolts.

Below right
Floor-to-ceiling glazing on the ground floor makes the public areas on the inside visible from the outside and provides, from the inside, views of the lush vegetation along the banks of the River Thames.

Giving Shape to Identity

One could argue that architecture, when compared with the apparent incoherence of contemporary politics, has a greater potential to capture people's imaginations and give form to national identity. In Britain, Scotland and Wales have recently gained their own devolved governments and are in the process of acquiring parliament buildings (see Scottish Parliament building, page 106). In both cases, the selection of an architect and the design seem to have attracted more controversy and public interest than the debates between the elected members of parliament. Large public projects are hard to pull off at the best of times but, with the added burden of political expectations, the buildings described in this chapter are in even greater danger of being marred by both political and financial difficulties.

Over the last decade the world map has been greatly transformed but the consequence of such political change is just beginning to be seen in the built environment. The fragmentation of the former Soviet bloc in Eastern Europe came to a head in Germany in 1989 with the collapse of the Berlin Wall. Almost nine years after reunification, on 1 July 1999, the German parliament met for the last time in Bonn. The following week, the entire operation moved to Berlin, into Norman Foster's revamped Reichstag. But this high-profile building is just one element of a huge programme of public and private works in the new capital. In the same year, for example, nearly 100 countries set up diplomatic missions in Berlin and many of those are in the process of building their own embassies. As the new Indian Embassy by Léon Wohlhage Wernik shows (see page 118), countries now use their embassy buildings to display their national characteristics, with the result that the diplomatic quarter is beginning to resemble an international expo, with a colourful display of global styles.

More stable nation states, such as the UK, have had their own share of fragmentation. There, the growing importance of the European Union and a palpable sense of disillusionment with traditional British values enabled Scotland and Wales to succeed in their demands for devolution. But the fragile identities that are emerging seem to be just as unstable as the disintegrating nation state. In Wales less than 50 per cent of the population turned out to vote in the referendum for devolution, and fewer than half of those voted positively. If trying to define Welsh identity is difficult in political terms, it is equally problematic in the realm of architecture. Welsh architect Jonathan Adams, who led the project to build the Wales Millennium Centre in Cardiff (see page 112), wanted to contribute to the 'process of political self-discovery'. 'It occurred to me that Wales has no distinctive architectural idiom,' he says, 'and the opportunity might be there to put forward an idea that might be regarded as characteristic of its regional origin.'[1]

In the absence of clearly defined political movements, architecture may have a greater than usual role to play in defining identity. Architectural writer Chris Abel argues that architecture has always been a strong element in the formation of identity and feels that it is one of the ways in which a society comes to know itself: 'Architecture is a way of being, just as science, art and the other major culture-forms are ways of being.'[2]

It is hard to determine whether the architecture of Imre Makovecz (see the Culture House, page 126) reflects the national identity of Hungary or has helped to define it. By pursuing his interests in local architectural techniques, language and folk art during the days of Soviet occupation, Makovecz became a national hero. While the regime forced architects to work in state-run practices using regulation system-build techniques, Makovecz worked on the fringes outside Budapest where he followed his own architectural principles, taking inspiration from nature and from the Hungarian language. However, in a fast-changing society such as Hungary, where the influx of Western capital is producing dramatic developments, organic architecture surely has a limited shelf-life. Like other proponents of the organic style, Makovecz believes that identity has a fixed, almost timeless essence, but as the political and economic situation changes the style is in danger of becoming a caricature, as architecture critics have pointed out.[3] A struggle has already emerged in Hungary between two schools of thought: the organic, typified by the work of Makovecz, and 'international', spearheaded by Joszef Finta.[4]

Architecture has also become a focus of public debate in Latvia, another fast-changing former-communist state, where the capital, Riga, is preparing for the most significant programme of building since the 18th century. Latvian-born architect Gunnar Birkerts, who for many years has run a successful practice in the USA, was asked to return to his homeland to design the country's first public building since independence. Like Makovecz, Birkerts sees his work in the tradition of the national romantic school and looks for the source of Latvian identity in the country's folklore, which he describes as the people's 'DNA'. In philosophical terms his views correspond almost to the ideas of the German particularist philosophers who believed in the *Volksgeist* – an unchanging spirit of a people refined through history. Such romantic notions are only tempered by Birkerts's interest in cutting-edge construction techniques, which represent a desire to bring Latvian architecture into the 21st century.

Ethnic origin is increasingly becoming one of the most important criterion for selecting architects for buildings of national significance. In this search for 'authenticity', it seems that architecture cannot be regarded as having any 'true' meaning unless the designer has roots in the culture. In July 2000 the tragic death of architect Enric Miralles cast a shadow over the Scottish Parliament building – but from the beginning many people had criticized his appointment because they thought a building of such importance should be designed by a Scot. This position was summed up by the Edinburgh-based architect Peter Wilson, who said: 'The Scottish Parliament arguably required an architecture more conditioned by an understanding of the nation's past, its cultural development and its position in the modern world.'[5]

The trend smacks of parochialism, although some local architects would suggest that they are simply defending lesser known practices against the hegemony of global 'signature' architects. It seems unfortunate that the valid promotion of young talent should be confused with an anti-rational argument that places the accident of birth above talent and experience.

Such a trend is a reflection of the increasing ownership of culture. Commenting on the Scottish Parliament debate, architecture writer Penny Lewis argues, 'I have always thought of culture as the accumulated knowledge and creativity of the whole of human society, not a component in the branding or self-affirmation of a particular region.'[6]

As the possibility of achieving truly fundamental social change became more remote in the 1990s, the emphasis of national movements was increasingly placed on the demand for the 'space' to express difference. The Tjibaou Cultural Centre (see page 132) on the South Pacific island of New Caledonia was funded entirely by the ruling French government as a sop to the independence movement, which had struggled for many years for democratic rights. After the assassination of its leader, Jean Marie Tjibaou, in an internal feud, the movement seemed content to accept an outlet for Kanak culture.

Architects have also shifted the balance of their ideas towards more particularist concerns. Renzo Piano, Italian

architect of the Tjibaou Cultural Centre, acknowledged the struggle involved in designing a building with such 'symbolic expectations'. Before beginning the design, his studio did significant research into New Caledonia's culture and climate and gave considerable thought to the philosophical issues. 'A mistaken concept of universality would have led me to apply my mental categories of history and progress outside the context in which they were developed, a grave error,' says Piano. For him, 'True universality in architecture can be attained only through connection with the roots, gratitude for the past and respect for the genius loci.'[7]

This is surely a redefinition of the idea of universality and an acquiescence of difference (and, therefore, of inequality) between the developed and undeveloped worlds. In reality it is impossible for an Italian architect to put aside the accumulated knowledge and experience of European culture and architecture. The brilliance of the Tjibaou Cultural Centre stems from the dynamic relationship between the particular aspects of the place and Piano's sophisticated grasp of architecture as the sum of mankind's achievement – not just the specific, localized aspects of Kanak culture.

Above top
Renzo Piano's Tjibaou Cultural Centre consists of elegant timber structures that echo Melanesian huts and use sea breezes to ventilate the building's interior.

Above
The Wales Millennium Centre in Cardiff by Percy Thomas Partnership attempts to find expression for Welsh identity in its use of form and local materials.

Opposite
The culture house in Mako typifies the organic architecture of Hungarian architect and national hero Imre Makovecz.

Year of completion
2002

Location
Edinburgh, Scotland

Architects
Enric Miralles and
Benedetta Tagliabue
with RMJM

In September 1997 the people of Scotland voted in favour of devolution from the UK's London government, and the process of finding a home for Scotland's first Parliament for 300 years began. Perhaps it is inevitable that such a historically and politically significant edifice should end up at the centre of controversy. From the start, almost every aspect of the Parliament building has been a battleground for the media, the Scottish architectural profession and, since an election in May 1999, the Scottish Members of Parliament (SMPs).

The first matter of controversy was the site chosen by the Scottish Office in January 1998: a dramatic spot at the foot of Edinburgh's Royal Mile, near the Palace of Holyroodhouse (the Queen's Edinburgh residence) and overlooked by the rocky Salisbury Crags of Arthur's Seat, a dormant volcano. Some argued that the Parliament should be situated in the centre of Edinburgh, within walking distance of the railway station, but at least the chosen site allowed the architects to exploit the drama of the landscape.

In July 1998 the Catalan husband and wife team Enric Miralles and Benedetta Tagliabue (EMBT), with RMJM as executive architect, were appointed following an invited competition. This provoked another, even more heated argument about whether the architect, in order to understand the nature of Scottish identity, should have been a Scot. Others argued that, as Catalans, from a region of Spain with its own distinctive identity, EMBT were in a good position to interpret the brief. The tragic death of Miralles in July 2000 briefly put a stop to the row, but it reappeared in new forms some months later. Then new questions were raised about who would see the project through to completion.

EMBT's concept, which it later worked up into a detailed design, was to link Scottish national identity with the land by allowing the Parliament building to open on to the landscape of Holyrood Park. According to Tagliabue, the idea emerged from a conversation between her and her husband when they were first searching for ideas to express the essence of Scotland, in which they joked about Scottish whisky. That led to more serious thoughts about peat and the flavour of the earth, and the pair developed

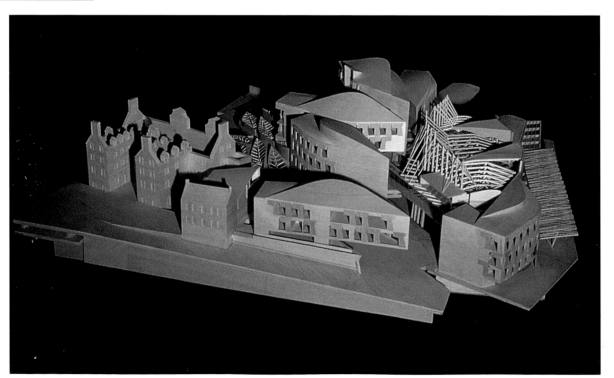

Opposite top
A model shows how
the Scottish Parliament
building relates to
existing buildings on
the site.

Opposite bottom
The Parliament has
an urban context at
the foot of Edinburgh's
Royal Mile, but is
inspired by Scotland's
mountains and rugged
scenery.

Below
Collage expressing the
architect's idea that
the building opens
onto the landscape
of Arthur's Seat.

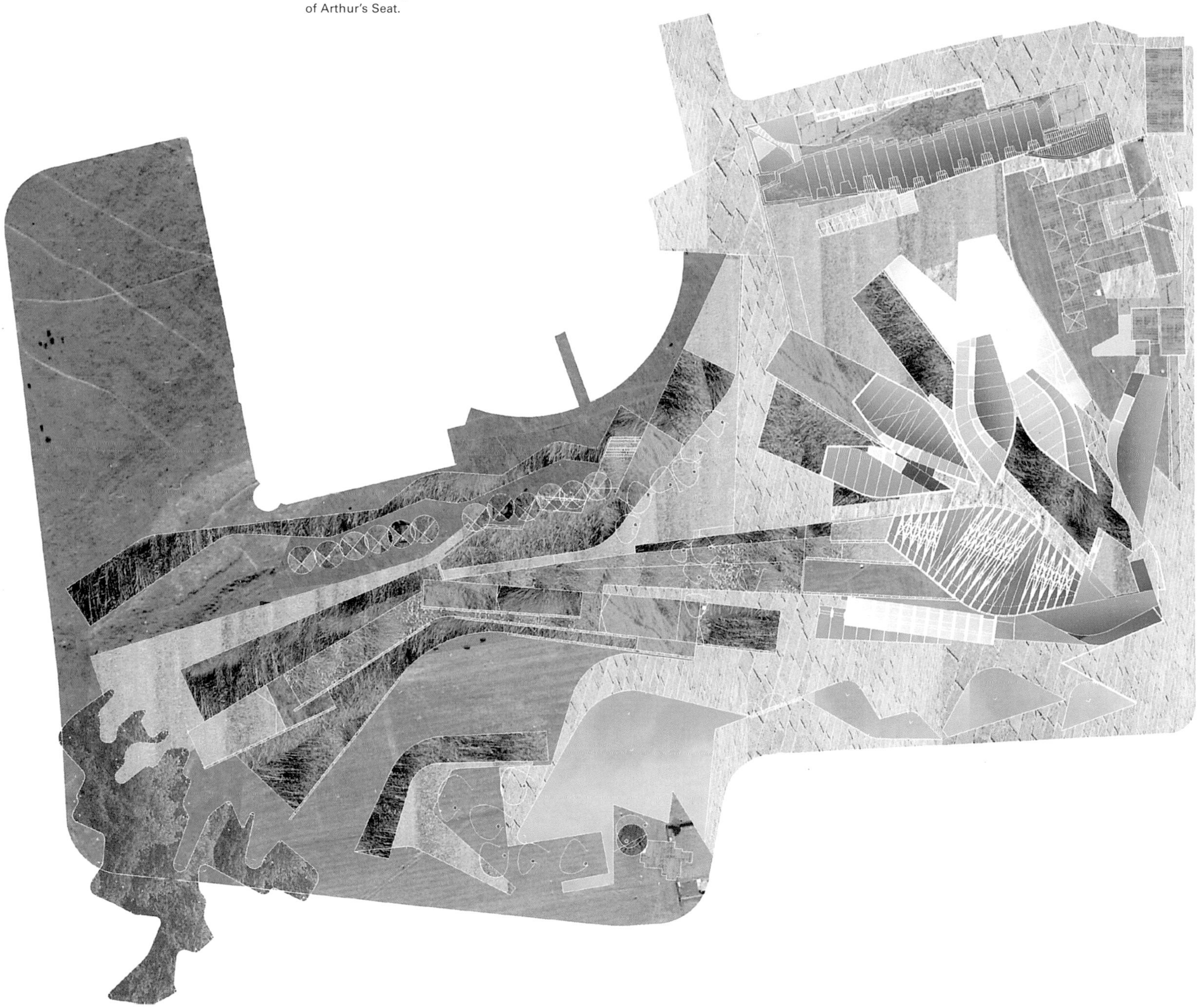

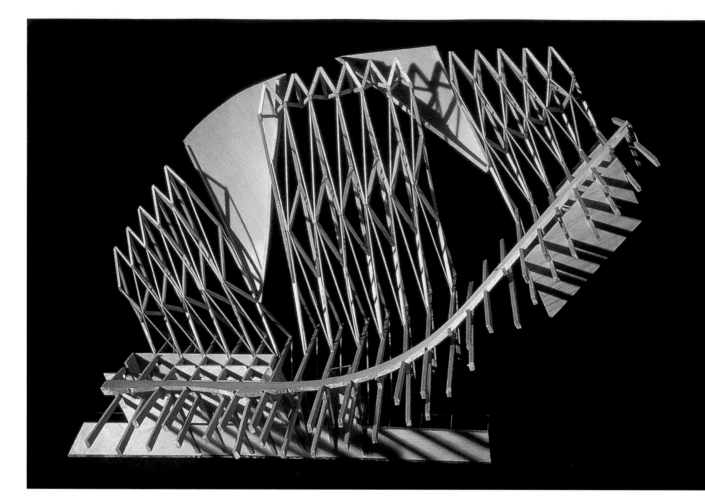

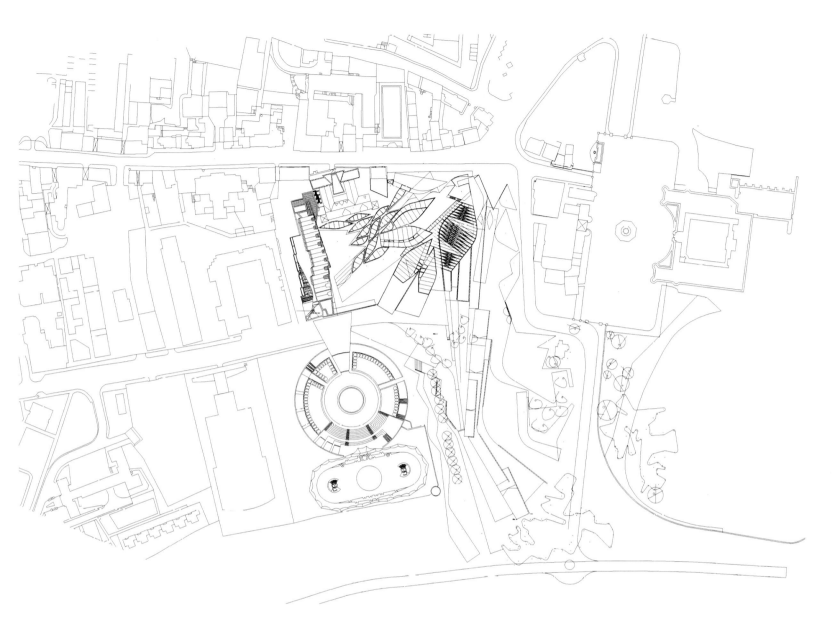

a design that symbolically linked Scottish identity with what they described as the 'immense presence of the landscape'. Miralles, who had studied English in Edinburgh as a child, described the location as 'ambiguous'. 'Our proposal is that Scotland is a land, not a series of cities,' he said. 'It demands a construction that is not monumental in the classical sense. The Parliament will be not in Edinburgh but in the land of Scotland.'[1]

In its orientation, the building was to relate not to Holyrood Palace, which has grounds that the architect said were in the 'gardening tradition', but to the Scottish mountains, represented by Arthur's Seat. While this was an appealing idea and went some way to make Scottish people feel included in the scheme, it left some architectural historians anxious about how the building would relate to the urban context and in particular to the neighbouring Queensbury House, built in the 17th century.

In June 1999 the progress of the design became a little more complicated with the arrival of the new SMPs, who then officially took over responsibility for the building from the Scottish Office. The building had already been

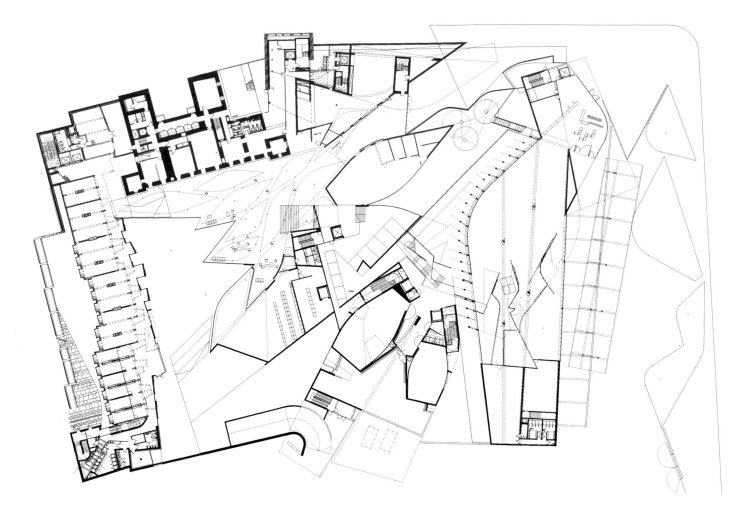

Above
'Garden' plan clearly
showing the leaf-
shaped elements of
the building, which
have glass walls and
roofs in order to flood
the public spaces
inside the building
with daylight.

Opposite
At fifth level the plan
reveals a complex
arrangement of glass
roofs, which in an
earlier design were
compared to the
upturned hulls of
Scottish fishing boats.

Right
A timber model show-
ing the foyer space
opening onto the
surrounding garden.

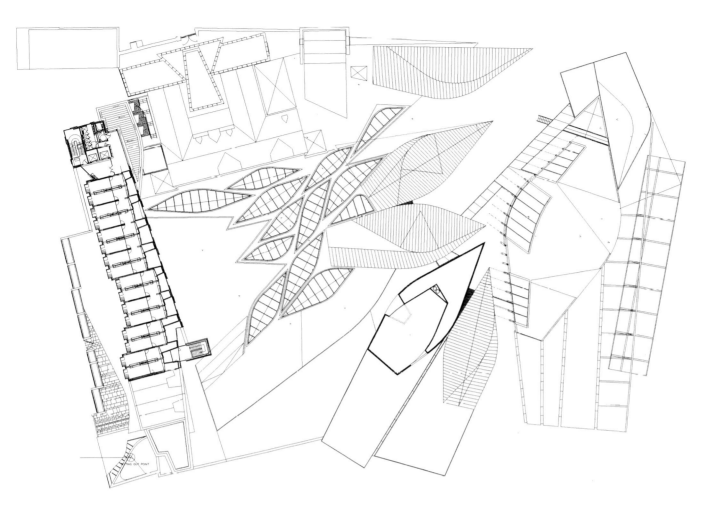

turned into a political football during the elections, but afterwards the hostility of some SMPs threatened to put a stop to it altogether. One of the hottest topics, which took three months to resolve, was the shape of the debating chamber, which eventually had to be changed from EMBT's original design. Then, in September 1999, the SMPs decided that they needed more space for staff and circulation, which again meant that the building had to be substantially redesigned.

Despite such complications, Tagliabue insists that the original idea remains intact. 'We tried to identify the idea of democracy in things other than the shape of the debating chamber,' she says.[2] The debating chamber, traditionally the heart of a Parliament building, is one of a series of oval rooms, which relate to each other as 'boats in a harbour'. Early on, many people took the idea of boats literally, and it was even said that the boatlike chambers were going to be prefabricated in a Scottish shipyard. Since then, the idea has developed along less literal lines, and the elegant oval shapes could almost be read as the leaves of a branch. Instead of the SMPs being the main focus of attention at the Parliament, the building orients itself towards an outdoor amphitheatre, carved out of the earth, representing the participation of the Scottish people.

Year of completion
2003

Location
Cardiff, Wales

Architect
Percy Thomas
Architects

Opposite top
Computer-generated
elevations showing the
distinct form of the
auditorium rising up
from a base of slate.

Opposite bottom
A mock-up of the
innovative slate wall,
which uses three
colours of waste slate
in strata-like bands
with glass sandwiched
between.

Below
Model showing the
Centre's setting close
to Cardiff Bay, a former
industrial area that is
currently undergoing
a programme of
regeneration that
includes the Welsh
Assembly by Richard
Rogers Partnership.

Certain buildings have the capacity to tell a story about the political and cultural struggles of their day, whether they have overcome great obstacles in order to be built, or have never got further than the drawing board. The Wales Millennium Centre is such a building, which, at the time of writing, is expected to be completed by 2003. It has achieved notoriety, even before its foundations have broken the ground.

In a previous existence, the proposed building was known as the Welsh Opera House and the competition to design it was won by Zaha Hadid. The Opera House had been controversial from the start. Labelled elitist and alienating by local politicians and critics, Hadid's design was dropped – to the outrage of (mainly English) critics. To many, the loss was a blow for contemporary British architecture and a lost opportunity, for it would have been Hadid's first built project in the UK. From outside Wales, it looked like parochialism – it seemed that local dignitaries did not like the thought of Wales's first national cultural institution for half a century being designed by an Iraqi-born woman.

Angered by this version of events, Welsh architect Jonathan Adams, who had worked in London for 20 years, returned to Wales to lead the design team of the reinvented project. He told the Institute of Welsh Affairs, 'Nothing more reminded me of my nationality than the casual assertions of the English press that, because it had bitten the hand that fed it, Wales was undeserving of the cultural tutelage offered by its neighbour.'[1]

The redesigned Millennium Centre is now described as a 'palace for the performing arts', and will have cultural facilities reaching beyond the opera-loving connoisseur – for example, hosting community groups as well as international travelling productions. Its architectural intention is to communicate something to the public about the state of the nation of Wales and about its hopes for the future.

From the beginning, Adams stated that, since there was no Welsh architectural idiom for such a building, the architecture would inevitably be unlike any that had gone before. He also felt strongly that it was an opportunity to move away from the trend for buildings to become collections of factory-made elements and features drawn from manufacturers' catalogues.

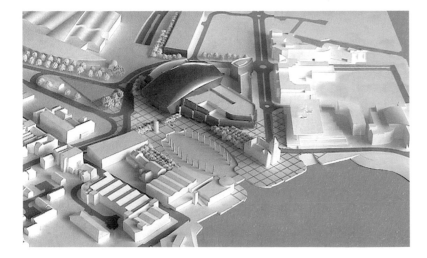

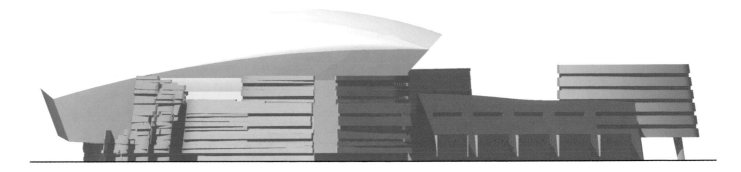

Above
The theatre and
flytower are expressed
as a distinct metal-clad
form, which the
architect intended
as a reminder of Welsh
manufacturing industry.

Opposite top
At night an inscription
in the wall of the
theatre foyer will light
up, and each letter
becomes a window
onto the inside.

Opposite bottom
The north concourse
has columns made
from cast metal with
patterns on the surface
echoing the floral
motifs that were popu-
lar in 19th-century cast-
iron work.

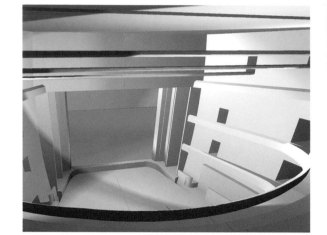

The façade, for example, rejects the ubiquitous glass curtain wall and instead takes inspiration from Welsh cliffs and stratified landforms. 'The layering of the strata of rock seems to symbolize the persistence of our nation through the passage of ages,' says Adams.

Slate production in Wales currently makes use of less than 1 per cent of the material taken from the hillside; the rest, which is rejected, litters north Wales, representing 'the toil of quarry workers going back to the last century,' comments Adams. As a memory to those people, the façade will use around 2,500 tonnes of waste slate recovered from spoil tips in north Wales, which will be cut and laid by stonemasons using rarefied masonry techniques. Panes of glass resembling natural veins in the rock will be laid horizontally on the slate, letting dramatic slivers of daylight into the foyer.

As a contrast to the slate 'cliff' façade – signifying the Welsh landscape – a curved, metal-clad form containing the theatre and flytower rises up through the rock. The reference here is to Wales's history of manufacturing: the bodies of blast-furnace vessels, with their overlapping seams and rows of rivets. Cut out of the metal will be an inscription (the exact words are yet to be chosen) based on the work of the Welsh artist David Jones. He in turn was inspired by letterforms engraved into stone by the Romans – a reminder of another era in Welsh history and a celebration of the convergence of literary traditions.

Each letter is also a window that will allow narrow shafts of light into the darkened interior during the day and will glow at night. From the concourse, the main social space of the centre, the routes to the different venues include open balconies made from layered indigenous hardwoods, picking up on the patterns of the external stonework. Columns are made of cast iron, with surface patterns that echo the floral motifs of 19th-century ironwork. In another reference to Welsh geology, the patterns are based on fossilized tree-ferns that can be found among mining spoil.

The architect's drawings and descriptions of the building are rich in the inventive use of materials and sensitive historical references, which no doubt will strike a chord with Welsh people. The building is unlikely to have the iconic international appeal of Zaha Hadid's opera house – but many people would argue that that is a good thing.

Opposite top
The centre houses many national and local arts groups and provides Wales with its first world-class Lyric theatre, with an auditorium seating up to 1,900 people.

Opposite bottom
In the concourses a glazed wall divides the back-of-house from the front-of-house, reflecting the curved balconies so that they look like an abstract model of the woodland from which they were formed.

Below
The reception area and box office.

Year of completion
2001

Location
Berlin, Germany

Architect
Léon Wohlhage Wernik

By the tenth anniversary of reunification, almost 100 countries had taken up embassies in Germany's new capital, Berlin. This is remarkable when you consider that, before the Second World War, when Berlin was previously the capital, only 33 countries had embassies there. Clearly this is a reflection of Germany's status at the heart of Europe, but it is also an indication that embassy buildings themselves have acquired new status. Many of Berlin's new embassies have been specially built, rather than occupying existing buildings, and more than ever before the architecture consciously reveals the customs and traditions of the home countries. One architectural guide to the city describes it as a 'gala location of the United Nations'. It goes on to say, 'Even minor states such as the Vatican and Iceland are building veritable festival houses.'[1]

In this competitive atmosphere most nations appointed a leading indigenous architect to design their embassies. India stands out as the only one to hold a competition restricted to German architectural practices. While the decision certainly reflects the desire to speed the project's passage through Berlin's notorious planning process, it makes the Indian Embassy particularly interesting in that the building attempts to reflect cultural identity from the point of view of an objective outsider.

The competition was won by Léon Wohlhage Wernik, a relatively young Berlin-based partnership. As with the practice's previous work, the architecture is derived from the immediate urban context and uses geometric shapes to create a composition of solids and voids. Konrad Wohlhage plays down the overt 'Indian touches' in the building, which are confined to the use of certain materials and techniques.

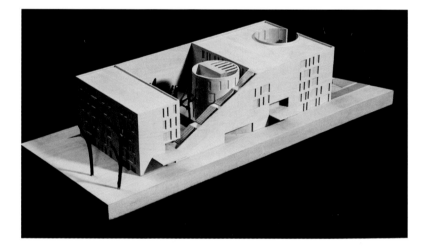

Opposite
Model of the embassy
showing how the
simple external form
conceals a complex
internal arrangement
of geometric forms
with a courtyard at the
heart of the building.

Below
The entrance is via
a cylindrical atrium,
which increases the
amount of daylight
entering the public
areas.

The Indian government was keen that the building should reflect contemporary India and wanted to present a very different image from that in the Western mind. Consequently, there was no brief to accommodate the Indian way of life or any specific aspects of Indian culture – except that, having recently celebrated 50 years of Indian independence, the government wanted to steer clear of architectural references to the British Raj.

The most obvious reminders of India are the outer walls, formed from rough-hewn blocks of red sandstone imported from Rahjistan and cast into large-format concrete panels supported on a concrete frame. The size of each panel, 2 by 5 metres (6½ by 16 feet), was specified by the architect and the stones were cut to size by traditional stonemasons in India. The only other traditional element are the window grilles, which are influenced by Islamic decorations and were designed in collaboration with Indian craftsmen. But the building is more subtly influenced by post-colonial Indian modernism, especially the work of Charles Correa, with its use of geometry and sequences of interconnecting internal spaces and open-air courts.

The 8,170 square metre (88,000 square foot) embassy occupies a plot of land in Tiergartenstrasse close to the embassies of Austria, Turkey, Japan and Italy, and adopts the same typology as the free-standing villas in the area. But its simple rectangular façade conceals a complex internal layout of steps, courtyards and water gardens. The only clue to what lies behind is a cylindrical void forming an atrium that appears through a narrow gap in the façade. This gap constitutes the main entrance to the embassy and gives access to public areas such as a multi-purpose hall and business centre.

Their expanded cultural role gives the new embassies a higher public profile. In the past a separate building would have been devoted to the promotion of indigenous culture; this function is now incorporated, making the range of facilities required all the more complex. Léon Wohlhage Wernik deal with the challenge by splitting the building into three distinct areas: staff residences, in a separate building to the south; offices and public areas, which are accessible from the street; and the ambassador's quarters, which are located in a cylinder (the 'positive' reflection of the cylindrical entrance atrium) amid gardens. The elements are all connected by a grand outdoor staircase, expressed with a dynamic cutaway on the east façade. Just as Correa incorporates open-air 'rooms' in his buildings, formal gardens are an integral part of Léon Wohlhage Wernik's design. The main garden courtyard is a realm of its own. Water flows around formal pools and the ambassador's cylindrical quarters stand aloof, like a garden pavilion.

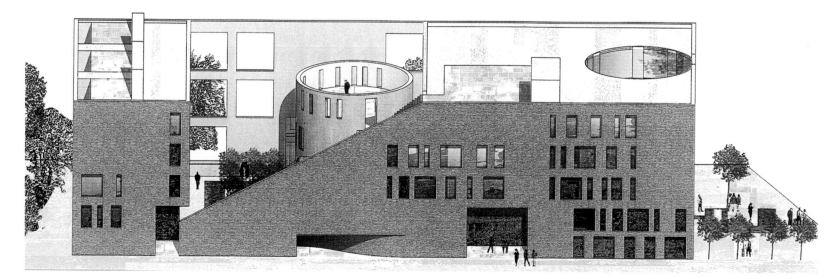

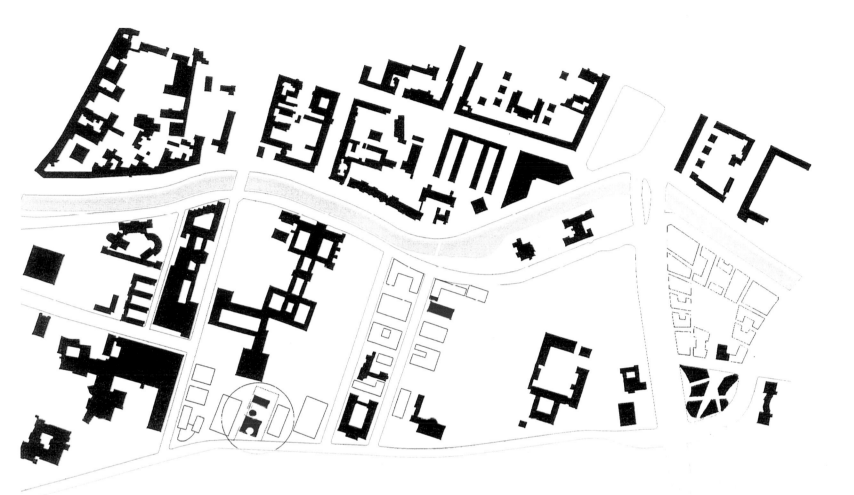

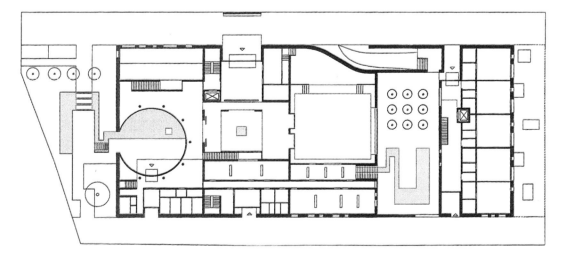

Year of completion
2005

Location
Riga, Latvia

Architect
Gunnar Birkerts
Architects

The Latvian National Library is becoming almost as much a part of the country's folklore as the fables that inspired its design. Since commissioning the design in 1989, the government has struggled to come up with the estimated $100 million needed to build it. The library is much more than a mere building in which to store books; it will stand as a potent symbol of Latvia's struggle for national freedom. Of course it was only appropriate that a building of such national importance should be designed by an indigenous architect. Although he had not lived in Riga since his youth, having escaped to Germany after the Soviet Union occupied Latvia in 1940, Gunnar Birkerts was the only Latvian architect with an international reputation and the necessary experience to see such a project through to fruition.

Since his move to the USA in 1949, Birkerts had worked with Eero Saarinen and established his own highly successful practice in 1963. But, like many émigrés to the USA, he had a strong sense of nostalgia for his birthplace and, although the project looked set to be fraught with difficulties, he was only too keen to take it on, describing the commission as a 'distinct honour and an immense responsibility'.[1]

That was more than ten years ago. The foundations of the National Library are now set to begin being laid on Riga's 800th anniversary, in the second half of 2001, when the government has released the first tranche of funding.

Even unbuilt, the library has as much potency as the finished building would have as a symbol of Latvia's struggle to express its identity, perhaps more – for, if it were never built, it would only add to the sense of victimhood that has become the basis for Latvia's self-image. Independence in 1991

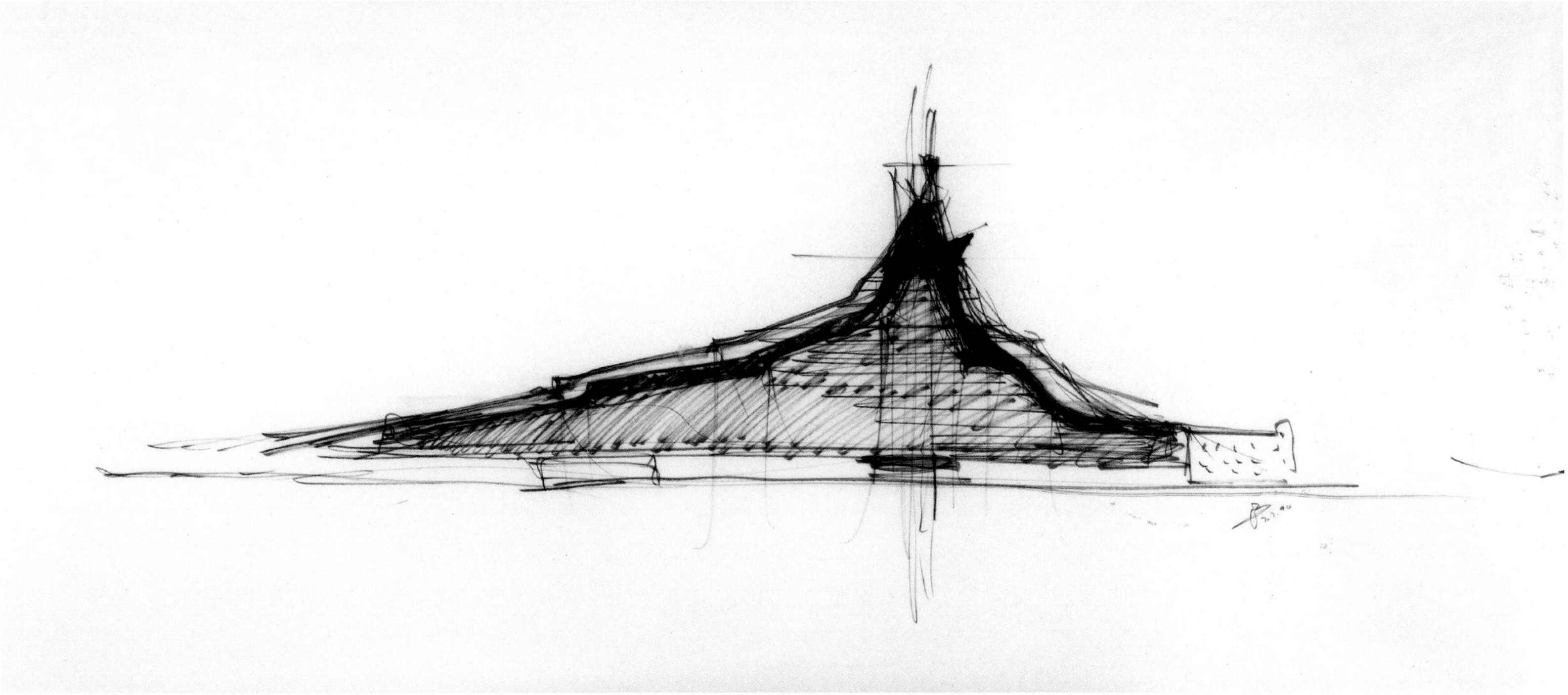

Opposite
Sketch describing the
form of the library,
which was inspired
by two Latvian folk-
tales about a castle
of light and a crystal
mountain.

Left
The building's protec-
tiveness and raised
position alludes to the
kletis, Latvian farm
storage buildings.

Bottom
The high-tech glass
construction is
representative of
Latvia's desire to
become part of the
modern computer-
dominated world.

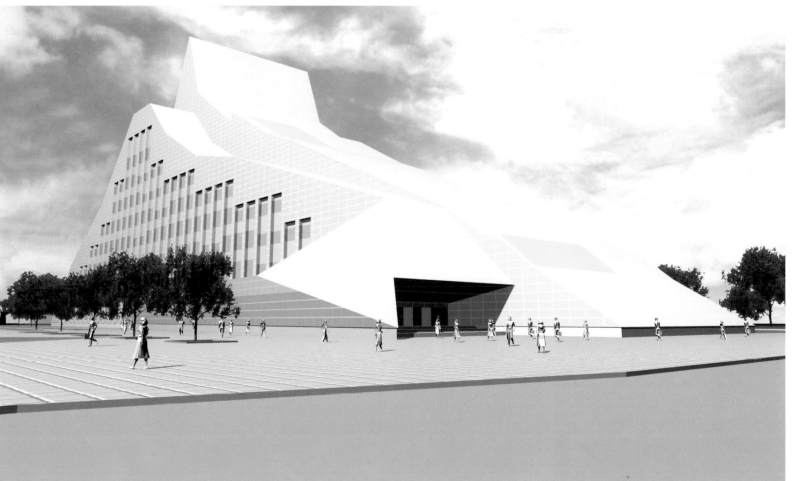

sparked a discussion on how architecture should be used to express the country's identity. For Birkerts, the answer was in Latvia's folklore – its songs, riddles, sayings, anecdotes and fables. Two such fables, the stories of the 'castle of light' and of the 'crystal mountain', became the inspiration for the form of the library.

According to folklore, during the 'bloody days of enslavement' a castle of light sank into a black Nordic lake, only to rise from the depths as a symbol of national strength when its name was invoked by courageous men. In the story of the crystal mountain, a hero struggles to ride up a mountain to awake a sleeping princess. Both tales are the allegories of Latvia's fight for freedom against various outside authorities, most recently the Soviet Union. The library's design is an interpretation of these stories, resembling a mountain covered with a skin of glass.

With a floor area of 46,000 square metres (500,000 square feet), the library will consolidate Latvia's national collection of 5.5 million books, which is presently scattered in 12 different locations around the city. Rising to a height of 60 metres (200 feet) at the 'mountain's peak', the library is a grand statement that will dominate the Riga skyline. Its impact will be modified by its location on the undeveloped left bank of the formidable Daugava river, which is crossed by two 600 metre (2,000 foot) wide bridges.

Apart from the mountain metaphor, the library makes direct references to Latvian agricultural vernacular – for example, threshing barns and farm storage buildings called *kletis*, which are raised on stilts to protect their contents from water.

Birkerts describes his architectural methodology as 'organic synthesis', meaning a natural process of combining various ingredients to find the most appropriate solution. Stylistically, he sees the library as fitting into the tradition of the National Romanticism of the late 19th century and the later regionalism of Alvar Aalto – Nordic movements that reacted against imposed formalism.

The way Birkerts uses materials and technology is, however, decidedly modern. The building's structure will be reinforced concrete covered with a skin of glass, merging the walls and roof into a continuous surface. The latest glass technology will be used to enable the skin to function in a variety of ways, shading the interior from ultraviolet light while supporting wind load and the weight of people walking on it.

Providing public access to new technology is a priority for the Latvian government which, along with many other European states, has declared its intention to develop a competitive workforce at the cutting edge of information technology. Birkerts remains sceptical of the power of electronic networks to tie cultures together, insisting that the main task of the library is to 'carry our literary and historical records and our folklore – our very DNA'.

Opposite top
Section showing a tall atrium at the heart of the building and 12 floors of books and archives accommodating 5.5 million volumes.

Opposite bottom
The vast scale of the library seems more appropriate when it is seen in context on the undeveloped left bank of the River Daugava.

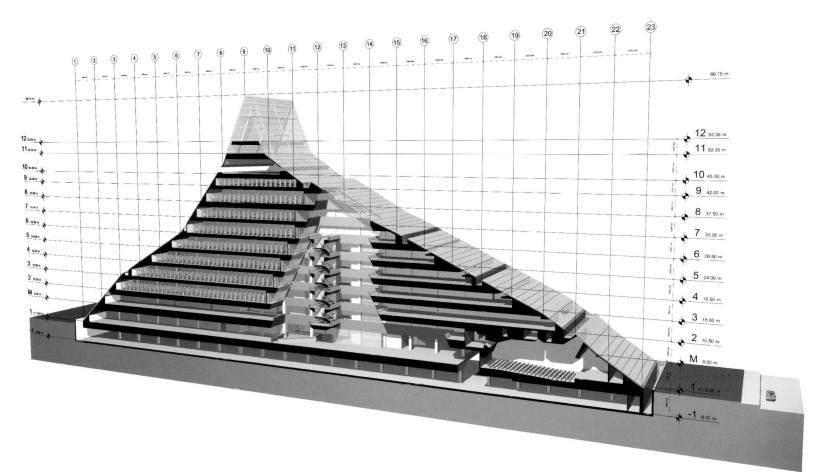

Culture House

Year of completion
1999

Location
Mako, Hungary

Architect
Imre Makovecz

Imre Makovecz's organic architecture has become a potent symbol of Hungarian nationality. He is probably Hungary's best-known architect, although for most of his 40-year career he has worked on the fringes of society, designing small community buildings in provincial towns. It is precisely this independent streak in Makovecz, and his rejection of the political and stylistic trends of the day, that made him so popular once Soviet influence had been removed from Hungary. The Culture House at Mako shows many of the characteristics of Makovecz's work, which has been remarkably consistent during his long career.

Influenced by the National Romantic architect Karoly Kos (1883–1977), Makovecz first experimented with the organic style in the 1960s. During the 1970s he established a reputation as a freethinker, continually breaking the communist regime's rules by designing handcrafted buildings that were defiant gestures against Soviet system-build techniques.

In the late 1970s his design for the Sarospatak Cultural Centre was the final straw: his licence to practise was withdrawn with the excuse that the building schedule had overrun. Exiled to a national park north of Budapest, Makovecz was reduced to designing holiday-camp structures and community buildings. Ironically, this situation allowed his interest in Hungarian folk tradition to flourish and confirmed his fears that the nationalization of land and state-run farming cooperatives were destroying Hungarian rural life.

But by the early 1980s the political situation was changing and Hungary had become the most Westernized economy in Eastern Europe. Taking advantage of a new market for private commissions, Makovecz set up his practice,

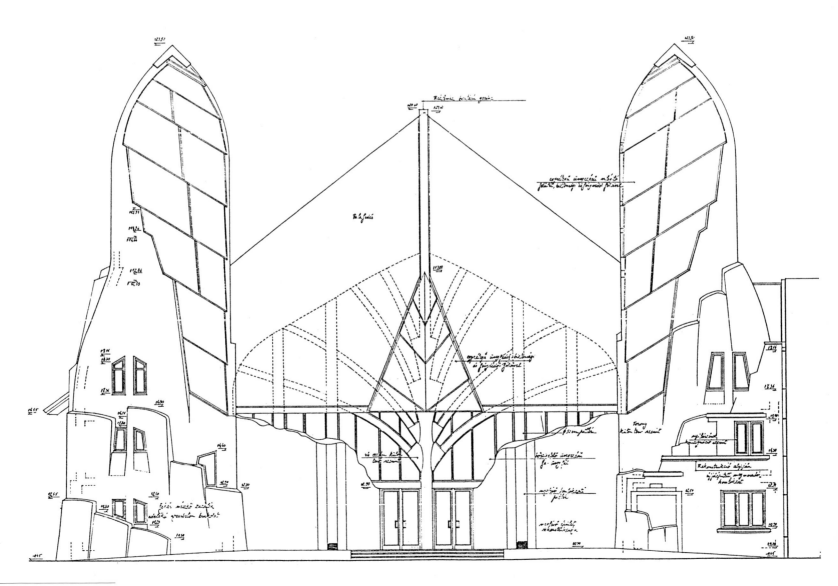

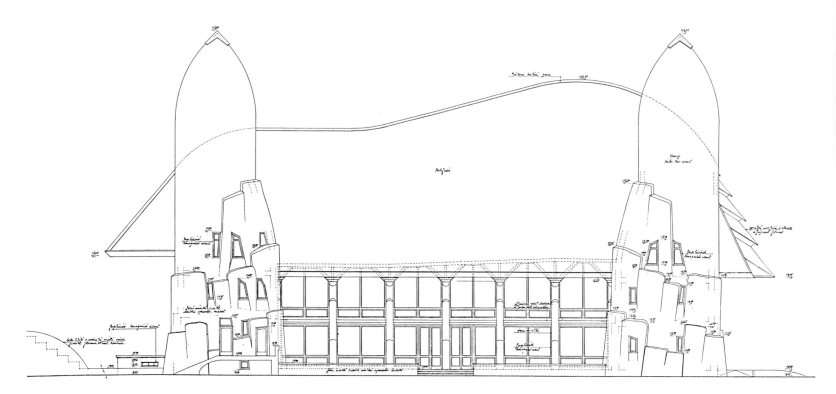

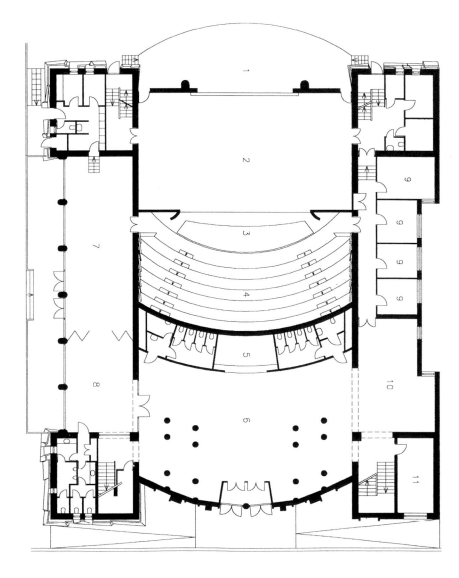

Above
Elevation showing the sculptural corners of the building on which sits the large dark form of the roof.

Right
Plan showing the auditorium at the heart of the building, which has a stage that can be opened up at the back for open-air performances.

1 Outside stage
2 Stage
3 Orchestra
4 Auditorium
5 Doors
7 Foyer
8 Lounge
9 Dressing rooms
10 Cloakroom
11 Office

Opposite left
A 'tree-trunk' column at the front entrance supports a mass of timber 'branches' forming a canopy.

Opposite right
The roof of the auditorium, which seats 600, resembles an upturned boat with curved timber ribs rising up from the plaster walls.

Makona, in 1983. By offering workspace and a training in the organic style to younger architects, he began to disseminate his ideas throughout Hungary.

Despite the political impact of his work and its strong links with Hungarian nationalism, Makovecz claims that his interest is spiritual and emotional rather than political. The Culture House at Mako, a small town in south-eastern Hungary, near the border with Romania, makes explicit references to nature and folk art, and to Hungary's forgotten architectural heritage. As a reminder of the site's history, the building incorporates the ruins of a 1930s cultural centre that was built by the town's onion-growers' association and demolished during the Soviet occupation.

The main function of the centre, commissioned by Mako's town council, is to house a 600-seat theatre. This dramatic space at the centre of the building is roofed with plywood and shingle slate. Above the entrance, the shingle gives way to glass and a skeletal timber structure is revealed. Inside the auditorium the roof resembles an upturned boat. At the sides curved timber ribs rise up from a base of moulded plaster and the back wall of the stage opens up for outdoor performances at the rear of the building.

Four glazed towers, which accommodate stairwells and reading rooms, stand at the corners of the theatre, recalling the region's white-painted Calvinist church towers. But these are the only reminders of Hungarian architectural heritage. 'It is typical of Hungary,' says Makovecz, 'that although we have a very rich history there are only a few material remains. If somebody wanted to see what Hungary looked like in the past, they would have to go to Slovakia or Romania.'[1]

Reflecting on what he describes as an 'invisible country', Makovecz takes his references from nature and from the vernacular language rather than from specific building forms. In his distinctive style, parts of the building are derived from anthropomorphism, where words that describe building elements are linked with features of animals – for example, doors are wings, a ridge is a spine, rafters are horns and windows are eyes.

Inside the Mako theatre twisting timber columns resembling tree trunks support the foyer roof. The tree, Makovecz says, is the 'most complete representation of life itself'. It not only has symbolic value – the root is a metaphor for the hidden, underground world of the unconscious – but also 'it ages and matures like wine'.[2] Timber is his material of choice for practical reasons as well. After the Second World War, Hungary was short of technology and technical building expertise to build. The only remaining craftsmen tended to be skilled in joinery techniques and, with the widespread use of prefabricated concrete panels during the 1960s and 1970s, timber became a symbol of defiance against the communist regime.

Given that so many aspects of Makovecz's architecture are linked to this spirit of resistance, it is hard to see how his work will evolve in a situation where it is accepted as the national style. But, with Western capital pouring into Hungary and most new commissions going to foreign architects, Makovecz continues to see himself as the underdog struggling for an authentic Hungarian architecture.

Left
A forest of tree-like columns supports the ceiling in the foyer.

Opposite
Timber is Makovecz's favourite material for symbolic as well as practical reasons: the tree signifies life, while joinery was the only craft skill available at one time.

Tjibaou Cultural Centre

Year of completion
1998

Location
Nouméa,
New Caledonia

Architect
Renzo Piano Building
Workshop Architects

The Tjibaou Cultural Centre was the last *grand projet* to be overseen by the late French President François Mitterand in one of France's remaining colonial territories. The building, which is located a short distance from Nouméa, the capital of New Caledonia, was the result of a political deal arranged between the French government and the New Caledonian independence movement following the assassination of its leader, Jean Marie Tjibaou, in 1989. Tjibaou had long campaigned for the restoration of indigenous Kanak culture and, following his death, as a concession to his supporters, the government agreed to fund an Agency for the Development of Kanak Culture (ADCK) in return for postponing independence.

As well as promising support for Kanak culture, the government pledged to invest some 200 million French francs, of which the Tjibaou Cultural Centre represented the first instalment. In 1990 a two-stage international competition was launched to find an architect for a building that would reflect the complexity of Kanak rituals and customs, its 28 languages and, most importantly, its desire for independence.

Renzo Piano came up with the most inventive and appropriate design. As an Italian, he was also politically acceptable – a French architect might have been seen as a further act of cultural imperialism. Piano is known for his sensitivity to place and his workshop approach, which involves exhaustive studies into climate and culture before a design emerges.

Piano's idea came from a complex reading of Kanak culture that reconciled his interest in technology with local Melanesian traditions. He even went to the lengths of enlisting the help of a social anthropologist and specialist in

Right
The Tjibaou Cultural
Centre stands on
a peninsula a few
kilometres from
the capital of New
Caledonia, Nouméa.

Below
The centre consists
of ten 'cases' –
narrowing structures
of laminated timber
that open at the
top in a comb-like
arrangement and
move in the wind
with the surrounding
trees.

Next page
As well as being a
visible landmark,
each of the ten cases
has a different
function, including
exhibition and
performance space
in which to celebrate
Kanak culture. The
cases together form
a connected public
space and a ritual
pathway.

Opposite top
Built from wooden joists and ribs, the curved structure of each case is loosely based on the form of the traditional Kanak huts, which were constructed from intertwined plant fibres.

Opposite left
Each case consists of a double structure with air circulating between the cladding of the exterior and interior glass skin. Openings exploit the trade winds from the sea and induce convection currents to help ventilate the interior.

Opposite right
Horizontal section through a case showing the Iroko timber ribs held together by steel rods.

Below
Section through a case, the tallest of which is 28 metres (90 feet) high, which shows how the steel structure tapers off towards the sky.

south Pacific culture, Alban Bensa. 'A true acceptance of the challenge took courage,' writes Piano. 'It meant taking off the mental clothes of the European architect and steeping myself in the world of the people of the Pacific.'[1] It also meant a struggle against what he describes as the 'trap of folkloric imitation, the world of kitsch and the picturesque'.

Perhaps surprisingly, he was helped by the fact that there is no Kanak building tradition to speak of, since the Melanesians constructed huts from perishable materials that were not intended to be permanent. This absence of a vernacular allowed Piano greater freedom to experiment with materials and forms and meant that his design represented the first attempt to create a distinctive architecture for the region.

The solution was not a single monumental building – which would have failed to respect the Kanak belief in harmony with nature – but an assemblage of 'villages', pathways and open spaces. The centre's most distinctive features are what Piano refers to as 'cases' – curved structures built from wooden joists and ribs, which are visible from far away above the trees. There are ten of these curious but elegant structures, each having a different height and function. At 28 metres (90 feet) high, the largest case is as tall as a nine-storey building and forms a visible landmark from far away. Its profiled wooden slats vibrate with the wind, merging with the surrounding vegetation and evoking the intertwined plant fibres of the local Melanesian huts.

The cases work so well because they are pure invention rather than a borrowed form. Loosely based on indigenous huts, an earlier design took a far more literal interpretation. But the final version is a more abstract reading, which avoids the dangers of kitsch. Their logic is based on Piano's investigations into the texture of materials and the local climate and experiments, which combined the use of natural materials and modern technology, using laminated wood and natural wood, concrete and coral, steel castings and glass panels, tree bark and aluminium. The cases also have a practical purpose, which is to provide an effective system of passive ventilation, exploiting the trade winds from the sea and bringing convection currents into the interior.

Beneath the towering fronds of the cases, the centre is organized into three 'villages' housing exhibitions about the history, community and natural environment of New Caledonia. There is also a 400-seat theatre, a multimedia library and other facilities of a modern cultural centre such as restaurant and offices. All the various elements are connected to each other and surrounded by a 1 kilometre (½ mile) pathway running from the edge of the lagoon to the tip of the promontory. Along this route, the 'pathway of history', is a series of metaphors for the Kanak representation of human evolution, including themes of death, rebirth and nature. The most important – creation – is represented by a water lily surrounded by flowing trees, and agriculture is depicted by fields of sweet potatoes and other local vegetables.

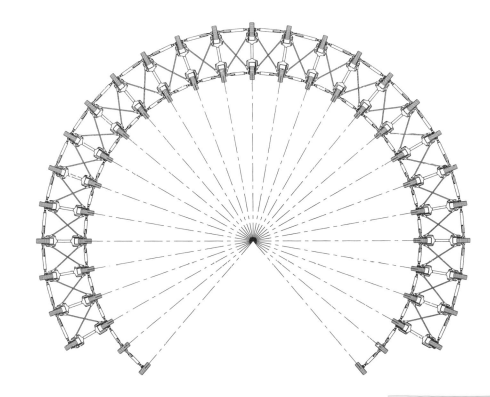

Building with the Landscape

Environmental consciousness, almost universal today, has added a new dimension to vernacular architecture. The current concern with the destruction of the environment has at its heart the notion that the natural world is a distinct object under threat from man's intervention. Yet one could argue that natural disasters in the developing world prove the reverse to also be true. Simon Schama, in his book *Landscape and Memory*, argues that man and nature are indivisible: 'Before it can ever be a repose for the senses, landscape is the work of the mind. Its scenery is built up as much from strata of memory as from layers of rock.... It is difficult to think of a single natural system that has not, for better or worse, been subsequently modified by human culture.'[1]

The projects in this chapter show particular sensitivity to the landscape, whether they reject the view that man should alter the landscape or, rather, see architecture and landscape in a dynamic relationship. The approach is fundamentally different from that of architects of the past, who viewed the landscape almost as something to be shaped and used by man. As Jacob Bronowski confidently put it in his influential television series *The Ascent of Man*, 'Man is a singular creature. He has a set of gifts which make him unique among the animals so that, unlike them, he is not a figure in the landscape – he is a shaper of the landscape.'[2]

In the latter part of the 20th century the pace of change, the use of new materials and fast-track building processes changed the time frame of architecture. Buildings could appear almost instantaneously and in some cities – for

instance, Tokyo – they were expected to last only for around a decade. Architects generally considered their buildings to be perfect at the time of completion, rather than envisaging what they would be like after decades of maturing and weathering. This latter view tends to be the preserve of landscape architects, who work with a different timescale. As the landscape architect Geoffrey Jellicoe pointed out in *The Landscape of Man*, 'It is the present that matters [now]. The imagination for example no longer cares to bridge the gap, peculiar to landscape, between the seedling and the tree.'[3]

Peter Salter is a rare example of an architect who thinks like a landscape architect, treating inert building materials as if they are alive. His Kamiichi Mountain Pavilion in the Toyama Prefecture of Japan (see page 146) reintroduces the idea of temporality into architecture. Salter projects into the future and considers what effect the snow, wind and rain will have on the pavilion, taking into account the geological processes of erosion and deposition, as if the building were an extension of the land.

Vernacular buildings have an 'undeniable logic', thinks Salter, born from their evolution over time. Architects can only get close to that logic by taking into account the objective factors and responding to them, rather than by mimicking the forms of the vernacular. Salter does not see a contradiction between the artifice of the architect and the unconscious process of the vernacular. Architects can learn from the vernacular or, as he puts it, 'go as close as they dare to it'.

This is an approach shared by the Australian architect

Glenn Murcutt (see the Arthur and Yvonne Boyd Education Centre, page 140). During the 1980s he documented the agricultural structures of the aboriginal people, noting the way in which woolsheds, for example, had evolved in relation to their function and interaction with the climate. The resemblance of many of Murcutt's buildings to these structures springs not from imitation but from what he describes as 'analogous inspiration' – a sensitivity to the landscape similar to that of the aboriginal people. Unlike Salter, whose buildings are firmly anchored in the land, Murcutt's 'touch the earth lightly' (an aboriginal phrase). The Arthur and Yvonne Boyd Education Centre rests on concrete piles that do not interfere with the flow of water beneath the site – a human intervention that does not disrupt the laws of nature. In Australia the landscape is more than simply scenery to be viewed through a window; it is a symbol of national identity or, according to Murcutt, 'almost an instrument of national reconciliation.'

The Norwegian architect Sverre Fehn is equally inspired by the landscape, although he describes his museum in west Norway (see page 164) as 'doing battle with the hillside'. By this he does not mean that the architecture is unsympathetic or incompatible with the landscape but that it is a counter-statement completing a dialectical whole. Fehn believes various types of Norwegian terrain have different characters that influence the form of vernacular architecture and even the temperament of the people living there.

Many of the projects described in this chapter are intended to be experienced as part of a journey through the landscape, in some cases as a symbolic reminder of the Chinese allegory of man's passage through the world to eternity. This is clearly the case with the Miho Museum in Japan's Shigaraki Hills (see page 158), which occupies a remote site accessible only by journeying through a tunnel and across a dramatic cable-stayed bridge. To comply with planning laws, which limited how much of the building could be seen above the ground, part of the museum had to be buried in the hillside, involving the excavation of thousands of tonnes of earth and rock. The planning laws reflect a belief that the landscape should be revered as an object to be viewed rather than as an ecosystem not be interfered with.

Antoine Predock's Science Center in Arizona (see page 152) – the only urban building featured in this chapter – brings the landscape of the desert to downtown Phoenix. Predock purposefully distances himself from 'Eurocentric' theoretical discussions, working in New Mexico where, he says, 'A person basically concerns himself with the direction of the wind, the movement of the sun and the form of the landscape.' Uninspired by the architecture of Phoenix, Predock modelled the Science Center on the forms and light effects of the Sonoran Desert, working at first with clay models to create sculptural land forms. The centre is also a journey through the urban landscape, turning the visitor into an active participant in the building, and incorporating them into the public spaces of the city. Although the building is a sensitive piece of urbanism, its rejection of urban forms reflects an ambivalence towards the enduring quality of civilization compared with that of the landscape.

Opposite
Antoine Predock's Science Center brings an abstracted interpretation of the desert to downtown Phoenix, Arizona.

Above right
With his Kamiichi Mountain Pavilion, Toyama, Japan, Peter Salter projects into the future, considering the effect snow, wind and rain will have on the structure.

Right
The Miho Museum in Japan's Shigaraki Hills is approached via a tunnel followed by a dramatic cable-stayed bridge over a deep valley.

Year of completion
1999

Location
Riversdale, Australia

Architects
Glenn Murcutt, Wendy
Lewin and Reg Lark

The buildings of Glenn Murcutt have come to define the style of contemporary Australian architecture. This is not because you can find one on every street corner – quite the reverse – but because they capture the essence of the Australian climate and landscape.

In contrast with his international reputation, Murcutt likes to keep a low profile, working alone from a studio near Sydney harbour. Since he started his own practice in the 1960s, he has mainly designed private houses and has established such a reputation that many of his clients are prepared to wait years for the benefits of his services.

The Arthur and Yvonne Boyd Education Centre breaks with that pattern, being a collaboration between Murcutt, his partner, Wendy Lewin, and a former student, Reg Lark. As his first public building for more than a decade, the centre also represents a break in terms of its scale, its client and its construction methods.

Murcutt's buildings generally reflect three separate influences: European Modernism, Australian agricultural vernacular, and the natural landscape. Over the years the last of those three elements has probably become his most important concern. Murcutt believes that human beings should act as custodians rather than as owners of the earth and its resources; he is guided by the aboriginal maxim 'touch this earth lightly'.

The Arthur and Yvonne Boyd Education Centre occupies a dramatic site above the Shoalhaven River near Nowra, a three-hour drive from Sydney. It was commissioned by the Bundanon Trust, an organization set up to administer the bequest to the state by the painter Arthur Boyd. Just months after the building was completed in 1999, Boyd himself died, having worked for many years from a studio in an old farm cottage on the site. The trust wanted a centre that combined communal teaching and social facilities with dormitories for 32 young students from Australia and the rest of the world.

The stunning landscape that had originally attracted Boyd to the site became the main inspiration for Murcutt and his collaborators, and in turn for the students who now come to the centre to learn to paint and draw. Remote and isolated, the centre perches on a rise overlooking the river, with

Above
The building stands
at a point where
rolling hills become
native bush – the
landscape that
originally inspired the
painter Arthur Boyd
to move here.

Opposite
The site is a dramatic
spot looking down on
the Shoalhaven River,
near Nowra, a three-
hour drive from
Sydney.

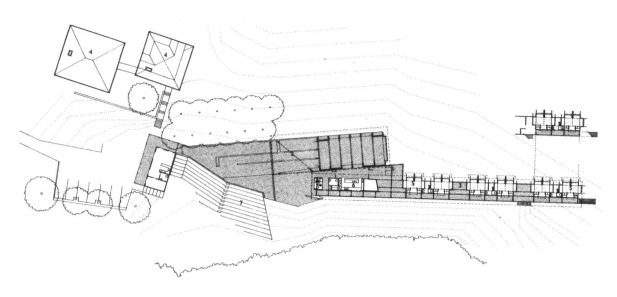

Left
Ground plan showing the building as a linear sequence starting with an older group of timber and stone cottages, and continuing with the communal spaces of the new building and then the dormitories at the south end.

Key
1   Main hall
2   Veranda
3   Dormitory block
4   Existing studios
5   Bedrooms
6   Kitchen
7   Steps up to veranda

Opposite
The accommodation is given a Spartan feel by the exposed concrete, and simple corrugated metal roofing (commonly used by Murcutt) evokes rural agricultural buildings.

Below left
Looking from the south, white fins protrude from the concrete façade and bounce morning light into the dormitories.

the native bush behind it and cultivated farmland rolling down to the river in front.

The accommodation is in a linear arrangement, with the entrance at the north end, and the building is only gradually revealed to the visitor. Arriving at an existing group of timber and stone cottages, visitors cross a large terrace paved with mushroom-coloured bricks set into a concrete plinth. This warm-toned surface unites the different areas of the building, running from the outside into the hall and along the corridor to the dormitories. At the south end, the building tapers off as the hill falls away, and the lowest step of a concrete staircase touches the ground as if it were a drawbridge.

This was the first time that Murcutt had used in-situ, or off-form, concrete. It was a practical necessity due to the need for fire walls to separate the rooms, but it also suited the site, hugging the ground as it rises from the river and giving the building a Spartan quality in keeping with the basic level of accommodation provided. Always keen to minimize disturbance to the landscape, Murcutt set the concrete foundations on piers in order not to disrupt the flow of groundwater. Waste water and sewage are recycled and rainwater is collected and stored in an underground concrete tank.

The corrugated-iron roof, characteristic of Murcutt's houses, simply rests on a series of timber beams and is exposed internally as if it were an agricultural shed. Between the thinness of the roof and the solid base of concrete is timber, also used for the doors, floors, bed supports and windows, and most of which is recycled.

Above
East elevation showing how the building adapts itself to the landscape rather than disturbing the natural shape of the hill.

Opposite
In the dormitories the scale and materials are more intimate. Beds closest to the window cantilever beyond the façade and timber casements frame the view.

Left
The roof slopes in two directions and rainwater is channelled into a steel downpipe.

The brief specified that the residents were to rise early, so Murcutt devised a way of bouncing morning light into each bedroom by means of white 'fins', which jut out from the façade. The fins break down the scale of the exterior and double as housings for the large sliding doors that subdivide the rooms.

Inside, the building frames a series of views. 'Just as a painter would frame a scene, so we have organized the building to look at different parts of the landscape', says Murcutt.[1] The largest 'frame' is the soaring roof at the north end, which covers the hall and an open terrace. Sloping in two directions, the roof funnels the prevailing north-easterly breezes up into the open-ended corrugated iron. In the dormitories the framing is on a more intimate scale. Bedboxes are cantilevered beyond the edge of the building and each one has a view framed by a composite window consisting of a fixed panel of glass below a timber screen that can be opened. 'We kept breaking down the scale into smaller elements,' says Murcutt, 'using screens to break down light levels and vistas.'[2]

Kamiichi Mountain Pavilion

Year of completion
1994

Location
Toyama, Japan

Architect
Peter Salter

Situated on a rocky spur at the edge of a meltwater river 2,500 metres (8,200 feet) up in the northern Japanese Alps, the Kamiichi Mountain Pavilion is visited more often by birds than by walkers, who occasionally pause to admire the scenery.

Peter Salter received the commission from the Toyama Prefecture after building a folly for the Osaka Expo of 1990. He was paired with a local firm to design a small structure in the national park of Mount Tsurugi. Unlike the Osaka folly, which was supposed to last only as long as the Expo, the Kamiichi Mountain Pavilion is as permanent as the harsh mountain climate will allow. Viewed from a path that follows the river's edge, the building seems at first to be part of the man-made infrastructure of the river: it sits on a concrete base resembling the weirs that control the flow of water down the valley; this prevents it from being washed away in the spring when boulders and branches crash down with the meltwater.

Above is a timber structure protected by two timber-latticed compression shells clad in dark copper tiles. Originally Salter wanted to clad the pavilion in corten steel so that streaks of rust would stain the concrete base over time. 'The idea of walking into a building that is undergoing a process of corrosion is very exciting,' he says.[1] But, as the local architect pointed out, since the building is covered in snow for half the year, the steel would have been unable to form its protective coat of rust. Copper tiles, however, patinate in their own way, turning from bright metallic to dark brown in just a few years.

For Salter, who is now head of the University of East London School of Architecture, the pavilion was an opportunity to put into practice the ideas he had developed while teaching at the Architectural Association (AA) in London during the 1980s. The project is one of just three built projects by Salter, although he has a large body of unbuilt competition projects, all of which explore the overt physicality of buildings, how they are built and the life process of the materials.

Before teaching at the AA, Salter had worked for some years with the British architect Peter Smithson, who used to tell him, 'Don't go and see a building till it's 12 years old.' Salter believes that the fact that buildings change over time links them to the landscape and makes them subject to geological processes similar to land erosion and deposition.

With its concrete base and patinated cover, the Kamiichi pavilion is firmly anchored in the ground. But it has an internal landscape that is quite different. ('It's important to have an inside and outside,' says Salter.) Visitors enter beneath a large gutter, which brings water into the building and acts as a sun canopy in the summer. The darkness of the interior focuses attention on the views down the valley and, from a second room above, up to the mountain peaks.

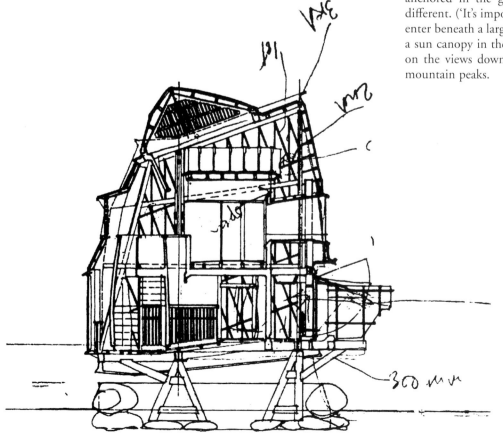

Left
Long section through the pavilion showing its timber structure and base of concrete and boulders.

Right
The pavilion is
protected by shells
covered in copper
tiles and is almost
entirely buried in
snow for several
months of the year.

Right
Plan of the pavilion
showing its snug
position within
the contours of the
hillside.

Opposite
North elevation with
the building perching
on the side of a
concrete weir.

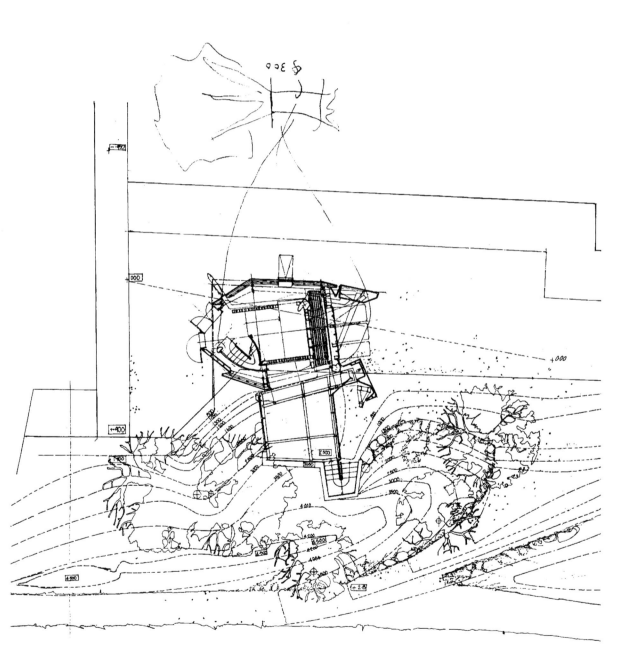

The building has no electricity or power of any kind. The only creature comfort provided is water from a hand pump. On the inside face of the shell-form walls the timber structure is revealed, and the sides of the staircase are made from traditional bamboo lattice screens. Each October, the river path becomes impassable, and for the following seven months the pavilion is boarded up and covered in snow. Since it is effectively submerged in frozen water, it seemed appropriate for the building to have a boat-like quality. The upturned boat is a favourite device of Salter's ('Boats are protective and carry everything you need,' he says). Here it is both functional, its shape resisting the snow, and symbolic, recalling the shape of the upturned hull of a curragh.[2]

Design decisions, such as the shape of the roof and the method of construction, were taken in discussion with the local Japanese architect, who had grown up in the national park and was familiar with the climate. He was also able to introduce Salter to local carpenters, who built the timber frame on site using Japanese tea-house techniques. The rest of the building was put together during the winter months in a large garage in Kamiichi using a mixture of traditional and modern materials.

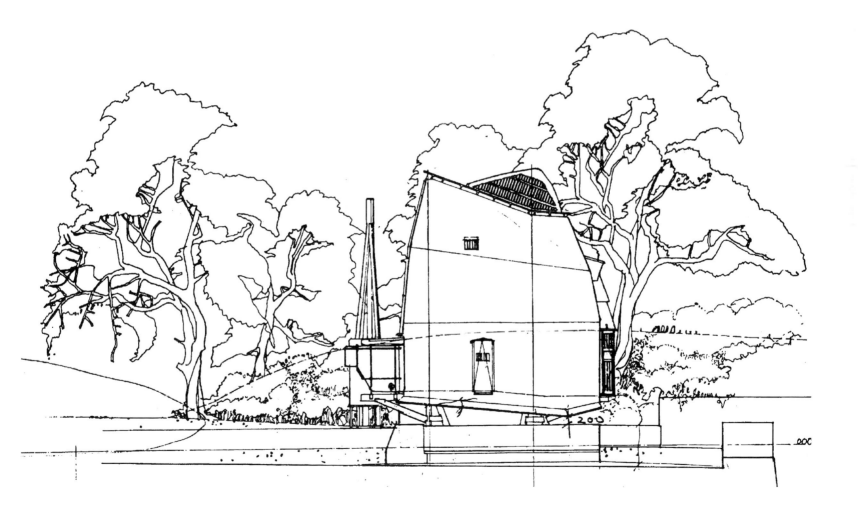

Right
Salter likes to build
with materials such
as these copper tiles
that change their
character with the
process of ageing
and weathering.

Below
South elevation
showing a gutter that
collects water, which
is fed into a tank near
to the entrance.

Opposite
A view of the entrance
and a panoramic
window above with the
copper water tank and
three overflow pipes,
which 'celebrate' the
gushing melted snow
in the spring.

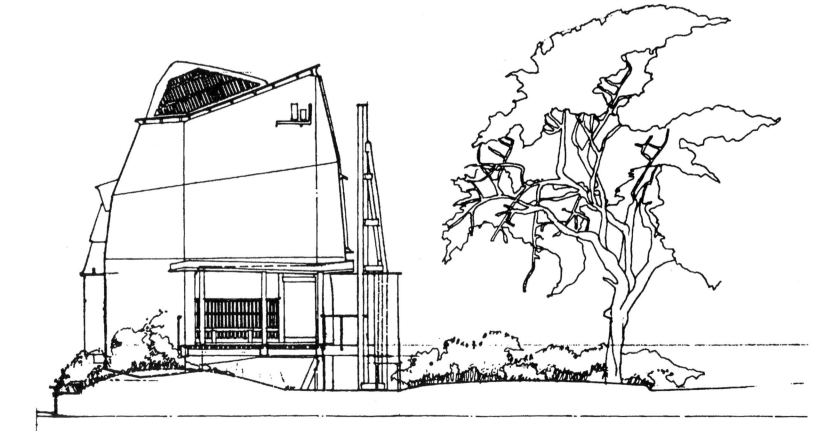

Year of completion
1997

Location
Phoenix, Arizona, USA

Architect
Antoine Predock

The Arizona Science Center is a like a small piece of the desert transported to downtown Phoenix. Practising from a remote studio in Albuquerque, New Mexico, Antoine Predock has for many years been fascinated by the relationship between architecture and the land. With not much in the way of history to inspire him in the city of Phoenix, he decided to treat the site as if it were outside the city and part of the landscape of peaks, valleys and canyons in the Sonoran Desert. 'I hate what is offered here. It's either a stylistic rehash or a denial of the desert,' he says, referring to Phoenix's kitsch 'cowboy movie' imagery or glass office blocks that could be anywhere.[1] 'There is still an absolute authority of the desert.'

Situated on a busy downtown road and bordered by warehouses, residential buildings and a convention centre, the Science Center is an enigmatic collection of monolithic concrete forms. Predock wanted to avoid institutional references in what is primarily a building for children. Instead he aimed for the 'power engendered by place'.

Although it was not inspired by the city, the building was designed as an integral part of the urban landscape. The spaces between the buildings are open 24 hours a day to passers-by, who can participate in the building even if they do not actually enter the museum itself. This permeable zone forms a new route through the city, with terraces, views and sheltered places to sit that belong as much to the nearby park as they do to the Science Center.

The building's function gave Predock a chance to experiment with his interest in dramatic use of light. Providing 3,000 square metres (32,000 square feet) of exhibition space, the main internal rooms are black boxes – a

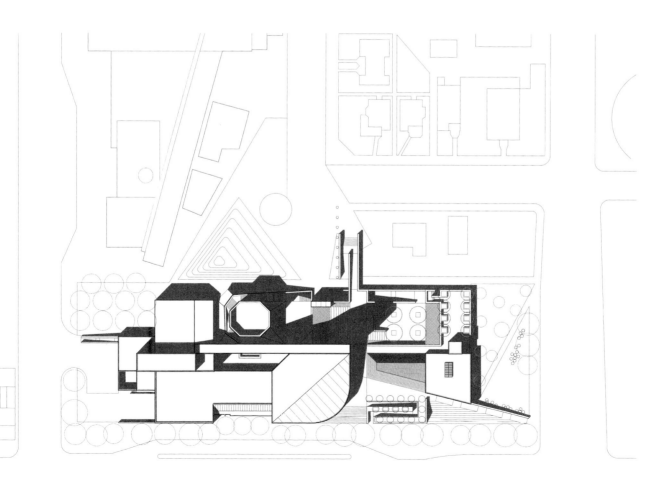

Opposite
Site plan showing
the location on a
busy downtown
street bordered by
warehouses, houses
a convention centre
and a public park.

Right
A flight of stairs,
curved around the
wall of the cinema,
leads from the street
level to the entrance.

Below
From above the
Arizona Science
Center is a series of
sculptural solids
formed from con-
crete.

Bottom
Section showing the
planetarium with sky-
viewing platform
above. Much of the
accommodation is
below ground level
to take advantage of
natural cooling.

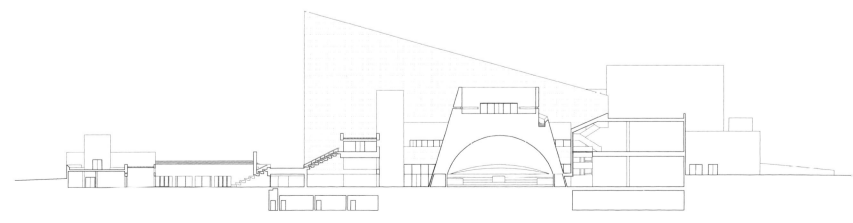

Above
Certain light effects give
the building the surreal
ambience of the desert,
with the aluminium-
clad, wedge-shaped
gallery appearing
almost like a mirage.

Opposite
Sunken courts provide
shade with dramatic
shafts of light being
admitted in places.

planetarium, a large-screen cinema and a theatre – enclosed by windowless volumes cast in reinforced concrete.

Predock develops his ideas by making clay models, which allow the building's form to emerge as if it were an extension of the ground. For the Science Center, he made a model in which the shapes created strong silhouettes against the southern sky. 'When people come to the desert they are amazed by the intensity and physicality,' says Predock. The Science Center provokes a similar emotional response; visitors are directed to enter from the north, where they are overwhelmed by the power of the building against the brightness of the sky.

Like a jagged rock, a wedge-shaped 'celestial gallery' clad in aluminium towers above the rough-textured concrete. Its appearance changing with the light, this metallic blade was inspired by desert mirages. In certain light conditions, the aluminium blade is invisible, while at other times, with the light coming from behind, the volumes become a series of abstract silhouettes. Eventually the celestial gallery will house an exhibition about the cosmos, but for now it serves as a lighting mast, with a door that pivots a bank of lighting, sending beams onto the plaza below.

From the street, the visitor climbs a flight of steps that follows the curved wall of the cinema to reach a platform from which the main elements of the building rise. No longer clear where ground is, the visitor descends into the earth through a covered entrance passageway. By rooting the building in the ground, Predock takes advantage of the sense of protection and the thermal stability and cooling it offers. He also emphasizes the difference between inside and out, and selectively provides light and shadows in semi-external spaces such as an internal canyon that forms an exhibit terrace. This reflects what he describes as 'the duality of sun and shadow that applies to desert realms'.

After being led on a mysterious journey through the building, the visitor finally emerges into a gallery above the planetarium with an irregular-shaped aperture open to the sky and a horizontal-strip window, which frames views of the city. Here, apparently, children like to camp out with sleeping bags and gaze at the starry night sky – the real version of the artificial sky projected on the dome of the planetarium below. The horizontal window creates the impression that the upper part of the planetarium is floating – a reminder of the effect of mirages on the desert horizon.

Opposite and right
The dome of the planetarium with a projected view of the stars...and the real thing – an irregular-shaped aperture opens the gallery above to the sky.

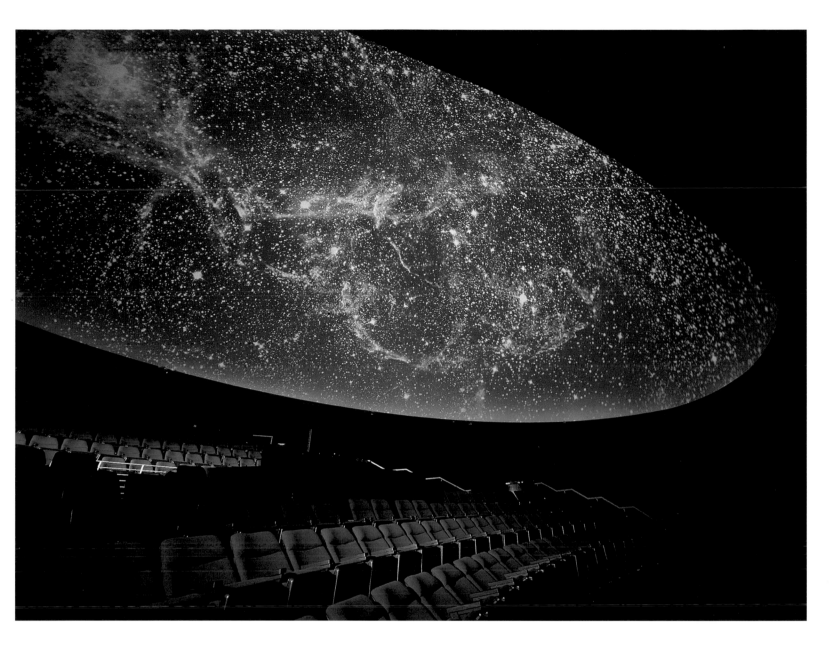

Year of completion
1997

Location
Shigaraki Hills, Japan

Architect
I M Pei

The design of the Miho Museum, Japan, echoes a favourite theme in Chinese literature: a difficult journey is a preparation for enlightenment. The journey in this case begins with an hour-long drive into the Shigaraki Hills from Kyoto. The visitor enters a 200 metre (650 foot) tunnel cut through the rock, along a path lined with spring-blossoming trees, and travels onward by foot or silent electric car. As the light at the end of the tunnel gets brighter, reflected on stainless-steel-clad walls, a stunning panorama of mountains and forests opens up. The last leg of the journey is the most dramatic: a 120 metre (400 foot) cable-stayed bridge over a deep gully, which leads finally to the temple-like ceremonial steps that go up to the entrance of the museum.

The journey is closely related to a 4th-century Chinese story, 'Peach Blossom Spring' by Tao Yuan Ming, in which a fisherman follows the course of a fragrant peach grove into a cave that opens on to a secret world of peace and harmony. For I M Pei, the tale offered a poetic solution to the practical problem of how to approach a site as inaccessible as a hilltop peninsula surrounded on three sides by a densely forested nature reserve. Tunnelling under the hill and bridging the valley was an expensive proposition, but nevertheless appealed to the client because of the sense of seclusion it would offer to the museum.

The museum's collection is a vast treasure trove built up over the years by Mihoko Koyama, the leader of the Japanese religious order Shinji Shumeikai. Traditional Japanese tea ceremony objects were the first to be collected in the 1950s. By the 1980s Koyama's collection had grown to include ancient Egyptian, Greco-Roman, Islamic, ancient West Asian and East Asian art.

Having completed an international review of world architecture in the late 1980s, Koyama and her daughter Hiroko Koyama decided that Pei would be the most suitable architect for what they had in mind. They first invited him to design the carillon bell tower at the Shumeikai headquarters a kilometre (two-thirds of a mile) west of the museum site.

Left
80 per cent of the museum is hidden beneath the earth so that it is assimilated into the landscape of the Shigaraki Hills.

Opposite top
The ceremonial steps leading up to the entrance door evoke the approach to a traditional Japanese temple.

Opposite bottom
Drawing of the museum within its protected forest environment showing the entrance via a tunnel and a bridge.

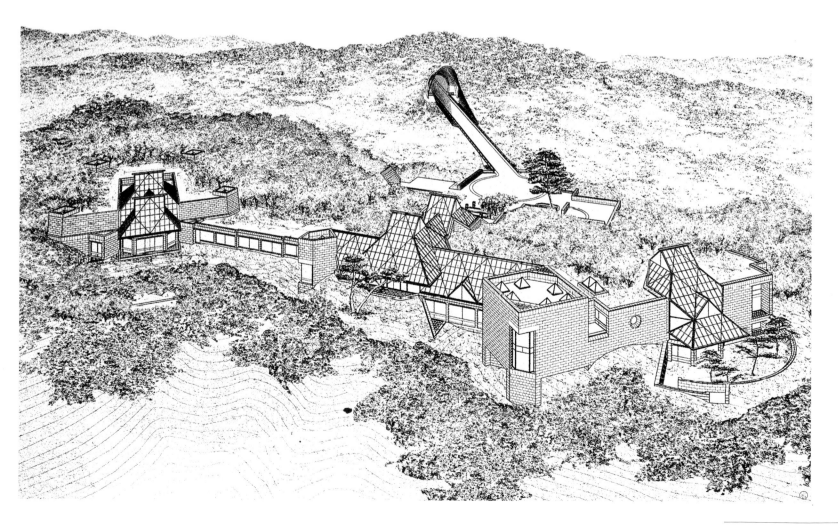

Pei's architecture is characterized by bold geometric forms – think of the Pyramid at the Paris Louvre or the Bank of China in Hong Kong – but at the Miho the geometry is tempered by concern for the natural surroundings. A national preservation code limited the visible roof area to 2,000 square metres (22,000 square feet), which meant that more than 80 per cent of the building had to be buried in the ground. However, this suited the remoteness of the museum and enabled Pei literally to merge the building with the landscape.

Inside, the journey continues across a sequence of paved terraces leading to the museum's main internal public space. The museum reveals itself by degrees as one passes from room to room, many of which have been specially designed for the exhibits.

From the outside, the building is visible only as a series of tetrahedral glass roofs sitting on French limestone walls, neither of which rise higher than 13 metres (43 feet) above the ground. While landscape and building are integrated as far as possible, the building does not mimic nature. The aim was to create an equilibrium between art and nature in the same way that

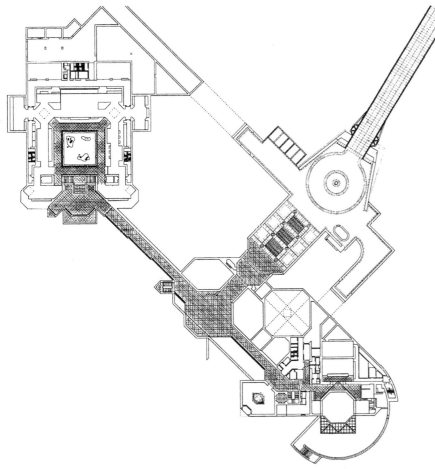

Above
Looking through the
tunnel to the arch
of the bridge, which
is supported by
tensioned steel
cables.

Opposite
The museum is only
accessible by
following a tunnel,
which emerges onto
a cable-stayed bridge
across a deep valley.

Left
Plan of the museum
showing a series of
galleries connected
by paved terraces
and light-filled halls.

traditional Japanese and Chinese landscape design explores the relationship between the artificial and the natural.

There is also a carefully created balance between traditional forms and new technology. The profile of the glass skylights is an abstracted version of the surrounding hills but also echoes the profile of thatched Irimoya roofs, which are common in this region. Japanese temples are recalled in the large cantilever of the space frame and the steps leading up to the entrance.

Within the steel space frame, a sunscreen made from metal tubes and etched with digitized images of the texture and grain of timber acknowledges timber's use as a traditional building material in Japanese architecture – real timber could not be used because of technical difficulties.

It would be wrong to suggest that Pei's interest in tradition is limited to particular symbolic forms. In common with many of the new vernacular architects, he is more interested in traditional builders' sensitivity to context, which he feels is being lost in contemporary Japanese architecture. 'If you look at all the ways Japanese temples were built in the landscape... you somehow find a harmony between their silhouette and the hills,' he says. 'I do not want to abandon that but to learn from it.'[1]

Right
The profile of the glass roofs is an abstracted version of the surrounding hills, and the space frame echoes the hipped shape of thatched Irimoya roofs, specific to this region.

Opposite
Sunscreens etched with digitized textures of the grain of wood acknowledge the traditional building material, although timber could not actually be used for fire safety reasons.

Year of completion
2000

Location
Orsta, Norway

Architect
Sverre Fehn

Apart from a few linguists and historians, the name Ivar Aasen is unlikely to be familiar to anyone outside Norway. But in his homeland, Aasen – a 19th-century poet and linguist – is as historically significant as Robert Burns is to the Scots or James Joyce to the Irish. Sverre Fehn, the architect of a government-financed museum dedicated to Aasen, is a similarly enigmatic figure abroad, even though a fine body of work dating back to the 1950s (mostly in Norway, Sweden and Denmark) makes him arguably one of the greatest Scandinavian architects.

The Center was in many ways the perfect commission for Fehn because he has used the work of Aasen as a philosophical framework for his architecture, through which he has consistently explored the relationship between Modernism and the character of the Norwegian landscape.

Born in 1813 in the village of Orsta in west Norway, Aasen rose to fame by single-handedly devising the grammar for a new national language – Nyorsk, or New Norwegian – to replace Dano-Norwegian. In linguistic terms his work was comparable with that of the romantic nationalists, emphasizing the virtues of rural life and 'rootedness' against the perceived affectations of *bok-mal*, the official language imposed when Norway was a mere province of Denmark. Today, New Norwegian is an official language and is used in about 25 per cent of national television and radio broadcasts, but more than 100 years after it was adopted it still symbolizes a counterculture of resistance.

The Center is located near the farm where Aasen was born and where his descendants live to this day. The surrounding landscape of steep hills and valleys that inspired his romantic poetry in turn became the guiding principle for Fehn's design. According to Fehn, each valley in Norway forms a kind of 'room', with its own dialect and vernacular buildings. The importance Fehn attaches to the Norwegian topography even stretches to a belief that a different terrain gives rise to different character traits in the people living there. 'I have built in a flat landscape,' he says, 'and there they are very calm. Here in Orsta they are very lively.'

Fehn believes that vernacular buildings have a timeless quality, which is reproduced by the best examples of modern architecture. 'The [primitive]

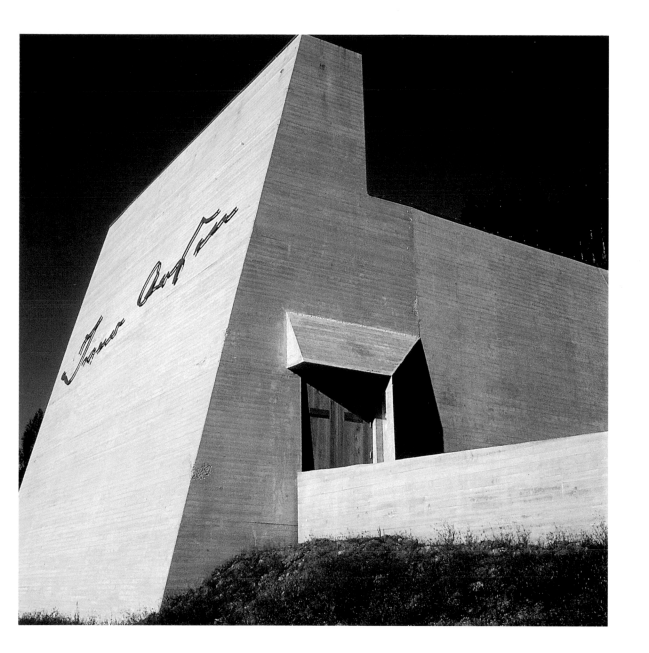

Opposite left
The Ivar Aasen Center, dedicated to a Norwegian literary hero, is near the village of Orsta in west Norway.

Opposite right
Both levels consisting of exhibition space above and a linguistic institute below, have south-east-facing glass façades to take advantage of natural light.

Left
The dynamic form of the auditorium echoes the terrain of steeply sloping hills.

Below
Site plan with contour lines showing the building's dramatic hillside setting and a dense forest behind.

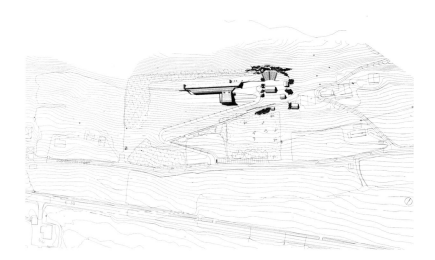

Opposite top
Basement plan show-
ing the rooms of the
linguistic institute,
which is buried into
the ground.

*Opposite middle
and bottom*
A curved white con-
crete wall continues
from the inside out
and bounces light
into the café.

Below
Ground floor plan
with display walls in
the exhibition space
in the shape of Vs –
like open books.

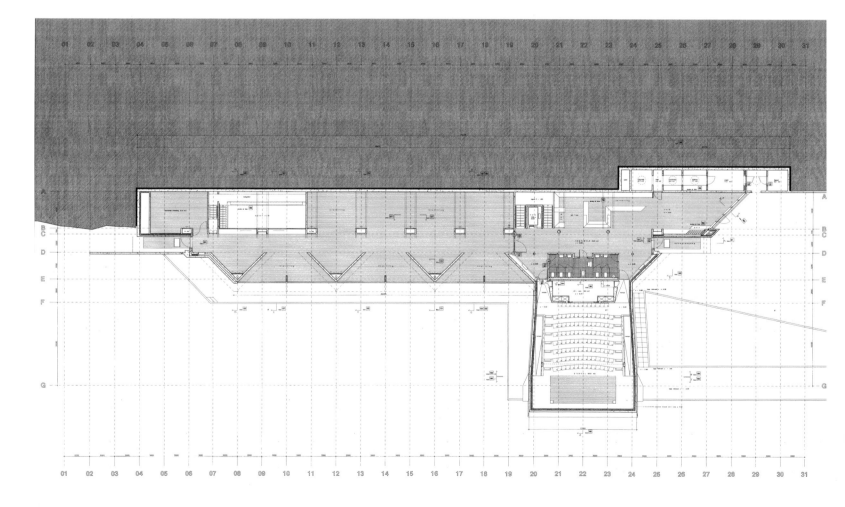

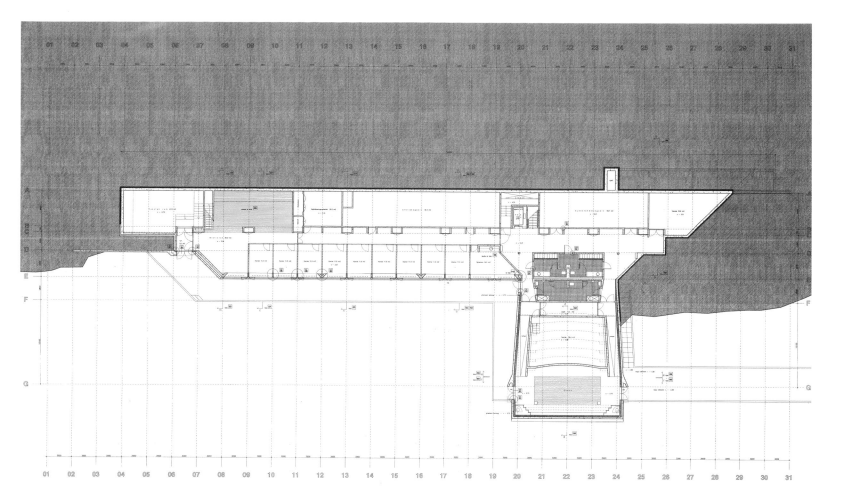

architecture works perfectly because it exists in a timeless space. Its signature is anonymous, for it is nature itself.' The museum attempts a new interpretation of this timelessness by responding to the context and site. Strung out along the contour of a steep hill, it looks almost like a piece of civil engineering, with raw concrete walls slanting in opposite directions, as if to emphasize its precarious position. Unlike the work of other architects inspired by the landscape – for example, the Australian regionalist Glenn Murcutt, whose buildings make a minimal intervention on the site – the museum is described by Fehn as 'fighting with the hill'. 'In a way it is in a battle with the landscape,' he says. 'At the back it is buried into the hill like a cave and at the front it opens up to the view.'

The main structure is white concrete, which carries the print of its timber shuttering 'as a kind of dialogue with old Norwegian architecture'. The building's form exploits the plasticity of concrete to the full – there are very few vertical walls and the core structure is internalized. These V-shaped cores reflect the museum's literary purpose and provide an organizational strategy for the space. Five Vs stand like the open pages of a book, propping the building up against the hill and providing exhibition space away from direct sunlight for displaying Aasen's manuscripts and personal possessions. On the reverse side of the 'open-book' walls, large areas of glazing give a vantage-point for appreciating the same view that once inspired Aasen's poems about the landscape. At one end of the linear plan an auditorium is positioned at the point of two Vs with its slanting concrete walls providing a compositional balance to the Center's glass façade. At the back, the museum building digs into the hill like a cave, and below the galleries is an institute for linguists studying Norway's languages.

Opposite left
The back of the museum is dug into the hillside and the curved wall appears to grow out of the landscape.

Opposite right
There are few vertical walls in the building, exploiting the plastic nature of concrete to the full.

Above left
The white concrete is imprinted with timber shuttering, reminiscent of local vernacular structures.

Left
Views of the landscape are an important part of the building because this was the original inspiration for Ivar Aasen writing in the 19th century.

Year of completion
1998

Location
Caminha, Portugal

Architect
Souto Moura
Architects

Eduardo Souto de Moura's 'exploded' axonometric of the Moledo House is more than just a technical drawing. It explains his idea of the house as a man-made concrete box and floating roof plane that have 'fallen from the sky' into place. Souto de Moura wanted the house to take maximum advantage of its dramatic view west over the Atlantic Ocean, without being obvious in the landscape.

In contrast with south and central Portugal, the region that includes the town of Caminha is hilly and occupied by subsistence farmers. Drystone retaining walls built from large irregular blocks of granite more than 200 years ago create the terraces that cover the hillsides; their purpose is to prevent soil erosion and allow the farmers to use every available slice of land.

As with Souto de Moura's previous work, which dates back to 1977, when he first established his practice in Oporto, the house has minimal impact on the landscape. 'I believe the greatest aspiration of an architect is to be anonymous, [to create] space that possesses the wisdom accumulated over thousands of years,' he says.[1]

But Souto de Moura is not cautious about making radical alterations to the landscape, even if the result is modest. Ironically, his intervention in Caminha makes the terrace walls appear almost to be modern rather than vernacular. Another reading is that the house has been inserted behind the old wall without changing a thing. In fact, the changes to the landscape were significant and actually cost more than the house itself. Owing to the complexity of the work and the loss of a building contractor, the house took seven years from design to completion.

Right
Emerging from a rocky hillside, the smooth concrete roof is a distinct man-made element in a natural landscape.

Opposite top
Section showing how the house is hidden behind a stone wall that continues the terracing of the hillside.

Opposite bottom
The hillside had to be recontoured to accommodate the house, but the stone was saved and replaced so that it would look almost as it did before. All that can be seen of the house from this angle is the glass façade.

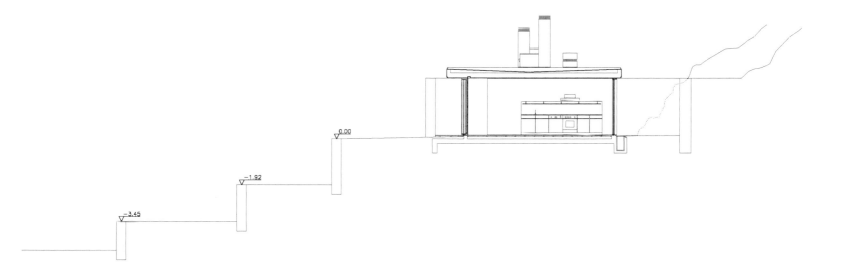

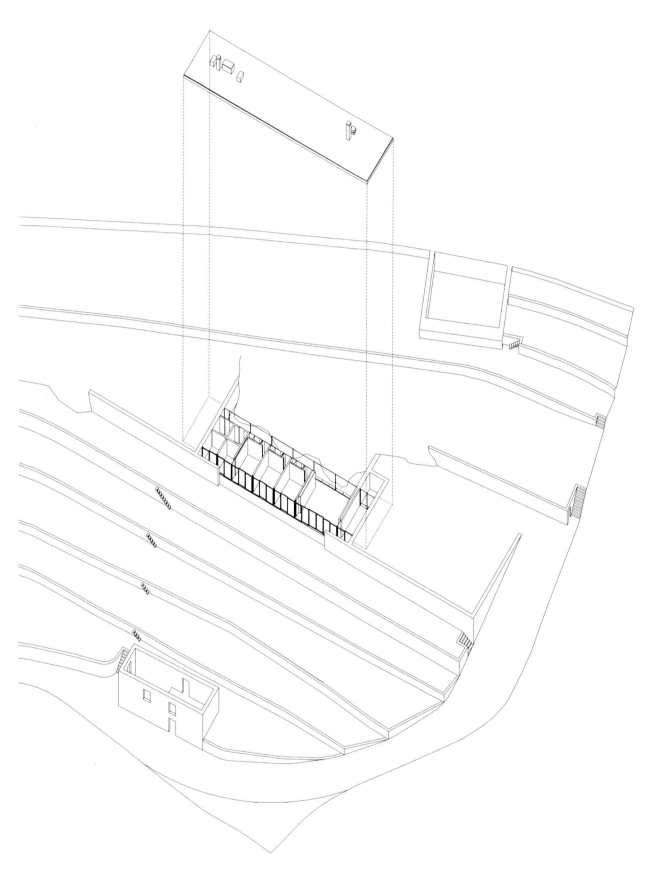

Left
Axonometric
showing how the
accommodation fits
neatly between the
stone retaining wall
and the rocks.

Opposite
At the back of the
house a glass wall
reveals the raw edge
of the hillside and
allows light into
the corridor.

The major task was to take down one of the terraces in order to make a wide enough ledge to accommodate the house. Before construction work started, the position of every stone was recorded in drawings and photographs, so that the wall could be rebuilt just as it was, using the traditional drystone-walling technique. At the front of the house an all-glass façade, which gives each room a seaview, emerges from a gap in the reconstructed retaining wall. Trees and creepers will eventually soften the impact of the glass, and moss will cover the smooth slabs of granite that have been used to form a platform outside the living room. The remaining original stones were used to create two side walls, with concrete behind, which are embedded in the rocky hillside and support the concrete roof slab. A timber deck made from dark hardwood forms a buffer zone between inside and out, sheltered by the roof and wrapped around at each end by the stone wall.

Inside, the planning is simple: the long rectangular space is divided by parallel cross walls into a living room, a kitchen and three bedrooms, with bathrooms and utility rooms located at the north end, concealed by the granite wall at the front. At the back of the house a long corridor runs alongside the glass, with the rocks emerging from the ground just behind, giving the impression of a cave. The kitchen is separated from the living room by a concrete cavity wall wide enough to accommodate a small hearth and fireplace, which pops up above the roof in a shiny aluminium chimney – one of six geometric objects sitting on the roof to conceal air vents and water tanks.

Like the house itself, the entrance is almost invisible, in keeping with the sense of seclusion that the client wanted to achieve. A steep road climbs the hill to the south of the terraced slope, leading to a flat area on the same level as the roof plane. Visitors have to walk back down the hill to a flight of stone steps, which leads to a paved pathway running along the terrace. The way into the house is through a sliding timber-framed glass door resembling the other glass panels in the front façade. This is not a house that welcomes unexpected visitors.

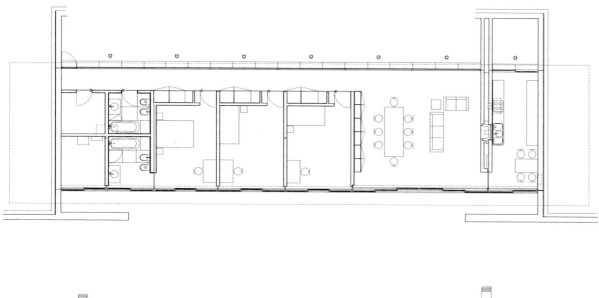

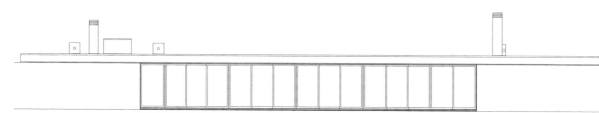

Left
Roof plan, ground plan and front elevation; respectively, they show the industrial minimalism of the chimneys, the modernist layout and the simple glass façade that emerges from behind the wall.

Opposite top
Slabs of smooth stone form a terrace and are the only indicators of the entrance to the house.

Opposite left
A glass façade takes advantage of the sea view to the west. A timber deck between the glass and the inner face of the stone wall acts as an intermediary zone.

Opposite bottom
The retaining walls were built to form terraces for growing crops at least 200 years ago using a drystone-walling technique.

Villa S

Year of completion
1998

Location
Grenoble, France

Architect
Herault-Arnod
Architects

'The story of a house is always the story of a situation,' say architects Isabel Herault and Yves Arnod, who set up their Grenoble office in 1990. At Villa S the situation in question consisted of two main components: a wonderful but challenging site and an ambitious client. Set on a steeply sloping hillside wooded with cedar trees, and with superb views over the valley of Grenoble and the Belledonne and Vercors mountains, the site already had a sense of drama. The client, who had requested a 'James Bond-type house', wanted to add more. A young businessman with a family, he was looking for a house that would provide him with a swimming pool, terrace and large bay windows, suitable for entertaining guests as much as for quiet meditation.

The site presented challenges other than its topography. In a wealthy area surrounded by large 1960s houses, the villa was subject to two sets of planning restrictions: those of the estate, which were not particularly burdensome, and the national land-use planning regulations, which caused a few more problems. The latter were the result of what the architects describe as a 'fever of standardization' that has resulted in regulations concerning the aesthetic appearance of buildings with the object of controlling a regional style. In this case, the restrictions had led to the paradoxical situation where the planners were trying to impose a neo-traditional architecture of coloured render and pitched roofs while the 1960s houses on the estate reflected the diversity of postwar freedom.

Refusing to toe the line, Herault and Arnod geared up for a battle with the planners with the full support of their pioneering client. Eventually they managed to escape the 'straitjacket of the regulations', after a process of education, meetings and presenting architectural references to local elected representatives.

Despite rejecting legislative controls on regional aesthetics, Herault and Arnod base their ideas and designs on pre-existing circumstances. 'Do not force, but reveal the strengths and specific nature of places,' is how they describe their approach. The Villa S derives its plan from the contours of the hill. Its three levels follow three successive strata that fan out towards the countryside and the view south-west over Grenoble.

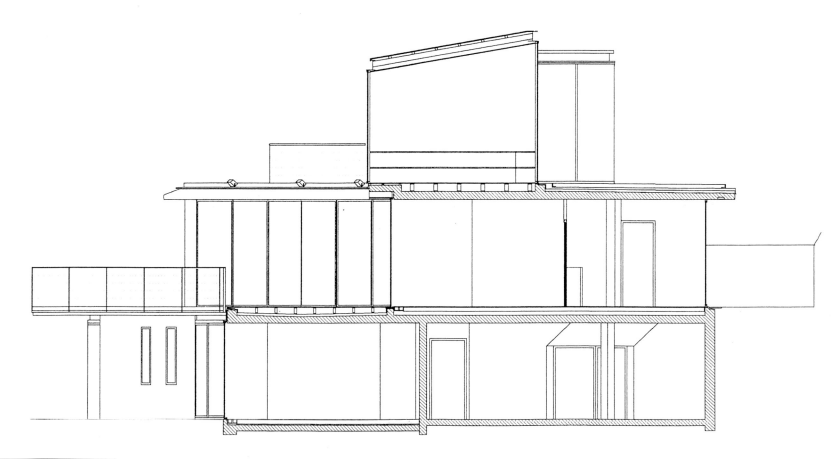

Opposite
Cross-section of the house showing how the three levels are stacked unevenly to create terraces and canopies.

Above
The cantilever of the second floor creates a carport, while the roof above becomes an outdoor terrace.

Left
An outdoor pool gives the impression of swimming amongst the trees.

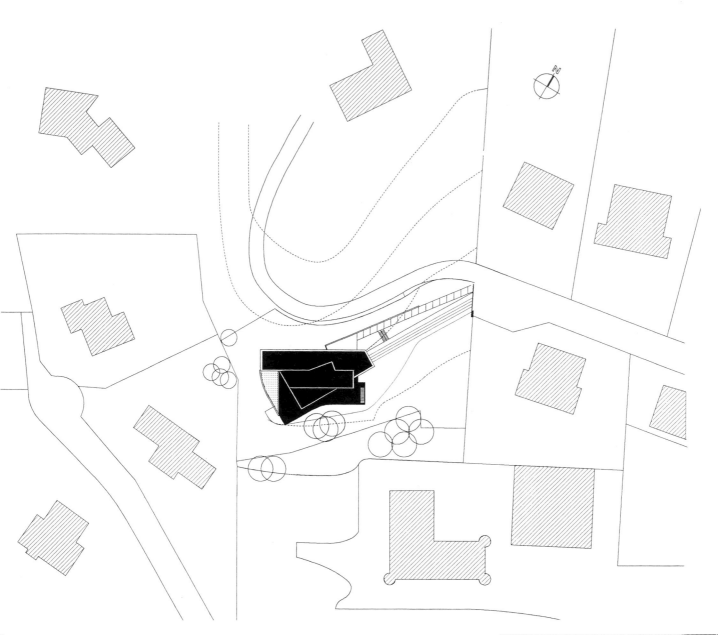

Above
Site plan showing the surrounding estate of 1960s private houses and the setting amongst the trees.

Right
Each floor takes its position from existing trees on the site and from the view south-west towards Grenoble.

Opposite top
The double-height living space has a mezzanine library.

Opposite bottom
The pool extends inside with the inner part being closed off by a sluice gate in winter.

The organization of each floor depends on the position of the trees, the view and the accommodation. The rooms are conventionally proportioned but open on to irregular-shaped canopies and terraces created from the cantilevers and exposed areas of flat roof that resulted from stacking the floors unevenly.

The ground floor contains the bedrooms, bathrooms and a garage dug into the hillside. The inward-tilting plan is largely determined by the layout of trees, so that the rooms which have floor-to-ceiling glazing benefit from a sense of proximity to nature. At the back of the house the forms are opaque – the ground floor is clad in stone blocks, the first floor in concrete with a ruled finish, and the north façade of the second floor and roof in verdigris copper. The overhanging end wall of the first floor forms a car port, while the main entrance is at first-floor level – a gate on the north side of the site opens on to a ramp leading to the front door and on to the living rooms, kitchen and swimming pool beyond.

The pool – the ultimate 'James Bond' idea – is both inside and outside, the inner part being closed off by a sluice gate in winter. With the water lapping right against the curved edge of the wall, the pool gives the feeling of swimming among the trees. In summer the large open-plan living room opens onto an expansive terrace (the roof of the floor below), which extends upwards to a mezzanine, with a library perched in the trees.

5

Civic Architecture and the Vernacular

What could a vast shopping centre in south-east England possibly have in common with a small school in rural India? These two buildings (see pages 182 and 192) exist at opposite ends of the social spectrum – one is the product of millions of pounds of private investment and caters for affluent Europeans, while the other is built with funds scraped together from aid agencies and provides the most basic level of primary education. But a closer look reveals ideas about the role of architecture in society that are common to both the developed and so-called developing world. These, and the other buildings in this chapter, adhere to the idea that the vernacular enhances a feeling of community and belonging by appealing directly to people's experience of place, as well as assisting in the regeneration and sustenance of local economies.

While architects of the Modern movement tended to have a transformative approach to society, the architects discussed here are generally concerned with preserving the status quo – even sometimes returning to past models. Embracing technological and social change is less of a priority for them than preserving the character and social traditions of a place. According to its architect Eric Kuhne, even Bluewater shopping centre – very much a late 20th-century phenomenon – is based on the medieval market town, where people came together as individuals to engage in commerce.

Both the Turkapally Primary School and the Swiss village of Vrin (see page 196) have used architecture as a means to preserve archaic social arrangements. In each case the architect has cast himself in the role of social

worker as well as designer, taking into account the effects of the building and the building process itself on the community. In Turkapally, P K and Peu Banerjee Das, architects from New Delhi, proposed traditional building techniques in order to train local people as bricklayers and maintain the prosperity of the village. The UK's Department for International Development, which funded the school, favours this approach. It also adheres to the policy of sustainable architecture put forward by the United Nations Conference on Human Settlements (often know as Habitat).

Sustainable architecture has its origins in the work of the Egyptian architect Hassan Fathy, a key influence on the work of P K and Peu Banerjee Das. In his book *Architecture for the Poor*, Fathy puts forward the argument that the world's poor would be best housed using materials they have immediately to hand.[1] Fathy first rediscovered traditional Egyptian mud-brick techniques in the 1930s. At that time it was virtually impossible to find labourers skilled at building traditional formless brick vaults, but Fathy assembled his own team of masons and began to establish a reputation for low-cost housing. In 1945 he started work on his most famous project, the village of Gourna near Thebes, where 7,000 peasants needed rehousing. The project failed because of bureaucratic red tape and his ideas remained on the fringes of architecture until recently, when they became a key influence on the policies of Western non-governmental organizations towards the developing world.

At Turkapally a Fathy-inspired approach was a means to deal with two problems: the shortage of jobs and the need for a new building. Here the building process itself became a kind of welfare for local people, and consequently the traditional, labour-intensive technologies were favoured. 'Extremely labour-intensive methods, such as traditional and modified earth construction, can be particularly helpful for job creation locally and for unskilled people,' says Graham Tipple, director of the UK Centre for Architectural Research and Development Overseas.[2] But Tipple also points out a dilemma: 'It can be argued that, if local development is achieved through keeping low-paid workers low-paid, this is exploitative.' One remedy is to promote 'skill-enhancing activities and on-the-job training' (as was provided at Turkapally). The danger remains, however, that villages such as Turkapally, which have no choice but to accept Western aid to finance local buildings, are thereby tied to a philosophy aimed at preserving the status quo, rather than finding a permanent way out of poverty.

Intensive labour also had its benefits in the Swiss village of Vrin, where local people were employed to construct new buildings as a means of gaining their support for the project and to keep wealth in the village. Architect and planner Gion A Caminada, who grew up in Vrin, sits on the local council and helps to determine the course of development – a role that links architecture with the economic processes of the village. Around half of the 280 inhabitants make their living from agriculture, and tourism – which dominates the region – has scarcely made an impact. But, although Caminada's buildings respect the existing fabric of the village, he is open to the possibility of change: 'For me an appropriate architecture is one that adjusts to normality, one that seeks to respect the needs of its time.'[3] As a consequence, his buildings are free from many of the nostalgic references of the other projects discussed here.

For Daniel Solomon, architect of Britton Courts, a housing project in a run-down neighbourhood of San Francisco (see page 188), being true to the time is far less important than being true to the place. 'Unlike the 19th century, nothing is threatening change, but the quality of places is very much at issue,' he says. Britton Courts, which replaced two demolished 20-storey housing blocks, is symbolic of a return to the urban grain of traditional clapboard housing. Solomon's approach owes much to the Congress for New Urbanism (CNU), which was established in 1993, which has shaped new developments such as Seaside and Celebration in Florida. CNU is a reaction against the 'placelessness' of American suburbs and the growing division of communities by race and income, and favours a style of architecture that takes account of local history, climate and building practice.

A similar approach is followed by the American architect Eric Kuhne, who designed Bluewater, although for him there was no ready-made vernacular model. Kuhne hopes that incorporating particular elements – for example, the form of oast-house roofs commonly used in Kent for drying hops – allows the building to speak more directly to ordinary people's experience. Bluewater, as its promotional literature explains, is much more than a shopping centre; it is almost a new town in itself. It has its own police force, community facilities such as a nursery, and exhibitions borrowed from London cultural institutions – and it has played a major part in the regeneration of the region, having the effect of raising property prices and creating jobs. Its success has led to a number of imitators, and as a paradigm for the new breed of socially responsible commercial development, it is likely to become a more important part of the contemporary landscape.

Opposite
The timber architecture of Gion A Caminada, who has helped restore and develop the Swiss village of Vrin, respects the fabric of local buildings.

Below
Bluewater shopping centre in south-east England has a variety of architectural references including the handkerchief domes here, inspired by Sir John Soane.

Bottom
Britton Courts, a San Francisco housing scheme by Solomon ETC (in collaboration with Michael Willis & Associates), returns to the tradition of clapboard housing.

Bluewater

Year of completion
1999

Location
Dartford, England

Architect
Eric Kuhne and
Associates

It is hard to find a vernacular precedent for a shopping centre, let alone a 180,000 square metre (2 million square foot) one. But American architect Eric Kuhne was determined that Bluewater should 'trigger an emotional response' in local people.[1] His inspiration for the shopping centre was the vision of a white unicorn surrounded by flowers that he had spotted on a tapestry and the White Hart depicted against a background of gold in the Wilton Diptych. Kuhne wanted Bluewater to emerge from the cliffs of the former Blue Circle cement quarry 'like a magical city chiselled out of the chalk'.

Bluewater is not like anything seen before in the UK, which has made it a difficult project to understand and criticize. Some critics have taken the line that, as a shopping centre, Bluewater is morally beyond the pale – even its high quality is seen as merely encouraging consumerism. But, commercially and economically, it has been a huge success, playing a part in the economic regeneration of part of south-east England, and even turning around the tarnished image of the out-of-town shopping centre – the *bête noire* of British urbanists and environmentalists during the 1990s.

Kuhne believes that the centre works aesthetically because the references to the region's heritage 'reach inside people's hearts'. The clearest regional theme – obvious immediately as you see the centre from above – is represented by dozens of conical structures sitting on top of the grey metal roof of the shopping malls. These are based on the Kent vernacular oast-house roof, a conical structure once used for drying hops. Here Kuhne has reversed the flow of air so that the cowling – traditionally made from timber – becomes an air-intake device, providing the malls with a gentle breeze.

The irony of Bluewater is that, although it gathers together dozens of references to the literary, artistic and architectural history of Kent, the overall effect is more typically American – for many visitors, this is precisely the source of its appeal. It is not simply that the shopping mall is a building type that has been imported from the USA, but that the structure's vast scale, quality of materials and finishes and generous exterior landscaping are all decidedly un-British.

Bluewater is more than a shopping mall; it is a new civic centre with all the amenities of a small town, and more. For example, it provides a nursery, employment and training opportunities for local people, and links with major cultural institutions in London that enable it to borrow artefacts and artworks for exhibitions. However, it is a privatized, highly controlled and entirely manufactured civic centre with little room for spontaneity or piecemeal development – an urban experience suited to an age when nothing is left to chance.

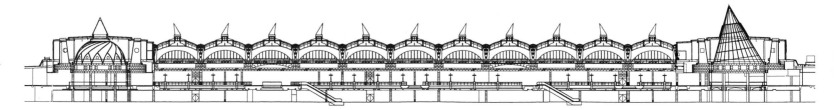

Above
Bluewater shopping centre is surrounded by the white cliffs of a former cement quarry. Seen from above, dozens of oast house-style ventilators break up the expanse of the roof.

Right
The Winter Garden is inspired by Decimus Burton's Palm House at Kew Gardens in London.

Opposite
Section showing the Sun Court connected to the Star Court by the Guildhall Mall, which is lit by daylight and ventilated by fresh air introduced at roof level.

Opposite top
The ceiling of the Guildhall was inspired by the 'handkerchief' domes at Sir John Soane's Bank of England trading rooms.

Opposite bottom
One of three distinctive civic spaces, 'The Village' has a 'townscape' design theme and literary quotations line the walls.

Next page
The Sun Court, one of three civic spaces that form entrances to the department stores.

Below
Plan triangulated by three large department stores, which are modelled on English country houses. They are connected by malls and civic spaces for meeting and relaxing.

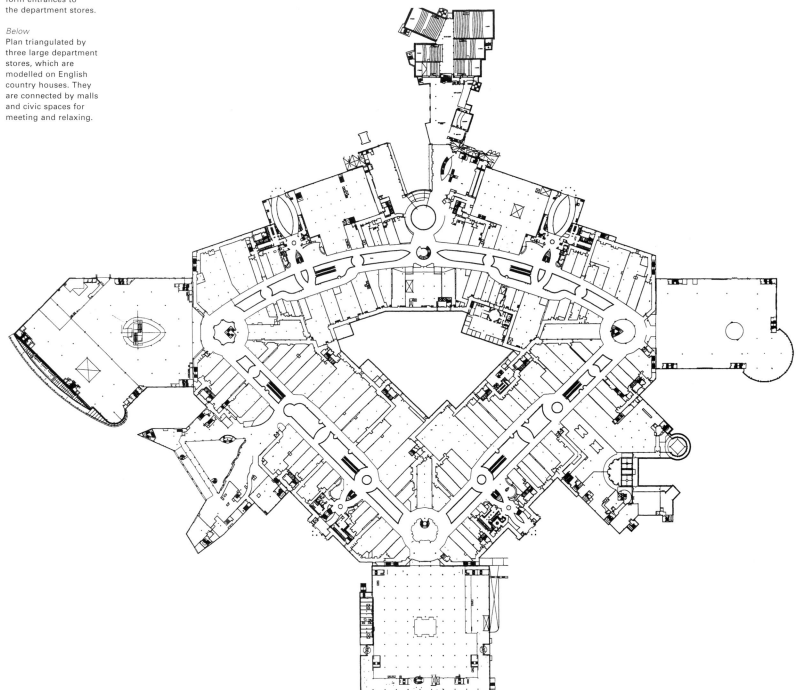

Bluewater is rich in historical detail, reflecting the huge efforts Kuhne made to research the heritage of the region. At each corner of the triangulated plan is a department store situated at the end of an avenue of oak trees – which, Kuhne says, is modelled on the English country house. Three malls connect these 'mansions', each one with its own character. The Western Mall is barrel-vaulted to recall English libraries and reading rooms; the Southern Mall has sail-like ceilings; and the Eastern Mall has a ceiling based on Sir John Soane's now demolished trading rooms at the Bank of England. At points along the malls, visitors can stop off at, for example, the Winter Garden – a 'botanical garden dining room' – inspired by Decimus Burton's Palm House at Kew Gardens in London, or at water gardens based on those at Blenheim Palace.

All the references are stitched together by what Kuhne describes as 'civic art': carvings of the 106 guilds of London positioned above the shops; a mosaic of the route of the River Thames laid into the floor; and quotations from writers who lived and worked in Kent written in large, calligraphic lettering on the walls.

For some critics, all this is too much, and turns the centre into a kind of Kentish theme park. But Kuhne rejects the criticism on the basis that everything he has done at Bluewater is authentic. He and his team of researchers and architects searched for accurate references that would really mean something to local people. 'It takes a long time to get all that right,' he says. 'Otherwise it could look kitsch and inappropriate. Unlike Disney, which imports culture, we haven't imposed anything.'

Year of completion
2000

Location
San Francisco, USA

Architect
Solomon ETC with
Michael Willis &
Associates

The controlled explosion that demolished one of the city's most troubled housing projects, Geneva Towers, made the front page of the *San Francisco Examiner* in May 1998. Two years later three new housing schemes, including Britton Courts, had replaced the 20-storey buildings that for years were notorious for their poor living conditions and high crime rates. Following the principles of the Charter of New Urbanism, Solomon ETC set out to create a place to live that was the inverse of the isolating and dangerous high-rise environment it replaced.

Britton Courts provides 92 units of housing for many of the former residents of Geneva Towers, as well as for new low-income residents. The site covers 1.5 hectares (3½ acres) and is located in the residential neighbourhood of Visitacion Valley, about a 15-minute drive from downtown San Francisco. The area is a tough place, with ethnic tension between the mainly Asian (Cantonese) community and African Americans. 'Even taking the photographs was dangerous,' says architect Daniel Solomon.[1] The main issue was how to provide security and safe communal areas for the residents without turning the scheme into a fortress.

The solution was an arrangement of two- and three-storey townhouses located around shared, secure courtyards. Each apartment or house has its own private garden, as well as access to communal space, with some houses looking out onto the street in order to encourage natural surveillance. The idea of courtyards continues the urban fabric of San Francisco, and in particular the typology of row houses built in the late 19th century.

Solomon ETC has specialized in housing from its San Francisco office for the past 20 years. In 1993 Daniel Solomon helped to found the non-profit organization called the Congress for the New Urbanism that has influenced much recent urban renewal and development in the USA. New Urbanism stands for the restoration of existing urban centres, the reconfiguration of sprawling suburbs into communities, the conservation of the natural environment, and the preservation of built legacy. Some of these principles echo those of the UK's Urban Taskforce set up by the architect Richard Rogers, although the emphasis on celebrating local history and building practice is peculiarly American.

Right
A site plan showing the arrangement of houses around shared, secure courtyards.

Opposite top
The houses are constructed from modern materials such as cementitious horizontal planks, which visually echo the traditional timber weatherboarding of local homes.

Opposite bottom
Many of the town houses front the street in order to encourage natural surveillance.

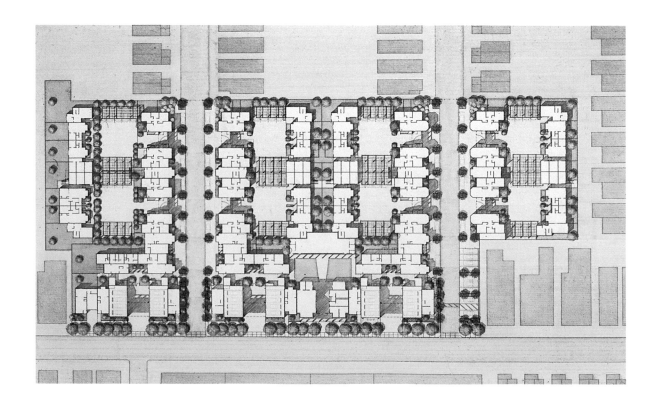

Britton Courts embodies Solomon's view that the primary task of all architecture should be the physical definition of streets and public spaces as places of shared use. One shift in practical practice that he believes has helped to revive public space is the supplanting of the term 'set back' with 'build to line'. The former, says Solomon, prescribes minimum distances from buildings to property lines, which implies 'buildings that float in a continuous matrix of undifferentiated space'. By contrast, build to lines – exemplified at Britton Courts – are 'specific prescriptions for the shapes of spaces defined by buildings'.[2] In this way, says Solomon, the principle of frontality is re-established and buildings become parts of larger ensembles defining the public realm.

Britton Courts is surrounded by small single family houses, known as Sunstream Homes after the developer which constructed many of them in the 1940s. Stylistically, Solomon describes these as a form of 'debased art deco and quite a difficult context to relate to'. For him, the importance of the vernacular in housing projects is twofold. Firstly, it is an important part of eradicating the distinction between public and private housing, since the use of avant-garde architecture in the 1930s and 1940s for low-income housing immediately made these homes identifiable. Secondly, Solomon believes in maintaining continuity and being true to place. 'The pressure to homogenize places is greater than the pressure of the homogenization of time,' he says.

In their construction, the houses reflect Solomon's concern to be true to place, using common West Coast techniques to give a 'vaguely craftsman-like character'. The main structure is a platform frame, which allows a relatively high degree of standardization. Plywood cladding provides stability in this earthquake zone, and cementitous horizontal planks echo the weatherboarding of the Sunstream Homes.

Above
As public housing, Britton Courts is not easy to distinguish from the surrounding private homes.

Left
Each housing unit has its own private outdoor space, whether a ground-level garden or, here, a patio at first-floor level.

Opposite
The reality of crime and violence means that communal space within the development must be secured by gates.

Primary School

Year of completion
1996

Location
Turkapally, Andhra
Pradesh, India

Architect
P K–Peu Banerjee Das

Since the late 1960s a series of government programmes in India has focused on rural development, and particularly on primary education and healthcare infrastructure. But such assistance is described by the architect P K Banerjee Das as 'like a little paint available to brush over a mile-wide canvas'.

One of these programmes is the Andhra Pradesh Primary Education Project (APPEP), which came to the help of Turkapally, a village of a few thousand inhabitants situated about 35 kilometres (22 miles) from the state capital, Hyderabad. Before 1996, one small building served as the primary school, with five classes (grades one to five) and around 40 children in each class. The lack of space often meant that classes were held outside under the trees, but this was difficult during the long rainy months. To make matters worse, there were only two teachers, although the community had voluntarily raised 800 rupees a month to pay for two additional teachers.

For some time, the villagers had been asking the council to fund a new school with four classrooms, and eventually the APPEP put 200,000 rupees (approximately £3,000) towards a new building. The architects, P K Banerjee Das and his wife Peu, worked out that, with a usual construction cost of 250 rupees per square foot, they could construct a building of about 74 square metres (800 square feet) with the available money. But the government standard recommended that the school be at least 135 square metres (1,500 square feet), so the challenge was to design a building with the maximum floor area using the minimum resources.

The approach they adopted is known in India as Cost Effective Construction Technologies (CECT). Its aims are that all parties involved in a building project should learn something from the process. The Turkapally school would be a kind of prototype involving monitoring of the costs and performance of certain materials and technologies. Before any decisions were made on the method of construction, P K and Peu Banerjee Das carried out what they describe as a 'resource-mapping' exercise to find out what materials and skills were available within the region. They also had discussions with the community about their needs and observed how the existing school was used. The research exposed the difficulties and expense of certain methods, but also the potential solutions offered by local resources.

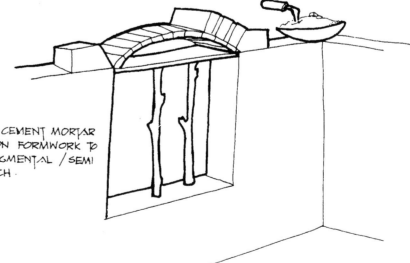

BRICKS IN 1:6 CEMENT MORTAR ARE PLACED ON FORMWORK TO CONSTRUCT SEGMENTAL / SEMI CIRCULAR ARCH.

Above
The school provides two classrooms and two verandas for open-air teaching and accommodates over 100 children.

Opposite left
Parents gave their permission for their children to help stack bricks to bring down the cost of construction.

Opposite right
Drawing showing the method of construction of segmental arches for the windows.

Right
The corbelled roofs were built using traditional techniques and locally produced bricks.

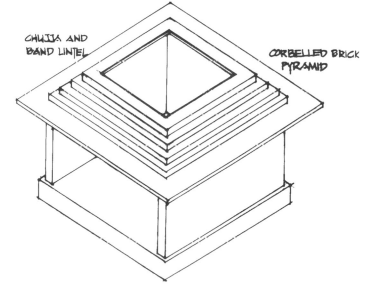

CHUJJA AND BAND LINTEL

CORBELLED BRICK PYRAMID

The first consideration was the climate – as one of India's southernmost states, Andhra Pradesh has an extremely hot and dry season, which lasts for six months, with heavy rainfall for the rest of the year. In these circumstances the close integration of internal and open-air space, common in traditional Indian architecture, made sense, so the architects designed a sequence of four 28 square metre (300 square foot) octagonal rooms, two of them fully enclosed and two semi-open. Both the walls and roof were constructed from brick, allowing the interior of the classrooms to remain cool in the hot dry season.

Steel and cement had been ruled out early on because these would have to have been brought from Hyderabad, which would have proved too expensive. Timber for shuttering was scarce, so concrete would not have been logical. There was, however, a nearby brickfield producing wire-cut bricks, and this seemed the obvious choice of building material. The corbelled stone temples of Orissa became the inspiration for the design and detailing.

The octagon works particularly well as a unit shape for a classroom. Its 2 metre (6½ foot) dimension provides just the right amount of wall space for blackboards, shelves, windows and walls, which, given the scarcity of books, are covered with educational paintings depicting, for example, the galaxy, parts of the human body and the action of water siphons. The building sits on a base of wide coarse-rubble stone blocks, with three steps leading up to the entrances between the verandas and the classroom. The roof, supported on brick piers, consists of four ziggurats of corbelled brick and one small four-sided corbelled brick pyramid in the centre to cover the remaining space – a passageway connecting the two verandas. Openings in the classroom walls were formed by placing bricks on formwork to produce segmental or semi-circular arches. Another advantage of brick was that, since it involved a relatively labour-intensive construction method, it offered the possibility of improving the skills of local people and retaining money within the village.

As part of the building process, bricklayers were trained on site, and even students assisted in the stacking of bricks to save money. By investing around a third of the construction cost on labour, the school generated employment for local people, which in turn acted as an income multiplier. For example, says P K Banerjee Das, a local painter who worked on the project earned about 10,000 rupees and employed five helpers, hence supporting about 25 children and adults for three weeks.

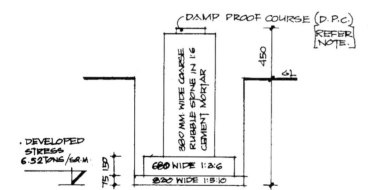

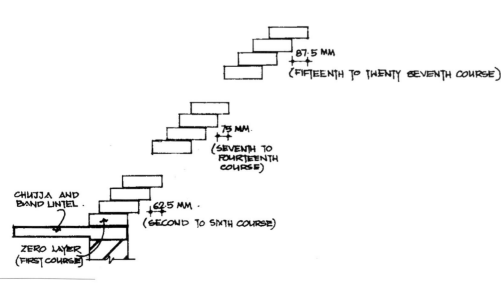

Above left
Interior of the school showing a typical class of 40 children and drawings on the wall in the place of text books.

Left
Drawings showing construction details.

Opposite top
Section of two classrooms with a passage connecting the two verandas between.

Opposite bottom
Plan of the school, which shows the octagonal classrooms and open-sided verandas.

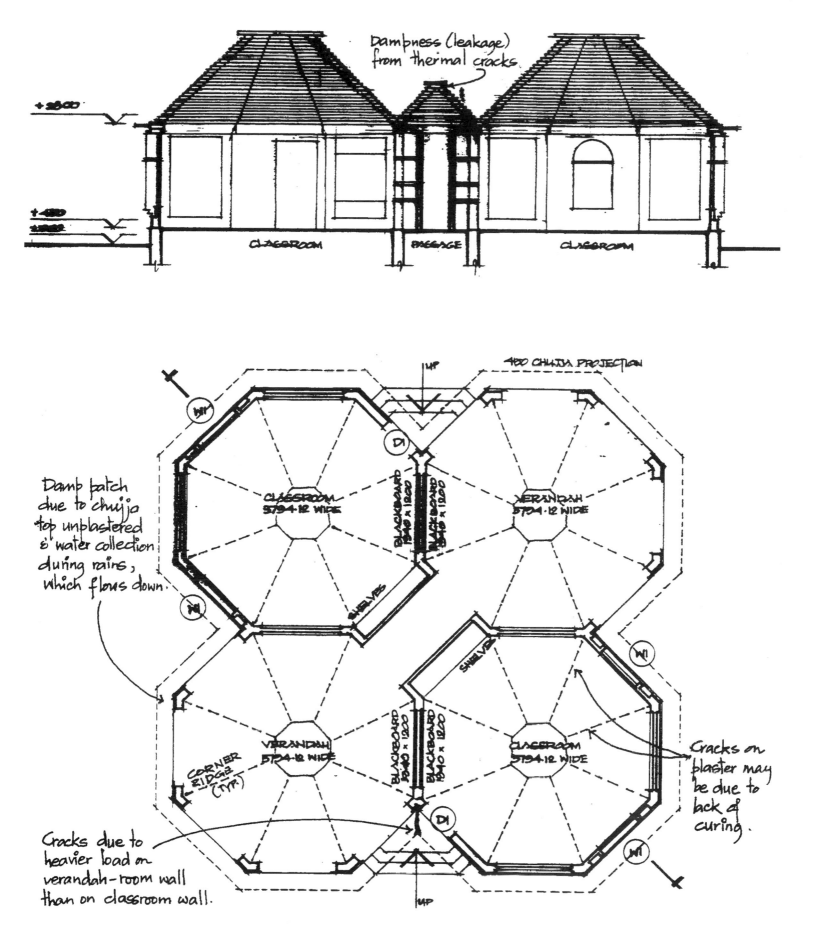

Dampness (leakage) from thermal cracks

CLASSROOM

PASSAGE

CLASSROOM

+2800

+480

480 CHAJJA PROJECTION

UP

D1

CLASSROOM
5794·12 WIDE

BLACKBOARD 1840 x 1200

BLACKBOARD 1840 x 1200

VERANDAH
5794·12 WIDE

SHELVES

Damp patch due to chajja top unplastered & water collection during rains, which flows down.

VERANDAH
5794·12 WIDE

SHELVES

CLASSROOM
5794·12 WIDE

BLACKBOARD 1840 x 1200

BLACKBOARD 1840 x 1200

D1

CORNER RIDGE (TYP.)

UP

Cracks on plaster may be due to lack of curing.

Cracks due to heavier load on verandah-room wall than on classroom wall.

Year of completion
1998

Location
Vrin, Switzerland

Architect
Gion A Caminada

The village of Vrin has around 280 inhabitants, the majority of whom are farmers. Tourism has hardly made an impact on the village and commercial life consists of a carpenter's shop, a building materials supplier, a locksmith, a bakery, three restaurants and a road-haulage Wrm. Vrin is situated in the valley of Lumnezia (the Valley of Light), with a series of hamlets, hermitages and churches scattered over the pastures and meadows. The village architect and planner, Gion A Caminada, is intimately involved in the life of Vrin, being a local councillor and having grown up there.

Caminada's buildings cannot be understood individually, or even as pieces of 'architecture'. They emerge out of the needs of the villagers and the traditional typology of timber farmhouses that characterizes the landscape. His work has much in common with the approach advocated by Adolf Loos in 1913 in his essay 'Rules for Those Building in the Mountains': 'Do not build in a picturesque manner. Leave such eVects to the walls, the mountains and the sun…. Pay attention to the forms in which the locals build. For they are the fruits of wisdom gleaned from the past. But look for the origin of the form. If technological advances make it possible to improve on the form, then always use this improvement. The Xail is being replaced by the threshing machine.'1

The villagers' ability to produce their own means of survival continues to be a decisive factor in the life of Vrin. Modern agricultural techniques have led many of the farmers to move into the centre of the village, leaving their farmhouses empty. In order to carry on the farming tradition (instead of turning the village over to tourism), Caminada has constructed a group of

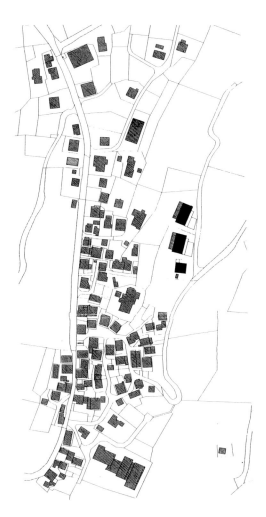

Left
The majority of Vrin's
inhabitants are farmers
and traditional timber
construction of the
cattle sheds was for
practical reasons rather
than for nostalgia.

Opposite left
Vrin is situated in
the Lumnezia Valley
(Valley of Light) and
consists of a series
of hamlets, hermitages
and churches scattered
over the meadows.

Opposite middle
The slaughterhouse
has a ground floor
or *socle* made from
local waste stone,
and an upper floor
of timber.

Opposite right
Site plan of Vrin
showing the location of
a group of cattle sheds
and a slaughterhouse
located on the outskirts
of the village.

cattle sheds and a slaughterhouse on the outskirts of Vrin. The Wrst of the group of three buildings is the slaughterhouse which, with its stone-clad ground Xoor or socle, acts as a link with the village. The upper Xoor is clad in timber, relating to the two cattlesheds next to it. Virtually all the materials came from nearby and were put together using local crafts. Caminada uses local materials for practical rather than nostalgic or symbolic reasons, and the stone came from a heap of waste that had accumulated over years from the demolition of old buildings, excavations and the building of roads. The construction techniques are intense, using the smallest quantity of prefabricated materials in order to involve the maximum number of people in the village in the building process. 'In this way,' says Caminada, 'the new building is much more readily accepted by the people of the village, even by those who have not beneWted from it directly.'2

For cattle sheds and other agricultural buildings Caminada uses system-building techniques, combined with traditional stacked log construction. The corners of the sheds are bonded and left exposed, with a cladding of planks covering an inner structure of roughly sawn logs.

The schoolhouse, Caminada's most architecturally distinctive building, was placed within a group of buildings in Duvin, a hamlet on the hill opposite Vrin, in order to preserve the traditional layout of the village. The second most important building in the community, apart from the church, is the village hall, which is attached to the old school and located on the edge of a steep hill at the boundary of the village. A masonry base anchors the building to the ground while the upper structure is clad in timber shingles. The interior is lined entirely with timber, with light entering through high-level windows. The roof is supported by an innovative system of trusses tied by cross members consisting of Wve 24 millimetre (1 inch) thick timber laths nailed together at the centre.

At the heart of Vrin, Caminada uses new buildings to reorganize the village's streetscape. For example, a new house was positioned on the main street to create an extra bend in the road to act as a traYc-calming measure. He has also repaired and extended many of the existing buildings and built his smallest intervention – a telephone booth built from narrow planks of timber – on the side of an old farmhouse.

The success of Caminada's work means that Vrin has gained a degree of independence from the planners in the capital of Graubunden, Chur. Although the village is unlikely to change dramatically in the future, Caminada recognizes that it cannot continue to be an island. 'We have to allow some things from the outside to have an inXuence; nevertheless we have the opportunity of reacting to those structures in a diVerent way and adapting them to our needs.'

Opposite
A new school
building in Duvin,
across the valley
from the Swiss
village of Vrin.

Right
The interior of the
school is entirely built
from sawn wood.

Below
A shed in Duvin.

6

New Directions in Regionalism

For most of the 20th century, architects were preoccupied with the apparent contradiction between the universal and the particular. This reflected the broader power struggles between unequal nations and societies. In his influential essay on critical regionalism in 1982, Kenneth Frampton expressed this connection between architecture and broader social consciousness by describing regionalism as an 'anti-centrist sentiment – an aspiration for some kind of cultural, economic and political independence'.[1] Frampton was attempting to find a way forward for Modernism, which had been discredited for its lack of specificity, at the same time as distancing himself from the nostalgia of post-Modernism.

At the beginning of the 21st century the old debate between the universal and the particular may have been resolved. It seems that we are all relativists now and the prevailing political culture embraces difference rather than equality.

Portuguese architect Álvaro Siza (see the Portuguese Pavilion, page 206) is a defendant of the idea of shared human values, believing there is no contradiction between the universal and the particular. 'Cervantes's Don Quixote is genuinely a work of universal relevance,' he says, 'but at the same time you are also reading about the Spanish culture without feeling that this is contradictory.'

While Siza has done most of his work in his own country, the Mexican architect Ricardo Legorreta has for many years taken his ideas further afield, particularly to the Mexican-influenced American Southwest. The Santa Fe Visual Arts Center (see page 218) has many of the charac-

teristics of Mexican vernacular, including the use of vibrant warm-coloured render and the importance given to walls as solidly grounded protective enclosures – a reminder of vernacular haciendas. Unlike Siza, who primarily responds to place, Legorreta raises the possibility of regionalism existing outside its regional context – the result, says Legorreta optimistically, of 'globalization creating the wonderful opportunity for exchange'.[2]

Siza's work forms a bridge between the first wave of 20th-century regionalists, notably his great mentor Alvar Aalto, and a younger generation of architects influenced by his contextual approach, in particular his use of light, which he treats almost as if it were a building material in its own right.

The Swiss Alpine canton of Graubunden is home to a dynamic strand of regionalism centred on the architect Peter Zumthor. The area's distinctive Romansh language and culture gives it a sense of coherent tradition, but its position at the heart of Europe, and its links with Italy, Austria and Germany, makes it unusually cosmopolitan for a rural area. The most interesting new architecture in the canton is far away from the over-exposed skiing resorts, in remote villages such as Paspels, where Valerio Olgiati has built a school (see page 228).

Olgiati, as well as many other innovative practices in the area, are interested not in following a Swiss style but in understanding the nature of the place. Olgiati responds to the drama of the mountains by reducing the form and details of the school to their most essential elements. The Battle of Seattle in December 1999 and subsequent anticapitalist protests gave new urgency to the sense that regional architectural differences were being lost in a world of corporate homogeneity. The buildings that were seen to epitomize globalization, and became easy targets for the protesters, were the city's air-conditioned glass offices and McDonald's restaurants. The protests seemed to capture the mood of our time, signalling an increasing awareness of social injustice and environmental damage. In this context regionalism is increasingly being replaced by a discussion about sustainability and community, particularly in the developing world.

The changing priorities of the Aga Khan Award for Architecture (established up in 1977 to foster architectural excellence in Islamic societies) illustrate this shifting emphasis. In its early years the award was widely seen as supporting a 'third way' in architecture, lying between Modernism and tradition. An important element of this third way was using regionalism as a form of resistance to Westernization. In his introduction to the 1998 award (see Charles Correa's winning Vidhan Bhavan, page 214), Indian architect and jury member Romi Khosla argues that in the new context of globalization (where modern architecture has become inseparable from economic development in Asia), it is less important for the award to focus on style and identity. Instead, he says, the Aga Khan Award should foster social concerns that might be globally relevant. 'Perhaps the award represents the only, and rather lonely, articulated position that holds that architects still have broader responsibilities in developing societies,' writes Khosla.[3]

The sense that regionalism has become, to a degree, a superficial stylistic concern is not a notion confined to the developing world. British architect David Lea has become known as a regionalist after many years of studying the vernacular of Wales and developing a contemporary response to it. But his recent work and writing illustrates a shift towards sustainability and environmental and social concerns. 'I believe in it [regionalism] less and less these days,' says Lea. 'It's being used by planners to make a Mickey Mouse world.'[4] The problem is by no means unique to Wales, as he points out: 'The British building industry has developed a "vernacular" costume to hide modern construction; its colours and textures can easily be adjusted to give a regional flavour.'[5]

Lea believes that local architectural identity should spring from a resource base of materials. The Segger House, an extension to a traditional Welsh farmhouse (see page 224), takes its timber frame from woodland owned by the client, its stone from a reopened quarry near the site and its natural-wool insulation from the farm's flock of sheep. Few people are in a position to 'grow' their own house, but Lea sees in the project the possibility for communities around the world to re-establish economic links with their own regions.

Above
The vibrant colours of Ricardo Legorreta's Santa Fe Visual Arts Center are inspired by the Mexican vernacular of the haciendas and pueblos where the architect grew up.

Left
A schoolhouse in the mountainous village of Paspels by Valerio Olgiati is part of a dynamic movement of Swiss regionalism.

Opposite
Álvaro Siza's Portuguese Pavilion provides a ceremonial plaza covered by an impossibly thin curved concrete roof.

Portuguese Pavilion

Year of completion
1998

Location
Lisbon, Portugal

Architect
Álvaro Siza

Opposite
The plaza is defined by a reinforced concrete roof just 20 centimetres (8 inches) deep, which seems to bend under the force of gravity and is supported by two porticoes.

Below
Elevation looking west showing the two aspects of the pavilion: a covered plaza and an exhibition building.

When it came to choosing an architect for its national pavilion at Expo '98, the Portuguese government dispensed with the usual competitive process and gave the commission directly to Álvaro Siza. But it was difficult for Siza to come up with a design because it was far from clear what the building was actually to be used for. The main requirement of the brief was to provide a flagship image for Portugal and a pavilion that would outshine all the others, although the building also had to be compatible with a subsequent urban role and a more permanent, unknown function once the Expo was over.

During a career of nearly 50 years Siza has explored the relationship between Modernism and the characteristic aspects of Portuguese architecture, being inspired in particular by the work of Alvar Aalto. But, despite this interest in the specifics of place, for the pavilion Siza was less interested in making a statement about Portugal than in ensuring that the building sat well on the site and responded to the conditions of light.

Like the Seville Expo of 1992, the Lisbon Expo had a long-term goal: to regenerate a large section of former industrial land along the banks of the River Tagus, north-east of Lisbon's city centre. In addition to the Portuguese pavilion, permanent Expo buildings – including a new rail and bus station by Santiago Calatrava, an aquarium by Cambridge 7 and an arena by SOM – formed the beginnings of a new section of the city.

Siza's first step was to obtain the permission of the Expo's chief architect, Manuel Salgado, to reposition the building to a site at the north-west corner of the dock, 'as if it were a great ship solidly anchored'.[1]

The pavilion was to consist of two parts: a ceremonial plaza and internal areas incorporating exhibition space, restaurants, reception rooms and services in the basement. But the pavilion is essentially one brilliant idea: a curving concrete roof plane of almost impossible thinness covering a vast ceremonial square. This canopy or slab has the effect of creating a powerful graphic image, but it also works as a new element of the city, generously framing views of the neighbouring buildings. Like a huge wave, it recalls the movement of water, and the downward pull of the catenary curve anchors the building to the site.

Above
The Portuguese Pavilion
stands on the north-west
edge of the quay in
Lisbon's former docks.
On the east façade,
a covered portico of
marble columns rises
from the quayside.
To the north is the multi-
purpose arena by SOM
and to the west, Santiago
Calatrava's Oriente
Station.

Designed in collaboration with the engineer Cecil Balmond, the slab measures 65 by 58 metres (210 by 190 feet) and is just 20 centimetres (8 inches) deep. It hangs from steel post-tensioned cables spaced at 50 centimetre (20 inch) intervals and at its lowest point is 10 metres (33 feet) from the ground. A gap between the canopy and the building reveals the steel cables and allows light to fall on the stone of the portico. Curving elegantly like a piece of fabric, it refers to the ephemeral nature of the Expo's tensile structures, but as a structural and spatial achievement is far more profound.

It is rumoured that Siza had an unlimited budget for the pavilion and indeed the quantity of local marble used suggests this was the case. The two huge porticoes supporting the ceremonial roof are clad in marble; seats and window reveals are made of solid chunks of marble; and large blocks have been used to replace the stone that lined the dock at the east side of the building. Here, facing the water, another portico provides a sheltered walkway alongside the water, and thin structural columns emerge out of the dock wall.

Within each alcove of the two main porticoes, the walls are covered in traditional Portuguese ceramic tiles, which reflect the light almost as if they were metal. The entrance beneath the curved roof and through a portico gives access to the exhibition spaces, which are organized around a central courtyard.

The combination of old materials and new technology or engineering is a common feature of Siza's work. Although his buildings have become synonymous with Portuguese architecture, he is not so wedded to the local that he ignores new possibilities. But, as shown by the Expo pavilion, he is interested in technology not for its own sake but as a means to an end.

Opposite top
Two marble-clad porticoes, inset with coloured ceramic tiles, support the roof canopy.

Opposite bottom
Early sketch by Álvaro Siza for the idea of a sheltered ceremonial plaza that would accommodate the festivities of Expo '98 and afterwards act as a new urban public space.

Right
Sketch showing the pavilion in relation to the dock and the multi-purpose arena to the north (above).

Below
Plan showing a complex internal arrangement of spaces grouped around an inner courtyard.

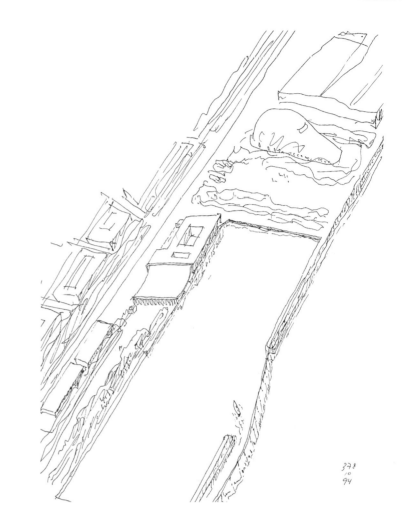

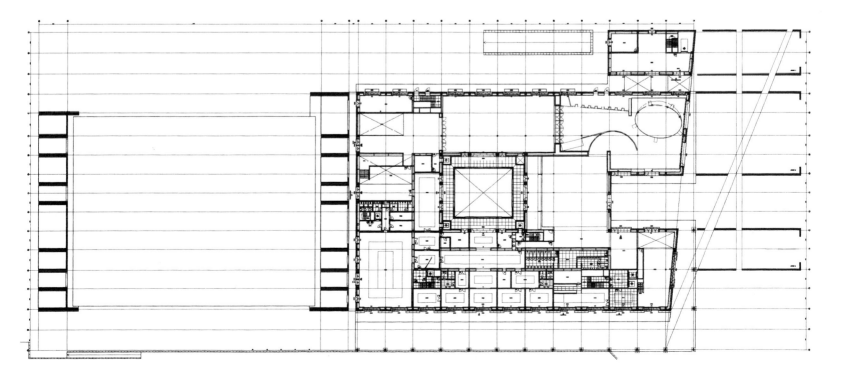

Above
View of exhibition space looking onto an internal courtyard.

Left
An internal courtyard brings daylight into the heart of the building, which accommodates an exhibition space, a reception area and restaurants.

Opposite
Marble columns of the eastern portico appear to rise from the stone edge of the quay. The ground is paved with traditional Portuguese limestone blocks.

Vidhan Bhavan (State Assembly)

Year of completion
1996

Location
Madhya Pradesh, India

Architect
Charles Correa

Bhopal, capital of the state of Madhya Pradesh, is known to most people as the city where the tragic Union Carbide disaster killed more than 2,500 people in 1984. Although the Vidhan Bhavan was planned long before the disaster happened, its completion twelve years after the event has helped to restore people's hopes in the future. Charles Correa won the project in competition in 1980 and construction began two years later. Beset by economic problems, the building took another 14 years to complete.

Vidhan Bhavan overlooks Bhopal from the top of the Arera Hill. It occupies the site of a colonial building that had served as a guesthouse for the viceroy of India before it was turned into an assembly building after the Indian States Reorganization Act of 1956.

Taking many years of Correa's attention, this large and elaborate building incorporates many of the architect's key design principles. After starting architectural practice in the newly independent India in the 1950s, following his training in the USA, Correa was committed to developing a strand of Modernism based on pre-Raj traditions and techniques. This has led him to incorporate many of the traditional symbols and graphic devices of India, as well as to respond to the more timeless influence of climate.

The most striking reference to Indian tradition is best appreciated in the plan, which is based on the *mandala*, a 'magic diagram' that forms the basis of temple planning and consists of a circle enclosing a grid of nine sections. As a well-known motif, the *mandala* makes the complex internal organization of the assembly – almost a town in itself – easier to understand. Two axes bisect the circular perimeter wall and lead the visitor through a sequence of five square courts. The remaining quadrants of the diagram house are the Vidhan Sabha, or Lower House, for 366 members; the Vidhan Parishad, or Upper House, for 75 members; the Combined Hall; subsidiary chambers; offices; and a library. This arrangement cleverly dispenses with corridors and leaves all circulation space open to the sky.

The perimeter wall holds all the elements together and presents a unified face to the town, with only the white dome of the Vidhan Sabha rising above it. But, although the enclosure is monumental in scale, it is not defensive or aloof; it is broken in three places, creating separate entrances for citizens, legislators and VIPs. The public entrance is the grandest, flanked by a pool in the shape of Madhya Pradesh. Through an expansive opening in the stone wall a formal patio leads to an open-air court with stepped-brick seating arranged in a geometric pattern. The walls are decorated with paintings of animals and birds by Jangarh Singh, a local artist.

'Disaggregating architectural forms into a series of separate but interdependent volumes is quite common in India,' writes Correa.[1] He points out

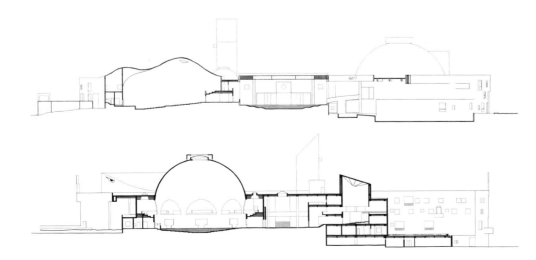

Opposite
Sections illustrate
the variety of forms
and spaces within
the circular plan.

Above
The Vidhan Bhavan
stands on top of a hill
overlooking Bhopal.
Its circular wall opens
in several places to
break down the
monumentality of
the building.

Right top
The entrance leads
first to an open-air
court with stepped
brick seating for
visitors and wall
paintings by local
artists.

Right bottom
The public entrance is
flanked by a pool in
the shape of the state
of Madhya Pradesh.

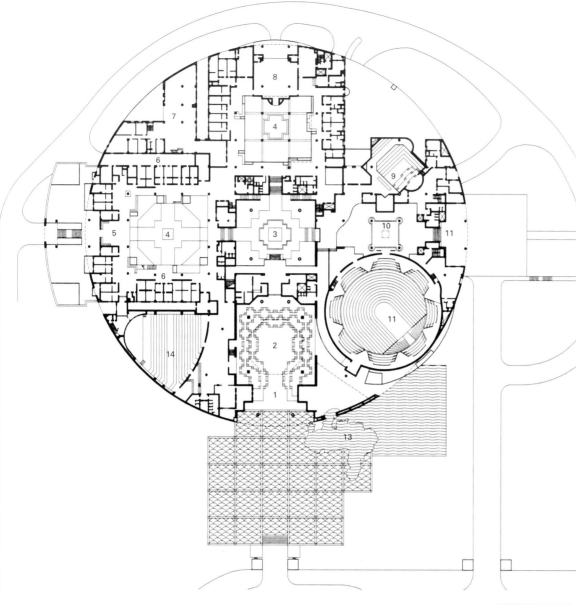

Left
The plan is based on the *mandala*, a magic diagram that is used for planning temples and consists of a circle enclosing nine sections.

1   Public entrance
2   Court of the People
3   Central Hall
4   Courtyard
5   Legislators' entrance
6   Ministers' offices
7   Library
8   Cabinet Room
9   Vidhan Parishad (upper house)
10 Legislators' foyer
11 Vidhan Sabha (lower house)
12 VIP entrance
13 Reflecting Pool
14 Combined Hall

Below
Many of the public spaces are only partially roofed to encourage fresh air to circulate around the building.

Opposite
The white dome of the Lower House is based on the dome at the Buddhist Stupa (temple) at Sanchi, 48 kilometres (30 miles) east of Bhopal.

that the assembly's sequence of interconnecting open courts and closed halls can also be seen in Indian housing, for example, where a series of circular huts focus on a central courtyard – 'a kind of nomadic living'.

At the assembly the 'nomadic' arrangement provides varying degrees of protection between the closed box and open courts, and creates a careful balance between the benefits and disadvantages of strong sunlight and air-movement for cooling.

The device of the *mandala* gives the building overall coherence while allowing Correa to create spaces with radically different materials, colours and atmosphere. In the central hall, which accesses the main chambers, the atmosphere is formal and the light strongly manipulated. The ceiling appears to stand free from the walls on four columns, with shafts of light flooding down the walls through roof lights around the perimeter. Steps from the hall lead to the Cabinet Court, which is partially roofed so that the sky is reflected in a central cruciform pool.

Beyond this central space is the grandest court in the building, the Legislators' Foyer, a double-height space articulated by four columns topped with Correa's interpretation of capitals in shining bronze. On opposite sides of the foyer, dramatic brightly coloured murals lead to the domed Vidhan Sabha, which is directly inspired by the dome at the Buddhist Stupa (temple) at Sanchi, 48 kilometres (30 miles) east of Bhopal, and, on the other side, to the Vidhan Parishad.

Correa's 'borrowing' of traditional architectural forms and motifs has been criticized by architectural writers, who have questioned why a democratic building should be furnished with symbolic forms of a past which 'knew little about freedom, transparency and openness'.[2] Correa argues that the references have little to do with what he calls 'grave-digging', and traditional forms are used only where they reflect contemporary sensibilities. 'Only a decadent architecture looks obsessively backward. At its most vital, architecture is an agent for change,' he says.[3]

Santa Fe Visual Arts Center

Year of completion
1999

Location
New Mexico, USA

Architect
Legorreta and
Legorreta

'In the vernacular there is no reason, just emotion,' says Ricardo Legorreta.[1] Although he was an apprentice to one of Mexico's purest Modernists, Jose Villagran, from 1948 to 1960, the lasting influence on Legorreta's work are the Mexican villages, haciendas, convents and churches in which he spent his childhood. Branching out in the 1960s with his own practice, Legorreta was strongly influenced by the Mexican architect Luis Barragan. Together they developed a regional interpretation of Modernism based on intuition rather than rationality, which they felt was more in keeping with the Mexican lifestyle and enjoyment of colour and light. The work of both architects is influenced by the vernacular: the use of walls to form protective enclosures, the treatment of landscape as an important element of a building and, most important, the exuberant use of colour.

While Barragan rarely built outside Mexico and concentrated on designing private houses, Legorreta's work has taken him further afield. In the summer of 2000 his first European building was completed – a fashion museum in south London – but most of his foreign projects have been completed in the Mexican-influenced American Southwest. The latest of these is the Santa Fe Visual Arts Center which, like his other buildings away from home, is a fusion of Mexican influences and elements inspired by the immediate context.

In recent years Santa Fe has become the USA's second most important centre for museums and art galleries. As a collaboration between the College of Santa Fe and the Art Institute, the Arts Center was intended to become one of the world's leading schools of art. Having an impressive new building was an important element in its bid to attract the best students and artist–teachers, who now include Larry Bell, Helen Frankenthaler and Fritz Scholder.

Phase one, completed in April 1999, lies outside the historic centre of the city and incorporates five departments: the Marion Center for Photographic Arts, the Art History Center, Tishman Hall, Tipton Lecture Hall and the Santa Fe Art Institute. Phase two, which is dedicated to three-dimensional arts, will follow within five years.

Opposite
Phase one of the Santa Fe Visual Arts Center is located on the outskirts of the city and forms a 'little pueblo' as if it were a small village.

Left
The rendered walls are painted in vibrant shades of orange and fuschia, a break with the local tradition of brown adobe.

Below
The horizontal emphasis and residential scale of the campus are balanced by this tower, which marks the entrance.

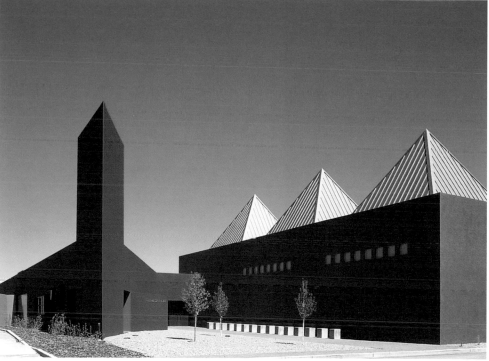

Instead of designing a single building to house the wide range of functions of the centre, Legorreta approached the building as if it were a small Mexican town, or 'little pueblo'.[2] This gave each department its own identity and fitted in with the college's diverse collection of existing buildings scattered around the campus.

Although it is not set in an urban context, the building adopts Santa Fe's residential scale and spreads out horizontally. Within the protective wall, each department building has its own courtyard providing open but secluded spaces and connecting it to other departments without the need for long stretches of corridor. Although the blank perimeter wall makes sense internally, from the outside the absence of features such as windows and doors gives the building a defensive posture in relation to the highway. The only concessions to the streetscape are the striking red colour, the animated roofscape made up of pyramidal metal roofs, a curved light monitor and, rising above the complex, a three-sided entry tower.

Walls in their various forms – patterned by small square windows, pierced by large protruding frames, layered and sliding past each other like floating planes – are one of the most important aspects of the Mexican vernacular. They form the backdrop for great muralists such as Diego Rivera and have social significance, maintaining the separation between public and private life. For Legorreta, walls are primarily a base for experimenting with colour, which he uses to elicit an emotional response. He takes inspiration from market stalls, Mexican folk art, self-built houses and the natural environment.

At Santa Fe, Legorreta strayed from the local vernacular of adobe walls, saying, 'What makes up Santa Fe is a way of living, not a brown colour palette. Santa Fe is prepared to experience other forms and colours. This is part of a process of growing and evolving.' Instead of the usual brown, the perimeter wall is two shades of red – one verging on ochre, the other more orange – inspired by the red rock of the mountains north of the city and the dazzling shifts of colour in the sky, 'from pink to purple to blue to charcoal'.[3] Although Legorreta says he tones down his colours when working outside Mexico, the interior of the Arts Center is a blaze of purplish-blue, fuchsia and lavender, giving each department its own personality.

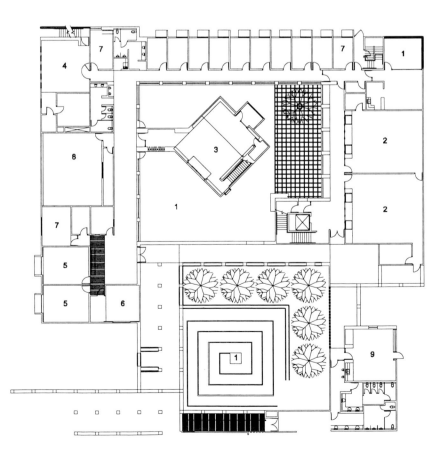

Opposite
Openings in the walls are sharply defined in three dimensions to make use of light and shade.

Opposite bottom
Ground plan of the Art History Center and Tishman Hall, with studios, seminar rooms and libraries, grouped around two courtyards.

1 Courtyard
2 Studio
3 Art History Library
4 Visual Arts Library
5 Seminar
6 Conference
7 Office
8 Classroom
9 Lounge

Above right
The Art Institute has courtyards for work and leisure and its studios are roofed by three pyramidal shapes, which bring in northern light.

1 Work courtyard
2 Leisure courtyard
3 Dormitory
4 Common room
5 Conference
6 Reception
7 Director
8 Studio
9 Master Artist

Right
The master plan of phase two of the campus showing the integration of open and covered space.

1 Art History
  Tishman Hall
2 Art Institute
3 Marion Center

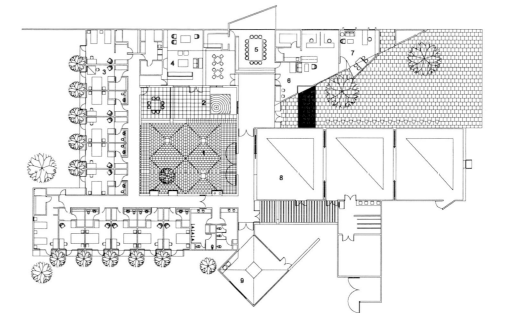

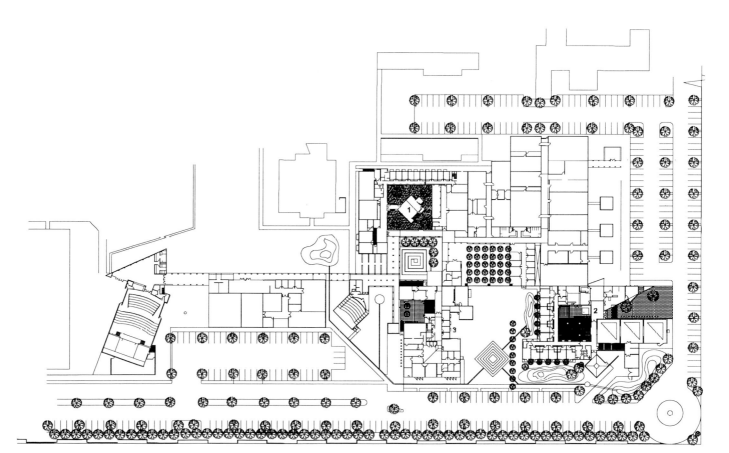

Left
The art studios open
onto a secluded
courtyard, which is
used by students
for meeting and
exhibiting their work.

Below left
Ground plan of the
Marion Center
incorporating the
main lecture theatre,
entry tower and
gallery.

1 Entry tower
2 Lecture hall
3 Darkroom
4 Seminar
5 Director
6 Gallery
7 Library
8 Faculty
9 Atrium
10 Laboratory

Below
Each department has
its own personality
and is connected by
semi-open cloisters.

Opposite
The Art History
Center wraps around
a courtyard with the
library sitting alone in
the centre, like a
sculptural object.

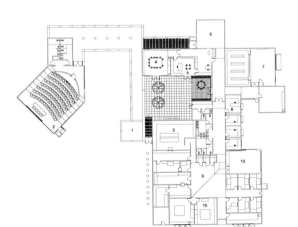

Segger House

Year of completion
1999

Location
Blaen Camel, Wales

Architect
David Lea

David Lea practises architecture with an attitude similar to that of the organic farmer for whom he built the Segger House. Peter Segger approached him to design an extension to his Welsh farmhouse after realizing that they shared a respect for the environment and the land on which they both depend. Having worked in rural north Wales for around 25 years, Lea takes inspiration from his close connection with nature (he combines architecture with running a smallholding) and from the knowledge of the craftsmen who built the cottage and barn where he lives.

This was the perfect commission for Lea to demonstrate his approach to regionalist architecture, which, he believes, should be based on local materials rather than on a notion of local style. In the spirit of self-sufficiency and living off the land, both he and his client wanted to build the extension from materials found on or near the farm. The family had a typical Welsh stone cottage with a pitched slate roof and chimneys at each end. Extending such a self-contained unit in an appropriate manner required great sensitivity, both to the character of the Welsh vernacular and the possibilities offered by modern architecture. The extension, which provides a new living room, bedroom, bathroom and office-cum-guestroom at the side of the old house, has two pitched roofs, which were arranged perpendicular to the existing roof. With its white rendered walls and floor-to-ceiling frameless windows, the extension does not try to blend in with the house but to complement it.

In Wales regionalism has been discredited in Lea's eyes by the ignorant planners and developers who want to enforce it as a catalogue of indigenous styles, even producing design guides that stipulate particular forms, styles and materials – which, he says, lead to the 'emptiness of Disneyland'.[1] Lea believes that 'Architectural identity springs from local identity, which springs out of a local resource base.'[2] In that spirit, the house extension is enclosed by a 'garden' wall made from stone taken from a quarry near the site. The stone provides an element of continuity with the farmhouse, enclosing the new addition at the back and sides and forming a low, solid base at the front. Timber for the structure and internal partitions was taken from trees owned by Segger, and even the insulation was made from wool provided by his sheep.

In plan, the new building is essentially a square divided into semienclosed rooms by partitions set in a grid of timber posts. But in section it reads as two halls defined by pitched roofs of different heights. Between and around the halls are lower bays topped with rooflights, which from the outside give the building a Modernist aspect, and provide sources of daylight and circulation routes for the interior.

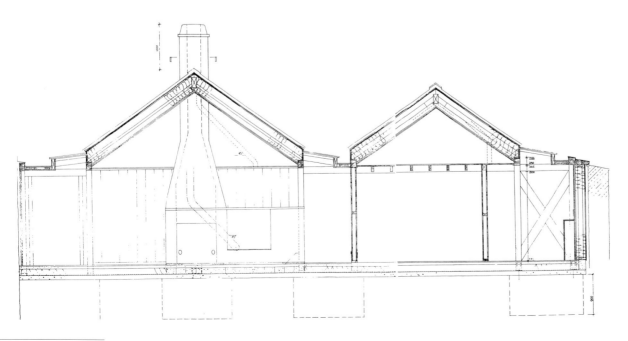

Opposite
Section showing the extension's two double-pitched roofs, which stand perpendicular to the roof of the cottage.

Right
The stone wall wraps around the side and back of the new building with an opening for a sheltered terrace.

Below right
David Lea's addition to a traditional Welsh stone cottage is made up of layers of horizontal, light-filled spaces. The outer walls are rendered and sit on a base of local stone, which provides a link with the old building.

Bottom right
Light enters through skylights and through full-height glazing at the end of the interstitial bays.

The bays have a structural as well as an organizational function. Stripped of the timber battens and render, the building is essentially a green oak frame. The timber skeleton and stone walls are independent structures that do not rely on each other for support. So, in order to provide the frame with the necessary strength, without using ties that would obscure the inner roof space, the lateral forces from the roof are transmitted to a series of timber crosses placed at the end of each minor bay.

The exterior of the building is clad with heavily insulated timber battening with a limewash render and a finish of white limewash. The client's flock of fifty sheep provided wool for insulation (supplemented by cellulose-fibre insulation), which was placed in the cavities by hand. Internal partitions – for example, to create an intimate bedroom aedicule – were formed from oak or ash boarding, all of which was left untreated.

Not all the materials are traditional, low-tech or even local. Lea believes in applying modern technology where it can have the maximum benefit. For example, there are full-height, doubled-glazed windows and low-emission double-glazed roof lights. 'Technology,' writes Lea, 'takes away craftsmanship and the art of decoration, but gives back the life-enhancing experience of living in nature.'³

Although the building represents almost a manifesto of Lea's ideas, he does not put it forward as a model (in any case, few clients can provide their own supply of timber or natural-wool insulation). The house does, however, demonstrate a way forward for regionalism that is not based on the imposition of a vernacular costume of style and form. In the bigger picture of a globalized economy, the building is Lea's own contribution to enabling people to re-establish economic roots in their own regions.

Opposite left
The structural frame, made of locally grown green oak, is exposed inside. Skylights create a feeling of openness and connection with the outside.

Opposite right
Intimate corners within the open plan are panelled with untreated oak and ash boarding.

Opposite bottom
Built-in furniture made from untreated timber organizes the space.

Right
One room flows into another and the living room space extends to an outdoor terrace sheltered by a wall of local stone.

Schoolhouse

Year of completion
1998

Location
Paspels, Switzerland

Architect
Valerio Olgiati

In a perfect setting such as the mountains of the Graubunden canton (also known as the Grisons) in south-east Switzerland, new buildings are seen with particularly sensitive eyes. Valerio Olgiati's schoolhouse in the small village of Paspels, which is an addition to an existing secondary school, completes the picture-postcard scenery and shows that rational, man-made architecture can be a far better complement to nature than an organic imitation. The building's cubed structure is made from carefully formed smooth white concrete and rests in a gently sloping wheatfield with its roof following the angle of the hillside. Positioned at the edge of the village, the building is incorporated into the farmland but oriented towards the existing school, although not visibly connected to it.

Paspels is a village of 400 inhabitants, which for the purpose of schooling links with nine small mountain communities in the area of Domleschg. Olgiati himself grew up in the Graubunden village of Chur, where his father, Rudolf Olgiati, was a well-respected architect.

While the exterior impact of the school seems particularly important in such a dramatic landscape, the building really explains itself when experienced from the inside. In plan, it is full of subtle surprises. For example, the slight distortion of the cube produces spaces that are as irregular as the traditional buildings in the village. Carefully crafted details mean that the building can be appreciated on different scales. Olgiati describes it as a 'stone' lying in the landscape, but the way in which the materials have been handled makes it a pleasure to spend time in. Entering beneath a cantilevered concrete slab, the visitor's first experience of this sensitivity is the

Right
The simple exterior conceals a complex plan, which varies on each of the four levels. The upper two floors have a cruciform circulation space with four classrooms at the corners, each with their own character.

Opposite top left
Section showing the basement level link to the existing school building.

Opposite top right
At basement level an underground tunnel connects the new building to the existing school.

Opposite bottom
A new schoolhouse sits in a field of swaying wheat with a dramatic backdrop of mountains and fir trees.

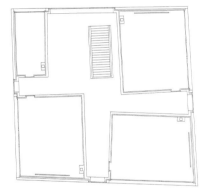

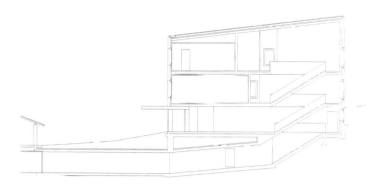

Right
A cantilevered concrete slab shelters the entrance and the main door is framed in patinated bronze.

Opposite top
Unlike the corridors, the classrooms are intimate spaces, panelled with larchwood and with large windows framing views of the landscape.

Opposite left and right
The walls, floors and ceilings of the circulation spaces are exposed, beautifully cast concrete, which reflects the changing tone of the light outside.

front door, made from bronze and glass, with subtle variations in the colour of the metal.

The floors, walls and ceilings of the circulation spaces are simply faced with smooth grey concrete, although light pours in to create subtly coloured washes at different times of day, the consistency of the material drawing attention to the variations in seasons and daylight. Inside no two rooms are the same, either in the plan, the quality of light or the floor-to-ceiling height, and the building becomes a kind of spatial exploration. At ground- and first-floor level the ceiling height is 3 metres (10 feet), while on the second floor the ceiling follows the slope of the roof, at its tallest point opening up to twice the height. The consistent feature linking the floor levels is the stair-case, which rises up from the basement, where a tunnel links the new build-ing to the old schoolhouse. A large window positioned close to the top of the stair on the first floor breaks down the separation between the interior and the surrounding fields.

The first- and second-floor plans are dominated by the shape of a cross, which is slightly different in each case. Olgiati has likened this space to the intersections of village streets, while he sees the classrooms as the parlours of local homes. The classrooms, which exist in the negative spaces around the circulation cross, have a completely different character from the concrete cor-ridors, with floors, walls and ceilings warmly panelled in larch wood. Large strip windows running the entire length of one side of each classroom frame the view as if they were paintings hanging on the wall. Olgiati has remem-bered that these rooms, in which children spend a large and important sec-tion of their lives, need to fulfil different needs: ideally, they should provide the warmth and security of home, while being different enough to create a setting in which children's minds are opened up to the world beyond. The irregular plan exploits the structural potential of concrete, but achieving this level of geometric complexity while maintaining razor-sharp edges and a smooth fair face required considerable commitment from the building team. As inspiration, and to convince them that he was not making inhuman demands, Olgiati took the whole team and the local council to see the fair-faced concrete at Peter Zumthor's Kunstmuseum in Bregenz. The reaction was better than he had expected. 'We can easily improve on that,' they said.

Year of completion
1999

Location
Riudaura, Spain

Architect
Aranda Pigem Vilalta
Architects

Before the addition of its new civic centre, Riudaura, in the Catalan province of Girona, had just two public buildings – a church and a town hall. Shared space for the 425 inhabitants to hold meetings, events and performances was limited, and even the school was confined to the lower floor of a house. Aranda Pigem Vilalta, a young practice based in the nearby town of Olot, had already built several community facilities in the area and had developed a certain sensitivity to the character of the place, without allowing local people's expectations to compromise the practice's ideas. The plan was to use the civic centre to define public space and to emphasize the qualities of the existing buildings in the village.

The site chosen by the local council was a plot at the entrance to the village, in a slight depression in the ground opposite the church. By its position and low-lying form, the building defines the square in front of the church; a separate area for sport has been created on the lower side of the sloping site behind the building. Capturing the environment without mimicking it, the architects have used the dark form as a horizontal line to emphasize the verticality of the church, which remains the dominant building in the village, towering over the smaller stone houses.

At first, the civic centre reads as a somewhat forbidding dark mass in contrast to the pale dusty ground and local stone. But in daylight its rusted and varnished steel cladding produces a reflective surface that allows it to sit quite comfortably in its surroundings. A series of semi-open spaces and terraces counteract the heaviness of the metal façades, and the building becomes almost an extension of the land surface. The east and west façades are dis-

Key
1 Zinc sheet roofing
2 Rusted and
   varnished steel
   sheeting
3 Transparent
   laminated glazing
4 Sliding window
5 Shaped metal
   sheeting with
   a rusted and
   varnished finish
6 Skylight
7 Glass screen with
   lighting inside
8 Bar counter made
   from pumiced
   Cabra stone
9 Artificial stone
   bench

Opposite
The Social Centre
is the third public
building in the town
of Riudaura, Spain. It
is designed to be a
horizontal line to
complement the
verticality of the
church tower on the
opposite side of the
square.

Left
The roof, clad in
rusted and varnished
steel, sails over the
glass front of the
building, providing a
sheltered place to sit.
At either end, covered
routes lead to the
sports field at the
back of the building.

Below
Cross-section
revealing the change
in levels between the
front and the back of
the building. Inside,
the space is not
divided by walls but
by stairs, which link
three different levels.

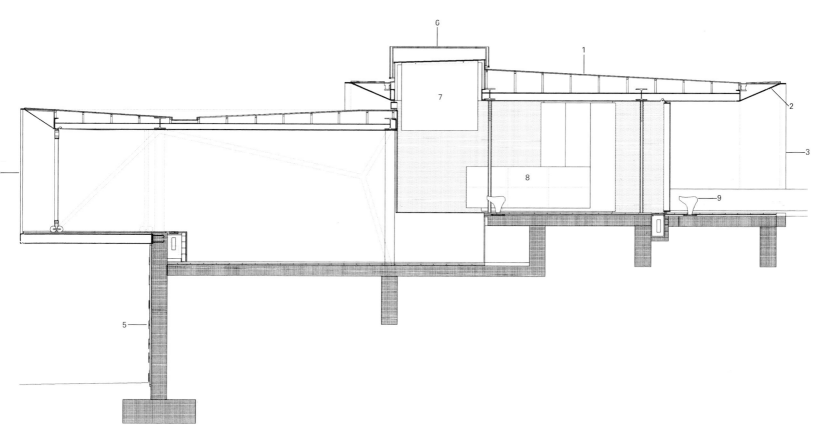

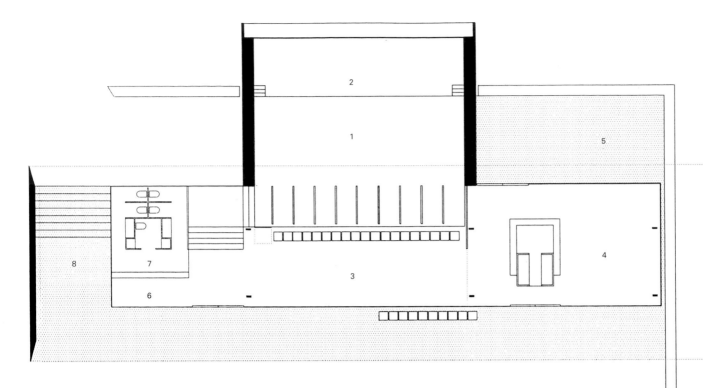

Above
Plan showing the
building as a series of
overlapping planes
and transitional open-
air spaces shaded by
the roof.

1 Multi-purpose
   space (drama,
   dance, lectures)
2 Reversible stage
3 Exhibition space
4 Bar
5 Outdoor terrace
6 Promotion and
   tourist space
7 Toilets
8 Access to public
   space

Opposite top
The east façade
overlooks a sports
area with a large
window cantilevered
one storey above the
ground, which can be
opened to form an
outdoor stage.

Opposite bottom
Elevations looking
north (above) and
south (below) show
the building's base of
shaped steel cladding
and the cantilevered
form that houses
the dance floor and
stage.

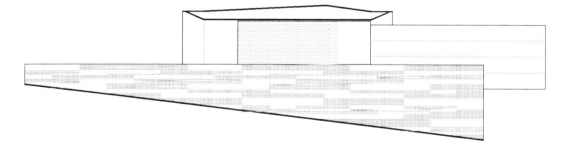

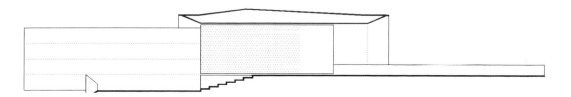

similar due to the change in levels. The over-sailing steel roof shades the glazed west façade, and stone benches provide a place to enjoy comings and goings in the square. On the other side of the centre, the shaped steel-clad base seems to grow out of the slope, and at the north and south ends the roof encloses two open-ended passageways connecting the village square with the sports field.

Inside, the accommodation is arranged in a T-shape and is divided into rectangular areas providing a bar, exhibition space, a multi-purpose space for dancing or theatre, and toilets. While essentially one large room without partitions, the space is cleverly organized, incorporating a change in levels that responds to the slope of the site. The space is unified by the central focus of a light box and skylight, from which a series of glass screens with fluorescent lighting hang down, transmitting a diffused light to the interior. Steps lead down from the entrance to the dance floor and at the far end of the space is an elevated stage. Together the dance floor and stage form a separate box-like element that emerges from beneath the roof and cantilevers above the sports field. From the inside a large sliding glass window at the back of the stage creates a picture frame for the view across the sports field and to the village beyond.

Aranda Pigem Vilalta's architecture typically reflects the local context in a subtle, rather than direct way – the use of materials is not restricted by an attempt to merge the building with its surroundings. Yet the building does not turn its back on the village. Instead, it provides places from which to contemplate the surrounding buildings and watch public activity. In that sense it is in the tradition of Catalan recreational spaces that are a focus for the life of the community. In philosophical terms, explains the practice, the civic centre is traditional because it is architecture for its time – whereas, paradoxically, 'Making ancient architecture would be anti-traditional.'

Opposite
A raised stage with
a glass sliding door
(on the left) can be
transformed into an
open air theatre, with
the audience outside
looking in.

Above
The exhibition space
with stone benches
dividing it from the
multi-purpose space
on a lower level.
Glass screens hang
above the space.

Sheep Field Barn
1   All quotes Roger Hawkins in conversation with the author, 15 May 2000

Flawil House
1   Correspondence with the author, 13 October 2000

2: Techniques and Materials
1   Robert Venturi, Denise Scott Brown, Steven Izenour, *Learning from Las Vegas: The Forgotten Symbolism of Architectural Form*, MIT Press, Cambridge, Mass, 1972
2   Charles, Prince of Wales, *A Vision for Britain: A Personal View of Architecture*, Doubleday, London, 1989
3   Kenneth Frampton, 'Rappel à l'Ordre: The Case for the Tectonic', *Architectural Design*, Vol. 60, No. 3–4, 1990

Teton County Library
1   *Architecture d'Aujourd'hui*, October 1996
2   The 1999 John Dinkeloo Memorial Lecture, published by the University of Michigan
3   Lecture by Will Bruder at University of Westminster, London, 26 September 2000
4   Correspondence to the author, 31 May 2000
5   Lecture by Will Bruder at University of Westminster, London, 26 September 2000

Self-Build House
1   All quotes from correspondence with the author, 5 July 2000

Orphanage
1   Conversation with the author, 27 September 2000

Sibelius Hall
1 Correspondence with the author, 2 October 2000

River and Rowing Museum
1   'Natural Selection', *Architecture Today* 49, pp24–29

3: Giving Shape to Identity
1   Talk for 'Global-blanding' seminar, Institute of Ideas, London, 17 June 2000
2   Chris Abel, *Architecture and Identity*, p154, Architectural Press, 1997
3   Catherine Slessor, 'Hungarian Ark', *Architectural Review*, September 2000
4   'Country Focus: Hungary', *World Architecture* 80, October 1999
5   Peter Wilson, 'No More Messiahs', *ARCA: The Journal of Scottish Architecture*, Issue 4, April 2000
6   Penny Lewis, 'Message from Edinburgh: No One Owns Culture', *The Independent*, 31 August 2000
7   From *Renzo Piano Logbook*, Thames & Hudson, London 1997

Scottish Parliament
1   Interview with Penny Lewis, 1 June 1998
2   Conversation with the author, 3 November 2000

Wales Millennium Centre
1   Lecture to Institute of Welsh Affairs

Indian Embassy
1 Ulf Meyer, *Berlin Capital City*, Jovis Verlagsbüro, Berlin, 1999

Latvian National Library
1   All quotes from written statements by Gunnar Birkerts, 31 May 2000

Culture House
1   Written statement to the author, 19 June 2000
2   *Architectural Design*, Vol. 63, November/December 1993

Tjibaou Cultural Centre
1   From *Renzo Piano Logbook*, Thames & Hudson, London 1997

4: Building with the Landscape
1   Simon Schama, *Landscape and Memory*, Alfred A Knopf, New York, 1995
2   Jacob Bronowski, *The Ascent of Man*, 1973
3   Geoffrey and Susan Jellicoe, *The Landscape of Man*, Thames & Hudson, London 1989

Arthur and Yvonne Boyd Education Centre
1   *UME*, No. 10, pp46–61, 1999
2   *Ibid.*

Kamiichi Mountain Pavilion
1   All quotes, conversation with the author, 25 July 2000
2   A traditional tarred fishing boat from the west of Ireland

Arizona Science Center
1   All quotes, conversation with the author, 29 August 2000

Miho Museum
1   Quoted by project architect Tim Culbert in *Orientations*, October 1997

Moledo House
1   Tom Heneghan, 'Souto Moura Arquitectos', *10x10*, p356, Phaidon, London, 2000

5: Civic Architecture and the Vernacular
1   Hassan Fathy, *Architecture for the Poor*, University of Chicago, 1973; first published as *Gourna: A Tale of Two Villages* in 1969.
2   Graham Tipple (Director of the Centre for Architectural Research and Development Overseas (CARDO) at the University of Newcastle-upon-Tyne, UK), 'Building Homes to Build Local Economies', *Habitat Debate*, Vol. 5 , No. 2
3   Gion A Caminada, *The Vrin Project*, a 50-minute film, directed by Christoph Schaub, 1999, quoted in 'Building in the Mountains: Recent Architecture in Graubunden', *2G*, No. 14, 2000

Bluewater
1   All quotes, conversation with the author, 21 August 2000

Britton Street Housing
1   Conversation with the author, 30 October 2000
2   Daniel Solomon, 'Block, Street and Building', *Charter of the New Urbanism*, 1999

Farm Buildings and Telephone Booth
1   Adolf Loos, 'Rules for Those Building in the Mountains', 1913, quoted in 'Building in the Mountains: Recent Architecture in Graubunden', *2G*, No. 14, 2000
2   'Building in the Mountains: Recent Architecture in Graubunden', *2G*, No. 14, 2000

6: New Directions in Regionalism
1   Kenneth Frampton, 'Toward a Critical Regionalism', *Perspecta* 20, 1982
2   *GA Document Extra* 14, 2000
3   Romi Khosla, 'The Conscience of Architecture', *Legacies for the Future: Contemporary Architecture in Islamic Societies*, (Cynthia C Davidson, ed.), Thames & Hudson, London, 1998
4   Conversation with the author, 2 March 2000
5   David Lea, 'Fake or Real', *Planet: The Welsh Internationalist* 138, December/January 2000

Portuguese Pavilion
1   Notes by Álvaro Siza, February 1998

Vidhan Bhavan (State Assembly)
1   Charles Correa, 'Transfers and Transformations', *Charles Correa*, Mimar, 1987
2   Gerd de Bruyn and Gunter Nest, *Domus*, October 1999
3   Charles Correa, 'Transfers and Transformations', *Charles Correa*, Mimar, 1987

Santa Fe Visual Arts Center
1   'The Architecture of Ricardo Legorreta', interview with John V Mutlow, May 28 1996
2   Correspondence with the author, 3 March 2000
3   *Ibid.*

Segger House
1   David Lea, 'Fake or Real', *Planet: The Welsh Internationalist* 138, December/January 2000
2   Conversation with the author, 2 March 2000
3   David Lea, 'Fake or Real', *Planet: The Welsh Internationalist* 138, December/January 2000

Introduction – Architecture in Denial
1   Nikolaus Pevsner, *An Outline of European Architecture*, Pelican, London, 1943
2   Paul Oliver (ed.), *The Encyclopaedia of Vernacular Architecture of the World*, Cambridge University Press, 1997
3   Bernard Rudofsky, *The Prodigious Builders*, Secker & Warburg, London, 1977
4   A W N Pugin, *The True Principles of Pointed or Christian Architecture*, London, 1841; quoted in Peter Davey, *Arts and Crafts Architecture*, Phaidon, London, 1995
5   John Ruskin, *The Stones of Venice*, Vol. II, 1853; quoted in Peter Davey, *Arts and Crafts Architecture*, Phaidon, London, 1995
6   Gertrude Jekyll, *Old West Surrey*, 1904.
7   Quoted in Margaret Richardson, *Architects of the Arts and Crafts Movement*, RIBA Drawings Series, Trefoil Books, London, 1983
8   Hermann Muthesius, *The English House*, trans. Janet Seligman, Crosby Lockwood Staples, London, 1979; quoted in Peter Davey, *Arts and Crafts Architecture*, Phaidon, London, 1995
9   William J R Curtis, *Modern Architecture since 1900*, Phaidon, London, 1996
10 Sigfried Giedion, *Space, Time and Architecture: The Growth of a New Tradition*, Harvard University Press, Cambridge, Mass, 1967 (fifth edition); first published in 1941
11 *Ibid.*
12 Kenneth Frampton, 'Toward a Critical Regionalism', *Perspecta* 20, 1982
13 'Universal Civilisation and National Cultures', Paul Ricoeur, 1961; quoted in Kenneth Frampton, *Modern Architecture: A Critical History*, Thames & Hudson, London, 1980
14 Alan Colquhoun, 'The Concept of Regionalism', in G B Nalbantoglu and C T Wong (ed.), *Postcolonial Space(s)*, Princeton Architectural Press, New York, 1997
15 *Ibid.*
16 Vittorio Magnano Lampugnani, 'What remains of the project of the Modern?', *Casabella* 677, April, 2000

1: Innovation from Tradition
1   'Looking back in appreciation', *Building Design* 29, September 2000
2   Helen Castle (ed.), *Modernism and Modernisation in Architecture*, p6, Academy Editions, 1999
3   'Tyranny of the New', *Blueprint*, May 1998
4   Conversation with the author, 19 July 2000
5   Conversation with the author, 9 August 2000
6   Robert Venturi, *Complexity and Contradiction in Architecture*, The Museum of Modern Art, New York, 1990
7   'The Feeling of Things', *A+T* 13, 1999
8   Letter to the author, 27 June 2000
9   Hans Iberlings, *Supermodernism: Architecture in the Age of Globalisation*, Nai Publishers, Rotterdam, 1998
10 Conversation with the author, 15 May 2000

Prototype Social Housing
1   Notes by Sergison Bates, January 2000
2   New towns were initiated by the New Town Act of 1946
3   Conversation with the author, 19 July 2000

Zachary House
1   All quotes taken from a letter to the author, 27 June 2000

New Art Gallery
1   All quotes, Peter St John in conversation with the author, 9 August 2000

Luis Ferreira Alves (170–75), Courtesy of Stephen Atkinson (36, 37 bottom), Mikko Auerniitty (87–91), Hélène Binet (20–25, 38–43), Peter Blundell-Jones (225–7), Sue Bolsom (12 bottom left), Courtesy Black Dog Publishing Ltd. and Peter Salter (139 top, 146–51), Richard Bryant/Arcaid (15), Meredith L Clausen (13 left), Eleanor Curtis (95), Lucia Degonola (180, 196–203), James Dow (74–9), Peter Durant/arcblue (181 top, 183, 185 top), Edifice/Darley (9 top), Guy Fehn (164–9), Dennis Gilbert/VIEW (18, 45, 47, 48 bottom, 49, 99–103), Jon Gollings (105 top, 132–7), Jon Gollings/ESTO (140–45), Courtesy Gunnar Birkerts (112–25), Heinrich Helfenstein (205 bottom, 229–31), Hannes Henz (50–55), Courtesy Hans Olav Hesseberg & Sixten Rahlff (62, 81–5), Anthony Hoete (63 bottom, 70–73), Timothy Hursley (2, 19 bottom, 32–3 top, 35, 37 top, 138, 139 bottom, 153–7, 158–63), Lourdes Jansana (105 bottom, 106, 108 top, 110 bottom), Lourdes Legorreta (205 top, 218–23), Paul M R Maeyaert, Mont de L'Enclus (Orroir), Belgium (13 right), Duccio Malagamba (204, 208–13), Sue Milton (98), Mags Mogensen (57–61), Grant Mudford (188–91), Newell & Sorrell (16 right), Garrick Palmer (10 left), Courtesy Percy Thomas Partnership (112–7), Erhard Pfeiffer (63 top, 93–4, 96–7), Courtesy PK-Peu Das (192–195), Eugeni Pons (232–7), Ram Rahman/Aga Khan Trust for Culture (215–7)Timothy Soar (48 top), 1999 Spectrum Colour Library – Digitally Enhanced Image (12 top), Courtesy of Starwood Hotels and Resorts (17), Szanto Tamas (104, 127–31), Hugo Timmerman (64–9), Rauno Traskelin (14 bottom), Philippe Ruault Nantes (27–31), Andrew Southall/arcblue (185 bottom, 186–7), Tripp/BB Goldings BV (16 left), Courtesy Léon Wohlage Wernik (118–21)

Project Credits

Arizona Science Center
Location: Phoenix, Arizona, USA
Design Architect: Antoine Predock Architect
Project Team: Geoffrey Beebe (Associate in charge), Karen King and Brett Oakes (Project Architects) Geoffrey Adams, Johjn Brittingham, Linda Christensen, Mark Donahue, Nancy Napheys, George Newlands
Executive Architect: Cornoyer-Hedrick Inc.
Project Team: Stephen Basset (Principal in Charge) Dave Lockrow (Project Director) Helen Bowling and Buck Yee (Project Managers)Randy McManus (Job Captain) Kris Floor (Landscape Architect) Robert Morris (Interior Designer) Jim Bolek (Graphic Designer)
Landscape Architect: Cornoyer-Hedrick Inc.
Subcontractors/Suppliers: Main Contractor: Sundtcorp, Structural Engineers: Robin E Park Associates, Inc., Mechanical/Electrical Engineers. Baltes/ Valentino Associates Ltd., Civil Engineers: Wood/Patel Associates

Arthur and Yvonne Boyd Education Centre
Location: Riversdale, Australia
Architects: Glenn Murcutt, Wendy Lewin and Reg Lark

Bluewater
Location: Dartford, England
Architect: Eric Kuhne and Associates
Design Architect: EKA
Subcontractors/Suppliers: Structural Engineers: Waterman Partnership, Cost Construction: Cyril Sweett & Partners, Landscape: Townsend Landscape, Construction Management: Bluewater Construction Management Team, Project Management and Development: Lend Lease Projects Europe, Lighting: Speiers and Major, Engineering: Battle McCarthy, Service Engineers: Roberts & Partners

Britton Street Housing
Location: San Fransisco, USA
Client: Housing Corporation and Development Corp, San Fransisco
Prime Architect: Michael Willis & Associates, San Francisco
Associate Architect: Solomon E.T.C, San Fransisco
Contractor: Bill Johnson, Joe Mazzetti, Nibbi/Lowe
Landscape Architect: Gary Strang
Structural Engineer: Steve DeJesse Associates, Inc.

Culture House
Location: Makó, Hungary
Client: Makó Town Council
Architect: Makona Kft, Makovecz Imre
Construction: Pond Kft, Pongor Làszlò, Harsànyi Csaba
Mechanical Engineers: Kovàcs Pàl és Tsa Kft, Kovàcs Pàl
Electrical Engineers: Villes Kft, Villànyi Làszló
Stage Technician: Vajda Ferenc
Furniture: Mezei Gàbor

Farm Buildings and Telephone Booth
Location: Vrin, Switzerland
Architect: Gion A Caminda

Farm Buildings
Collaborator: Thomas Settler and Toni Pfister
Contractor: Societad Mazalaria Vrin
Master Builder: Caminada SA Vrin
Engineer: Fanchini/Perez Bonaduz
Timberwork: Alig & Co. Vrin
Construction: Betonkonstruktion, Naturtsteinmauerwerk, Holzmassivbau geschichtet

Telephone Booth
Collaborator: Thomas Settler
Construction: Holztappelbau
Timberwork: Alig & Co, Vrin

Flawil House
Location: Flawil, Switzerland
Architect: Markus Wespi with Jerome de Meuron
Engineer: Braunschweiler & Jackli AG
Wood Engineer: Fritz Alenbach
Building Physics: IBE Institute Bau & Energie

House near Sarzeau
Location: Sarzeau, France
Architect: Eric Gouesnard
Engineers: Ingetec Nantes

Indian Embassy
Location: Berlin, Germany
Client: Republic of India
Architects: Léon Wohlhage Wernik, Prof. Hilde Leon, Konrad Wohlhage, Siegfried Wernik
Assistants: Abdullah Motaleb, Anne Kleinlein, Bettina Storch, Johannes Muller Baum, Jochen Menzer

Ivar Aasen Center
Location: Orsta, Norway
Client: Statsbygg (Directorate of Public Construction and Property)
Architect: Sverre Fehn
Collaborators: Henrik Hille, Ervin Strandskogen
Contractor: AS Veidekke
Structural Consultant: Terje Orlien

Kamiichi Mountain Pavilion
Location: Toyama, Japan
Architect: Peter Salter
Project Team: Arata Isozaki and Shuichi Fujie: Urban Factory; Mayor of Inami; Mayor of Kamiichi; Peter Beard; Tom Heneghan and Kazuhiro Ando: Architecture Factory; Toshiki Kato: Kato Associates; Tamura Associates: Site Architects, Kamiichi; Tsune Umene: Asrata Isozaki Associates

Latvian National Library
Location: Riga, Latvia
Architect: Gunnar Birkets Architects
Structural Consultant: Leslie E. Robertson Associates
Mechanical, Electrical Consultant: Joseph R. Loring

Miho Museum
Location: Shiga Prefecture, Japan
Client: Shunei Cultural Centre, Shinji Shuneika
Architect: I.M.Pei, New York City
Project Team: I.M.Pei (Principal) Tim Culbert (Project Architect) Perry Chin (Building envelope) Chris Rand (Initial Design) Carole Averill, Price Harrison, Hubert Poole.
ATE Architect: Kibowan International, Tokyo. Principal in charge: Osamu Sato, Principal Administration: Hiroyasu Toyokawa, Project Team: Hitoshi Maehara, Fumio Ozaki, Masa Sato, Yasuhiro Sonoki, Miho Toyoda
Consultant: Fisher Marantz Renfro Stone
Subcontractors/Suppliers: General Contractor: Shimizu Corporation, Landscape Architects: Kohseki and Akenuki Zoen, Noda Kensetu, Engineers: Leslie E Robertson Associates, Aoki Structural Engineers, Nakata & Associates, Whole Force Studio (Structural) P.T. Morimura

Miramar Hotel
Location: El Gouna, Egypt
Client: Osracom Touristic Establishments
Architect and Interior Designer: Michael Graves & Associates, New Jersey USA
Associate Architects: Rami El Dahan & Soheir Farid Architects
Interior Design Coordinator: Ibrahim Nagi
Landscape Architect: Hydroscapes Egypt
Structural Consultant: Hamza Associates
Engineering Consultants: Bakry Engineers

Moledo House
Location: Caminha, Portugal
Client: António Reis
Architect: Eduardo Souto de Moura
Collaborators: Manuela Lara, Pedro Reis, Nuno Rodrigues Periera
Structural Consultant: Jose Adriano Cardoso

New Art Gallery
Location: Walsall, England
Client: Walsall MBC
Architect: Caruso St John
Project Architects: Laurie Hallows, Alun Jones
Design Team: Martin Bradley, Adam Caruso, Andres Martinez, Peter St John, Silvia Ullmayer
Main Contractor: Sir Robert McAlpine
Project Team: Structural and Services Engineers: Ove Arup and Partners, Façade Consultant: Arup Façade Engineering, *Access:* David Bonnet Architects, Art Handling: Bruce McCallister, Graphic Design: Michael Nash and Associates, JANE, Landscape: Lynn Kinnear, Artists: Richard Wentworth, Catherine Yass, Project Management: Citex

Orphanage
Location: Chhebetar, Nepal
Client: SCH-Chidren's Home with Krishna Ghimre
Architects: Hans Olav Hesseberg and Sixten Rahlaff with Eli Synnevåg
Contractor: Svaviman Construction/Mahendra Shrest
Engineering Consultant: Krishna Pokhrel

Portuguese Pavilion
Location: Lisbon, Portugal
Client: Expo '98
Architect: Álvaro Siza
Principal in Charge: Rui Castro
Project Team: Daniela Antonucci, Hana Kassem, Luiz Diaz-Maurio, Taichi Tamura, Luis Antas de Barros
Contractor: Abrantina SA
Subcontractors/Suppliers, Design Phase: Ove Arup & Partners, Structural Engineers, Electrical Engineers: Mike Gilroy, Air Conditioning: Martin Walton, Water Systems: Rod Green, Security: Andrew Minson, Acoustics: Malcom Wright
Execution Phase: STA Lda, Structural Engineers: Segadaes Tavares, Ana Bartolo, Electrical Engineers: Vieira Periera, Air Conditioning: Carlos Palma, Water Systems: Carlos Palma, Security: Viera Perieria
Landscape Architecture: Joao Gomes da Silva.

Primary School
Location: Turkapally, Andhra Pradesh, India
Client: Government of Andfra Pradesh, Government of India
Sponsors: Overseas Development Administration, UK, the BritishCouncil Division, British High Commission, India
Architects: PK-Peu Das, New Delhi, India
Contractor: Babiah Marigela
Masons: Laxminarayan, Hanumantha

Prototype Social Housing
Location: Stevenage, England
Client: William Sutton Trust
Architect: Sergison Bates Architects
Project Team: Stephen Bates, Sally Richards, Cornelia Schwaller, Jonathan Sergison, Mark Tuff (Project Architect)
Structural Engineer: Baldock Quick Trust
Cost Consultant: Philip Frank Partnership
Contractor: Willmott Dixon Housing Ltd.

River and Rowing Museum
Location: Henley-on-Thames, England
Client: The River and Rowing Museum Foundation
Architect: David Chipperfield Architect
Structural Engineer: Whitby Bird and Partners
Services Engineer: Furness Green Partnership
Landscape Architect: Whitelaw Turkington
Quantity Surveyor: Davis Langdon Management
Enabling Works Contractor: Laing
Main Contractor: Norwest Holst Construction
Exhibition Designer: Land Design Studio Ltd.

Santa Fe Visual Arts Center
Location: Santa Fe, New Mexico, USA
Architects: Legorreta and Legorreta
Contractor: Loloyd and Tryck
Interior Design: Legorreta & Legorreta, Lloyd & Tryck
Photography: Lourdes Legorreta

Schoolhouse
Location: Paspels, Switzerland
Architect: Valerio Olgiati
Client: Politische Gemeinde Paspels
Planning: Iris Datwyler, Gaudenz Zindel, Raphael Zuber
Contractor: Peter Diggelmann
Engineer: Gebhard Decasper

Scottish Parliament
Location: Edinburgh, Scotland
Architect: Enric Miralles, Benedetta Tagliabue Associates Architects
Collaborators: RMJM Scotland Ltd, M A H Duncan, T B Stewart, Ove Arup & Partners Scotland, Steve Fischer
Project Leader: Joan Callis

Segger House
Location: Blaen Camel, Wales
Architects: David Lea, Tom Miller
Structural and Energy Calculations: Pat Borer
Main Contractor: CLS Construction
Sub Contractors/Suppliers: Alpine Boilers (Boiler Supplier), Cambrian Alarms Ltd (Electrical Contractors), Rod Bird (Plumbing and Heating Engineer), Cwt y Bugain Slate Quarries (Roofing Slates), Clive Davies (Specialist Iron work), Wayne Elridge (Roofing Contractor), Fiddes & Sons (Pigments), Farr and Harris Ltd (Plumbers Merchants), Glenhurst Roofing (Specialist Leadwork), Hall & Co. (Builders Merchants), Mick Jones (Timber), Stephen Medland (Stone Mason), Mid Wales Underfloor Heating, Penycoed Construction (Warmcell), Pren (Sawyer), Ridegway Timber (Mobile Sawyer), HMC Concrete, Ty Mawr Lime, Uginox (Steel Gutters), Ron Valentine (Glazier), Witney Sawmill (Chestnut Lathe).

Self-Build House
Location: Motiti Island, New Zealand
Client: Hoete Whanau O Motiti
Architect: Anthony Hoete
Subcontractors/Suppliers: Main Contractors: Graham and Kathy Hoete
Carpentry Assistance: Billy Hoete, Building Surveyance: John Meads, Catering: Kathy Hoete and Delwyn Howe, Contingency: Roly Hei Hei, Structural Engineers: Chris Rose Assocs., Localized Building Conditions: Peter Townsend (JTA) Chris Adams and Glenn Watt (Technopolis)

Sheep Field Barn
Location: Henry Moore Foundation, Perry Green, England
Client: The Henry Moore Foundation
Architect: Hawkins Brown
Project Team: Roger Hawkins, Russell Brown, David Bickle, Seth Rutt, Nicola Chambers, Wayne Glaze, James Gosling, Andrew Groarke
Planning Consultant: Adrienne Hill
Quantity Surveyor: Stern and Woodford
Structural Engineer: Price and Myers
Mechanical and Electrical Engineer: Michael Popper Associates
Landscape Consultants: Dan Pearson
Main Contractor: John Mowlem

Sibelius Hall
Location: Lahti, Finland
Client: City of Lahti
Architect: Hannu Tikka, Kimmo Lintula
Project Team: Elina Alhdeoja, Risto Häapoja, Karo Hautalahti, Paula Holstrom, Tony Kajasviita, Rainer Lindeborg, Matias Manninen, Mika Saarikangaas, Juha Salmenpera, Katriina Teravuori
Subcontractors/Suppliers: Contractors: Ncc-Puolimatka, Kaakois- Suomen Tuloskksikkö, Olli-Pekke Teerijoki, Jaako Sainia, Risto Varjola, Antii Saari, Peeke Karpinen, Juha Kosonen, Seppo Viinikainen
Project Management: Engel rakennuttamispalvelut Oy.
Interior Designer: Markki Liukkonen
Structural Design: Turun Juva Oy
Glu-Lam Structures: Paijat Suunittelu Oy
Electrical Design: YSP Oy

Social Centre
Location: Riudaura, Spain
Client: Riudaura Council
Architects: Rafael Aranda, Carmen Pigem, Ramon Vilalta Arquitectos
Design: A Saez
Structural Engineers: A. Saez, A. Blazquez, LL Guanter
Construction Leader: RCR/ M Subrias

Strawberry Vale School
Location: Victoria, British Columbia, Canada
Client: Greater Victoria School District
Architects: Patkau Architects
Design Team: Grace Cheung, Michael Cunningham, Michale Kothke, Tim Newton, John Patkau, Patricia Patkau, David Shone, Peter Suter, Allan Teramura, John Wall, Jacqueline Wang
Subcontractors and Suppliers: Structural Engineer: C.Y Loh Associates, Mechanical Engineer: D.W Thompson, Electrical Engineer: Reid Crowther & Partners, Landscape Design: Moura Quale/Lenarc, Environmental Materials: Ray Cole, UBC

Teton County Library
Location: Jackson, Wyoming, USA
Client: Teton County, Wyoming
Architect: William P. Bruder-Architect Ltd
Project Team: Will Bruder, Wendell Burnette, Tim Christ, Jack DeBartolo III, Ben Nesbitt, Brett Oaks
General Contractor: Continental Construction
Subcontractors/Suppliers: Brieckey, Rudow & Berry (Structural Engineers), Clark Engineering (Mechanical Engineering), C.A Energy Design (Electrical Engineering). Nelson Engineering (Civil Engineering), Bob Rolhf (Library Consultant), Floor and Ten Eyck (Landscape Architect)

Tjibaou Cultural Centre
Location: Nouméa, New Caledonia
Client: Agence Pour le Développement de la Culture
Architect: Renzo Piano Buiding Workshop, P Vincent, Senior Architect
Design Team: D Rat, W Vassal (Architects in Charge) with A El Jerari, A Gallissan, M Henry, C Jackman, P Keyser, D Mirallie, G Molodo, J B Mothes, M Pimmel, S Purnama, A H Temenides, J P Allain
Consultants: A Bensa (Ethnologist), Agibat MTI (Structure), GEC Ingenieure (MEP engineering and cost control), CSTB (Environmental Studies), Scène (Scenography), Peutz & Associés (Acoustics), Qualiconsult (Security), Végétude (Planting), Intégral R Baur (Signing)

Vidhan Bhavan (State Assembly)
Location: Madhya Pradesh, India
Client: State Government of Madhya Pradesh
Architect: Charles Correa
Project Team: Hema Sankalia, Nidish Majmundur, Satish Madhiwala, Suneel Shelar, Andrew Fernandes, Rahul Mehrota, Viren Ahuja, Mnaoj Shetty.
Contractor: M/S Sood
Structural Engineer: Mahendra Raj
Mechanical Engineer: S.K.Murthy
Acoustical Engineer: Gautam Suri
Interior Designer: Satish Madiwhala
Landscape Architect: Ksihore Pradhan

Villa S
Location: Grenoble, France
Architects: Herault-Arnod Architects
Main Contractor: Zephyrin
Subcontractors/Suppliers: BSI: Structure Engineer; Thermibel: Fluids Engineer; Acem: Façade Waterproofing; SDCC: Roofing; Loiodice: Carpentry

Vistet Fritid Prototype House
Location: Malmö, Sweden
Client: The Vistet Foundation
Architect: Thomas Sandell
Project Architect: Thomas Sandell and Anders Landstrom
Project Management: Bertil Harströmer
Constructor: Mazur

Wales Millennium Centre
Location: Cardiff, Wales
Client: Wales Millennium Centre, Ltd
Architects: Percy Thomas Architects
Project Architect: Jonathan Adams
Project Director: Rob Firman
Structural/ Services and Acoustic Engineers: Ove Arup and Partners
Theatre Consultant: Carr and Angier
QS and Project Management: Citex

Zachary House
Location: Zachary, Louisiana, USA
Client: John and Brenda Atkinson
Architect: Studio Atkinson, Cambridge, Massachusetts
Construction Team: John Atkinson and Bill Roe

Index

Making Gardens

A CELEBRATION OF GARDENS AND GARDENING IN ENGLAND AND WALES

from the National Gardens Scheme

Edited by Erica Hunningher

Horticultural Consultant Elspeth Napier

CASSELL&CO

ABOVE Sudeley Castle was one of the twenty-three Gloucestershire gardens that opened in June 1927. Jane Fearnley-Whittingstall guided the restoration of the rose garden in 1989. FRONTISPIECE Nuns Manor, Cambridgeshire, designed, created and maintained by Ann and Bob Brashaw and their son Philip, first opened for the National Gardens Scheme in 1991.

First published in the United Kingdom in 2001 by Cassell & Co
Overall text copyright © NGS Enterprises 2001
Text contributions copyright © the individual authors 2001
Photographs copyright © the photographers as listed on page 336
Design and layout copyright © Cassell & Co

British Library Cataloguing in Publication Data
A CIP catalogue record for this book is available from the British Library
ISBN 0 304 355 97 6
9 8 7 6 5 4 3 2 1

Design director DAVID ROWLEY
Designed by KEN WILSON
Project managed by
 CATHERINE BRADLEY & CAROLINE BROOKE
Copyedited by RUTH BALDWIN
Index by INDEXING SPECIALISTS
Typeset in 10/13PT ADOBE CASLON
Printed in Italy by PRINTER TRENTO S.r.l.
Planting plan illustrations by WENDY BRAMALL
 (Wildlife Art Illustration Agency)

Cassell & Co
Wellington House
125 Strand
London WC2R 0BB

Contributors

Barbara Abbs
is a freelance garden writer for *The Garden* and *Gardens Illustrated.* She is the author of *The Conservatory Month by Month* and *Gardens of the Netherlands and Belgium.*

Louise Allen
is the Procuratrix at the University of Oxford Botanic Garden, coordinating a team of gardeners and communicating with visitors. She trained at Kew and Wisley and has an MSc in horticulture from the University of Reading. She writes for *The Merlin Newsletter.*

Stephen Anderton
is a writer and broadcaster. He is gardening correspondent of *The Times,* author of *Rejuvenating a Garden, Urban Sanctuaries* and a contributing author to *Gardens of Inspiration.* He writes for many magazines, including *Gardens Illustrated, Garden Inspirations, The Garden, American Horticulture* and *Country Life.* He lectures widely at home and abroad.

Rosie Atkins
is the Editor of *Gardens Illustrated,* which she launched 1993, and formerly a journalist on *The Sunday Times.*

Jinny Blom
is a writer and freelance garden designer. She has created many designs for gardens in the UK. From 1996–2000, she worked closely with Dan Pearson, assisting him with commissions such as Althorp Park. She writes for *Gardens Illustrated.*

Val Bourne
is an organic cottage gardener with three main plant passions – hardy perennials, snowdrops and vegetables. She writes for the *Daily Telegraph, The Garden, Gardens Made Easy, Country Home and Living* and *The English Garden,* and for specialist journals and websites. She lectures widely and broadcasts on radio and television.

Kathryn Bradley-Hole

is Gardens Editor of *Country Life* and was for ten years a gardening correspondent for the *Daily Telegraph*. She is the author of the BBC's *Garden Lovers' Guide to Britain*, *The Daily Telegraph Book of Weekend Gardening* and *Stone, Rock & Gravel*.

Daphne Foulsham

is Chairman of the National Gardens Scheme and, with husband John, opens her garden at Vale End in Surrey. She lectures at home and abroad, promoting the NGS and enthusing audiences with her passion for gardening born from her life-long love of wild flowers.

Trudi Harrison

is a writer, broadcaster and gardener. She writes for the *Chichester Observer* and the *Daily Express*. She has appeared in several television and radio programmes and is much in demand for her knowledge and personal experience of gardening on an inauspicious site on the Sussex coast. Her garden opens for the NGS.

Bryan Hirst

is the co-founder with Anthony Archer-Wills of Waterlands Productions Ltd, water feature specialists. Traveller, builder, lecturer and consultant to many eminent garden designers and their clients, Bryan considers water the primary energy in any garden.

Geoff Hodge

is a writer and broadcaster with ten years of experience of writing about gardening, and eight years' experience of gardening on clay. He has written for many gardening publications – but his current interest is in web-based gardening. He is the Editor of the Royal Horticultural Society website: www.rhs.org.uk

Christopher Holliday

is a writer, garden designer and a National Collection holder of New Zealand flaxes at Charney Well in Cumbria, a subtropical-style garden that opens for the NGS. He writes for *The English Garden*, *Gardens Illustrated* and *Garden Inspirations*.

Tim Ingram

is a plant scientist turned nurseryman with a particular interest in dryland species. His garden at Faversham in Kent opens for the NGS.

Susanna Longley

is a researcher, editorial consultant and writer who has contributed to gardening television, magazines, partworks and books including *The Weekend Gardener*. She has a degree in horticulture from Wye College and lives with her family in Suffolk.

Anthony Noel

is a writer and garden designer with a reputation for style in small spaces. He is the author of *Terracotta* and *Great Little Gardens*. He writes for newspapers and magazines, including the *Daily Telegraph*, *The English Garden* and *Garden Inspirations*. His tiny garden in South London opens for the NGS.

Barbara Segall

is a garden writer and horticulturist. She edits a quarterly magazine for professional horticulturists and is the author of seven books, including *The Ultimate Herb Garden*. Her garden in Suffolk, which is exposed to biting winds and earth-cracking droughts, opens for the NGS.

Patrick Taylor

became a garden writer and photographer after a career in publishing. He is the author of a dozen books, including *Gardening with Roses* and *Gardening with Bulbs*. He writes a column for *Gardens Illustrated* and has contributed articles and photographs to many newspapers and magazines.

Expert Insights

Rosemary Alexander

is a garden designer and head of The English Gardening School at the Chelsea Physic Garden. She is the author of *The English Gardening School* and *A Handbook for Garden Designers*. From 1989 to 2000 she restored and maintained Stoneacre, a National Trust garden in Kent.

Anthony Archer-Wills

is a specialist on water features. Many NGS garden owners have consulted him on the design and construction of pools, from small urban ponds to vast lakes. He is the author of *The Water Gardener* and *Water Power*.

Chris Baines

is national vice-president of The Wildlife Trusts, president of the Urban Wildlife Partnership and a trustee of the Heritage Lottery Fund. In 2000 he co-presented a six-part TV series on wildlife gardening. He is the author of *How to Make a Wildlife Garden*.

Jill Billington

lectures widely and her books include *Planting Companions*, *Really Small Gardens* and *New Classic Gardens*. A formal training as a sculptor and a passion for plants has been the foundation of her garden design career. She works closely with Barbara Hunt and their design practice has won many show awards.

John Brookes

is a designer of dynamic living spaces and closely involved in the professional training of garden designers. His garden in Sussex opens to the public. His books include *Room Outside*, *The Small Garden*, and *The Book of Garden Design*.

Beth Chatto VMH

opens her world-famous garden and nursery in Essex for the NGS. Her books include *The Dry Garden*, *The Damp Garden*, *Dear Friend and Gardener* (with Christopher Lloyd) and *Beth Chatto's Gravel Garden*.

Nigel Colborn

is a former nurseryman and now a writer and broadcaster. He is the author of *Shortcuts to Great Gardens, Annuals and Bedding Plants, The Container Garden* and *The Garden Floor.*

John Foulsham

an architect by profession, shares his enthusiasm for butterflies and vintage cars, as well as compost-making and construction projects, with visitors on open days. The garden he and his wife Daphne have created at Vale End in Surrey has opened for the NGS for eighteen years.

Fergus Garrett

is the Head Gardener at Great Dixter in Sussex, which opens for the NGS. He studied amenity horticulture at Wye College. His articles have appeared in *Gardens Illustrated.*

Martin Gilbert CBE D.Litt

is one of the foremost historians of our time, the official biographer of Sir Winston Churchill and the author of more than sixty books, his most recent being *Letters to Auntie Fori: The 5,000-Year History of the Jewish People and their Faith.*

Penelope Hobhouse VMH

is a garden designer and writer and a former NGS County Organizer. Her books include *Colour in Your Garden, Garden Style, Penelope Hobhouse's Garden Plans* and *Plants in Garden History.*

Hugh Johnson

is the author of *The International Book of Trees* and *The Principles of Gardening,* as well as many books on wine. For twenty-six years he has written Tradescant's diary in *The Garden.* The garden he and his wife Judy have created at Saling Hall in Essex has opened for the NGS for twenty-five years.

Mary Keen

is a writer and garden designer. She is the author of several books, including *Creating a Garden,* which features the restoration and transformation of her garden in the Cotswolds that opens for the NGS.

Noel Kingsbury

is a garden designer and writer. His books include *Designing with Plants* and *The New Perennial Garden.* He is a leading exponent of contemporary naturalistic design. His garden in Hereford opens for the NGS.

Carol Klein

is a writer, television presenter, lecturer and nurserywoman. She has won ten RHS Gold Medals for her plant exhibits. Her garden in Devon opens for the NGS. She writes for numerous magazines, including *BBC Gardeners' World* and *The English Garden.*

Stephen Lacey

is a broadcaster and writer, with a regular column in the *Daily Telegraph.* His books include *The Startling Jungle, Scent in your Garden* and *Gardens of the National Trust.*

Robin Lane Fox

is a Fellow of New College, Oxford, Gardening Correspondent of the *Financial Times* for which he has written a weekly column since 1970. As well as books on classical history, he is the author of *Better Gardening* and *Variations on a Garden.*

Joy Larkcom

has travelled all over the world studying vegetable growing systems and has written and lectured for many years on organic gardening and being adventurous with vegetables. Her books include *Creative Vegetable Gardening, Oriental Vegetables* and *The Salad Garden.*

Christopher Lloyd OBE VMH

writes weekly columns for the *Guardian* and *Country Life.* He is the author of many gardening books, including *The Well-Tempered Garden, Christopher Lloyd's Garden Flowers* and *Colour for Adventurous Gardeners.* His garden at Great Dixter has opened for the NGS since 1929.

Mirabel Osler

writes books that are idiosyncratic and personal. They include *A Gentle Plea for Chaos, A Breath from Elsewhere, In the Eye of the Garden* and *The Secret Gardens of France.*

Adam Pasco

is editor of *BBC Gardeners' World Magazine,* launched in 1991. He has an honours degree in horticulture, is a regular radio broadcaster, and has made numerous television appearances. He writes for books and magazines.

Anna Pavord

is a broadcaster and the author of the highly acclaimed *The Tulip.* Her other books include *The Flowering Year* and *The New Kitchen Garden.* She is Gardening Correspondent for the *Independent.*

Dan Pearson

is a garden designer and columnist for the *Sunday Times.* He is the author and presenter of *The Garden,* about the making of Home Farm, and, with Terence Conran, the author of *The Essential Garden Book.*

Sue Phillips

began her horticultural career as a grower, producing crops under glass and polytunnels. For the past eighteen years she has lived on the south coast and is almost self-sufficient in vegetables from a small polytunnel. She is the author of over twenty gardening books, and contributes regularly to magazines.

Nori Pope

and his wife Sandra garden at Hadspen in Somerset, which opens for the NGS and is a centre of plant introductions, demonstrating the design skills of a great gardening partnership. They are the authors of *Colour by Design.*

Sarah Raven

is a gardening columnist for the *Daily Telegraph* and the author of *The Cutting Garden* and *The Bold & Brilliant Garden.* She has a seed catalogue, specializing in cut flowers and vegetables.

Graham Rice

is the Gardening Correspondent of the *Evening Standard* and author of fifteen books, including *A Gardeners Guide to Growing Hellebores* (with Elizabeth Strangman) and *Discovering Annuals.* He and his wife, photographer Judy White, divide their time between Northamptonshire and Pennsylvania.

Brita von Schoenaich

designs 'natural' gardens and landscapes with her business partner Tim Rees. They designed the perennial border at Ryton Organic Gardens, Warwickshire, which opens for the NGS.

Pamela Schwerdt

trained at Waterperry Horticultural School. From 1959 to 1991, she and Sibylle Kreutzberger were Head Gardeners at Sissinghurst, first for Vita Sackville-West and from 1967 for the National Trust. In retirement, they have created a garden in the Cotswolds.

Anne Scott-James

made a well-known cottage garden on the Berkshire Downs. She has written many gardening books including *The Cottage Garden*, *Sissinghurst: the Making of a Garden* and *Gardening Letters to My Daughter*. She is a former member of the RHS council.

Peter Seabrook

is a former nurseryman and now a writer, broadcaster and adviser to the garden centre industry. His books include *Shrubs for Everyone* and *The Complete Vegetable Gardener*. He is President of the Garden Writers Guild and holds the Guild's Lifetime Achievement Award.

Gay Search

is a writer and broadcaster, and a champion of the NGS. She is the author of many books on gardening in small spaces, the most recent being *The Healing Garden*.

David Stevens

is a garden designer, broadcaster and winner of eleven Chelsea Flower Show Gold Medals. He is Professor of Garden Design at Middlesex University and Consultant to the Chelsea America Foundation. He is the author of many books, including *The Outdoor Room*, *Gardens by Design* and *The Garden Design Sourcebook*. He is a contributing author to *Gardens of Inspiration*.

Tom Stuart-Smith

is a landscape architect and garden designer working in London and winner of four Chelsea Flower Show Gold Medals. His garden in Hertfordshire opens for the NGS.

Katherine Swift

is a tenant of the National Trust at Morville Hall in Shropshire, where her garden at the Dower House opens for the NGS. She writes for *Hortus*, *The Countryman* and other publications.

Anne Swithinbank

trained at Kew. She is a broadcaster and the author of *The Conservatory Gardener*, *The Gardeners' World Book of House Plants* and *Container Gardening*.

Elspeth Thompson

writes the weekly 'Urban Gardener' and 'Country Gardener' columns in the *Sunday Telegraph Magazine*: journals of her gardening experiences in a shady back yard and an organic vegetable garden on the south coast. Her garden in south London opens for the NGS.

Alan Titchmarsh

has written more than thirty gardening books, including *How to be a Super-gardener*, as well as being the main presenter of BBC2's *Gardeners' World* and *Ground Force*. He gardens on a chalky hillside in Hampshire.

Rosemary Verey OBE VMH

was a writer, plantswoman and garden designer. Her books include *Good Planting* and *The Making of a Garden*. The garden at Barnsley House opens for the NGS.

Robin Williams

is a garden designer and winner of Chelsea Flower Show Gold Medals. He is the author and illustrator of *The Garden Planner*, *The Garden Designer* and *The RHS Garden Planning*. He designs and lectures widely at home and abroad.

Beric Wright MB FRCS MFOM

started the Institute of Directors and BUPA medical centres, was a Governor of BUPA and practises a holistic approach to health and disability. He is Treasurer of the Buckinghamshire NGS, his wife Sue is County Organizer and together they garden on heavy clay soil.

Helen Yemm

is a broadcaster and writer, author of *Gardening in Your Nightie* and a contributor to the *Daily Telegraph*. She opens her Sussex garden for the NGS.

Photographers

Jan Baldwin
Mark Bolton
Clive Boursnell
Nicola Brown
Jonathan Buckley
Brian Chapple
Val Corbett
Eric Crichton
Melanie Eclare
Michael Edwards
Valerie Finnis
Fergus Garrett
Martin Gilbert
John Glover
Jerry Harpur
Marcus Harpur
Charles Hawes
Bryan Hirst
Caroline Hughes
Tim Ingram
Nada Jennet
Andrew Lawson
Patrick Lichfield
Marianne Majerus
Alan Munson
Jackie Newey
Clive Nichols
Picturesmiths
Vivian Russell
Derek St Romaine
Rosalind Simon
Philip Smith
Elizabeth Tite
Michael Warren

Contents

Foreword

by Daphne Foulsham

How appropriate it is to mark the seventy-fifth anniversary of the National Gardens Scheme with a book that includes hundreds of gardens in England and Wales open for charity and draws on the expertise of many of our garden owners. Their generosity and dedication is the foundation of the NGS's charitable purpose and success since 1927, as Rosie Atkins so ably demonstrates in her introduction. We are enormously grateful to Rosie for delving into our archives and weaving the jewels she unearthed into the fascinating story of gardens and gardening in our lifetime.

We are a nation of gardeners and our favourite topic of conversation is the weather. So how right it is that *Making Gardens* focuses on the challenges (and joys) of our temperate climate, degrees of wetness and drought, exposure to sun, sea and wind, different soil types and on the problems of planting on inauspicious sites (surely the greatest challenge of all). With increasing conurbation, we need to savour the pockets of green in our towns and cities and to cherish for future generations the trees that grace our island. The contributors address all these issues and offer a wealth of practical advice gleaned from NGS gardens and garden owners. Their in-depth chapters are enhanced not only by the work of the best garden photographers but also by the host of experts who have so generously given their personal insights.

Behind every endeavour there are people who are key to its success who wish to stay in the shadows. As well as to those whose names appear in *Making Gardens*, we owe an enormous debt of gratitude to the staff at NGS Head Office and at Cassell & Co, and to the Publications Panel who have steered the project. They have succeeded in transforming a bright and ambitious idea into a book that celebrates our heritage and our future. *Making Gardens* is a mine of vital information for every gardener.

A sun-baked border at Vale End, Surrey, the garden created by John and Daphne Foulsham on light, sandy soil (see pages 80–3). The millpond provides a soothing background to a tapestry of flowers, which includes plumes of *Macleaya cordata*, pink and red *Phlox* 'Starfire', *Veronica spicata*, *Achillea* 'Coronation Gold' and *Clematis* 'Perle d'Azur', with self-seeded sisyrinchium and *Alchemilla mollis*.

ROSIE ATKINS

with expert insights by
MARTIN GILBERT
ROBIN LANE FOX
ANNE SCOTT-JAMES

1 Gardens of England and Wales: for Charity's sake

How nice to have a place so large
That you can make a shilling charge
And ask your neighbours in to see
How good their gardens ought to be.
How nice to see them stroll about
When all your flowers are coming out;
To mark the envy in their eyes
Whose gardens are not half the size.
How nice to note the deepening gloom
Caused by your splendid Spanish Broom;
To see them cringe with grief and shame
Because they cannot do the same.
But how much nicer still to know
That all your toil with spade and hoe
With pruning knife and garden rake
Was done for Charity's sweet sake.

REGINALD ARKELL
in *Gardens Open List*, 1948

What a clever idea to combine a nation's obsession with gardening (and our natural curiosity for what's happening on the other side of the fence) with raising money for 'Charity's sweet sake'. The National Gardens Scheme (NGS) has been doing just that for as long as most of us can remember, for seventy-five years to be precise. *Gardens of England and Wales Open for Charity*, the annual guide known affectionately as the Yellow Book, bears witness to massive changes in our society in what amounts to a single lifetime. When the NGS started in 1927, most of the gardens that opened to the public had been handed down with estates through the generations. Victorian high fashion in garden design might have stretched to a garden influenced by Miss Gertrude Jekyll and the Arts and Crafts Movement, but most gardens owed their style to the eighteenth-century 'lords of landscape design', like Humphry Repton and 'Capability' Brown. We have all seen demands on leisure time change and watched the transition from high- to low-maintenance gardening, from labour-intensive seasonal bedding schemes and highly manicured bowling-green lawns to 'naturalistic' perennial borders incorporating ornamental grasses. Gardening has become a pursuit to be enjoyed by all, and the gardens that open for the NGS now include thousands of privately owned suburban plots as well as the rolling acres attached to stately homes. Today those who open for the NGS are more likely to have designed their gardens themselves.

But how did the National Gardens Scheme come about? Well, back in 1926 a committee of the Queen's Institute of District Nursing, chaired by the Duke of Portland, was discussing how to raise money to develop the district nursing service and provide for retired nurses. It decided to link fundraising efforts to an appeal in the memory of Queen Alexandra, the Institute's late patron. Miss Elsie Wagg suggested that money could be raised by charging the public admission to see private gardens. Tradition has it that she said, 'We've got all these beautiful gardens in this country and hardly anyone except their owners and friends ever sees them.'

We don't know if this inspired idea was met with enthusiasm or shocked silence. At the time Britain was still reeling from the effects of a General Strike and the thought of inviting anybody and everybody on to your private property would have been pretty radical; but word may have got around that in 1924 Lady Loder had made the handsome sum of £170 from charging the public to see her garden at Leonardslee in Sussex. Whatever the reaction of that committee, Elsie Wagg found a supporter in Lady March, later Duchess of Richmond and Gordon, who used her considerable influence to persuade her noble friends to open their gardens during the month of June in 1927, charging one shilling a head to raise money for the fund. (In 1927 a shilling, five pence in decimal currency, was a gardener's wage for a morning's, or afternoon's, work.)

The list of owners of the 349 gardens who took part in the June garden opening in 1927 reads like the pages of *Debrett's Peerage*. The King opened his garden at Sandringham in Norfolk and the Duke of Devonshire opened Chatsworth in Derbyshire. The Marquess of Salisbury opened both Cranborne Manor in Dorset and Hatfield House in Hertfordshire. Well-known gardeners were also invited to take part. Miss Ellen Willmott, the first woman member of the Linnean Society, who gardened on a lavish scale (she employed a hundred gardeners at Warley Place in Essex), seemed happy to show off her garden. William Robinson, the influential author of many gardening books, including *The English Flower Garden*, agreed to open his newly acquired home, Gravetye Manor, near East Grinstead in Sussex.

Elsie Wagg's idea was so well supported that the committee decided to continue the scheme throughout the summer. Altogether, 609 gardens opened that year, raising £8,191. With the entrance fee set at one shilling, simple arithmetic suggests that nearly 164,000 people took advantage of the opportunity to enjoy gardens that had never been open to the public before. Special rail and coach trips were laid on and visitors even travelled from abroad to enjoy the spectacle.

When the Queen Alexandra Memorial Fund was disbanded, it was decided that the garden opening should be handed over to the Queen's Institute as a permanent way of raising money to help district nurses. The Gardens Committee was formed, with the Duchess of Richmond and Gordon as its Chairman and a network of well-

PRECEDING PAGES The ponds in spring at Benington Lordship, Hertfordshire, one of the 349 gardens that opened on 8 June 1927 when the NGS was inaugurated. Laid out in a mixture of formality and wildness by Lilian Bott in the early years of the twentieth century, the garden is now owned by her grandson Harry Bott and his wife Sarah. The drawing is of Sandringham, the Norfolk home of King George V, which also opened in 1927 and continues its openings today. It appeared on the cover of the sixtieth Anniversary edition of the Yellow Book 1987, by gracious permission of Her Majesty the Queen.

RIGHT Pamela Schwerdt and Sibylle Kreutzberger, the Head Gardeners at Sissinghurst in Kent from 1959 until their retirement in 1990. Vita Sackville-West wrote her books and articles in the Tudor tower.

ANNE SCOTT-JAMES

'The shillingses' at Sissinghurst

In 1930 Vita Sackville-West and Harold Nicolson fell in love with a neglected Elizabethan castle in Kent – Sissinghurst – and started creating a celebrated garden. Shortly before the war the Nicolsons felt confident enough to open it under the charitable auspices of the National Gardens Scheme. It was open on two days in the summer of 1938, on four days in 1939, on six days in 1940, and thereafter it was open daily throughout the spring and summer. The entrance fee was a shilling. The customers, known as 'the shillingses', put their coins in a bowl left on a table at the entrance. The gardeners got an extra half-crown for doing Sunday duty.

Vita would talk gardening for hours to interested outsiders who came to see the plants. Many a visitor, seeing this tall, handsome woman working in the garden, wearing a brown jacket and breeches and with secateurs tucked into her boots, would stop to ask her questions, and she would answer patiently and with enjoyment.

She wrote affectionately about 'the shillingses' in an article in the *New Statesman* in 1939. 'These mild, gentle men and women who invade one's garden after putting their silver token into the bowl, these true peacemakers, these inoffensive lovers of nature in her gayest form, these homely souls who will travel fifty miles by bus with a fox-terrier on a lead, who will pore over a label, taking notes in a penny note-book – those are some of the people I most gladly welcome and salute. Between them and myself a particular form of courtesy survives, a gardener's courtesy, in a world where courtesy is giving place to rougher things.'

It must be reported that Harold, on the other hand, was apt to be brusque with strangers and that many walked away feeling snubbed.

Gardens of England and Wales

Beatrix Havergal MBE VMH (1901–80) founded Waterperry Horticultural School in 1932. It was one of several establishments set up to train young women to be gardeners. The school where the students boarded closed when Miss Havergal retired in 1970 but the 20-acre Waterperry Gardens at Wheatley in Oxfordshire survive and are open several times a year for the National Gardens Scheme.

connected local organizers was set up to convince people like Sir Henry Hoare, who owned Stourhead in Wiltshire, and Major Lawrence Johnston of Hidcote to continue to open their gardens. Lady Pamela Digby, the Honorary County Organizer for Dorset for the first forty years of the NGS, is quoted as saying that it was one thing to get owners to open their gardens on a 'once-ever' basis, but quite another to persuade them to open annually. However, the Honorary County Organizers must have been very persuasive. On 8 May 1929 the Right Honourable David Lloyd George MP opened Bron-y-de, at Churt near Farnham, and raised £27 16s 6d for the NGS. (If all the money donated was from the 'gate', nearly a thousand people must have visited.) And in August later that year Nathaniel Lloyd at Great Dixter in Sussex opened his garden, little knowing that one day it would bring universal acclaim to his son Christopher, then eight years old.

The number of gardens open to the public grew and grew (in 1931 Ralph Vaughan-Williams opened his at Leith Hill, Dorking), attracting more than a thousand by 1932. In 1934 £12,225 was raised for charity, despite the fact that two million people were unemployed and Britain was in a state of economic collapse. By 1938 the 1½-acre roof garden designed by Ralph Hancock on the sixth floor of the London department store Derry & Toms had opened and soon became a major attraction with its Spanish garden, complete with canal, a Tudor garden and even a traditional English wood.

'Digging for Victory' took its toll on ornamental gardening as well as fundraising but, somehow, the NGS struggled on during the Second World War, producing a much-reduced list of gardens (with the emphasis on vegetables) that continued to open. Records show 1941 to be the worst year, yet the NGS still managed to raise £3,000. Some owners never surrendered, including the former Prime Minister, Lloyd George, who opened Bron-y-de every May throughout the war. The final opening in 1944, the year before Lloyd George died, yielded a contribution of £10 16s.

By 1946 the total sum raised annually by the NGS was back above £10,000. But in the aftermath of war the British gentry faced higher taxation and death duties.

Wage increases imperilled the future of many of Britain's great country houses and garden maintenance was neglected. That same year the Chancellor of the Exchequer decided to use his powers to accept houses and land in payment of death duties by turning them over to the National Trust. Cotehele in Cornwall was the first to be taken over by the Trust in payment of death duties in 1947 and Blickling Hall in Norfolk, which had opened for the NGS in June 1927, soon followed. Both gardens still open for the Scheme.

The one remaining copy of the 1947 list of *Gardens Open in England and Wales* in the NGS archive offers a glimpse of war-torn Britain. This rare and coverless book is printed on paper so thin you can almost see through it. The Organizing Secretary, Mrs Powell, who lived in Putney, must have had a hard time finding garden owners willing to open. I can just imagine her picking up one of those heavy black phones and asking the operator to put her through to Waterperry's gardening school near Oxford to finalize the arrangements for opening with the legendary Miss Havergal. The next year the National Health Service was set up and local authorities became responsible for supplying a home nursing service, threatening to make the NGS redundant. However, money was still required by the Queen's Institute of District Nursing to look after the welfare of elderly and retired district nurses, and the fundraising continued.

Lady Daphne Heald CBE joined the NGS committee in 1947 when she and her family moved to Chilworth Manor near Guildford after being bombed out of their London house. Having been involved in nursing charities for many years, she soon became the Honorary County Organizer for Surrey and, four years later, took over the chairmanship of the NGS from Ruby Fleischmann of Chetwode Manor, Buckinghamshire, who had succeeded the Duchess of Richmond and Gordon. Lady Heald, who was born in 1904, has seen many changes and delights in the fact that people today have a much wider circle of friends. 'In my day sultanas never mixed with currants, but now it's a rich mix of sultanas and currants,' she laughs. She remains a great supporter of the NGS and continues to opens her glorious house and garden for charity. It is incredible to think that, throughout her

MARTIN GILBERT

The garden at Stour

On Sunday 9 June 1963 Winston Churchill's son Randolph opened his garden for the National Gardens Scheme. His pink house, Stour, at East Bergholt in Suffolk, overlooked the Vale of Dedham, Constable country. For the previous year and a half Randolph – or the Boss as we knew him, until a telegram with a typing error in the address caused him to be called 'the Beast of Bergholt' – had been preparing the groundwork of the official biography of his father, then envisaged as a four-volume work (after his death it grew to eight).

Stour became the powerhouse where the Churchill papers were lodged in a specially built strong room next to the house, and where we whom he called his 'ghosts' worked day and night to satisfy his literary demands. His great love was the garden. When the weather allowed, and sometimes when it did not allow, he would dictate to a secretary or a ghost while pacing up and down the terrace, sometimes in his dressing gown.

The pride of the garden, other than the magnificent tulip tree – about whose characteristics Randolph engaged in a massive correspondence with at least a hundred other tulip tree owners – was his arched avenue of roses. This led from the terrace down a gentle slope. One night, during a severe storm, one of his great trees (not the tulip tree) was blown over and dragged the avenue with it: he was devastated. The repair was never fully completed.

Guidance on the roses, and on all aspects of the garden, came from his Essex neighbour across the county border, the artist and sculptress Natalie Bevan, and also from the gardening correspondent of the *Daily Mirror*, Xenia Field, whose strong opinions on what needed doing in the garden often conflicted with his, but while he was strong-willed, she, it seemed to us ghosts, was stronger-willed.

As well as the rose avenue, there were magnificent rose bushes on the terrace. At the Boss's request, I spent many hours away from the archive room, deadheading. One day Loelia, Duchess of Westminster, was his guest. As her car was drawing up in the driveway, he remembered that the roses had not been deadheaded that week. These included one, 'The Duchess of Westminster', which he wished to show off to Her Grace. We ghosts were shooed out to the terrace to get to work, even as Randolph was welcoming the Duchess at the front door.

I remember the June 1963 opening of the garden at Stour for the National Gardens Scheme, the first of five consecutive openings. Ghosts were instructed to wear suits, and Randolph sported a fine cravat. According to the NGS archive, the garden was to have opened a sixth time on 30 June 1968, but the entry has been crossed out. The Boss had died on 6 June. The opening was cancelled. But I remember how well the garden looked on the day of his funeral: Harold Macmillan and Aristotle Onassis were among those who gathered on the terrace and wandered across the lawn.

I was proud to see in the NGS archive that on one of his openings Randolph raised £237. It is pleasant to feel that the arrival of the public at Stour – an event which gave him such pleasure, for he did so love his garden – is now to be remembered.

TOP The pink house, Stour, at East Bergholt in Suffolk, photographed in February 1965. The strong room that housed the Churchill papers during the 1960s can be seen on the far left. To the right of the photograph is the sloping lawn leading to the rose avenue, the pride of Randolph Churchill's garden.
ABOVE 'The Beast of Bergholt' on the terrace, setting off for a stroll down the rose avenue.

twenty-eight years as Chairman, Lady Heald had the help of only two secretaries, but her 'team' was very successful. It must have been something of a *coup* when Mr and Mrs Lanning Roper had the first opening of their Chelsea garden in Onslow Square in 1954.

Lady Heald's job was made a lot easier with the arrival of Rachel Crawshay who was appointed Organizing Secretary in 1956, a job she held for twenty-seven years. 'Rachel was a brilliant organizer,' Lady Heald recalls. Also she 'always knew which of the Honorary County Organizers weren't speaking to each other, so I could make sure they didn't sit next to each other at our annual conferences'. Lady Heald remembers how people started to enjoy life much more after the Queen's coronation in 1952; and then came cars and television. 'When you open your garden today, it's not just the people you have to accommodate but their cars.'

As a child in the 1960s, I remember my parents' first car, a black box on wheels with the all-important Automobile Association badge displayed on the front. Whenever we had the misfortune of breaking down, which seemed to be quite often, a uniformed mechanic on a motorbike would miraculously turn up to rescue us. These smart chaps would salute us as we motored past, but their attention to duty didn't end there. On request, they were able to produce a NGS guide book from their side-car and, if they had nothing more pressing to do, would even escort you to the nearest garden displaying the distinctive yellow sign, 'Garden Open Today'. In some cases the public were just as interested in catching a glimpse of the owner as admiring their flowerbeds. However, celebrities like Beverley Nichols at Sudbrook

ABOVE Margery Fish (1892–1969) in the garden at East Lambrook Manor (the dry corner by the gate). A journalist on the *Daily Mail*, Margery Fish took up gardening in her late forties when she and her husband Walter moved from London to Somerset. She wrote about her exploits in eight much-loved books, including *We Made a Garden*. The garden, now owned by Robert and Marianne Williams, opens for the NGS.

ROBIN LANE FOX

Memories of the Dower House

The gardens of The Dower House in Northamptonshire, which opened for the NGS from 1973 to 1986, were a charming double act, a famous marriage of two talents. Sir David Scott had lived there since 1946 and his subjects were fine trees and shrubs. In 1970 he enlarged the garden by marrying Valerie Finnis, well-known as plantswoman, photographer and a guiding hand behind the grand old Waterperry Horticultural School, near Oxford. As part of her dowry, she brought one of the country's finest collections of small hardy plants, some potting compost and, by courtesy of the removal men, a bucket or two of their resident compost worms.

On to Sir David's framework of trees and shrubs his wife grafted informal beds of unusual hardy plants, a host of cold frames and a wall garden – rectangular raised beds filled with grit and garden soil and retained by a low wall of railway sleepers. I remember the violas and pulsatillas, pinks, phlox, shade-loving bloodroot, rare primulas and saxifrages, all delighting in these beds' improved drainage and circulation of air, while allowing their gardeners to weed them accurately without pulling a muscle.

The Scotts looked after the entire 2½ acres and many thousands of cuttings in pots without the help of a regular gardener. Life, they told me when I visited in 1983, consisted of a morning exodus, armed with a packed lunch and the necessary knee-pads. They returned at dusk, having covered their ground and left themselves with a host of small details to discuss in peace. Wet days were spent potting up cuttings – about 10,000 each year – for sale to keen Yellow Book visitors each April and June.

One plantsman attracts others; a pair is twice as effective. Memories of The Dower House are of a monument to plantsmanship and happy combinations, white hellebores among the Scotts' named blue form of hepatica and, not least, of the two gardeners themselves.

Cottage, Ham Common, were not put out by curious visitors. Mr Nichols wrote to Rachel Crawshay saying that he could have a thousand people in an afternoon at his annual opening and have less to clear up than if he had had a few friends to tea.

As Britain emerged from post-war gloom, the rolling acres attached to castles and stately homes which opened for the NGS began to be outnumbered by suburban gems and small plots behind terraced houses. There was a chance of climbing up the social ladder if you were prepared to move house. As the upwardly mobile upped sticks, children lost touch with grandparents and had no one to teach them the difference between a delphinium and a dahlia. The sixties had started swinging and young people were into music and mini skirts and experimenting with almost everything but gardening. I was lucky and picked up a good deal of practical gardening knowledge as the unpaid assistant to the two gardeners my parents employed to grow vegetables and flowers for the almost self-sufficient Georgian hotel where we lived in Kent. Watching these competitive and highly skilled men, I noticed that, like good cooks, good gardeners were always after good results – results reflecting personality and taste. I was fascinated and saw gardening as an interesting art form but, as it was also considered a form of manual labour and definitely not encouraged as a career, I went off to art school.

So what was happening in garden design in the 1960s? Many would agree that Russell Page's *The Education of a Gardener*, first published in 1962, heralded a great new awakening of interest in the subject. There were other beacons, like the great architect and philosopher Sir Geoffrey Jellicoe, who redesigned Sutton Place in Surrey and, until his death, was working on a park dedicated to garden history in Texas. Very few gardeners in Britain would have been aware of the work of American

designers like Fletcher Steele and Thomas Church. Nor would many have known about the German nurseryman Karl Foerster, who had been promoting the use of perennials, ferns and grasses as the central component of the garden since the 1920s. However, there were those who had a finger on the international pulse and spread the word by opening for the NGS. Among them was Alan Bloom of Bressingham fame, now in his nineties, who pioneered the use of perennials and introduced the idea of the island bed to Britain.

By the 1970s the number of column inches devoted to gardening in national newspapers and magazines seemed to double and books on gardening began to compete with cookery books in popularity. John Brookes' *Room Outside*, published in 1969, was way ahead of its time. He started a revolution, encouraging people to think of their garden as an outdoor room. For some it meant nothing more than buying a set of white plastic chairs, for others it involved an outing to a famously smart garden to seek inspiration. Barnsley House in Gloucestershire became a magnet for

LEFT Valerie Finnis VMH in the potting shed at The Dower House, Boughton House, Northamptonshire, where she and her husband, Sir David Montagu Douglas Scott KCMG OBE (1887–1986), propagated plants. Valerie, who trained at Waterperry, is known for her immense plant knowledge, her garden photography and her candid portraits of well-known horticultural figures, many of whom were her friends.

ABOVE Alan Bloom with members of his family, Fred Whitsey of the *Daily Telegraph*, Sir David Scott (seated on the wall) and Arthur Shackleton of Dublin at Bressingham Hall in Norfolk in the 1960s. Alan Bloom opened the gardens for the NGS from 1954 to 1985. He started Bressingham Nurseries in 1964, specializing in herbaceous perennials. He introduced new cultivars to Britain and promoted the island bed.

those who wanted to copy Rosemary Verey's elegant parterres and potager.

Property booms resulted in a rush for mortgages and as soon as you got your mortgage you were planning your next move. Time for gardening was limited – gardens didn't evolve; they were created in a rush. Low-maintenance gardening became the buzzword and instant gardens were the rage. To meet the demand, garden centres sprang up everywhere, trying to market mass-produced plants as you might sell baked beans.

While some garden owners went for dwarf conifers and the 'planting by numbers' option, others continued to seek inspiration and information from visiting gardens. In Northamptonshire Valerie Finnis and David Scott propagated thousands of plants a year for open days under the NGS and each year attracted more than 1,500 visitors who came from around Britain to see their meticulously kept garden and to buy plants that were available nowhere else. At the Chelsea Flower Show Beth Chatto's exhibits won Gold Medals and her garden in Essex became a mecca for visitors seeking inspiration from a living catalogue of unusual plants. The NGS continued to flourish and by 1973 over £1 million had been raised for charity. The Scheme's Golden Jubilee in 1977 coincided with the Queen's Silver Jubilee. The occasion was marked by all NGS garden owners contributing to a garden seat for the Savill Garden, as well as to a selection of winter-flowering shrubs for the royal garden at Frogmore in Windsor, which had first opened in 1946.

Penelope Hobhouse, the well-known garden writer and dedicated supporter of the NGS, was Honorary County Organizer for Somerset in the late 1970s. Years later her abiding memories are of getting into 'terrible difficulties' when garden owners offered to open their gardens, rather than waiting to be invited to take part. 'I used to find it impossible to tell someone their garden wasn't up to scratch,' she recalls. Like the County Organizers today, she had been told that a garden had to provide 'at least forty-five minutes of interest' in order to get into the Yellow Book. 'Thankfully, there was always Rachel Crawshay to deal with the complaints from both disappointed visitors and insulted owners.'

In 1980 the NGS became a charity in its own right as the National Gardens Scheme Charitable Trust under the patronage of HM Queen Elizabeth the Queen Mother. A major part of its funds continued to be donated to nursing charities, but now over two hundred other national and local charities also benefited, since garden owners were able to allocate a share of what they raised to a charity of their choice. By 1986 over two thousand gardens opened and producing the Yellow Book, now a best-selling paperback, had become a Herculean task.

In the late 1980s the country was hit by an economic recession, house prices began to fall and unemployment figures went up. People's faith in property was shattered and they began to give more consideration to their environment and quality of life. Because people were no longer moving house every few years, they felt it was worth paying more thought to the garden. 'Toil with spade and hoe' was even considered therapeutic – an antidote to stressed lives. There was an insatiable need to demystify gardening, which was wonderfully addressed by Geoff Hamilton whose garden at Barnsdale in Rutland featured regularly on television. Chris Philip computerized the Hardy Plant Society's card index system and, in April 1987, published *The Plant Finder*, containing details of where to find nearly 30,000 plants. The plant snob was born and every keen gardener had a hope of visiting an NGS garden, which might have a specialist nursery attached. Many nurseries catering for the connoisseur gardener were the offspring of opening for charity. Audrey Vockins of Foxgrove in Berkshire opened her garden for the NGS and became so successful at propagating plants that she and her daughter Louise turned their hobby into a business and have been regular medal winners at Royal Horticultural Society shows ever since. Even in the recession of 1988 garden visiting figures topped one million and the entrance fees were rarely more than 50p.

By the 1990s gardeners had also become keen to garden organically and garden design was at last a respectable profession. Schools for garden design were proliferating up and down the country and courses were being laid on in every adult education institute. In 1991 *BBC Gardeners' World Magazine* was launched and gardening magazine circulation figures never looked the

Nancy Lancaster (1897–1994), with her dogs for company, deadheading the borders at Haseley Court in Oxfordshire, which opened frequently for the NGS. The trellis cone which she designed, and painted pale grey, typifies her garden style. Many of the plants came from nearby Waterperry Nurseries, where Nancy Lancaster loved to visit Beatrix Havergal and Valerie Finnis, who took this photograph.

same again. Then, in 1993, *Gardens Illustrated* was created to stimulate new ideas and celebrate the fact that gardening is an international language. Other gardening magazines came (and some went), as gardening became outrageously fashionable. Television went gardening mad, offering everything from Dan Pearson's thoughtful explorations to the 'make-over' programmes which were pure entertainment. By the end of the decade Britain was waking up to the pleasures of natural planting schemes inspired by the Dutch designer Piet Oudolf, and to modern garden design practised by the American-based

partnership of Oehme/Van Sweden. Enthusiasm was also mounting for initiatives which benefited from the Millennium Fund, like the Seed Bank of the Royal Botanic Gardens Kew at Wakehurst Place, West Sussex, which is preserving our botanical future and Cornwall's Eden Project which explores the plant world.

As the new millennium gets under way, and the NGS celebrates its seventy-fifth anniversary, the Yellow Book lists over 3,500 gardens in England and Wales, the majority of which are not normally open to the public. (And, significantly, *The Plant Finder* now contains references to over 70,000 plants.) The NGS provides an invaluable link to the past as well as to the future. Members of the royal family have opened their gardens for the NGS annually since 1927 and many other families have opened their gardens for more than sixty years and, we hope, will continue to do so. The owners of Munstead

Wood, near Godalming in Surrey, generously allow visitors to roam the 10 acres of garden which Gertrude Jekyll created on a sandy heath. I also know of young owners who are busy planning gardens which they hope will be good enough to go into the Yellow Book in the future.

All these gardeners see opening their gardens as an honour and a worthwhile endeavour, allowing visitors to experience a vast diversity of gardening styles. Writer and garden designer Mary Keen has noticed important changes in her attitude to garden opening, having welcomed NGS visitors for the past fifteen years. 'When I used to open once a year, I would go purple in the face getting ready. Now I open all the time with the help of two unskilled girls (two mornings a week) and a contractor to cut hedges and mow when needed. The garden is much rougher around the edges, but I don't feel it has to be immaculate any longer – it is more about the atmosphere and people seem to love it.'

It is impossible to predict what our gardening aspirations will be in the future, but in the next decade buying plants on the internet may take the place of buying plants at garden centres – it is certainly a way of conserving fuel. Then there are the obvious concerns about genetically engineering plants and worries about climate change, which look set to have an enormous effect on the way we garden. By 2020 winter frosts in south-west England could disappear altogether and research shows that oak trees are already coming into leaf earlier because of the increased temperatures. This may sound like good news to some, but many plants and trees are already finding it difficult to cope with the drought and the pests and diseases in frost-free gardens. There is no doubt that everyone will have to think about new ways to conserve water and energy if we want to continue to have beautiful gardens for future generations.

With the help of the NGS, and the expertise of the garden owners who support it, we can 'stroll about' in thousands of gardens to keep abreast of new ideas. We can learn, too, how gardeners cope with heavy or light soil, damp conditions or drought and a host of other watery-weathery-soily issues, and have fun at the same time. Long may the NGS promote a nation's favourite pastime for Charity's sweet sake.

ABOVE Her Majesty Queen Elizabeth the Queen Mother with Sir Harold Hillier (on her left) at The Hillier Arboretum, Hampshire, 8 May 1978. Her Majesty became Patron of the NGS in 1980.

RIGHT Bryan's Ground, Herefordshire, the 7-acre garden created since 1994 by David Wheeler and Simon Dorrell on the Welsh border, first opened to NGS visitors in 1996. Here, in the orchard, *Iris*

sibirica is massed either side of the sinuous lawns lining the gravel drive – a modern and ingenious interpretation of Edwardian formality and an evocation of the lavender fields of Provence.

Seventy-five years of the National Gardens Scheme

1927
Following a suggestion from Elsie Wagg, a council member of the Queen's Institute of District Nursing (now known as the QNI), 609 gardens raise £8,191 for the Queen Alexandra Memorial Fund. The Gardens Committee is set up, with Lady March (later Duchess of Richmond and Gordon) as Chairman.

1928
The QNI makes garden opening an annual event. The Gardens Committee appoints County Organizers and Peggy Smith becomes Secretary, a post she holds until 1945. 727 gardens, including Harewood House in Yorkshire, home of Princess Mary and the Earl of Harewood, raise £6,806.

1929
The QNI prints 5,000 copies of the 'Gardens Open' list. Each county produces its own leaflet.

1930
901 gardens open, raising £10,000.

1931
Scotland's garden scheme is founded.

1939–45
Some counties manage to open gardens (especially those with vegetable gardens) throughout the war years. These include Coppins in Buckinghamshire, the home of the Duke and Duchess of Kent. In 1941 only £3,000 is raised.

1946
Queen Mary opens her private garden at Frogmore for one day a year. Christopher Stone gives the first BBC Home Service (now Radio 4) broadcast on the new season of garden openings.

RIGHT *Ruby Fleischmann, a great rose grower, in her garden at Malcolm House near Moreton-in-Marsh, Gloucestershire.*

The National Gardens Scheme
GARDENS OF ENGLAND & WALES OPEN TO THE PUBLIC
GENERAL LIST 1954
Illustrated Edition 1/6

1954
The Yellow Book 1954 (left) with a drawing of Cottesbrooke Hall, Northamptonshire, the first cover by Rowland Hilder.

1955
Pembrokeshire gardens close because of damage suffered by winter gales, but 1,115 gardens open, raising £19,000.

1965
'Gardens open frequently' is introduced. Garden owners set entrance fees.

RIGHT *An NGS party at Chilham Castle, Kent, in 1956.*

1932

Country Life magazine publishes an illustrated guide – costing one shilling – to 1,079 gardens open for charity, with a green cover and an introduction by its editor, Christopher Hussey.

RIGHT *Cranborne Manor, Dorset, which opened for the tenth year running in 1937 and is still open today.*

1934

Sussex opens more gardens and raises more money than any other county. 10,000 illustrated lists and 40,000 free general lists are printed. The total amount raised is £12,255.

1938

Sissinghurst opens and continues to open throughout the war.

1947

Reginald Arkell mentions the NGS on television. Ruby Fleischmann of Chetwode Manor, Buckinghamshire, succeeds the Duchess of Richmond and Gordon as Chairman of the Gardens Committee. The NGS has its first stand at the Chelsea Flower Show, but the second is not until 1957.

1948

The National Health Service is inaugurated and the money raised from the NGS goes direct to nurses. A joint committee of the RHS and the National Trust is set up for the preservation of gardens, which agrees to link garden opening with the NGS. A proportion of NGS takings is given to the National Trust.

1949

Princess Elizabeth and the Duke of Edinburgh open their garden, Windlesham Moor in Surrey, for the second year running.

1950

The first guide book with a yellow cover is published.

1951

Ruby Fleischmann hands over the chair to Lady Daphne Heald of Chilworth Manor in Surrey.

RIGHT *Chilworth Manor*

1956

Rachel Crawshay is appointed Organizing Secretary and produces the Yellow Book (from a small flat in Lower Belgrave Street) with just a manual typewriter.

LEFT *Barnwell Manor, home of the Duke and Duchess of Gloucester, on the cover of the 1956 Yellow Book.*

1958

Lady Heald suggests floral decoration displays in houses opening for the NGS.

1959

A 'New Owner' sign is introduced in the Yellow Book. Fisons produces *Gardens for Britain*, a forty-minute film about NGS gardens.

1964

The last Yellow Book with a cover by Rowland Hilder is published. The admission price to gardens is no longer a standard one shilling and owners are able to charge more.

1966

The first general map of English counties appears in the Yellow Book, which has its first cover by Val Biro (right). Fisons produces a twenty-minute film, *In Search of an English Garden.*

1970

1,234 gardens open, raising almost £52,000.

1973

Total revenue since 1927 is over £1 million, despite the average admission charge still being one shilling.

1974

The style of the Yellow Book changes from chronological list to diary, with gardens presented alphabetically and descriptions included.

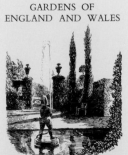

1975

County boundaries in the Yellow Book are adjusted to reflect local government changes. Somerset becomes South Avon. A triangle symbol is used to mark gardens which open for other reasons on other days.

LEFT *The Fireboy Fountain at Plas Brondanw, Merioneth, on the Yellow Book 1966, the first cover drawing by Val Biro.*

27

Gardens of England and Wales

1976

The NGS hires professional help to publicize the scheme and (the following year) employs an agent to sell advertising in the Yellow Book. The QNI assumes responsibility for the Nurses' Welfare Service.

RIGHT *Frogmore, Windsor (by gracious permission of Her Majesty the Queen), on the Golden Jubilee Yellow Book.*

1977

The NGS Golden Jubilee. A rose named after Rachel Crawshay marks her twenty-one years of service as Organizing Secretary.

1978

1,402 gardens open, raising £130,000. The index dropped from the Yellow Book, as economy measure (reintroduced in 1993).

1979

Carolyn Hardy becomes Chairman. The QNI gives consent for NGS to become a charity in its own right and provides a loan to start it off. A black spot in the Yellow Book indicates gardens that open regularly, such as Bressingham Hall in Norfolk and Hever Castle in Kent.

1981

The first trowels are presented to owners who have opened regularly for more than twenty-one years. Carolyn Hardy goes to the USA on a trip organized by the English Tourist Board. The first computer appears in the NGS offices. The number of gardens listed in the Yellow Book now stands at 1,504.

1982

The first Yellow Book to be produced on a computer is published.

LEFT *Her Majesty the Queen receiving an award trowel from Carolyn Hardy (Lord Aberconway, President of the RHS, is on her right).*
RIGHT *Rachel Crawshay admiring euphorbias.*

1986

Angela Azis (Vice President since 1984) succeeds Carolyn Hardy as Chairman. 2,071 gardens are listed in the Yellow Book, including Gardeners' Sunday gardens.

1987

The NGS Diamond Jubilee. *Gardens Open Today* by Alison and Martyn Rix is published to celebrate sixty years of garden visiting. Some gardens that had opened in 1927 open for the Diamond Jubilee. The Yellow Book costs £1. Over £600,000 raised brings the total revenue since 1927 to £4.5 million. The NGS moves from the QNI premises in London to Hatchlands, near Guildford in Surrey, as a tenant of the National Trust. Australia launches its Open Garden Scheme with 63 gardens.

1991

Sue Phillips gives the last in a series of BBC Radio 4 broadcasts given annually since 1946 by well-known celebrities announcing the start of garden visiting for the year.

1993

Daphne Foulsham succeeds Angela Azis as Chairman.

1999

Untold numbers of trowels are awarded: 145 forks to owners of gardens open for 40 years, 28 trees for 60 years and 49 long-service badges for gardeners who have worked for the NGS for 21 years. Carr Sheppards Crosthwaite sponsors the setting up of the website, www.ngs.org.uk. Rachel Crawshay MBE dies.

2000

The Yellow Book costs £4.50 and lists over 3,300 gardens, raising £1,534,860, including £700,000 for Macmillan Cancer Relief. Frogmore opens for the fifty-fifth year. NGS Enterprises is set up.

LEFT *Margaret Fuller of The Crossing House (see page 216), with a silver trowel award.*

1980

The NGS becomes an independent charitable trust with HM the Queen Mother as Patron and Princess Alice as President. The Nurses Welfare Service (NWS) separates from the QNI. A total of 1,455 gardens open, raising £188,705. Owners are able to nominate charities – a system to become known as Additional Charity Nominated by Owner (ACNO). Edward

Wagg (nephew of Elsie Wagg) organizes the Rose Walk in St James' Park as a gift from the NGS to HM the Queen Mother on her eightieth birthday.

LEFT *Dame Jean Maxwell Scott and Princess Alice, President of the NGS and 'a great weeder', says Valerie Finnis (who took the photograph), at The Dower House, Boughton House, Northamptonshire.*

1983

Elizabeth Lonsdale succeeds Rachel Crawshay as Organizing Secretary. Rachel Crawshay becomes a Vice President. The new NGS logo is used in the Yellow Book.

1984

The NGS makes the first donation to Macmillan nurses (now Macmillan Cancer Relief).

1985

The Gardeners' Royal Benevolent Society (started in 1956) and The Royal Gardeners' Orphan Fund become NGS beneficiaries. Gardeners' Sunday merges with the NGS.

RIGHT *The Gardener's Sunday Organisation, part of the Royal Gardeners' Orphan Fund.*

1994

The title of Administrator is changed to Director of NGS. Carr Sheppards (now Carr Sheppards Crosthwaite) sponsors the Yellow Book, which contains 3,000 gardens open in England and Wales.

LEFT *Daphne Foulsham, Chairman of the NGS, photographed in her garden at Vale End by Patrick Lichfield.*

1996

Marie Curie Cancer Care, Crossroads Caring for Carers and Help the Hospices become NGS beneficiaries.

1998

More than £1.4 million is raised and distributed to a dozen charities. The NGS begins funding National Trust Careership Bursaries for training gardeners.

2001

Nearly 50 of the 600 gardens that opened in 1927 still open for the NGS, but only the Queen's home at Sandringham, Norfolk, has opened every year. Garden openings are affected by winter floods and foot and mouth disease. An exhibition is mounted with the Museum of Garden History, entitled 'A Nurturing Nature'.

2002

The seventy-fifth anniversary of the NGS. Carr Sheppards Crosthwaite sponsors the Yellow Book for the ninth year and the website for the fourth year.

LEFT *'Charity', bred by David Austin and named on behalf of the NGS in 1997, has true Old Rose character with a myrrh fragrance.*

LEFT Cottesbrooke Hall Gardens in Northamptonshire, which has opened for the NGS for sixty years. BELOW Shrubland Park, Suffolk, was the home of the Lord de Saumarez in 1927 when the garden first opened for the NGS. RIGHT Frogmore Gardens, Berkshire, the royal family's private gardens, opened for the first time in 1946, giving the Gardens Scheme a much-needed post-war boost, and continue to open to this day, by gracious permission of Her Majesty the Queen. RIGHT, BELOW Blickling Hall, Norfolk, opened in 1927 and continued to support the NGS after ownership transferred to the National Trust after the war.

As well as the gardens Rosie Atkins unearthed from the archives, here are others that have contributed to NGS charities for fifty years or more.

Bedfordshire
Luton Hoo Gardens
Southill Park

Berkshire
Englefield House
Hurst Lodge
Odney Club

Bristol & South Gloucestershire
Lyegrove

Buckinghamshire
Ascott
Nether Winchendon House
West Wycombe Park

Cheshire & Wirral
Manley Knoll
Thornton Manor

Cornwall
Glendurgan

Cumbria
Dallam Tower

Derbyshire
Tissington Hall

Devon
Dartington Hall Gardens
Mothecombe House
Tapeley Park

Dorset
Minterne

Durham
Raby Castle

Gloucestershire North & Central
Batsford Arboretum
Hidcote Manor Garden
Kiftsgate Court
Misarden Park
The Old Rectory
Sezincote
Stanway Water Garden
Westonbirt School Gardens

Hampshire
Bramdean House
Exbury Gardens
Hinton Ampner
Jenkyn Place
Moundsmere Manor

Pylewell Park
Somerley
Wyck Place

Herefordshire
Dinmore Manor

Hertfordshire
Knebworth House Gardens
St Paul's Walden Bury

Isle of Wight
Woolverton House

Kent
Chevening
Hole Park
Knole
Ladham House
Northbourne Court
Sandling Park
Scotney Castle
Sissinghurst Garden

Leicestershire & Rutland
Prestwold Hall

London
Walpole House

Norfolk
Sandringham Grounds

Northamptonshire
The Cottage
Deene Park

Nottinghamshire
Thrumpton Hall

Oxfordshire
Barton Abbey
Blenheim Palace
Buckland

Kingston Bagpuize House
Kingstone Lisle Park
The Manor House
Wardington Manor

Powys
Powis Castle Garden

Somerset
Barrington Court
Tintinhull

Surrey
Chilworth Manor
Feathercombe

Sussex
Bignor Park
Borde Hill Garden
Chidmere House
Cooke's House
Cowdray Park Gardens
Great Dixter
The Manor of Dean
Mountfield Court
Newtimber Place
Nymans Garden

Warwickshire
Ilmington Manor

Wiltshire
Conock Manor
Corsham Court
Fonthill House
Iford Manor
Stourhead Garden

Worcestershire
Overbury Court
Spetchley Park Charitable Trust

Yorkshire
Ampleforth College Junior School
Sleightholme Dale Lodge

31

*Gardens
of England
and Wales*

GEOFF HODGE

with expert insights by
PENELOPE HOBHOUSE
ADAM PASCO
BERIC WRIGHT

2 Wrestling with clay

As solid as a rock in summer and a soaking-wet quagmire in winter, clay soil causes severe heart- and backache for gardeners. The soil type that I get more questions about than any other is the cold, stodgy mess that, when in poor condition, just passes for soil. Patience is the key. If trouble is taken to make the soil more workable, clay is a fertile and water-retaining soil type.

Pick up a handful of soil and squeeze it gently in the palm. If it forms a solid ball that won't break up easily, it is clay. Other tell-tale signs include boggy, waterlogged areas in winter and deep fissures and cracks in summer. The problem for gardeners often comes with a brand-new house. The builders usually scrape off the good topsoil before they start building and sell it. Months of wear and tear from contractors' machinery and heavy boots leave behind a material more suited for making bricks than a garden. This is then usually covered with turf or a bark mulch to hide the hard panned soil and brick rubble the day before the builders leave the site. So, if you are buying a brand-new house, brush back mulches to see if the soil below is cracked. Make sure that the contract states you will be left with a proper garden and good topsoil; if it does not, get it written in. I know several people who have done this and have been thankful they did.

But if your garden soil is based on clay, take heart – it has the potential to be an excellent growing medium and the best soil you could possibly have. At 46 Long Meadow Road in Derbyshire the flower borders and a mixed

vegetable, fruit and shrub garden are flourishing on what was once a thin layer of heavy clay covering a pile of building rubble. And I used to garden in a town that was an island before the Fens were drained – an island formed from a huge lump of clay left behind by the Ice Age. The soil took some hard work when I first moved there, but it soon became workable and an excellent growing medium for just about any plant.

Taking care of the soil and working with it – rather than against it – is the key to success. John and Sue Dinenage's garden at 8A Castle End Road in Cambridgeshire was once a field on heavy clay. They have been gardening there since 1979, adding their own compost and loads of mushroom compost and horse manure. 'Improving it', John and Sue told me, 'is a continuous process.' But it now grows good plants, and many seed freely, including *Anemone blanda*, dierama, snake's-head fritillaries (*Fritillaria meleagris*) and annual poppies. The main difficulties are digging up plants and weeds and planting new specimens. 'If we don't make big planting holes and incorporate compost in and around new plants, they become isolated in a cylinder of potting compost, surrounded by cracks. Then the roots dry out and the plant suffers.'

Throughout Britain there are NGS gardens on heavy, unforgiving soils. The owners I talked to, whether they garden in Dorset or Kent, Yorkshire or Lancashire, all agree on one point: to turn clay soil into a fertile oasis takes hard work, and keeping it in good condition is an on-going process. Julia and Tim Wise at Rustling End Cottage in Hertfordshire admit to finding out the hard way. They planted in heavy clay, but soon the plants were struggling and many were starting to die. There was nothing for it but to dig up all the plants that were still alive, pot them up and spend time on improving the soil. Within two years the herbaceous borders were established, the potager was flourishing and the garden was ready for visitors.

A glance at the directory of gardens on clay on pages 52–3 will dispel the misconception that all clay soils have a low pH value and are best for growing acid-loving rhododendrons, camellias, pieris, summer-flowering heathers and other lime haters. These plants certainly thrive at Woodside in Lancashire and at Sherwood in Devon. But as well as being acid, clay can be alkaline or neutral depending on the parent rock from which the soil was formed. The pH value is more stable than that of other soils. John Tordoff's garden at 17A Navarino Road, London, is on neutral clay, but he grows ericaceous plants, such as dwarf azaleas and rhododendrons, in plastic buckets plunged into the soil.

PRECEDING PAGES Once Judy and Raymond Brown had worked organic matter into the cold, clay soil at Old Farm, Buckinghamshire, they were able to plant delphiniums among the roses and alstroemerias. The tall spikes echo the dreaming spires of Oxford in the distance, across the Vale of Otmoor. The drawing of Ilmington Manor, Warwickshire, is from the 1992 Yellow Book.

ABOVE In the shady, oriental part of his 25 x 7m/80 x 22ft London garden, John Tordoff has created an undulating carpet of baby's tears (*Soleirolia soleirolii*) on either side of a narrow stream.

RIGHT Roses and other shrubs are interplanted with perennials and annuals such as cosmos and cleome in the Staceys' 32 x 9m/ 105 x 30ft mixed border on alkaline clay at Gorsehill Abbey Farm, Worcestershire.

Wrestling
with clay

Advantages and disadvantages

There are several advantages of gardening on clay. Whereas sandy and chalky soils drain rapidly in summer and, especially in the case of sand, leach out in winter or during periods of heavy rains, clay soils are neither hungry nor thirsty. Clay particles lock in nutrients and moisture and, therefore, are naturally very fertile. They are also rich in beneficial soil-dwelling insects and other animals, including earthworms, as well as micro-organisms, all of which are vital for maintaining soil fertility. Unfortunately, slugs are also usually more prevalent in clay soils, especially the soil-dwelling keel slugs which feed on potatoes and other plants with thick, juicy roots and tubers.

In their vegetable garden at Gorsehill Abbey Farm in the Vale of Evesham, where the clay soil is very heavy and alkaline, Michael and Diane Stacey grow mainly potato varieties like 'Charlotte' and 'Kestrel' that are reasonably resistant to slugs. 'These second earlies', says Diane, 'have the added advantage of being harvested before blight becomes prevalent, and also store well.' The old maincrop salad potato 'Pink Fir Apple', though slug resistant, succumbs to blight in a bad year. Voracious slugs and snails, as well as the cold, wet clay soil, have put paid to delphiniums, lupins and crown imperials. Penstemons, however, though they succumb in waterlogged soils and cold winds, are totally slug-proof and these are grown where the drainage can be improved sufficiently. The Staceys tried various slug deterrents, including bonfire ash, which 'though deterring them when dry, ceases to be effective after rain'. The most successful deterrent is bran, purchased inexpensively in large quantities from agricultural merchants. 'The bran works as a distraction rather than a deterrent,' says Diane. 'On damp evenings I gather the marauding creatures and put them in salt water.'

Densely planted ground cover stops the heavy soil from baking solid in summer in Jackie Barber's garden, Deanswood, in Yorkshire. Colourful-stemmed willows, elders and bamboos are luxurious backdrops to living-willow arches. Jackie made these by planting long rods of *Salix viminalis* 'Bowles' Hybrid' 15cm/6in apart on either side of the grass walks and criss-crossing them to join overhead. She tied the crossing points with tarred twine until, after two years, the stems had united. Pruning and weaving in the new shoots is done during the winter, cutting side shoots not used for weaving back to three buds.

One drawback of clay soils is that they are 'cold', so they take longer to warm up in spring than sandy soils. Delay seed sowing until the soil has started to dry out, warm up and become workable. On the other hand, deep clay has an advantage – making a pond or bog garden is a matter of excavating a hole and puddling the clay base to a waterproof finish. Jackie Barber took advantage of a natural stream and solid, waterlogged clay by developing three ponds in her garden, Deanswood, near Ripon.

Understanding clay soils

The particles that make up clay are very fine and generally flat in profile – like plates – and they tend to clump together one on top of each other when wet. They are also very sticky and, because they prefer to stick to each other rather than anything else, they form large lumps that prevent air and water moving through them – which is why clay is used in pottery. As roots need oxygen, air spaces in the soil are essential for healthy root growth: without them plants struggle and either become unhealthy or die.

In badly drained clay the roots sit in water in winter and rot. In summer, because the particles prefer to stick together, they tear apart when they start to dry out, producing the characteristic soil cracks. This tearing or ripping can physically damage any roots in the vicinity, again leading to poor growth. In severe conditions, especially in the lower subsoil layers, the plate-like stacks become almost glued together to form solid, impervious layers. These become very hard and prevent further water from passing through them, so the winter waterlogging problem becomes worse. They can also be too difficult for roots to grow through and, because there is so little air

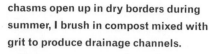

ADAM PASCO

Heaps of magic

More by default than desire, I have gardened on clay soil for the past seventeen years in one home or another. It has its virtues and its drawbacks, but on balance I'm happy. The secret is to learn to live with it, go with the flow and slowly, very slowly, improve your lot. I've tried creating high-rise beds to improve drainage, flocculating the soil with gypsum and, top of the list, combining it with compost.

In the world of gardening make-believe on television, barrowloads of compost turn up programme after programme as if from a magic heap. Advice to dig in copious quantities of homemade garden compost wears thin when you haven't got any! Mushroom compost is the solution. When I moved to my present home in 1990, a year before I launched *BBC Gardeners' World Magazine*, a truck full of mushroom compost almost followed the removal van down the road to make its first delivery of many. I spread it liberally over all bare areas. The thick mulch keeps down weeds, and I let the worms do the job of taking the compost down into the soil. Why bother digging when the worms can do it for you?

Of course, I now make as much compost as I can, and have four heaps plus a worm bin in the corner of the greenhouse, but even this isn't enough. Surface mulches soon disappear underground and you quickly realize how hungry clay soil is for more. If wide chasms open up in dry borders during summer, I brush in compost mixed with grit to produce drainage channels.

Everyone says roses love clay, and they do, but you cannot create a garden with roses alone. Star performers on my clay soil include *Ceanothus* 'Cynthia Postan', *Euphorbia characias* subsp. *wulfenii*, *Rhamnus alaternus* 'Argenteovariegata', *Solanum crispum* 'Glasnevin', *Humulus lupulus* 'Aureus', plus spiraea, liatris, campanula, stachys, hedera, flag iris and epimedium. A firm favourite is *Phygelius* × *rectus*, the Cape fuchsia, which establishes well and spreads in a controllable fashion.

Everyone thought that the late Geoff Hamilton's garden at Barnsdale, just up the A1 from me north of Rutland Water, had a garden composed of friable potting compost. Oh, how the television deceives! The reality was a soil of boot-caking clay, and only a great deal of work over a number of years transformed it into perfect garden soil, with bountiful rewards.

present, plants become stunted and generally unhealthy. At Tinpenny Farm in Gloucestershire the clay goes down at least 1.8m/6ft and a day or two of rain leaves water on the surface of the soil for a week or more. The ground is often under water until the end of April. 'Then in summer it looks like a lunar landscape,' says the owner, Elaine Horton, 'with plates of clay surrounded by deep cracks. After three days of a drying wind, I'm left with concrete.' Elaine advises never planting anything that has been grown in peat as the roots are too fine to penetrate the clay. Everything is started in a soil-based compost or is planted bare-rooted. And after planting she makes a slight mound around the plants to throw off the water.

The topsoil may also form an impenetrable layer after compaction by heavy rain or excess water from a hosepipe. Luckily, this is easy to break up with a hoe or soil cultivator. Because clay soils are easily compacted, especially when wet, it is essential that you don't walk on them or use rollers or similar heavy machinery when they are very wet. Otherwise the weight will compact the soil even more and squeeze out the air introduced by cultivation, so ruining the structure that you have painstakingly tried to create.

In Hans and Elizabeth Seiffer's summer garden at Garden House Farm, Suffolk, a deep border on well-worked clay displays clouds of *Crambe cordifolia*, *Rosa* 'Blairii Number Two' (on the trellis), *R.* 'Tour de Malakoff' and *R.* 'Gypsy Boy', with astrantias, alliums and *Papaver* 'Patty's Plum'. At the front of the bed a froth of pink *Phuopsis stylosa* merges with *Campanula takesimana* 'Elizabeth'.

Improving clay

You can start to make the soil more workable by roughly digging it over in autumn. The action of wind, rain and frost will break apart the large, dense clumps into smaller lumps. Adding hydrated lime or gypsum – a natural rock – at the rate of 550g per sq m/1lb per sq yd, or calcified seaweed at the rate of 135–270g per sq m/4–8oz per sq yd to the roughly dug soil will help break down the large clods even further, reducing the particles' desire to clump together. Lime and calcified seaweed will raise the soil pH, making it more alkaline and unsuitable for lime haters; gypsum does not affect soil pH, so should be used where lime haters are to be grown. Any thick, impenetrable layers of clay lower down in the soil need to be broken up with a garden fork or, in some cases, a pickaxe. If you have a large garden and can't tackle this all in one go, concentrate on an area at a time and give it your full attention, rather than skimping over the whole garden.

One word of caution: subsoil. All soils have a low-lying subsoil which is more like the parent rock from which the soil was originally formed and this is even more compact, containing no air, organic matter or nutrients. In clay soils the subsoil can be yellow or contain rusty brown streaks or, at the worst, either has blue streaks or is grey-blue in colour, indicating it is high in iron content but low in oxygen. It is important never to bring the subsoil to the top of the soil – either leave it where it is or, where practical, dig it out and remove it. If you leave it *in situ*, first break it up and add plenty of organic matter directly on top to help break it down and prevent it from re-forming, and then replace the topsoil.

Conditioning with humus

Whenever I get a question on plants growing badly and the soil is clay, I can almost guarantee that the gardener has not improved the soil with humus. My answer is nearly always to throw lots of organic matter at it – so much so, that a local radio station I work for has christened me Geoff 'Bulky Organic Matter' Hodge! But I don't mind. A good soil is the route to becoming a good gardener.

After roughly digging over the soil and allowing frost to work on the large, clumping boulders, you need to increase the humus content to improve it further. Humus – the dark brown or black substance produced by the slow decomposition of organic matter by bacteria and fungi – is the soil's lifeblood. It will work its way between the fine clay particles, creating air spaces through which water can percolate and through which roots can grow. As well as helping to separate the soil particles, humus also holds nutrients and moisture and is the food of many micro-organisms and soil-dwelling insects and animals.

It doesn't matter what bulky organic matter you use, as long as it is well rotted and you can get a plentiful supply of it. A very poor clay soil may need a wheelbarrow load for every 2–3 sq m/2–3 sq yd of soil. But it is a great way of building up muscles and giving you a healthy glow on cold days. Manure of all sorts – farmyard or stable manure (the latter is usually mixed with straw or paper which, when rotted down, are also excellent soil conditioners) – and mushroom compost are cheap and readily available; the producers are usually only too happy to get rid of the stuff. You can also use homemade or proprietary compost, leafmould, dried seaweed, bracken litter or spent hops. Even shredded newspaper mixed with grass clippings and allowed to rot down for a few months before digging in provides excellent humus.

The organic matter has to be well rotted. The high nitrogen and other nutrient levels in fresh manure will scorch plant roots. Using fresh grass clippings and other unrotted green material will rob the soil of nitrogen, as the bacteria used in the breakdown processes will have to absorb the nutrients they need to decompose the raw materials. Proprietary concentrated manures are also best avoided as these are not bulky enough and contain too many nutrients to be used in large quantities. They are best applied as a general fertilizer top dressing as they will burn plant roots if used in bulk. And because mushroom compost contains lime, it should not be used as a soil conditioner where lime haters are going to be grown.

Finally don't forget the lawn. Many people think that lawns can look after themselves and don't need plenty of soil improving to do well. Wrong! The soil should be improved before you sow seed or lay turf by digging to a depth of 15–23cm/6–9in and applying plenty of bulky organic matter, and sharp sand if necessary.

Spend every penny

It is always better to economize on garden features and plants rather than on soil preparation and improvement, as a garden will never be quite as it should be if the soil is unworkable. Also in heavy soil you, the gardener, will have to endure the backbreaking task of difficult digging every time you plant and gardening won't be fun.

Thorough preparation is vital to turn difficult clay soil into viable loam. In my garden at Bettiscombe, I was faced with heavy Dorset clay, waterlogged in winter and drying out into cement-like blocks in summer.

Before initial planting, I recommend double digging and incorporating mushroom compost (which contains gypsum, a clay breaker) and grit to improve soil structure. Thereafter, I find it best to avoid digging but to add handfuls of 6mm/¼in grit whenever I plant. I mulch the beds with more mushroom and homemade compost in both autumn and early summer.

I grow vegetables in raised beds and for plants needing humus-rich, well-drained soil to a substantial depth – the foxtail lilies (*Eremurus*), for example – it is worth bringing in new topsoil. It is expensive, but worth every penny you can afford.

The walled garden of The Coach House in Bettiscombe, Dorset, is a sea of colour, structure and form, thanks to traditional clay pipe drainage, topsoil mixed with gravel and further gravel mulching.

41

Wrestling with clay

Improving soil structure

If the soil is very heavy clay, you may need to do more than add humus. Because the aim is to break up the layer upon layer of flat particles, adding more rounded ones adds to the ease with which water and air can penetrate and percolate. So you can use sharp grit or gritty sand to improve the structure further; don't use builder's sand as its particles are too smooth and will increase the problem rather than reduce it. In practice this means adding a 2.5cm/1in-thick layer of the sharp grit on top of the soil and then a thick layer – 23–30cm/9–12in – of organic matter and forking both of them into the top 45cm/18in of soil. This is the ideal depth for most perennial plants, although for vegetables and annuals you can get away with 23–30cm/9–12in of good soil. If your soil is not so deep, you will have to amend this accordingly. In this case you may want to try to increase the depth of soil by raising it above ground level (see 'Raise your expectations' on page 47).

You may have read or heard about magic clay cures or clay breakers: powders you add that claim to turn clay into a workable soil. Sadly, this isn't the case. They can be used to help the conditioning process, but won't solve the problem on their own. They are based on gypsum and should be applied at the rate of 275–550g per sq m/10oz–1lb per sq yd.

Mulching

Unfortunately, one initial application of organic matter will not be the end of the process. It is amazing how quickly clay soils 'eat' organic matter and soon it will seem as if nothing has been added. So you have to keep topping it up. The easiest way to do this in planted beds and borders is to keep the soil well mulched with an annual top dressing of more bulky organic matter. Not only does this help top up the soil's organic content and continue the conditioning process, but it also helps fill in the cracks that form as a matter of course in dry weather.

Rather than using something like ornamental bark chips, which are very popular as a mulch, you want a material that will break down more quickly and become incorporated into the soil. One of the best for this is composted bark, but compost, leafmould or whatever you used in the first instance as a soil conditioner will be fine. Use the mulch at least 7.5cm/3in thick and top it up annually. Over time worms and other animals will help incorporate the organic matter into the soil, improving it all the time.

In the vegetable garden, annual borders and any other area that may be left bare in winter, further organic matter can be added at any time when the crops are removed and the soil is worked over. Alternatively it can be used as a mulch around growing plants. Judith and Tony Bradshaw at Cherry Tree Lodge in Lancashire were lucky enough to

have soil in reasonable heart when they moved to Catforth in 1984, but they still mulch heavily with well-rotted cow and horse manure and leafmould from the end of March through April. 'We find this traps in the moisture for the summer,' they told me. It also 'keeps weeds at bay and makes those that do appear much easier to pull out'. Jackie Barber at Deanswood mulches during the summer months to overcome the problems of cracking. Mulches also insulate roots from frost in winter.

In 'bare soil' situations, some gardeners also sow green manures – quick-growing, leafy plants, such as alfalfa, agricultural lupins, agricultural mustard, clover, tares and Hungarian grazing rye. These are a quick, easy and beneficial way of increasing soil humus content. When the plants have produced plenty of leafy growth, dig them into the soil to rot down naturally. The roots improve soil structure, work their way between clay particles, so helping to break up larger clumps, and bring up nutrients from the lower layers of soil. Many are legumes which produce their own nitrogen in root nodules and this is released when the plants are dug in, increasing fertility.

Planting precautions

Bearing in mind that patience is the key, don't get carried away and start planting up your garden as soon as you can – clay soils need time. Get the soil into shape first and worry about planting later when conditions have improved. The Staceys at Gorsehill Abbey Farm spread the strawy bedding from the farm's cattle and sheep sheds and leave it to rot down for a year before digging it in and planting their borders. The result is a profusion of colour from the roses and perennials that relish the fertility of heavy clay.

Planting in heavy clay should never consist of digging a hole and simply putting in a new plant. Clay surrounding friable soil/compost will act like a sump, water will accumulate within it and the plant's rootball will be sitting in a bath of water. Unless it is an aquatic or bog plant, the roots will soon start to rot. To test for drainage, dig the hole and fill it with water. If the water does not drain away, rather than digging a hole big enough for the plant, dig over an area of at least 1 sq m/1 sq yd to a depth of 45cm/18in, incorporating compost or composted bark.

Roughly fork over the sides and bottom of the hole: if they become smeared, this could be the start of an impervious clay 'pan'. Fork over the soil below the rootball and add more organic matter to encourage the plant's roots to grow down rather than back up to escape the horrible conditions below. Make sure that the rootball is completely covered, but only just: burying the stems in cold, wet soil may lead to them rotting. As Elaine Horton advises, after planting make a slight mound around the plants to throw off any excess water.

Winter flooding

If your garden becomes heavily flooded in winter because of poor soil drainage, you may have to consider installing a sump or even underground drainage pipes to take away excess water. Connecting pipes to the main drains or a similar drainage route is a difficult and time-consuming job and usually best left to an expert.

A sump is easier. Find the lowest point of the garden or an area that always floods and dig a hole about 60cm/2ft square and as deep as needs be to get past any impenetrable layers which will need digging over, but probably in the region of 1.2–1.8m/4–6ft deep. Once it drains reasonably freely you can fill the hole with brick rubble and stones. If you have to dig the sump in the borders or in the lawn, you can lay a planting or landscape membrane over the rubble and cover that with soil, or soil and turf. Remember that this area will be more prone to drying out in summer. You could place a large plant container over it.

LEFT Long grass in the orchard at Weeks Farm, Kent, is studded with daffodils and drifts of naturalized *Fritillaria meleagris*. The cold, Wealden clay retains moisture in winter and dries out in summer when the snake's-head fritillaries are setting and dispersing seed. Robin and Monica de Garston apply a high-potash lawn feed when the blooms have faded and delay mowing the grass until July.

ABOVE At The Menagerie, Northamptonshire, yellow flag iris (*I. pseudacorus*) colonize the boggy margins of the pond, created in a natural clay quagmire to complement the native wetland garden.

Wrestling with clay

ABOVE At Dunstarn Lane in Leeds, Richard and Joyce Wainwright grow more than sixty varieties of delphinium, including 'Chelsea Star', 'Circe', 'Cupid' and 'Tessa'. The borders are fed with high-potash fertilizer in spring and with granules 'little and often' through the summer. These are left on the surface as even gentle hoeing might damage the delphiniums' shallow roots. Feeding the already rich clay soil encourages sturdier stems, but tall plants with heavy flowering spikes are vulnerable to wind and rain. Each stem is individually staked – a painstaking task but one that ensures a magnificent display.

Dr H. Beric Wright

Be kind to your back

I write this as an active octogenarian, custodian of a 2½-acre garden which opens to the public for the **NGS**. My younger wife is the 'plantsperson' and I do produce for house and sale. We do have a little outside help, but there is always more than enough to do and we never quite catch up. Madam has to watch her back and is often

encouraged to stop for tea.

I am, luckily, one of the few people I know who has never had any of the back trouble which afflicts so many, perhaps even the majority, of other folk. A frozen shoulder, from throwing logs many years ago, has been my only major physical problem. Why this should be is probably a mixture of good or the right genes, luck and knowing how to grow old gracefully – and successfully.

Simplistically backs, or their owners, can be divided into three categories. First, there are those with really bad and limiting backs requiring medical supervision. They are beyond the scope of a short article. Second, there are people with a vulnerable back which, perhaps because of a previous event like a prolapsed disc or other mild trouble, has to be treated with some respect but, with minor limitations, should allow a fairly full range of physical activity. There are several causes of this vulnerability, one of which is being tall and unusually thin and possibly a bit hyperactive (ectomorphic). The tall are vulnerable because they don't get an extra vertebra for being taller – the same anatomy, bones, joints and so on are stretched over a greater area, so there is greater leverage when they are exerted. To minimize risk, gardeners with vulnerable backs must be disciplined about maintaining muscle strength with regular use/exercise – see below.

For the rest of us, the reasonably fit and actively inclined, there are a few sensible rules, largely related to 'growing old gracefully' in physical and mental terms. A vital rule for survival is 'use it or lose it' – and this goes for brain as well as muscles and joints. Flexibility is maintained by regular exercise, or

use. Thus the key and the discipline for the gardener's back, and indeed the rest of him or her, is to keep up activity levels by regular demand. Regular exercise means all the year round and not just during the gardening season. In winter swimming is ideal because it is non-weight-bearing exercise; as is using a static bicycle, a good, all-weather challenge.

Given twelve months' reasonable activity, there is no need to be frightened off gardening, whatever your age. But be sensible about it: don't over-exert by unusual pushing, pulling or lifting (there are good health rules about heavy lifting in most manuals on health and safety). Mechanize as much as you can afford: it leaves energy for other things. Don't dig for too long at a time and always stop when tired. When pottering in the greenhouse, potting shed or elsewhere, work at a comfortable height. I have an old table that leads a mobile life in the yard for special or unusual activity.

For weeding, get comfortable – kneeling is often more so than bending. Special two-height stools can help. Momentary giddiness is natural when standing from kneeling, because it takes several seconds for the blood supply to the brain to readjust. If it lasts longer, it might be wise to have a medical check.

The message, then, is: remain fully physically and mentally involved in life and gardening, exploit good genes if you have them, watch your weight and, above all, keep fit all the year. Take no notice of anyone (and this may include an over-sympathetic doctor) who tells you to take it easy 'because of your age'. You have to be tired to sleep well.

ABOVE The raised beds at Brudenell House in Buckinghamshire, give root crops room to develop in a more free-draining soil (made of seven parts topsoil, three parts peat-substitute and two parts horticultural grit) than the garden's heavy clay. Raised beds warm the soil more quickly in spring and allow Sue and Beric Wright to garden and harvest their produce more comfortably.

RIGHT At Tinpenny Farm in Gloucestershire, Elaine Horton's stone-edged beds lift plants above the clay soil, which is often under water until the end of April, and introduce changes in level.

Raise your expectations

If the soil in your garden is really problematical and you cannot face digging down to improve it, why not raise it above normal soil level? The Bradshaws at Cherry Tree Lodge told me: 'Although our heavy, yellow clay soil is overlaid with about a spade's depth of good loam, the clay holds water in winter and the beds become waterlogged. So we raise beds to give better drainage.'

The raised-bed or 'no-dig' method of gardening is becoming very popular for growing vegetables as you can crop heavily from a relatively small area. But it can be used anywhere in the garden for any plants, especially alpines which need particularly good drainage. (The Bradshaws hold a National Collection of hardy geraniums and grow the alpine types in raised beds.) You never have to dig over the soil once the bed has been built – just lightly work it with a fork now and again and top dress annually with organic matter.

The soil in the raised bed should never be walked on if you can help it, so make the beds of a size that allows you to reach in to the plants from the sides. The vegetable garden at Gorsehill Abbey Farm has been maintained with minimal cultivation for eighteen years. The Staceys got rid of the weeds by covering the narrow beds with carpet and black polythene, dug them over thoroughly once, and every year enjoy an impressive range of well-flavoured and colourful produce, including purple-podded peas and mangetout 'Bijou'.

There are several types of material you can use to create a restraining wall to 'box' in good topsoil above normal ground level. There are the ever-popular railway sleepers. Mini-sleepers, available from most good garden centres, are more expensive but, being less bulky, are often more appropriate for small gardens, and unlike railway sleepers they don't leak tar. Log roll – short pieces of wood attached to a length of galvanized wire – is flexible and especially useful for making curved beds, but it generally comes in short lengths and is not tall enough to form a good high bed. It works out quite expensive if used over a large area. I prefer to buy lengths of half-round larch, which enables me to build beds of any height and length. Both log rolls and larch are held in place by banging in wooden stakes at corners and at appropriate points along the sides; the log roll or lengths of larch are then nailed to these. Another alternative is to buy lengths of round wood, cut them to size and hammer them into the ground or set them in concrete.

If stone, brick or rock fits in better with the look and feel of the house, you can make your raised beds from these, but they will be more expensive.

Shady border on clay soil

This planting combination contains some stalwarts that will thrive in a shady spot in nearly all clay soils. Backed by a fence, clothed with hardy wall shrubs, the border measures 6 x 1.5m/20 x 5ft and the plants will provide many months of colour.

1 *Cotoneaster horizontalis* 'Variegatus'

2 *Pyracantha* 'Navaho'

3 *Chaenomeles speciosa* 'Nivalis'

4 *Digitalis* × *mertonensis*

5 *Aucuba japonica* 'Crotonifolia'

6 *Anemone* 'Honorine Jobert'

7 *Mahonia* × *media* 'Winter Sun'

8 *Geranium* 'Ann Folkard'

9 *Vinca minor* 'Variegata'

10 *Iris sibirica* 'Butter and Sugar'

11 *Potentilla fruticosa* 'Eastleigh Cream'

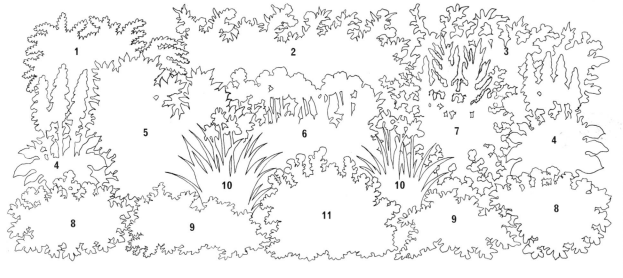

ABOVE *Iris sibirica* 'Butter and Sugar' with variegated *Hosta* 'Frances Williams' at Glen Chantry in Essex. The Siberian flag irises will grow in sun or partial shade in almost any retentive soil.

RIGHT In the Rose Garden at The Menagerie, in Northamptonshire, *Geranium* 'Johnson's Blue' and sweet williams complement a variety of different types of shrub rose. Foxgloves provide colourful vertical accents. A neat edging of box defines the planting and prevents plants from flopping on to the lawn. The border is mulched regularly to keep the heavy soil in good condition and to reduce weeds.

Plants for clay soils

Most of the NGS gardeners I talked to have arrived at 'best plants' by trial and error, and with a positive attitude. At first Diane Stacey planted 'anything and everything' in a Jekyllian colour scheme, but most of the silver and grey plants rotted away. The Bradshaws also discovered the conditions were useless for silver-leaved plants, though *Lychnis coronaria* thrives, for a relatively short time. They lose achilleas and monardas in very wet winters, but the damp conditions do provide one advantage: 'We don't have problems with mildew!'

Almost every gardener on clay has success with roses. All types do well in clay soils and there are myriad flower colours, shapes and scents. Heights vary from a few centi-metres with ground-cover varieties to several metres in the ramblers. Jackie Barber lost roses in very wet areas at Deanswood but some survive and 'Paul's Himalayan Musk' does exceptionally well up an old apple tree. She had an idea of what to expect when she moved to Potteries Lane – they still dig clay for the pottery just 390m/430yd away. It took six years to transform the pony field and, Jackie says, 'The soil is still a challenge. I'm still actively working on it by improving the drainage and applying mulch.' She buys only plants that will tolerate the soil. Her main-stays are the colourful-stemmed dogwoods, willows (*Salix daphnoides*, *S. alba* subsp. *vitellina* 'Britzensis' and *S. purpurea* 'Nancy Saunders') and elders (*Sambucus nigra* f. *laciniata*, *S. n.* 'Guincho Purple' and *S. n.* 'Aureomarginata').

Japanese anemones and asters at The Arles, Worcestershire.

Perennials

Anemone. The herbaceous Japanese anemones bring a ray of light to late summer and autumn borders with their open, saucer-shaped blooms. *A. hupehensis* var. *japonica* 'Bressingham Glow' (60cm/2ft) bears semi-double, rose-red flowers. Of the hybrida types, white 'Honorine Jobert' (1.2m/4ft) is the cream of the crop.

Digitalis. The foxgloves bring woodland charm to any garden. The common *D. purpurea* colonizes easily, but there are other excellent forms. *D. lanata* has small flowers best described as buff; *D.* × *mertonensis* has flowers the colour of crushed strawberries; and 'Sutton's Apricot' needs no further description.

Geranium. The long-flowering hardy cranesbills are a variable group but generally good in sun or part-shade and make effective ground-cover plants. The new 'Rozanne' produces masses of iridescent, multi-toned-blue flowers; 'Ann Folkard' has strong magenta-purple flowers with the added attraction of yellowish foliage.

Geum. Long-flowering throughout summer and colour-ful, geums will help add a splash of yellow, orange or red to borders. 'Borisii' forms dense hummocks covered in pure orange flowers. 'Lady Stratheden' with pure warm yellow, double blooms and her flaming-red counterpart, 'Mrs J. Bradshaw', should be widely grown.

Iris. The common yellow flag (*I. pseudacorus*) luxuriates where the soil remains damp. 'Variegata' (75cm/2½ ft) is the one to choose for its striking yellow-striped foliage. The flowers and foliage of *I. sibirica* (90cm/3ft) looks more delicate, and 'Perry's Blue' and 'Butter and Sugar' (illustrated on page 48) are good choices.

Ligularia. If you have a moist soil and a shady spot then you have to grow the stately ligularias which reach a height of 1.2m/4ft. Their large, deeply cut leaves cover the ground and in summer the yellow or orange daisy-like flowers make a column of colour. *L. dentata* 'Desdemona' has leaves that are mahogany-red beneath; 'Gregynog Gold' prefers some sun.

Lythrum. Purple loosestrife prefers a humus-rich or moist soil and produces tall spikes densely packed with pink or red, starry summer blooms. These are often followed by startling autumn foliage colours. Look for named varieties like *L. salicaria* 'The Beacon' (crimson) and 'Firecandle' (rose-red); both reach 90cm/3ft.

Papaver. The oriental poppies, growing to 90cm/3ft high, bring gardens to life from May to early July with their large papery blooms. Afterwards they can look a bit untidy, so the foliage is best cut back or hidden by other plants. Look out for 'Mrs Perry' (salmon pink), 'Perry's White' (greyish-white) and the gorgeous 'Patty's Plum'.

Phlox. The border phlox (up to 1.2m/4ft) are a summer mainstay, producing colourful and scented blooms in a wide range of vivid colours over a long period. Good choices include *Phlox paniculata* 'Balmoral' (rose-lavender) and 'Starfire' (red), and for extra colour go for 'Harlequin' with purple flowers and gold-varie-gated foliage and 'Pink Posie' with white variegation.

Rodgersia. This is a superb choice for moist soils and part-shade where the large leaves and plumes of small flowers will provide a summer stunner of a focal point. *R. pinnata* 'Superba' (up to 1.2m/4ft) has pink flowers; *R. aesculifolia* is larger, bears white flowers and the leaves have a metallic, bronzy sheen.

Vinca. The ultimate ground-cover plant, especially in awkward spots where the soil is dry and the aspect is shady. In time, when well established, plants may even become rampant. *V. minor* is the best choice where space is limited and produces its blue flowers all summer. 'Variegata' is more colourful.

Trees & shrubs

Aucuba. The spotted laurel is a versatile evergreen that grows in sun and even deep shade and can reach up to 2.4m/8ft high. Male and female varieties exist – the females bear winter berries when pollinated by a male. 'Crotonifolia' is one of the best males, boldly spotted and blotched with gold.

Berberis. A large genus of evergreen and deciduous varieties for sun or light shade. All produce masses of yellow or orange flowers in spring. *B. thunbergii* 'Rose Glow' is a superb small, colourful, deciduous variety reaching 1.5m/5ft. The leaves are purple, mottled silver-pink and bright rose, later becoming purple.

Chaenomeles. The Japanese quince is an easily pleased shrub which grows well in sun or shade and is perfect as a wall shrub up to 1.8m/6ft. Spring flowers in a range of colours from white to red, depending on variety, are followed by yellow quinces in autumn.

Cornus. The colourful-stemmed dogwoods brighten up winter gardens with their thicket of shoots up to 3m/10ft high. *C. alba* 'Sibirica' has the best crimson winter shoots; *C. sanguinea* 'Midwinter Fire' is aptly named with its orange, yellow and red stems; *C. stolonifera* 'Flaviramea' adds a splash of yellow to winter time.

Cotoneaster. A large group of versatile evergreen and deciduous species and varieties, producing masses of white flowers in June followed by yellow, orange or red berries. *C. horizontalis* 'Variegatus' with cream-edged leaves is excellent for covering banks and is invaluable for north- and east-facing walls.

Hamamelis. If you have room, a witch hazel (3m/10ft) is a must for the winter garden. The highly scented, spider-like, yellow or reddish flowers, produced on bare stems from early winter to early spring, withstand the severest weather. 'Pallida' is one of the most popular.

Hypericum. A tough shrub with large, saucer-shaped, golden flowers in summer. 'Hidcote' (1.5m/5ft) is the standard one to go for, but *H. × moserianum* 'Tricolor' (45cm/18in) has leaves variegated with white and pink and *H. olympicum* 'Citrinum' (20cm/8in) has lovely pale sulphur-yellow flowers.

Mahonia. Architectural evergreens with spiny leaves and sweetly scented, yellow winter flowers. *M. aquifolium* (1.2m/4ft) produces bunches of flowers, but the long panicles of hybrids like *M. × media* 'Charity' and 'Winter Sun', which reach 2.4m/8ft, are the best.

Philadelphus. On a warm summer's day you'll fall in love with the scent from the white flowers of the mock orange. This deciduous shrub is deservedly popular, but larger varieties like 'Virginal' often need to be pruned so hard to keep them within bounds that this results in lack of flowers. So try smaller varieties which reach up to 1.8m/6ft, such as 'Manteau d'Hermine' or even 'Beauclerk'; *P. coronarius* 'Aureus' has yellow foliage.

Potentilla. The mound-forming deciduous shrubby potentillas (60cm–1.5m/2–5ft, depending on variety) are excellent choices where flower power is needed, especially in light shade. Often starting to flower in May, plants can be covered in blooms, which range in colour from white through yellow and tangerine to red, until November. *P. fruticosa* 'Tangerine' is aptly named, as are 'Goldfinger' and *P. f.* 'Eastleigh Cream'.

Pyracantha. The firethorns are valuable evergreens, producing masses of white flowers in June followed by yellow, orange or red berries in autumn. Although they can be grown as shrubs, they come into their own for covering north- and east-facing walls up to a height of 3.6m/12ft. 'Navaho' has orange-red berries; other good ones include Saphyr Rouge and Saphyr Orange.

Ribes. Flowering currants may not be everyone's bag, but they provide valuable spring flowers on 1.8m/6ft stems. Normally pink or red, but white- and yellow-blooming varieties are available. 'Pulborough Scarlet' has deep pink flowers; *R. sanguineum* 'Brocklebankii' has golden-yellow foliage and needs shade. *R. odoratum* bears yellow, clove-scented flowers.

Rosa glauca. Most roses are grown for their sumptuous blooms, but this beauty (previously called *R. rubrifolia*) is also grown for the fine foliage which covers 1.8m/6ft stems. As the name suggests, it has a delightful glaucous/purplish sheen. The pink, single, slightly fragrant flowers are short-lived, but they are followed in autumn by clusters of dark red hips.

Spiraea. These popular deciduous shrubs can be split into spring- and the summer-flowering varieties. Spring types, such as *S. × cinerea* 'Grefsheim' (1.5m/5ft), produce white flowers, whereas the summer ones like *S. japonica* 'Anthony Waterer' and 'Goldflame' (75cm/2½ft) tend to produce pink/crimson ones; the latter boasts orange-and-yellow foliage too.

Syringa. The lilacs are popular, summer-flowering, generally large shrubs or small trees grown for their usually highly scented flowers, which come in a range of pastel colours. *S. × josiflexa* 'Bellicent' (4.5m/15ft) bears masses of rose-pink flowers; *S. vulgaris* 'Madame Lemoine' (3.6m/12ft) is a superb white; *S. pubescens* subsp. *microphylla* 'Superba' is medium-sized (1.5m/5ft) with rose-pink flowers.

Viburnum. A big group of evergreen and deciduous shrubs which, if chosen carefully, could give a splash of white/pink flowers all year round. Many have the added bonus of heavenly scent. *V. carlesii* (1.8m/6ft) produces white, scented flowers in spring and gorgeous autumn foliage; *V. odoratissimum* (4.5m/15ft) is a summer counterpart; *V. × bodnantense* 'Dawn' (3m/10ft) is your winter choice.

Weigela. A late spring- and summer-flowering deciduous shrub (up to 1.8m/6ft), covered in flowers that are usually pink or red. *W. praecox* 'Praecox Variegata' has creamy-white-variegated leaves and honey-scented rose-pink flowers; Briant Rubidor with yellow leaves and carmine flowers is good in shade; 'Mont Blanc' is white and scented.

OPPOSITE, ABOVE Jill and Martin Leman's back garden at
1 Malvern Terrace, London, is decorated with seasonal plantings
in containers. OPPOSITE, BELOW A magnificent sweet gum
(*Liquidambar styraciflua*) frames one of the many unexpected vistas
at Coton Manor Gardens in Northamptonshire.

Here is a handful of the hundreds
of Yellow Book gardens on heavy
soil to add to the ones Geoff Hodge
has tracked down.

Bedfordshire
Broadfields
88 Castlehill Rd
High View

Berkshire
Foxgrove
Meadow House

Bristol & S. Gloucestershire
Portland Lodge

Buckinghamshire
Ascott
Ashton, East & Botolph
*   Claydon Gardens*
Brudenell House
The Manor Farm,
*   Little Horwood*
Old Manor Farm, Cublington
Old Vicarage, East Claydon
Watercroft, Penn

Cambridgeshire
Sutton Gardens

Cornwall
Eden Project
Penjerrick Garden

Denbighshire & Colwyn
Plas Nantglyn

Derbyshire
The Gardens at Dobholme
*   Fishery*
46 Long Meadow Road

Devon
1 Feebers Cottage
Milland Farm
Sherwood
Sunrise Hill

Dorset
Cothayes House
Knitson Old Farmhouse
Salopean Rise
Vine Cottage

Essex
Writtle College

Glamorgan
Llanvithyn House

Gwent
Plas Cwm Coed

Hampshire
Appletrees
Flintstones
Forest Edge
Forest Gate
Holly House
The Ricks

Herefordshire
Darkley House
Huntsman's Cottage

Hertfordshire
Cockhamsted
Patchwork
Pelham House
Queenswood School
Rustling End Cottage

Kent
Forest Gate
Leydens
Marle Place
Old Buckhurst
Slaney Cottage
Waystrode Manor

Lancashire
Chilsworthy
Weeping Ash

Leicestershire
Barnsdale Gardens
Chestnuts
Orchard House
Stone Cottage

Lincolnshire
Guanock House
Hall Farm
Holly Tree Farm

London
33 Balmuir Gardens
Eccleston Square
The Ferry House
8 Grafton Park Road
Harold Road Gardens
239a Hook Road
13 Queen Elizabeth's Walk
5 St Regis Close
Tewkesbury Lodge Garden
*   Group*
Waltham Forest Register Office
66 Woodbourne Avenue

with expert insights by
NIGEL COLBORN
PAMELA SCHWERDT

3 Living with chalk and limestone

Maps are marvellous things, not merely for the mundane but essential jobs like tracing routes, but also for the way they can be so revealing about all sorts of other aspects of life. Any wine lover who pores over Hugh Johnson's masterly *World Atlas of Wine* will have a vivid idea of how cartography illuminates an understanding of the delicious glass of wine in your hand. One of the great cartographic masterpieces is the Ordnance Survey geological map of Britain which shows, in a controlled explosion of knicker-bocker-glory colours, the amazingly complicated patterns of our geology. The story is complex but the meaning for gardeners is more straightforward.

Chalk land, shown in an encouraging lettuce green on the map, runs in a great diagonal swathe across the country, from mid-Dorset, round about Dorchester in the south-west, all the way to the north Norfolk coast, with a hiccup at the Wash, north of which it continues into the Lincolnshire and Yorkshire Wolds. Two slender fingers of chalk run east of Dorset and Hampshire – one across West Sussex to the coast round about Brighton and the other wriggles its way across Surrey and Kent ending – where else? – at the white cliffs of Dover. Limestone country also follows a diagonal pattern, in essence running to the west of the chalk belt. It starts on the west Dorset coast, runs west of the Wash and straggles up to North Yorkshire, curling round in an easterly hook to the coast at Scarborough. That is the broad picture but the geology of England sometimes presents a bewildering pattern and there are substantial outcrops of limestone outside the major belt – for example, in the Lake District of the north-west.

What is the relevance of all this to gardeners? The degree of alkalinity of your garden soil is usually closely related to the underlying geology – or what soil scientists call the 'primary material'. However, decaying vegetation, especially of leaves in woodland, will increase the acidity of the soil. At its simplest, though, both chalk and limestone signify alkaline soils: the alkalinity may vary but it will always be there. The story is made more complicated by the fact that England is, geologically speaking, such a complex and intricately varied country. Thus, in the limestone country of south Somerset, where I live, you find in many places seams of deep, diggable acid greensand immediately adjacent to dense, alkaline clay. The same is true of chalk country. In Sussex, for example, the fabulous greensand that has allowed the creation of so many notable woodland gardens rich in rhododendrons is ringed with chalk. The geology is, however, only the underlying fact of your garden soil – much can be changed by cultivation. In many parts of English chalk downland – in Wiltshire and Sussex, for example – the soil has been transformed over immense periods of time by cultivation and grazing. The rich pastures of the South Downs in Sussex, which produce those marvellously well-fed sheep, acquired their fertility and luxuriant growth only through farming.

Another factor relevant to farming and gardening, independent of the underlying geology, is that of alluvial soil. Rivers and streams carry in their flow all sorts of organic material and silt which builds up over the centuries along the banks.

In alkaline soil there are limitations to what you can grow. Essentially, most ericaceous plants need acid soil. These include enkianthus, heathers, kalmias, pieris and rhododendrons. However, one genus of plants in the Ericaceae family, the important and very beautiful tribe of strawberry trees (*Arbutus* species), will flourish in alkaline soil. Also, some major plants such as camellias, although not ericaceous, require acid soil. Certain alpine plants will not thrive on alkaline soil. Such autumn-flowering gentians as *Gentiana sino-ornata*, for instance, demand neutral to acid soil. Alpine treasures of this kind are really for dedicated specialists and for most gardeners the limitations to what is possible in alkaline gardens are small. The possibilities, as I shall show when I discuss individual gardens, are enormous.

Cultivating the soil

Whatever the nature of your soil, cultivation can transform it. In the garden, as I know from my own practical experience, dramatic changes can be wrought in the soil. Early in my gardening life I lived in limestone country in the Mendips near Shepton Mallet. In much limestone country the soil is very heavy clay. I spent many days of one winter digging a new kitchen garden in an old orchard. The soil was glistening, pale toffee-coloured clay, hard enough to get your spade into and harder still to remove it, making that sloppy sucking sound as it came out which all clay diggers know so well, each spadeful unbelievably heavy. I double dug a large area, introducing both well-rotted manure and spent mushroom compost which immediately improved the texture of the soil and greatly increased the biological activity – worms find it hard burrowing through heavy clay. However, the soil was naturally sufficiently alkaline to make an excellent medium for growing vegetables: one of the delights of gardening in limestone country. Elsewhere in the garden all ornamental planting was made in holes with well-loosened bottoms

PRECEDING PAGES In Denny Wickham and Peter Fox's garden at the Clock House in Coleshill, Oxfordshire, free plantings of often self-sown plants create veils of colour. Here, inky purple lupins intermingle with scarlet corn poppies. The drawing from the Yellow Book 1989, shows the eighteenth-century Gothic stable block of Conock Manor, Wiltshire, whose garden has opened for fifty years.

NIGEL COLBORN

Cabbages fit for kings

Alkaline or limy soil is too frequently seen as a curse rather than the rich blessing that it is. Glance at a European flora and you will discover that limestone habitats have not only the richest numbers of species, but also many of the prettiest. Where I live in Lincolnshire, such gems as pyramidal orchis, dropwort, alpine milk vetch and meadow cranesbill grow in profusion on the oolitic limestone of our parish. Within a short bicycle ride, we see such delectable rarities as wild pasque flowers. And in gardens near here, clematis seem to shout out: 'We were made for lime!' Members of the pink family thrive, too, often exhibiting better, brighter colour than on acid soil. As for the best of the hardy annuals, planted in soil beefed up with organic matter they seed around with such abandon that the first packet is the only seed we Limeys have to buy.

When it comes to edible crops, lime is the gardener's best friend. Apart from blueberries and cranberries, most fruit and all vegetables give good results if you manage the soil well. Have access to manure if you can, and compost every scrap of organic material, constantly building up the humus content of your ground. Then, if your more ericaceous acquaintances feign pity that you cannot enjoy camellias and rhododendrons, remember that they will invariably suffer clubroot, whereas your cabbages will be fit for kings.

ABOVE Vegetable-growing gardeners bless their luck in possessing naturally alkaline soil. In the formal kitchen garden of The Old Rectory at Sudborough, Northamptonshire, burgeoning cabbages echo standard roses and the plump topiary of clipped box. The potager was designed by Rosemary Verey and developed by Rupert Golby with the owners, Annie and Anthony Huntington.

for drainage, filled with compost to which had been added about one third by volume of coarse limestone grit.

In the case of chalk the problem is different, with a lack of both nourishment and anything to retain moisture. The addition of humus provides the nutrition that is lacking and, crucially, builds up water-retentive ingredients. My father-in-law, an expert gardener, in his retirement made a garden from scratch in a pure chalkland field on the Berkshire Downs north of Newbury. He was especially fond of shrub roses – species and old cultivars – and planted a giant bed of them in chalk immensely enriched with manure and his own compost. I cannot remember ever seeing roses look happier.

The splendours of chalk

The classic book on the many splendours and few miseries of gardening in chalk is F. C. Stern's *A Chalk Garden*, published in 1960 but remaining an essential guide to the subject, a rare classic of gardening literature. Best of all, Stern's garden, Highdown, at Goring-by-Sea in West Sussex, opens for the NGS and you can go and see exactly what he achieved. Sir Frederick started gardening here in 1909 on what had been a chalk pit with cliffs of chalk rising 9m/30ft high. The expert advice he received about gardening in such a place was 'don't even bother to try'. By much trial and error he discovered the astonishing range of plants that would flourish. He looked at a geological map of the world and noticed that while Japan has generally acid soil, so no Japanese maples, China has beautiful maples like *Acer griseum*, and many Chinese shrubs would do well at Highdown. Another major area with generally alkaline soil is the Mediterranean. The sharp drainage and long hours of sunshine at Highdown allow many Mediterranean plants to thrive. Sir Frederick discovered that, as he wrote in his book, 'A great number of beautiful plants have no dislike of lime, and will grow perfectly if the chalk is broken up and cultivated.'

The head gardener at Highdown, Chris Beardsley, who took over here in 1976, knows as much about chalk gardening as anyone in the country and is emphatic about its delights. He thinks of Highdown as 'the perfect spring garden' and told me that early bulbs 'love chalk because it warms up so quickly'. Aconites, crocuses, *Cyclamen coum* and snowdrops flourish here, followed by waves of narcissi and species tulips, and later in the year lilies and colchicums perform outstandingly well. Of shrubs, says Chris, 'the possibilities are endless'. Here are many berberis, buddlejas, cistus, cotoneaster (Roy Lancaster says their *C. serotinus* is the biggest in the country), daphnes, roses, viburnums and much else. Tree peonies were a special love of Sir Frederick's and here is a superb original *Paeonia suffruticosa* subsp. *rockii*, with great silky white flowers and deep maroon blotches, one of his original plantings in the early 1920s. Chris emphasises the importance of one of Sir Frederick's golden rules of planting in chalk. When planting a shrub or tree, excavate a good, deep hole, and when you hit the chalk pan, break it up with a crowbar which will both allow drainage and permit roots to grow deep down where there are permanent sources of moisture. Then fill in with compost – at Highdown they use much spent mushroom compost. Many ornamental trees have been established there in this way, among them cherries, dogwoods, *Koelreuteria paniculata* and rowans, as well as the Chinese maples.

Grow with the soil

Susan Brooke of Overstroud Cottage, at Frith Hill in the Buckinghamshire Chilterns, underlines one of the essential principles of gardening on chalk or limestone: 'Things that I couldn't grow just wouldn't look right in the garden.' Some gardeners on alkaline soil dig pits full of acid soil in which to grow rhododendrons but, as Susan emphasizes, however they flourish they will always look wrong in the context and 'It's best to grow with the soil.' When she came here in the 1960s, she inherited an attractively designed garden on two levels. There were some good trees, among them a row of the handsome wild service tree, *Sorbus domestica*. The winter-flowering cherry, *Prunus × subhirtella* 'Autumnalis', is a success here, as are crab apples. One of Susan's favourite trees is the Chinese *Malus sargentii* (now correctly *M. toringo* subsp. *sargentii*) – 'always lovely and absolutely glorious in spring' with its exquisite white flowers. Susan does not do well with modern roses, both Hybrid Teas and the David Austin English Roses languishing here. Species, such as semi-double *Rosa nutkana* 'Plena', and near-species such as the *R. × alba* cultivars do well. She finds that some climbing roses of wild character, such as *R*. 'Paul's Himalayan Musk' and *R. filipes* 'Kiftsgate', are very successful with her.

Overstroud Cottage has a floriferous winter garden with *Cyclamen coum*, Lenten hellebores (*Helleborus orientalis* cultivars), snowdrops and winter aconites. Many shrubs do well, and Susan Brooke is especially successful with buddleja, deutzia, lilacs and viburnums. For some reason the precious winter-flowering daphne, *D. odora* 'Aureomarginata', has never been successful and she has lost it on three occasions. Of the herbaceous perennials she can count on aconitums, hardy geraniums, peonies (especially the lovely pale yellow *Paeonia mlokosewitschii*, known as "Molly the witch"), primulas and pulmonarias. In her ornamental kitchen garden she grows many herbs, several different Italian lettuces, runner beans and spinach, but she is not successful with brassicas and peas which she feels need heavier soil.

Susan Brooke attaches great importance to the thoroughness with which she plants trees and shrubs. She excavates a deep hole, removing chalk, and fills in with homemade compost mixed with some of the old soil and enriched with bonemeal. She finds it essential to keep an eye on any new plantings in dry weather the following summer and, if necessary, waters vigorously. She is a believer in the use of mushroom compost as a mulch, but she finds it is sometimes excessively rich in lime. To remedy this she leaves it in a heap for at least six months to reduce the alkalinity.

PRECEDING PAGES The temple at Springhead in Dorset is glimpsed through a screen of cosmos. At the head of the garden, clear spring water bubbles from beneath the chalk. In the upper garden Rosalind Richards used massed annuals in beds chocked with ground elder and is gradually introducing perennials to create mixed plantings to replace labour-intensive herbaceous borders.

A champion of chalky soil

Jane Sterndale-Bennett moved from London to White Windows in Longparish, Hampshire, in 1980. She moved from the thin neutral soil of a London garden to a former chalk quarry, a garden of chalk and flint which had been neglected for some time. All her gardening friends commiserated: 'Oh you poor thing, you won't be able to grow very much.' When she started she found it very hard to get good advice, and she has had to learn by trial and error. Her experiences have turned her into a 'champion of chalky soil'. Her soil is not merely chalky, but it is also full

of gravel and flint – 'stick in a spade and it bounces straight back,' she told me. It is free draining but it was also lacking in nutrients. She makes her own compost, on a three-bin system so that there is always some home-made compost available. With this she is able to mulch most of the garden flowerbeds once a year, occasionally bulking up supplies with mushroom compost. Her compost, too, is an essential addition to any new planting. Although her free-draining soil might suggest that many Mediterranean plants would flourish here, the garden is 61m/200ft above sea level, in a valley and subject to late

---

LEFT The Rambler rose 'Wedding Day' frames a view of the double borders at The Manor in Hemingford Grey, Cambridgeshire. Diana Boston's garden has 200 old varieties of roses.

ABOVE *Paeonia mlokosewitschii* and *Euphorbia palustris* are among the many finely grown plants in Carol and Malcolm Skinner's Eastgrove Cottage Garden, Worcestershire. Behind the statuesque cardoon,

Cynara cardunculus, is *Prunus* 'Okumiyako' (syn. *P. serrulata* 'Longpipes') and, to the left of the bench, *Cornus alternifolia* 'Argentea'.

frosts. She grows an immense range of plants and there are very few which she is unable to grow whose absence she regrets. 'Small woodlanders', for example, such as trilliums, which she loves, simply will not flourish, even if planted in a shady place and with the addition of leaf-mould. Ordinary primulas, of the primrose kind, do well, but she is unable to grow the exotic Himalayan kinds. Such lilies as *Lilium regale* and *L. candidum* do enjoy the conditions, while those of a woodland character that like deep soil are unsuccessful. She finds that brunnera, euphorbias, geraniums, hemerocallis and potentillas flourish. Sometimes it is hard to identify why a particular plant or group of plants is unhappy. She is generally unsuccessful with dicentras except for *D.* 'Stuart Boothman' which is thoroughly established. Among trees and shrubs that do well for her are birches, caryopteris, daphnes, berberis (especially *B. koreana*), osmanthus (especially the lovely holly-like *O. heterophyllus*), sorbus and viburnums. One of the things she particularly relishes about her fast-draining soil is that she can work in the garden in almost any conditions. And as she describes herself as 'a-little-and-often gardener' this is of great importance, for she can always nip out and do a quick bit of gardening as the spirit moves her.

A limestone paradise

A fascinating National Trust garden, which also opens for the NGS, is Sizergh Castle near Kendal in the Lake District. The soil here is loam on underlying limestone and, a key factor in the sort of planting that is successful here, the rainfall is high, with around 1,270mm/50in per annum. To the north-east of the castle a local firm, T. R. Hayes of Ambleside, laid out in the 1920s a rare garden that has now become a historic period piece – a rock garden of natural limestone. This in itself is a rarity, for so many rock gardens have been made from rock imported from a geologically completely different area and, for that reason, often look horribly alien. Here is a quarter of an acre, a great stone-lined bowl scooped out of the ground, with a pool at the centre, fed by streams from a natural lake at a higher level. The chief plantings are conifers (seventy-five species and cultivars, mostly of a miniature kind), Japanese maples (mostly *Acer palmatum* cultivars) and a collection of well over a hundred hardy ferns. The garden holds several National Collections of ferns, among them that of *Asplenium scolopendrium*, the wild hart's tongue fern, so familiar in damp hedgerows but also a highly ornamental garden plant. The single species has many cultivars of which no fewer than thirteen may be

seen at Sizergh, with ruffled leaves, forked tongues or golden foliage. Another collection held here of special interest to gardeners is that of buckler ferns (*Dryopteris*) with fifteen species and twenty-eight cultivars. The rock garden is handsomely laid out, with narrow paths winding between rocks, and the banks of the pool are thick with *Lysichiton americanus*, primulas and rodgersias. Gardens of this sort, fashionable in the early part of the twentieth century, are an admirable way of displaying the particular plants that relish such conditions.

The Wild Garden below the rock garden is a delightful display of wild limestone meadow flora, among them the native daffodil *Narcissus pseudonarcissus*, several different orchids, including the greater butterfly orchid (*Platanthera chlorantha*) which smells of vanilla, *Geranium pratense* and many others. In the more formal parts of the garden there are other plantings of special interest to limestone gardeners, including an avenue of the handsome mountain ash, *Sorbus aucuparia* 'Beissneri'. For anyone who gardens in alkaline soil, with high rainfall, Sizergh is a precious showplace of interesting plants.

Not only chalk

Water is so attractive, and adds a new dimension to a garden, that few gardeners can resist. Lynn and David Penfold garden in chalk country at The Thatch, Littlewick Green in Berkshire. They have created an artificial cascade and stream in the hollow of their garden, taking advantage of the moist banks to cultivate many marginal plants: arum lilies, candelabra primulas, ligularias, lysichitons and rodgersias, all of which do well in the moist soil overlying the chalk. Lynn made the surprising discovery that she could grow watercress here – she simply planted a few bits of root taken from a supermarket packet.

The Penfolds' garden is curious in that the soil has, intermittently, both clay and chalk, with a 25cm/10in layer

of clay between the topsoil and the underlying chalk. When making a planting hole, the clay subsoil must either be mixed with plenty of grit and humus or disposed of and replaced with compost. They have been successful with many trees, among them *Catalpa bignonioides*, the pretty Judas tree (*Cercis siliquastrum*), the winter-flowering cherry (*Prunus × subhirtella* 'Autumnalis') and walnuts. Lynn discovered that *Eucryphia × nymansensis*, one of the most beautiful flowering shrubs of late

LEFT The well-watered garden at Melplash Court in Dorset gives many opportunities for using moisture-loving plants. In the stream garden the banks are densely planted with irises (*I. pseudacorus* 'Variegata'), rodgersias (*R. aesculifolia*), hostas, *Lysimachia ephemerum*, *L. clethroides* and candelabra primulas (*P. prolifera*).

ABOVE A lemon tree, *Citrus × meyeri* 'Meyer', makes a central feature in the sunny herb garden at Mead Cottage, Dorset. Janet Bolton made the 1-acre garden from scratch and has created areas in different styles, such as a formal garden with topiary by the house and what Janet describes as 'English country style' in what was once a field. The soil is fertile clay over limestone and allows her to grow a wide range of plants.

PAMELA SCHWERDT

Mouse psychology

If you live in a limestone area and grow clematis, you may well have drystone walls. Now here is a warning: drystone walls make comfortable living quarters for mice of all kinds – and mice abso-lutely *love* eating clematis, especially in spring when the shoots are young and tender. Even when the shoots have grown up the wall a bit, the mice are athletic enough to go after them and remove their tips. This may be bene-ficial once or twice, as it is, in effect, stopping the plant and encouraging bushy growth, but there comes a time when they go too far and start removing potential flowers or demolishing the whole plant.

So watch out in February and March and do not just meekly wonder why your clematis has not started into growth. If you see any signs of damage, take precautions: get a cat, perhaps, or a mousetrap or some bait to use in those safe little boxes and set them along the foot of the wall. Mouse psychologists say their routes favour the protection of a wall in preference to open spaces. Peanut butter makes excellent bait for traps as it has an alluring smell (to mice) and cannot easily be detached like cheese. To ensure the safety of birds, put the trap in a drainpipe or lean a seedbox against the wall over it, making sure there is clearance for the trap to spring.

summer, is one of the very few members of the genus that will flourish in alkaline soil and its lavish white flowers are a feature of her garden. The Penfolds' garden had been an orchard in the past and there are still some fine fruit trees surviving, among them damsons and apples. Roses are a great love of Lynn's, especially the old shrub varieties. Mildew is a problem, particularly for roses grown against the wall of the house. She has found that this is often a sign of thirst and that a good dousing of water is the answer. Herbs are often very successful in chalk gardens, the sharp drainage providing the conditions which encourage flowering and scent. The Penfolds' herb garden is full of lavender, rosemary, sages and thymes. Lynn tries to garden organically, mulching the beds every year with her own compost, to which she sometimes adds bought-in organic compost. Apart from the lack of ericaceous plants – and azaleas and camellias are grown in pots – the Penfolds find no limitations in gardening on chalk.

David and Valerie Keeble at Stansfield in Oxfordshire garden in alkaline soil at the foot of White Horse Hill.

The 1¼-acre garden is windy and they created it from scratch – 'just a field when we started thirty years ago'. To give wind protection and seclusion they have planted many trees – beeches, birches and oaks – and hedges of yew and hornbeam. A hedge of Leyland cypress proved a problem as it soaked up any moisture in the soil. However, they have made a 'grass border' with such decorative grasses as *Carex elata* 'Aurea', *Miscanthus sinensis* 'Gracillimus' and *Stipa gigantea*, the bamboo-like *Nandina domestica*, the Californian tree poppy (*Romneya coulteri*) and many other shapely plants that relish the dry soil. The Keebles as far as possible garden organically, making their own compost and shredding clippings. David has recurrent yearnings for rhododendrons and other ericaceous glories, but their flowery, interest-packed garden gives the impression of being deficient in nothing.

Because of the complexity of the geology of England it is perfectly possible to have abrupt changes in alkalinity in a single garden. At Boveridge Farm, near Cranborne in Dorset, the garden made by David Dampney, now tended

---

66

Living with chalk and limestone

ABOVE The beautifully fashioned drystone walls of Hestercombe, Somerset, designed by Edwin Lutyens and Gertrude Jekyll, may provide a happy home for mice as well as crevice-dwelling plants. The platt, shown here, is a sunken garden displaying the Lutyens/Jekyll magic. Triangular beds planted with china roses ('Mevrouw Nathalie Nypels') and delphiniums are edged with bergenias.

RIGHT Repeated blocks of *Nepeta grandiflora* 'Bramdean', *N.* 'Six Hills Giant' and *Geranium psilostemon* establish a rhythm of colour and texture in Victoria Wakefield's perfectly balanced herbaceous borders at Bramdean House, Hampshire. *Thalictrum flavum* 'Glauca' and *Cynara cardunculus* give height and structure. The gates lead to the walled garden and on to the apple house in the orchard that terminates the vista.

by his son-in-law and daughter, Michael and Tina Yarrow, is chalk at one level and precisely neutral in the upper half where there is a drop of 12m/40 ft. The chalk part of the garden has good drainage, with lumps of chalk under the topsoil before you arrive at solid chalk. Here all sorts of trees have done well, including a magnificent *Paulownia tomentosa*, with extraordinary purple foxglove-like flowers and the decorative sycamore, *Acer pseudoplatanus* 'Brilliantissimum', whose newly opened foliage is a dazzling pink-cream. Here, too, are some exceptional magnolias. Two outstanding cultivars of *M. × loebneri* are 'Leonard Messel' with the palest pink, narrow-petalled flowers of great elegance and 'Merrill' with pure white, star shaped flowers. In gardens of more or less solid chalk, such as Highdown (page 59), it has proved difficult to establish flowering shrubs of this sort.

One of the finest gardens to open for the NGS is Bramdean House in Hampshire. Its 6½ acres are a triumphant vindication of the art of gardening on thin chalk soil. With a backdrop of old beeches and limes, a series of gardens is strung together on an axis leading from the door behind the house up a gentle slope, ending in the splendid eyecatcher of an eighteenth-century apple house. On the way you pass between dramatic mirror-image herbaceous borders planted by Victoria Wakefield to provide continuity of interest from the spring deep into autumn. Wrought-iron gates lead to the walled garden where the scent of old-fashioned sweet peas and perennial carnations fills the air. Here, vegetables, herbs, annuals and perennials are planted in V-shaped beds, backed with free-standing espaliered pears and apples interspersed with clematis. Beyond the walled garden is an orchard with flowering cherries underplanted in spring with waves of daffodils. Among many fine plants is the rare Chilean evergreen tree, *Maytenus boaria*. It has elegant, almost olive-like, leaves and forms a handsome upright shape. It loves chalk – Sir Frederick Stern planted it at Highdown.

Plants for chalk and limestone

The essential limitation is that almost all ericaceous plants will refuse to grow in alkaline soil; the exception is the genus *Arbutus*, the strawberry trees. Apart from the pH of your soil, the other essential factor is its physical nature. Soil in limestone country is often heavy clay, and frequently in parts of the country, such as the West Country, with high rainfall it is vital to improve the drainage (see Chapter 2 for information on improving clay soil). In the case of chalk, which is characteristically free-draining, it will often be necessary to build up the moisture-retentive properties of your soil by enriching it with humus. It is also worth bearing in mind what might be called the Highdown rule when planting shrubs: the planting hole must be well prepared (see page 59). The limitations in what you can grow are minor; the possibilities are immense. Here is a list of plants with which gardeners on chalk and limestone have been very successful.

Trees, shrubs and climbers

Acer. The maples are a big group of often very beautiful trees, many of them small enough for even the most diminutive garden. The Japanese maples (*A. japonicum* and *A. palmatum*, and countless cultivars of both) are slow-growing, distinguished trees whose foliage is often of surpassing beauty. Sir Frederick Stern found that Japanese maples would not grow in his chalk garden, but many gardens on limestone, such as that of Sizergh Castle, for example, have no problems. *A. griseum*, the Chinese paper-bark maple, has distinctive peeling bark, making a striking winter ornament. Its newly opening foliage is handsome, with tones of cream and pink, and the leaves have brilliant autumn colours of red and orange. It makes a very good-looking, upright shape (10m/33ft).

Arbutus. The strawberry trees are among the most beautiful of broad-leaved evergreens. The most commonly seen *A. unedo*, the Killarney strawberry tree of hedgerows in western Ireland, grows to a height of 8m/25ft and is decorative in any season – but dazzling when covered in its strawberry fruits. The Greek hybrid with the forbidding name, *Arbutus × andrachnoides*, has the additional charm of peeling bark, a glowing caramel colour.

Berberis. Many gardeners on chalk and limestone say how successful they are with these shrubs with their decorative flowers, foliage and berries. The genus is a very large one with well over four hundred species and countless cultivars, many of which are stocked by most garden centres.

Buddleja. B. alternifolia has graceful, swaying branches covered in diminutive, lilac-blue flowers with a wonderful, honey scent. A cultivar with distinguished, silver leaves is *B. a.* 'Argentea'. *B. colvilei* is the most unusual of the genus, with brilliant red panicles of flowers, but is not hardy in colder gardens. *B. crispa*, for warm gardens only, has soft grey-green leaves with white undersides, and plumes of well-scented, pale lilac flowers from June to the first frosts; it is very successful trained against a sunny wall.

Clematis. The native traveller's joy or old man's beard (*C. vitalba*) is naturally found in chalk and limestone country. All species of clematis will grow well, although it is a myth that they will do even better if you add lime. They do need nourishment and moisture, which may sometimes be a particular problem in chalk gardens. I've never seen an ugly clematis, and many of the summer-flowering kinds have the virtue of taking up little room, scrambling through shrubs or small trees and scattering their flowers aloft.

Cotoneaster. The many cotoneasters with brilliantly coloured berries, striking foliage and often excellent autumn colour are precious shrubs. *C. atropurpureus* has leaves that turn a distinguished plum-purple in autumn with dazzling orange-red fruit. *C. horizontalis* has spreading growth, making it a fine structural plant, and scarlet berries much loved by birds. *C. meiophyllus* forms an upright bush with red berries.

Koelreuteria paniculata. One of the finest of ornamental trees (6m/20ft), this has elegant pinnate leaves flushed with pink as they emerge. Cascades of golden-yellow panicles of flowers in summer are followed by autumn colours of warm yellow.

Malus. The highly decorative crab apples are valuable ornamental trees. The Japanese *M. toringo* subsp. *sargentii* (6m/20ft) has clusters of white flowers in profusion and decorative red fruit.

Osmanthus. This genus is one of the most beautiful of broad-leaved evergreens with dark green, glistening foliage and scented flowers in spring. *O. delavayi* has hanging clusters of white flowers with a sweet almond perfume. *O. × burkwoodii* is similar to *O. delavayi* in all respects, including height (6m/20ft), except it has longer, more elegant leaves. *O. heterophyllus* looks like an aristocratic holly with large leaves with pointed lobes and is suitable for hedging; cut back after the fragrant, white flowers in autumn.

Paeonia suffruticosa cultivars. The tree peonies (2.2m/7ft) have a short flowering season but exceptional beauty of flowers, and elegantly divided foliage adds to the charms. Many cultivars are available, especially those from China. *P. suffruticosa* subsp. *rockii*,

Paeonia suffruticosa cultivar at Kiftsgate Court, Gloucestershire.

with white, crushed-silk flowers splashed with deep maroon at the centre, is hard to find.

Prunus. P. × *subhirtella* 'Autumnalis' (8m/25ft) forms a characterful spreading tree with delicate, white flowers in mid-winter. There is also a pink-flowered cultivar, P. × s. 'Autumnalis Rosea'. *P. serrula*, a great sight at Highdown where it grows to 10m/33ft, is a Chinese cherry of upright habit with bark which peels away in gleaming, mahogany scrolls.

Roses. Virtually all roses will flourish in a pH range of 6.0–8.0. Indeed, gardeners on acid soil often need to add chalk or ground limestone. Some species from Japan (such as *R. rugosa* and *R. wichurana*, and their hybrids) are less tolerant of alkaline soils. Chinese species (such as the magnificent *R. moyesii*) and their hybrids positively prefer alkaline soil.

Styrax japonicus. One of the most beautiful of all medium-sized flowering trees (10m/33ft), this has an elegant form of growth, exquisite, hanging, white, bell-like flowers in late spring and butter-yellow autumn foliage. It does not like cold winds.

Herbaceous perennials and bulbs

Allium. The onion tribe produces many decorative plants. *A. hollandicum* (formerly *A. aflatunense*), especially in its selection 'Purple Sensation', is a dramatic plant – a 90cm/3ft stem crowned with a rich and vivid violet sphere, 'the sort of colour a rather racy cardinal might wear', as someone wrote. *A. cristophii* is much shorter but with flowerheads 25cm/10in in diameter with a metallic purple sheen.

Corydalis. The English native fumitory, *C. lutea*, is found in limestone country. Its finely cut, glaucous foliage with trusses of lemon-yellow flowers will colonize moist places in an uninvasive way. *C. ochroleuca* is similar, with less exciting, putty-coloured flowers. *C. flexuosa* is a Chinese fumitory with flowers of an intense blue. All are about 30cm/1ft tall.

Cyclamen. The winter-flowering *C. coum* (pink-purple or white flowers) and the late summer *C. hederifolium* (also pink-purple or white flowers) are two essential garden plants for gardens on chalk and limestone. The foliage of both is attractive, that of *C. hederifolium* outstandingly so. The spring-flowering magenta-pink *C. repandum* is slightly less hardy than the two above but adds to their charms the most delicious, sweet scent.

Dianthus. Many gardeners on dry chalk gardens do very well with the pretty, clove-scented cottage-garden pinks which in wet, heavy clay are so unhappy.

Euphorbia. The pretty but hideously invasive *E. cyparissias* is an English native found on chalk soils. *E. c.* 'Fens Ruby' has red-flushed youthful foliage, a fine effect. *E. characias* subsp. *wulfenii*, with glaucous foliage and columnar heads of flowers, has great character. *E. griffithii* is a creeping, suckering plant whose cheerful red or orange stems enliven the spring scene.

Geranium pratense. The meadow cranesbill is an English native found especially in chalk soils. It is a delightful plant and there are several decorative cultivars: *G. p.* 'Mrs Kendall Clark' has pale grey-blue, finely veined flowers of ghostly delicacy; *G. p.* 'Plenum Violaceum' has small but very double violet blues; *G. p.* 'Striatum' is white with irregular splashes of blue. Geraniums, rightly so, are fashionable plants and a very wide range of species and cultivars is available.

Iris. Many gardeners on chalk and limestone say that irises of every kind are very successful. Apart from recommending the unbeatably lovely winter-flowering *I. unguicularis*, all I can do is to suggest a visit to your garden centre to choose the ones you like.

Lilies. Many lilies are suitable for alkaline soil. The white, sweetly scented madonna lily (*Lilium candidum*) and white, equally sweetly scented *L. regale* are excellent. In semi-shade both *L. pardalinum*, a brilliant orange Turk's cap, and *L. martagon* with plum-coloured or white flowers, will often establish themselves well.

Pulmonaria. The English native lungwort *Pulmonaria officinalis* – 'soldiers and sailors' because of its simultaneous red and blue flowers – is a limestone plant. *P. o.* 'Bowles' Blue' is a good pale blue form; 'Sissinghurst White' is excellent in a shady corner.

LEFT Sweetwell at Fiddleford, Dorset, is Ann Hay's 1-acre cottage garden which was started from scratch in 1981. It is rich in old roses, borders of shrubs and perennials and drought-tolerant plants along the gravel drive. RIGHT, ABOVE Richard and Norma Bird's garden at Stocks in the village of Blewbury, Oxfordshire, lies on the spring line of the Berkshire Downs – the soil is chalky but rarely dries out. Plants in profusion include *Lathyrus grandiflorus*, *Geranium pratense* 'Plenum Purpureum' and *Symphytum × uplandicum* 'Variegatum'. RIGHT, BELOW The Plantation Garden in Norwich, Norfolk, is a rare Victorian city garden being restored by volunteers, with flint and brickwork (including a Gothic fountain) and informal planting.

As well as the owners who Patrick Taylor has met, many NGS gardeners live with chalk or limestone – a few of their gardens are listed here.

Bedfordshire
88 Castlehill Rd
Valley Forge

Berkshire
Briar Rose

Buckinghamshire
Bucksbridge House
Great Barfield
The Manor House, Bledlow
West Wycombe Park

Cambridgeshire
The Crossing House
Docwra's Manor
Mill House
Nuns Manor
Pampisford Gardens
Sawston Gardens
Whittlesford Gardens

Cumbria
Holker Hall Gardens

Devon
Rock House Garden

Dorset
Cranborne Manor Garden
Down End House
Hookeswood House
Millmead
Salopean Rise
Stanbridge Mill
Welcome Thatch

Essex
Clavering Gardens
Glen Chantry
Saling Hall Lodge

Gloucestershire
25 Bowling Green Road

Gwent
Castle House

Hampshire
Abbey Cottage
Brandy Mount House
71 Church Close
Clibdens
Fairfield House
The Forge
Hinton Ampner
Little Court
Meadowsweet
Mylor Cottage
Ulvik
Wades House
The White Cottage

Isle of White
Badminton

Hertfordshire
Odsey Park

Isle Of Wight
Badminton

Kent
Goodnestone Park
Olantigh
Rock Farm
Thornham Friars

Lancashire, Merseyside & Greater Manchester
Lindeth Dene
The Reginald Kaye Garden

Lincolnshire
Gunby Hall
Harrington Hall

Norfolk
Gayton Hall

Oxfordshire
Ashbrook House
Carpenters
Church End House
The Cuckoo Pen Nursery
Green Bushes
Hall Barn
Hethersett
Mill Lane House
Nottyngham Fee House
Stocks

Suffolk
Mildenhall Gardens

LOUISE ALLEN

with expert insights by
JOHN FOULSHAM
STEPHEN LACEY
TOM STUART-SMITH

4 The challenge of sandy soil

My first experience of working with sandy soil was as a trainee gardener at the Royal Horticultural Society's Garden at Wisley in Surrey. Each spring, hour after hour, day after day was spent barrowing tonnes of mushroom compost. Applying the spent compost from the mushroom industry as a thick mulch around herbaceous plants, young trees and mature shrubs throughout the garden was the 'Wisley approach' to improving hungry soil. It is not the only method and gardeners who open under the NGS have adopted a variety of techniques for making fine gardens on sandy soil.

For some gardeners, discovering that their garden is on sandy soil comes as an unpleasant surprise. Although Pam and Nicholas Coote were led to believe that the soil at Greenways, Oxford, was very good, they found it was sandy soon after buying the house in the late seventies and setting about making a garden from scratch. It is worth assessing the soil by digging down and taking a handful when it is moist. If it feels gritty and is impossible to roll into a ball, this indicates a soil lacking the structure and nutrients that are vital if plants are to succeed over a period of many years. A sandy soil has a low proportion of the clay particles that help to bind the soil together, so that it tends to wash away, especially during heavy rain.

Sandy soil is notoriously poor and hungry, and when nutrients are added, often in the form of fertilizers, they can be quickly washed through the soil, a process referred to as leaching. Sandy soil is also prone to drought: coarse pores between the soil particles indicate that water is readily available, especially compared with clay soils, but it also means that the soil is free-draining, drying out quickly, especially in periods of drought. Lack of water retention makes the establishment of young plants, whose limited root system depends on a plentiful supply of water, a particular problem for gardeners on sandy soils. Also, plants with shallow roots will struggle because of lack of water on the surface of the soil.

So the challenge the gardener faces is fourfold: hunger, drought, unstable soil and the difficulty of establishing, and keeping, young and shallow-rooted plants. This makes life on a sandy soil sound difficult but, as eighty-year-old Joyce Salisbury-Jones at Bumble Cottage in West Chiltington, Sussex, points out, she can get out her spade at any time of the year and plant up her garden, even after a thunderstorm. Sandy soil is certainly the least problematical as far as backache is concerned. A further advantage is that the soil warms up quickly at the beginning of the gardening year, so when gardeners on clay cannot step outside, except on hard surfaces, for fear of compacting the soil, those on sandy soils may have been gardening for weeks. At the other end of the gardening year, the soil remains relatively warm and well aerated, enabling gardeners to grow plants that elsewhere would perish during the depths of winter.

The challenge of sandy soil

PRECEDING PAGES
Magnolia × soulangeana is one of thousands of plants on sandy soil at Great Comp in Kent. The drawing of Stanton Harcourt Manor, Oxfordshire, is from the 1957 Yellow Book.

RIGHT *Kniphofia* 'Bees' Sunset', cannas and dahlias at Munstead Wood, Surrey, the garden created from a sandy heath by Gertrude Jekyll which is now owned and tended by Sir Robert and Lady Clark.

STEPHEN LACEY

Making leafmould

Although my soil is not as sandy as some, it can get a little too dry in summer for certain plants, especially woodlanders like rhododendrons and witch hazels. So we take our leafmould making seriously, with three large bins of the stuff tucked under the beech tree. This is spread as a mulch over all the shady beds during winter.

My first attempt was a disaster. I was told to pack the leaves into black plastic bags, seal them up, puncture a few holes in the sides and wait two years. I did. It was like opening a time capsule. Not the slightest bit of decomposition had taken place. The missing piece of information was that the leaves had to be damp.

Now we have a completely different regime. The leaves that fall on the lawn are collected with the lawnmower, which means there are grass clippings mixed in; these generate some heat and speed up the rotting process. The smaller the leaf pieces, the quicker the decomposition, so we also pass a fair quantity of leaves through the shredder; alternatively, you could put a rotovator into your heap (beware of hibernating hedgehogs). But if you are not in a hurry, all this is optional.

The leaves are stacked, with no disturbance, in simple, post-and-chicken-wire bins, open to the elements. We usually use the mould after eighteen months. And delicious it is, too – as appetizing as chocolate cake.

A gateway leads to the leafy courtyard at Moleshill House, Surrey, which is packed with pots of pelargoniums and fuchsias that came (unnamed) from the flower market. Throughout the garden, and especially in borders designed for drought tolerance, flower arranger Penny Snell improves the sandy soil by applying copious quantities of horse manure (supplied by a friend), home-made leafmould and the compost she makes in five 'serious' bins at the end of the garden. 'After fifteen years of constant nurturing, most of the soil is pretty good', says Penny, but she goes on 'adding and adding, lest it should revert'.

Garden compost

Gardeners throughout the NGS have long recognized the need to give sandy soils a constant source of food and that garden compost is the most economical of all soil additives. Not only is it completely free, but it also solves the problem of what to do with garden waste.

For many gardeners time seems to be of the essence when producing garden compost, but those who boast how quickly they produce compost usually have large amounts of material available. In small gardens, where compostable material is limited, the compost heap may virtually disappear in a few days, which indicates that the carbon/nitrogen ratio is out of balance. Green material, such as annual weeds and grass clippings, increase the nitrogen level and cause the material to rot down too quickly and the heap to give off unpleasant odours. Adding carbon-rich material, such as shredded woody material, dried leaves and even straw, will slow down the decomposition process. However, if the heap contains too much woody material, the carbon level will be too high and the heap will never rot down. Achieving the right balance of carbon/nitrogen depends on using both green and woody material.

If space allows and you have a steady supply of compostable material, have more than one compost bin, three being ideal. They come in all sorts of shapes and materials, but the important factor is size: at least 1 cubic m/yd so that the heap generates sufficient heat to encourage the compost to break down, killing any weed seeds. It is also vital to cover the heap to conserve heat. Add compost in layers – too many grass clippings will inhibit air movement, so include different types of garden waste: green material, shredded branches and plane leaves, moss, annual weeds, fruits, shredded paper and cardboard (minus the sellotape), straw and wood ash. Add leaves other than plane, if you like, but it is better to save them for leafmould. The following should never be added: very fibrous or woody material, perennial weeds (such as dandelion, bindweed and nettles), weed material treated with herbicide, cooked food which will attract vermin, and coal ash.

Keep the heap moist and, if the compost ingredients are very dry, water them in. As layers of compost ingredients are added to the heap, include extra nitrogen to speed up the composting process, in the form of a compost activator, artificial nitrogen fertilizer or manure. Manure has the advantage of bringing with it lots of beneficial soil organisms.

Turning the heap is essential to keep it well aerated for effective composting. It is also good fun on a cold and frosty morning. Never walk on the heap, the aim being to keep the compost light and fluffy. When turning the heap, remember to watch out for wildlife – hedgehogs and mice will enjoy its warmth, especially in the depths of winter.

When the compost is ready to use, remember to use it well. It is free, bulky and nutritious and will make gardening on sandy soil much easier.

Other bulky soil additives

Well-rotted farmyard manure is like gold dust in many areas, but Jean Venning at Grove Lodge in Bedfordshire, whose garden resembled a giant sandpit when she bought it, is one of many NGS gardeners who negotiate with farmers to deliver this precious soil additive. To provide the fertility that plants need to survive on a sandy hillside, Jean has trailer loads brought regularly to her garden via a neighbour's field. Her supplier stacks the manure for up to a year before delivering it to Grove Lodge, so Jean knows it is well rotted before she digs it into her beds and borders. Fresh manure gives off ammonia, which can be toxic to plants, so it is essential to ensure it is not green.

Even greater care is needed with poultry manure, which is well known to be exceptionally strong. Applying it directly to the garden can cause similar problems to using very green farmyard manure. Ideally it should be layered within the compost heap to reduce its strength and provide greater substance to compost made of garden waste.

Mushroom compost can be used as an additive or mulch and is an effective alternative to well-rotted farmyard manure. It tends to be alkaline in pH, so should not be used for too many years running. At Vale End in Surrey, a garden with an acid soil, the Foulshams apply mushroom compost every three years.

If there is one soil additive that turns people green with envy it has to be leafmould. Mary Eastwood has known her garden at Heyes Lane in Timperley on the edge of Manchester since childhood and remembers her father digging for sand for her to play with. Each autumn she calls upon her neighbours in Heyes Lane to give her their leaves which she turns into leafmould to enrich her sandy soil. Only the Cootes of Greenways on the out-skirts of Oxford can beat that trick. They collect the leaves in their garden but also those that have fallen in the

road outside their house and from the hospital grounds just across the road. Nicholas Coote is well used to the strange looks he receives on winter evenings as he collects the leaves by streetlight. He is convinced that local residents think the council are working overtime.

Even the smallest garden can produce leafmould. Either stack damp leaves in a heap for at least a year, or enclose them in black polythene bags which quickly generate the heat needed to rot them down. On a larger scale the twelve oak trees surrounding Grove Lodge create generous amounts of leafmould each year. The leaves rarely finish falling until just after Christmas. 'We collect and dry them and then use a shredder to speed up the process,' says Jean Venning. And of course the best thing of all about leafmould is that around the time that gardeners start using it, another load of leaves is begin-ning to fall off the trees.

Using soil additives

Textbooks often tell us that manure should be applied to the soil at the start of winter and then allowed to break down through the winter months. On sandy soils this is rarely a good idea, as the manure has usually disappeared by the time the growing season begins. It is better to incorporate bulky additives when starting to plant in a garden on sandy soil, and to continue the practice when-ever the soil is cultivated. The age-old adage 'Spend a shilling on the plant and a pound on the hole' could have been formulated for gardeners on sandy soils.

As well as adding well-rotted farmyard manure or garden compost to the soil whenever they plant, many NGS gardeners sing the praises of the spring mulch. A 10–15cm/4–6in mulch of garden compost, well-rotted farmyard manure, mushroom compost and/or leafmould helps to regulate soil temperature, discourages weeds and, most importantly, encourages mois-ture retention. Mary Eastwood at Heyes Lane gardens organically and has adopted a no-dig policy. An annual mulch of garden compost is vital, she says, if the no-dig policy is to succeed. The garden at Greenways in Osler Road was last dug in the early 1980s – the thick mulch of leafmould being the Cootes' preferred solution for conditioning the soil.

Concentrated fertilizers can also be used to boost the lack of nutrients in sandy soils, and are a valuable addition to every planting hole. Although they can never take the place of bulky additives, the two together can be effective. Blood, fish and bone, bonemeal, Vitax and Growmore are all popular, so when a fertilizer works in your garden the best advice is to stick with it. Most gardeners feed in spring, just as the plants are starting to grow, but with leaching a problem on sandy soils, a controlled-release fertilizer will maintain nutrient levels throughout the growing season. The Cootes make extensive use of a foliar or liquid feed and the phenomenal growth rate of plants at Greenways shows the effect of well-managed nutrient levels.

ABOVE *Clematis* 'Niobe' scrambles up *Rosa* 'Swan Lake', trained against a flint wall at Baconsthorpe Old Rectory, Norfolk, the 3-acre garden owned by Tessa and David McCosh. Tessa describes herself as a 'compulsive compost-maker, forever adding muck to retain moisture in the dry, hungry soil'. Rainfall in this part of East Anglia rarely exceeds 700mm/27½in in a normal year.

RIGHT At Pettifers in Oxfordshire, *Stipa tenuissima* and self-seeded *Nectaroscordum siculum* subsp. *bulgaricum* grow among traditional herbaceous perennials, such as red-hot pokers (*Kniphofia* 'Jenny Bloom'), *Sedum* 'Herbstfreude' and *Achillea* 'Terracotta' to give a contemporary effect. Else-where in the garden, the soil is naturally fertile, but Gina Price has to feed and mulch the light soil on this free-draining bank.

John Foulsham

Compost making at Vale End

There is nothing so good for the growth of the compost heap as opening your garden to the public. In the haste to tidy up before open days, we can amass spectacular amounts of garden waste. One Sunday we sported a heap almost 3m/10ft high, with a ladder leaning against it to reach the top! It was eyed with amused and incredulous wonder by our visitors, as well as with some knowing nods. That was when we just used to pile up green matter in a far corner of the vegetable garden. It made poor compost, lumpy and difficult to use, and the couch grass beneath it thrived. Being in a sunny patch, it was a breeding ground for slow worms and grass snakes whose leathery white egg cases surfaced from time to time.

Something had to be done. On the concrete base of an old shed I built three bins, reserving an area at one end for farmyard manure, which has to be tractored across a neighbour's field. I used five courses of concrete blocks to make walls 1.2m/4ft high and 1.8m/6ft deep, with plenty of weep holes in the bottom course to prevent waterlogging. The fronts are made of gravel boards slotted into grooves and the roof is corrugated sheeting fixed to an old beam. The outer two bins are 1.3m/4¼ft wide and the centre one 90cm/3ft wide, the theory being that when a big bin is full

and has been left to stand for four to six months, it is turned into the small one. Turning traps the air that encourages aerobic action. It has another advantage – the recovery of old friends, be it spoon or peeler, which disappeared many moons before with the vegetable waste from the kitchen.

I derive pleasure in sorting green matter and making a neat and orderly heap. I try to fork grass cuttings down into the last layer and to cover them with fresh waste. I add poultry manure from our own hens between layers. With our light, sandy soil scarcely any earth clings to roots of plants, so the heap never becomes heavy or sodden. Woody bits are thrown on to the adjacent bonfire heap and nasties like couch grass and bindweed, sorted into a bucket at the weeding stage, have a small side heap of their own where they eventually rot down. I ought to use a shredder as they do at Wisley, but hide

behind excuses such as its screeching noise and my lack of time.

I keep the working bin tightly covered with a double layer of bubble plastic, weighted down round its edges with heavy boards. The temperature generated can be almost too hot to put your hand on. I'm always surprised at how much the heap has rotted down in six months and reflect on the concentrated goodness it must contain.

I do not claim to make the best compost in the world, yet it is very rich and gives much-needed bulk and nutrients to our light and hungry sandy soil. It is by no means seed-free and can raise a beautiful crop of foxgloves and poppies if we don't catch them before they go to seed. Daphne prefers to dig compost in when replanting in the flower garden, but I enjoy the rogue seedlings among my vegetables. Between us we must use at least 4 cubic m/140 cubic ft of recycled material a year.

LEFT & ABOVE Lettuces – 'Lobjoit's Green' Cos, 'Tom Thumb' (small hearting type) and 'Cerise' (red/bronze hearting type) – look decorative around a pot of lavender in the ornamental potager at Vale End, Surrey. The vegetable garden provides John and Daphne Foulsham with bountiful crops, due to the addition of large quantities of organic compost, made in three sturdy bays (above). Evening primroses, poppies and sisyrinchium are welcome volunteers among the peas, runner beans and sunflowers, adding a relaxed note to the geometric layout of raised beds intersected by gravel paths.

Overcoming hunger

Daphne Foulsham, Chairman of the NGS, and her husband John have become masters at feeding the hungry soil at Vale End in Surrey and have some of the smartest compost bins in the country. Unlike most gardens with sandy soil, theirs has a plentiful supply of water from a series of wells. The problem is soil structure and the need to improve the soil's water-retentive properties. As well as garden compost and mushroom compost – although not every year – they use leafmould, well-rotted farmyard manure and poultry manure.

The gentle sound of clucking contributes to the feeling of relaxation in the garden, but it is not intended as therapy for the adults. Chickens are kept to entertain and enlighten the grandchildren and to supply eggs for the family but, most importantly, to provide further valuable organic matter to improve the light, sandy soil. The hens have a large run and become very free-range in autumn when they have the run of the whole garden and are not confined again until plant growth starts in spring. 'We have the obvious bonus of their litter for composting,' says John Foulsham, 'but they serve another practical purpose too, considerably reducing slug and snail damage. Surprisingly, our hens do little harm to plants and shrubs, though I banish them from the fruit cage and the brassica patch as they are too fond of the brussels sprouts and scratch out the strawberries for the worms underneath.'

The Foulshams started gardening the 1½-acre site in a beautiful setting overlooking a millpond (illustrated on pages 10–11) in the 1960s. Birch trees, well suited to sandy soils, contribute to the garden's structure, and a yew hedge planted just ten years ago creates a background to informal planting. In the early days they were not particularly successful with plants and Daphne admits to learning the hard way that plants do not succeed if they are just pushed in where there is a gap. Selective weeding is the key to what grows where. A reliance on self-seeders and a childhood love of wildflowers works well, the choice of plants further influenced by John's fondness for butterflies. Herbs have thrived in the garden, but the Mediterranean garden plants often suggested for sandy soils are rarely used, as the garden is located in a frost pocket. Plants are moved about, especially if they are not growing well, with a move of just a short distance sometimes making the difference between success and failure. Daphne's love of the informal is apparent as she describes what grows well: 'no smart roses' but alliums, *Salvia sclarea*, catmint, irises and love-in-a-mist to create the much-loved cottage-garden feel.

The ornamental vegetable garden provides the family with produce. In this productive part of the garden, soil additives are essential if notoriously hungry vegetable plants are to thrive and succeed. Shallow-rooted brussels sprouts, cabbages and other brassicas are often difficult to get established and the Foulshams go so far as to stake these plants to prevent them falling over, giving the roots a chance to get down deep into the soil.

Overcoming drought

'To water or not to water' – that has become the big question since the summer droughts of the late 1980s and early 1990s and the introduction of regular hosepipe bans. Gone are the days when gardeners watered whenever the weather turned dry and sprinklers in action were a common sight. Already aware of the environmental implications of

applying gallons of water to gardens, many gardeners are now reminded by domestic water meters of the cost of every drop they use. So the problems of drought on sandy soil have to be overcome by means other than tap water.

At Grove Lodge, Jean Venning acknowledges that if plants are never watered they may simply die, and no gardener lets that happen willingly. She waters newly planted or young plants until they are established, but allows

ABOVE In a container with free-draining compost, *Echeveria elegans* survives most winters in Richard and Elizabeth Tite's ¾-acre garden at Field Cottage, Littlethorpe Gardens in Yorkshire. Most of their hard work is done early in the year: to improve the garden's loam over gravel, Richard digs in tons of mushroom compost in January and applies more mushroom compost as a surface mulch in April. This enables the Tites to grow more exciting plants, such as the tender evergreen sub-shrubs *Isoplexis canariensis* and *Teucrium fruticans,* and a collection of *Erysimum,* as well as plenty of hardy perennials.

mature plants to fend for themselves. At Heyes Lane watering in the first year is seen as the key to success; but plants are reviewed after a couple of years and those that have not done well are removed. Mary Eastwood also aims to keep as much of the soil as possible covered with plants to help reduce moisture loss.

Joyce Salisbury-Jones believes her plants must be watered to succeed and she achieves this by conserving rainwater in butts fed by drainpipes from the roof of Bumble Cottage. The water is channelled into a series of pools, which act as reservoirs and also as an attractive water feature. A plant in need of water is given a drink straight from the pool via watering cans. The result is a garden that must rank as one of the most colourful open for the NGS. Life in warmer parts of the world and experience of gardening in countries where dry sandy soils are commonplace has influenced Joyce's choice of plants and, after spending twenty-one years at Bumble Cottage, she knows what grows well in her dry garden.

Joyce started by removing many of the mature Scots pines that surrounded the garden and soaked up the limited water supply. Shrubs and conifers now provide the framework, with herbaceous perennials, hardy and half-hardy annuals bringing splashes of colour. In the shady parts of the garden, dry-loving ferns such as *Asplenium scolopendrium*, grow alongside *Euonymus fortunei* and an abundance of rhododendrons. In the sunnier areas, climbing roses thrive but Joyce avoids the Hybrid Teas because of their hungry nature. Plants that like extra water are in or around the three pools, which makes watering easy.

Reducing water loss

Mary Eastwood's father was responsible for building the houses in Heyes Lane and at Number 35 is the garden where she grew up. As well as a no-dig policy, it is managed entirely organically. Although relatively narrow (27 x 10m/90 x 33ft), it is packed with a diverse range of plants. Unusual plants that do not thrive in the sandy soil are grown in pots and provided with the conditions they need. In beds and borders Mary grows many plants well-suited to sandy soil – shrubs like *Phlomis fruticosa* and *Tamarix ramosissima* alongside annuals and biennials such

as *Cerinthe major* 'Purpurascens' and *Oenothera biennis*.

One of the most striking parts of the garden is home to a productive patch of fruit trees and bushes. Fourteen different kinds of fruit are grown, including raspberries, blackcurrants, redcurrants, pears, apples and loganberries alongside plum trees that date from the time when this part of the garden was an orchard. The bushes rely heavily on the garden compost that is added to the soil in thick layers each spring to reduce water loss by evaporation.

Stabilizing the soil

Building raised beds is another way of preventing water loss and at the same time stabilizing the soil. At Bumble Cottage soil movement on a massive scale was carried out initially to reduce the dramatic fall in the land and a series of raised beds was built.

At Grove Lodge a neighbouring quarry came in useful when the 1½-acre garden was created twenty years ago. It provided stone for the series of terraces that Jean Venning and Peter Wareham felt were the only way to cope with the steep, sandy garden. They planted shrubs such as cotoneaster, holly, hypericum and ivy all the way along the hillside and these knitted together to prevent heavy rain washing the soil down the sloping site. The three terraces enabled them to get young plants established and, as these have matured, the terracing has become almost invisible. The garden's centrepiece appears to be a vast, sweeping double herbaceous border, but actually they are mixed borders whose visual impact is enhanced by the changes in level. A visit to Bressingham Gardens in Norfolk and the individual gardens of Alan and Adrian Bloom many years ago inspired Jean's initial experiments with conifers and heathers as well as perennials. Unlike the approach at Bressingham, however, her choice was to combine these three groups of plants: the conifers to give the garden structure during the winter months; the heathers to provide texture throughout the year; and a wide range of herbaceous perennials, in abundance, to create sweeps of colour in spring and summer. Annuals and prize-winning specimen plants are avoided as they compete for nutrients, which are not plentiful enough to create the 'big is beautiful' effect.

OVERLEAF Repeat plantings of standard wisterias establish a rhythm in the mixed double borders designed by Penelope Hobhouse for Baron Sweerts de Landas Wyborgh at Dunsborough Park in Surrey.

At the front, *Alchemilla mollis* and silver-leaved *Stachys byzantina* flourish in the dry, light soil, spilling over the stone edging and completing the repetition of colour and texture at ground level. The yew hedge

provides a dramatic background to echinops, *Acanthus mollis* Latifolius Group and *Lychnis coronaria*. Golden yews form a centrepiece where the path broadens into a circle around a sundial.

Tom Stuart-Smith

The sap is rising

Self-seeded annuals and biennials loom large in my garden over the summer months. Opium poppy, various mulleins, clary sage, *Eryngium giganteum*, teasel and foxglove are the main players. For me they inject not just drama but an important element of randomness and unpredictability. The garden becomes like a wayward child, who sometimes delights, sometimes disappoints and always has some direction of its own. When I am recasting a bit of the garden I normally plant some year-old mulleins and so on, to give the new area continuity with the rest of the garden; I also scatter some seed about. So it is in the second year that biennial chaos really lets rip. At that stage I have to be careful not to let these beautiful brutes swamp the perennials, which are sometimes squashed like infants on a rush-hour tube. Over the next two or three years the proportion of ephemeral plants decreases as the perennials colonize

The challenge of sandy soil

and the planting takes on a more settled look. This might be appropriate in some circumstances, but I find that this is often the time to go in and shake things up a bit and get the cycle restarted.

If I gardened on a gumboot-sucking clay, things would be very different. I would fill the place with sombre eupa-toriums and glistening helianthus. But given my stony sandpit in Hertfordshire, many of the most effective tall plants that succeed here are short-lived.

In June, surveying the wilder bit of the garden, with spires of white and yellow dotted across quite a broad canvas, I think of those early-eighteenth-century views of London, with the spires of the city churches floating above a sea of more lowly buildings, and all circumscribed by low hills. Beautifully contained and settled, yet bristling with vigour, variety and change. Looking at the decrepit chaos that is my garden in March, the ana-logy seems far-fetched. But the sap is rising again.

The challenge of sandy soil

Mediterranean plants

Visiting Greenways, Oxford, is a little like taking a holiday in Italy – visions of ornate garden statues, lush green foliage, enormous terracotta pots and low box hedging. The Cootes decided on structural plants for the bones of the garden, describing their aim as being to make 'a green garden where shapes, patterns and colours are provided by evergreen foliage that offers year-round interest'. The ⅔-acre site is divided into a series of 'rooms', the structure of which has remained constant during the owners' twenty-four years in Osler Road but, as the garden has evolved, the planting within has become more adventurous. Mediterranean species feature highly in what is a relatively warm garden, with literally hundreds of tender plants in pots being brought out of the greenhouse for the summer months to accentuate the exotic feel.

For warm, sandy gardens Mediterranean plants are the natural choice. Lavenders, euphorbias, *Teucrium fruticans*, *Brachyglottis* Dunedin Group 'Sunshine' (syn. *Senecio greyi*), and *Prunus laurocerasus* will thrive in free-draining, sandy soils, even in those that are not that warm. But imagine being able to grow olive trees alongside honey-scented *Euphorbia mellifera*.

Tucked to one side of the house at Greenways is a border that gives hope to any gardener who despairs of being able to grow anything in dry, sandy shade. It is planted with *Prunus laurocerasus* 'Otto Luyken', gently clipped to provide the perfect backdrop for large terra-cotta pots containing the white form of *Agapanthus africanus* – simplicity at its best and proof, if proof were needed, that life on sandy soil is not really all that bad, especially if you work at it.

The challenge of sandy soil

PRECEDING PAGES Self-seeded verbascum among *Papaver orientale* help Tom Stuart-Smith to achieve an element of randomness in the 1-acre garden, The Barn at Abbots Langley, Hertfordshire.

ABOVE In poor soil by the house wall *Albizia julibrissin rosea*, the silk tree with mimosa-like foliage, casts dappled shade on to the gravel path at Greenways, Oxford.

Plants for sandy soils

Trees, shrubs & climbers

Betula albo sinensis. Birch is a common sight on sandy soils throughout the British countryside. This species creates interest in winter when the bark stands out and almost glistens in low sunlight. The colour of the bark can be very variable, so always go to the nursery to choose a good form. Avoid mature specimens of any tree as younger transplants find it easier to grow away quickly. This is particularly so with birch which grows very fast to 10m/33ft.

Cistus ladanifer f. *albiflorus.* The rock roses from southern Europe thrive in well-drained, sandy soils as long as they are not exposed to extreme cold and very wet conditions in winter. When happy, *C. ladanifer* f. *albiflorus* produces a profusion of big, white flowers in early summer. It is not long-lived, but is easily propagated by cuttings which will ensure survival.

Ercilla volubilis. Botanically interesting is a description that could be applied to the rather discreet, greenish flowers of this evergreen climber. But don't let this put you off, especially if you are trying to find something a little unusual. It even grows well on a north-facing wall.

Hippophae rhamnoides. The distinctive orange berries of the sea buckthorn (6m/20ft) are a striking sight when they first appear in autumn. It tolerates salt-laden winds in coastal gardens, but is just as happy growing inland. Ironically the birds inland do not eat the berries, unlike their relatives on the coast who obviously recognize a good meal when they see one.

Hydrangea aspera subsp. *sargentiana.* This plant will stop even the most experienced of gardeners dead in their tracks when it flowers in late summer. It will thrive against a wall in a dry, shady, sandy spot and the downy foliage and violet lace caps provide the perfect backdrop to the flowers of *Anemone × hybrida*. Plant deep green ivy behind to solve the problem of what to do with a north-facing wall.

Lavandula angustifolia. Take the advice of the Provençal growers and cut lavender back with shears as soon as you have collected the flower spikes. This creates a tight bush that will thrive year on year, producing an annual crop of long, arching stems of flowers. If your plant does become tall and leggy, forget pruning and take cuttings instead. They are the easy way to replace plants that have grown unsightly.

Mahonia aquifolium 'Atropurpurea'. This much-neglected, vigorous ground-cover shrub (90cm/3ft) requests little of gardeners but gives much back in return, especially in winter when the foliage turns the colour of a red burgundy wine. It will grow in even the poorest of soils and combines well with the equally vigorous ground-cover woodland spurge, *Euphorbia amygdaloides* var. *robbiae.*

Teucrium fruticans. This fast-growing, silver-foliaged shrub works well alongside other Mediterranean plants such as cistus, rosemary and sage. In Beth Chatto's garden it is planted with *Tropaeolum tricolor* whose red-and-black flowers create the illusion of tiny red and black fish swimming through the silver foliage. It grows to 1.2m/4ft, so when it gets too big for the border, simply take cuttings and start all over again.

Perennials, biennials & annuals

Acanthus spinosus. There is something majestic about walking down a set of stone steps with magnificent flowering specimens of *Acanthus spinosus*, 90cm/3ft tall, lining the journey. Whenever possible give it a permanent home as it is a nightmare to eradicate the roots if you try to move the plant in later years. It will thrive in a hot, dry, sunny spot, which will remind it of its Mediterranean origin.

Alchemilla mollis. Just because a plant is common does not mean that it doesn't a deserve a place in our gardens. In fact plants are often common simply because they are good garden plants. And as Gertrude Jekyll once said, every good garden should include at least one drift of the billowing, lime-green flowers of lady's mantle. It can be particularly effective when repeated at the front of a herbaceous or mixed border, carrying the eye along and often pulling the whole picture together.

Allium hollandicum 'Purple Sensation'. As spring ends and summer beckons the drumstick-like flower heads of *A.* 'Purple Sensation' slowly rise above the perennials in the border and burst into bloom. These deep lilac balls fade as summer progresses and their straw-coloured flower heads persist into late summer, giving the border an air of faded gentility, a little like that which a well-loved great aunt would give to a family portrait.

Anemone × hybrida 'Geante des Blanches'. A dry, shady corner can be a nightmare for the gardener trying to choose a plant that will grow well, but this is just the spot for the tall, late-flowering *Anemone* hybrids (1.2m/4ft). They have a thuggish nature, spreading quickly through the garden if not kept under control, yet the sight of the crisp clean white flowers of 'Geante des Blanches' will enable even the most strict of gardeners to forgive its enthusiasm.

Sandy soil: borders in shade and sun

The design is inspired by borders in the Cootes' garden, one of which faces south-west and consists of Mediterranean sun-lovers; hostas provide the backbone to the other, north-west-facing bed. The palm set in a sea of nasturtiums (right) draws the eye to the house entrance.

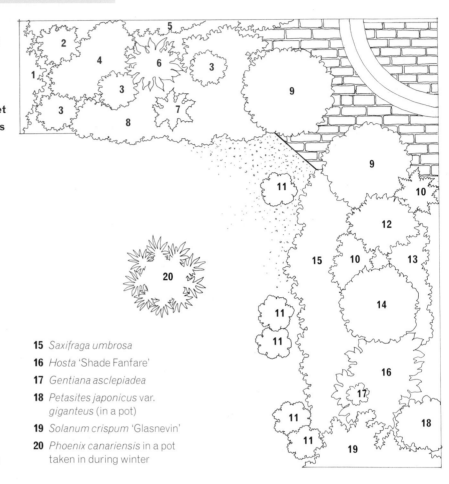

1 *Actinidia kolomikta*
2 *Mahonia acanthifolia*
3 *Euphorbia characias* subsp. *wulfenii*
4 *Euphorbia mellifera*
5 *Robinia hispida* 'Rosea'
6 *Strelitzia reginae* in a pot taken in during winter
7 *Agave americana* 'Variegata' in a pot taken in during winter
8 *Brachyglottis* Dunedin Group 'Sunshine'
9 *Hydrangea* 'Générale Vicomtesse de Vibraye' (in stone urns)
10 *Athyrium nipponicum* 'Pictum'
11 *Geranium maderense* in gravel
12 *Kerria japonica*
13 *Hosta* 'Pearl Lake'
14 *Hydrangea aspera* subsp. *sargentiana*

15 *Saxifraga umbrosa*
16 *Hosta* 'Shade Fanfare'
17 *Gentiana asclepiadea*
18 *Petasites japonicus* var. *giganteus* (in a pot)
19 *Solanum crispum* 'Glasnevin'
20 *Phoenix canariensis* in a pot taken in during winter

Anthemis punctata subsp. *cupaniana*. Silver-foliage plants often feature in sandy, Mediterranean-style gardens and this low-growing perennial is an absolute must. A crop of bright white daises with deep egg-yolk centres contrasts well with the finely cut, silver foliage, acting as a sign that summer has almost arrived. Plant alongside the golden-foliaged *Origanum vulgare* 'Aureum' and the buttercup-yellow flowers of *Anemone ranunculoides*.

Calendula officinalis 'Indian Prince'. Hardy annuals often add much-needed summer colour to borders and containers. This cultivar of our common corn marigold is best sown directly into the ground where you wish it to flower. Use sand to mark out where annuals have been sown so that you do not inadvertently hoe off the young seedlings. To keep annuals such as marigolds in flower, deadhead them as soon as the flowers start to fade.

Cercis siliquastrum. If it is true that behind every good plant there is a good story, in the case of *Cercis siliquastrum* it is said to be the tree on which Judas Iscariot hanged himself, following his betrayal of Jesus. In Britain it makes a good, small tree (8m/25ft) for a small garden. The tiny, cerise-pink flowers appear in spring before the foliage, coming directly from the bark and stems.

Eryngium giganteum. Miss Willmott's ghost, as *Eryngium giganteum* is popularly known, prefers a garden that is not too tidy where it can seed about without the risk of its young seedlings being dug up and destroyed. The silvery-green, thistle-like flowers are at their best in late June.

Eschscholzia californica. This Californian annual is a plant for life as, once established in your garden, it will reseed in the same place each year. The flowers range in colour from egg-yolk yellow through to almost blood-orange red, appearing throughout the summer months. It looks effective seeded among black-

foliaged *Ophiopogon planiscapus* var. 'Nigrescens'.

Euphorbia characias subsp. *wulfenii*. In the world of euphorbias this is among the largest (90cm–1.2m/ 3–4ft) and sturdiest, verging on being a shrub rather than a herbaceous perennial. The distinctive green spurge flower heads start to form in the winter months and as soon as the warmer spring days arrive they open to create a perfect backdrop for the yellows and blues of spring. To propagate take cuttings; never try to divide the plants as this will finish them off completely.

Nepeta 'Six Hills Giant'. Loved by gardeners and cats alike, this is the most vigorous of all the catmints and should survive the attention of even the most persistent of felines. Plant either side of a path to create an illusion of distance and, if you can bear it, cut back immediately after flowering to encourage a second flush of flowers later in the summer.

Papaver orientale 'Beauty of Livermere'. If you are limited in space and wish to include just one of the oriental poppies, this deep blood-red cultivar will easily live up to its name. The flowers are all too brief, but this just makes them even more special. Other perennials can be planted to cover up the dying foliage.

Salvia sclarea. This is a short-lived perennial or biennial, depending on the growing conditions in your garden. It is occasionally referred to as the hot housemaid or sweaty Betty, but as long as you do not inhale the scent it should not affect your enjoyment of the lilac bracts and white flowers. It is easily propagated by seed.

Verbena bonariensis. Many plants benefit from repeat planting and in the case of this verbena it should be regarded as essential – one could even go so far as to say the more that are planted (or self-seed), the better. It is most effective when allowed to grow up through other perennials, enabling its flowers to wave about in the breeze. It is a memorable sight among the majestic grass *Stipa gigantea*.

The challenge of sandy soil

The following list is a dusting of Yellow Book gardens on light soil, in addition to those Louise Allen explores.

ABOVE Herbs in pots make a central feature in Lesley Kant's and Stephen Cunneen's scented courtyard at The Old Vicarage, Carbrooke in Norfolk. RIGHT, TOP Acid-loving conifers and heathers grow around sand pits to give year-round interest in David and Mary Bowerman's garden at Champs Hill in Sussex. RIGHT, BELOW Hundreds of herbaceous perennials flourish in the grand double borders at Newby Hall, Yorkshire, where the gardeners feed the light sandy soil with homemade compost.

Bedfordshire
The Old Vicarage
Orchard Grange
Southill Park
Swiss Garden

Berkshire
Blencathra

Ceredigion/ Cardiganshire
Henblas

Cheshire & Wirral
Dunham Massey
Orchard Villa

Denbighshire & Colwyn
Bryn Celyn
Trosyffordd

Derbyshire
Eastview

Devon
The Pines
Powderham Castle
Yonder Hill

Dorset
Dominey's Yard
6 Malmesbury Road
Minterne
Toad Hall
24a Western Avenue

Essex
Glen Chantry
Tudor Roost
Wickham Place Farm

Glamorgan
Nant-y-Deri

Gwynedd
Bryniau

Hampshire
March End

Herefordshire
Ash Farm
Elmtree Cottage, Linton Gardens
Kingstone Cottages

Hertfordshire
Wickham Hall

Isle of Wight
Cassies
Northcourt Gardens

Kent
Beechmont

Lincolnshire
4 Ringwood Close
2 School House

Norfolk
Baconsthorpe Old Rectory
Magpies
Wretham Lodge

Oxfordshire
Headington Gardens
9 Rawlinson Road

Shropshire
Wollerton Old Hall

Staffordshire
Arbour Cottage

Suffolk
12 Borrow Road
Euston Hall
The Old Hall, Barsham
Treaclebenders
Wyken Hall

Surrey
Appletrees
Arden Lodge
Dovecote
Heathfield

Heathside
22 Knoll Rd
6 Upper Rose Hill

Sussex
Alcheringa
Champs Hill
Parham Gardens
Stonehurst
Whydown Cottage, Ansty
*   Gardens*

Wiltshire
Home Covert
The Old Vicarage

Worcestershire
Cedar Lodge
Dial Park
Harvington Hall
Ivytree House
9 Low Habberley
Stone House Cottage Gardens

Yorkshire
Blackbird Cottage
Hotham Hall
The Old Priory

The challenge of sandy soil

KATHRYN BRADLEY-HOLE

with expert insights by
JILL BILLINGTON
MARY KEEN
DAVID STEVENS

5 Stony issues

Within its small area Britain reveals a diverse range of
rocks, as a result of a varied lifetime spent on the borders
of shifting continental plates. It has undergone periods of
volcanic eruptions, scorching desert, submergence under
tropical seas and crushing beneath sheets of ice. There are
granites, slates, sandstones and volcanic remains in the
west and north; old, hard limestone forms the bulk of the
Pennine ridge from the Midlands up to the Scottish border;
and younger, softer limestones run diagonally from Dorset
to Yorkshire. The south and south-east of England consist
largely of chalks, flints and gravels. So there are rocks in
abundance in our Isles, on which stand houses for people –
and stony homes for many fine plants.

Stony soil

Garden soil that is peppered with stones is more often thought of as a curse than a blessing. Stones make digging difficult: they are jarring on the joints when using garden tools and, for all the stones that you remove, more of them are forever coming to the surface, so it is a battle which is never truly won. You could, of course, build raised beds over a tough, permeable liner and fill them with rock-free imported topsoil; this is a good way round the problem for anyone who finds gardening too strenuous, or for people with limited mobility. Making raised beds is also a good solution for a stony kitchen garden. They make cultivation easier and reduce the likelihood of producing malformed root vegetables (choose 'stumpy' carrot varieties instead of long types if you wage constant battles with rocks).

Gardens on very stony soil such as gravel beds can also be poor in nutrients, due to the fact that rainwater easily percolates through the ground, carrying away with it the minerals and trace elements necessary for plant vitality. In this case the problems are gradually corrected by applying a thick annual mulch in autumn or winter of well-rotted farmyard manure or garden compost, and applying a slow-release dose of lime (such as calcified seaweed) every three years or so, to maintain a balanced, near-neutral pH. The extra organic matter from such mulches also increases the soil's capacity to retain moisture, further improving the chances of plants growing successfully.

But surely the most creative way of dealing with rocks is to use them to your advantage, with rockscapes, drystone walling or screes; or indeed, the now fashionable gravel garden, which is also discussed in chapter 12. If you garden on thin soil over solid rock, there isn't really any choice but to go with the flow of what is there. At Highdown, on the Sussex coast (illustrated on page 59), for example, the garden was made in a former chalk quarry – a startling example of how creative thought has made a virtue out of terrain that could have been considered a serious drawback; its planting is composed of lime lovers, such as peonies, bearded irises, ceanothus and buddlejas. I believe that rocks should be admired and appreciated as part of the very fabric of the garden.

Refined stonework

Rock gardening has long been a popular pastime in Britain. In the eighteenth and early nineteenth centuries, the gardens of the Picturesque movement echoed, and to an extent were inspired by, the ancient Chinese method of imitating idealised landscape paintings. Rockwork clearly implied the 'bold roughness of nature' and was a Romantic gesture, in tune with the poetry of Byron and the unrestrained paintings of Turner. Admirable examples survive in the thrilling caves, follies and grottoes of Hawkstone in Shropshire, in the great quarried rockscape of Belsay Hall in Northumberland and the mossy springs in the grotto of Stourhead in Wiltshire.

A widespread passion for collecting and displaying hardy ferns during Queen Victoria's reign generated yet more requirements for rocky landscaping. Those who could afford it would show off ferns in a contrived shady rock garden with, perhaps, some dribbling 'springs' of water, or among tranquil pools, as at Waddesdon Water Garden in Buckinghamshire. Extensive collecting of Himalayan and alpine plants through the late nineteenth and early twentieth centuries inspired a desire for yet more rocks and screes, and this time, thanks to the popular writings of Hibberd, Robinson and Farrer, the trend caught on in a major way. There are fine examples of naturalistic rock gardens throughout England, from Trebah, in the south-western reaches of Cornwall, to the steep landscape of Cragside in Northumberland and the rhododendron-enclosed rockeries of Parcevall Hall, in a remote part of Wharfedale in Yorkshire.

At the start of the third millennium, garden makers are being inspired by contemporary artists and sculptors who challenge our traditional notions of how to use stone outdoors. The trademark stone circles made by the British contemporary artist Richard Long, the poet Ian Hamilton-Finlay's carved inscriptions at Little Sparta, his home in the Scottish borderlands, and sculptor Andy Goldsworthy's rocky walls and cairns (such as at Grizedale Forest Park in Cumbria) inject new vitality into ancient themes. Wherever stone is abundant it can be put to good use in the garden. When used well it enhances our connection with the natural world and the garden's sense of place in its surroundings.

PRECEDING PAGES Classic rock-garden plants such as the tough dwarf willow, *Salix* 'Boydii', alpine dianthus and *Armeria maritima* 'Bloodstone', grow out of crevices in limestone at Glen Chantry, Essex.

Sue and Wol Staines also grow wood anemones, saxifrages, campanulas and *Aruncus aethusifolius* in this well-drained area. The drawing of Hodges Barn, Gloucestershire, is from the 1964 Yellow Book.

MARY KEEN

Our stony soil

The soil was appalling when we came to this garden in Gloucestershire, so stony that in the first year we filled three skips with rocks, as well as building all the terrace walls and putting in foundations for paths with those we removed. Planting was hard work, which invariably needed a pickaxe – often it took half an hour to make a hole big enough for a tree or shrub. Sometimes a large rock seemed to be locked into position by a smaller stone, but after a long struggle it was disappointing to discover that the culprit was not as large as the effort it took to dislodge it.

We still have to resort to the pickaxe for deep planting holes, even though years of improving the soil, by adding manure, bark and homemade compost have made the ground more workable. There is a downside to this, I suspect, that by adding so much humus we may have sacrificed some of the free-draining properties of stony soil. The garden is high and in winter it is the dry areas that survive hard weather best. I could have left the ground unimproved and majored in Mediterranean plants, but I cannot resist large and greedy flowers like roses, peonies and dahlias. We don't use everyone's favourite mushroom compost as a mulch because its lime content would increase the alkalinity of our soil, whose parent rock is limestone. All sorts of quite ordinary things like the favourite roses can

become chlorotic with too much lime.

Stones still rise to the surface like the raisins in muesli, especially after frost. In the beginning I was very fussy about removing them all. Now I don't bother with anything smaller than 8 or 10cm/3 or 4in in diameter. One can't aspire to better advisers than Pam Schwerdt and Sibylle Kreutzberger, the former head gardeners at Sissinghurst, who also garden on Cotswold brash. Their view is that, as long as the stones are too small to inflict root damage, they help with the drainage. Larger stones come in useful for mulches around newly planted trees, to keep them cool and conserve moisture.

ABOVE In the quietest corner of the Summer Garden at The Old Rectory at Duntisbourne Rous, Gloucestershire, *Rosa* 'Heritage' flowers above *Mimulus guttatus*, which, says Mary Keen, 'is supposed to prefer a wet place, but grows perfectly well here'. The salvia-like *Nepeta sibirica* 'Souvenir d'André Chaudron' is invasive but worth growing for its long season of beautiful blue flowers and *Salvia* 'Indigo Spires' repays the trouble of taking cuttings. A *Cosmos* 'Versailles' looms out of the copper at the centre of the garden and is 'the best crimson cosmos, if you can find it'. Self-seeders are carefully 'edited' to achieve the relaxed effects Mary loves but she never has the heart to weed out the self-sown black mullein, which is native to the Cotswolds and makes itself at home everywhere in the 1½-acre garden.

A style to suit the site

Successful stone and rock gardens are those where the owners have considered the local geology, climate and the gradient of the site, as well as the atmosphere they want to convey and the types of plants that interest them. At Glen Chantry in Essex the limestone rock garden is a habitat for alpine plants – hummocks of thrift (*Armeria maritima* 'Bloodstone') and plumes of *Aruncus aethusifolius* relish the dry conditions. The shady moss garden at Windy Hall in Cumbria is quite different in feel, the stone slabs standing like ancient monoliths in a woodland glade. The 'steppe' rock garden at Lady Farm

garden, near Bath, flows into the Somerset hills. Here Judy Pearce, in collaboration with horticulturist Mary Payne, planted a sunny slope with grasses including blue fescues and the airy *Stipa tenuissima*, accompanied by fairly low-growing, drought-tolerant perennials in a fluid and naturalistic style. The plants are widely spaced and sit well among the Cotswold limestone boulders and chippings from nearby Cirencester. It is, in effect, a Mediterranean-style rock garden, reminiscent of the dry, garrigue landscapes you can see on the hillsides of Greece.

While sloping ground (and certainly gardens with very steep inclines) can be difficult to landscape in a formal way, hilly terrain is ideally suited to creating a rock garden. Whether shallow or steep, a gradient allows more opportunities to replicate nature. Sloping ground also has better drainage and there is less likelihood of the need for major earth moving.

An open, bright and sunny site is essential for growing many of the more traditional rock-garden plants, particularly alpine types, and few of these will thrive where water drips off branches after a shower, or where fallen leaves may gather and rot. However, shade does not rule out a rock garden: rather than fight the gloom, make a virtue of it by planting woodland flowers. Ferns, foxgloves and candelabra primulas feature in the exquisite rock garden at Bide-a-Wee Cottage in Northumberland; its shady nooks are also planted with saxifrages and blue and orange forms of meconopsis. Elsewhere, on the cliff walk, sun-loving thymes and small sedums spill on to gravel paths.

A level site is often particularly suited to making a raised bed or stony scree. If the chosen position is exposed, you may need to plant a screen of mixed shrubs and evergreens to help filter wind. A shrubby background is often visually pleasing anyway, providing a green backdrop which complements the stones. At 18 The Avenue, Ipswich, shrubs and trees contribute to the topography of the front rock and gravel garden.

Rock-garden plants

While there are plenty which are not too fussy about soil alkalinity or acidity, rock-garden plants often show marked preferences, as a result of having adapted to growing in specific habitats. Plants that choose to live on limy soils (known as calcicoles) and avoid soils lacking lime (calcium carbonate) include clustered bellflower (*Campanula glomerata*), hardy annual larkspur (*Consolida regalis*), the common spotted orchid (*Dactylorhiza × fuchsii*), round-headed rampion (*Phyteuma orbiculare*) and hairy violet (*Viola hirta*).

As well as many rhododendrons and most members of the heather (*Ericaceae*) family, acid-loving plants which will not tolerate lime in the soil (known as calcifuge) include arctic birch (*Betula nana*), creeping dogwood (*Cornus canadensis*), *Shortia uniflora* and *Gaultheria procumbens*. Even in the contrived habitat of the garden, it is easy to see when their needs are not being met. Often their leaves show yellowing patches and perhaps some brown areas along the leaf margins. When lime is present it inhibits their uptake of iron and manganese and other trace elements. Gardeners can try to correct this deficiency by feeding plants with fertilizers to overcome the shortfall, or buying ericaceous (lime-free) soil, but the best solution is to plant according to your soil type rather than fighting it.

ABOVE Shady conditions and a climate with high rainfall provide ideal conditions at Windy Hall, in Cumbria, for a garden of mosses. Stones, in an eclectic arrangement, stand like monoliths amid the greenery.

RIGHT In Daphne and Godfrey Royle's ½-acre garden at Home Farm in Oxfordshire, wisteria and *Abutilon × suntense* clothe the house walls. In the rockery *Helianthemum cupreum* 'Fire Dragon' and *Erysimum cheiri*

'Harpur Crewe' are followed in August by brilliant orange *Zauschneria* 'Dublin' and yellow *Allium flavum*. Digging the stony soil requires a pick and getting rid of bindweed was a nightmare until Daphne

discovered how to get down to the roots: 'Let the weeds grow to 45cm/18in and shove the tips into a jam jar sunk into the ground, filled with a weak solution of glyphosate and covered with a slate lid.'

Plants for different habitats

The average rock garden offers a range of habitats suited to different types of plants. The vertical crevices between rocks are ideal for rosetted plants such as saxifrages and lewisias, which resent having water sitting around their necks or puddling into the leaves. Level parts of the rock garden suit upright perennials – aquilegias, shooting-stars (dodecatheons) and many primulas. Level areas are also ideal for planting diminutive bulbs, including cyclamen, dwarf daffodils and crocuses such as *C. chrysanthus* cultivars, *C. c.* 'Saturnus', *C. tommasinianus* and autumn-flowering *C. speciosus*. Tulips, too, should be selected carefully; *Tulipa biflora*, *T. dasystemon* and *T. tarda* are dainty species that have the right ambience.

Mat formers, such as thymes, *Lithodora diffusa* and mountain avens (*Dryas octopetala*) will also favour planting into flat surfaces of the rock garden, and look especially effective when they have grown large enough to tumble like green waterfalls over the edges of the rocks nearby. It is worth including among the mat selection the ground-hugging, dwarf willows *Salix retusa* and tiny-leaved *S. serpyllifolia* for their fluffy, spring catkins, and the creeping forms of cotoneaster for their scarlet, late-season berries and, in some cases, rich red autumn tints in the foliage.

Dwarf shrubs and trees can also invigorate the planting scheme by providing added overall structure, or foliage detail, or simply a green backdrop against which some of the bulbs and perennials may be seen more effectively.

In Judy Pearce's sloping 'steppe' garden at Lady Farm, Somerset, plants are widely spaced and randomly planted among stones and gravel. Grasses are mostly *Carex buchananii*, *Stipa tenuissima* and *S. gigantea* with colonies of self-seeding verbascums and metallic blue *Eryngium bourgatii* 'Picos Blue' and kniphofias giving vertical structure. As it is a 'hot spot', silver plants, such as santolina and *Artemisia alba* 'Canascens', and Californian poppies are prominent. The clay sub soil has never been dug or prepared in any way. 'Hand weeding is minimal', says Judy. 'and the area is never watered, fed, stocked or divided.'

JILL BILLINGTON

Go with the flow

On our initial visit to the Weir House at New Alresford in Hampshire, both Barbara Hunt and I responded instantly to this dynamic riverside site. We knew at once that flowing water would inspire the overall design, but had to respect the hot, dry, south-facing situation behind the house, on alkaline soil of gravely loam. Here, stone for the terrace, brick for the widely curved, shallow steps and fine gravels for the path, all laid with flowing lines and serpentine curves, would echo the meandering watercourse.

Clear streams divide around the house, flowing smoothly from a watercress farm. The house is reached by crossing a ford through which the water flows into the high-walled kitchen garden where the gradient forces the water to race. The rear garden is open, wide and flat and here the river is a slow flow of cleanly transparent water, maintaining a constant level with the sweeping lawn and almost enclosing the area by completing the encircling boundary of the old brick wall.

To us this watercourse seemed so precious that we chose it to express the essential spirit of the design. We maintained the open flatness of the site and replaced the existing rectangular balustraded terrace with a widely curving, spaciously paved area that provides an uninterrupted link with the river. Only wide box hedging, clipped 5cm/2in higher than the flagged level, edges this sweep of terrace. Beyond it we designed a 'Flow Garden' of widely winding 'Breedon' gravel paths, crossed by ribbons of brick, sinuously flowing through the serpentine planting.

Free-draining soil but a fairly high water table influenced the choice of plants – those that would sustain themselves without irrigation once they matured. Flows of santolina, lavender, heuchera and small reedy day-lilies like *Hemerocallis* 'Summer Wine' emphasize the layout, infilled with textures of wispy stipas, oaty deschampsia and huge, fluffy miscanthus and the subtle colours of bronze-leaved carex, silvery artemisias and many greens. Randomly dotted tulips, *Allium sphaerocephalon*, *Knautia macedonica* and *Geum* 'Borisii' make seasonal appearances. Pleasingly, the gardener has confirmed that the 'Flow Garden', planted in 1996, is easy to maintain.

Because yew is part of the iconography of the local Hampshire landscape, large, clipped wedges, radiating from a round bay window, block the flows with rigorous formality, allowing light to penetrate different areas as the sun moves around the house.

Select evergreens for their different shapes and textures. Some people admire dwarf and slow-growing conifers, although I would use them very sparingly, if at all, in the confines of a small rock garden, except for the very compact forms of *Pinus mugo*, such as 'Gnom' and 'Mops', dwarf cultivars of *Pinus heldreichii* and some of the smaller junipers. These are good companions to heathers particularly. Likewise, if you aim to achieve a tranquil and semi-natural scene, be sparing in your use of variegated-leaf plants and those with golden foliage, although both of these can be charming as subtle highlights.

Whereas traditional rock gardens tend to include few annuals, largely because most true alpine plants are perennial so as to be suited to the short growing season in high mountain habitats, there are plenty of subtle annuals to bring added interest to rock gardens in summer. There is the Venus's navelwort (*Omphalodes linifolia*), with tiny, white flowers held on slender stems, for example, *Helipterum roseum*, with greyish-green leaves and pink flowers, and fast-spreading *Nemophila menziesii* which carries blue flowers with white centres for many months in summer. Brightly coloured argemones, eschscholzias, dimorphotheca and portulaca add vibrant notes.

The small scale of many traditional rock-garden plants and bulbs means that a wide range of plants can be grown in a small space. If the texture and character of the rocks themselves have special appeal, a limited palette of plants will be the means of enhancing them.

ABOVE & FOLLOWING The 'Flow Garden' at Weir House, Hampshire, is on a hot and dry south-facing slope, with gravel paths winding sinuously through low mounds of sun-loving shrubs, including lavender, santolinas and rock roses, reminiscent of a Mediterranean landscape. Designers Jill Billington and Barbara Hunt interspersed generous clumps of grasses (*Stipa gigantea*, *S. tenuissima* and large arcs of miscanthus) with shots of crimson scabious, purple alliums and grey santolina to create a naturalistic landscape in tune with Janette and George Hollingbery's riverside site.

Making use of stone

Building an informal rockscape can be a very satisfying way of making use of stone in the garden. If you need to import materials, always choose local stone as a first principle, whether it is for making a rock garden, building new walls or other substantial features. As well as for practical reasons – transportation from a nearby source will be easier and much cheaper – selecting local materials is more likely to enhance your garden. If the local stone is soft or crumbly textured and breaks into fairly small pieces, it could be ideal in raised beds or screes. If you can get large, characterful rocks from a nearby quarry and you have the space, you could introduce dramatic rockwork to the scene, creating a mini-gorge or cliff-face with the help of machinery and skilled labour. Many quarries have 'waste' piles of stones which are rejected by the building industry but ideal for gardens.

Detailed planning is essential for any rock-garden project to run smoothly. Plan the sequence of operations before the stone arrives, bearing in mind that any excavations – perhaps for a pond or other water feature, or for site levelling – should be completed in advance. If plants are to be removed for replanting elsewhere, this must be done ahead of time too, and preferably in the dormant season when they will suffer least, with evergreens best moved in spring or autumn.

Check out access for delivery of any new rocks: stone is very heavy and should be set down close to where it will be used. The larger the rocks, the more effective the result, but heavy machinery will almost certainly need to be hired to move them into place (you can hire the driver too). Lumps of stone heavier than 25kg/55lb should be moved with wheeled assistance such as a sack truck, preferably with broad tyres which are less likely to sink into the ground. Never try to cart big stones in wheelbarrows: they are too unstable for the job and can easily overturn. Some stones may be round enough to be rolled into position. Flatter or rectangular slabs may be trundled from one spot to another by lifting up one and 'walking' them along on the bottom two corners. Have plenty of strong timber boards, ropes and rollers to hand to facilitate moving stones into position. Choose a period of dry weather, to avoid ruining the soil structure and handling wet, slippery stones. Gloves and protective footwear are essential.

If necessary, sharpen up the drainage on low gradients by replacing the top 15–20cm/6–8in of soil with a layer of brick rubble or large gravel stones. Lay inverted turves or permeable geotextile membrane on top to keep loose soil out of the rubble base, then replace some of the topsoil.

Spread out the stones nearby so that you can see their shape, size and strata. Use a hosepipe or string to mark out the chosen areas for each 'outcrop' layer of rocks, working from the bottom upwards. The aim is to achieve as natural an effect as possible. Use a crowbar to arrange the largest stones first, wedging them firmly in place with pieces of brick or rock underneath. They should be one-third to one-half buried in the soil, and tilting backwards slightly, with any visible strata lines running horizontally. Aim to avoid random 'dotting' of stones over the area, which produces a 'currant bun' effect.

Infill large gaps with topsoil, firmed in to avoid air pockets. Use sharp, gritty soil in planting areas between the rocks and for planting into crevices. Larger plants may be inserted during the course of building but care must be taken not to crush them.

If all of this is too daunting and you do not have a team of strong helpers on hand, it is best to call in a skilled landscaper to manage the project for you, since there will still be the opportunity to plant the rock garden yourself, at leisure after it has been built.

Planting the rock garden

Some gardeners favour planting the rock garden during the course of its construction, poking in plants here and there while the rocks are still being arranged. Others carry out planting immediately the construction stage is over. The advantages of planting while you build are far outweighed by the disadvantages. If you start watering in plants as you go, the site will become a muddy quagmire. You may find you have put plants – or even stones – in the wrong place and disturbing it all will cause the plants a good deal of stress. There is also the strong likelihood that plants already set into their homes will get trampled upon during continued construction.

Delaying planting for a couple of weeks after building

DAVID STEVENS

Using rocks

Rock: elemental, solid, stony, rugged, smooth, dry, wet and oh so often wrongly used!

Stone is one of the building blocks of our world, infinitely variable in its composition and rich in design potential. The trouble is that many people use it simply for the sake of doing so, always a dangerous precedent, without taking due regard of how it can contribute positively to a particular composition. Rock is, or should be, one of the most integral garden elements, whether it is used as rugged outcrops or carefully chosen as a sculptural point of interest. Because of its inherent power rock should figure high in the planning process and never as an afterthought, when it becomes instantly devalued.

The use of rock falls into two broad classifications, naturalistic and artificial, both having the ability to become major players in the garden layout. The first revolves very much around creating features that echo nature as closely as possible, perhaps a cascading upland stream using the largest possible pieces of local stone set to regular strata or 'bedding planes'. Water will dash and tumble over a boulder-strewn bed with deep pools and shallow beaches adding to the realism. Building such features takes skill, sensitivity and an eye for the way

nature does it, which is the real point.

Artificial features, on the other hand, use stone in a rather different way, but with no less sensitivity. Here we might look at rock as standing stones which can form sculptural focal points of the highest order, either set within a soft shawl of planting or as lone sentinels on a sweep of lawn. Alternatively a smooth, water-worn boulder set at the turn of a path deflects the eye and doubles as an occasional seat.

Much modern garden design uses the charisma of stone, often in conjunction with water, as the Japanese have done for centuries, as a minimalist foil for elegant architectural planting.

With rock, as with planting, shape, form and texture are everything and, like plants, no two rocks are exactly alike. Character is therefore paramount, so choose and use rock carefully, but if you have a mind to experiment, as I did in my controversial garden at the Hampton Court Show (1998), you might just paint them a colour – why not red!

will give the rocks and soil time to settle so that cracks and depressions can be topped up with more soil. (Use a hose 'sprinkler' for a few hours in the interim period if there is no rain, to encourage the settling process.) When the stone building is completed first, you can set plants in position and rearrange at leisure, getting an overall picture before beginning planting.

Water all potted plants well, an hour or two ahead of planting, to ensure turgidity in the roots, and water again when the plants are in. Be wary of overcrowding plants,

mat formers especially, by placing them too closely. Mulch the surface with a 2cm/¾in layer of washed horticultural grit to aid drainage and prevent mud-splashes. Water young plants regularly.

Working with gravelly ground

In Britain gravel beds occur chiefly in the south-east, a region which lacks the great quantities of solid stone that feature in the rest of the country. Land extraction of

Rugged boulders rise out of untamed grass and bracken at Penns in the Rocks in Sussex. A large, wild and romantic area makes use of natural rock formations of Tunbridge Wells sandstone and contrasts with the rest of the garden, with its neatly clipped hedges and flights of steps flanked by Irish yews. The old walled garden is packed with perennials, roses and shrubs.

gravel has therefore long been a controversial issue, since the south-east is heavily populated (nobody wants a noisy, ugly gravel pit on their doorstep). From the gardener's point of view, 'gravel' may also be crushed quarried stone, supplied as various limestones, sandstones, granites and other stone chippings. Both chippings and dredged gravel are sold in 5kg to 25kg bags at garden centres and builders' merchants, or bulk quantities are delivered by lorry. The colours of garden gravels and chippings are as varied as the colours of stone itself, from pure white through pink, beige, grey, green, cream and brown to nearly black. When you choose gravel, try to get local stone. If it is not available, at least choose gravel that matches your home and surroundings in colour and texture.

Beth Chatto's virtuoso gravel garden in Essex, created on 'soil' consisting of a mixture of gravel, stones and yellow sand, provides endless inspiration in creating harmonious plantings. On a much smaller scale, garden designer Marie-Elaine Houghton has used the local gravels at 80 Old Charlton Road, Shepperton, on the outskirts of West London, to make a grass-and-herb centrepiece within her long, narrow plot. And in Helen Yemm's walled gravel garden at Ketleys, East Sussex, honey-coloured stones radiate the warmth of Mediterranean climes.

The drystone wall

The technique of drystone walling is an ancient one, born out of necessity. In regions such as upland moors and dales where there is plenty of rock to hand, stones have been gathered together to provide field boundaries down the centuries. Building walls was a way to use surface stones cleared from fields and pastures, and use a material that was free and immediately to hand. Such walls are especially valued in areas where the soil is too thin or the climate too harsh to make boundaries out of hedges, or where the ground is rocky and too hard to sink fence-posts.

ABOVE In the open and sunny gravel garden of Ketleys in East Sussex, Helen Yemm makes use of dry conditions by planting drought-tolerant species, such as rich blue agapanthus, fennel and verbascum. Ancient roses, purple sage, lavender and blue mallow (*Malva sylvestris*) form the backbone, while grasses, such as *Stipa gigantea* and *S. arundinacea* provide constant soft movement. Helen encourages self-seeding in the gravel but the seemingly random drifts are dependent on the culling of over-energetic seeders and the encouragement of others. 'The garden ebbs and flows,' says Helen, ' – subtly different each year.'

In the garden there are many ways that these walls can be put to excellent use. They may offer protection from wind or cold, radiating absorbed heat so that rather tender plants can grow nearby. And, as well as the aesthetic value of a well-built stone wall, it also offers plenty of opportunities for growing plants. Climbing plants may creep over the surface and a good range of species can be poked into the cracks. Typical alpine and rock-garden plants are among the best for this treatment. Many of the retaining walls and stone step risers at Great Dixter in Sussex are colonised by pendulous cushions of aubrieta, which, says Christopher Lloyd, 'will even tolerate a north aspect, if required to'. The Mexican daisy (*Erigeron karvinskianus*) is 'a wonderful do-it-yourself plant' in walls and paving cracks, needing a hard cut back in late winter or early spring. In pollution-free areas lichens may handsomely decorate the stone face. Walls in damp and cool regions can harbour liverworts, cushion mosses, ivies and ferns.

A section of drystone wall may also be a miniature wildlife zone, even before you begin to plant it. Birds such as wrens, wheatears, swifts and flycatchers may make themselves temporary homes in crevices and cavities and they will certainly discover well-stocked larders of insects lurking in the cracks. Toads, voles, field mice and lizards are among the small creatures that will find suitable living accommodation among the footings and fillings.

Wall patterns

Lots of different styles are employed in building drystone walls. They have developed over many centuries of trial and error and, because stone types are extremely varied, one region's building method can be very different from that of another. In regions such as Scotland and Wales, where granite is readily to hand, traditional local walls are single-stone thickness, built from substantially sized boulders in a mixed, rather unkempt pattern. This suits granite, since it is very dense and heavy, with an abrasive

ABOVE RIGHT *Erigeron karvinskianus* and red valerian *Centranthus ruber* sow themselves into nooks and crannies in the old retaining walls at Great Dixter in Sussex, thriving in meagre conditions.

surface, so the wall, although not thick, is likely to last. In regions of slates and shales where the stone breaks into small, flat pieces, walls will be of double thickness, often filled out with soil in the interior and laid in neat rows or 'herringbone' patterns which help to give them strength and some weather resistance. Cornwall is famous for its herringbone-patterned stone 'hedges' and can be seen at Headland, the cliff garden, Polruan (illustrated on pages 184–5).

When coachloads of tourists are trundled through the narrow, undulating lanes of the Cotswolds, you may pause and wonder what it is they have come to see. Chocolate-box pretty villages, certainly. But what they are really admiring is the local oolitic limestone, pale honey-grey and beautifully laid by generations of craftsmen, fashioned into mile after mile of house, garden and field wall, just as they have been for centuries. Since this limestone characteristically breaks into small, irregular and quite shallow pieces, a local style has evolved whereby the longest side of each stone is visible in the wall-face, with smaller rubble pieces filling up the interior. The effect is of a wall built up in fairly neat, horizontal bands, usually with a tight row of upturned 'coping' stones along the top. You can see good examples of this at Rodmarton Manor, at Snowshill Manor, and Bourton House, all in the Gloucestershire part of the Cotswolds, to name just a few.

A drystone terrace wall in Pam and David Pittwood's 2-acre garden at Radnor Cottage, Shropshire, retains the soil on a south-facing slope. It provides sun and the sharpest drainage for succulent alpines such as sempervivums and sedums, including *S. spathulifolium* 'Cape Blanco' and *S. s.* 'Purpureum'. Drought-loving rock-roses, which Pam grew from a mixed packet of seeds, tumble over the top of the wall, enlivening the colour scheme. Over higher sections of the wall, she grows cistus: *C.* 'Grayswood Pink', *C. crispus* 'Sunset' and *C.* × *hybridus*.

Crevice-dwelling plants

These hardy perennials are suitable for planting or sowing into cracks and crevices between stones or for poking into walls. Choose young, small plants and make sure there is soil in the gap between the stones. Where crevices are narrow and too small to accommodate a rootball, put seeds on a piece of paper folded into a V-shape and use a drinking straw to blow them into the gap. Alternatively, roll the seed into a ball of clay soil and push that into the crevice with a spoon handle or dibber.

Pack in more soil after planting and place a slender wedge of rock over the soil to guide rainwater into the recesses of the crevice. Pour a dribble of water into the crack after planting or sowing and keep plants lightly watered until they are established.

For sunny positions

Androsace lanuginosa. In summer the spreading rock jasmine produces pretty, pink, five-petalled flowers clustered on leafy stems above the rosette of woolly foliage (10cm/4in).

Arenaria montana. The showy, white flowers of mountain sandwort look like drifts of snow in June with clustered heads on wiry stems above grey-green foliage (10–20cm/4–8in).

Aubrieta 'Doctor Mules'. Deep violet, single flowers are borne in profusion on dense, spreading cushions (15 x 60cm/6 x 24in). It will grow in partial shade as well as in sun and likes to colonize limestone walls.
A. 'Silberrand' has blue flowers and wedge-shaped leaves outlined in white.

Aurinia saxatilis. An evergreen sub-shrub, with soft stems, woody at the base, yellow alyssum or gold dust produces small clouds of tiny, clear yellow flowers above mounds of grey-green foliage in spring and early summer, making this a good companion to aubrieta.

Erodium × *variabile* 'Roscum'. Long-flowering from spring to late summer, this has dark rose petals pencilled with crimson veins (5 x 20cm/2 x 8in).

Helichrysum milfordiae. A South African evergreen perennial (10 x 20cm/4 x 8in), this needs full sun and protection from winter wet. Its crimson buds open in response to sunshine to reveal brilliant white daisies.

Iberis sempervirens. Tiny, brilliant white flowers smother the familiar candytuft, a spreading, evergreen sub-shrub, in spring and summer. 'Schneeflocke' and 'Weisser Zwerg' are good, compact forms for crevices (15–30cm x 30–60cm/6in–1ft x 1–2ft).

Sempervivum spp. Houseleeks (5cm/2in) make spreading, evergreen rosettes of fleshy, pointed leaves, fascinatingly geometric in their structure. The foliage of some species, such as *S. arachnoideum*, has a cobweb-like, hairy covering. Some flower in summer. They are drought-tolerant and dislike wet conditions. As well as for sunny crevices, they are ideal in troughs and screes.

For shade and partial shade

Asplenium scolopendrium. The hart's-tongue fern is a tough and characterful evergreen (55 x 35cm/22 x 14in). Its shiny, strappy fronds are particularly attractive in new growth in spring. It suits damp crevices among limestone, as does the smaller maidenhair spleenwort, *A. trichomanes*, with slender fronds.

Campanula portenschlagiana. With dark lavender-blue bells clustered on relaxed, leafy stems, this spreads densely. It is a thug but can be used as a mat-forming plant in partial shade (15 x 50cm/6 x 20in).

Erinus alpinus. The fairy foxglove is a free-flowering and self-sowing dainty evergreen perennial (6cm/2½ in). Usually pink, but *E.a.* var. *albus* is a pretty, white form, flowering in May and into summer.

Lewisia spp. This is valuable for its bright flowers from spring to summer in a range of colours, including peach, magenta, pink and white, which spring out of a low rosette of foliage (8–20cm/3–8in). It resents any water settling in the rosette.

Linnaea borealis. The twin flower (5 x 8cm/2 x 3in) has wiry stems bearing fragrant, pale pink and white flowers in early summer. A hardy sub-shrub requiring a low pH (acidic soil conditions), it thrives in peaty, shady conditions.

Mentha requienii. Fragrant, creeping Corsican mint (1cm/½in high x indefinite spread) spreads widely but hugs the surface, preferring moist soil in shade. Tiny, purple flowers appear in summer.

Directory | **stone and rock gardens**

As well as the places that have delighted Kathryn Bradley-Hole, here is a list that skims the surface of NGS gardens where stone is an issue.

BELOW Stone walls at Apple Tree Cottage in Sussex provide raised planting beds for a riotous collection of perennials. RIGHT Foxgloves sow themselves into nooks and crannies of the cliff walk at Bide-a-Wee Cottage, Northumberland, a garden made on the site of an old sandstone quarry. OPPOSITE, ABOVE Large cobbles set among the gravel enhance the stony setting for a potted arrangement of echeverias, sempervivums and purple-leaved heuchera at Old Buckhurst, in Kent. OPPOSITE, BELOW At Cerney House, Gloucestershire, an old drystone wall of the local Cotswold limestone separates garden and woodland.

Bedfordshire
Grove Lodge

Berkshire
Blencathra
Sandleford Place
Whiteknights

Bristol & South Gloucestershire
Barum
Highview

Buckinghamshire
Manor House, Hambleden

Carmarthenshire & Pembrokeshire
Tyfri

Cheshire & Wirral
Lynwood, Burton Village Gardens
Tulip Tree Cottage
Withinlee Ridge

Cornwall
St Michael's Mount

Cumbria
Browfoot
High Cleabarrow
High Rigg
Windy Hall
Wood Hall
Scarthwaite

Denbighshire & Colwyn
Arfryn
Golygfa'r Llywelyn
Rhyd Tan y Cae

Derbyshire
Fir Croft
Hillside

Devon
Castle House
Manaton Gate
The Water Garden
Westpark

Dorset
Chesil Gallery
Fernhill House

Essex
Beth Chatto Gardens
Glen Chantry

Saling Hall Lodge

Flintshire & Wrexham
Chirk Castle

Gloucestershire North & Central
Bourton House Garden
Pitt Court
Rodmarton Manor
Snowshill

Gwent
Castle House

Gwynedd
Bont Fechan Farm
Haul-a-Gwynt
Treffos School

Hampshire
Beechenwood Farm
Durmast House
60 Lealand Road
Macpennys Wood
22 Springvale Road

Herefordshire
Abbey Dore Court
Ivy Croft
Kingstone Cottages
The Nest
The Picton Garden

ANTHONY NOEL

with expert insights by
MIRABEL OSLER
GAY SEARCH
ELSPETH THOMPSON

6 Urban shade

Much as I love London, in June, when the streets are hot, noisy and tiring, I can think of nothing lovelier than going through my dark, shuttered house into the green-and-white garden beyond, where the fountain plays on the crumbling stone urn. How grateful I am for this leafy place. Gardens do not come much shadier than this north-facing plot in Dulwich and in summer I wouldn't have it any other way. My former garden in Fulham, west London, where I cut my teeth as a gardener and designer, faced south and was sunny for most of the day and I just longed for one shady corner where I could sit and read the newspaper or have a cup of coffee. So, if you are a town rat like me, be grateful if your garden is on the shady side. There is nothing more restful.

When others are luxuriating in spring sunshine or enjoying the glory of an Indian summer, I do long for more light in the garden. We are lucky in these islands to have a temperate climate that allows us to grow plants from all over the globe, but the shade cast by buildings, walls and fences, and often by trees as well, limits the range we townies can grow. However, one of the advantages of urban gardening is that the air temperature can be several degrees higher than that of the surrounding countryside – so, while shade restricts, a favourable microclimate extends the palette of plants that survive in town and provide year-round interest. It is a question of choosing the right plants for the type of shade and soil your garden offers.

Then there is the fact that the best gardens do not depend entirely on plant interest. A strong, simple, elegant frame is important, and especially so in a plot surrounded by buildings where the cityscape of angular roofs and straight lines tends to be overwhelming. With the infinity of the sky dictating the scale, design at its most successful is as generous as possible: wide steps, deep beds, as large a terrace as the site can accommodate, big pots and decisive planting. And no clutter! The very best gardens are smart – well maintained and kept as neat and clean as a well-run ship – without losing their soul.

Often it is clever architectural solutions that single out the great from the run-of-the-mill, and there are plenty of NGS urban gardens to visit for inspiration. Many show how to create interest in the shade, frequently without a flower in sight. Some owners manage to transform the awkward 'dog's leg' outside the back door of many terraced houses into a charming introduction to a town garden. Others demonstrate the use of architectural plants, trelliswork, mirrors and paint to trick the eye into thinking the space is larger. Elspeth Thompson, for example, at Rattray Road, Brixton, has varied the levels to make her tiny garden seem bigger. At 30 Westwood Park, Jackie McLaren has trellis panels framing a mirror to give an illusion of space. Perri Morton

uses mirrors at 32 Victoria Street in Nottinghamshire to reflect dense planting in her narrow, 25m/80ft plot.

Urban gardeners with plots ranging in size from a pocket-handkerchief to as much as half an acre can learn, too, from large, country gardens open to the public, from the simple elegance of the White Garden at Sissinghurst Castle, Kent, for example, or the geometrically laid-out walled garden at Saling Hall in Essex. Both have areas in shade. In their ¼-acre plot at 239a Hook Road, Chessington, moments away from the busy A3, Derek and Dawn St Romaine have created a series of garden rooms, including an elegant potager, inspired by larger, grander

PRECEDING PAGES Opulent hydrangeas are framed by pale papery birch stems set in the lawn at Eccleston Square, London. The 3-acre communal garden run by Roger Phillips and the residents shows what can be grown where drought, fumes and shade are the challenge, and includes a National Collection of ceanothus. The drawing is of Little Lodge, Thames Ditton, from the 1990 Yellow Book.

ABOVE Blue trellis panels swathed in climbers frame a mirror that doubles the light levels and increases the illusion of space in Jackie McLaren's garden at 30 Westwood Park, London.

ABOVE RIGHT Beneath a pergola of Tuscan columns, wreathed in variegated ivy and scented *Jasminum beesianum*, Malcolm Hillier has planted shade-loving ferns around a pot at 101 Cheyne Walk, Chelsea.

GAY SEARCH

Ways with shade

Some shade in town gardens is un-avoidable, from surrounding buildings, neighbours' trees and so forth, but some is self-inflicted – from large shrubs that take up not only a lot of light but also much valuable ground space. One answer here is to 'standardize' them, removing the lower branches to create a small tree. I did this with a large ceanothus in my last garden, making a mushroom-shaped tree and giving me space underneath it to plant shade lovers. I have seen this done very successfully with evergreen *Magnolia grandiflora*, pruned to a lollipop shape.

If you have inherited untouchable trees which make the soil directly underneath so dry and root-filled that it is almost impossible to plant, try a real toughie like Irish ivy (*Hedera hibernica*) at the edge of the canopy where there is a little more light and train the growth in towards the trunk. In the Cambridge University Botanic Garden they have it growing very successfully under ever-green holm oaks which cast an almost Stygian gloom. Alternatively find a large and handsome pot and place it on the bare ground under the tree. If you insist, you can plant it with shade lovers – big, bold hostas perhaps; or, for a very stylish option, just leave it unplanted.

gardens. The extensive gardens at West Green House in Hampshire are brimful of ideas for urban gardeners. Here, in the shadowy stable walk, Marilyn Abbott has pots planted with white winter pansies to 'capture every ray of light' and add sparkle late in the season.

Degrees of shade

The sort and amount of shade your garden receives will directly affect your soil and the plants you can grow there. Most town gardeners would gladly put up with some shade from trees in return for the beauty and setting they provide – evergreens for a sense of permanence and stability, and deciduous for a feeling of life renewing itself each spring. However, trees casting heavy shade may need to be professionally thinned or pruned. Summer pruning to lighten the leaf canopy (as opposed to winter pruning which stimulates the tree, because the sap, the following spring, forces in new growth) can transform oppressive shade into pleasant, dappled shade. Check, though, with your local council, the law on trees in your area: you often need permission to prune them over a certain height. And remember that the people from the town hall are only doing their job and are there to help. Removing a tree may get you into trouble with the law and, anyway, is a

last resort – when it has gone, all that maturity, and beauty, may take another hundred years to restore. Some trees can be trained like a venerable bonsai specimen. I once opened up a silver-leaved willow and made a raised bed of reclaimed bricks around it, bound together by cottage rock-plants such as aubrieta, mossy saxifrage and London pride.

Evergreen trees, whose needles can turn the soil sour in the immediate vicinity, are the most difficult ones under which to grow smaller plants and ground cover, closely followed by beech – especially copper beech – which has a dense leaf canopy. Given a good start, varieties of wild cyclamen, which offer flowers almost every day of the year, will grow beneath the darkest conifer or densest beech, as will many ferns and moss: there are excellent examples of moss carpets in the Savill Garden at Windsor Great Park. On the edges, where the canopy is thinner, you can grow shrubs, herbaceous plants, climbers and bulbs. Improve the soil by adding organic matter, keep the plants well watered and fed in the early years, and the odd branch of a happy shrub might even stray under the canopy. Beneath deciduous trees and large shrubs you can have fun with spring bulbs and hellebores, which revel in the shady protection they receive during warmer months. Some plants, such as

rhododendrons, azaleas and the exquisite blue Himalayan poppy (*Meconopsis betonicifolia*), need a light overhead canopy to survive. The light shade and leafmould provided by an ordinary English oak is their ideal. (Large leaves such as sycamore do not make good leafmould as they take too long to rot down.)

More common in town, though, is shade cast by buildings, walls and fences. My garden gets some sun in the summer, especially at the far end, but, because there are high buildings on one side, receives none at ground level in the winter. There are still plants – box, yew, pulmonarias, Solomon's seal, hostas, euonymous, hydrangeas, cordylines, to name just a few – for north-facing borders. Even in south-facing gardens there is bound to be an area facing north which gets virtually no sun in winter and which in summer receives light early and late in the day when the sun shines from the side. Here, the range is opened up considerably to include dicentras, phlox, tradescantia, tricyrtis, sedums, primulas, monardas, campanulas, aubrieta and even certain roses.

Soil matters

Gardens are so different that, to some extent, planting is a matter of experimentation, but one thing is clear: shady soil is usually dry and often impoverished, so good cultivation and generous watering make all the difference. The soil at the foot of house and boundary walls can be drier or wetter than soil in the open, either because the border is in a rain shadow or because rain runs down the wall and soaks the earth at its base. Adding organic matter to dry soil and horticultural grit to wet areas will help alleviate the problem.

As a general rule, it is better to work with the soil you have than try to change it, unless of course it is polluted with a petrol-based product or some other toxic substance that will have to be dug out and removed. The same applies to a garden full of builders' debris: remove the worst where you want to make beds and borders and ensure that there is at least 23cm/9in of soil on areas to be grassed. Otherwise, choose plants to suit the soil. Heavy clay, for instance, is very fertile and, with the addition of plenty of organic matter to make it workable, is fine for

hostas, hellebores, honeysuckle and day-lilies, and ideal for roses, which are especially good in town because the sulphur in the air discourages blackspot. Stony, well-drained soil in partial shade will allow you to grow melianthus, silvers and herbs. Likewise, if you have a penchant for lime-hating plants, such as camellias, rhododendrons and azaleas, give in to it only if your soil's pH is below 5.8 to 6, or grow these plants in containers filled with an ericaceous planting medium. Soil-testing kits are no more complicated to use than using a new egg-poacher and are well worth the effort.

Planting time is your chance to get some good earth underneath the subject and, eventually, you will make an overall improvement to soil structure. Plunge the plant in a bucket of water while you double dig the area to break up the soil and mix in organic matter and general-purpose compost. Firm the area with your foot before digging a hole big enough to accommodate the plant. Allow the water to run through the plant before removing it from its pot, teasing out any pot-bound roots and placing it in the hole, firming it in and watering again.

Trees and shrubs for structure

Even in the smallest, shadiest places, it is possible to have trees and shrubs as structural elements. By their historical associations, box, holly, yew and bay, ready-grown as pyramids, cones or mop-heads, lend a certain gravitas to a garden. Clipped trees on stilts are fun too. Easy-going hornbeam is excellent for this purpose; you have only to

LEFT Black bamboo, timber decking and glass walls set in black frames make a chic combination in this modern design by Vivien Fowler and Tom Jestico at 5 Garden Close, London. The dappled shade

provided by the rustling bamboo is always changing – dramatized by the reflections in the glass and the strong lines of the decking, which has been constructed well above ground like a pier or jetty.

ABOVE Pleached limes bring living architecture to Andrew and Briony Lawson's town garden at Gothic House, Oxfordshire. The overhead tree canopy evokes the classical *bosquet* used by Renaissance

designers to create the experience of stepping from light into shade. The hostas appreciate the shade, too, and are beautiful alongside the small pleated leaves of *Alchemilla mollis*.

look at the ones at Hidcote Manor in Gloucestershire to see how stylish they are, and what a useful screen they can make at quite a high level.

The crisp effect of trained trees works well with buildings. At the Ferry House, Old Isleworth, on the Thames, Lady Caroline Gilmour has pleached limes forming elegant, semi-circular ends to her terrace. In a corner of the shady end of Andrew and Briony Lawson's garden in Charlbury, Oxfordshire, a *trompe l'oeil* view of the Hartland peninsula leads to a short but stylish pleached lime walk, where hostas and lady's mantle

flourish at the base of the limes' slim trunks. With a little sun, laburnum trained as an arch or modest walk is stylish too, and against a wall is as distinguished-looking as any wisteria. I like the way the late Nancy Lancaster trained fruit trees into goblet shapes in her garden at Haseley Court in Oxfordshire. With a little more room and, like any tree, kept well away from foundations (if in any doubt, consult a qualified surveyor), flowering crabs and cherries will bring glamour with spring flowers and rich leaf colour in the autumn – in the case of flowering crabs, decorative berries too. Mulberries (especially *Morus nigra*, the black mulberry) not only bear delicious fruit, architectural leaves and eventually a picturesque outline, but because of their longevity also bring a lovely feeling that you are planting for the future.

All the magnolias bring quality to a place, too, with their large leaves and elegant structure, to say nothing of the flowers. The spring-flowering ones will take some shade, indeed they are happier if they can be protected from the early-morning sun, but the summer-flowering *Magnolia grandiflora* really needs to be baked. Remember that frozen buds and blossoms may be damaged by quick defrosting and position spring-flowering shrubs on a westerly or north-westerly aspect so early-morning sun does not strike them.

The Judas tree, *Cercis siliquastrum*, produces pink or white (*C. s. f. albida*) sweet-pea-like flowers on the bare branches before the leaves – a lovely, spreading tree this, that creates the perfect amount of dappled shade for planting beneath. In Beth Chatto's scree garden (see page 251) it forms the centrepiece to one of the island beds, casting a network of shadows on drought-tolerant treasures. In the south of France they train the Judas tree on pergolas, an idea worth trying. And small trees do not come much prettier than *Sorbus cashmiriana* with its soft green leaves lined in grey-green, and palest pink flowers in May, followed by even paler pink or white berries which persist well into winter, long after leaf fall. Surprisingly, all of the sorbus family are not only elegant, but also unfussy, both in their soil and situation requirements.

Prune specimen trees and shrubs in summer to reduce leaf and branch area. Pollarding (cutting back to a branch-stump) and coppicing (annually cutting to the ground) will increase leaf size, and in the case of catalpa and paulownia the results will be dramatic.

Architectural plants

Plants with distinctive outlines and strong forms play an architectural role in town gardens, complementing the lines of the house. The hardy Chusan palm (*Trachycarpus fortunei*), cordylines, phormiums and silver astelias from New Zealand bring a dash of the exotic to the shade. In his shaded sunken terrace in Cheyne Walk, Chelsea,

118

Urban shade

ABOVE Paul Kelly softens the strict geometry of his 10 x 50m/35 x 120ft garden in Wimbledon with large-scale foliage plants such as cannas.

RIGHT *Fatsia japonica*, stone balls and box globes in terracotta pots furnish the terrace in Andrew Harman and Jonathan Norton's 9 x 28m/30 x 90ft garden at 68 Mortimer Road, London. The great interior

decorator Nancy Lancaster would have approved of the blue, French-looking folding chairs and table – it was she who said how white garden furniture reminded her of 'great big aspirins'.

Malcolm Hillier has tree ferns growing in pots to suggest warmer climes. I grow exotic-looking grey-and-white-striped agaves (*A. americana* 'Mediopicta Alba') in huge stone urns, set on tall plinths, in my garden in Dulwich. Two metres/six and half feet up, they get sun for at least part of the day. I fill the urns with a fifty/fifty mixture of gravel (for good drainage) and John Innes No.2 compost for nourishment and the necessary bulk to keep the mighty agaves stable in a high wind.

Reliably hardy, the ornamental fig, castor-oil plant or Japanese aralia (*Fatsia japonica*) is an underrated shade-tolerant shrub or small tree, as easy-going as you please. Its huge, shiny leaves look wonderful in conjunction with buildings. Planted as an elegant evergreen screen, edged in low box hedges, the foliage looks like waves on the sea.

Elspeth Thompson believes large pieces of furniture, even in small rooms, bring character and style, and her tiny garden at Rattray Road is proof of how large plants, such as tall bamboos and the magnificently over-scaled leaves of acanthus (said to have inspired the design of ancient Greek Corinthian capitals or column tops) do the same outside. 'I find a few large plants with interesting shapes and textures are more restful on the eye than fiddly, fussy planting,' says Elspeth. 'And because the plants have a fair amount of shade they don't grow as uncontrollably huge as they might in full sun.' Even the slightly tender, grey-leaved *Melianthus major* does well for her in quite a shady spot. Cut down on Easter Day, it produces another crop of leaves (which are the main point of this plant) and flowers, which are curious rather than beautiful.

A window to another world

I am always amazed by people who buy a house or flat without finding out which way it faces. Yet even the most careful can come a cropper. I was pleased that our small garden in south London faced south-west, but had not foreseen that its high brick walls and the tall neighbouring buildings would throw it into almost total shade for all but a few months in high summer.

When you have a small, shady garden, you have to decide whether to devote your main area of sun to sitting or plants. I chose the former, leaving a wide raised bed at the base of the rear wall for the principal area of planting. Ever the optimist, I put in cistus and potentillas, hoping that they would somehow be **OK** – the horticultural equivalent of buying size 6½ shoes because you can't bring yourself to admit you take a 7 (something else of which I have been guilty for years). They did not do well, and I lost these and a lot of other plants in the first few years, simply because I would not own up to the fact that I was dealing with full shade.

On the other hand, I have had some success with plants that are traditionally said to like a little more sun. *Acanthus mollis*, which I always imagine on sun-baked Greek hillsides, has done extremely well, and its white, candelabra flowers glow against the backdrop of its dark, glossy leaves. The gorgeous, grey *Melianthus major*

has also thrived, against the advice of all the books: Architectural Plants in Sussex, who supplied it, say they now recommend this plant for sheltered shade. And the honey spurge, *Euphorbia mellifera*, has held its own – the fact that it hasn't reached the size it would have in full sun is something of a blessing. A bronze *Phormium tenax* also seems happy enough, but has remained thankfully compact, and in summer the buff plumes of *Macleaya cordata* wave high above their beautiful, glaucous leaves.

Traditional plants for shade which have done well here include the Corsican hellebore, *Helleborus argutifolius*, whose acid-green flowers light up a dark corner in the dead of winter; the graceful, gold-stemmed bamboo, *Phyllostachys aurea*; and a variety of ferns. For ground cover I have lots of ivies, lamiums, *Geranium phaeum* 'Samobor' and 'Album' and a little creeping rubus with purple-and-silver leaves (*Rubus pectinellus* var. *trilobus*) that I found at Crug Farm Plants, the shade specialists in Caernarfon, North Wales.

The effect is now pleasantly jungly in summer, but with enough evergreen structure to carry it year round. The turning point – for both myself and the plants – was when I installed a 2m/6½ ft square mirror on the back wall. It may not actually bring in any more direct sunlight, but it opened up the space like a window to another world. And the plants seem to enjoy the illusion as much as I do.

Elspeth Thompson uses bold architectural planting – *Astelia nervosa, Acanthus mollis* and *Macleaya cordata* – to balance neighbouring buildings at the shady end of her 6 x 6m/20 x 20ft courtyard at Rattray Road, Brixton. Elspeth has saved the sunny area for people – and a few sun-loving plants such as *Eucomis* – and used shiny metal grilling and containers, as well as a mirror, to reflect precious light by the back door.

*Urban
shade*

Versatile trellis

However pretty the plants and flowers, they need a backdrop to lend an air of settled tranquillity. Good boundaries also provide privacy and shelter. In an ideal world we would all have ancient garden walls of mellow brick, but trellis panels, supported by stout 10 or 12cm/4 or 5in square posts and topped with large, turned, decorative finials such as acorns, pineapples or spheres, make a good alternative and can be used against fences, to increase the height of brick walls or on their own. Inexpensive, easy to install, natural yet stylish – the square module enhancing all plants – trellis is the answer to an

urban gardener's prayer. Where it is impossible to grow anything at all, perhaps under a porch, balcony or roof, trellis treated like wallpaper is chic. At 17 Church Lane, Wimbledon, Paul Kelly, who believes in design based on strict geometry, softened by effusive planting, has trellis inset with bamboo panels to establish the mood of the oriental side passage and to separate this area from the garden beyond.

At the far end of Malcolm Hillier's garden in Chelsea a high trellis creates an understated backdrop to the whole garden. A pergola complete with Tuscan stone columns makes a subtle balance to the house and provides privacy. The area beneath a pergola, draped in wisteria or jasmine, is a delightful place to give a summer lunch or supper party. Malcolm Hillier's is reached by a sweeping path of

unusually small bricks laid in a herringbone pattern.

Trellis pyramids are a good way of bringing height to an urban space where there is no room for a tree. I paint my pyramids in either French grey, which is warm and Parisian-looking, or powder blue – the same curious faded turquoise as old French chairs. Both paints are exterior eggshell, which nicely shows up the grain of the wood. I basket-weave old-fashioned roses on the pyramids, training most of the shoots in a horizontal or diagonal manner to get a generous flowering. The bushy Bourbon rose 'Honorine de Brabant', with shocking-pink-and-white striped flowers, thrives in the shade. At the far end of the garden, where there is some sun in summer but precious little in winter, another more upright and very prickly Bourbon, 'Variegata di Bologna', delights with flowers resembling blackberry fool into which a generous amount of double cream has been stirred. Bologna likes a cool root run and plenty of feeding and responds to generous watering. For extra excitement, to one pyramid I shall add the twining variegated climber *Jasminum officinale* 'Argenteovariegatum', with cream, pink-and-white leaves and a delicious scent; and to the other, the perennial white sweet pea, *Lathyrus latifolius* 'White Pearl', who will wrap her delicate tendrils around the trellis with a tenacity that belies her fragile beauty. Both jasmine and sweet pea are fine in the shade.

Climbing beauties

Trellis makes the perfect vehicle for climbers, plenty of which do well in shade. Variegated ivy, especially the marbled grey-, green-and-white type *Hedera canariensis* 'Gloire de Marengo', brings sparkle to the dullest boundary. I love to interweave ivy with all manner of flowering climbers, especially clematis and *Cobaea scandens*. Although usually treated as an annual, the cobaea will come through the winter in a protected urban

PRECEDING PAGES An iron pergola frames the view down Susan Berger's long, narrow, 21m/70ft garden in Bristol. This structure defines and shades the area by the house, which is furnished with box globes. An arch leads to a shady part of the garden, where plants are mostly green, or green and creamy yellow, such as *Tellima grandiflora* and *Hosta crispula*.

environment and have a head start the following summer, flowering quite as well in the shade as in full sun and producing an earlier crop of outrageous 'cathedral bells' in white, green or soft purple. Cobaeas are moisture lovers and need to be watered frequently.

Clematis are moisture lovers too and, even in the shade, a couple of bricks on top of the soil around the roots will conserve moisture, and stop puddling. If you can find them, mossy old pan-tiles make a pretty alternative. Should the plants get dry, thoroughly soak them by leaving the hose dribbling on the protecting bricks for a couple of hours. As with cyclamen (which thrive in dry shade), it is possible to have a clematis in flower from February to November. There is *Clematis cirrhosa* var. *balearica* (December to March), with scented, cream flowers and delicate, ferny foliage. The alpinas (April to May) flower on the previous season's growth and, despite their exquisite flowers, tolerate cold, exposed conditions. The rapid-growing montanas (May to June) will grow anywhere and need pruning only if they get out of bounds; they will scale a boring old conifer of 9m/30ft in two or three seasons, and the scent, especially of the pale pink *C. montana* var. *rubens* 'Elizabeth', is out of this world. Early season, large-flowered clematis cultivars (May to September), such as 'Nelly Moser' and 'Niobe', are the ones most susceptible to wilt, but that should not stop us growing them. *C.* 'Niobe' has enormous, wickedly dark claret-coloured flowers which are a dream growing through yellow-flowered, grey-leaved honeysuckle (*Lonicera tragophylla*). Hard prune these large-flowered beauties to about 15cm/6in from the ground in February or March. The late-flowering species, texensis and viticella types (July to September), are splendid value and give the garden a lift just when everything can be beginning to look rather tired. *C. viticella* 'Purpurea Plena Elegans' (reminiscent of Parma violets), *C. texensis* 'Etoile Rose' (an expensive-looking shade of pink) and *C. viticella* 'Etoile Violette' (a smudgy and decidedly uncheap-looking purple) are terrific. *C. orientalis*, with flowers reminiscent of orange-peel and fluffy seedheads, will climb up to 6m/20ft, flowering until November, and should be pruned hard in March to about 30in/2ft above soil level. 'Bill MacKenzie' is the best.

Give clematis roots a good start by loosening them slightly, forking good compost into the base of the generous and well-drained planting hole and enriching the soil with bonemeal. Clematis need to be planted with the top of their rootball at least 5cm/2in below the soil level, mainly as an insurance against clematis wilt. If this should strike, cut the plant back to healthy tissue, drench with a good fungicide and generously water and feed with liquid manure once a week. The plant will revive, producing more shoots from below the ground.

Janet Goodyer at 55 Rawcliffe Drive is a clematis-aholic, growing nearly a hundred different varieties in her 30 x 10m/100 x 33ft back garden in York. 'In the sun', she says, 'the paler colours tend to bleach out – 'Nelly Moser' is especially susceptible – and they are all better grown in semi-shade. But in total shade,' she continues, 'some of them will never develop colour at all. For instance, last year the flowers of 'Guernsey Cream' remained pale apple green, which actually was rather pretty!' Janet reckons that clematis take up about 4.5 litres/1 gallon of water a day in hot weather, and benefit from a high-potash feed, such as tomato fertilizer, once a week – except when in full bloom, as this encourages the flowers to fade and thus develop seedheads more quickly.

Sparkling silver and white

There is a surprising number of silver-leaved plants that are happy in shade, as long as the soil is free-draining. Both *Artemisia* 'Powis Castle' (which keeps away greenfly), and elegant *Santolina pinnata* subsp. *neapolitana*, which is the best form, can be clipped into silver globes. Penny Snell's walk of silvery, pleached whitebeam (*Sorbus aria lutescens*) in her garden at Moleshill in Surrey, tolerates a great deal of shade cast by mature oaks and beeches. The avenue is underplanted with thousands of snowdrops followed by wild daffodils (*Narcissus pseudonarcissus*) to make an early spring carpet. 'Don't despair', says Penny, 'if these understated flowers, which I have seen growing by the million in the woods of northern France, are shy to flower for the first three years. Once they are established they will blow your mind.' Penny plans to add pink and white *Cyclamen hederifolium*, whose corms will eventually

ABOVE, LEFT The garden at The Ark in Lambeth Road, London, was co-designed by Anne Jennings under the auspices of the Museum of Garden History. The layout is modern, simple and confident, yet well founded in the classical courtyard tradition, with a lily pond in a central, sunny position. Metal arches, painted pale grey, bring a sense of enclosure without adding to the shade cast by high walls. The path, with tile insets to reflect light, imitates a carpet unfolding down the centre of the garden – its diagonal pattern subtly echoing the diamond-shaped trellis and enhancing the sense of space.

be the size of dinner-plates. In another part of her garden a silver-leaved weeping pear is underplanted with lamb's lugs (*Stachys byzantina*), an elegant idea for the smallest space, if necessary using a tub and clipping the pear into a giant silver lollipop.

White flowers bring a garden alive and are particularly life-enhancing in the shade. *Anemone × hybrida* 'Honorine Jobert' seems to thrive on neglect, flowering in the gloom over a long season. In Islington, north London, Diana Yakeley's garden is an essay in foliage textures and shades of green. All the flowering plants are white – cyclamen, lilies, hydrangeas and agapanthus – and many are planted in containers so they can be arranged for maximum effect.

House walls

For sunless brick walls, pale or pastel colours will reflect light, but rather than paint them brilliant white, which in England can look cheerless and glaring in unrelieved expanses, choose colours to introduce the warmth of the Mediterranean. John Fowler of Colefax and Fowler recommends adding a little black, raw or burnt umber stainer to any paint to give it 'depth', a tip that is especially useful out of doors, where distressed surfaces are appropriate. In my garden I find 'Fowler Pink', a natural shell-pink, particularly effective for warming up the drabbest aspect, and it flatters any plant. In the secret courtyard garden at Cobble Cottage in Whixley, Yorkshire, the walls are painted a warm stone. The colour creates a peaceful setting for the central focus: a maple in a fine terracotta pot. Recognizing that strong colours are best kept to a minimum, Malcolm Hillier has painted one wall in the shadiest part of his garden a rich red, reminiscent of Suffolk cottages.

Even if few of us have brick garden walls, all of us have house walls on which to train wall plants, many of which will grow on a shady aspect. Plant them in compost, enriched with Vitax Q4, and make the planting hole at least 30cm/12in, or better still 38cm/15in, away from the wall and angle them in. For training climbers on masonry, 12cm/5in flat vine eyes with medium-gauge horizontal wires stretched between are the most satisfactory system, allowing air to circulate around the stems. Set the eyes into the wall 90cm/3ft apart in rows for every six courses of bricks. Attach climbing stems to the wires to make fan shapes, using twists of flexible, plastic-coated wire.

Wisteria, which flatters any house and tolerates a surprising amount of shade, needs to be planted well away from the house walls as the roots can damage the foundations. Dig a large planting hole and line the side nearest the house with a couple of flagstones to encourage the roots to grow away from the building. *Akebia quinata* is a pretty, twining climber, with fascinating, claret-coloured flowers, that will shin up three or four storeys in a couple of seasons. *Hydrangea anomela* subsp. *petiolaris* is a self-clinging beauty that foams in June. As well as the many clematis already mentioned, there are the honeysuckles, all of which tolerate shade.

Roses, as long as they are combined with other plants to lend interest or structure when they are not in bloom, are perfect for urban gardens. Apart from loving heavy clay soil, they enjoy the shelter of town gardens and the sulphur in the city air discourages blackspot. There are quite a few that will tolerate different degrees of shade, including: 'Gloire de Dijon', creamy straw suffused with pink; 'Madame Alfred Carrière', soft white, flushed with pink; and the cream butterflies of the classic, semi-evergreen 'Mermaid'. At Sissinghurst, trained over the central iron pavilion in the White Garden, is the vigorous rambler *Rosa mulliganii*, which at the end of June is festooned with thousands of tiny, banana-scented, single, white flowers.

Trained against a wall, the sweeping herringbone fans of *Cotoneaster horizontalis*, with leaves that turn salmon pink in autumn, nicely anchor a house and, at ground level, disguise boring paving. And what could be more cheering on a winter's day than fountains of primrose-yellow winter jasmine (*Jasminum nudiflorum*)?

It pays dividends to observe your garden at different times. The sun might surprise you and make a shaft of light, just where you need it. The golden hop, for instance, needs some sun to maintain the colour of the leaves, but it is an energetic beauty and will make a column of gold up a drainpipe to light up the corner of the house. And in the autumn the little, musk-scented flowers bring a breath of the country to the heart of town.

At ground level

One advantage of a shady situation is that it is so easy to
grow moss and ferns on brick paving, on walls and between
paving stones and, with a little help in the form of a thin
application of milk, lichens develop quickly on flowerpots
and retaining walls to give a charming weathered look.
The little, pink-and-white daisy beloved of Gertrude
Jekyll, *Erigeron karvinskianus*, black aquilegias, *Viola*
'Bowles' Black', creeping mint (*Mentha requienii*) and
Soleirolia soleirolii will all furnish the cracks between
paving stones. Tender bulbs such as nerines, acidanthera,
crinum and irises all like the protected conditions found
at the foot of a wall. But they will not be happy in total
shade, and will do well only if there is some summer sun.

Schizostylis, however, as long as it is grown with plenty of
sand or gravel, is the exception that proves the rule.

Bold planting is effective in small spaces and thinking
of each area as a foil to one performer is the best way to
redress the balance in a garden surrounded by buildings.
For instance, a wisteria could be planted in a square of
black *Ophiopogon planiscapus* 'Nigrescens', or the equally
wonderful painted clover, *Oxalis triangularis*, in lime,
maroon and black. A sea of quilted, grey-blue *Hosta
sieboldiana* var. *elegans* could be underplanted with snowdrops for spring and interplanted with tall alliums for
summer interest. The marbled leaves of *Arum italicum*
subsp. *italicum* 'Marmoratum' could take over between
November and February.

In a paved front garden in
Malvern Terrace, London,
shade-tolerant trees and shrubs,
such as Japanese maples and
conifers, grow in the acid clay
soil. The garden is a gorgeous
sight for passers-by, especially
in April and May when long
mauve racemes of wisteria
clothe the house. As is proved
by many a town basement,
this climber will grow in the
dankest position, as long as it
eventually reaches the sun.

MIRABEL OSLER

Bottoms first

There are many ways of visiting a garden for the first time. We have our methods. Some are intent on plant rarities; others on ticking addresses off their list; others on hard facts, on inspiration, on plant sales, or on hedonistic indulgence. Whatever it is that sets you off on marking down a garden from the Yellow Book as quarry to be pursued on Open Days, there are no preliminary ground rules; rather it's a matter of individual attitudes. For myself, I like to approach a garden bottom first. A quick glance round tells me what sort of gardener owns it by the number of sitting places there are.

Proper gardeners – the dedicated, the serious, the single-minded plantsmen or women – do not sit in their own gardens. How could they? No caring, cherishing gardener can sit if they see a weed to be pulled, a climber freed from its moorings, or a head to be deaded. That – a lack of seats – is an immediate pointer. I know then the

kind of garden I am entering and adapt my sights accordingly.

If there are places to sit – whether benches, cushioned arbours, or perching planks – then the gardener is someone inviting me to pause. They are telling me that I needn't hurry, that what is on show is to be lingered over. They are offering an extended hand to

me, the visitor, to take my time. To sit and ruminate; to savour scents; hear the wind in the trees; or watch the dappling of shadows across grass long before the moment to start crouching over plant labels. That comes later when – if they are willing – it is the moment also to meet the owner of the garden and ask: why?

But sitting in a college garden is a different experience altogether. Entering through a portico you enter another world: a haven of repose replaces the bombardment of noise and pollution. The effect is instant, dramatic. Through the centuries visitors have sat in courtyard gardens set within the perfectly proportioned buildings of Oxford's colleges. Nathaniel Hawthorne enjoyed serenity under 'heavy clouds of foliage'. In spring John Ruskin found 'almost an ideal of earthly Paradise' and wrote in *Country Life* '... to walk ... into the garden is to lose all memory of conflict'. For those with time to meditate, these oases of peace perpetuate the timeless value of sitting in a garden.

Great containers

In the same way as smart dressing depends on simplicity, so plants in containers, in sun or shade, are best limited to one or two varieties. This is more effective and makes it easier to provide the right conditions and the appropriate watering and feeding regime. For most containers John Innes No. 2 is the ideal planting medium, being well aerated and containing a balanced supply of nutrients. Water generously every evening or early in the morning before the sun has become strong to avoid burning the leaves. And once a week feed with a high-potash liquid feed such as tomato fertilizer. For plants needing a leaner diet and freer drainage, mix in one or two parts grit. Never use ordinary garden soil, or you will introduce pests that

are impossible to control in a small space. Even if worms, the gardener's best friend elsewhere, wriggle into containers, gently put them back into the border as they over-aerate the soil in the confined space of a container. I break up polystyrene trays into pieces and use these as crocks in the bottom of containers. It not only keeps the drainage holes free but also helps to keep the plants' roots warm – important for those who are not reliably hardy.

A few big containers are always more effective (if in doubt, over-scale – large scale looks expensive in gardens and even half beer-barrels appear smart, as long as the scale and colour are right), than lots of small flowerpots (have the flowerpots too, but as detail) and look better in the context of buildings and paved areas, as they take on

LEFT Many of the flowering plants in Diana and Stephen Yakeley's garden at 13 College Cross, London, are in carefully grouped pots, and all are white – tobaccos and busy lizzies, hydrangeas, lilies and

agapanthus, and cyclamen for winter. Diana exploits shades and textures of foliage, and uses many evergreens to clothe the walls and to create the elegant 'bones' of her shady green and white garden.

ABOVE A comfortable wooden bench in the blessed shade of a tree at Corpus Christi College, Oxford, which overlooks Christchurch Meadows, is the perfect place for meditation on a hot summer's day.

an architectural role. And the larger the container, the less likely it is to dry out. Box and bay (*Laurus nobilis*) lend height and structure all year round to large pots. In winter you could surround them with cream pansies with black splodges, reminiscent of pandas. Box balls in terracotta flowerpots, arranged in rows, are as smart as a line of toy soldiers. Incorporate controlled-release fertilizer into the soil-based compost and topdress with a little Vitax Q4 in spring. Hostas thrive in the shade and, in pots, remain glamorous given a three-weekly liquid feed, with a top-dressing of gravel and a ring of Vaseline around the rim to deter slugs and snails. You can move and split these gorgeous plants at any time of year.

The flowering tobaccos, *Nicotiana alata*, which is especially scented, and *N. langsdorffii* with elegant, greenish-white trumpets and architectural leaves, lend distinction. The humble busy lizzie (the doubles are prettiest) will flower extravagantly until November in a sheltered, urban garden, as will the small-flowered begonias (again, the doubles are best) as long as they are fed and watered regularly. Mop-heads of fuchsia are successful in the shade too, one of the loveliest varieties being the old cerise-and-white 'Checkerboard'. All mop-heads bring a gentle Parisian humour to a town garden, a bit like poodles. Fuchsias should have frost protection in winter, but within reason things should take their chance, and if they need replacing – *c'est la vie*. Of the regal pelargoniums, the ancient 'Lord Bute' is especially tolerant of shade, with sumptuous flowers that combine beautifully with small-leaved, grey helichrysum (*H. microphyllum*).

Tulips, as long as they are not too close together, are fine in the shade. The white lily-flowered ones are lovely, as are 'Black Parrot' and 'Queen of the Night'. Plant tiny white cyclamen with shocking-pink centres in other pots, troughs or, if you have it, an old, stone sink, as long as they are well-drained – they will flower all winter, with no sun, an occasional watering and weekly deadheading.

Pots are useful, too, for dressing up a garden for a special occasion. Second-hand galvanized florist's buckets, with drainage holes drilled into the base, provide a setting of simple elegance for sweetly scented lilies in white (*L. longiflorum*), pale pink ('Casa Blanca' and 'Mona Lisa') or deeper pink ('Star Gazer'). They will add an opulent touch, as classy as a turn-of-the-century film set in Paris or Mayfair.

But surely the ultimate in container gardening is the fuchsia walk at 9 St Lawrence Road, Chesterfield, Derbyshire. The area is 6m/20ft long x 1m/3ft wide and shaded by a wooden-slatted roof. In summer you can barely pass through for the thousands of flowers. 'The reason we made the walk in the first place was to give the greenhouse some shade,' says Julian Waring. 'At the end of April, each year, we bring out the plants and place them in wooden troughs which are on two levels – trailers on top and the bushy varieties below.' Julian and Judith, ably assisted by their ten-year-old daughter, Rebecca, religiously deadhead and water the plants, of which there are about eighty, every night from May to the end of September. Rebecca has loved gardening and planting since she was two years old, and not only does she take fuchsia cuttings, but also breeds her own native butterflies, which are successively released into the garden as the summer progresses. Who says there is no hope for the future?

Smart practices

Urban gardens need an element of smartness. There is no room for muddles. And one should be ruthless with plants that are poor performers, or don't look nice. A garden is a living work of art and we all tend to overplant. We should not be afraid to take away a plant that outgrows its place. Whereas in the country one can get away with a bit of untidiness, in town every dead flower should be removed and every leaf brushed away.

It is worth buying the best quality stainless-steel tools. Save using precious garden space for storage by keeping tools to the minimum and installing shelves and hooks in the cupboard under the stairs indoors. A telescopic (easy to store) long arm is handy for reaching wayward climbers.

Gravel is anathema to carpets and polished wood floors. So arrange paving of some kind near your garden door, and have a large mat inside. A couple of washable cotton dhurries inside the house aren't a bad idea, either – that way, you will not have to bother to remove muddy boots when you want to make a cup of tea to drink outside in your shady haven.

Pots crammed with cyclamen or cream and black pansies, and ornamental cabbages massed like chocolates, are luxurious in autumn. In his London garden at 26 Thompson Road, Anthony Noel plants the cabbages in September, around box mop-heads (where *Pelargonium* 'Lord Bute' has flowered all summer). The cold improves their colours but, by November, they are past their prime and are replaced with hyacinths and 'Black Parrot' tulips. 'Through the winter,' says Anthony, 'when the only bit of sun going is on the striped agave high up in the urn, I dream of the scent of hyacinths in the cold spring air.'

Flying border

At 7 Cloncurry Street, London, Mrs Adams and I designed a border around white-leaved willow (*Salix alba*), subtly pruned to open up its structure. The tree casts dappled shade on to a 'flying bed' 6m/20ft long and 2m/6½ft wide, built of old bricks in front of it. Hart's-tongue ferns (*Asplenium scolopendrium*) are planted in the shady, damp area between the raised border and the boundary fence, where they will self-seed. This 45cm/1½ft gap also serves

as a pruning gulley for the wisteria trained on the dark green trellis fence.

Box spheres and mop-heads lend living structure to the border throughout the year, while 2m/6½ft wrought-iron rose stands, copied from the Bagatelle in Paris, contribute height. These are decorated with *Cobaea scandens* and the shade-tolerant, striped rose 'Honorine de Brabant'. In spring a mass of snowdrops and *Narcissus* 'Tête-à-Tête',

Plants for shady town gardens

Trees, shrubs & climbers

Buxus. Clipped box – spirals, hedges, pom-poms, cubes, obelisks, mop-heads – can provide the structure without which a garden is incomplete. Box will tolerate quite a bit of shade, but does not like too much overhead watering, lack of air movement, or to be grown under trees. To keep box happy and less likely to succumb to box blight (*Cylindrocladium* and *Volutella*) apply the occasional liquid seaweed feed or a sprinkling of blood, fish and bone.

Cordyline australis. Torbay or New Zealand cabbage

palm, to give this glamorous creature a couple of its every-day names, is an easy way of bringing a Mediterranean and therefore sunnier look to the dingiest outside area. Cordylines will grow as small trees, unprotected in sheltered gardens in the British Isles, often reaching 3m/10ft or more. Happy in the shade, they also look splendid grown as younger plants up to about 1.2m/4ft tall in containers, where they are unfussy about soil. The most beautiful variety is the cream-and-green-variegated 'Torbay Dazzler' which does need some sun and more shelter than the others. The traditional way of protecting the heart of cordylines in winter is by tying them into a sheaf using which are often out together, appear through the under-planting of **Alchemilla mollis** and **Ophiopogon planiscapus** **'Nigrescens'**, which furnishes the border for much of the rest of the year. Then, in high summer, this base planting is hidden beneath the feathery foliage and the white, pale and shocking-pink flowers of **Cosmos bipinnatus** **'Sonata'**, planted up in the third week of May.

1 *Box globes*
2 *Box mop-heads*
3 *Rosa* 'Honorine de Brabant'
4 *Salix alba*
5 *Wisteria sinensis*
6 *Aubrieta,* London pride and *Convolvulus*

althaeoides on retaining brick wall
7 *Ophiopogon planiscapus* 'Nigrescens' x 24
8 *Alchemilla mollis* x 48 (24 in each square)
9 *Asplenium scolopendrium*

a couple of their dead leaves in place of twine or string.
Hedera canariensis 'Gloire de Marengo'. Indispens-able in a shady garden, whether you need to disguise an ugly shed or fence, arrange the easiest ground cover between shrubs, or make a marbled evergreen trellis boundary. The yellow ivies, such as *H. colchica* 'Sulphur Heart', are too strong-looking as anything other than a spotlight plant, whereas grey-, cream-and-green 'Gloire de Marengo' can be used in large quantities. It also makes an excellent host plant in which to weave twining plants, including clematis.
Prunus cerasus 'Morello'. Against a north wall as a fan-trained tree, the Morello cherry flowers and fruits

well. Being self-fertile, only one plant is necessary to achieve good fruit. It tolerates most soils, as long as they are well drained. Keep well watered for the first year or two and give the occasional feed with a high-potash liquid fertilizer such as tomato food. Let the fan grow to between 2 and 3m/6½ft and 10ft high and across; it will bring a dash of French country charm to your shady kitchen wall.
Rosa × odorata 'Viridiflora'. This peppery-scented, 'green rose' from China always attracts comment. Happy in medium shade, it should be grown on its own, perhaps on the edge of a terrace between paving stones, or in the angle between two low box hedges. It

Alchemilla mollis with *Chamaerops humilis*
and *Blechnum spicant* in Mhairi and Simon Clutson's
garden at 26 Kenilworth Road in south London.

makes a bush about 90cm/3ft high, flowers from June
to November, and makes a wonderful cut flower.

Rosa 'Honorine de Brabant'. Striped roses are
delicious, and one which will grow in shade, scale a
3.3m/11ft pyramid and flower in June and autumn is
a very special plant indeed. All these qualities apply to
the Bourbon rose 'Honorine de Brabant'. The flowers
are quartered and cupped, and flaked in deep lilac/
raspberry on a white-flushed-with-pink background.
Train the new shoots on the pyramid in a horizontal
to diagonal slant (horizontal training encourages all
roses to flower), water well in the first couple of years
and give a generous mulch of manure in March, and
your garden will start to develop some of the
gorgeousness of Sissinghurst.

Rosa 'Madame Alfred Carrière'. This beautiful,
nineteenth-century climbing rose will grow up to
6m/20ft on a house wall, of which there is no better
example than the cottage at Sissinghurst. Perfectly
happy on a northerly aspect, it will produce its pretty,
white flowers suffused with pink in June and again in
September. This rose combines beautifully with the
expensive-looking pink bells of *Clematis texensis*
'Etoile Rose'. Give the host plant a couple of years to
get established before you add the clematis, though.

Rosa 'Mermaid'. The huge, soft, single, yellow flowers
of this early twentieth-century rose will reach the
eaves of a house in around five years, as long as the
position is fairly sheltered – an attribute of most
urban gardens. A north wall suits this rose, as it does
Clematis viticella 'Etoile Violette' with which it combines excellently. 'Mermaid' will flower from June till
December if happy, the clematis enhancing it from
July to September.

Perennials & ephemerals

Alchemilla mollis. The lady's mantle is lovely as under-
planting to hostas and old-fashioned roses; never
growing more than 15cm/6in high, it will cheerfully
tolerate the toughest clay. The small, pleated leaves,
of the freshest light green, combine with the lime-
coloured flowers to give an expensive, understated
effect. When the first crop of flowers is over in July, cut
the whole plant to the ground and within six weeks it
will produce flowers all over again with brand-new
leaves to show them off.

Anemone × hybrida 'Honorine Jobert'. A superior,
old, French form of the white, herbaceous Japanese
anemone, this variety is well worth seeking out. The
large, single flowers are whiter and the leaves very
slightly darker, so 'Honorine Jobert' literally sparkles.
It thrives on neglect and is not without flowers from
July to November. Up to 1.5m/5ft high in full bloom.

Asplenium scolopendrium. The hart's-tongue fern
(45–75cm/18–30in) is one of those plants that, once
established, lends quality to a garden, suggesting that
it has been in existence for at least four hundred years.
Plant the fern near water and let it grow between
paving, in an old brick wall or at the back of a border,
perhaps behind hostas, where it will come into its own,
like hellebores in early spring. If you find the rare
variety 'Crispum', with crimped leaves, buy it without
delay, and plant it in old brick paving. The effect
is like a starfish made out of green Petersham ribbon.
Particularly, do not let 'Crispum' dry out.

Astelia nervosa. This easy-going, perennial beauty
will tolerate sun or shade. The leaves are reminiscent
of a tattered, silken, silver flag, not unlike those of
a phormium, but they have much more quality and,
never reaching much above 60cm/2ft, are better at
lighting up a small space. Astelias are excellent container subjects and if they should be cut down to the
ground by very rough weather will shoot again from
the base.

Cobaea scandens. You can germinate the seeds of these
climbers in polythene-covered pots on a warm window-

sill or on the middle shelf of the airing cupboard. Check them every day and the minute they have germinated, remove the polythene and gradually harden them off. Alternatively, you can buy plants at garden centres in early June and plant them out. The huge, bell flowers come in green, gridelin purple and the more unusual white. Give the plants plenty of water and feed once a week with liquid tomato feed.

Helleborus orientalis. The best way to buy hellebores is to see them in bloom at a nursery in February or at one of the RHS flower shows. Only then will you really know what you are getting, and a truly black one is a treasure that should move house when you do. It looks terrific near a fountain of winter jasmine on a shady wall, or at the back of a border to come into its own when the summer flowers have died down. It sounds obvious, but as with snowdrops, if you can arrange to plant this dusky beauty somewhere that you often pass, you will double the thrill. Hellebores, being woodland plants, love a shady situation, with plenty of moisture-retaining humus added to the soil at planting time.

Hosta sieboldiana var. *elegans.* Wonderful for the shadiest spot, if happy, these magnificent plants with their quilted leaves can grow up to 90cm/3ft high and as much across. Insist on *elegans* as the ordinary *sieboldiana* is not worth having. Topdress in the border with sharpest grit to keep those beastly slugs and snails away, to whom all hostas are champagne and caviar, then you will need to use slug-bait only in an emergency. Moisture lovers, hostas do well near water.

Impatiens walleriana 'Double Carousel'. Double busy lizzies are as pretty as miniature gardenias, and much more interesting than the singles. Snap them up when you see them at garden centres in early summer. No matter how dense the shade, with watering, deadheading and feeding they will flower without stint right up to the first frosts.

Melianthus major. The most beautiful of foliage plants, bringing to the smallest space all the grandeur of a cedar tree framing a Georgian manor house. Grey foliage is so smart, but much of it demands full sun: not *Melianthus*, which is happy in sun or shade (*major* is far superior to *minor*). Give it a couple of shovels of grit or gravel at planting, and cut the previous year's growth to the ground each Easter Day. It will reach 18m/6ft in a season.

Mentha requienii. This mossy, creeping mint enjoys the same rather dank conditions as soleirolia, and will give out a delicious mint fragrance when you walk on it as it sprawls over a path or terrace. It has tiny, stemless, purple flowers in summer.

Ophiopogon planiscapus 'Nigrescens'. This black-leaved, creeping grass enhances just about any plant, flower, tree or shrub you care to mention. Imagine standard 'Iceberg' roses in square beds of it with the outlines defined by low box hedges flanking a mellow brick path leading to a front door. Or you could have it as permanent ground cover between box balls, alternating with *Alchemilla mollis*. Push between it pink, white and cerise cosmos or shocking-pink-and-white-striped petunias for the summer, with tiny, bright yellow 'Tête-à-Tête' narcissi coming up to welcome the spring. Apart from a little watering at first, ophiopogon needs little or no attention, and will grow just about anywhere.

Pelargonium 'Lord Bute'. Raspberry flowers picoteed in black are borne from the end of May until early November. Pelargoniums flower better for being a little root-bound, so if yours are going to ring a large container where there is a free root-run, leave them in their plastic pots, trimming away the tops with secateurs. Water thoroughly two or three times a week when the weather is hot, and feed them once a week with a high-potash tomato feed.

Soleirolia soleirolii. As long as your garden is not too cold, this soleirolia, helxine, mind-your-own-business or baby's breath is wonderful for disguising dodgy paving or cheap-looking brick, or for giving a well-founded look to recently laid, nice paving too – especially in the shade. It loves moisture, and the odd sprinkling of Growmore. It is rampant, though, and if you get it into a lawn, you will never get it out. Vary the regular emerald with the lime and, especially pretty, grey varieties.

Trifolium repens 'Purpurascens'. As long as it does not dry out, this charming little chocolate-, black-and-lime four-leaved clover will quickly make thick mats of ground cover. No more than 10cm/4in high, it is grown for its foliage, but unlike other clovers never becomes a nuisance. It looks particularly good at the base of a 'Mermaid' rose, with something grey or one of the black-flowered violas or aquilegias nearby.

Viola 'Bowles' Black'. This little viola is one of those 15cm/6in treasures no garden should be without. The masses of tiny flowers are true black, and as long as no other viola is in your garden it should always be true to seed, and will come up just where it is needed. Weed out any that are not true black. That great gardener Lady Salisbury grows it in the most chic manner among grey-leaved pelargoniums in great terracotta swag-pots, which decorate the courtyards of the Tudor palace of Hatfield House.

LEFT The warm stone colour of the courtyard walls at Cobble Cottage, Yorkshire, flatters the plants and a mirror gives an illusion of space. BELOW A potted azalea and *Rosa × odorata* 'Mutabilis' bring scent and colour to Graham Leatherbarrow's tiny garden at Stanley Road, Cheshire. OPPOSITE, ABOVE Mirrored red lacquered doors reflect a fantastical temple at 5 St Regis Close, the London garden designed by Earl Hyde and Susan Bennet. OPPOSITE, BELOW A sundial is glimpsed through a beech arch at Magnolia House, Suffolk, the small village garden designed by Mark Rumary (also illustrated on page 222).

Nearly all NGS urban gardens include plantings in shade and here are some to add to those that have soothed Anthony Noel.

Bedfordshire
King's Arms Path Garden
Seal Point

Berkshire
Briar Rose
17 Oaklands Drive

Bristol & South Gloucestershire
13 Goldney Road
4 Haytor Park
18 Queens's Gate
The Urn Cottage
Wellington House
West Tyning

Buckinghamshire
14 The Square
Turn End

Cambridgeshire
Clare College, Fellows' Garden
Crowden House
Emmanuel College Garden & Fellows' Garden
Trinity College, Fellows' Garden

Cheshire & Wirral
Greyfriars
The Mount
2 Stanley Road

Cornwall
Bosvigo
Kingberry
Moyclare

Cumbria
Acorn Bank
Station House
Tomarobandy Gardens

Derbyshire
Ash House
334 Belper Road
100 Wellington Street
26 Wheeldon Avenue

Devon
Collepardo
Little Cumbre
Meadowcroft

Dorset
2 Curlew Road
The Priest's House Museum & Garden
Prospect Cottage
St Annes

Essex
Canonteign
19 Stewards Close

Glamorgan
19 Westfield Road

Gloucestershire North & Central
The Chipping Croft
13 Merestones Drive

Hampshire
53 Ladywood
60 Lealand Road
Romsey Gardens

Hertfordshire
20 Park Avenue South
23 Wroxham Way

Kent
The Beehive
25 Crouch Hill Court
Weald Cottage

Lancashire
480 Aigburth Road
89 Southbank Road

Lincolnshire
21 Chapel Street
2 School Lane
15 Vicarage Gardens

London
31 Belsize Park
9 Birkdale Road
21 Brunswick Street
5 Burbage Road
9 Caroline Close
11 Cavendish Avenue
36 Downs Hill
56 Drakefell Road
286 Earl's Court Road
Edwardes Square
73 Forest Drive East
29 Gilston Road
7 The Grove
252 Haggerston Road
767 Hertford Road
Holly Cottage
72 Holmleigh Road
125 Honor Oak Park
10A Hoveden Road
46 Lincoln Road
1 Lyndhurst Square
56 Middleton Road
9 Montpelier Grove
Myddelton House Gardens
Flat 1F Oval Road
53 Ringmore Rise
31 Roedean Crescent
1 Rosslyn Hill
12 Westmorland Road
4 Wharton Street
11 Woodlands Road

Norfolk
3 Cromer Road
The Exotic Garden

Northamptonshire
Bungalow no 5, Main Street
Terracend
Wisteria Cottage

Northumberland
70a The Gables

Nottinghamshire
Darby House

Oxfordshire
Christ Church Fellows' Garden
Christ Church Masters Garden
Corpus Christi
Exeter College, Rector's Lodging
2 Fortnam Close
Holywell Manor
Merton College Fellows' Garden
New College
Pumpkin Cottage
1 Stoke Place
Trinity College
Wadham College

Powys
Kyber Khoti
Tyruched Garden Nursery

Somerset
Byways
Fernhill
190 Goldcroft
Henley Mill

Staffordshire
Silverwood

Surrey
Culverkeys
10 The Glade
Knightsmead
50 Milton Avenue
Pathside
9 Raymead Close
69 Station Rd

Sussex
Amerique
Tanner's Plat
93 Wayland Avenue

Warwickshire
Ashover
38 Augusta Road
37 Belvedere Road
The Coach House
65 School Road

Worcestershire
21 Bittell Lane
94 Fairfield Road
21 Swinton Lane
The Walled Garden

Yorkshire
Bankfield
The Mews Cottage

137

Urban shade

VAL BOURNE

with expert insights by
HUGH JOHNSON
CAROL KLEIN
NORI POPE

7 Woodland shade

I was mesmerized by flowers from an early age, but the leaf took longer. I grew to love the pattern, the shine and the veining much later on. Strangely, my conversion didn't happen in a garden. It was a pre-Raphaelite experience, built up over countless visits to the Birmingham Art Gallery. The inspiration was a painting called *The Long Engagement* by Arthur Hughes. The young couple gazing longingly at each other didn't hold my attention, but the rich, green ivy in the foreground (placed there to represent everlasting attachment) grew more interesting with each visit. The seeds of my woodland garden were sown there and then. I wanted to re-create the soothing peace of green leaves in dappled settings for myself.

Once I became the owner of a garden, I soon noticed that the gardening year made its debut under the shelter of leafless trees. Snowdrops bravely defied the weather in the weeks following the shortest day, producing the first real flowers of the year. A succession of jaunty flowers and bulbs followed and by early May, when the leaf canopy had unfurled, the early show was almost over. That is the value of a woodland garden – it performs while most of the garden still sleeps, like an eagerly awaited warm-up act for the real performance ahead. In early spring the pure, clear colours of woodland flowers are deepened by low-level sunshine and enhanced by tiny droplets of moisture. Later, in the intensity of high summer, woodland gardens provide peace and cool respite.

Cast your shade

Few of us are lucky enough to be blessed with mature woodland carpeted with bluebells or wood anemones and we have to create our own shade. One mature tree can support over a hundred different woodland plants, providing shelter for a range of fragrant shrubs, evergreens and flowering bulbs, perennials and annuals. The arboretum at the Bluebell Nursery and Woodland Garden in Derbyshire has open days for the NGS throughout the year and offers visitors a chance to watch trees and shrubs, planted by Robert and Suzette Vernon over the last eight years, mature and change.

I use hazels, witch hazels (which should not thrive on my limy soil, according to the gardening books) and fruit trees, and deciduous viburnums for winter scent as well as shade. To maximize their impact, fragrant plants should be close to paths or on the corners of a planting. And because a woodland garden performs early in the year, ideally it should be visible from the warmth of the house. Big blowsy flowers would soon be ravaged by wintry weather, so early flowers tend to be small and compact. Yet these inconspicuous blooms still have to attract pollinators – and scent will lure the gardener too.

Though many woodland plants are spring-flowering, their leaves linger. Mixing the textures give the best all-year effect. Plants adapt to the lower-than-usual light levels found under a tree by making less chlorophyll. The leaves of most pulmonarias are dappled and spotted, those of dryopteris and dicentra finely divided and those of *Symphytum* × *uplandicum* 'Variegatum'. Arums and trilliums produce stunning, but short-lived, glossy leaves early in the year, dying down completely with the bulbs. Then later-flowering plants – geraniums, epimediums and violas – expand to cover these gaps. But, to go back to the start of the gardening year, the performance begins in February.

The glories of snowdrops

Late February sunshine can be surprisingly warm and the days are just long enough for visitors to make their first forays into Yellow Book gardens. Three gardens close to Bourne in Lincolnshire welcome visitors every spring. Manor Farm (Keisby), 21 Chapel Street (Hacconby) and 25 High Street (Rippingale) have large collections of snowdrops and lie within 8km/5 miles of each other. Autumn will find their gardeners meticulously tidying their snowdrop beds, then giving them a gentle feed of blood, fish and bone to help them on their way. The owners wait anxiously, hoping that their snowdrops will peak in the third week of February, when over a thousand people visit the gardens.

Gill Richardson, of Manor Farm, grows over 300 different snowdrops in her ½-acre garden, which she intersperses among oriental hellebores. They vary in height, flowering time, leaf colour, flower shape and the number of petals. There are neat doubles, pixie-hats, wide-open snowdrops and large, globular 'pearl droplets' in her garden, which has heavy, cold soil. She confesses to liking 'the oddities', but many of her rare snowdrops are impossible to buy. Gill, who has been growing snowdrops for over twenty-five years, recommends the following easily available varieties. *Galanthus* 'Atkinsii' is a tall, slender snowdrop, which opens its three outer petals wide. It makes large clumps and flowers early in the year. The Greatorex double 'Dionysus' is a tall, upright snowdrop with a dark green, inverted heart-shaped mark on the outside of the rosette. It is the strongest of many Greatorex doubles, most of which carry names from Shakespeare or classical myth. *Galanthus plicatus*, a later snowdrop with wide, green leaves, also thrives here on Gill's heavy soil.

Woodland shade

PRECEDING PAGES Three hundred varieties of snowdrop are among the early spring sights in Ian and Angela Whinfield's ½-acre garden, Snape Cottage, in Dorset. Here is *Galanthus* 'Magnet', with a deep green V-shaped mark at the tips of its flowers, which is vigorous enough for naturalizing in grass as well as beneath trees. The drawing is of Hackwood Park, Hampshire, from the 1979 Yellow Book.

RIGHT Rhododendrons, azaleas and other lime haters thrive in the woodland garden at Goodnestone Park in Kent (see also page 206) where a band of greensand runs through the chalk.

*Woodland
shade*

My own Cotswold soil is lighter and the handsome, grey-leaved snowdrop *G. elwesii* is superb here – but it needs good drainage. It has very bold, clean-cut, dark green markings on the inners and forms huge bulbs. Placing them on a bed of grit helps in heavy soils and they should always be planted on the sunnier woodland edge. Another stunner, *G.* 'Magnet', may seem fragile as it sways in the wind on wiry stems, but it clumps up quickly and always looks fresh. I am also a fan of 'S. Arnott', a tall, mid-season, honey-scented snowdrop with a very heavy, bulbous flower. Snowdrops were commonly known as white violets until the seventeenth century when fashionable German ladies began to wear large pearl

droplet earrings as their favourite accessory. The fashion spread through Europe, then to Britain. *Schneetropfen* became 'snowdrop' and the word began to be used to describe the plant itself. 'S. Arnott' is the snowdrop most like a large, white pearl; 'Brenda Troyle' is a look-alike.

E. A. Bowles was probably the greatest galanthophile who ever lived. He grew and collected snowdrops for sixty years and many of the fine snowdrops bred in the late nineteenth and early twentieth centuries would have been lost to cultivation but for him. *G.* 'Augustus', which bears his middle name, has outer petals with the bumpy texture of seersucker and can be seen in the 4-acre garden he created at Myddleton House in Enfield, Middlesex. Another great performer with large flowers, 'Ketton', was introduced by Bowles from a gardening friend who lived in the Leicestershire village of the same name. It is a robust grower. Bowles' famous advice 'to stir them up' by dividing clumps every third year kept his stocks healthy

and allowed him to be generous with his bulbs too. Gill Richardson's excellent advice is to move them around if they are not thriving and to split up clumps as soon as you can. Do this and you'll give your snowdrops the maximum chance of survival.

Early shade lovers

As snowdrops fade, other woodland plants come into their own. The spring-flowering *Cyclamen coum*, though not enjoying deep shade, performs well on sunnier edges. The silvered, round leaves are often very prettily marked. These cyclamen will grow in very dry situations among mature tree roots. Wood anemones (*Anemone nemorosa* – a British woodlander) emerge in late March and enjoy leafy, friable soil. The more usually grown *Anemone blanda* is a Mediterranean plant of rocky places and scrub which sulks in shade. *A. nemorosa* 'Vestal', an enduring plant, is a neat, white double with very dark leaves. The mauve-blue form 'Robinsoniana' was named for the Victorian gardener William Robinson after he spotted it growing at Oxford Botanic Garden. The neatest of all is *A. n.* 'Allenii', a lavender blue with very regular outer petals. Wood anemones spread slowly – at a rate of 1.8m/6ft every hundred years – so you have to be patient. The closely related hepaticas enjoy the same conditions and obligingly self-seed in my garden. *Hepatica nobilis* comes in shades of dark blue, white and deep pink. There are also doubles and large-leaved forms, like *H. × media* 'Harvington Beauty'.

Ways with hellebores

Lenten hellebores (*Helleborus orientalis*) are one of my top ten garden performers. They thrive in semi-shade and have large flowers in shades of white, yellow, green, pink, plum, slaty black, apricot and white. The flowers can be streaked with green, spotted and blotched, or elegantly plain. Some have large nectaries, some perfectly round, open flowers; others are pendent, some bell-shaped, others frilled and double. The variations are endless. Their unique flower structure, in which the 'petals' are actually tough sepals, enables them to endure for many

ABOVE *Ranunculus ficaria* 'Brazen Hussy' makes dense ground cover with *Anemone nemorosa* in Beth Chatto's Wood Garden in Essex. Wood anemones open their flowers and set their seed before the canopy of leaves makes the woodland floor a dark, uninviting place for pollinating insects. Unless bright conditions prevail in spring, the celandine's foliage will lose its dark bronze-brown colouring.

weeks, if not months. They are a vital source of nectar and pollen for solitary and bumble bees – an important consideration in a productive garden.

It is worth buying hellebores when they are in flower, so that you can select the colours and forms you like. Once you have a good plant, leave it alone. Hellebores do not respond well to division and it is quite possible to lose the whole plant. If you do have to divide, take very small 'noses' and pot them up in pots of good, friable compost. I don't let my hellebores set seed, because I prefer the plant to put its strength into developing a larger crown, not into producing possibly dubious seedlings. If you want to experiment with growing hellebores from seed, the important factor is to sow the seed as fresh as you can. Several gardening friends of mine almost run from plant to pot. Once the seed is sown, place the round 7.5cm/3in pot in a cool place and wait. The seed should germinate in the

following spring and each seedling will need pricking out into its own individual pot, before planting outside in September. After three or four years your plants will flower for the first time.

The leaves of hellebores can succumb to a fungal disease which is similar to blackspot on roses. Leaves develop patches, then turn dull and dark brown, finally falling off. The disease is spread by tiny spores on the soil and the best way to prevent it is to cut away most of the outer leaves of each hellebore in late October, meticulously tidying the area underneath the plant. This removes any old leaves and helps the air to circulate through the plant, as well as showing off the flowers. Remove any spotted leaves as soon as you see them and your plants will stay healthy. In bad cases of fungal disease, remove all the leaves and destroy them – never put diseased foliage on a compost heap.

ABOVE A classic spring combination of yellow, white and blue in one of Peter Aldington's garden rooms at Turn End, Buckinghamshire, with broom, *Tulipa* 'Spring Green' and drifts of bluebells.

FOLLOWING PAGES *Galanthus nivalis*, Lenten hellebores and *Cyclamen coum* at Manor Farm, Lincolnshire. Gill Richardson grows more than 300 named snowdrops and a large collection of hellebores.

If you go down to the woods today

Most of the plants in our nursery are herbaceous and spend the winter resting, but there is one group which hibernates much earlier – the woodlanders, which are perfectly adapted to life under the trees. As soon as the first watery spring sunshine hits the sodden leaves, plants begin to stir. Here and there among the all-prevailing dun of last year's leaf litter, green shoots push upward. Once they are through it's a race against time. Rushing to take advantage of increasing day length and warmth, leaves unfurl, buds swell and burst into flower.

These first flowers are so precious, psychologically, to us, but much more importantly as the source of life-giving ambrosia to early bees and other insects. Overwintered butterflies are sometimes on the wing as early as February and desperately need a nectar fix.

Suddenly the woodland floor is thick with flowers, a brown backcloth embroidered with a rich tapestry of green, white and yellow, as primroses and wood anemones burst into bloom under the bare trees. Act One, Scene Two: carpets of wild garlic and bluebells. But by mid-summer the play has come to an end. The canopy closes in, tree leaves have opened and expanded, depriving the ground underneath of direct light. Pollinated by their earlier visitors, plants have set seed, accomplished their purpose and bowed out until next year's performance.

Few of us are lucky enough to have a wood, but most of our gardens will support at least one tree. Even a few large shrubs, or the shade cast by buildings, which is an obligatory feature of most urban gardens, can provide the perfect place for woodland plants to thrive. With some decent humus worked into the soil and a mulch of chipped bark to keep their roots damp, woodland plants should feel perfectly at home. Most of them are colonizers, they have to be pragmatic to take advantage of every opportunity to grab a bit more space and survive. To this end many live in the top few centimetres of the soil, their fibrous roots questing horizontally to find food and water between the layers of rotting leaves. Others, like wood anemones and snowdrops, have rhizomes or bulbs to keep them going until the next spring.

When it comes to the plants there are three choices: using indigenous woodland plants, going for shade lovers from other parts of the world or having a mixture of both. Obviously, native birds and insects are going to find native plants the most useful, and aesthetically they are unbeatable. What could surpass the simple beauty of a primrose? Pale perfect petals with an enticing egg-yolk centre, held aloft on fragile stems the colour of pink skin, nestling in a rosette of fresh green leaves. And with the sweetest perfume imaginable, redolent of spring. Primroses can be grown from seed: once you have one plant you can produce hundreds of others in a season. Sow the seed green, on the surface of loam-based compost, grit over the top, water from underneath and stand your tray outside. Bluebells too will seed profusely and naturalize very quickly.

Once you've acquired a few wood anemones, you can encourage them to ramble by breaking up the little rhizomes and replanting them close and a few centimetres deep, with a little extra compost to settle them in. If I had to choose only one wood anemone, I'd have to plump for the wild species, *Anemone nemorosa*. Delicate, arching stems support modest flowers, their heads bent to protect their pollen from fierce showers. When the sun shines they turn their faces upwards, revelling in its warmth, their open white flowers following its progress across the clear spring sky.

If you front your woodland planting with a few of the subjects you associate with the edge of woodland or hedgerow – foxgloves, ferns and betony perhaps – they can take over later, leaving your woodland beauties to die down and sleep for the rest of the year until they are called upon next time to herald the spring.

Omphalodes cappadocica 'Cherry Ingram' and snake's-head fritillaries are tucked under *Narcissus* 'Thalia', which light up the damp woodland area at Carol Klein's Glebe Cottage, Devon. Carol describes the omphaloides as a plant to 'write sonnets about: like super forget-me-nots with little dimpled centres (hence 'navelwort', its vernacular name), its vivid blue flowers unfurl from tight, rounded buds, expanding into sheets of sheer heaven'. Irises, geraniums and shade-loving tellima are waiting in the wings.

147

Extending the season

Many of our garden plants grown in sunny herbaceous borders are found naturally in woodland or on the fringes and thrive in semi-shade. Dicentras, or bleeding hearts, flower into May. Ignore the showy Dutchman's breeches type (*Dicentra spectabilis*) – it is short-lived, rather brash and often damaged by hard frost. Instead choose the demure, white form, *D. formosa alba*, a cool combination with green, ferny leaves and smaller, white lockets. There are grey-leaved dicentras – but they jar against the spring freshness of other green leaves. Add *Viola cornuta* Alba Group and dark-leaved heucherellas on the fringes. In summer the hellebore-leaved *Astrantia maxima* gently creeps through the woodland patch. It produces pale pink flowers edged with a collar of pale, papery bracts.

Longthatch (illustrated on page 160), the 3½-acre Hampshire garden of Peter and Vera Short, has the sparkling River Meon (one of Hampshire's premier chalk streams) running through it. The Shorts have gardened here for forty-five years and Peter planted the poplar, silver birch and willow trees which now make up the canopy of the woodland garden. The garden is fed with natural rills and streams and is permanently damp. In early spring hundreds of different hellebores are in flower – part of the National Collection is held here. Large numbers of pulmonarias are followed by hostas and several species of bog primula, which extend the season well into summer. Peter deals with the slug problem on hostas by 'tackling it early and putting down bait before the new shoots emerge'. He continues to be vigilant for the following four weeks and by then 'the worst is over'.

The moist microclimate and the neutral soil allow Peter Short to succeed with Himalayan poppies (*Meconopsis*), which depend on cool, moist air during early summer. The natural covering of leafmould, from the overhead trees, also helps to make the soil light and airy. A top dressing of manure is applied in November because hellebores and other woodland plants are greedy feeders. The woodland garden at Longthatch is colourful for many months and the borders close to the house also contain some rare specimen trees. The nursery attached to the garden sells many hellebores to admiring visitors and the garden opens throughout the year.

In early summer, *Lilium martagon* var. *album*, peonies and *Campanula lactiflora alba* take over from spring bulbs and light up the dappled shade cast by *Robinia pseudoacacia* 'Frisia' in Patricia and Clive Hardcastle's 3-acre garden, Old Rectory, Southacre in Norfolk. Later in the year, scented *Nicotiana alata* and sedums (*S.* 'Ruby Glow' and *S. telephium* 'Matrona') continue the season of interest.

Damp woodland slopes

Two star attractions just west of the Dorset-Hampshire border lie only metres apart, yet have evolved into two totally different types of garden. Kenneth Potts of Chiffchaffs worked at Bedgebury National Pinetum in Kent, which reputedly has the finest conifer collection in the world. Kenneth told me that when 'I came to look at Chiffchaffs over twenty years ago, I chose the soil before I chose the house'. He realized as soon as he arrived the potential of the damp slope circling the house – the bracken indicated an area of acid soil. Twenty years later the steep-sided woodland garden, set away from the house and overlooking the Vale of Blackmore, is full of acid-loving magnolias, camellias and eucryphias. The whole hill is spring-fed and moisture-loving bamboos, primulas, hydrangeas and showy flowering cornus grow well. This garden also contains some prize trees, including many oaks and some fine conifers – as you'd expect from a former employee of Bedgebury. Kenneth and his wife, Gudran, have put their heart and soul into making this

lovely garden which also has a good nursery attached. The gardens surrounding the house are packed with flowers.

Within yards of Chiffchaffs another husband-and-wife partnership, Ian and Angela Whinfield, work hard at a traditional cottage garden on a south-facing slope. Snape Cottage has a tract of woodland close to the house which brings a host of birds into the garden. The tally in 1999 was fifty-nine species and attracting wildlife into this perfectly maintained garden is a priority. Ian, a practical man, makes and sells bird feeders, lard logs and ladybird houses. Angela, who lectures on plant history, is a plantswoman and together they have created a garden without gimmicks – it relies on plants well grown. A generous 100cm/40in of rain and natural springs flowing into the garden allow them to grow many moisture-loving plants, including a magnificent 2.4m/8ft gunnera. This organic garden, which boasts three hundred varieties of snowdrop, almost a hundred pulmonarias and countless hellebores, named lesser celandines and wood anemones (all meticulously and clearly labelled) is a learning experience and a visual treat. The low stone walls on the boundaries make a moist bed for ferns and astrantias. Angela has a passion for pulmonarias, which are grown both for spring flower and summer leaf. In the shade of the house the variegated *Pulmonaria rubra* 'David Ward' produces red flowers. This plant, which was a sport discovered in Beth Chatto's garden by her propagator David Ward, needs very shady, sheltered conditions. Full sun would scorch the green leaves edged in cream. *P. rubra* is the earliest of all to bloom and the tomato-red flowers mix well with the apple-green flowers of *Helleborus argutifolius* (the Corsican hellebore). Both are large plants and are not suitable for the smaller garden.

Pulmonarias are promiscuous plants and cross-breed readily, hence the huge numbers of named hybrids. Angela leaves her pulmonarias to self-seed and they produce an array of offspring. Their leaves vary in both shape and markings. The flowers range from white, mauve and light blue through to dark blue and there is often that hint of pink and blue about the clusters. This is where the common name 'soldiers and sailors' comes from – when soldiers wore red and sailors blue. Among her named favourites is the narrow-leaved *Pulmonaria longifolia* 'Bertram Anderson', a late-flowering

ABOVE Rhododendron 'The Hon. Jean Marie de Montague' brings dramatic colour to the woodland garden of Gudrun and Kenneth Potts at Chiffchaffs in Dorset. A natural greensand band of acid soil overlying gault clay supports camellias, stewartias and numerous acers above a spring carpet of bluebells. Further down the south-facing slope, primulas, gunnera and astilbes grow in the dappled shade of 20m/67ft alders.

OPPOSITE Among emerging hostas, yellow tulips, Welsh poppies and narcissi light up the perfectly managed shade cast by beech trees in the walled garden at Hadspen in Somerset.

Hugh Johnson

Green thoughts in a green shade

Look aloft in the great woodland gardens, the showpieces of British horticulture, voluptuously hosta-ed and sweet with azaleas, and what do you see? Tall, deep-rooted oaks, light-branched larches, Scots pines with all their foliage far above the ground on salmon-red trunks. If you can choose your shade, that is ideal: a broken canopy far above your head, creating lovely shafts of light. Delve in the leaf-mould and plant what you like.

What is the worst shade? Heavy, dense-branched conifers, creating constant gloom.

Garden woodland shade is usually somewhere between the two: the result of mixed ornamental trees which affect the garden not only with their shade but also with their roots.

Some of the greediest trees, alas, their roots snaking near the surface, even breaking it, are our favourite flowering cherries, grafted on wild cherry roots, and those graceful birches which seem so ideal as lightweight cover. Leyland cypress, of course, is notorious. The soil within a couple of metres of a mature one is permanently dust-dry and infertile. Beech sucks the surface dry too, and eucalyptus tries to turn your garden into Australia.

The friendly trees for gardening under, oak, larch and pine apart, happily include some of the most beautiful. I rate magnolias and maples at the top; slow-growing perhaps, but never over-powering. I used to believe the books that said Japanese maples need acid soil, moist but free-draining … the usual daunting formula. They don't in Essex, even on chalky clay, where *Acer palmatum* in its many forms needs only some shelter from other trees to form the perfect woodland understorey. Magnolias are almost equally willing, late frost being their principal enemy.

Instead of cherries, we have learned to plant flowering crabs – *Malus* in its many species. And *Sorbus*, especially the Chinese mountain ashes, not so much for spring flowers as for early autumn fruit and later turning leaves.

Above all we have learned to be master of all our trees, to fell or tame the bullies, prune the misshapen and slowly raise the crowns of almost every one by gradually removing lower branches.

The rewards are more space for gardening, more even light and very often the pleasure of a smooth or craggy, papery or shiny trunk. Trunks are the architecture of woodland gardening; the pillars of the green shade.

154

Woodland shade

RIGHT A glade among tall trees at Saling Hall in Essex provides perfect conditions for plants of the woodland edge. A pool gives it life, and a simple fountain jet sets off the monu-mentality of a towering swamp cypress (*Taxodium distichum*). Many rarities are included in Hugh Johnson's collection of trees that is on basically alkaline clay (pH 7.5) but has patches of sandy gravel with lower readings.

Dappled shade beneath mature trees

The entire garden at 53 Ladywood, Hampshire, is over-shadowed by mature trees – ancient birch and oak wood-land that was part of a large farming estate. The modern house (built in 1979) has a plot just 12m/40ft square, sub-divided into smaller areas, where Sue Ward has created one of the prettiest, most feminine gardens I know. She has used three simple devices to make the garden appear larger: a meandering path, screens to provide hidden areas and masking the far corners by placing a seat at an angle across one and a summerhouse across the other. Pale pastel colours also help to open up the garden. Strong, strident colours would shorten the vistas, bringing the eye up short.

The heavy clay soil lies wet and cold in winter and then dries out in summer so, although the garden is meticulously tidied in autumn, planting and division have to wait until spring – a necessity on clay soils. If this were not enough, birches are shallow-rooted, greedy trees and it is difficult to plant among the network of surface roots. Sue's garden was entirely lawn until, in 1986, she began removing areas of turf and burying it beneath the soil, raising the flowerbeds by several centimetres. She also added coarse grit to improve drainage and the beds are now (after several years of adding compost) 30cm/1ft higher than the lawn. They are edged in neat stone walls and every year more compost is added, plus two feeds of pelleted chicken manure in March and June. Organic matter helps to retain moisture, but the driest areas under the birches are kept moist by a seep-hose laid beneath the soil, allowing Sue to grow a wider range of plants.

The birches cast dappled shade and as the sun moves through the sky it spotlights areas of the garden, changing the mood at different times of the day. The papery, white trunks add a coolness of their own, enhanced by the foliage which 'goes on for ever'. Flowers 'play second fiddle', says Sue, 'they're little stars that come and go'. Amazingly, there are 1,800 discreetly labelled plants in this small garden. The shrubs and perennials are constantly dead-headed and tidied, so it always looks fresh and young. Hardy geraniums and violas ('Rebecca' is a favourite) flower for months rather than weeks and phloxes produce a second flush of flower.

Decaisnea fargesii – to provide shelter for ground cover beneath the old oaks and birches, giving them a good start with plenty of organic matter worked into the root-infested earth. Nurtured with compost and irrigated during their first year of growth, *Arum italicum* subsp. *italicum* 'Marmoratum' (syn. 'Pictum'), *Vinca minor* 'La Grave' and *Lamium maculatum* 'White Nancy' now make carpets penetrated by snowdrops, aconites and narcissus. Foliage contrasts include big-leaved brunnera and hostas with finely cut ferns and American woodlanders, such as tiarellas, tellimas and heucheras. 'The overhead leaf canopy at the height of summer', says Beth Chatto, 'pre-serves good foliage and the ground remains a symphony of shapes and textures of green.'

The sun casts patterns of light and shade at 53 Ladywood in Hampshire. Sue Ward uses a seep-hose to give plants such as *Lythrum salicaria* 'Blush', *Phlox paniculata* 'Rosa Pastell' and *Astrantia major* 'Ruby Wedding' the moisture they need among shallow-rooted silver birches. In this area Sue also grows *Palmonaria* 'Cotton Cool', *Anemone × hybrida* 'September Charm' and *Tiarella polyphylla* 'Skeleton Key'.

lungwort with a mop-head of dark blue flowers. *P. longifolia* tolerates drier conditions and makes tight mounds rather than spreading plants. Two very compact and pretty pulmonarias with longifolia blood are the pale pink 'Mrs Kittle' (a shy grower) and the stronger and more floriferous powder-blue 'Roy Davidson' – both ideal for small gardens. Another favourite, 'Sissinghurst White', has heart-shaped, green leaves spotted with silvery white, which Angela likens to 'flocked wallpaper'. It too is a gentle spreader.

I prefer to deadhead my pulmonarias, thus preserving named cultivars – but the choice is yours. After flowering, I also cut off all the leaves and water on a high-nitrogen liquid feed to promote fresh growth. The new leaves, which appear within two weeks or so, add another dimension to the woodland garden. The leaves of 'Majesté' and 'Cotton Cool' light up dark areas and remain silvered throughout the year. Others are strongly marked, a mixture of silver and green. The old cultivar *P. saccharata* 'Leopard' has vibrant brick-red flowers and distinct silver splashes. Many pulmonaria leaves change through the year, the individual markings joining together, but the aptly named 'Leopard' keeps its distinct spots. There are also plain-leaved pulmonarias, but these tend to have flowers of a deeper colour. *P. mollis* has dark green leaves all year, topped by plum and garnet-red flowers. 'Blue Ensign' (discovered as a seedling at Wisley) has the deepest blue flowers of all, but emerges late after disappearing for the winter and is not a robust doer here. It is a form of *P. angustifolia*, a species that disappears during the summer, leaving an annoying gap.

Cool plantings for deep shade
When you are visiting Snape Cottage in Dorset, it is worth having a good look at the north-facing border, which is devoid of sunshine until late afternoon. In this shady area, full of rich greens and silvers, there are cool white flowers: the floppy, black-stemmed *Aster divaricatus* (one of Jekyll's favourites) and the tall, autumn-flowering *Anemone* × *hybrida* 'Honorine Jobert'. However, the border relies on a rich mixture of dark green leaf and occasional splashes of white and silver variegation. Important lessons

can be learned. First, variegated foliage falls into two spectra – the cool whites and the warmer golden yellows – and the rule is: don't mix them. Golden leaves will light up a dark corner and mix best with blue flowers, but if cool peacefulness is desired, whites and silvers set among greens are more soothing. The other important lesson is that variegated leaves need lots of green leaf to harmonize with and weave them together. Clipped box, evergreen sarcococca (a powerfully scented, winter-flowering shrub, ideal for fragrancing doorways and paths), glossy green ivies and quince are used here. Silver splashes of leaf come from various pulmonarias, *Lamium maculatum* 'White Nancy', variegated silvery privet, stripy *Molinia caerulea* 'Variegata' and green-and-white hostas. Specks of gold appear only occasionally, courtesy of the self-seeding (but non-invasive) Bowles' golden grass (*Milium effusum* 'Aureum') which produces beaded heads that glisten and shine as they move on the wind. The ultimate lesson, though, is that many plants can thrive in shade.

Dry shade beneath trees
Barren areas of dry shade beneath trees are the gardener's toughest challenge. Ivies and periwinkles are easy to establish. Epimediums are often recommended as dry-shade plants, but to flower well they need moisture and friable soil. The plants I find do best are self-seeders which can establish themselves quickly. Honesty (*Lunaria annua*) is a biennial to my mind, despite its name. It will happily inhabit the driest soil and there are variegated forms available from seed companies. It is also worth sprinkling a little aquilegia seed about too, but this plant prefers moist soil. Comfreys also do well and I treasure the blue *Symphytum caucasicum* and the white *S. orientale*, although both are invasive. *Geranium phaeum*, the mourning widow, will self-seed and thrive in dry areas too, delighting you when flocks of greenfinches arrive to devour the seeds in mid-summer.

The impoverished soil in her Wood Garden in Essex has not stopped Beth Chatto from creating a masterpiece with dry-shade lovers. She planted evergreens, such as mahonias, box and privet, and small deciduous trees and shrubs – dogwoods, sorbus, eucryphias, viburnums and

NORI POPE

On light

Let there be light – and there was!

Not to complain, of course, but sometimes there was too much or too little, too strong, or too watery. What is this bright shade but not direct sun that we are supposed to provide for our planty pets? Hostas and their illumination springs to mind. These are in fact very tough and tolerant plants, but we're not talking survival here but perfection. We want waist-high 'Frances Williams' with an unblemished creamy margin surrounding the undulating glaucous-blue-and-green central area, the tiny beads of wax which give the bloom on the leaf its iridescent quality.

Hostas and many other shade plants enjoy the full impact of a sunny spring day, 10 per cent shade by the end of May and about 30 per cent shade by mid-summer. Ah, the idyllic sylvan glade! As you see in Andrew's photo of the hosta walk at Hadspen Gardens, the thin overhang of the attenuated beech allows plenty of light through to tulips and the emerging hostas.

As the season progresses, though, the dappled light turns to a flat shade, robbing the charm from the leafy underlay. Out come the long-handled pruning hook and the camera with a light meter. I can prune out branches until an even canopy of bright shade has been opened up and, by walking out into the unfiltered sun, check that the perfect balance has been reached.

leaves; the double blue *G. pratense* 'Plenum Caeruleum' also flowers over many weeks in mid-summer; and *G.* 'Dilys' has soft magenta flowers from June into late autumn. To Sue's list I would add 'Salome', a sprawling, late summer performer with dark-veined, smoky-lavender flowers which persist well into October. Bellflowers also do well: *Campanula latifolia* 'Buckland' (milky-white with a dark purple centre), pale blue *C. lactiflora* 'Prichard's Variety' and pale pink 'Loddon Anna' enjoy some shade. Subtle oriental poppies like *Papaver* 'Witchery' (a pale pink which fades to white) and *P. orientale* 'Graue Witwe' (literally grey widow) are followed by many different phloxes. Sue chooses 'Cool of the Evening' (a deep blue) and 'Monica Lynden-Bell' as favourites. Both are hard to find, but Sue discovers the latest offerings by visiting nurseries and scouring seed catalogues.

A change of pace

Veddw House in Gwent, owned by Charles Hawes and Anne Wareham, is full of imaginative touches, including beehive-shaped compost bins. The 4 acres include a woodland garden on the hill, giving glimpses of the sun-drenched area below. The nearby Plas Cwm Coed, a 5-acre garden set in a wooded valley, is the perfect place to grow ferns. (Their open days coincide.) John Humphries and his wife Eliana moved to Plas Cwm Coed eight years ago and when they've both 'lost their patience' with their large herbaceous borders, they go down to the fern garden 'for a change of pace'. The shelter provided by this ancient woodland, which is carpeted by hundreds of wood anemones, bluebells and violets, is full of native ferns. Encouraged by an Australian friend, they have begun to add Japanese and Australasian tree ferns to accompany their summer-flowering astilbes, rodgersias and aruncus. John told me, 'I use a bark mulch to suppress weeds after the wood anemones have retreated underground.' He and Eliana gain a great deal of comfort from this area, especially on hot summer days.

NGS gardeners who extend the gardening year by planting early woodlanders agree. Woodland shade should never be viewed as a problem area — it is the perfect opportunity for inspired planting.

Sue Ward has a unique way of training her shrubs. She cuts off the lower branches to leave a bare stem 60–90cm/2–3ft high, creating a little woodland microclimate. This means that she is able to plant right underneath each shrub – an important consideration in a small garden. She enhances the effect of foliage plants by using clusters of three similar plants, set at different heights. One of her cool combinations consists of a white-and-cream dogwood, *Cornus alba* 'Elegantissima', on the upper level, a pot of variegated ground elder (strictly contained) at mid-level and at ground level the toning *Pulmonaria rubra* 'David Ward'. Another trio has a gold theme: holly (*Ilex* × *altaclerensis* 'Golden King') and *Choisya ternata* 'Sundance' with a golden ivy climbing through.

Over one hundred hardy geraniums thrive here. Sue recommends the following star performers for shady conditions: *Geranium* 'Sue Crûg' flowers from May to August and has large, magenta-pink flowers and green

At Plas Cwm Coed, Gwent, in the damp Welsh hills, native ferns such as *Dryopteris affinis*, *D. filix-mas* and *Asplenium scolopendrium* relish the cool shade beneath a canopy of ancient trees.

Woodland border

This border (3 x 6m/10 x 20ft) is shaded by shrubs and a mature apple tree. High fences screen the eastern and southern edges, adding further shade. As well as snowdrops, wood anemones and *Cyclamen coum* (not shown) mingle among the hellebores and many different pulmonarias. Late-flowering tulips, 'White Triumphator', 'Queen of the Night' and 'China Pink' are planted in groups.

1 *Asplenium scolopendrium*
2 *Viburnum x bodnantense* 'Dawn'
3 *Sarcococca confusa*
4 *Pulmonaria spp.*
5 *Viburnum tinus* 'Eve Price'
6 *Geranium spp.*
7 *Symphytum x uplandicum* 'Variegatum'
8 *Skimmia japonica* 'Fragrans'
9 *Helleborus argutifolius*
10 *Iris foetidissima*
11 *Skimmia x confusa* 'Kew Green'
12 *Galanthus spp.*
13 *Viburnum burkwoodii*

14 *Viola cornuta* Alba Group
15 *Symphytum orientale*
16 *Dicentra formosa alba*
17 *Helleborus orientalis*
18 *Epimedium x versicolor* 'Sulphureum'
19 *Dryopteris filix-mas*
20 *Daphne odora* 'Aureomarginata'
21 *Lamium maculatum* 'White Nancy'
22 *Magnolia x soulangeana*
23 *Astrantia maxima*
24 *Epimedium perralderianum*
25 *Euonymus planipes*
26 *Dryopteris affinis*

27 *Malus domestica* 'Bramley's Seedling'
28 *Hamamelis x intermedia* cultivars
29 *Vinca minor*
30 *Viburnum x carlcephalum*
31 *Hepatica x media* 'Harvington Beauty'
32 *Daphne laureola*
33 *Heuchera* 'Eco Magnififolia'
34 *Helleborus x sternii* Blackthorn Group
35 *Heucherella* 'Quicksilver'
36 *Anenome nemorosa* 'Vestal'

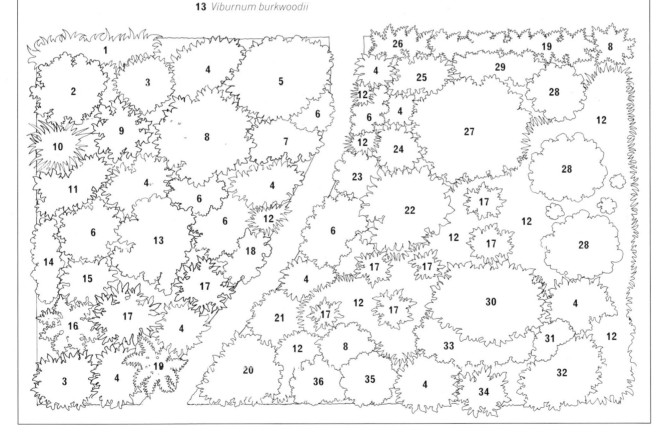

Plants for woodland shade

Trees & shrubs

Daphne. The low-growing spurge laurel (90cm/3ft), *D. laureola,* has shiny, green rosettes of foliage and, from December to April, small, green flowers that are scented to attract pollinators. It can thrive in deep shade. The cool greenness is an ideal foil for all spring-flowering plants. *D. odora* 'Aureomarginata' is the hardiest pink-flowered daphne. It needs a sheltered position which gets some sun. It forms a wide-spreading bush that reaches 2m/6ft when mature. Each green leaf is edged with silver and the very fragrant flowers are clustered at the top. The marginated form is much hardier than the green form and the fruity scent isn't subdued by low temperatures.

Euonymus planipes. Spindle trees, deciduous members of the euonymus genus, are really large shrubs, *E. planipes* reaching 3m/10ft. By mid-September the leaves have turned a rich red. They drop to reveal bright, winged fruits in two-tone red and orange. Outward-curving stems give good winter shape.

Hamamelis × intermedia. Shortly after Christmas this small, branching shrub with fist-like buds begins to show flashes of colour. By the end of January the spidery ribbons unfurl to produce clusters of flowers along each bare branch. Find a sheltered spot, because on still days there is a hint of spicy fragrance in the air. The delicate flowers are indestructible, resisting heavy rain, frosty weather and strong winds. After several weeks they fade and thick, mid-green leaves unfurl. 'Arnold Promise', a yellow bred at Arnold Arboretum, flowers well. 'Jelena' is a warm orange and 'Diane' a rich red. 'Pallida', an old cultivar, has the best scent – like freesias – but is harder to grow. These grafted plants are expensive, so buy them in bloom to make sure of an abundance of good-size flowers in your desired colour. All are slow-growing, eventually reaching 3m/10ft. The crucial factor for these (and all Himalayan plants) is to provide a cool root run in the shade of other, smaller shrubs where, because the flowers form six months before they open, the sun will ripen their branches.

Magnolia. These are understorey trees in their native habitat. Placing them beneath a mature tree in the garden helps to protect the large flower goblets from frost damage, which turns the large, pink-tinged white 'tulips' into wet, brown mush. *M. × soulangeana* cultivars are the least fussy about soil, and have a spreading habit that makes the flowers easier to appreciate than those of more upright species.

Blooming in April on bare wood, they mix well with plum-pink hellebores and lily-flowered tulips. Prune after flowering to restrict the size to 2m/6ft.

Sarcococca confusa. This low-growing (60cm/2ft) member of the box family has shiny, pointed, rich green leaves and tiny, sweetly scented cream flowers which are followed by black berries.

Skimmia × confusa 'Kew Green'. Skimmias need good soil and a sheltered position. The buds are formed and make an attractive feature long before the flowers. 'Kew Green' (90cm/3ft) has free-flowering conical heads of fragrant, creamy white flowers on a mound of glossy foliage. *S. japonica* 'Fragrans' is taller (1.5m/5ft).

Viburnum. The best viburnum for winter flower is *V. × bodnantense* 'Dawn', beginning in November when still in leaf and continuing to display a mixture of pink-and-white flowers throughout the winter, although severe weather will turn the flower heads brown. It is a tall, upright shrub (3m/10ft) with a strong hyacinth scent. *V. × burkwoodii* (2.4m/8ft) is an evergreen with a branching, balanced habit. It has glossy, leathery leaves and heads of white flowers (held in pink buds) in late spring. *V. × carlcephalum* (6m/20ft) produces highly scented flowers in late spring, coinciding with May tulips. *V. tinus* 'Eve Price', the large, evergreen laurustinus (3m/10ft), is good for the outer edges of a woodland border. It looks like a loose-leaved privet bush in summer; by late autumn the pink buds are opening to produce clusters of star-shaped white flowers encased in pink buds.

Perennials

Asplenium scolopendrium. The hart's-tongue fern (15cm/6in) has good green winter leaves and is a useful plant for shady corners.

Astrantia maxima. The hellebore-leaved astrantia (45cm/18in) is a summer-flowering perennial that creeps about the woodland garden. Each pale pink pincushion is surrounded by a neat collar of jagged bracts which stands proud of the cushion. Very subtle and easy.

Dryopteris. In late spring the unfurling fronds, or fiddle-necks, of *D. filix-mas* and *D. affinis* (90cm/3ft) emerge and cover spent snowdrops and other bulbs, remaining handsome for at least six months. Sheltered, shady conditions suit ferns and these two, once esatablished, tolerate dry shade.

Epimedium perralderianum. This handsome winter foliage plant (40cm/16in) is capable of growing right up against a tree trunk but needs friable, fertile soil to flower well. Bright yellow, spidery flowers on wiry stems appear in late spring above the heart-shaped, evergreen leaves. In *E. × versicolor* 'Sulphureum' the flowers are pale yellow and the leaves tinted red. Gardeners are often told to remove the leaves in late winter to expose the flowers, but use your judgment: if the leaves are shabby, remove them; if they look handsome, leave them alone.

Geranium. Many hardy geraniums enjoy semi-shade. *G. macrorrhizum* (40cm/16in) produces a loose covering of low-growing stems which stay in leaf all year long and cover large areas. Once established, it tolerates dry shade. It is often described as aromatic, but the pungent smell of tom cat sends me rushing to wash my hands. In late spring 'Bevan's Variety' has deep pink flowers and 'Ingwersen's Variety' is an apple-blossom white. *G.nodosum* is a summer performer that enjoys shady conditions, produces purple flowers with paler centres over many months and self-seeds moderately. It has glossy, three-lobed leaves on wiry stems (40cm/16in). *G. phaeum,* mourning widow, flowers in that awkward gap between the spring bulbs and the main flush of perennials. Dying down in winter to brown knuckles, it puts out green leaves with zoned markings followed by tall, slender stems (90cm/3ft). The darker colours are almost black and there is a clear white with green leaves. They self-seed rather too freely, producing some wishy-washy crosses which need weeding out. 'Lily Lovell' is a large, lilac-flowered form. 'Samobor' has very zoned leaves, darkly marked, with dark flowers. *G. wallichianum* 'Buxton's Variety' emerges from mid-summer onwards. The attractively mottled leaves make a handsome addition. It revels in shade and is easily grown from seed, flowering in its first year. The intensely blue flowers each contain a pale eye topped by black stamens.

Helleborus. Starting to flower in February and maintaining a presence until May, hellebores underpin the woodland garden. Friable, moist soil is ideal but drier soil, well mulched in late spring, will serve. They are greedy plants and benefit from a dressing of fertilizer in September. *H. × sternii* Blackthorn Group is shorter and more compact (60cm/2ft) with marbled foliage and apple-pink flowers, and not as hardy as oriental hellebores.

Hepatica × media 'Harvington Beauty'. Most hepaticas tend to get lost in the woodland border unless planted at the edges. This is a large hepatica (30cm/1ft) with substantial, green leaves and lots of clear mid-blue flowers.

Heuchera. The heucheras have excellent winter leaves and summer flowers. 'Eco Magnififolia' (30cm/1ft) has large, pale-green-and-silver-leaves flushed with red – very fetching against bare earth. Heucherellas, the result of crosses between heucheras and tiarellas, have daintier leaves and flowers. × *H.* 'Quicksilver' (20cm/8in) has mottled-silver-and-purple leaves which mix well with cyclamen and hepaticas.

Lamium maculatum 'White Nancy'. This silver-leaved dead nettle (20cm/8in) has small leaves with green edges – among the most perfect in the garden during winter – and white flowers.

Lilium martagon. The Turk's cap lily (90cm/3ft) thrives in shade on lightish soils. It has rich dusky purple flowers in July and seedlings if you're lucky.

Symphytum orientale. This green-leaved upright comfrey (60cm/2ft), which seeds down in a controlled way, has pure white flowers without any hint of dinginess. It enjoys damp shady corners. *S. × uplandicum* 'Variegatum' is a taller (90cm/3ft), non-spreading plant; its leaves have bold white margins to light up dark corners, followed by mauve-blue flowers.

Viola cornuta Alba Group. This long-lived viola (20cm/8in) has white, winged flowers and bright green foliage. It enjoys damp edges, where it will scramble through taller plants.

Vinca minor. Small periwinkles (25cm/10in) are valuable allies and well worth growing for their evergreen leaves and early flowers and their ability to grow right up to the foot of a tree. This less invasive species comes in shades of white, red and blue, in single and double forms.

Hellebores and pulmonarias at The Old Rectory, Burghfield, Berkshire.

LEFT *Helleborus orientalis*, with *Carex* and celandine in the riverside garden at Longthatch in Hampshire, where Peter and Vera Short hold part of the National Hellebore Collection. BELOW The woodland garden at Windy Hall, Cumbria, was developed from a wilderness. Diane and David Kinsman cleared the sessile oak, birch and mature Christmas trees and underplanted with camellias, rhododendrons and hydrangeas. The male fern (*Dryopteris filix-mas*) self-seeds in the moisture-laden climate of the Lake District. RIGHT Trees cast semi-shade where foxgloves grow on disturbed soil in one of the informal areas of Mair and David Lloyd's 5-acre garden at Edenbridge House in the Kent Weald. This plantsman's garden also has an arboretum that includes *Ginkgo bilboa* and *Gleditsia triacanthos* 'Sunburst' and *Acer platanoides* 'Crimson King'.

Hundreds of NGS gardens make a virtue out of shade cast by trees and shrubs and here are a few to add to the ones that have excited Val Bourne.

Bedfordshire
King's Arms Path Garden
Manor Farm
Tofte Manor

Berkshire
Blencathra
Braywood House

Bristol & South Gloucestershire
Sherborne Garden
Special Plants, Cold Ashton
West Tyning

Buckinghamshire
Blossoms

Carmarthenshire & Pembrokeshire
Ffynone
Hilton Court Nurseries
Llysnewydd

Ceredigion/Cardiganshire
Coetmou
Farmyard Nursery Woodland Garden
Llwyncelyn
The Mill House
Pant-yr-Holiad

Cheshire & Wirral
Briarfield
Dorfold Hall
The Old Parsonage

Cornwall
Bocconoc
Pencarrow

Cumbria
Browfoot
Stagshaw
Wood Hall

Denbighshire & Colwyn
Donadea Lodge

Derbyshire
Bath House Farm
The Bluebell Nursery and Woodland
Kedleston Hall
The Riddings Farm
Shatton Hall Farm

Devon
Dippers
Wolford Lodge

Dorset
Frankham Farm
The Old Rectory, Litton Cheney
Welcome Thatch

Essex
Fairwinds
Little Myles
Olivers
Wickham Place Farm

Flintshire & Wrexham
Chirk Castle
Pen-y-Bryn
Tir-y-Fron

Glamorgan
Clyne Gardens

161

Woodland shade

STEPHEN ANDERTON

with expert insights by
ALAN TITCHMARSH
ROBIN WILLIAMS

8 The trials of slopes

People say that gardeners are a good crowd, that they are kind, generous folk who would wish no one ill. By and large it is true. But speak to one on a bad day, at the end of the day and the end of the bar, at the moment for a lifetime's regrets, and a gardener will tell you that the green thought in the green shade is nothing more than the little god of jealousy. With life to live over again, the flatlander would have hills, and the hill people would have the level plain. Gardeners, whatever anybody may say to the contrary, are just like everyone else. They are never satisfied.

The grass is always greener.

So are you a hillsman or a flatlander? In my time I have been both, and I tell you this, the gardener with a sloping garden has much more to worry about, a deal more problems to solve, than the gardener on the plain. Solving those problems makes for interesting gardening, of course. But then interesting was never easy.

House and garden

Most provoking of all is a sloping garden's relationship to its house. Either the garden drops down out of view, or it rears up in front of you. Or both. You are offered the garden as a map on the wall, or as a bird's-eye view to look down upon. Private places are hard to achieve because everywhere is visible from the house in the same eyeful. Flatlanders have to build towers or gazebos, at considerable expense, to be able to look down on things. But gardens on a slope automatically come with a view.

At Marsh Lane, the garden outside Harlow made by Sir Frederick Gibberd, there is a gazebo which beautifully shows the flatlander's passion for a prospect. Essex is pretty flat here, and the garden slopes only gently down to a meandering valley bottom. The gazebo is built into the slope and bridges two levels. Its upper storey is on the level of an upper lawn and pool. It looks just like a summerhouse from here. But enter it and you realize you are in the upper storey of a two-storey building. It is made of concrete and is utterly charming. Romeo and Juliet would have been perfectly at home clambering up and down it. It has turned the transition from upper to lower level into a moment of interest in itself.

Slopes are intrinsically and pleasurably unstable too. It is that dynamic of the fall which pushes gardeners towards rock gardens centred on a plunging stream, or to screes of slithering shales. These miniature artificial landscapes solve the problem in the sense that they are appropriate to the terrain if not to the full-size house which sits behind them. But they are difficult to garden. Gardeners of steep screes require strong backs and mountaineers' calves as they scramble about spider-wise across the face of their slopes, tucking in an androsace here and a dianthus there. God always finds the maintenance of these natural features far easier, of course, working from above.

To terrace or not to terrace?

The alternative answer to gardening on steep slopes is that unashamedly man-made construct, the terrace. We have been making terraces for thousands of years, either to stabilize roads or build houses or even to build gardens. Terraces make life infinitely easier. They offer the gardener the chance to stand up and straighten his or her back, and also the chance to focus down on to plants close by, instead of being perpetually distracted by the view. It makes a haven, where you feel safe enough to concentrate on gardening rather than on the wider landscape.

The steeper the slope and the deeper the terrace, the more terraces become a monumental construction. They must be well drained at the base so that the retained soil does not become waterlogged and mobile. Sometimes walls may be battered (sloped backwards) for even greater solidity. Whatever their size, they must have generous foundations. They must be built to last, so that whatever you plant against them can have a lifetime without unnecessary disturbance.

It is not surprising that good terracing is expensive to make, because it has so much to hold up. Look at the terrace at Harewood House near Leeds. The house sits on the brim of a slope, and under it, for its entire length, is a vast terrace big enough to land a light aircraft. It is flat enough to make the formal parterre which lies upon it seem perfectly comfortable, yet in reality the whole terrace sticks way out from the hillside. It has two jobs to do. First, it gives a visual anchorage to the house, so that, when seen in the landscape, it looks more stable perched at the top of a slope. But the terrace also acts, when you are in it, as an almighty viewing platform from which to see the 'Capability' Brown park down below. If ever the Devil feels the need to tempt me in a high place, this is where I'd like it to be done.

Steps and stairs

It is a brave move to make such a monstrous single terrace to deal with a drop in levels. For the bigger the single drop, the mightier must be the construction. Most of us settle for a series of more modest terraces to cope with a slope. Most of us, too, wish to maximize the growing

PRECEDING PAGES A seat on a higher level, like this one at Winkworth Arboretum in Surrey, tells you there is an enticing outward view waiting for you up there beyond the azaleas. In a flat garden it would merely be a reverse view. The drawing of the ruined stone keep on the site of a prehistoric hill fort at Harwarden Castle, Clwyd, appeared on the cover of the 1995 Yellow Book.

opportunities of terracing, and the more warm walls we have to plant against, the happier we are.

The pay-off is that the more terraces you make, the more effort you have to put into building steps which link them. At Port Lympne in Kent is one of the grandest garden staircases you will ever see. In fact it is a tall set of narrow terraces held together by a grand central staircase. Flanking it are pairs of monumental hedges and, at one time, a pair of Roman temples. Gardens do not come more theatrical than this. It is pure Hollywood. Today you can mount this stair and see at the top, in the woods at either side, tigers roaming under the trees (behind fences – this is John Aspinall's zoo). I cannot help thinking they ought to be walked down the staircase on jewelled leads by oiled gladiators, every twenty minutes or so. The visitors would love them to death.

But on rising terraces, connecting stairs do not have to go straight up the middle. You can put them where you like. They could be to one side of the terraces, under an ascending pergola. Or they could be on alternate and opposite sides, so that as you progressed up the slope, you could walk right along one terrace, left across the next, and so on. Or you could play the Italian card in the Powis Castle manner, and go for curving, balustraded steps, centrally placed on one terrace, to the sides on the next, and so forth. Or the whole path could snake informally through the terraces, cutting through walls and borders as it goes. The terraces themselves could be informal, narrow and numerous, as in the Edwardian gardens set high above the river Wye at How Caple Court in Herefordshire, with a path weaving up through them all, sometimes stepped, sometimes not.

Think of a terrace balustrade, and a whole new area of interest opens up. Here is an opportunity for some high-quality modern design, for a balustrade is no more than a perforated wall or railing. You could make one in any number of sizes, materials and styles, from rustic wooden to steel to glass to rope. It is all there to be played with.

ABOVE Deep terraces such as Powis Castle, Welshpool, give the feeling of both stability and strength. They also provide fine views from the balustraded viewing platform – out to the Severn Valley and down to borders containing sophisti-cated herbaceous planting. The high sheltering walls of terraces, the south-east-facing aspect and well-drained soil allow for a collection of rare and tender shrubs and climbers.

Resolving your slopes on paper

We gardeners are a contrary lot. Well, some of us are! When we have a flat garden, we are anxious to make it slope – at least in parts. When it slopes, we have a craving for the flat. The happy gardener is a slope dweller who recognizes that a sloping garden, provided it is not too steep, has greater potential to be interesting than one which is level.

Whether you are redesigning a sloping garden or starting from scratch, a proper survey of the site is essential, particularly if you intend to include steps, terraces and local level areas. A professional land surveyor will take superficial measurements and also record the levels. Both sets of information need to work in combination. Unlike with a flat plot, you need to compare horizontal and vertical measurements at every stage of the design process. Draw sections of existing slopes on graph paper and overlay this with tracing paper on which your proposed section is drawn to the same scale. You need not be an expert draughtsman – just make the drawing as clear as possible. Draw in 'stick' people to give a sense of the human scale.

Many years ago my schoolteacher told me that most geometrical problems could be solved diagrammatically – and how right he was! For example, if you want to put a flat terrace of a certain size on your slope, drawing it on the tracing paper overlay will tell you if it will fit, and show you how many steps you will need to get from one level to another. It will also give an indication of how much of the ground needs to be built up or reduced and the quantity of soil to be moved. With this information, calculating the cost will be easy.

Digging out soil at the high side of the slope and transporting it to the low side to make a flat area – for children's play, as a seating area or to function as a path – known as 'cut and fill', is less expensive than removing or importing soil. Remember that there is always a 'price' to pay when you create a flat surface on a slope because, at some point, the existing slope will be even steeper – at the periphery of the new flat area, for example. No apologies for repeating this: it is always better to resolve your slope problems on paper than on the ground, where it can be both expensive and embarrassing if you get it wrong.

Never gauge a slope by eye. This is far too risky because your eye 'follows' the slope to some extent and it is almost impossible to check that you are looking horizontally, so the degree of the slope is usually underestimated. Remember, too, that slopes can vary up and down and from side to side – another reason for a proper survey.

The main problems of slopes – to do with access, maintenance and the loss of view of the garden as a whole – can also be addressed on paper. The orientation and degree of the slope will have a bearing on the choice of ground cover: whether to use plants, grass, paving, bark or gravel. Unsupported slopes or embankments should not be more than 40 degrees, otherwise erosion is likely to be a problem and a serious one on light, sandy soils. Garden style, too, will be dictated by the slope: it would be difficult, for example, to create a symmetrically formal design on an uneven slope.

The vertical measurements in combination with the horizontal will show that a retaining wall higher than eye level will allow very little, if anything, to be visible beyond it, so it is better and safer to have two or more shallow retaining walls than a single high one. As long as the terracing is not overdone, thereby creating areas that are completely hidden, the view down a sloping garden allows you to see most of what lies before you. On the other hand, a slope which goes up from the house leaves you standing or, worse, sitting without much to see. And one of the worst situations is where a house is built into sloping ground leaving a small area between the embankment and the windows or doors. Cutting back into the slope to create a level space may not be feasible or would be too costly. Such a potentially claustrophobic situation is one where you need to make a virtue out of necessity by designing the area to look interesting throughout the year.

Many slope dwellers have told me that unless the part of the garden furthest away from the house is even more interesting and useful than the areas in immediate view, there is little incentive to visit. But gardens which combine slopes and flat areas, linked with steps or ramps, provide a wonderful opportunity to explore with both the intellect and the feet. And your plan and section drawings will tell you in advance what is possible and what is not. As the saying goes, 'There are no such things as problems – only opportunities.'

In a flat garden, you can add interest by digging down for privacy as well as building up for views. The shaded sunken area in Malcolm Hillier's garden at 101 Cheyne Walk, Chelsea, is overhung by tree ferns and has a separate character of its own. Go up the steps and you reach lush planting, redolent of the tropics, where less dense shade extends the range of plants you can grow.

Planting on slopes

However you handle falling ground, a slope or terracing are the basic alternatives, and both systems share many common problems of cultivation.

For instance, the aspect of the slope will make an enormous difference to how you plant it. If your house looks on to a rising south-facing slope, you will see the best-clothed or the most floriferous side of all the plants, which is good. Not so if you are looking at a north-facing slope, or, for that matter, if you are looking down south-facing terraces at the backs of south-facing plants. Then you will always feel that the best views are from outside the garden looking inwards – that heavenly angle again. Stand north of a cistus in full flower, or even a mound of yellow heather, and you will see what I mean.

Hot slopes

South-facing slopes or terraces take all the sun going and can be very hot and dry, especially at the foot of retaining walls. So consider whether you want to garden in a way which may require irrigation and if so, install it, preferably at the start when you construct the terraces. Or choose to garden with drought-resistant plants, perhaps with a focus on grey foliage, and settle for a less sumptuous style of planting.

Some gardeners discover that terraced slopes in their particular climate need shade to make them pleasant. They find themselves planting the terraces as a series of rising pergolas, or, if a simpler effect is required, as a series of walks under stilted hedges or between lines of espaliered trees.

You may think that, having made terraces, it would be crazy to hide the view from them with espaliered trees. But remember that you do not have to have every view for twelve months of the year. Variety is the spice of a garden's life. Why not see the view in summer filtered by a light screen of beautifully trained espaliers – fruit trees, perhaps – or beyond the regular, clean trunks of a stilted hedge? After all, slopes with commanding views often are very exposed places which require shelter for plants to thrive, as well as some shade. I know a seaside garden in the Canaries where all that separated the path from a drop out to sea was a chain-link fence. But the fence was interleaved with old palm fronds, set vertically like long, narrow feathers, and the effect, looking through to slits of blue sky or to ships in the harbour below, was delightful.

Many a sloping garden enjoys a good distant view, perhaps to hills or the sea, but has a muddled unpromising middle ground to the view. This is when planting to create your own horizon can quietly wipe out all that foreground muddle, and lift up the prospect to concentrate on the better part of the view. Those lines of espaliered or cordon apples would do it, or a balustrade of spiky phormiums. Such opportunities in gardens – to make a whole view and a whole horizon – are rare indeed, and should be worked for all they are worth. You are going to see that horizon 365 days a year. It is what you will see during breakfast on the terrace or smoking a sunset cigar. So the style of plants or balustrade is everything. Make it your own stab at perfection.

Terraces also provide an opportunity to create a tightly controlled view down from one terrace to the next. Looking down on to that picture is as controlled an eyeful as you are ever likely to encounter, which is why for centuries terraces have been the place where gardeners have made geometric parterres. But you can also put water on those terraces, and pull down a moment of serene blue sky into the garden, by its reflection. Parcevall Hall, in my native Yorkshire dales, has just such a pool. It provides a still, calm centre to a busy set of terraces.

I once found myself in a tearing hurry and having to plant bulbs at dawn outside Mount Grace Priory in Yorkshire. It has a little Japanese pool surrounded by Japanese maples below the terraces where I was working, and suddenly, there in the middle of the pool, was the great white moon, captured by the light and glimmering on the floor of this small area of water. Imagine pulling back a bathroom curtain in the middle of the night and seeing that! These are the kinds of effects gardeners should plan for, as well as flowers.

Terrace housekeeping

Think hard about grassed terraces. The idea of grass is pleasant, but it involves lugging mowing machinery up and down, and afterwards clippings. Otherwise you need

ABOVE Deep beds on a slope offer the opportunity to make receding seas of planting in which the plants can all be visible from below. From the conservatory at Ash Tree House, Yorkshire, however, the grass path is hidden from view in summer, and the mixed naturalistic planting appears to flow across it and onwards up the slope. *Cistus × purpureus*, hardy geraniums and white foxgloves enjoy the open site.

OVERLEAF When a view of ancient hills comes right into the garden, as it does at Parcevall Hall in Yorkshire, then it is good to match that view with similar simplicity – with strong but unsophisticated walls, paths and hedges, and one gentle old cherry tree. What more do you need – apart from the three years it took thirty men to haul all the rock and stone from the moors to construct the terraces.

169

The trials of slopes

ALAN TITCHMARSH

Planting inclinations

My favourite seat in my favourite county is on the top of a cliff in Yorkshire. The grassy slopes on either side of the steep gully leading to this resting place are studded with wild Farndale daffodils in spring, then sheets of blue aquilegia and yellow Welsh poppies in June. I come up here to the Cliff Garden at Parcevall Hall for the breathtaking view across Troller's Ghyll, home to a legendary hound which reputedly howls at night. But, on the way up, I think of all the gardeners who contend with slopes – great for visitors who want a bit of exercise, but planting and maintaining a slope isn't easy, and can be tough on the calf and thigh muscles.

Grassy banks, studded with trees and shrubs, are romantic, though mowing in between can be tricky. Strimmers are easy to use, but the gardener and the trees must be protected – goggles for you and plastic guards at the base of trees. Ground-cover planting is often a better option.

A problem on slopes – especially steep ones – is erosion. Close planting helps: the closer the plants, the more rapidly they will spread and merge to inhibit weed growth. But steep slopes are usually dry, especially if they are in

full sun on light or stony soil. So, to consolidate loose surfaces, choose plants that enjoy good drainage and which sucker or take root as they spread – ground cover like ivies and periwinkles and spreading shrubs such as *Ceanothus thyrsiflorus* var. *repens* and *Cotoneaster microphyllus*. Give them a good start with plenty of organic matter in the planting hole and mound up the soil in a curve around the plant to catch water and prevent it running off down the slope. Alternatively sink a large flowerpot into the ground on the higher side of a plant and direct the hosepipe or irrigation into the pot so that the water goes into the soil instead of running off.

Oh yes, slopes can be tricky, but they are worth the effort, especially when they lead to a seat and a little bit of heaven.

a mini compost-heap per terrace, and somewhere to hide a machine. The same mechanical hassle comes from plants on terraces which require major annual pruning. All the prunings will have to be got away somehow, and you need adequate access for the job.

Yet far be it from me to put you off from such gardening on terraces and slopes. Only remember that it involves the kind of heavy work which, though it may be worthwhile, will reduce the time and energy you have to spend elsewhere in the garden. In the end – of course – any hard work in a garden is worthwhile, if it gives you the effect you want. The crowning glory of gardening is that it is all so wonderfully unnecessary. So the only good way of doing it at all is to put your heart and soul into it, and to make it exactly what you want. People who merely want clean, open spaces beside their houses are not gardeners in any sense of the word. Cleanliness, on its own, must surely be next to deadliness.

Sloping lawns

We have talked a great deal so far about terraces, and rightly so. They are the most business-like way to make a steep slope manageable. But less severe slopes offer more opportunity to relish the flow of the land as it is, and to make a more naturalistic virtue of its gradually changing contours. Gardeners lucky enough to have broken, falling ground, perhaps focused on a stream or boulders, already have a logic to the space, and will make a means of getting sideways across the space relate to the existing features. A zigzag via a boulder perhaps, or a streamside path with an occasional bridge crossing from one side to the other.

It is much harder to make sense of

an odd patch of sloping grass with no particular logic of its own. There are ways, however, of giving a *raison d'être* to such spaces. At Stowell Park in Gloucestershire head gardener Neil Hewertson is proud of his grass. There are fine terraces filled with the kind of roses-and-perennials gardening which is so deliciously, achingly Cotswolds. There is grass on the upper and lower terraces. And to one side beyond high stone walls, bridging the slope between the terraces, is a little triangle of sloping lawn

Grass is the perfect material with which to make a path that slopes from side to side and yet still looks satisfactory. A hard path at The Garden House in Devon would have needed major landscaping to level up side-to-side, but here the grass flows happily with the land – a former paddock transformed by Keith and Ros Wiley. The 8 acres at The Garden House are inspired by the 'new naturalism' style (see pages 231 and 257).

The trials of slopes

leading to a dovecote – also achingly Cotswolds. This triangle could be truly boring – a patch of no-man's-land leading to non-ornamental areas of the garden. But not so. It is carefully mown in stripes, which swing around the falling bowl of grass, following the contours, and at the same time providing a perfect invitation to walk around the slope to the dovecote, and, who knows, perhaps collect a few achingly Cotswold eggs. This is clever, painstaking gardening, simple but effective, and worth all the effort. It is also a great contrast with all that macho terracing, and contrast in gardens is always a good thing. (An even greater contrast is the walled kitchen garden at Stowell Park. This garden, and that at West Dean near Chichester, have probably the best peach houses in the country. Never did you see so much loving care made fruity flesh.)

The bottom of the hill

One of the problems of slopes is what to do at the bottom. How do you handle the change to level ground? How do you satisfactorily slow up all that downward momentum? Motorways have escape lanes of loose gravel, but you can hardly have those in a garden. The happiest way to do it is to arrange for there to be some level ground of your own at the foot of the slope. Instead of making the whole slope into terraces, or instead of letting the slope roll right down to the boundary, create an area at the bottom which is level. Even if you have a fine drystone wall as a boundary and unspoilt fields beyond, make yourself at least some flat space inside it, even if it is only a path. This is your escape lane. This is your centre of gravity.

There are other reasons too for wanting some flat space of your own at the bottom of the slope. If, for instance, a garden slopes steeply down to a blockade of trees and the land runs away underneath them, there is very little temptation to go down there and the space is wasted. Wouldn't it be better – if possible – to cut a slot through the trees, either to a view or to the level ground? If you can see under the trees, but not pass beyond them, there is an even greater feeling of denial, especially if the focus of that slope, the place you are being pushed towards, is out of reach and beyond the garden.

My garden was just like that. It sloped very gently eastwards to tall trees at the fence, so that by evening the only patch of sun was in the field beyond, and my garden was in the shadow of my house. By building a summer-house-cum-sculpture-wall in front of the trees, raised up just a few centimetres from the sloping lawn, I have turned round the run-away prospect and made it somewhere you want to go, somewhere to reflect the evening sun. Such slope as there is, perhaps a fall of 90cm/3ft, is exaggerated by a moraine of topiary balls which have come to rest at the bottom and sides of the slope.

Building at the foot of a slope can be one of the best ways to stop a sloping garden fizzling out. What would you do, for instance, if you had a gully rock garden, centred on a stream, running down to a fence, with a field of houses beyond? The change from detailed rock gardening to houses would look ludicrously unnatural and abrupt. So would the sudden change from rock gully to agriculture, however bucolic your image of the countryside. So what to do?

At Kiftsgate Court in the Cotswolds, a steep woodland garden lures everyone to the bottom with glimpses of blue swimming pool. Hascombe Court in Surrey uses a different trick. In 1906 the designer Percy Cane, a pupil of Edwin Lutyens, made a Japanese rock garden here, at the top of a deep gully, and erected a curving Japanese teahouse loggia right across the bottom of the garden, to hold back the momentum of the gully and the transition to countryside below. Windows were put into the loggia, so that, once down there, you could sit and look down to the valley bottom through a framed view. The loggia's size and volume gave it enough mass to arrest the momentum of the gully, and its gentle curve, and fall from one side to the other, stopped it looking as if jammed across the gully. Chris Evans lives at Hascombe now.

The top of the hill

In a similar way, at Penpergwm Lodge near Abergavenny, Catriona Boyle has erected a wall to make a focus at the top of a slope. Lacking a walled vegetable garden, she has made the next best thing and planted a rectangle of hedges on a south-facing slope. The north side only, at the top of the slope, has been made with a brick wall. The paths within the garden are cruciform, dividing the whole area into quadrants, and because the main north-south axis focuses on the wall at the top, you feel to all intents and purposes as if you are in a garden surrounded by brick walls.

The wall is a great place for growing tender ornamentals, and Catriona takes full advantage of it. But more than this, the wall establishes a firm place from which all the garden flows outwards. And when you look up the garden towards it, your eye focuses not on the vague line where ornamental trees meet sky, but within the space itself, at the foot of the wall, and at a place for sitting. A horizon of varied trees at the top of a slope is interesting, yes, and perhaps looks fine against a blue sky or with the sunset behind. But the top of a slope is not a great focus for a garden. It needs something on or preferably just under the horizon to focus and anchor the prospect.

Aqueous solutions

Perhaps the greatest trick waiting to be played with slopes is the one using water. Think of Chatsworth and Buscot Park, and of the exotic oriental water garden at Sezincote. A slope is the classic place for a waterfall, and that is why decade after decade rock and water gardens have continued to appear at Chelsea Show, eliciting cries of delight from the visitors and cries of horror from more innovative designers. In the right place, where waterfalls are part of the vernacular, naturalistic rock and water gardens look fine even today of course. As stick-on style statements, however, in urban or arid areas they can look pretty silly and be ecologically profligate. But in the right place, if you can design one to look at home in the ways I have described above, with some direction – somewhere happily to go from and to – such gardens will look good.

Naturally falling land makes the temptation to have moving water irresistible, but there are so many ways of doing it formally, rather than with a naturalistic rock garden. You might terrace the slope and make fountains tall enough so that you can look through their spray on the terrace above. You might choose sheets of water slowly tipping in a line over a clean terrace lip of stone or steel or glass, like air before the wing of an aeroplane. You might choose to put a line of galvanized buckets down a staircase, each fitted with a spout to pipe it into the next. You might plumb a pouting lion mask into an under-terrace grotto or dribbling into a cistern at the foot of the terrace wall. Down a more shallow slope you might run rills on either side of a set of steps, with a patterned or textured lining to make the water ripple and foam. You might create rills, or even wider water tanks, to flow sideways along the length of a terrace from each end, falling beside central steps into more rills on the next terrace, and running outwards again to the sides. Think of water as play. Make of it what you will. Work it hard, for its sounds and movement and its ability to hold light, both natural and electrical.

The beauty of water in a sloping garden is that it can act as a logo for the general dynamic of the garden – the stillness of terrace or pool, the descent of wall or waterfall. It is a parallel medium which you can manage to create the same effects. It is a combination those gardeners in the flatlands would give their right arms for, would give their wide-open skies for – to be able to play with the opportunities afforded by a sloping garden. So make the most of it.

ABOVE Slopes can by their very inaccessibility offer temptation. At High Cleabarrow, Cumbria, how do you find your way down to the luxuriant borders and that delicious green space below, which you keep glimpsing through the trees? Planting such steeply sloping terrain is a challenge. Richard and Kath Brown anchor logs laid horizontally with stout wooden pegs to retain shallow terraced beds on the banks.

RIGHT A falling naturalistic watercourse offers the chance to make many kinds of different movement – water falling smoothly over a broad lip, trickling between stones or pausing to widen into a calmer pool. In their hillside garden, Dolwen, Flintshire and Wrexham, Bob Yarwood and Jeny Marriott have ferns, foxgloves, astrantia and *Rodgersia pinnata* 'Superba' beside the tinkling stream.

As well as the slopes Stephen Anderton has scaled, here are a few more of the hundreds of NGS gardens that are not on the level.

Bedfordshire
88 Castlehill Rd

Berkshire
Little Harwood

Bristol & South Gloucestershire
15 Goldney Road
Highview
44 & 46 Old Sneed Avenue
Portland Lodge
Sherborne Garden

Buckinghamshire
Baker's Close
Barry's Close, Long Crendon
Concordia
North Down
The Old Crown

Cambridgeshire
15 Back Lane

Carmarthenshire & Pembrokeshire
Ffynone

Ceredigion/Cardiganshire
Bronwydd
Llwyncelyn
Pant-yr-Holiad
Plas Llidiardau

Cheshire & Wirral
Bank House
Laneside Cottage
Rode Hall
St Davids House
Sandymere

Cornwall
Cotehele
East Down Barn
Readymoney Cove

Cumbria
Copt Howe
High Cross Lodge
High Dixon Ground
Lindeth Fell Country House Hotel

Denbighshire & Colwyn
Golygfa'r Llywelyn
Llys-y-Wiwa

Derbyshire
Cashel
The Gardens at Dobholme Fishery
Hillside
The Riddings Farm

Devon
Bickham House
Hamblyn's Coombe
The Moorings
Pikes Cottage

ABOVE Narcissi on the sloping grass beside the leat at Docton Mill, Devon, where a tumbling stream follows the boundary of the 8-acre hillside site. RIGHT Expensive major earthworks have made Buscot Park, Oxfordshire, a fine example of a serenely sloping garden, the water offering a gentle and continuous sense of purpose to the vista. FAR RIGHT A light pergola over the steps in Joan Taylor's south-facing garden at 30 Prospect Road, Birmingham, adds just enough sense of a tunnel to separate upper and lower terraces most effectively.

177

*The trials
of slopes*

TRUDI HARRISON

with expert insights by
SUE PHILLIPS
ANNE SWITHINBANK

9 By the sea

The coastal gardener epitomizes the nation's resourceful spirit, battling on when all around are crumbling at the knees. Not only does this valiant trooper have to tackle problem soils in awkward spots like his inland counterpart, but he or she must also contend with year-round pests and diseases and scorching, spiralling salty winds that tunnel through defences on a mission to destroy, uproot and flatten everything in their path. Yet, despite all this, alone and stumbling in the dark, our seaside gardener persists. Those who can stand being frustrated and deflated by countless losses in beds and borders will come through with a feeling of triumph. There is nothing to touch the feeling of achievement when you create an oasis in a barren landscape.

As well as a nation of gardeners, we are after all an island nation, surrounded by miles and miles of coastline. So pack your cossie, towel and shades (and a waterproof, just in case) and go visit a seaside garden near you. It will offer a treasure trove of information and inspiration, not just for the fellow seaside gardener but for all gardening enthusiasts. Even in winter you can gaze in wonder at front gardens where plants grow happily outside in the balmy climate influenced by the sea's warmth – plants that would require a greenhouse elsewhere. And, if possible, talk to the owners and hear about their unique discoveries. All of them will tell you theirs isn't the easiest of gardens, but you must keep on trying as the dividends are bountiful when you do succeed.

Salt winds

The amount of salt in the wind varies from coast to coast and place to place. Gardens at or below sea level are more exposed to salt than those on a cliff top, for example, salt being heavier than air. Sometimes the wind brings salt several miles inland. Whatever the reason, the difference in salt levels is vast, so visit other people's gardens in your area and make a note of which plants are doing well. Frequently lavender is recommended for a coastal situation but in my neighbourhood in Sussex it fails: out of ten

plants in my garden, six died the year I planted them and two more failed the following year after the winter storms. I kept trying to establish a lavender hedge till I met a lavender specialist who explained that, coming from hot, dry Mediterranean regions, lavender couldn't tolerate extreme exposure and the only one that might survive and become established was *Lavandula angustifolia*. It was too risky to recommend other species.

Shelter

The most important task when setting out to create a seaside garden is erecting some form of protection from salt winds, either with trees and shrubs or man-made materials. Some gardens nestle behind massed plantings of oak, ash, sycamore, lime, willow, hawthorn and alder, all of which are generally salt-tolerant and effective for screening. The folk on the hill at Bronclydwr, Gwynedd, have used native trees to the full to shelter their seaside haven, with its fine views of Cardigan Bay. A stroll through the Bishtons' woodland offers a good opportunity to see trees that most seaside gardeners can plant with confidence to shield their plots.

Other gardeners are restricted to planting only one or two specimens that are able to cope with the volume of salt and sand hurled at the garden at a moment's notice. At the Long Cross Victorian Gardens, Trelights, Port Isaac in north Cornwall, 50kg/1cwt of salt is deposited per acre each year. Here shelter is provided by maze-like plantings of Monterey pine (*Pinus radiata*), one of the few trees able to withstand England's windiest area. Behind these windbreaks, parts of the garden are in total calm as the trees sift and slow the wind's path. Created more than a century ago, Long Cross is an example of the pioneering work of the Victorians who brought new and exciting alternatives to the more traditional ideas of the day. After decades of neglect, the garden has

PRECEDING PAGES At Charney Well in Cumbria, Christopher Holliday and Richard Roberts know only too well how quickly this idyllic scene can change to chaos when storms tumble in from the Irish Sea. They hold the National Collection of phormiums (see pages 273–7) and enjoy the way these strappy evergreens dip and toss in the wind. The drawing of Trebah, Cornwall, is from the 1991 Yellow Book.

ABOVE & RIGHT *Geranium palmatum* and *Echium pininana* at Tapeley Park, Devon, flourish by the sea when sheltered from prevailing winds. As sea mists creep over Hector Christie's Italianate garden, recently restored and replanted under the guidance of Carol Klein and Mary Keen, *Verbena bonariensis* and evening primrose appear luminescent in the soft light that occurs only by the sea.

undergone massive restoration, which has included replanting gaps in the windbreaks. For, unfortunately, the Monterey pine has a life span of only a hundred years, and where the oldest trees have died you can observe the wind's work as it tries to carve its way to the main garden.

Walled gardens have their own special problems because, rather than slowing the force of the wind, they deflect it, leaving it to land on the other side with such force that plants are literally tunnelled out by the roots. Although many enclosed gardens have walls high enough to deflect the wind outside their boundaries, sometimes even they become unstuck. Protected from south-westerlies by a wall of local granite, the gardens at Tregenna Castle Hotel in St Ives, west Cornwall, are exposed to north-north-easterly winds that often reach storm force 10. These have been known to uproot plants just as they were flowering, mainly because the rebound off the wall increases the wind's speed so much that nothing can stand in its wake. Christopher Griffin, head gardener since 1996, has encountered another problem: the garden inclines to the north-west and leaves a slight

frost pocket in one corner. He plans to overcome this by creating a hole in the wall to allow the cold air to escape. Highly experienced in the practice of coastal gardening, Christopher has a wealth of hints and tips for the novice gardener, such little gems as pinching out the tips of plants to encourage a more compact, bushier growth.

Screens and hedges

Of course, this sheltering behind large trees or massive walls is all well and good if you have acres to plant. But with more and more gardeners vying for a patch of seaside heaven, large trees and high walls are an impossibility. We need to find alternative ways to screen our gardens, remembering that solid barriers lead to turbulence on the lee side. The ideal screen, whether made of latticework, bricks or stout timbers, should be built to a ratio of 60 per cent solid to 40 per cent aperture. A 1.2m/4ft screen made to this specification provides some shelter from wind for an area up to twenty times the height of the barrier but 10m/33ft from the screen, wind speed will increase and

Visitors who take the circular walk at Trelissick find themselves in a sheltered, stream-fed dell among plants such as Australian tree fern (*Dicksonia antarctica*) that would not survive on sites exposed to

heavy salt winds. Like many Cornish gardens on acid loam and benefiting from the mild and moist climate influenced by the Gulf Stream, Trelissick has tender shrubs, and groves of camellias – cultivars of

C. × williamsii and *C. japonica*. There is also a succession of magnolias, hydrangeas, rhododendrons and azaleas to enjoy while taking in the chocolate-box views of Falmouth harbour.

subsidiary screens will be needed. My own garden is sheltered by Rokolene wind netting, which I have decorated with swags of rope and chains to create a seaside effect. Netting is also indispensable for establishing hedges and other plants while they adapt to the exposure.

It is best to buy or grow young saplings, rather than mature trees, in a coastal garden. The roots of a mature specimen will take longer to get a grip in the ground, whereas a sapling will establish quickly and outgrow a larger tree in a matter of years. It is a good idea to give newly planted trees and shrubs some protection until they are established, but traditional ways of staking trees can prove to be a frustrating and futile exercise, the continuous motion of the wind rendering the stake useless over time. I have found that a short (30cm/1ft), stout stake, secured with tree ties that adjust as the tree's girth increases, is the most effective method. Old tights rot away in a matter of months and are no substitute for proper ties. You can create a protective cage or teepee around a plant by driving stakes into the ground and attaching hessian or wind netting, using a staple gun.

Be sure to keep hessian well away from the plant, as it is absorbent and could cause mould. For winter protection, plants such as cordylines, with strappy leaves, should be tied upwards, using a length of rope like a lasso.

Shrubs and hedging plants that work well in coastal conditions are on the whole silver-leaved, hairy-leaved, shiny-leaved or sticky to the touch, each working in its own special way to prevent the salt from reaching its core and killing it. Often when these plants are subjected to extreme conditions they become wind-shaped and stunted in growth as the tender, young, spring shoots are exposed and burnt back, by either cold northerlies or blustery south-westerlies. As unattractive as this may seem, they do a vital job providing shelter, the point that must be remembered at all times when trying to establish a garden in extreme conditions.

Trebah in Falmouth, Cornwall, is another nineteenth-century wonder, reflecting the plant introductions around the 1830s. Among the fine collection of rhododendrons, tree ferns (some of them a hundred years old), camellias, bamboos, hydrangeas and unusual conifers, there is a hill

ABOVE A collection of hydrangeas at Trebah, Cornwall, covers 2½ acres of a south-facing ravine over- looking the Helford estuary. Although not exposed to fierce south wester-lies, the gardens include many other plants that tolerate coastal conditions, as well as rare trees and shrubs. The experts claim hydrangeas thrive only on sandy acid soil but they do well on limed clay at Peerley Road, Sussex.

OVERLEAF Like a tribe of warriors' spears, these South African aloes rise through the cliff face at Headland, Cornwall, naturalizing happily with other succulents in the free-draining conditions.

SUE PHILLIPS

Veg. growing by the sea

Salt winds, driven sand and flung spume do not make for easy vegetable gardening, but by the coast at least there is bright light all the year round and a climate whose summer and winter extremes of temperature are evened out by the proximity of the sea – that's if you live within ½ mile of it.

Veg. gardening isn't so hard if you stick to fast-growing summer stuff like lettuce, spinach, radish and spring onions. It is worth making a humus-rich bed of pure compost, if your soil consists mainly of coastal ballast, and short crops can easily be sheltered by temporary hurdles. Then, when the holidaymakers have gone home and the windy season starts, you can just clear everything away so there's nothing to be blown about. There is

even the odd veg., like asparagus and beetroot, that actually enjoys a spot of salt in its diet. And seakale will put up with grotty soil and a stiff sand-blasting by the wind – since it lives wild on pebbly seashores, your garden will strike it as positively luxurious.

But the real answer lies in buying a plastic tunnel. It is true that tunnels are not exactly beautiful, but their aero-dynamic shape means they withstand gale-force winds far better than fragile greenhouses, and you can always park one at the windward end of the garden where it will shelter something else.

The mild coastal climate and the uniquely buoyant atmosphere under plastic mean that you can grow veg. crops all the year round under cover, and it also makes for much more pleasant working conditions when the going is rough outside. In summer a poly-

tunnel is perfect for humidity-loving cucumbers and melons; it is also ace for peppers and aubergines, indoor and outdoor tomatoes, and early courgettes. At the end of summer you can plant overwintering spring onions, spring cabbage and oriental leaves, plus early cauliflower and 'Carouby de Maus-sanne' mangetout peas for an early bite. Then in early spring put in first early potatoes, your first salads and some calabrese plants, and between them you'll have something to pick at for most of the year.

Choosing a polytunnel for a coastal garden is simple: go for the one with the thickest steel hoops, as it will be the strongest, and pay the extra for the thickest-grade, heavy-duty **UVI** plastic – mine lasted seven years before the cover needed replacing. I wouldn't be without it now.

---

affectionately nicknamed 'the deathbed' where, although it is sheltered from the prevailing westerlies, exposure to the colder easterlies has proved a problem. Rather than throwing their arms up in despair, the owners have seized the opportunity to experiment and now proudly boast a collection of quick-growing shrubs, mostly from New Zealand, such as *Olearia traversii*, so rapid in growth that it requires regular pruning to prevent it from falling over. Senecios, elaeagnus, *Arbutus unedo* and other New Zealand wonders adorn this hill, along with the perennial succulent *Carpobrotus edulis*, otherwise known as the Hottentot fig, scrambling through the rocky walls. *Muehlenbeckia complexa*, a twining climber that looks like a verdant piece of fine lace, with tiny, greenish-white flowers in mid-summer and pretty, white berries in autumn, is planted to shroud a boundary fence. This garden is an exceptional day out for all and, with access to the private beach, you can almost imagine that you have been transported to an exotic wonderland.

Climbers for height and interest

Trees and large shrubs are not an option in a tiny seaside plot, so how does our valiant trooper clothe fences, arbours and pergolas? Fortunately there are some beautiful climbers and wall shrubs that are well able to withstand the elements. Again the trick is to get them established and through the first year. By the second year they will put up with a certain amount of wind damage and by the third most will have settled into the swing.

However much the books and television presenters extol the virtues of planting in the autumn, this does not apply to the coastal garden – there is no way a newly planted climber can build up enough strength and stability to face the onslaught of winter by the sea. Instead, plant in early spring to allow the plant a long season to get established and help it along by keeping it covered in the first winter with hessian or netting as described above.

Some plants require patience as well as initial cosseting. It took five years for my *Rosa* 'Compassion' to show signs

---

Eccremocarpus scaber (Chilean glory vine) scrambles up a sheltered house wall at Peerley Road, Sussex, reaching 3m/10ft in the first year of sowing seed and sometimes continuing to produce its orange-red flowers

in the depths of winter. In the salt-laden atmosphere, garden string and twine rot, and twist-it ties rust, so Trudi Harrison uses fishing line to tie in climbers, which has the advantage of being invisible. Salt-tolerant

Hemerocallis and moisture-loving *Impatiens glandulifera* enjoy the shade cast by the house walls. The impatiens self sow but the salt kills the seedlings that pop up in exposed places.

of climbing, after which time it shot up to become a crowd pleaser. Its salmon-pink, slightly scented blooms go on for ever and there are plenty to pick for the Christmas table. When the wind gets up and fries the flowers, there are still many buds waiting to perform. I grow this rose with *Clematis* 'Huldine', which has upright, lavender-tinted white blooms that do not seem to brown in the wind and rain.

Pyracanthas also take time to get going, and for four years mine lost its leaves and never flowered. Eventually, it proved its worth, softening the hard edges of the house walls and producing fiery fruits that cheer the spirits in winter. Another stalwart is *Solanum crispum* 'Glasnevin' which clothes the front of my house, with nothing between it and the sea. In an area where you have to wash the salt off the windscreen before driving the car, it is amazing how the Chilean potato vine stands up to it all. It does lose its leaves in winter, but is quick to sprout in early spring and soon drips with sprays of blue flowers.

Making the most of views

Many NGS gardens on the coast boast wonderful views of the sea in all its moods – from peaceful to playful, joyful to tumultuous. Even when the vast expanse of water and sky is dark, still and sombre, it is a shame not to be able to see it. Gardens in sheltered bays and coves, protected from prevailing winds by hills and woodland, often need some shelter, while for those on very exposed sites some form of protection is vital. There are still ways to enjoy the view. One option is to establish a framework of hedging and then create 'windows' to reveal glimpses of favourite vistas. Another is to group the toughest, salt-tolerant, front-line defence plants so that they 'frame' the view. A planting of fully grown cordylines, for example, will transport you to sunnier climes on distant shores. For a more formal style try 'box-type' hedging with plants such as Japanese spindle (*Euonymus japonicus* 'Macrophyllus'), real box, *Buxus*, being unsuitable in exposed areas. Toughies like privet (*Ligustrum*) can be clipped into topiary shapes, perhaps surrounding clear pools of water to echo the sea.

Improving the soil

A simple trip to the washing-line is ample proof, if it were needed, of the drying effects of the wind and we all know how much better our washing dries on a breezy day. The same principle applies to the soil – even my heavy clay can turn in an instant from a soggy quagmire to hard-baked biscuit in a matter of hours, sun and shade having played little part in the process. Only too often in coastal gardening the salt wind gets the blame for a plant's demise, when in fact it is the gardener's failure to observe the constantly changing conditions of the soil. It will take three to five years for a plant to establish properly in exposed sites, as the constant buffeting from extreme winds produces its very own special problems. Casualties will occur. There is nothing 'instant' in producing a seaside garden.

Coastal gardeners deal with a varying range of soils, from sandy to heavy clay, chalky to peaty, and each has their own problem to confront, combated in their own special way. Let's start with sand. Having practically no nutritional value to a plant whatsoever and unable to lock in moisture, this soil type can be a nightmare to any novice gardener, let alone those who regularly receive the constant drying breezes from the sea. However, beefed up regularly with copious amounts of organic matter, sandy soil can be a very workable property. Some gardeners use seaweed to make compost – it must be washed thoroughly first as the salt content harms plants. I like to add seaweed to my existing heap at the end of the season, as the stench of it rotting is unpleasant and attracts flies. Rich in nitrogen, iodine and potash, seaweed can also be used as a mulch on very sandy soils. Applied thickly (in a layer of about 7–8cm/3in), it helps to conserve moisture in the soil and feeds the plants as it rots down. Digging sand is no work at all, so every time you plant, make a hole three times as wide and twice as deep as the rootball and add two thirds compost and manure to one third of the excavated soil. Pour a few buckets of water into the planting hole and leave it to soak in. Soak the rootball for thirty minutes. Then half-fill the hole with the compost mixture, plant firmly and fill up the hole. Give the ground another good soaking. Then it is a question of watching out for dryness over the following six weeks, by which time the roots should be romping away and getting a good grip.

Yuccas, ginger lilies and cannas naturalize on the Devon riviera. Here at Overbecks, perched above the Salcombe estuary, thanks to the shelter offered by the cliffside and surrounding woods, the National Trust gardeners enjoy exploring a large range of exotic and rare plants. These include subtropical camphor trees, huge banana specimens and many different types of tender perennial.

On sandy soil, Mottistone Manor on the Isle of Wight boasts a wide range of plants in a 6-acre garden. Herbaceous borders, kitchen gardens, shrub borders, trees and a wild garden thrive. The head gardener, Robert Moore, says that fighting nature can be a fruitless task, but there are many plants that cope with coastal conditions and sandy soils. He cites some more of my favourite plants, like kniphofia and cistus, as highly suitable.

Gardening on sandy loam, the Bookers at The Gate House, Devon, also prove the benefits of adding heaps of farmhouse manure to the soil. The 21/2-acre garden is only a few minutes' walk from the sea and yet boasts a wide collection of plants, despite frequent showers of spume (the froth from the sea foam) depositing itself there at a moment's notice.

I myself at 33 Peerley Road, Sussex, garden on heavy clay and, with most of my garden facing north-east, I was perplexed for years as plant after plant died on me. I could not understand why these supposedly salt-tolerant plants expired after every winter. Then I realized it wasn't the salt killing them. They were drowning in the soggy soil. Of course, I now take every step possible to remedy that. And since I have adopted a no-dig policy, which has been in operation some seven years now, my garden has become a different place in which to practise horticulture.

It also stops the soil compacting and, gradually, as it becomes more friable, casualties caused by winter rot are rare. The thick layer added in January also helps to keep the soil warm (clay being so slow to warm up in spring), allowing plants like canna to naturalize with such gusto that they are almost a weed! Of course, I have to dig when I've got a new plant to put in, adding plenty of grit to every planting hole.

No-dig gardening is simple: instead of turning the soil over, every winter I apply a layer of homemade compost, manure and grit to the top and allow the worms to carry it beneath the ground. This mulch works in several ways. It does not disturb the fibrous roots of overwintering perennials and shrubs, so it allows them to get a good grip in their growing season, reducing wind rock to a minimum.

Gill James of 11 Eastcliff, Swansea, gardens on a limestone cliff, where the soil is only some 15cm/6in thick. By adding compost and manure to make up the beds, she has created a loamy, alkaline soil that, although still very thin is just enough to support plantings of euphorbias, eryngiums, phlomis, ozothamnus and other beautiful architectural plants that can take your breath away. Plant

South Green Farmhouse in Essex looks across windswept marshes and an estuary to Brightlingsea and Mersea Island. Delphiniums and the tree lupin (*Lupinus arboreus*), standing tall and upright, show how the hedges surrounding Zélie Jopling's garden provide shelter from the cold east winds that would stunt or kill young growth. Every coastline is different: plants that grow on one may not survive on another.

combinations like *Geranium psilostemon* 'Bressingham Flair' with *Nepeta* 'Six Hills Giant' would be the envy of any inland garden, but here it shows just how very attractive a coastal garden can be when using the right plants in the right place, with the right soil preparation.

Proving the benefits of continuous applications of compost and manure, the owners of Jasmine Cottage, Clevedon, have actually noticed over the last twenty years that in their loam-over-limestone garden overlooking the Bristol Channel the pH has altered to relatively neutral. Avid plantaholics, Michael and Margaret Redgrave built their home and garden on a plot of land that was in such poor condition most folk would have given up on the garden years ago. In fact they were planting potatoes and runner beans around the builders' hut as they waited for their home to be completed. Such is the nature of the seaside gardener – nothing will stop them.

Pots and baskets

Having hanging baskets or pots on the coast can be very testing. If the wind isn't picking them up and throwing them about like a Tasmanian devil, it is constantly drying them out. One stormy night, my window boxes were deposited in a neighbour's garden three doors away. Fixings rust in salty conditions and it is wise to check them at the start of the season.

When preparing baskets for planting, double the manufacturer's recommended amount of water-retaining granules and add chicken manure to the planting medium. Pouch containers are better than baskets as they hold on to the moisture and sit better in the wind. I reinforce the handles with tape to prevent the wind tearing them. If they dry out, I rehydrate the pouches by immersing them in a bucket of water to which I add a few drops of washing-up liquid – this helps the water cling to the compost.

Choose container plants adapted to sea breezes, such as *Felicia amelloides* and marguerites (*Argyranthemum*), whose natural habitat is the South African coast. Small sedums and sempervivums are evergreen and never look tired or untidy in pots. Apply a thick mulch of gravel, shingle, slate or pebbles to pots to help prevent the soil drying out too quickly.

Pests and diseases

Seaside gardens never sleep and neither do common pests and diseases. Greenfly and leafhopper breed all year round in our warmer gardens while their natural predators like ladybirds and lacewings hibernate. There is only one way to deal with them and that is by being vigilant.

The key to growing strong and healthy roses near the sea is to choose disease-resistant varieties, like the climber 'Dublin Bay', and to prune promptly at the end of the season to prevent wind rock. I do this around November, leaving a few healthy-looking stems to bloom for Christmas. I prune those in early January. Regular watering and feeding with proprietary rose food in spring and autumn also makes for a much stronger plant, and the stronger the specimen, the more resistant it is to disease. Roses displaying signs of rust or blackspot are dealt with immediately: in summer by pulling off the affected leaves and spraying with a systemic fungicide; in other seasons by hard pruning and disposal of every leaf. Do not add diseased leaves to your compost heap as they cross-infect – they must be burnt or disposed of at your local tip. Removing every leaf from your roses means that the spores of blackspot have nowhere to overwinter and neither do the greenfly and leafhoppers. Spraying insecticide two or three times during the winter significantly reduces the aphid population: I rarely have to use sprays in the growing season now.

I have also noticed that aromatic plants like artemisias seem to keep pests at bay. Plantings of *Artemisia* 'Powis Castle' beneath concentrated 'pest delicacies', such as apple trees and roses, leave choice plants virtually pest-free.

Slugs and snails

These tenacious creatures never stop. Inlanders get a break from them in the winter as frost and snow set in, but in mild gardens they just keep on eating. Using grit or gravel around precious plants is a waste of time. I worked out why when I became interested in sailing and was advised to rub my hands with salt to make them tougher: slugs and snails exposed to salt are toughened to the point where grit does not work, nor does a bucket of salty water. Vigilance in this case involves venturing out at eleven o'clock at night, even on warm winter nights, armed with a torch

ANNE SWITHINBANK

Plants with stamina

My memories of seaside holidays are punctuated by plants. The springy turf of Cornish cliffside pastures spangled with yellow bird's-foot trefoil and edged by leaning, wind-battered sloes. Hydrangeas and montbretias in the sheltered valley by the campsite. Or drifts of viper's bugloss, teasel, horned poppy and clumps of sea campion above shingle shorelines. Seaside gardens can be gardens on the coast or inland creations inspired by a whim.

Creating the real thing requires stamina from gardener and plants alike, as everything has to be vetted first, to make sure it can survive the front line of salt-laden winds and scouring sand. Windbreak plants have to be well adapted to withstand severe conditions, yet those basking in the shelter they create often benefit from milder temperatures than those experienced inland and at higher altitudes.

Classic windbreak plants like sea buckthorn (*Hippophae rhamnoides*) are all the more beautiful for being the right plant in the right place, especially when groups of female trees have a male pollinator, ensuring plenty of matt orange berries. They root happily into sand, producing silvery leaves all summer. Milder coastlines boast posh windbreaks of unusual New Zealand daisy bushes (olearias) and oddities like the scandent Duke of Argyll's tea-tree (*Lycium chinense*), belying its tender appearance by growing in the teeth of the gales.

Inland shingle gardens make good homes for seaside plants, whose resilience comes in useful for poor, sun-baked sites. Gardeners on the trail of such plants need only look for the sea in their names. Sea kale is fantastic, with its almost undulating, blue-green leaves and white flowers. Sea hollies are a remarkable bunch, of which the perennial *Eryngium* × *oliverianum* is one of the smartest and *E. agavifolium* is all the rage. But if you like a challenge, try raising the stunning *E. proteiflorum* from seed.

Put thrift (or sea pink, *Armeria maritima*) and sea lavenders (*Limonium latifolium*) against shimmering mounds of cotton lavender (*Santolina chamaecyparissus*) and you can almost hear the gulls.

and a knife. But for hostas and other snail delicacies, a ring of WD40 (petroleum distillate, so take care not to breathe it in) sprayed on the ground acts like a fence around my precious plants (so does garlic water if you and your visitors can stand the smell).

Do not throw snails over a fence. The little monsters have a homing instinct second to none. Get on top of them before they get on top of you. If you can't bear to kill them, encourage wildlife into your garden: frogs, hedgehogs and thrushes will do the job for you. One January I removed 120 slugs and snails from 1 square metre of flowerbed – I dread to think how many I would have had in my garden by the summer if I had left them to breed.

Extending the range of plants

Putting the right plant in the right place is a good idea in any garden, but it is crucial to the seaside gardener's success. Coastal gardeners around the country sent me lists of their favourite salt-tolerant plants and, quite amazingly, all quoted a similar top ten: *Fatsia japonica*, hebes, cordylines, phormiums, griselinia, senecio, olearia, elaeagnus, yucca and escallonia. So, wherever you are situated, these plants will work.

However, in the balmy climate acquired by the sea's warmth, it is also worth experimenting with less stalwart plants. For one of the most positive aspects of being a coastal gardener is the climate. Warmed by the Gulf Stream and continental breezes, our maritime climate is a positive paradise for many Californian and Mediterranean plants, as well as for those from New Zealand, Japan, Chile and South Africa. Though we do not receive as much sun in the summer as these places, our plants soon adapt to the summer rain. With proper drainage and shelter from biting winds, our gardens are able to grow plants that the inlander would have to bring indoors in the winter. This is what makes the coastal garden one of the most exciting places on earth. Once we have combated the shelter problems, we can go on to explore the possibilities of being different from the rest. We can chuckle with glee as we watch the inlander go through tedious routines of lifting and storing summer bulbs for the winter. We can sit on our terraces, sipping our gin in the last of the autumn sun, enjoying our cordyline palms and the low lights shining

Close planting helps prevent wind-borne salt penetrating the soil. At Scypen, Devon, John and Ann Bracey use low-growing plants, such as dwarf hebes, bergenia, dianthus and eryngiums, to weave intricate textures and patterns. They employ many tricks in their ½-acre garden from which seaside gardeners can learn – for instance planting lavender in the lee of the phormium and the wall, where it escapes the wind's worst work. Paths take visitors past unusual features – a thyme sundial, a concrete revolving globe made for the millennium and a pool with a fountain of intriguing design based on a DNA double helix.

through our phormiums, knowing that we have all winter to enjoy ourselves.

Tomarobandy in Cumbria is a plantsman's paradise where Tom Wrathall has created a series of thirteen exciting gardens within his 1½-acre plot – from alpine to herbaceous sites, sunken to raised areas, incorporating pergolas and all manner of unusual planting themes. Inspired by a visit to Compton Acres in Bournemouth, he realized that once windbreaks provided shelter his garden could be a place to display the wide range of plants a seaside gardener can have with relative ease and he set to it with great imagination.

Sir Walter and Lady Lutterell of Court House, Somerset, started making their 5-acre garden in 1992. The views are breathtaking – across Bridgewater Bay to Wales and of the Quantock Hills to the south. The garden is bombarded by winds from the north and south-west and a still day is rare and somewhat ominous, the silence almost deafening and generally hailing another storm. Gales weed out trees on a regular basis and favourites like poplars are often lost. Fifty years' experience has taught them to view this as a bonus bringing new-found light to the woodland floor. Like many coastal gardeners, the Lutterells have discovered that close planting reduces wind damage as the violent whipping action of a single plant is moderated to a gentle roll. It also helps prevent weeds, retain moisture and keep the plants warm in the colder months, as the heat they release overnight remains trapped under the thick carpet of foliage. Plants are not static, of course, but should they become overcrowded it is simple to lift and divide them in the cooler months without any harm being done. This is a practice I have adopted in my own garden for many years with great results.

For nearly forty years a Kentish gardener, Major Harvey Blizard of Sea Close in Hythe, has been experimenting with a virtually frost-free plot, growing stars like *sophora*, *Melianthus major* and a *Leptospermum* that is twenty-five years old and 3m/10ft high. So enchanted is he with his 1-acre site that he has put pen to paper and writes books about it. He must be injected with an overdose of energy by all that extra warmth because, despite frequent water shortages on a slope that dries out constantly, you will find him watering by hand during hosepipe bans – no mean feat in a garden that size.

The jewel of the Solent, the Isle of Wight, boasts many gardens of note on a wide range of soils, considering that it is such a small island. Ventnor has more sunshine hours than any other part of England and many unusual plants bedeck gardens there in a kaleidoscope of colour, form and texture. Native plants alongside foreign imports self-seed on beaches and cliff tops and in hedgerows. A journey across the water to visit the NGS gardens is like a trip abroad without the hassle of planes and passports and, whether dreaming of your own seaside garden or looking for ideas for something different, is sure to be inspiring.

In another plantsman's paradise across the Solent at Sowley House, Hampshire, Catharina van der Vorm makes full use of the sheltered microclimate and neutral soil. A marsh of native flora, including orchids, flowers in the spring with breathtaking beauty. On the shore sea hollies (*Eryngium maritimum*) and the yellow horned poppy (*Glaucium flavum*) flower profusely in the pure clean light. Wild flowers found on sand dunes and shingle, such as sea kale (*Crambe maritima*), sea aster (*Aster tripolium*), sea lavender (*Limonium vulgare*) and sea buckthorn (*Hippophae rhamnoides*), add to the seaside gardener's palette. And with so many English native species endangered as we overdevelop the coastline, gardeners can play a role in conserving coastal habitats and encouraging the return of wildlife.

For most people, the seaside conjures an image of a gloriously sunny day when baskets of pelargoniums sway to and fro in the breeze and candyfloss-pink lavateras peek over whitewashed walls. They see themselves ambling along a bustling promenade, licking ice creams, and envying the folk who live there. Even in winter, they imagine the coastal gardener basking in the sun, tempered by the gentlest sea breeze. Nothing could be further from the truth. We may not get the frost but winters are harsh and often very destructive, but on rare days when the pale lemon sun shines on tortured trees and exploding phormiums, there is beauty like no other and it is little wonder that the British gardener is the envy of the world and coastal gardens must be the envy of the British gardener.

At Holker Hall Gardens in south Cumbria, the healthy young growth of *Rosa sericea* subsp. *omeiensis* f. *pteracantha* shows how well roses can do in coastal climates, in spite of the pure sea air being a perfect breeding ground for blackspot, rust and mildew. Before pruning, watch the weather forecast, aiming for at least three frost-free, calm days in which the cut can heal, so neither salt nor cold damages the wound.

Gravel border in full sun

This evergreen planting for neutral to alkaline soil will withstand the worst the weather can throw at it. Easy to care for, it is suitable for the garden of a holiday home or for gardeners in their twilight years for whom labour-intensive gardens are out of the question. The design reflects the dips and curves, ripples and patterns in the sea. It is for an area 4 x 2.5m/13 x 8ft.

1 *Phormium tenax* 'Yellow Wave'
2 *Festuca glauca*
3 *Erigeron karvinskianus*
4 *Helichrysum italicum* subsp. *serotinum*
5 *Euphorbia myrsinites*
6 × *Halimiocistus wintonensis*
7 *Aloe aristata*
8 *Silene maritima*
9 *Ophiopogon planiscapus* 'Nigrescens'
10 *Eryngium variifolium*
11 *Mertensia maritima*
12 *Sempervivum arachnoideum*
13 *Felicia amelloides*
14 *Thymus* × *citriodorus* 'Silver Queen'

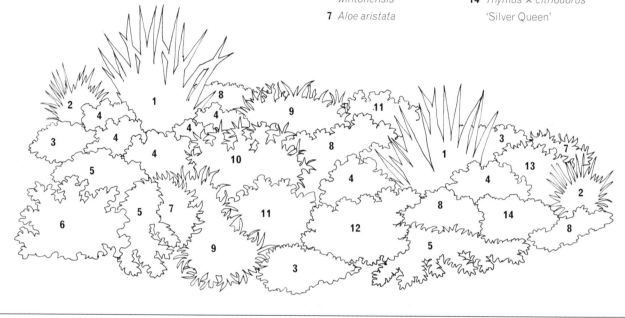

Plants for seaside gardens

Shrubs & climbers

Aucuba japonica 'Gold Dust'. A superstar shrub from Japan, underrated because of its extensive use in hedging, that can take sea winds and remain evergreen. 'Gold Dust' is a favourite as a specimen plant because its young foliage, which emerges in late winter and early spring, is such a bright yellow that the sun looks pale in comparison. The rich red, jewel-like berries provide amusement for us all in winter, as we giggle at the antics of the birds trying to feed on them. Give it a light prune in spring to keep it to the size you require (unchecked it will reach 3 x 3m/10 x 10ft).

Cotoneaster horizontalis. I like to call this 'God's very own fireworks display' – its deep red berries glow with fire and passion in the darkest months of the year. It will withstand some shade and is salt-tolerant, making it a valuable foundation plant (90cm/3ft high and 1.5m/5ft wide) for the shady seaside border.

Euonymus fortunei 'Silver Queen'. This shrub makes a good climber against a wall or fence, reaching as much as 6m/20ft in maritime conditions. It may get its leaves stripped in winter, but is quick to recover. The variegated, oval leaves make a good backdrop to colourful plantings.

Fatsia japonica. This lovely shrub dances and shimmers in the breeze and is unaffected by 80mph winds in winter. In summer it provides a wonderful backdrop for brightly coloured plants. The white berries against the glossy, dark green foliage bring pleasure in the winter months. Originating from the coastal forest of Japan, it is a great plant for shade. Keep it to size with a light prune in spring (left unchecked it will grow to 4 x 4m/13 x 13ft).

× *Halimiocistus wintonensis*. A hybrid of cistus and halimium, this shrub is a delight in summer, with white flowers that have a yellow-and-red centre blushing like a strawberry. It grows to about 60cm/2ft.

Helichrysum italicum subsp. *serotinum*. Cut into soft mounds about 40cm/16in high and 75cm/2½ft wide, this has a sturdy yet gentle presence in a border. I cut mine three times a year. If you can't stand the smell of curry, try *Santolina* 'Lemon Queen' which is smaller and prettier than *Santolina incana*.

Ligustrum ovalifolium 'Aureum'. Clip privet to any shape you like for quick and easy topiary. Although some of its leaves may be lost in winter in exposed sites, it quickly fills out again in spring. In my shady north-facing garden it maintains its golden glow throughout the year. Unchecked it will grow to 2 x 2m/6½ x 6½ft.

Pyracantha 'Orange Glow'. A thorny evergreen which can reach as high as 5m/15ft, providing a place for wildlife to party all year. 'Orange Glow' has fiery berries that last all winter. For red berries try 'Watereri' and for yellow 'Soleil d'Or'. Trim away some of the leaves in late summer to expose these jewels.

Thymus × citriodorus 'Silver Queen'. With adequate drainage, this thyme remains evergrey in the coastal garden. In those rare moments when the wind drops, the scent wafts in the air along with the smell of the sea breeze to whet your appetite. As well as being useful for cooking, the foliage is silvery white and soft; fluffy, lilac flowers are a summer bonus.

Perennials

Aloe aristata. An exotic-looking South African succulent which makes a dark-green-and-white stripy rosette about 10cm/4in high and produces terracotta spikes and flowers in June–July. It would have to be in a greenhouse inland, but thrives outside on the coast.

Erigeron karvinskianus. This little perennial has a constant smile, a self-seeding, long-flowering frothy addition to the border that no seaside gardener will want to be without. It is easy to grow from seed and forms evergreen mats in winter. The white, daisy-like flowers start in March, turn pink as the season progresses and keep going till December.

Eryngium variifolium. A wicked and undemanding perennial (45cm/1½ft tall), with jagged, green-and-white-marbled evergreen foliage and flowers like shooting stars of silver and blue in July.

Euphorbia myrsinites. Crawling out of the border like a cubist snake, this evergreen, salt-proof perennial is constantly beautiful. It supports the brittle stems of the crocus and *Iris reticulata* I plant underneath its glaucous foliage and which set off the euphorbia's yellow flowers to perfection.

Farfugium japonicum 'Aureomaculatum'. From the seashores of Japan comes this evergreen, semi-tender perennial of incredible beauty, with the prettiest kidney-shaped leaves splashed with gold. The flowers

appear between autumn and winter when all around is looking drab and forlorn. It seems too good to be true and will lift a shady corner. It has a height and spread of 60cm/2ft.

Felicia amelloides. Sold as bedding in garden centres, this is actually a sub-shrub from South Africa. Give it good drainage and a warm spot and it will produce blue flowers above bright green leaves non-stop.

Festuca glauca. If you can get past the cliché status this seaside grass has acquired, its blue-green tufts (10cm/4in) are pretty, especially in drifts with slate shingle.

Helleborus foetidus. I grow this in a very windy, exposed border and yet it still surprises me in late January with creamy nodding flowers. All year round, the foliage looks good, strange and exotic, as if it belonged on some distant planet. If you are exposed to extremely cold northerlies, however, give it a miss. But for most of us, the extra few degrees of warmth by the sea mean that this is a star, 45 x 45 cm/1½ x 1½ft.

Stalwart silvers at Peerley Road, Sussex: *Elaeagnus angustifolia*, cordylines, senecios and santolinas.

Border for dappled shade

This open border is for neutral to alkaline soil in an exposed shady garden. It includes yellow foliage plants most of which are evergreen, to lighten a dull corner. This design is for an area 3.5 x 2m/11½ x 6½ft.

1 *Fatsia japonica*
2 *Cotoneaster horizontalis*
3 *Helleborus foetidus*
4 *Milium eVusum* 'Aureum'
5 *Farfugium japonicum* 'Aureomaculatum'
6 *Ligustrum ovalifolium* 'Aureum'
7 *Aucuba japonica* 'Gold Dust'
8 *Hemerocallis* 'Golden Chimes'
9 *Pachysandra terminalis*

Hemerocallis 'Golden Chimes'. Day-lilies are incredibly tolerant of shade and salt and, because the flowers last only a day, if they get blitzed by bad weather one day there are more to enjoy the next. I love to see their sword-like foliage poking through the earth in spring. A big swathe 75cm/2½ft tall can look dramatic in mid-summer.

Mertensia maritima. Why this perennial (10–15cm/4–6in) is overlooked, I know not: its fleshy, silver-blue foliage and flowers of a gentle aquamarine have a luminescent appearance. It does best in poor soil, well guarded from slugs which think it is delicious.

Milium effusum 'Aureum'. 'Sunshine in the shade',

born in a regal profusion of fine, grassy leaves that explode this way and that. It has a marvellous texture, fine to see dancing in the wind at any time of year. The slender, nodding, greenish-yellow flower panicles appear in spring to late summer, making this a must-have plant, 60cm/2ft tall and with a spread of 30cm/1ft.

Ophiopogon planiscapus 'Nigrescens'. This black 'grass' reflects the shadows and depth in the sea. Grey-mauve spikelets shoot up in summer and look good mirroring the blue in *Eryngium variifolium*.

Pachysandra terminalis. For a carpet of tough, evergreen foliage (10cm/4in), one cannot go wrong with this plant. It makes a very good support for spring

flowers like grape hyacinths (*Muscari*) and, until the storms get a grip, for autumn crocus (*Colchicum*). Able to withstand dry shade, this is another Japanese star.

Phormium tenax 'Yellow Wave'. A striking plant at all times of the year, in low winter sunlight the stiff leaves of the New Zealand flax positively glow. *P.* 'Yellow Wave' (3m/10ft) picks up the colours of × *Halimiocistus wintonensis* and *Euphorbia myrsinites* in the plan on page 196. Other good forms include pink 'Maori Sunrise' and, my favourite, 'Sundowner', with bronze-green leaves with dark rose-pink margins.

Sempervivum arachnoideum. Cobweb-like filaments cover fleshy leaves in many shades of red and green,

looking too precious and unusual to put in a border that will get beaten about in winter. Yet the houseleek, the Mother Teresa of the plant world, remains constant and untroubled.

Silene uniflora 'Druett's Variegated'. The variegated sea campion (formerly *S. maritima*) is a beauty, with tiny white flowers that seem to go on for ever as a bonus to the evergreen foliage in white, yellow and green. It requires a free-draining soil (dig in loads of grit if on clay) and a sun-baked site. Plant it in large amounts (say, thirty plants 10cm/4in apart per square metre/yard) to make stunning carpets that stay fresh all year round.

The garden at Peerley Road is just a stone's throw from the sea, protected from the fiercest winds with sturdy trellis and wind netting. Secondary winds bouncing off the surrounding houses can still cause havoc, yet the climate is balmy and tender plants like cannas, *Hedychium* (ginger lily), dahlias and yuccas can be left *in situ* for the winter. These and evergreens like *Phoenix canariensis* form the backbone to this north-facing border. Deep mauve *Verbena bonariensis* and pink *Impatiens glandulifera*, along with scented white lilies and spider flowers (*Cleome hassleriana*), add sparkle in August when daylight hours are diminishing.

ABOVE A gravel path runs north to south between the double herbaceous borders in the old kitchen garden at Somerleyton Hall, Suffolk. Fine trees, such as monkey puzzles and the dawn redwood, stand tall and straight on this favoured site four miles from the coast. RIGHT Grasses, *Salvia confertiflora* and *Dahlia merckii* make a tapestry of soft colours and textures at Clent Cottage, Dorset. BELOW Agapanthus and yuccas line the steps leading to the Mediterranean Garden at The Old Vicarage, East Ruston.

In addition to the gardens in which Trudi Harrison has tasted the salt, here are some of the Yellow Book gardens near the coast.

Bristol & South Gloucestershire
Barum
Canok Garth
Highview
Jasmine Cottage
The Manor House, Walton-in-Gordano
Queen's Gate Gardens

Carmarthenshire & Pembrokeshire
Brynheulog
Hean Castle

Ceredigion/Cardiganshire
Nantcellan
Plas Penglais, University of Wales

Cheshire & Wirral
St Davids House

Cornwall
Polgwynne
St Michael's Mount

Cumbria
Hazel Mount

Denbighshire
Plas Heaton

Devon
Churchpark Cottage
Coleton Fishacre
Docton Mill and Garden
The Gate House, Lee
Old Rectory, East Portlemouth

Dorset
Abbotsbury Gardens
Chesil Gallery
The Manor House, Abbotsbury
Smedmore
Studland Bay House
24a Western Avenue

Essex
Springvale

Glamorgan
The Botanical Gardens
Clyne Gardens
9 Willowbrook Gardens

Gloucestershire
Threeways

Gwent
Tredegar House & Park

Gwynedd
Crug Farm
Henlys Lodge
Pentre Bach
Plas Newydd

Hampshire
Alverstoke Crescent
Garden
Littlewood, Hayling Island

Isle of Wight
Crab Cottage
Hamstead Grange
Highwood
Kings Manor
Northcourt Gardens
The Old Church House
Pitt House
Woolverton House

Kent
The Pines Garden

Lancashire & Merseyside
Lindeth Dene
The Reginald Kaye Garden
Speke Hall Gardens & Woodland

Norfolk
The Dutch House
Felbrigg Hall
Sheringham Park

Somerset
Court House
190 Goldcroft

Suffolk
Aldeburgh Gardens
Stanford House

Sussex
51 Carlisle Road
Cleveland House, Winchelsea's
*   Secret Gardens*
Dale Park House
64 Old Shoreham Road
14 Roedean Way
18 Tongdean Avenue

Yorkshire
Manor Farm, Hunmanby
Rudston House
Saltmarshe Hal

201

BARBARA SEGALL

with expert insights by
CHRISTOPHER LLOYD
PETER SEABROOK
ROSEMARY VEREY
HELEN YEMM

10 Exposure

Exposure has a tabloid ring to it, and certainly if your garden is exposed to the elements or to traffic noise, neighbourly gaze and/or unsightliness, you might well find that you are experiencing much the same as the hapless victims of the ravaging media pack – the twin troughs of vulnerability and revelation. In the garden these conditions are quite literally rained in and blown in upon us by the weather, not the antics of the press pack. Wind, sun, rain, cold: excesses of any of these will cause plants to suffer and the garden will look and be a less attractive place.

In the perfect garden the perfect plant would have all its requirements of nutrition, light, water and shelter met and there would be no external problems of pest, disease or weather to worry about. But then, the Garden of Eden is a place that we left behind some aeons ago. And anyway, where would a gardener be without a challenge or two!

Gardening on an exposed site has challenge a-plenty. But as with all garden problems, there are ways and means to overcome those of exposure. There are plants for the purpose as well as non-plant solutions that will provide shelter and therefore reduce the level of exposure. Time, energy and cost are the main inputs and once exposure has become enclosure, the benefits will be visible in an increased palette of healthy-looking plants. Indeed, so enclosed might you become that, like Beth Chatto who, after protecting and sheltering her plant jewels for some thirty years against the desiccating wind that sweeps across flat Essex, now finds herself thinking about removing some mature, shelter-belt trees, so that she can find clear skies. There are hundreds of Yellow Book gardens in which exposure is dealt with so effectively that the need for protection is no more than a memory. But for most of us starting out on the metamorphosis from an open site to enclosure, the thought of removing trees is a long way in the future.

The wind factor

Strong, drying or chilling winds, or a combination of all three, affect gardens and plants in several ways, and strong winds may physically damage plants, snapping stems and taking off branches.

Wind damages plant growth because of its drying action on the foliage. It causes an increase of evaporation of water from the leaf which, if it happens too fast and too much water is lost, prevents the roots from replacing the water in the plant's vascular system, and so it is weakened and, in extreme cases, dies. Such damage, if the plant survives, will stunt its growth, causing it to grow in a misshapen way. Wind pressure on the stem or trunk of a plant will eventually loosen the plant's roothold, causing wind rock, and you should always check that plants are secure in winter. Roots and leaves are paramount for a

plant's survival; for our enjoyment in the garden, more than just survival is demanded. We want our gardens to look ravishingly healthy. If a plant is struggling to keep its roots attached to its natural source of moisture and nutrition, and its leaves, the powerhouse of its conversion of the sun's energy into food, are being mutilated and losing moisture too rapidly, it will be first casualty in the morning of the long loppers!

Leaves, whose role in a plant's life are so critical, have evolved and adapted to manage and control the way climatic factors affect them. Shape, texture and size of leaf have a bearing on the plant's survival in certain conditions. Evergreen foliage often has a shiny, almost leathery and tough exterior. Small foliage offers a reduced size of area for evaporation. Grey, felted foliage, juicy, succulent foliage and thin, aromatic leaves withstand the effects of drought and therefore are suited to exposed, hot gardens. Wind wreaks damage by tearing to shreds plants with large leaves and snapping those with top-heavy flower stems. Providing support for plants can be a losing battle until your defences are in place – better to choose carpeters, such as sempervivums, alpine phlox and acaenas, and the many members of the grass family that bend and sway in the breeze and survive the strongest gales without snapping. Some plants actually benefit from the wind: *Spartium junceum*, for example, becomes bushier and tends to give a better show of flowers in an exposed garden.

What is more, windy conditions discourage the pollinating insects that are essential if fruit trees and certain vegetables are to crop and certain flowers are to set seed. And, of course, spraying against pests is a waste of time. Wind also has a drying effect on the soil and, combined with low rainfall, transforms clay into cracked biscuit and light soil to dust. David and Anke Way's garden at Southover in Kent is on river alluvium, and the combination of low rainfall and an exposed site means that the ground dries out very quickly in protracted periods of drought. Thuja and yew hedges enclose and shelter the cottage garden and these green walls have another benefit: they hold the scent of the old-fashioned roses and fragrant flowers, so much so that visitors comment on the nosegay effect enjoyed from their bedroom windows.

As well as mulching beds and borders with homemade

PRECEDING PAGES Although sheltered from the wind, plantings around the lowest of three pools that descend to the rock garden at Mindrum, Northumberland, are in a frost pocket and Virginia and Peregrine Fairfax are used to the casualties of harsh winters and the excesses of the east wind – 'the great blaster'. The drawing of Preston Tower, Northumberland, is from the 1997 Yellow Book.

RIGHT As well as their protective role, the hedges at Southover, Kent, are a foil for plants in the deep borders. Here *Buphthalmum salicifolium*, *Achillea* 'Moonshine' and *Helenium* 'The Bishop' dazzle in the foreground; *Kniphofia* 'Painted Lady', *Hemerocallis* 'Stafford' and *Lysimachia ephemerum* burnish the back of the border. Anke and David Way make use of the hedge clippings as mulch.

compost and leafmould to hold moisture for the plants, David and Anke have many strategies to deal with their exposure to prevailing winds. The latest of these are what they call 'eco hedges': shelter barriers that have functional value, remove the need for bonfires and are havens for insects and therefore a larder and refuge for small birds. The first eco hedge, made from a hundred tree stakes gleaned from a nearby orchard that had been grubbed up, encloses and camouflages the compost heap, and yet it looks very natural. The stakes are piled one on top of each other parallel to the ground and held in place by a pair of vertical stakes at each end. The second eco hedge consists of two rows of stakes set at 2.5m/8ft intervals and 1m/3ft apart along the length of the rows. Into this open container David and Anke pile all the prunings and trimmings, branches and other garden debris. By this device they keep up with European practice and don't burn or otherwise make any energy input, other than clearing the prunings and so on. This decaying screen is a haven for insects and therefore for birds. It is on the border of their property and the adjoining farm and footpaths, and has become an effective and eye-catching barrier against the east wind and any agrochemical spray that might drift into their garden.

Defence against wind

Even the most minimal shelter, such as a mesh fence with a light covering of a scrambling plant like nasturtium, will reduce the flow of wind and increase the suitability of a border for a wider range of plants. With a substantial hedge the shelter will be even more effective and the force of wind much reduced. The taller the screening you can provide, the greater will be the area that it can protect from the wind. That said, you have to balance the size of the screening with the size and style of the garden. In large country gardens a line of tall-growing trees can be accommodated, yet in an urban setting they would not only be out of place, but their massive root systems would also make them a positive hazard, being in such proximity to house walls.

So defence is the answer and the way wind works will influence the way you choose to thwart it. When wind meets the resistance of a solid structure, such as a wall, or a dense planting, it pushes upwards and over the barrier. Then it sweeps on, coming downwards more turbulently and causing damage to anything in its wake on the leeward side of the barrier. If wind is able to pass through a barrier, it will be filtered and its ferocity, and therefore its potential to damage, will be reduced. The solution,

CHRISTOPHER LLOYD

Cold frames are the answer

I would far rather be gardening on an exposed slope than in a sheltered frost hollow. However, those of us who do, have to admit that wind is our greatest enemy. For young plants needing protection, cold frames are the answer.

Not only does the cold frame protect against wind; if properly made, it retains warmth far into the night. It maintains a humid atmosphere when this is needed to promote the rooting of cuttings and their faster growth, once rooted. In winter young stock can be kept snug against all weathers and, if the temperature is below freezing, the frame can be covered with mats or hessian and its contents be kept in total darkness for days, even weeks on end, till the temperature rises, and light and air can be admitted once more.

The essential, found in commercial models, is that the frame should have solid walls for the sake of insulation. It is easy to make a frame yourself, on the premises, or to have one made for you. The lights can be of glass or plastic

and they need to be light in weight and easily removed. They also need to be easily secured in a closed position in the face of high winds. Being at a low level, a frame is not nearly as vulnerable as a greenhouse.

You can root cuttings into a bed composed of a suitable, well-drained and open-textured rooting medium or insert them into pots and stand these on the floor of the frame. Seeds can be germinated in pots or other containers. Young plants, newly potted up, can be given a start, to get them established, in a closed frame; ventilation is gradually admitted until the youngsters are fully hardened off. In winter slightly tender plants that will benefit from a frame's protection can be kept in it till early spring, when the frame will again need to be used for raising young stock. And we use ours for this purpose all through the summer. You always need to have young plants coming on for

one purpose or another, especially if you want your garden to keep on looking fresh and lively right into autumn.

The frame will also come into its own for starting dahlia and canna, begonia and certain salvia tubers, when they are taken out of storage. If you want to propagate them from cuttings of young shoots, ideal material will be provided out of the frame.

Don't just sit back and be content with cucumbers and melons in summer: there are far more intensive uses for a cold frame, at any season, than that. For most purposes you'll have no need of artificial heat. The sun and the frame between them will do the work for you.

then, is to choose plants that withstand the damaging effects of wind and allow it to flow freely through them.

The first piece of armoury in the defence against exposure is a shelter belt, usually provided by a staggered but quite close planting of trees, such as birch, pine, willow or Lombardy poplars, that will provide some ornament in the shape of their outlines, flowers or fruits, and, more importantly, will filter the wind. Trees planted closely tend to become bare of lower branches, so often a row of shorter trees or a hedge is needed for protection.

Some gardeners are prepared to put in temporary shelter belts of conifers that will grow away quickly. These trees become 'nursemaids' to a permanent enclosure of a

slow-growing hedge of yew, for example. When the yew no longer needs protection, the 'nursemaid shelter' is felled and, eventually, the yew grows tall, strong and mature enough to be the first line of defence.

At Shore Hall in Essex, Denny Swete has such an arrangement. A shelter belt of thuja and hornbeam is the nursemaid to the yew hedge on the north side of her ravishing ornamental and productive kitchen garden. Yew, thuja and hornbeam were all planted at the same time, and the young yews had the extra protection of a woven netting barrier fixed to stakes. Once the shelter plants were up and growing, this was removed. In a few years' time the thujas will be removed. The hornbeam will

LEFT Lord & Lady FitzWalter have been restoring the 14 acres at Goodnestone Park, set in rippling Kentish countryside, since 1955. The walled garden is surrounded by sheltering hedges and ancient trees.

In the foreground, snaking across the full 36m/120ft of the inner wall and enjoying the warmth and protection it provides, is *Wisteria sinensis*. The woodland garden is illustrated on page 140.

ABOVE The cold frames at Great Dixter in Sussex, made to Christopher Lloyd's specifications, have solid walls and double glazing: horizontal inner lights and sloping outer lights to throw the rain off.

Shelter at Barnsley House

We always open for the NGS on the last Saturday in April when the garden is full of bulbs, primroses, polyanthus and hellebores, and on the first Saturday in June when lots of visitors come to see the laburnum tunnel wreathed in wisteria and *Allium aflatunense* in flower under the canopy of yellow and mauve. Everyone enjoys the peace and tranquillity, but few are aware of the shelter that surrounds and protects our Cotswold site.

The high stone wall, built in about 1770 on three sides of the garden, contains the property and is essential to its character. A shelter belt of fine trees – a sycamore, a majestic Turkey oak, an evergreen oak, a copper beech, a sweet chestnut and yews – was planted on the west side of the garden about 150 years ago. We have planted more trees (including a Norway maple, a dawn redwood and a giant sequoia) to make sure it is an effective windbreak from the strong west wind.

On the north side, two old London

plane trees, a horse chestnut and more yews protect us from the icy blasts from Russia in winter. When I first came to Barnsley more than fifty years ago, Mr Archer's milking cows went to and fro past the house twice a day quite safely. Nowadays the trees also muffle the noise of the traffic pounding through our village.

The old trees must have attention. After a hot summer followed by an exceptionally cold spell and hard frosts, the evergreen oak (*Quercus ilex*) probably planted in the 1830s, lost all its leaves and looked as though it was dead until June and July when new leaves formed. I was advised to take up circles of turf under the farthest spread of the branches and add bonemeal and bull's blood to feed the roots. This worked wonders and revitalized a venerable friend doing the vital job of giving the garden a feeling of maturity.

remain and fill out, and to provide a sort of backstop in the longer term (about thirty years) to the whole area Denny has planted a row of holm oaks.

At Mindrum in Northumberland the hilly site that Peregrine and Virginia Fairfax garden at the foot of the Cheviots is exposed on all sides. There is some natural protection from prevailing south-westerly winds offered by a natural bank, for this garden is in a gully. Tall Scots pines on the ridge withstand the wind and add extra protection to the shrubs on the bank itself and still allow for breathtaking views along the Bowmont Valley. Virginia has the usual suspects in place for long-term shelter for the garden as a whole, but to enable plants to thrive she has made numerous internal enclosures. Yew is the main choice for these but she also uses briar roses clipped to form hedges. Large shrubs are another of her ploys. They double up as protectors and beautifiers, providing additional structure too. She prefers to use

deciduous shrubs, which she finds offer less overpowering blocks of green, such as *Viburnum* × *bodnantense*, *Rosa rugosa*, *Kolkwitzia* and *Weigela*, which she allows to grow to great size.

Although the prevailing winds are westerlies, the main damage in winter comes from what Virginia describes as 'the real blaster', the east wind. It just breaks plants apart, tears them off walls and crushes the supports of wandering, waving wands of roses such as 'Paul's Himalayan Musk'. But then, as in all gardens there are surprises, such as her collection of wonderfully coloured abutilons, which you would not credit surviving these rigorous conditions. Not only do they come through most winters, but Virginia has noticed that they also provide shelter for smaller shrubs such as hebes and cistus.

In this garden at 90m/300ft simply surviving is a great achievement, and Virginia chooses from plants known for their hardiness, but she has another survival strategy – her

PRECEDING PAGES Shore Hall's various garden areas are worn like a mantle around the ancient domestic buildings, and are well protected from ravaging winds. In the semi-walled side garden massed ranks of *Allium*

hollandicum 'Purple Sensation' stand to attention, their drumstick heads held high above the low box edging of the beds.

ABOVE Frost has painted the flat surfaces of the knot garden at Barnsley House, Gloucestershire, the double tiers of 'Golden King' hollies standing guard at the corners. In the distance is the shelter belt that

holds the key to this tranquil scene. Transcending its practical purpose, it is now a majestic plantation of mature trees, with younger additions planted by Rosemary Verey.

greenhouse. It has a double function: it is the storehouse of the subjects that won't get through the winter and, in addition, it is packed with replacement plants grown from cuttings and seeds, including some two dozen abutilons, waiting in the wings.

Mixed-species hedges

Documentary evidence shows that hedges consisting of native plants, such as hawthorn, hazel, holly, hornbeam and blackthorn, usually in a sequence of planting, have been part of the British landscape since at least Roman times, when they were used as boundary markers and stock enclosures. Then, as now, these barriers provided a habitat for many species of wildlife, offering shelter, food and breeding sites. A hedge of glossy holly or dark hawthorn, with their respective prickles and thorns, is as impervious to burglars as it is to wind.

A mixed hedgerow brings extra ornament for the garden, too, with a lovely flowing shape and an appearance that changes through the seasons, as flowers and foliage are followed by berries, nuts and fruits. To start a wild-looking hedge, choose bare-root plants, set 60cm/2ft apart, combining wild roses and spindle with hawthorn, blackthorn, hazel and holly. Closer planting, 45cm/18in apart, will create a thicker, more formal effect. When planting small hedging whips, remember that soon they will have grown to fill the space and you should try to leave room between the hedge and the boundary on one side and between the hedge and the border it shelters on the other. In these two corridors you will have enough space to walk so that you can maintain both the hedge and the back of the border.

While they are young even the toughest of hedge plants will need protection from wind. You can provide this with a shelter-belt planting of living trees or with a temporary windbreak made from hessian or a light-mesh horticultural netting. Hurdles of woven willow are also useful as a temporary, moveable and attractive screen.

Tapestry hedges of similar species but different forms, such as two colours of *Rosa rugosa*, copper with purple beech, or berberis with privet, can also be useful in an informal setting. Choose species that grow at a similar rate so that they can be clipped or pruned at the same time and plant them alternately to make a single or a double hedge. Informal hedges can be free-flowing and don't have to be clipped within an inch of their lives.

The dazzling, 60m/200ft-long tapestry hedge at Town Place in Sussex is kept well in hand. Some twenty years old, the plants – *Thuja plicata* 'Zebrina' and *Chamaecyparis lawsoniana* (Lawson's cypress) – give an effect, say garden owners Anthony and Maggie McGrath, of 'golden flames leaping through the green'. At its edges the hedge curls away in the shape of two rather modernist letters 'C'. Although it does shelter the garden from the prevailing south-westerly, its main function is as a backdrop for the dramatically long herbaceous border. To enclose their secret garden the McGraths have planted a shorter hedge of 'Zebrina' thuja and Lawson's cypress and, after a mere five years, have a well-structured, golden flame burning. The rest of their property is protected by native mixed hedges, except for the herb garden which is walled. The walls, say the McGraths, buffet the wind and make fierce eddies in and around the herbs. They have planted trees outside the walls, as well as a walnut inside, to filter the wind.

Green architecture

In a formal garden it is best to use one species of plant such as beech, box or yew to gain a uniform effect. There are, of course, exceptions that prove the rule: the fine mixed hedge of matt box and light-reflecting holly at Rodmarton Manor, near Cirencester, could hardly be less formal.

Yew (*Taxus baccata*) is one of the most desirable and adaptable hedging plants: its dense growth keeps out wind and intruders, it is most amenable to cutting and shaping, the foliage makes an effective backdrop for flowers and statuary and it will grow in most soils. Dark and golden yew may be grown together.

Another advantage of yew is its ability to regenerate from old wood, so hedges in need of restoration can be rejuvenated by cutting right back to the central stems. It is wise to feed the hedge the previous year as growth can be patchy unless yew is in good health. In addition, yew clippings are sought after by a number of firms involved in the production of a cancer-treating product. Once established and shaped by regular cutting, yew becomes less plant and more garden architecture.

At Montacute House in Somerset there are two 50m/165ft-long yew hedges that roll in free fall away from their intended lines of duty. Once bastions of shelter and enclosure, these formerly majestic hedges had an additional function of screening from garden view the pedestrian activities of the servants. However, perhaps in sympathy with a changing society, but more likely as a result of heavy snowfall in the notorious winter of 1947, the hedges were pushed out of shape into their bulging, rather surreal undulations. Even so, today's gardeners at Montacute clip them, albeit following their new curves.

Mammoth yew arches and topiary pieces people the garden at East Bergholt Place, Suffolk. Rupert and Sara Eley maintain and add to the sheltering hedges and trees, plantings which provide protection sufficient for the mature magnolia and camellia plantations, many of which were established by Rupert's great-grandfather, Charles Eley, the first secretary of the Rhododendron Society and a subscriber to George Forrest's plant-hunting expeditions in China and Tibet. Rupert and Sara have replanted many of the mature trees torn down in the gales and storms of 1987 and 1990. It is a slow task re-establishing shelter, but the spring displays of plants that would seem more secure in the West Country are proof of their own good plantsmanship. Holly and cotoneaster hedges provide berries for winter decorations, food for birds and wildlife and a formal shelter belt around the walled garden which the owners have transformed into a nursery.

For speed of establishment there is nothing to beat the Leyland cypress for handsome green walls, and fifty-five million have been planted in the United Kingdom. However, in recent years it has been the subject of many an unneighbourly dispute because, if not regularly clipped and shaped to a reasonable height of, say 1.8–2.5m/6–8ft, it becomes a huge, light-blocking tree. The result of a hybrid cross of two substantial forest conifers, the Leyland cypress displays the hallmark vigour of hybrid crosses and rushes to prodigious heights, just doing what comes naturally! In suburban situations this type of plant thuggery is frowned upon, especially if it casts dense

Without the shelter belt of trees planted by his father, Robin Compton is certain that little would have survived at Newby Hall, Yorkshire. In the Autumn Garden, the original flimsy wattle fencing has been replaced by decorative walls. Here, backed by mature hedges of amelanchier, tender plants thrive, including *Salvia uliginosa*, *S. candelabrum* and *Ozothamnus rosmarinifolius* 'Silver Jubilee'.

is clipped at least twice a year now and if the spring clipping is left too late, I wait until the nestlings have fledged!

The downside of a well-maintained Leyland hedge is that it is a greedy feeder and keeping the plants that are grown too near the hedge healthy is a battle. Irrigation and mulching will help to keep them moist, but it is better to leave the area nearest to the hedge plant-free. Instead, it can be used as an access path behind borders and other plantings. Even the hedge clippings are put to use and shredded to make a mulch for the access path.

Box is another hedge stalwart. It is good for tall, medium and low hedges and can be shaped into straight lines or whimsical topiary forms. Free-flowing cloud shapes offer the same filtering enclosure, but in a comfy way, rather like an armchair that the garden nestles up against. In herb gardens and parterres, box is the plant of choice for edging and delineating shapes. Sadly in the late twentieth century many hedges of the low-growing box, *Buxus sempervirens* 'Suffruticosa', succumbed to a fungus called *Cylindrocladium*. It is not easily visible, but its effects are seen as brown patches on leaves and black streaking on stems. Eventually the leaves fall off, making the plant helpless and the hedge very ugly. At The Old Vicarage, Hill, Gloucestershire (illustrated on page 223), the Longstaffs had to replace their box hedges with the more resistant *Buxus sempervirens*.

Evergreens have their upsides and downsides too. *Lonicera nitida*, one of the smallest, neatest-leaved, shrubby hedging plants, makes a dense hedge yet grows so vigorously that it needs to be cut two or three times during the growing season. At Shore Hall in Essex it gives stylish shelter but Denny Swete rues the day it was planted because of the high level of maintenance – four cuts a year is what

shade across neighbouring gardens.

At Holly Cottage, my ½-acre garden in Suffolk, I was the inheritor of an 18m/60ft run of very unruly and over-grown Leyland cypresses. Kind cuts were made and in no time their height had been reduced so that, while the hedge continued to provide shelter from south-westerly winds, its upper limit is just below the line of evergreen and deciduous shrubs that soften the relentless green of its coniferous foliage. It filters the wind and provides privacy. In addition it is a haven for wildlife, small birds diving into it for cover in danger, and in nesting time it becomes a twittering, shrieking mass of small mouths waiting for the next morsel from worn-out parent birds. It

ABOVE At Holly Cottage, Suffolk, tall perennials such as *Lysimachia* 'Firecracker', *Thalictrum aquilegiifolium*, lilies, lupins and *Digitalis lutea* send flower spires skywards without recourse to supports, thanks to a neatly trimmed Leyland cypress hedge, plus a shelter belt of mature hedgerow trees. The heated greenhouse is the protector of countless seed-lings in spring, particularly of basil, a herb that Barbara Segall cannot do without. It is also the overwintering quarters of tender lavenders and sage, as well as four standard lemon verbenas and an olive tree.

Plant protection

Where a few bushy twigs are left on the lawn for a few weeks over winter you will see that the grass grows greener and stronger – a simple demonstration of how reducing wind speed warms a localized area.

This natural means of providing protection can be used to the gardener's advantage; for example by surrounding autumn-sown hardy annual flower and vegetable seedlings such as sweet peas, cornflowers and broad beans with twiggy sticks from November to March. On a larger scale, taller sticks arranged wigwam fashion around frost-tender, woody perennials will give several degrees of frost protection. Pushing dry leaves around the base of the plant between the sticks gives an even greater temperature lift.

Avoid wrapping polythene and plastic sheets around plants in winter, as they hold moisture, heat up rapidly in sunny spells and increase the chance of damage to soft roots. Instead, use a man-made woven material, sold as horticultural fleece, which breathes and gives drier, safer frost protection.

In spring both fleece and clear polythene sheet may be used to warm the soil. Strong plants growing beneath them will lift the cover as they grow – this is a good way to harvest early potatoes. Be careful when covering newly sown seeds with translucent mulches, however, as emerging seedlings such as carrot can be scorched in a few hours of bright sunlight. It is safer to support the mulch on wire hoops to give a larger volume of air above the seedlings.

Once they reach the desired height to give protection, quick-growing hedge plants, such as Leyland cypress, privet and thorn, are easily, and safely, controlled with growth retardant. Cut hedges in May and spray with Cutlass. It shortens the length of stem between leaves and makes the hedge denser, thus doubling the period of time between trimmings and halving the workload.

this vigorous hedging plant demands to keep it in trim.

With its wonderful spring transformation from old leaves and new buds to a crinkly state of fresh, tender leaf, beech is a delight through the summer and fires up in autumn, but its almost overnight loss of old leaf in spring may make it the butt of the leaf sweeper's temper. Like beech, hornbeam, another admirable hedging plant, will fill your leaf-litter bays to the brim in spring.

Maintaining the hedge, whether it is of ramping Leyland cypress or leafy beech, is part of the annual round of garden work, and a well-kept hedge will not become bare at its skirts, as Leylands are prone to do, thus nullifying its enclosing properties somewhat. It is the maintenance that may dictate just which plants you choose for enclosure.

Of course, once you have your hedge in place, you may be driven by some manipulative imperative to give it more than just a straightforward clip. Straight-topped, wedge-shaped hedges are the norm, but castellated battlements are possible, as are round tops, and some gardeners go further, leaving promising shoots unclipped. Then, like some lesser Michelangelo of the topiary shears, they can clip a whimsy in the shape of a peacock, squirrel or architectural finial, to individualize their enclosure.

Cold comfort

Although the soil in a sheltered garden may not be frozen as deeply as in an exposed area, the fact that you have successfully filtered out the wind may be a factor in creating frost pockets. Frosty air tends to roll downhill into hollows and to well up, like water in a dam, against solid objects such as hedges, walls and fences, damaging plants that are above the barrier.

At Magnolia House (illustrated on pages 137 and 222), Suffolk, Mark Rumary finds that the privacy and shelter provided by high brick walls (in places up to 3.6m/12ft) are a mixed blessing. The total enclosure that these mellow walls offer to his relatively small garden area has distinct disadvantages. As garden owners of similarly smallish, walled properties will know, solid brick walls create additionally turbulent eddies. But at Magnolia House the high walls make it impossible for extremes of cold or hot air to escape, thus creating frost pockets in winter and hot spots in summer. As a result temperatures inside either drop or rise far in excess of the temperatures beyond the walls. Mark deals with the situation by protecting tender plants in winter, either bringing them in or covering them *in situ*. To help parched moisture-loving plants through the summer he waters well, applies thick mulches to conserve moisture and keeps the soil in good condition so that plants have a healthy start. Shelter-belt trees would improve the situation greatly, but in the small space available such a strategy is a non-starter.

If the barrier is of living plants, thinning or removing part of the windbreak can help cold air to drift further downhill away from the garden. The absence of air movement tends to increase the duration of frosts, adding extra incentive to choose a permeable wind barrier rather than a solid one. And you can make a hedge earn its keep in every way, even when you have to maintain it. A fitting end for foliage and branches cut from the hedge is recycling as an anti-frost blanket for border-line plants that need extra winter protection. You can use laurel, conifer, lonicera or any other evergreen plants that need trimming as you do your autumn clean-up. Push the stems into the ground and fluff the foliage around the plant in need of protection – it works and it blends well into the garden's winter look.

Shelter for privacy

Shelter brings with it tranquillity and privacy and in many gardens exposure is not confined to climate. In some cases it reveals ugly views and unappealing neighbours. It can also expose you and your garden's outdoor living areas to the unwanted and uninvited gaze of passers-by – even, in the case of The Crossing House at Shepreth, to that of commuters on the Kings Cross-to-Cambridge railway. Margaret and Doug Fuller and John Marlar are devoted

to their garden and even though eight trains an hour whizz by, they seem hardly to notice. Perhaps it is that Doug is the former crossing keeper and the trains are part of their life, or perhaps exposure can simply be avoided by the distraction – or is it abstraction that these enthusiasts feel. I like to think that the commuters are calmed and distracted too by the wonderful seasonal entertainment of colour from bulbs, trees, shrubs and herbaceous plants that they catch a tempting glimpse of as they speed through Cambridge-shire to and from home.

It may be that you need a barrier between the garden and a noisy street or simply want to screen from view the areas that you want to enjoy for sitting and entertaining. A light screening of trees such as one or two birches (*Betula pendula* or, in wet soils, *B. pubescens*), will help to create a delicate filter between you and views or neighbours. Birches are deciduous, shapely trees and although they will provide an effective lace-like curtain between you and the offending view and/or the neighbours, they won't appear to take up much space, nor will they dominate the site where you plant them.

For country gardens, hurdles woven out of wattle, willow, wicker, bamboo and heather are as attractive and effective as they are expensive. They are good-looking enough, however, to leave unadorned by plants, merely to serve their semi-permeable, enclosing purposes. The ultimate in woven shelters can be seen at Ryton Organic Gardens in Warwickshire – a weave of living willow twigs. These root very quickly, growing to form a thin 1m/3ft barrier in a year, and are a decorative solution for screening off unsightly areas of the garden. Of course they should not be planted near to house walls, as willow roots are notorious for unseating foundations and heaving walls.

Pergolas and arbours are the meeting points of plant and hard-landscaping solutions to exposure. A well-constructed pergola will support climbers that provide shelter from sun, prying eyes and to an extent, once clothed with plants, from wind. Pergolas and arbours offer sheltered sitting areas as well. Ann James at the Thumbit in Suffolk, describes the wide pergola at the side of the cottage as 'multifunctional'. It supports roses, provides shade for seating, gives protection from wind, screens neighbouring sheds and offers a route through the garden.

ABOVE The ¼-acre garden at The Crossing House, Cambridgeshire, is exposed to the gaze of countless high-speed eyes but Margaret Fuller (seen on page 28 with her NGS award trowel) gardens

undisturbed. In July a border by the railway has evening primroses and deep red holly-hocks where the beds are full of crocuses, aconites, snowdrops and hellebores in spring.

RIGHT Sheared and shaped so that they are more architecture than plant, the yew bulwarks, planted at right angles to the brick walls that line the double borders at Arley Hall, Cheshire, provide protection from wind

and weather for magnificent stands of sky-blue delphiniums, giant scotch thistle and blowsy heads of opium poppies. They also offer punctuation and rhythm to a long border.

Helen Yemm

Rabbit talk

As big as dogs, as bold as brass, cavorting all over the garden – when we said goodbye to mains drainage and street lamps, we said hello to **RABBITS**.

At first we would stamp our feet, clap our hands, mutter about an air gun and applaud **Mr Grumpy**, the cat, who was partial to frequent baby bunny breakfasts. And then it dawned on us that this was a real war, and if we seriously wanted to replant this drought-damaged, rabbit-ravaged garden, we would simply have to fence the area close to the house that we cared about, and protect individual plants or plant rabbit-proof ones beyond.

Largely concealed behind a holly hedge, the fence was built using 90cm/ 3ft-wide 2.5cm/1in gauge chicken wire, with the bottom 30cm/1ft buried horizontally under the turf on the rabbits' side. Picket gates were meshed at the base and kept shut. We have become accustomed to living under siege, and it works – so far. (As I write, dusk approaches. Oh horrors – have I left a gate open somewhere?)

Outside the fence in Rabbitland, most damage is done in spring. Similarly afflicted gardeners leave old shoes around, scatter human hair, or construct

miniature fences made of string soaked in creosote (which rabbits detest). I put my trust in physical barriers: trunks of new trees wear plastic spiral guards, and unobtrusive chicken-wire fencelets around roses in the rough orchard grass protect vital new shoots from the nasty nibblers. I have also devised a method of making anti-rabbit cloches by moulding chicken wire into domes around (ironically) my salad spinner – much easier than making them 'freehand' – to put over special favourites in my bog garden. It all sounds most unsightly, but – like stakes in the border – everything 'vanishes' in high summer.

So far, so good. Unprotected buddlejas, azaleas, viburnums, dogwoods and various elders have remained untouched, and our rabbits thankfully have no taste for primroses, bluebells, ox-eye daisies, campions and other wild essentials. But then, nor will they eat ground elder, nettles, bindweed, thistles and hogweed.

Such shelters, out of wind, rain and sun, provide the gardener with an additional, almost intangible benefit. Even the most basic shelter offers a place for reflection and separation from the garden – a place where you can take a moment to stand back and 'see' the garden, almost as if you were seeing it for the first time.

Non-plant enclosures

Although roof-top gardens endure a buffeting from winds at a higher level, they share similar conditions with patios and courtyards. All can become oases of calm through the use of a variety of non-plant and non-living plant materials, some of which may be able to support plants.

Trellis is the most open of the non-plant screens. Being a lightweight, rather flimsy material, it needs to be securely fixed to posts if it is to carry the weight of climbing plants. Attached to the tops of walls you share with neighbours, trelliswork panels offer a little extra height of filtered screening and, when climbers such as honeysuckle and clematis have twined and twisted their stems through, the garden area will have added privacy.

Post-and-rail fencing, although more open than walls and timber fencing, will be similarly dual-purpose in effect, reducing wind damage and offering support to plants. In a country garden split chestnut paling may be more in keeping than chain-link fencing, often used in urban settings.

Bamboo panels and rolls of lightweight bamboo screening can be fixed to walls in a similar way to trellis, but are not suited to supporting plants. As they are permeable they will help to reduce wind action and improve shelter. Although lightweight, they are not as open as trellising, so will cut out a percentage of light to the area, which may restrict your choice of plants.

ABOVE At Ketleys, East Sussex, Helen Yemm and Chris Craib keep meshed gates closed from dusk to dawn. In the herb and vegetable patch and in borders near the house, they are free to grow rabbit caviar. Outside the gates, wildflowers take their chances along with shrubs and roses 'pruned' the rabbit way – all new outward-facing shoots neatly removed. Delicacies such as *Lobelia cardinalis* in the bog garden are individually meshed.

RIGHT Lines of shrubs act as baffles against fierce westerlies to create a sheltered corner at Windy Ridge, Yorkshire. The garden is on a one in three slope down to winter water meadows and is inclined to flood.

Jacqueline and John Giles find that in a normal year most plants survive but in the autumn and winter of 2000–1 parts of the garden were under 2m/7ft of water for up to three weeks, resulting in losses.

If you prefer the permanence of a wall to enclose a garden, it will require secure and substantial foundations and you need to remember that solid walls will add to the problems already caused by wind. If you can put in a wall which has a gaps in it, a semi-open arrangement of brick-work, leaving 40–50 per cent of the structure open or gapped, you will be able to reduce the effects of the wind. If not, there will still be turbulent, windy eddies in the garden.

However, if the garden invaders that you wish to repel are of a four-footed nature, you will need to put in place a secure rabbit-proof fencing system. This means digging the fence material in about 60cm/2ft below ground level, and laying the buried bottom section parallel to the ground, at right angles to the upright section. This prevents rabbits digging their way underneath.

The benefits of enclosure

Windbreaks and hedges offer many benefits besides the reduction of the wind's drying, chilling and damaging effects. Among them is the raising of the soil temperature during the day which, especially in spring, helps to get seedlings and transplants better established. Shelter belts and hedges will also assist in soil stability and prevent erosion, often problematic on windy, exposed sites.

In addition shelter provided by hedges and non-plant enclosures offers opportunities for gardeners to grow a range of shade-loving plants that might not have suc-ceeded in the windy, sun-burned site prior to enclosure. Other effects, some less tangible and others incidental, add considerable impact to any garden. Hedges create

havens where colour, light and fragrance hold sway. The undisturbed air within the garden room seems to capture the perfume of flowers and aroma of foliage at head-height, like a herb-filled pomander or nosegay, ready for you to bury your nose in its wonderful bouquet of scents.

Well-maintained green walls, like those at Anglesey Abbey lining herbaceous borders and dividing sections of the garden, become the perfect background for plants, allowing herbaceous plants such as delphinium and *Crambe cordifolia* to grow to prodigious heights in a hostile, windswept and once-open Cambridgeshire land-scape. They are also the green architecture against which classical statuary nestles, appearing to be set in carved niches. Anglesey's hedges are 4km/2½ miles long and the combined annual clippings of this green framework weighs 15 tonnes.

At Sissinghurst in Kent similarly well-kept hedges hold monochromatic garden schemes together. The green walls of the hedge become the foil for plant interior-exterior decoration. Herbaceous perennials look good against this green background where the colours seem to strengthen and deepen.

Surprise is another of the intangible elements that await transformed exposed gardens. Once sheltered within its plant walls, the open aspect of an exposed garden is forever put aside, and the element of surprise or curiosity about what may be around the corner prevails.

When exposure has been combated, the contained world of the enclosed garden is yours to enjoy, free from turbulent battering by rude wind and weather … but no doubt, as is the nature of all things gardenish, some other problem will arise!

Plants for exposed gardens

Trees, shrubs & bamboos

Elaeagnus × ebbingei. This is a prince among shrubs, with a height and spread of 15ft/4.5m. Exquisite, scaly stems of a curious, silvery ginger arc out and become clothed with equally pretty, scaly, silver leaves. In autumn its demure flowers offer sweet perfume.

Hebe pinguifolia 'Pagei'. Tough enough to survive in exposed conditions and attractive with it, this hebe is a useful, low-growing (15–30cm/6–12in) shrub. Its intensely grey-green leaves are neatly arranged on short stems and when it flowers in May and June its froth of pure white provides a confetti-like shower at ground level. It grows equally well in sun or shade and can be used as a ground cover, an informal edge or hedging plant, or as an accent at the front of a border.

Ilex × altaclerensis. This holly is a great asset in exposed and seaside gardens. In addition it is capable of growing lustily in polluted situations and areas of meteorological challenge. Although slow to establish, as a windbreak or a specimen tree it is hard to beat. Vigorous growth and attractive, virtually spineless leaves are among its attributes. It can reach a height of 15m/50ft. 'Golden King' is a variegated cultivar and, despite its name, is a female holly bearing red berries.

Juniperus squamata 'Blue Carpet'. This is a ground hugger, capable of hanging on to a windy bank and smothering it in glaucous foliage. In time it can cover an area up to 6–8m/20–26ft across.

Lavandula angustifolia 'Hidcote'. A neat and well-shaped lavender, the leaves are the attractive, silvery grey of the species *L. angustifolia*, but more compact and better-looking in winter. The flowers are produced on uniform stems and are of a deep purple.

Olearia × haastii. The New Zealand daisy bush (3m/10ft) is a trooper in terrible conditions. It will tolerate wind and pollution and, perhaps because of this, many miserable specimens are seen in nasty locations. However, it is a real treasure when treated well. It is evergreen and unassuming, then it flowers, bursting into a shower of scented, white daisies in mid-summer. The undersides of the leaves are felted white.

Ozothamnus rosmarinifolius. This shrub (3m/10ft) is extremely beautiful for a warm, dry, open situation. The leaves are narrow and needle-like, reminiscent of rosemary. It is at its most dazzling when the pinky red corymbs are in bud. They persist for a couple of weeks before revealing their fragrant, white flowerheads.

Pleioblastus auricomus. Variably variegated with a tendency towards yellow, this little bamboo brings light to shady areas. Cutting it to the ground each winter encourages fresh, young growth in spring. It may burn in very open, windy locations, but despite its delicate and slender appearance it is pretty tough.

Rosa 'Fru Dagmar Hastrup'. Anyone who has walked the East Anglian coastline in winter will appreciate what a north-easterly wind can do to a human being's ears. Imagine, then, a plant that seems positively to thrive in these circumstances – how perverse! The rugosa rose is that plant. Roses are not supposed to like poor, gravelly soil; these do, and how. The foliage is always in peak condition, rough and shiny and characterful. Then there are the flowers – delicate, single pink with crinkly, paper-thin petals like moiré silk, a delectable scent and big autumn hips.

Salix fargesii. If you have the space, this willow will expand to fill it, growing to a height and spread of 3m/10ft, and in the process will offer year-round delights. Its spring shoots are green at first, maturing to a ruddy bronze. In winter its striking, red buds encase soft catkins. Once the winter show of male catkins is over, the female catkins dance in the wind at the same time as the foliage bursts along the stems.

Sasa veitchii. A splendid, slow-growing bamboo (1.5m/5ft), *S. veitchii* is ideal for running through a shelter belt. For a Japanese feel, mix it with evergreen pines and rhododendrons. It will cope with shade and damp ditches and is particularly lovely when the leaves develop white edges, giving it a painted look.

Spartium junceum. No exposed garden should forgo the endless delights of Spanish broom. Originating in Mediterranean regions, it does like warm, dry soil but is generally uncomplaining and very tough. By the sea it is a lovely sight; in urban situations it has great charm. Flowering from June to the first frost, it offers a dancing display of fragrant, yellow, pea-like flowers. It will reach 3m/10ft and can be trimmed in spring.

Tamarix. The thin, wispy stems of tamarisk allow any amount of wind through them, withstand gales and yet allow you glimpses of the view. *T. tetrandra* has pink, frothy flowers in spring. *T. ramosissima* flowers in autumn. Eventually these plants become small trees, 6m/20ft tall. They are never a nuisance, as they cast virtually no shade and yet create shelter.

Perennials

Aconitum carmichaelii 'Arendsii'. Thriving at the woodland fringe, aconites are ideal planted at the base of a shelter belt. Tall (1.5–1.8m/5–6ft), robust and imposing, with beautifully structured autumn flowers, but do not expect these to withstand a windy corridor.

Artemisia ludoviciana. A clump-forming perennial (1.2m/4ft) this has woolly white leaves early in the season and in an exposed situation will stay that way. Originating from the steppes and plains, it seems purpose-designed for a tough life. If planted in soil that is too rich, it turns a dreary green.

Bergenia cordifolia 'Purpurea'. Leathery bergenia has had a tough time of late, falling from favour as an overused edging plant for 'difficult' situations. It can cope with hard times as it comes from Siberia and in the right place will reward you with healthy foliage that glows in winter sunshine and spring flowers that are much undervalued. *B. c.* 'Purpurea' (45cm/18in) is one of the best, with leaves tinted purple and madder in the winter cold and tall spikes of pale rosy flowers in spring.

Brachyglottis (Dunedin Group) 'Sunshine'. One of numerous New Zealand plants that are tolerant of harsh conditions and a group worthy of further exploration, this is a very worthwhile backbone plant, growing to 1.5m/5ft tall. Sometimes the arrival of the sunshine-yellow flowers in June is a shock on a plant with softly textured, silvery-green, oval leaves. The yellow is a cheery shade but, for many, it may seem at odds with the moonlight tone and texture of the foliage.

Crambe maritima. Known as sea kale, this has a double life. If the stems are blanched, it becomes a vegetable for adventurous gourmets. If allowed to grow naturally, it reveals its 'tough-as-old-boots' character, thriving on gravelly surfaces even in the most inhospitable winds. The leaves are glaucous and leathery with attractive, fluted edges. From this beach-hugging base rises a 60cm/2ft tall mound of frothy, scented, white flowers, mimicking the foam on the waves.

Dianthus 'Gran's Favourite'. Most pinks are capable of surviving extreme conditions and have proved amenable to breeding without losing this inherent characteristic. 'Gran's Favourite' is an old-fashioned form with a low, spreading habit and clove-scented, raspberry-ripple-laced flowers.

Eryngium giganteum. Silver sea holly is deservedly popular as a border plant and is a superstar in difficult, windswept locations. It self-seeds randomly, providing unlooked-for but welcome combinations. It is at home in poor, gravelly or sandy soils with little winter wet, but also grows on heavy clay with added grit. It is a 'go-anywhere' plant, growing to 75cm/2½ft high.

Kniphofia triangularis. The red-hot poker is indigenous to South Africa and occupies areas as diverse as damp meadows and streamsides through to rocky banks and open grassland. It is a strong grower, provided it has moisture and a reasonable degree of warmth. It grows well on the western seaboard in Britain. *K. triangularis* (60–90cm/2–3ft) is a pretty, slender variety with coral-red racemes of flower. It is subtler than the big bruisers, such as *K.* 'Prince Igor'.

Rudbeckia fulgida var. *sullivantii* 'Goldsturm'. This moist meadow or woodland-edge plant from the USA (illustrated on page 288) is a thrilling shade of sou'wester yellow. The shorter, bushier stems of 'Goldsturm' (45cm/18in) make it more tolerant of exposure than other rudbeckias. Mass with like-minded compatriots to give a late-summer show.

Stachys byzantina. Well-known as lamb's ears, this soft and furry edging plant (30–38cm/12–15in) has silver, thickly felted leaves and, in summer, pale lavender flower spikes that moderate hot colours of neighbouring border plants. Very strong-growing, if left to romp freely it will form an impenetrable mat. *S. b.* 'Silver Carpet' is a smaller (12cm/5in), non-flowering form.

Brachyglottis (Dunedin Group) 'Sunshine' provides protection for *Salvia sclarea* var. *sclarea* at Mindrum, Northumberland.

LEFT At Magnolia House, Suffolk, Mark Rumary has created a silvery focus around a sundial using the spiky *Eryngium giganteum*, *Dictamnus albus* var. *purpureus* and poppies. BELOW At Montacute House, Somerset, the 50m/164ft long yew hedge is maintained with annual clipping. RIGHT At the Old Vicarage, Hill, Gloucestershire, Kate and Andrew Longstaff's potager is enclosed by walls punctuated by a moongate – a deep, round window – framed by *Rosa* 'Sander's White Rambler', which gives tempting views of vegetables growing in beds edged with *Buxus sempervirens*.

Hundreds of NGS gardeners have devised ways to create sheltered havens and here are gardens to add to those that have inspired Barbara Segall.

Bedfordshire
Grove Lodge
High View

Bristol & South Gloucestershire
The Brake
Camers
High View
Portland Lodge

Buckinghamshire
Fielding House
Hall Farm
Leap Hill
Quenington House

Cambridgeshire
Hardwicke House,
* Fen Ditton Gardens*
Mill House

Ceredigion/Cardiganshire
The Old Vicarage,
* Llangeler*
Plas Penglais University of Wales
* Aberystwyth*

Cornwall
Headland Garden
Long Cross Victorian Gardens
Manaton
St Michael's Mount, Penzance

Cumbria
Chapelside
Holker Hall
Tomarobandy Gardens

Denbighbighshire & Colwyn
Arfryn

Derbyshire
Monksway

Devon
Andrews Corner
Churchpark Cottage
Honeyway Farm
Newton Farm
Southcombe House

Dorset
Chesil Gallery
Holworth Farmhouse

223

Exposure

Jinny Blom

with expert insights by
John Brookes
Noel Kingsbury

11 Wild effects

To my mind, there is nothing finer in our native landscape than a fully flowering apple tree up to its knees in cow parsley. It amazes me that I ever progressed from rapt adoration of this simple sight to the full-blown joys of wild gardening and, eventually, to a conviction that planting effects that emulate or improve on nature's finest achievements are what gardening is about.

At some point in history, which is almost certainly lost to us now, nature ceased to be nature and the garden was born. It is still possible in remote areas of Europe to see the functioning husbanded landscapes of old and to witness the high level of regard and attention these receive from the people who tend them. There are hedgerows, unchanged over the centuries, which on close examination reveal the skilled techniques of coppicing and clearing to protect their valuable fruit and nut crops. There are pockets of hay meadow, humming with a huge variety of plant species – cattle raised on a diet of this stuff couldn't fail to thrive. Herbs and useful plants roam wild on the hillsides. Every-day crops and medicinal plants congregate nearer to dwellings. The land, for as far as the cattle and sheep can graze it, is part of the tended scenery, part of a living chain of health and wealth. Flower meadows may be hundreds of years old, handed on through generations. A slow, regular cycle of growing, scything, drying and clearing ensures a balanced evolution. The natural landscape is liberally bestowed with plants that are a joy to behold. Gradually, perhaps, these treasures began to be collected for their own sake, to take their place by the house. Gardens began to evolve.

With increased urbanization, the jewels of nature became more and more alluring. The Victorians, for example, stripped the countryside of ferns, orchids, primroses and violets to satisfy the whims of fashion. For every sort of plant, a specific tool was created to lift it, a marvellous marketing device for the burgeoning mass gardening market. The great red-brick mansions of the newly wealthy trade families, complete with conservatory, grotto and fernery, imprisoned the tender flowers of our wild landscapes. Perhaps this mass consumerism triggered the beginnings of eco-awareness, once populations of familiar plants began to dwindle. Then mechanized farming, unrestricted use of chemicals, grubbing up of hedgerows, population explosions and encroaching built landscapes gradually completed the erosion of the very commodity which used to be the source of our bread and butter.

This, in part, explains why collectively we may feel increasingly drawn to wild planting effects in our gardens. Perhaps even more than farmers, gardeners are fully in touch with the diurnal motion of the seasons and feel that subtle sense of rhythm is being swamped. Whether we are trying to create beautiful, wild and wilful pictures with plants, evolving a modest area for our own absorbing interest or cultivating arks to carry fragile species through to the future, gardening can redress that sense of loss. Even if our goal is to strike out as modernist gardeners, thrusting forward into a bold, new tomorrow, the flowery wayside is more than a romantic vision of lost pleasures.

Ah, wildflower meadows

When daisies pied and violets blue,
And lady smocks all silver white,
And cuckoo buds of yellow hue
Do paint the meadows with delight.
WILLIAM SHAKESPEARE

How delightful is the sight of a wildflower meadow and how impossibly trying for the impatient gardener. Meadows require a simple but unavoidable maintenance regime and the curbing of wild desires to recreate unseasonably complex combinations; something that once caught your eye in a tapestry in the Cluny Museum in Paris, for example. Being seduced by fields of nodding, dew-spangled snake's-head fritillaries is dangerous – at least until you have a firm grasp of the basics.

The best way to understand wildflower meadow gardening and its vagaries is to visit gardens and quiz the owners. Pam Lewis at Sticky Wicket in Dorset has devoted the last thirty-five years to understanding grasslands and is passionate about meadows. She started creating her current meadow in 1996, using seed collected from a local 'mother' meadow, a unique and important piece of land that includes 180 species. Pam's 'baby' has thirty species from the donor meadow and *Dactylorhiza* orchids imported from another meadow that was threatened with destruction. Many more species will appear in time. An important point to remember is never to take plants from the wild. The purpose of wildflower planting is to conserve what little is left and not to cause further destruction through well-meaning but ill-thought-out and, in some cases, illegal attempts at conservation.

Pam scraped off 15–20cm/6–8in of the richly fertile Dorset loam to provide suitable conditions for her

PRECEDING PAGES A perfect evocation of the naturalism at which British gardeners excel, in the gardens of Westwell Manor, Oxfordshire. Only the gate, half buried in the hedge, indicates that this is not just a wild wayside but a thoughtfully considered garden area, adjacent to crisp yew hedges and topiary specimens. The drawing of Flintham Hall, Nottinghamshire, is from the cover of the 1996 Yellow Book.

meadow and used the topsoil as a 'fertile mound for the goats to graze'. She had tried in vain to create meadows on the fecund local soil and, in the end, felt there was no option but to strip it. As a dedicated advocate of England's nearly extinct meadows and grasslands, Pam feels we must all be encouraged to try to have even a tiny patch of our own in order to foster not only the plants but also our understanding of this intricate web of life. 'All you need', she says, 'is an open, sunny area.' The rest, as can be seen by a visit to Sticky Wicket, is magical: yellow rattle, cornflowers, orchids and myriad other species jostle contentedly together. Seeing them makes me happy, as I feel certain that their custodians will see to it that they survive for as long as possible.

Visits to gardens and ancient protected meadows local to you will offer inspiration and advice that is likely be specific to you and your requirements. At Vann in Surrey early camassias and fritillaries are enchanting. Winllan in Cardiganshire is owned by botanists who are clearly devoted to their wild garden and very willing to share their knowledge. The meadow at The Old Vicarage, East Ruston, in Norfolk, is a pageant of annual colour in drought-prone East Anglia. Inspiration is free to the observant traveller. On my regular trips up the M1, I am thrilled to see miles of newly laid hedges, with thick carpets of primroses studding the man-made banks in spring. Railway sidings provide conditions stingy enough to allow abundant flowerings of wild lupins and reseda, and pulling in to Liverpool's Lime Street Station is made memorable by these artless beauties.

The uncrowned king of domestic meadows, Christopher Lloyd, at Great Dixter in Sussex, has tended

ABOVE Combined with the dense flowerheads of *Eryngium agavifolium*, cow parsley demonstrates its value as a garden plant at Yews Farm in Somerset, giving a hint of wild meadow in a modern border.

his areas of 'rough grass' all his life – in fact he did not even plant them. His mother's inspiration was William Robinson's *The English Flower Garden* and Christopher has written that her taste for wild gardening within the more formal architectural elements at Dixter was 'probably derived from Robinson'. It was she who started growing snake's-head fritillaries in the (well-drained) upper moat and planted all the spare polyanthus to make the first meadow garden. Elsewhere, from spring to autumn, there are areas studded with crocus and narcissus, ox-eye daisies, red clover and hawkbits, wood anemones, camassias and sweet grasses.

One of the casualties of the loss of old meadows is the orchid. A friend explained how problematic and particular the germination process is for orchids: the seed relies on a symbiotic relationship with a fungus present in the soil; only after the two come into contact can the seed become viable and germinate. It may take years before the plant shows any top growth, let alone flowers. How many meadows will sit undisturbed in order for these processes to be realized? At Great Dixter green-winged orchids (*Orchis morio*), early purples (*O. mascula*) and common spotted orchids (*Dactylorhiza × fuchsii*) have been growing in abundance since the 1930s. Christopher Lloyd says, 'One thing I have learned is that you can expect to be able to naturalize the species that would grow wild in your locality, but not those that come from quite different habitats, like, in our case, the bee, fragrant and pyramidal orchids from calcium-rich soils.'

Meadows in gardens need careful siting to give of their best. I love to see long, flowery meadow grasses contained within a formal setting. Christopher Gibbs, who gardened until recently at The Manor House, Clifton Hampden, Oxfordshire, made wonderful wild grassy areas. One of the best features is a room of tightly clipped hornbeam with a mound of wild grasses, studded with cowslips, almost filling the space. The atmosphere created by strong shapes coupled with these simplest of native flowers is really exciting. He, and his thoughtful and experienced gardener Terry Johnson, have also experimented with succession bulb planting in long grass. This is a fraught exercise, by all accounts, and is best approached by trial and error until a balance appears. 'Nothing later than narcissi,' says Terry,

referring to the summer-flowering long-grass lozenges beyond the pergola. He also made the salutary observation that it took a great deal of manpower to cope with the mowing and clearing of the meadow. Both the cutting of long grass, with machines less capable than the scythe, and the arduous task of clearing by hand, make this area of the garden a significant luxury.

Sowing and reaping

It is a recent affectation to include meadows in gardens, rather than as part of farming practice. Grazing animals are adept at keeping grasses short, thus allowing flowering plants a less competitive environment in which to thrive. Pernicious weeds are also controlled in this way. Without the necessary animals it is a question of replicating these effects by hand or machine.

LEFT Electric blue *Eryngium planum* and magenta *Allium sphaerocephalon* conjure an image of jewel-encrusted embroidery in one of Pam Lewis's wild plantings at Sticky Wicket in Dorset.

ABOVE The cuckoo-pint or lords and ladies, *Arum maculatum*, is one of many native plants that have been allowed to naturalize at Stowe Landscape Gardens in Buckinghamshire. As well as grand vistas and manicured

lawns, Stowe has wilder areas, such as William Kent's Elysian Fields and the Grecian Valley – a meadow full of massed cowslips and other wildflowers which dates back to 1746 and 'Capability' Brown.

The purveyors of meadow seed mixes offer a range to suit most soil types but wildflowers generally thrive only on impoverished soils – otherwise they are swamped by vigorous grasses. Chalky downland, rocky hillsides, maritime cliffs and gravelly soils all offer the necessary spartan conditions. To re-create these in a garden where the topsoil is rich and deep, or high in nutrients, as is clay, takes some preparation. Reducing the fertility of your soil involves stripping away topsoil until only a thin scraping covers the subsoil. Some gardeners recommend reducing fertility by growing potatoes for a couple of seasons.

The fundamental rule is to clear your allotted patch entirely of weeds. Ideally keep it weed-free for a year prior to sowing in the autumn. Then, depending on how much space you have and your ultimate aims, you can sow either a permanent meadow or an annual cornfield mix as bright as a child's drawing. A meadow mix for general use on a broad range of soils will be weighted 80 per cent grass species to 20 per cent flowers. The grass mix will be of fairly fine, slow-growing wild grasses, such as common bent (*Agrostis capillaris*), crested dog tail (*Cynosurus cristatus*) and red fescue (*Festuca rubra*). The more vigorous species, such as perennial rye grass (*Lolium perenne*) and rough meadow grass (*Poa trivialis*), are generally excluded as they may swamp the growth of gentler species in the vital early years while the meadow establishes.

The first year after sowing will see an astonishing explosion of growth. This first flush, in a perennial meadow, tends to be a show of annuals and pioneer species, like waist-high perennial ox-eye daisies, and will give way over successive years to a quieter and less volatile evolution of the perennial seed bank. Essentially, for the first year or so it is necessary to hand weed, or spray out, pernicious weeds such as docks, thistles, nettles and so forth. These commonly afflict the richer soils. An annual hay cut in July (after checking that seeds of desirable plants have been shed), followed by hard mowing or grazing in late summer and autumn on rich soils, helps keep the weeds and grass species in check.

Yellow rattle (*Rhinanthus minor*) is the meadow maker's companion. Sowing fresh seed into the meadow in autumn allows this pretty plant to establish its parasitic relationship with vigorous grasses and hold back their

Wild carrot (*Daucus* sp.) sways in the breeze among *Lychnis coronaria* and *Verbena bonariensis* in the Cretan meadow at The Garden House, Devon. More than 350 different species grow in the undulating landscape of slightly raised beds covering a ¼-acre area. Rather than those that grow in Crete, Keith Wiley's choice of plants is dictated by the exposed, north-facing slope, high rainfall and acid loam.

choking effects. It goes without saying that a meadow never should be fed. Over time the fertility level will drop and the flower bank become richer for it.

It is best to let things settle down for a few years before adding bulbs and plugs of meadow plants such as cowslips and greater knapweed. Once you have an instinctive understanding of the rhythm of life in the meadow, you will know what to add, and when. Then your mowing regime will include a close cut in November, before the young snouts of early spring bulbs are peeping through the turf.

Improving nature

'Should one mix together, in one's decorative arrangements, wild and cultivated flowers?' It seems to me that the answer in brief is: 'Why not, if they look well together?'
CONSTANCE SPRY

There would be little point in gardening if we did not try to emulate, or improve on, nature's finer moments. There is mounting interest in the possibilities of using herbaceous plants with our more naturalistic shrubs and trees outside the confines of the herbaceous border.

The unwitting advocate of this approach in Britain is John Brookes. He has taught generations of gardeners through his lectures and books to think carefully about their garden's design. John's passion for highly structured Modernist architecture found its 'loose overflowing' when he worked in the offices of Sylvia Crowe. He put the two together in his own inimitable style – 'discipline under looseness' is his own succinct description. He found his gardening match in Joyce Robinson who owned and gardened at Denmans in Sussex. Together they created a garden outside the usual constraints of lawns, box hedges and paths. Its evolution since the late 1970s demonstrates the maturing of John's modern approach. Claiming an un-English lack of interest in flowers and colour combining, he started by focusing on leaf shape and texture. Becoming more and more fascinated by native landscapes and plants in natural settings, he began to build up a carefully thought-out framework of trees and shrubby plants and to mass garden plants to reinterpret the surrounding landscape. These are the ideal background for the grasses, such as the elegant *Cortaderia richardii*, teamed with

perovskias and eryngiums. Elsewhere the planting is cool lemon and silver, white and acid green, the colours singing out in the deeper green shadows of the surrounding trees. John teaches the value of remembering that our British landscape is one of trees and shrubs, not just flowers and grasses. He uses free-flowing gravel shapes, where appropriate plants, well chosen for their beauty and structure, are allowed to self-seed randomly. Gardening within this framework is a looser, more intuitive activity. The thoughtful removal of self-seeded plants allows the picture to change subtly each year.

Had John Brookes concentrated only on the fleeting beauty of herbaceous plants and intuitive structuring of the landscaping, there would be a lot less of a legacy for the future. There is something in the atmosphere evoked at Denmans which hints at the flora of other countries. John is a great traveller and his feeling for alien plant communities, particularly those of South America, echoes in his own garden.

Back at Sticky Wicket, as well as sublime meadows, there are wonderful plays of colour in a broad and unbridled area of mixed planting, using rich magentas, soft pinks and electric blue. The egg-shaped heads of *Allium sphaerocephalon* combine with eryngium, salvias and opium poppies to create an effect as rich as the robes of a Russian Orthodox priest or the lavish ceiling of a tzarist stateroom. Nothing like this could ever appear in nature surely? Yet the overall effect is of an utterly bewitching mythical landscape.

Mannered wild planting

Oh give me land, lots of land, under starry skies above,
But don't fence me in.
Let me ride through the wide open country that I love,
But don't fence me in.
COLE PORTER

The world-famous, highly photogenic style of mannered wild plantings pioneered by the American duo, Wolfgang Oehme and James Van Sweden, has influenced a more natural approach on an international scale. Great drifts of miscanthus, interwoven with rudbeckias, calamagrostis, sedums and eupatorium, form huge, billowing masses of

In sun-baked gravel, pale pink *Watsonia merianiae*, lemon yellow evening primroses and purple foxgloves are behaving as nature intended under the guiding eye and hand of John Brookes at Denmans in Sussex.

Trees and shrubs form the permanent backdrop to the pictures John paints with ephemeral flowers. Naturalistic plant combinations are capable of unexpected depths of colour.

Thinning nature out

The first thing I learned in my natural gardening experience was not to feed, which was against my whole previous experience and training. What I do is to improve the water-holding capacity of the soil by conditioning it with the addition of organic matter in autumn. Then I select plants that prefer my type of soil. I have learned a lot about them by walking my dogs twice a day locally and really seeing what grows hereabouts. I don't necessarily then plant natives alone – many are terribly rampant, though some I do use.

We have such an amazing range of deciduous trees and shrubs, and some evergreens too, and we should use them. I'm getting just a tiny bit tired of prairie flowers and grasses. The technique of using them is fascinating, but we need to interpret this with our own rich palette of woody plant material. Then all the herbs love my gravel, being Mediterranean, and of course I can extend my palette that way as well, being on the south coast.

I have a nagging need to use plants which have architectural shapes or have architecturally shaped leaves, which are particularly necessary in association with a building and to punctuate my wilder groupings. This runs contrary to the wilder way, but I think that there are compromises – hellebores for instance, *Euphorbia characias* subsp. *wulfenii*, iris with some grasses and so on. And obviously the site matters – an urban situation will be very different from a suburban or rural one. It is all a matter of degree.

So, rather than attempting to 'improve nature', it is more a matter of adapting to natural ways or thinning nature out. Left to its own devices, the garden would not be a habitat for me, although it might be well stocked otherwise! Just go away for a week or two and see what happens – you'll know what I mean. But suppose you left your garden for a year or two – purely hypothetically – and then saw what had gained dominance, what had come in and what gone out. I think that that might be a learning experience. For so much of what we strive to eradicate from our gardens is just the spivs, who move in quickly where they see a bit of bare earth. Work through them and you really see what nature favours you with, according to light, sun, moisture availability and soil type. It is perceiving this without the chore of doing it that gives the clue to what you can grow, and then edit that.

Instead of improving nature, I feel it is more of a working relationship, for it is still my garden and I'm still the boss!

colour and texture through the four seasons. They have adapted their style for urban planting in parks and, with greater floral detail, for many large private gardens. Inspired by the American prairies, these plantings are a fascinating evolution of a style culled from the wild. The prairies themselves are a great source of inspiration to the gardener keen on going wild. So many of our beautiful herbaceous garden plants are prairie weeds, plants such as *Echinacea, Lysimachia, Ratibida, Helianthus, Gaillardia, Liatris, Monarda, Oenothera* and *Lupinus.* Unlike a native

meadow, a prairie-style planting on rich soil will reward with a superabundant floral display. Shut your eyes and imagine the effect spreading out over thousands of acres. Spires of white veronicastrum intermingled with the mauve pokers of liatris. Buffalo grazing in the distance, surfing tidal waves of colour. Not a tree or shrub in sight.

The urge to create a garden of this kind, where the ground is covered in towering, flowering herbaceous plants and grasses, is irresistible, if space allows. At Lady Farm in Somerset, Judy and Malcolm Pearce have made a large area of prairie and steppe planting. The rolling Somerset countryside dissolves before your eyes to become a tranche of the open grasslands of Wisconsin. A sure hand and a

practised eye have combined to create a truly exciting garden. On a gentle slope there are drifts of rudbeckias mixed with great care with upright *Calamagrostis* 'Karl Foerster', white echinaceas (*E.* 'White Lustre'), wild yellow yarrows and statuesque eupatoriums. The whole effect is remarkable, beautiful and gives every appearance of being natural. The desire to ornament the planting with species not strictly from the chosen wild palette has been carefully monitored, and the inclusion of plants such as eryngium and echinops doesn't jar the picture.

At The Menagerie in Northamptonshire (illustrated on pages 43 and 49), the stylized bog garden was inspired by the stature of the American herbaceous landscape. Vast stands of *Miscanthus sacchariflorus* rustle and whisper in the wind, swathes of eupatorium, lysimachia and the wonderful rusty pink *Filipendula rubra* 'Venusta' are underplanted with *Iris sibirica*, ferns, camassias and ajuga. For structure there are large, suckering stands of *Sorbaria kirilowii*, trees in the form of the swamp cypress, *Taxodium distichum*, and shrubby ones such as the shimmering silver coyote willow, *Salix exigua*. The effect is not whimsical but bold and shapely – a garden animated by the wind and the sky. The initial intention was to build up a self-sustaining and self-mulching matrix of ornamental herbaceous plants. The unromantic reality has been that nature really is natural. Plants rot down at different rates, leaving a thatch of unsightly, tough flower stems into the next season. Leaving fallen leaves on the iris to rot down over winter provided the perfect habitat for field mice, but they also enjoyed the handy snack of fresh young shoots that appeared in spring. So, while the garden teems with life – bees, butterflies in abundance on the eupatorium, finches on the seedheads – not all of it is welcome, and the gardener has, more or less, reverted to traditional methods of clearing, mulching and selective deadheading.

ABOVE Damp areas are a treat for wild gardeners. At The Mill House in Cumbria the huge leaves of *Petasites* are artlessly mingled with luminous umbellifers, showing that a little colour goes a long way.

RIGHT The bold and the beautiful combine in the moist and fertile soil at Elm Tree Cottage, Noel Kingsbury's Herefordshire garden. *Inula racemosa* rises from a mist of *Geranium phaeum* 'Lily Lovell'

growing in rough grass. Both plants are robust enough to compete with vigorous grasses once they have been nursed through the first year or two. By July the *Inula* will have clusters of yellow daisy flowers.

OVERLEAF The prairie at Lady Farm, Somerset, is home to this brilliant fusion of *Agastache foeniculum, Echinacea, Rudbeckia, Helenium* and *Achillea*, all tied together with *Calamagrostis* 'Karl Foerster'.

NOEL KINGSBURY

Wild-style planting on fertile soil

It is easiest to grow British wildflowers on dry and infertile soil, something which many gardeners find quite counter-intuitive. But what if you want to create a wild-looking planting on fertile soil? Whilst there are ornamental natives that will flourish, such as meadowsweet and purple loosestrife, the emphasis will have to be on choosing non-native species plants. I stress species, rather than hybrids, as the double flowers, enhanced colours and flower sizes of the latter will detract from the carefree naturalistic effect that you probably want to achieve. However, many cultivars still manage to keep the elegant proportions of their wild parents.

A wild-style perennial border must be made of plants that are chosen to suit the site, which means thoroughly researching the cultural needs and the longevity of the plants. Watch out for seductive but short-lived things like the achillea varieties which usually die after the first year in a wet British winter, or plants like *Gaura lindheimeri* which are not only tender but lack the tough clump-forming habit needed to survive in a competitive growing situation. Strong-growing plants will get the most from a fertile soil, and anything less than vigorous will not survive. Late-flowering American prairie species such as solidago, aster, rudbeckia, monarda and eupatorium are a good start. Geraniums are indispensable for early-season colour. Grasses, such as miscanthus, calamagrostis and molinia are vital for the wild look.

To get a naturalistic effect, never plant in clumps. Buy multiples of a limited number of varieties you know to be reliable and aim to blend and intermingle them, getting a balance between low clump-formers, such as geraniums, and taller upright growers, like asters.

Maintenance basically consists of a late winter cut-back of dead growth, which makes valuable compost material, or which can be shredded and used as a mulch. Keeping on top of weeds is absolutely essential, with the January to May period the crucial time for doing this, before the perennials link up and cover the ground. Unless you have the time, forget 'organics', and use a glyphosate-based weedkiller. It is pretty safe and makes life much easier. Wood chip mulch helps reduce weed seed germination too.

In order to accommodate wildlife, other areas at the Menagerie are left virtually uncultivated to provide habitats for overwintering. Even in fairly small gardens it is possible to introduce a measure of calculated untidiness to encourage natural predators. It is fascinating to see how many well-known garden perennials behave when left to their own devices and take on wild and woolly characteristics. Small creatures love the warm, cosy, fibrous mats of dead foliage or the safety of hollow grass stalks. Others, such as lizards and toads, like to nest in crevices in walls and will be your best allies against slugs. Why not try an experimental area over a few seasons and see how it works?

In harmony with the landscape

On the light, rich, silt soil which collects in the flat lands at the base of the Ridgeway in Oxfordshire is a small country garden devoted to plants. The ancient, swift-flowing Letcombe Brook runs through the garden at Lower Mill and under the mill house. There has been a mill here for a thousand years. Until a few years ago, it sat in an aged orchard grazed by horses and cattle which drank at the water's edge. Placing a garden into such a location needs to be done without upsetting the harmony with the landscape. Calls to Wisley and Kew ensured that no plants would be included that might escape and overwhelm the native flora, an important point to consider when gardening in proximity to a native landscape. (We all know about the misery of bindweed, knotweed and ragwort. Although it is hardly in the same league, I have seen a Devon valley overcome with *Lamium,* and *Acanthus mollis* naturalizing on a railway bank.)

A decision was taken to design the garden almost entirely with plants using the red-brick colouring of the mill as the tonal inspiration. A simple mixed hedge of hawthorn, wild roses, wayfaring tree and wild privet bound the garden to blend in with the orchard and local hedging species. Within the garden, at the base of the

hedge, is a thick band of *Geranium phaeum*, the mourning widow geranium. This acts as a visual buffer zone between the garden and the open countryside. The deep blue and red brick of the mill inspired the use of smoky purple-black *Sambucus nigra* 'Guincho Purple'. As a close relative of wild elder, this looks lovely in spring with its pinky-cream plates of flowers against dusky foliage. As a contrast there are pollarded *Salix alba* subsp. *vitellina* 'Britzensis' with sealing-wax-red shoots that look like starbursts above the herbaceous plants. The garden is packed with billows of planting in shades of plum, copper, rust and mauve. *Monarda* 'Prairie Night' blends into creamy *Aruncus dioicus*, with *Symphytum caucasicum* and *Dryopteris filix-mas* carpeting under the sycamore.

In the open areas of the garden are fine filigree stands of bronze fennel set with tapering spires of *Digitalis ferruginea* and rich red pincushion heads of *Cirsium rivulare*. For structure and body there are hummocks of unruffled, brick-red *Euphorbia griffithii* 'Dixter' and *Sedum* 'Herbstfreude' (Autumn Joy). Softer mounds of pink *Chaerophyllum hirsutum* 'Roseum' blend into *Achillea* 'Salmon Beauty' and *Panicum virgatum* 'Rubrum'. Along the bank of the brook are *Euphorbia palustris* and sparkling white *Iris sibirica* 'Alba'. All in all, and in spite of the lavish use of ornamental garden plants, the garden feels very much a part of the landscape and not a recent interloper.

Management of this sort of garden depends on a bold approach and keeping a reasonably open mind, especially when dealing with the river bank. Where there is water there are weeds in abundance and this garden suffers from creeping buttercup and ground elder. Periodically areas are sprayed off or dug out and replanted. Otherwise regular tidying keeps the worst of the weeds at bay. The density and health of the herbaceous planting helps suppress weed growth, as does leaving on most old growth over winter. A thorough cut-back in February, coupled with a short but intensive period of weeding and hoeing and a hefty mulch of well-rotted horse manure, sets the garden up for the coming season.

Weird and wild

However incredulous the reader may be, I must still carry him a step further, and tell him I have not enumerated one-half of the uses to which the bamboo is applied in China.

From *A Journey to the Tea Countries*
by ROBERT FORTUNE (1852)

Perversity makes us do rash things. Plants on the border-line of hardiness are particularly appealing and anything which grows slightly out of our reach becomes addictively alluring. For example, I have an affection for echiums and a passion for returning on Eurostar with bags bristling with silvery rosettes of new and thrilling finds. I have travelled many miles to nurseries to buy seed and seed-lings of rare and wonderful echiums. I do not, however, garden in the warm Canary Islands on the volcanic soil which they love. Nevertheless, even in the autumn, when their flowers are spent and their towering silhouettes look just plain weird, I won't get rid of them. I am attempting to marry my naturalistic urges in the garden with these alien characters. To this end, the naturalism I espouse is fast becoming a multicultural mix of naturalized foreigners. I favour warm climates and the plants that thrive in them. In my garden in London drifts of white agapanthus, planted like weeds, mingle with *Phlomis italica*, the annual tulip poppy (*Papaver glaucum*) and verbascums of all denominations. A particular favourite is *V. creticum*, with large, sweetly scented flowers. Rearing up through this

LEFT Deep crimson *Knautia macedonica* highlights bronze fennel and *Digitalis ferruginea* at Lower Mill in Oxfordshire. Hummocks of *Sedum* 'Herbstfreude' buffer the edges of the planting and add structure into autumn. Rich soil and abundant moisture from Letcombe Brook ensure the garden remains lush and inviting all summer. Many of the plants self-seed, subtly changing the look each year.

ABOVE Jinny Blom defies any-one to spot that her wild hilltop garden at 56 Drakefell Road is in the middle of London. A wooded railway embankment allows a long view to be incor-porated into the design.

ground plane like demented flagpoles are echiums: *E. wildpretii, simplex, boissieri, pininana*. In tubs are *E. fastuosum* and, planted to mimic the Russian steppes, *E. russicum* with the delectable feather grass, *Stipa pennata*.

For the shrub layer, I looked to Virgil. In the exuberantly evoked landscapes of the *Georgics*, rich with vines, hazelnuts, olives and the good things of life, lay all the inspiration needed to complete the scene. Mounds of scented myrtle and box blend with the rounded shapes of the honey-scented *Euphorbia mellifera*. Cyclamen, ajuga and hellebores at the feet of *Cercis siliquastrum* conjure up Mediterranean woodland. Foxy-brown foxgloves, *Digitalis parviflora*, svelte and demure, add spikes of interest. In spite of the heavily foreign influence, the garden blends easily into the surrounding native woodland of poplar, cherry and hawthorn. Careful use of colour has helped sustain the balance, nothing too extreme. The editing process continues apace and each autumn plants unsuitable to the evolving wilderness are removed. Out from this hot dry garden go the veronicastrum, and, hovering on the brink of expulsion, the dearly loved *Thalictrum rochebruneanum* – really rotten luck as the neon-mauve flowers look tantalizing beside *Corylus maxima* 'Purpurea'. They were planted in a moment of moral weakness when the soil was damp and forgiving; however, watching them shrivel over the summer was too much to bear. Having adopted a ruthless no-watering policy has had its drawbacks, but I am keen to persist and see how the plants and I manage.

A few streets away from my south-east London garden is another exponent of the weird, wild look. You could be forgiven for thinking that you had washed up on the shore of a strange fantasy island in Biddy Bunzl's garden at 57 Breakspears Road. Here there are very few herbaceous plants and the garden reflects a flora utterly alien to Europe and the Americas. The front garden alone produces exclamations of disbelief from passers-by. Strangely teetering spiky *Pseudopanax* lurch skywards, emerging from tussocky *Stipa arundinacea*, silvery astelias, chunks of slate and drunken driftwood palisades. Most noticeable are the colours: these plants are rusty, black, coppery, buff and a deep waxy olive green, not those usually associated with our climate or countryside.

The source of this extraordinary landscape is found in the amazing talent of its creator, James Frazer. James is a New Zealander and Biddy's partner. Clearly he loves the flora of his native land and the temperate British climate allows him to grow most of it here. 'The grassy path is just like the desert road we took through the Tongariro National Park,' says Biddy. 'It's like having New Zealand here in my back garden.' The Tongariro Park is an area of volcanic plateaux, so it represents a very specific environment, not typical of suburban London. Remaining from the previous garden was a grotty old conifer which has been cleverly pruned so that it resembles a starkly beautiful manuka tree. Blending in with the rich mix of tussock grasses, *Chionochloa rubra*, *Calamagrostis brachytricha* and *Pennisetum macrourum*, are pollarded *Catalpa × erubescens* 'Purpurea', the huge leaves creating drama when seen close up. There are plants, such as the beautiful, candle-shaped pennisetum, which are not New Zealand natives, but they are so cleverly adapted to the scheme that they blend in perfectly. Car loads of pumice were brought in for the paths to replicate the volcanic landscape. Curiously, in spite of the outlandish planting, the garden feels very appropriate to its location. The answer lies in the absolute confidence and conviction with which it has been made. An innate understanding of this plant community in the wild has passed into the garden with seamless results.

An expansive attitude

It is the confidence with which all these wild gardens have been created which makes them so exciting. There is something inherently beautiful in seeing a few plant varieties thoughtfully chosen and then massed together over a generous area. With the strictures of time and space affecting most of us at every turn, there is a sense of bountiful release in this expansive approach to gardening. The freedom to experiment with it is there for every size of garden and budget. From a cheap packet of cornfield annuals in a small backyard to massive steppe plantings on umpteen acres, there is a wild effect to suit every plot and every purse. Go wild in the garden and enjoy the feeling of liberation it brings.

Is it the Tongariro National Park? No, it's Brockley, south London. *Pseudopanax, Chionochloa rubra*, cacti, bananas and alliums jostle together in Biddy Bunzl's garden, created by New Zealander James Fraser. The addition of driftwood palisades and rough-hewn decking makes this garden an exciting wild experience for the visitor who teeters along a wobbly plank to reach the sitting area.

Tuning into the wilderness

This scheme for rich, retentive soil is designed to work in association with the surrounding countryside. Bounded by a stone wall (14), a buffer planting of indigenous hedging (13) is maintained at about 1.2m/4ft to allow views into the garden from the footpath (15) and views out to open meadowland and orchards.

Beneath a belt of silver willows and black-leaved elders, dense ground cover merges into a mixed planting of tall perennials, with added structural perennials such as sedums. The planting is designed to provide interest through the year and is augmented with bulbs and self-sown annuals.

Herbaceous plants, grasses and trees

1 *Aruncus dioicus*
2 *Knautia macedonica*
3 *Chaerophyllum hirsutum* 'Roseum'
4 *Sedum* 'Herbstfreude'
5 *Miscanthus sinensis* 'Gracillimus'
6 *Achillea* 'Salmon Beauty'
7 *Foeniculum vulgare* 'Purpureum'
8 *Verbena bonariensis*
9 *Panicum virgatum* 'Rubrum'
10 *Eupatorium purpureum* 'Atropurpureum'
11 *Salix exigua*
12 *Sambucus nigra* 'Guincho Purple'

Tall perennials and ground cover beneath trees

Digitalis ferruginea
Dryopteris Wlix-mas
Euphorbia griffithii 'Fireglow'
Geranium phaeum 'Samobor'
Symphytum ibericum

Bulbs

Camassia leitchtlinii 'Alba'
Fritillaria meleagris

Gladiolus communis subsp. *byzantinus*
Narcissus poeticus var. *recurvus*

Hedge to boundary (13)

Crataegus monogyna (hawthorn) 60 per cent

Ligustrum vulgare (wild privet) 10 per cent
Rhamnus catharticus (purging buckthorn) 10 per cent
Rosa rubiginosa (sweet briar) 10 per cent
Viburnum lantana (wayfaring tree) 10 per cent

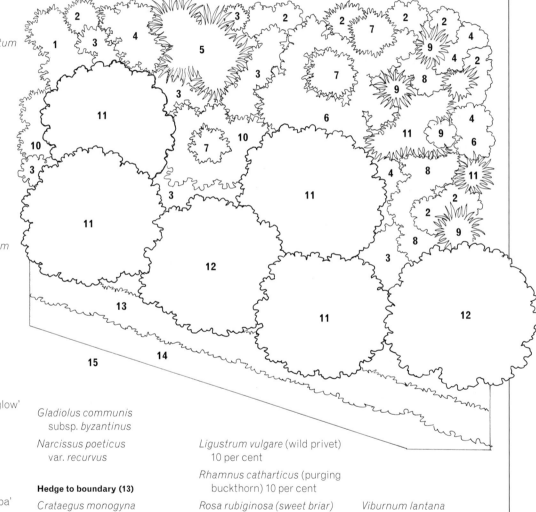

Shrubs, perennials & grasses for wild effects

Achillea 'Salmon Beauty'. Achilleas are especially effective in wild plantings on an open site. They prefer reasonably good soil, not too heavy. If planting them in clay soil, add grit or mulch with fine grit to keep keel slugs at bay. The cultivars, such as 'Salmon Beauty', 'Cerise Queen' and 'Walter Funke' (all 60–90cm/2–3ft) seem to hate any competition and need to be treated with more respect than the big old favourites such as 'Gold Plate'. For a long summer display (May to August), plant achilleas in well-drained soil in sun.

Aruncus dioicus. An easy and finely rewarding plant for retentive soil, the graceful aruncus has few rivals. It has far greater poise than astilbe, even though it flowers only white, in June to July. The leaves are beautiful and held attractively on tall stems (1.2m/4ft) which in winter turn nut brown and keep their form for a fair while.

Camassia. All camassias deserve a place in wild gardens – from tall and startlingly blue *C. leichtlinii* Caerulea Group to the equally stunning white form (90cm/3ft) illustrated (right) and the smaller *C. quamash*. Any retentive soil in an area of only moderate slug and snail infestation should reward the gardener with a fine display in May. Plant in autumn and, if they are to naturalize, give them a good start by preparing the ground well. Camassia will grow well in grass, but does enjoy a cultivated border.

Chaerophyllum hirsutum 'Roseum'. An aristocrat of the wild garden, this beautiful cow parsley has flowers at the dusty lilac end of pink. In a mild winter, ferny foliage hugs the ground, always looking fresh and beguiling. It is ideal for tiny bulbs to grow between and wonderful in association with *Geranium phaeum* and *Helleborus foetidus*. It grows to 60cm/2ft and by May is breathtaking in full flower. In principle it flowers once, but may have a second flush if well cared for. Keep an eye out for wood louse damage to the stems and cut back spent foliage to keep it fresh.

Digitalis ferruginea. Another must-have plant, reaching 1.2m/4ft in height. From June to August tall and slender spires of foxy-brown mini foxgloves with ochre netting spring from handsome rosettes of deep green evergreen leaves. This is a migratory self-seeder and will chose its own preferred position in the garden in time. Don't let it get smothered by other plants of a more rampant nature. Be careful how you site the colour – great with reds, buffs and grasses, revolting near purple filbert foliage (my mistake!).

Camassia leichtlinii subsp. *leichtlinii* at The Garden House, Devon.

Fritillaria meleagris at The Coppice, Surrey.

Eupatorium purpureum 'Atropurpureum'. A statuesque beauty for well-prepared, rich, deep, retentive soil. Give it the conditions it loves and prepare to be amazed. Over 2m/6½ft tall, the stout, dark purple stems with whorls of rough leaves are most graceful and become more so as the flowers develop in September to October: huge, rounded plates of rich purple almost 60cm/2ft across and bristling with butterflies. The flowers last for ages. So potent is this autumn-flowering plant that serious consideration must be given to its companions or it will look unbalanced. Try it with the coyote willow, *Salix exigua,* whose silvery leaves clothing slender, wand-like stems associate so well with herbaceous plantings (to encourage long stems and less suckery growth, cut the willow back hard, taking out a third of the old growth, every three years). It also looks lovely with the rusty spent flowers of a hydrangea, such as *H. paniculata* 'Unique'.

Euphorbia griffithii 'Fireglow'. For mass planting this euphorbia (90cm/3ft) has no equal for vigour, and for that exciting, slightly unnatural, waxy leaf. The new shoots are thrilling as they emerge in spring and when in full spate (May–June) the bright orange inflorescence is sensational. *E. g.* 'Dixter' is a deep orange-red and equally exciting. Planted in a massed herbaceous scheme with sedums and grasses, its beauty is set off to perfection. The only downside is that when it goes over there is a gaping hole which is hard to fill except by shipping in late-flowering tender plants such as *Salvia guaranitica* or *Nicotiana sylvestris.*

Foeniculum vulgare 'Purpureum'. Loved and loathed in equal measure, bronze fennel is ideal for the committed lazy gardener. If you plant it and ignore it, you are rewarded with a mirage of deep bronze foliage crowned with mustardy plates of flowers from July to September. In an open site on deep retentive soil in full sun, these can reach unexpected heights (1.7m/5½ft). In drier stony soil it will cut its cloth accordingly, becoming finer and shorter with a tendency to less deep colouring and scorching of lower leaves as the year progresses. It is a competent self-seeder, so be brutal if you wish to limit the takeover bid.

Fritillaria meleagris. The well-known and much-loved snake's-head fritillary (30cm/1ft) is well worth planting. Make sure the bulbs are fresh and plant early in the autumn in well-prepared ground. Look to nature to see what they need to succeed: a moist site which does not dry out in summer. The plant is a damp meadowland native, and if the conditions are not right then you can expect no miracles.

Geranium phaeum 'Samobor'. The straight native *G. phaeum,* or mourning widow, a modest plant and nonetheless satisfying, is treated to a burst of excitement in the cultivar 'Samobor', identified by dark, smudgy blotches on the leaves. From a dense mass of soft leaves rise tall stems (60cm/2ft) of small, deep dusky purple flowers over a long period in spring (April–May). A prolific self-seeder and thriving in shade, this is a very useful plant for beneath the skirts of shrubs or tree canopies. Cutting the plants hard back after flowering rewards with a fresh crop of leaves. The plants maintain a neat crown, making it easy to chop them up with a sharp spade to divide them.

Gladiolus communis subsp. *byzantinus*. Another essential plant is this magenta-flowered species gladiolus. A native of southern Spain, it is now widely cultivated. Provided it has warmth, it will reward with lovely flower spikes from May to June on 75cm/2½ft stems, and will bulk up well if happy. It is an excellent colour and many hours of fun are to be had inventing new combinations.

Knautia macedonica. Rapidly becoming ubiquitous, this deep crimson scabious (60–75cm/2–2½ft) has a pleasantly wild-and-woolly vibe. It will flower for months on end and, apart from mildew if it gets too dry, has no problems to speak of. Deadhead it to keep it fresh and flowering – the easiest way is by cutting the long-stemmed flowers for the house: they look lovely in wild arrangements culled from the hedgerow or field. It is a shame that plants go in and out of fashion and it is to be hoped that the new-found joy of knautia goes on as long as the flowering season. Bees and butterflies will arrive in hordes.

Miscanthus sinensis 'Gracillimus'. From gigantic *M. sacchariflorus* (3m/10ft) for deep, retentive soil to the tiny *M. sinensis* 'Yakushima Dwarf' (60cm/2ft), there are many miscanthus to choose for wild effects. A great all-round garden variety is *M.* 'Gracillimus'. It is of medium height (1.5m/5ft), the very fine foliage with a central silver spine making it graceful and spangly when covered in dew. It flowers reasonably well (September–October) when allowed to get warm enough. A good accent plant and a bit of light relief in among heavier shrubs, it is also good with tall aconites or *Digitalis ferruginea*.

Narcissus poeticus var. *recurvus*. The old English pheasant's-eye narcissus is so unbelievably pretty that it must be planted at every opportunity. The variety *N. poeticus* var. *recurvus* (50cm/1ft 8in) is an old garden species and flowers from April to May, later than most other narcissi. It is not always a keen flowerer but that just makes it more wonderful when it does appear; be not dissuaded.

Panicum virgatum 'Rubrum'. One of the loveliest grasses, simple and unassuming with a gentle character (90cm/3ft). Panicum is not, in my experience, a rampageous grower and is suited as a punctuation plant among more static growers, such as sedums or *Salvia officinalis* 'Purpurascens'. Plant it where low light will catch in the miasma of spangly seedheads that follow its August–September flowers.

Sambucus nigra 'Guincho Purple'. Beauty and indestructibility in equal measure. The metallic black foliage of this elder is complemented by plates of soft pinky flowers in April and May. Later the colour fades from the leaves and they turn a deep bottle green with blackened edges. This doesn't detract from the plant and offers the chance to wind a moody clematis through it, such as *C.* 'Gravetye Beauty' or *C.* 'Niobe'. For a cooler combination, try the late-flowering *C.* 'Alba Luxurians'. How to prune elder for the best effect is a matter of trial, error and personal preference. If cut hard back each year, it may grow to as much as 4m/13ft but lose some character. Try pruning more gently and aiming for a natural shape. Every few years it could be cut hard back to rejuvenate. Experiment with a clear conscience as it is impossible to kill.

Sedum 'Herbstfreude' (Autumn Joy). Cutting around the roots is reputed to prevent sedum from flopping about like a walrus on a beach at the end of summer. Apart from flopping, this has no vices and is a good plant for almost any circumstance (60cm/2ft). Never bother trying to hold it up unless you are an expert scaffolder as it weighs so much. Plant near a path edge where the unruliness is rendered irrelevant and enjoy months of interest: lots of bees and butterflies, wonderful flowers from August to September, curious rosette formations of new leaves and, in winter, deep mahogany stems and old flowerheads. An important structural herbaceous plant.

Symphytum ibericum. If you have space then this charming white-flowered comfrey is an essential ground-cover plant. The dense, rough foliage smothers all but the worst weeds (such as ground elder) and creates a living mulch. From mounds of foliage rise unfurling stems (45cm/1½ft) of white flowers in April to May. It is beautiful in shade with ferns which can cope with it, such as *Dryopteris filix-mas*. The manner in which the flowers form along the stem is intricate and beautiful, lodging in the infantile imagination until adulthood.

Verbena bonariensis. Stately yet refined, the verbena's whippy stems (1.5m/5ft) are topped with vibrant purple flowers for a very long season (June to September). It has recently had a good run of interest as it is a 'very good rent payer', as a friend once put it. In a good, retentive soil on an open site it has no equal. In France it is often used as a huge bedding plant and associates well with many other plants. It does need companions of equal endurance, as it may overpower with its enthusiasm. A prolific self-seeder and a must for a wild garden.

LEFT *Iris sibirica, Dactylorhiza × fuchsii* and *Ranunculus acris* - all bound together with sweet meadow grasses – on one of the Great Dixter meadows which, to a besotted wild gardener, are more fascinating and complex than the galaxies. BELOW This is a scene of great simplicity and excitement: looking across the natural lake towards Elsing Hall in Norfolk, instead of the anticipated roses against the house, there are dramatic stands of giant hogweed (*Heracleum mantegazzianum*). RIGHT *Stipa gigantea* in the experimental meadow planting at The Cuckoo Pen Nursery, where innovative planting on a patch of waste ground in Oxfordshire offers inspiration for many dry and marshy wild effects.

Many gardeners share Jinny Blom's love of meadows and naturalistic plantings – here are a few more of the hundreds of NGS gardens with wild effects.

Bedfordshire
88 Castlehill Rd
37 Rectory Lane

Berkshire
Bear Ash
Farley Hill Place Gardensl
Little Harwood
The Old Rectory, Peasemore

Bristol & South Gloucestershire
Algars Mill
16 Gordano Gardens
Tranby House

Buckinghamshire
Hall Farm
2 Kingswood Cottages
Kingswood House
Rose Cottage
21 Station Rd

Cambridgeshire
*Cambridge University Botanic
    Garden*
The Old Post Office
*Private Nature Reserve, Shingay
    Gardens*
South Farm
Tadlow House

**Carmarthenshire
& Pembrokeshire**
Glandwr
Great Griggs

Ceredigion / Cardiganshire
Cae Hir
Old Cilgwyn Gardens

Cheshire & Wirral
Bluebell Cottage
Long Acre
31 Moss Lane
Poulton Hall

Cornwall
Carwinion
The Old Mill Herbary
Penjerrick Garden

Cumbria
Acorn bank
Browfoot
Copt Howe
High Beckside Farm
High Dixon Ground
Newbiggin Hall

Denbighshire & Colwyn
Rûg

*Wild
effects*

247

*Wild
effects*

TIM INGRAM

with expert insights by
BETH CHATTO
JOY LARKCOM
DAN PEARSON
BRITA VON SCHOENAICH

12 Withstanding drought

The weather is a particularly British topic of conversation. For gardeners it rules our lives and, although rarely behaving as we would like, it allows us to grow a breathtaking variety of plants. Clear signs of greater extremes in our climate, probably the result of global warming, have focused minds more than ever on the influence of weather on our plants and gardens. And of all extremes, drought must be one of the most fundamental and constraining – yet it is also an extreme that demands novel solutions that have stretched the boundaries of planting design and taken garden artistry to new heights.

Drought is not only a function of rainfall. The poor, sandy and chalky soils in parts of the south, and the free-draining, gravelly soils in East Anglia and elsewhere, add to the effects of low rainfall. Even more of a challenge is drought resulting from competition for moisture by other plants, in particular by evergreen trees and shrubs such as conifers and by greedy surface-rooting deciduous trees like cherry and birch. Such areas of dry, impoverished soil are common to many gardens, and occur in those with otherwise adequate rainfall. However, they may give opportunities to grow plants, such as bulbs, that would be difficult to establish in open ground. Rain shadows cast by buildings and walls lead to local planting areas which remain dry and warm. Exploiting such spots can often surprise us. In my own garden, Copton Ash in Kent, a south wall is home to the Chilean bromeliad, *Fascicularia pitcairniifolia*, and the tree lupin, *Lupinus albifrons*, from California.

The prevalence of drought

After the severe flooding of autumn 2000, it is extraordinary to recall recent years of drought. And yet the years 1989 to mid-1992 were some of the driest on record and had a profound influence on many gardens and gardeners. Even though such sustained dry weather is rare – probably the closest comparable period was 1740 to 1743 – spells of even a few weeks without rain occur regularly and can lead to quite severe stress for many plants, particularly when coupled with hot, dry winds in summer. Few of us will forget the summer of 1976. Such weather can test gardens to the extreme and lays down strict limits on the range of plants that will succeed without supplementary watering. Gardeners in the south-east of England are well used to these dry spells, but hosepipe bans in Yorkshire and other areas show that drought can hit the country more widely too. Only in the north and west of Britain is rainfall usually sufficient to maintain moisture levels in the soil throughout the summer months. To keep a traditional English garden, with flowery borders and green lawns, looking its best requires 25mm/1in of rain every ten days. In the driest counties, east of a line from the Humber to the Solent, an average 150–230mm/6–9in of rain is required to overcome the soil moisture deficit by

the end of a normal summer. A considerably higher deficit will build up in years of drought.

Nonetheless, even in the very driest years on record, such as 1921 when Margate had the lowest ever recorded annual rainfall (just 236mm/9⅓in), the overall rainfall in the British Isles was no less than 70 per cent of the long-term average. In the years 1989 to 1991 rainfall was only 15 to 20 per cent below the norm. Relatively small absolute changes can have large visible effects on our gardens. Across the country as a whole, considerably greater variation than this exists and much of the west of Britain receives at least twice the rainfall of the south-east. Shoeburyness in Essex, which has the lowest rainfall in the British Isles (averaging less than 500mm/19in), is a desert when compared with parts of Snowdonia where rainfall can exceed 2,500mm/100in! Even within the south-east itself there is a marked variation with, for example, up to 50 per cent more rain falling in the south of Kent compared with along the Thames coast in the rain shadow of the North Downs. Such variation can often be extremely local and helps give our gardens their wonderful individuality, if not adding to the frustration of many gardeners.

Although we normally think of drought as a problem in summer when temperatures and plant transpiration are at a high, extended dry weather in winter prevents replenishment of ground moisture levels and can have long-term repercussions. Even after the drought broke in the early 1990s, many trees continued to show signs of stress for a further year or more until moisture levels deep in the soil were renewed. In the south-east a general trend to milder and wetter winters and drier summers is likely to alter our landscape in a subtle way. On a small scale this can be seen in changes in the range of rare native species like the lizard orchid (*Himantoglossum hircinum*). But there will also be effects on dominant species like our hedgerow trees.

Though gardeners are a resourceful lot, ultimately we must live with our natural rainfall, whether this is 500mm/19in or 2,500mm/100in. Drought will affect us in different ways and is not so much a period of low rainfall as a period of rainfall lower than we expect. Many gardeners mediate its effects by artificial watering and in the

PRECEDING PAGES This planting of honeysuckle and *Rosa* 'Buff Beauty' against The Manor House at Birlingham in Worcestershire is replete with scent and colour. David and Jane Williams-Thomas

encourage plants to cascade on to the gravel path, juxtaposing informality with the rigid architecture of the house. The drawing of Redisham Hall, Suffolk, is from the 1994 Yellow Book.

ABOVE A fine Judas tree, *Cercis siliquastrum*, stands in the centre of the largest of Beth Chatto's scree beds in her Essex garden casting shadows across her collection of drought-tolerant plants. The five island

beds are home to many small treasures, such as sempervivums and raoulias, and to grey- and silver-foliage plants like *Helichrysum stoechas* 'White Barn' and *Lavandula angustifolia* 'Nana Alba'.

more western regions of England and Wales this is a good solution. However, in the east where drought is so much more severe, this option is expensive and sometimes not possible. Far better to make a virtue out of necessity and look to those plants that not only withstand drought but thrive under such conditions.

Hills and dales

Our native chalk downlands are an example of the unexpected diversity and beauty of a flora adapted to poor and dry soils. Plants such as the pasque flower (*Pulsatilla vulgaris*), maiden pink (*Dianthus deltoides*) and juniper (*Juniperus communis*) are favourites in many gardens. Limestone hills like the Mendips are home to other valuable garden plants, including bloody cranesbill (*Geranium sanguineum*) and rock rose (*Helianthemum canum*). To these we can add small herbaceous plants and alpines from similar places elsewhere: species of campanula, aquilegia, gypsophila, scabious, linum, origanum, potentilla, veronica, thyme, poppy and many more. Grown in raised beds and open sunny spots, these small perennials make a colourful picture in the driest of years. Dwarf conifers and small shrubs like hebes, plus a range of bulbs flowering from autumn to spring, keep interest right through the chill days of winter. Beth Chatto's scree garden epitomizes the success of such a planting, with sedums and the stunning American mint *Agastache barberi* 'Firebird' standing out against the silvers and greys of artemisias and perovskias.

On the outskirts of Maidstone in Kent, Mike and Hazel Brett's garden, Old Orchard, has a fascinating variety of small, drought-tolerant perennials grown in raised beds, troughs and more informal rock gardens. Mike and Hazel have a special interest in the Drakensburg Mountains of South Africa, home to species of diascia, dierama and

BETH CHATTO

Adaptation to drought

Droughts for us in Essex are a regular feature, not an occasional disaster. A desiccating east wind seems to blow endlessly across the garden all spring and half the summer. Added to which, the soil is gravel and sand to a depth of about 6m/20ft, overlying clay. We choose plants adapted by nature to the conditions we have to offer.

Among our stalwarts are the greys and silvers. Some wear shirts of wool and silk, just as we might protect our skin from sun and heat. These plants have a coating of fine hairs which, as summer progresses, form a felt-like covering that protects the green leaf beneath and reduces moisture loss through transpiration. They include the almost white-foliaged *Helichrysum stoechas* 'White Barn', which makes a bush similar to a lavender; the shining buds open to small pale sulphur-yellow flowers in mid-summer. *Stachys byzantina* 'Silver Carpet' spreads its silver-grey lamb's ears for yards and the flowering form, *S. b.* 'Cotton Boll', has stems heavily buried in white wool. We grow a curious form of sea holly, *Eryngium variifolium*, to make a striking impact among these soft, woolly plants. From a basal rosette of heavily veined, dark green leaves rise upright branched stems with leaves and flowerheads reduced to long, narrow spikes, so silvered they look as if they have been cut out of shimmering metal.

The sedums are another of nature's clever adaptations and are among my best-loved drought resisters. The icy-smooth foliage also makes a fine contrast to the velvety lamb's ears. Their fat, succulent leaves store water when it is available, and many are coated with a protective, waxy bloom. Some are at their best in hungry soils such as ours, making compact, free-flowering plants.

Early dormancy – dying down almost immediately after flowering – is another strategy in nature's armoury against drought. Oriental poppies die down after flowering in mid-summer, to conserve strength. Bulbous plants emerge for a short and brilliant season, and then their leaves return nourishment to the bulb, corm or tuber below ground, to be stored until the next burst of growth the following year.

osteospermum, which regularly experience spells of hot, dry weather. The opportunities are endless and such plantings allow the adventurous gardener to try out different soil types and aspects to grow a remarkable variety of flowers from dry hills and mountains the world over. With perfect drainage, it is possible to grow some quite eccentric plants, including species of agave and several cacti, a theme I will return to later on. These plantings are ideally suited to small gardens and in more formal areas next to the patio or driveway and can become of absorbing interest.

Mediterranean plants

Some of the most reliable and well-known plants for the dry garden come from around the Mediterranean, where they have evolved under mild, moist winters and long, hot summers. Indeed, the description 'Mediterranean garden' evokes a warm sense of wellbeing, even though the summer heat can become unbearable. Under such conditions plants simply stop growing or die down until the rains of autumn start the cycle of growth again. Many flower early in the year, often for many months when temperatures are low. Euphorbias are a prime example and *de rigueur* in dry gardens. If forced to choose I would go for the glowing golden heads of *E. characias* subsp. *wulfenii* in one of its selected forms such as 'Lambrook Gold'. But the wonderful Turkish *E. rigida*, which ends its flowering in a blaze of orange and red, would come a photo-finish second.

A lack of dense vegetation allows bulbs to flourish and many of these require summer drought to thrive in our gardens. The beautiful madonna lily (*Lilium candidum*) grows nowhere better than parts of East Anglia in sunny, calcareous soils. And in the walled garden at Felbrigg Hall, near Cromer, conditions are ideal for the National Collection of colchicum. *C. tenorei* grows here *en masse*, showing an obvious liking for the compacted, sandy soil and maritime climate (the North Sea is only 3.2km/2 miles away). For gardeners less concerned with summer colour, an area devoted to small bulbs like the famous spring walk at Sissinghurst is quite magical.

Silver and grey foliage plants provide an essential motif

in the dry garden and give an entirely different feel from the rich greens we are more used to. Some like *Artemisia* 'Powis Castle' and *Convolvulus cneorum* glisten in the hot summer sun, but phlomis and lavender have a velvety texture that seems to soak up the heat. The blue foliage of rue and *Euphorbia nicaeensis* meld perfectly with a soft apricot kniphofia in my own garden. Such foliage has been quite literally 'made' by tens of thousands of years of blazing summers and is proof against the severest droughts. Against it colours have an extra vibrancy, the brilliant reds late in the year of *Zauschneria* or the surprising 'rabbit's ears' of French lavender. Gardeners in mild areas may consider planting an olive, as at the Chelsea Physic Garden where a large, old tree graces the corner near the glasshouses. In colder areas silvery *Elaeagnus angustifolia* might take its place, or even *Eucalyptus pauciflora* subsp. *niphophila* with its exquisite white-and-grey-mottled bark. This is one of the hardiest of the Australian gums, surviving −23°c/−9.4°f in Northumberland in the winter of 1981–2.

No Mediterranean garden could be complete without cistus. In poor, well-drained soils, these can be long-lived and reliable and belie their reputation for tenderness. Bob Page, who holds one of the National Collections, lives at Rawdon just north of Leeds and is trialling many species and varieties at Harlow Carr Gardens, Harrogate. Several of the good recent introductions, such as *Cistus* 'Snow White' and *C.* 'Peggy Sammons', were bred by the late Eric Sammons from Walsall in the Midlands. One of the species, in particular, *C. ladanifer*, has deep green leaves which exude a resin, used in perfumes and incenses, and weight for weight is more valuable than gold! This plant has large, white flowers with a central blotch of maroon and has introduced the feature into many fine hybrids.

Aromatic and resinous leaves are an appealing property of many plants from the Mediterranean, in part an adaptation to the heat but also a deterrent to grazing. Another method, spines, is seen in a selection of 'hedgehog' plants, many of which have been given the specific epithet '*spinosum*', among them *Euphorbia*, *Bupleurum*, *Alyssum* and *Verbascum*. My personal favourite is *Erinacea anthyllis*, a rare and special sub-shrub with violet-blue pea flowers.

LEFT By July the flowerheads of *Stipa tenuissima* have bleached to the colour of straw in Beth Chatto's gravel garden in Essex. Soon the stems will be cut down to encourage new growth and avoid a rash of

seedlings. *Eryngium giganteum* seeded among the grasses, and *Verbena bonariensis* forming an airy screen, subtly change the picture each year. At the front are the yellow daisy flowers of *Anthemis* 'E.C. Buxton'.

OVERLEAF A peaceful scene at Sticky Wicket in Dorset shows the value of simple and open planting. The use of few species and small, quiet flowers evokes the natural beauty of a woodland clearing in summer.

An artist's eye

In her book *The Dry Garden*, published in 1978, Beth Chatto introduced a whole generation of gardeners to these Mediterranean plants. Her exceptional gravel garden takes this theme to a new level of artistry and will convert all who see it to the positive value of poor, dry soils. Here, just east of Colchester in Essex, the soil is deep glacial gravel and sand, overlying clay. Even drought-tolerant plants need a helping hand and, although the garden is not irrigated, its ability to retain moisture has been improved by copious additions of compost before planting. The resulting crop of weed seedlings was controlled by hoeing in the first season and, thereafter, the beds were mulched with 12mm/½in gravel, about 25–50mm/1–2in deep, and with baled straw beneath tree and shrub plantings. 'Once a mulch is laid', Beth Chatto advises, 'it should be disturbed as little as possible.' As a garden develops, a natural cycle of leaf fall and turnover helps maintain a more fertile 'soil'.

Structure and height in Beth Chatto's gravel garden are provided by trees and shrubs like the incomparable Mount Etna broom, *Genista aetnensis*, and smoke bush, *Cotinus coggygria*. In summer the dying seedheads of *Eryngium giganteum* and *Allium cristophii* merge with tall *Verbena bonariensis*. Brilliant blue agapanthus, encouraged by the mild and moist spring in 2000, were the best I have ever seen. A useful late-flowering euphorbia, the Balkan *E. seguieriana* subsp. *niciciana*, sprawled lazily across the gravel path. And a delightful detail was *Origanum laevigatum* growing out of a carpet of *Phyla nodiflora*, the latter dotted with tiny clusters of scented, lantana-like flowers. Sedums, grasses and autumn bulbs carry the garden on, and in winter the different textures of shrubs, brilliant red leaves of bergenias and vertical clumps of dried grasses are a picture in themselves.

Aromatherapy

The Mediterranean has also been the source of many herbs which are indispensable in the dry garden, their aroma and attraction for bees and butterflies as valuable as their uses in the kitchen. Although many gardeners grow them in a formal herb garden or in pots, they also happily mingle with more colourful plants in sunny borders. One of my favourite families, the umbellifers, gives a great variety of leaf textures and shapes, as well as flowers, from parsley to fennel and coriander. They are among the plants longest in cultivation. Mint and thyme, rue and sage can all play their part and are easily accommodated in raised beds in gardens with heavy and wet soils.

At Hexham Herbs in Northumberland, the National Collection of thymes grows in a series of south-facing, brick-sided cold frames, filled in with poor, sandy soil. Herbs are also especially suited to walled gardens which trap the sun and scents of summer, well expressed at Hollington Herb Garden at Wootton Hill in Hampshire.

Southern-hemisphere plants

Gardeners can also look to several other regions of the world with Mediterranean-like climates. South Africa is rich in bulbs and related plants, many of which, like agapanthus and kniphofia, are tolerant of periods of hot, dry weather, though they naturally experience isolated summer rainstorms. The autumn-flowering bulbs *Nerine flexuosa* and *Amaryllis belladonna* are especially good in gardens which provide the warmth to encourage flowering. At Felbrigg Hall, for example, the amaryllis produces its pink funnels beneath apricots and peaches on a south-facing wall.

California has been less looked to but, like South Africa, has a very rich and interesting native flora. Tree lupin and ceanothus are widely planted in this country, along with fremontodendron and eschscholzia. At both Dunster Castle in Somerset and Dunham Massey in Cheshire the tree poppy, *Romneya coulteri*, is a great success, although I and other gardeners find it frustratingly difficult to establish. Recently Dutch bulb growers have been successful at increasing some of the lovely Californian bulbs, including the beautiful Mariposa lilies (species of *Calochortus*), and these may make more of an impact in our gardens in future years.

Fewer still plants from the matorral of central Chile or heathland bush of Australia have become widely established in our gardens. Alstroemeria is one exception, even though many of the large-flowered hybrids are far removed from the native species of the southern Andes.

DAN PEARSON

Thyme Persian carpets

Water, it is said, will become one of the most valuable resources of the twenty-first century. A strange thing to consider in Britain maybe with its moist climate, but it is always prudent to garden with drought in mind, particularly on thin light soils or in exposed situations.

Planting the right plant in the right place is a mantra that all good gardeners follow. Vita Sackville-West resorted to a wonderful thyme planting in two windswept beds at Sissinghurst to resolve the problem of exactly this situation and she called them her 'Persian carpet laid flat on the ground out of doors'.

I have been inspired by these low, aromatic plantings and have used thyme *en masse* to cover ground in hot, dry situations where irrigation is not only inappropriate but also unnecessary. Hailing from free-draining, mountainous slopes in the Mediterranean, thymes prefer to be grown 'hard' with full sun and plenty of air. Placed where there is too much moisture, they will dwindle away and rot in winter.

Although they prefer to grow with little nourishment, it is best, as with any new planting, to give thymes a good start. Choose the hottest, brightest spot available and prepare the soil with compost if it is free-draining, or with a mixture of compost and grit if the soil is heavy so that it is open and never waterlogged. After planting, keep the plants watered in the first few weeks, and the area weed-free, and they will soon mesh together to form a weed-suppressing ground cover.

There are literally hundreds of

varieties to choose from. *Thymus serpyllum*, the wild thyme, is a creeping plant and its varieties, which vary from white to strong pink, hug the ground close. My favourite creeping thyme is woolly *T. pseudolanuginosus*, with furry, silvered foliage.

The creeping thymes are best kept together. Bush-forming varieties, such as *T. citriodorus* (lemon thyme), *T. herba-barona* (caraway thyme) and varieties of *T. vulgaris*, have a different growing habit, forming low mounds of woody stems. I grow several of these

together for contrast, massing the dark mauve-flowered 'Porlock' with the pale-leaved 'Silver Posie' in informal drifts. The lightness of 'Silver Posie' adds a lift to the carpet when the plants are not in flower. 'Porlock' flowers first, in early summer, and paler-flowered 'Silver Posie' neatly follows on. As soon as they have flowered, they should be trimmed back by a third – but never into old wood. This is one of the most delightfully aromatic tasks of the summer and should be reserved for a hot day to savour the moment fully.

A massed planting of aromatic thymes and small spreading alpines at The Garden House, Devon, makes a colourful alternative to the omnipresent English lawn on a sun-baked, well-drained site.

The yellow *A. aurea* can often become a weed, but the soft sunset colours of the *ligtu* hybrids are better behaved and are superbly combined with macleaya and *Crocosmia* 'Lucifer' in a corner below the tower at Sissinghurst. Some very attractive dwarf species of alstroemeria also have great potential, two successful with us being *A. presliana*, a rich, warm rose, and *A. pallida*, which is pale, ethereal pink. Gold prospectors in the Australian outback may have looked out for 'digger's speedwell', *Parahebe perfoliata*. This unique plant, with its eucalyptus-like leaves, is a surprisingly hardy and distinct addition to the dry garden, perhaps appropriate planted beneath the red bottlebrush, *Callistemon linearis*.

The plants of the southern hemisphere have a fascination drawn from unfamiliarity. A consequence in my own garden is an area devoted to them, dominated by several eucalypts and underplanted with pittosporum, *Luma apiculata* (syn. *Myrtus luma*), grevilleas and callistemon. The extraordinary New Zealand pseudopanax and wire-netting bush, *Corokia cotoneaster*, add a surreal touch, and other inhabitants include the silvery-leaved Tasmanian *Leptospermum lanigerum* and winter-scented *Azara microphylla* from Chile. These are interplanted with hebes, phormiums, astelia, olearias, prostanthera and senecio, woven together by carpets of acaena. The emphasis is on foliage textures and colours in contrast to the flowers, which are often small and insignificant. These plants have proved drought-tolerant and hardy over five or ten years, though no doubt a particularly severe winter would cause losses.

Daring experiments with drought

One of the most remarkable gardens I have seen experiments even more daringly with drought. The Old Vicarage at East Ruston, home to Alan Gray and Graham Robeson, lies close to the north-east coast of Norfolk. Winters here are relatively mild, similar to those in Devon and Cornwall, and probably warmer than further south where the closer land mass of continental Europe can bring quite severe frosts. Rainfall is low at around 640mm/25in. Visitors are faced with an astonishing collection of plants grown in a series of discrete gardens, delineated by hedges and walls to give shelter and warmth. Several of these are designed

Succulent species of *Cotyledon* and *Agave* from Africa and America combine with New Zealand *Phormium* and *Astelia*, loosely planted with grasses and ground cover, at The Old Vicarage at East Ruston, Norfolk. Elsewhere black *Aeonium* 'Zwartkop' and electric-blue *Puya* dazzle the visitor. A variety of form and leaf colour makes for an exciting scene in which the play can be changed every year.

JOY LARKCOM

Vegetables in a drier world

The climate-change alarm bells began ringing for me in 1991, when the annual rainfall in our East Anglian garden fell to little over 40cm/16in. For weeks on end there was not a drop of water in the rain gauge, and as I entered yet another blank on the rainfall chart, I would empathize with growers in Africa and truly arid regions of the world, scanning the mocking blue sky day after day for signs of cloud. The prediction that global warming could mean wet areas becoming wetter and dry areas drier gave an urgency to my thinking on how to grow vegetables in a drier world.

The first step was to save the natural rainfall. The gutters on every roof – house, barn, greenhouse and shed – were repaired and downpipes allied to water storage tanks and rain butts. We even attached guttering to the metal frame of our outsize polytunnel (a converted Nissen hut), piping the collected water through a slit in the polythene into a pair of tanks inside the tunnel. It is astonishing how much water can be garnered from a large expanse of roof in a summer shower.

Next the question of conserving water in the soil. As organic gardeners we have been working organic matter into the soil for over thirty years. This breaks down into humus, which, among numerous assets, has the ability to absorb and retain moisture. It makes a huge difference. But there is no let-up: organic matter has to be added continually year after year.

The real culprit in losing water is not drainage, but evaporation. To minimize evaporation it is essential to keep the soil surface covered: in other words, to mulch. We use organic mulches – up to 7.5cm/3in of mushroom compost and well-rotted straw, and rotted reeds from the pond one year. Or we plant through inert mulches, such as polythene films or, in the case of large plants like pump-kins, squares of old carpet. In some arid zones plants are mulched with gravel, stones or sand. I remember pushing my fingers through a deep sand mulch in Spain and feeling the unbelievably cool, moist soil beneath. The thing to remember is that mulching maintains the *status quo*, so always mulch when the soil is moist and just pleasantly warm, not cold. We generally water when we plant, and then mulch.

How you water is important too. Abandon wasteful overhead spraying in favour of trickly hose or permeable tubing laid, for preference, in the soil. Limit watering to a plant's 'critical periods'. In the case of legumes and 'fruiting' vegetables this is when they are flowering and podding. Watering then, if at no other time, will ensure a reasonable crop. Never water 'little and often', which encourages superficial rooting; occasionally but thoroughly encourages roots to grow down and utilize those deeper reserves of water in the soil.

Deep roots are one factor in determining which plants are drought-resistant. From my observations this includes rhubarb, the chard family, rather than spinach and chicories. One dry summer I planted a long bed with several varieties of lettuce, and a plot of 'Sugar Loaf' chicory. All were heavily mulched at planting, then left to their fate. The lettuce struggled and was poor, but the chicory, with its long tap root produced large, leafy, flavoursome heads – admittedly less sweet than lettuce, but lush and crunchy. Try them for salads in dry times.

A potato-and-feather bird scarer in the vegetable garden at Yews Farm, Somerset, is an effective and amusing piece of garden sculpture. The idea came from the walled kitchen garden at Normanby Hall in Lincolnshire. Vegetables are particularly vulnerable to drought and Louise and Fergus Dowding mulch heavily and use horticultural fleece to reduce evaporation in dry periods.

specially with plants from dry climates in mind.

The 'sunk' garden was created by excavating down to 1.5m/5ft, banking up the spoil around three sides and building retaining walls to make a warm and intimate area. At the lowest level all the topsoil was removed to leave starved, sharply drained, semi-alpine conditions. Here plants such as creeping thymes and winter-flowering *Iris unguicularis* have been established alongside colonies of self-sown pinks. Above them, *Dierama pulcherrimum* casts its delicate papery-pink bells on grassy stems. Elsewhere Alan and Graham have made use of low retaining walls to trap and reflect the heat in the sunniest part of the garden. Many relatively tender plants thrive in these well-drained terraced beds: the intensely scented lemon verbena, *Aloysia tirphylla*, communes with the bold red and orange flowers of *Aloe aristata* and *Mimulus aurantiacus*. A colony of soft pink *Echium boissieri*, established along the base of one of the terraces, amazes with its army of slender, vertical spires. *Euphorbia glauca*, a rare and none-too-hardy New Zealander, makes a 90cm/3ft-wide bush in front of *Melianthus major*. And appropriately perhaps for the flamboyance of the planting, *Phormium* 'Jester' in red and green grows in the central gravel path.

However, the surprise of this garden doesn't end with this Mediterranean plantsman's paradise. A narrow gap in the hedge leads to an extraordinary and challenging scene, created in imitation of a desert wash in the United States. A wide area of stone, gravel and boulders is sparsely planted with a great variety of yuccas, agaves and desert plants, overlooked by palms such as the heat-loving Mediterranean chamaerops and Mexican brahea. Strong-flowering clumps of berkheya, South African thistles with large, daisy-like flowers in white and soft purple, and more traditional plants too, such as onopordum, Californian poppies and *Linaria purpurea*, make bold isolated specimens.

Self-seeders

Sometimes the most successful plantings are arrived at naturally. Foxgloves, many umbellifers, the beautiful, soft yellow *Oenothera stricta*, *Verbena bonariensis* and Canary Isle *Geranium palmatum* are all examples that self-sow widely in my own garden. Indeed such plants will rarely stay where they were first planted. This tendency can be encouraged by careful management. In the Bolton Percy Cemetery in Yorkshire judicious use of herbicides to control aggressive weeds and open up new areas for colonization allows a range of garden plants to naturalize. Among them are dicentras which despite their fragile appearance are tolerant of extremely dry soils in sun or shade, growing away again from fleshy roots as conditions allow. At Abbotsmerry Barn near Penshurst in Kent paved and gravelly areas are softened with a profusion of self-sown plants, in particular the incomparable Mexican daisy, *Erigeron karvinskianus*, along with geraniums, poppies and *Campanula persicifolia*. Such areas with poor, dryish soils can be left to their own devices with only minimal maintenance and will give a great deal of pleasure year after year.

A corner of the Bolton Percy Cemetery in Yorkshire basks in spring sunshine. Roger Brook's management of the area, covering nearly 1 acre, is based on a understanding of the ecology of garden plants, coupled with timely weeding and judicious use of glyphosate herbicide. Planting and maintenance cause minimal disturbance to the established setting and take fewer than three hours per week.

Inspired by the prairies

Perennial plantings inspired by the natural rhythms and plant combinations of wild open landscapes are a low-maintenance alternative to the traditional border that relies on labour-intensive double digging, incorporating barrowloads of manure and irrigation in times of drought. The key to success is to choose vigorous, drought-tolerant plants that have compatible growth patterns so they are not competing with one another.

The North American prairies are known for their plant diversity but it is worth widening the range by using strong species from other continents that thrive in similar open habitats. Perennial species that have a natural appearance, including cultivars with single flowers and sturdy stems (that do not need staking), combine well with the sculptural grasses – tall clumps of *Miscanthus sinensis* and the arching stems of *Stipa calamagrostis* and *Calamagrostis × acutiflora* – that provide the backbone to a prairie border and give it its fluidity. An approximate guide is to plant one grass to five perennials.

To achieve a naturalistic effect, create bold plant groupings and use repetition to enhance the impression of self-seeding. Tall plants in the foreground, especially airy species such as Russian sage (*Perovskia* 'Blue Spire') and *Salvia nemorosa*, perform the role of a see-through screen to allow glimpses of plant associations beyond. Create layers of interest with towering kniphofia and echinacea emerging from ground-covering anaphalis and persicaria. Aim for contrasts of form, leaf shape, colour and texture, such as the velvety-grey leaves of *Phlomis samia* to rise up through *Origanum laevigatum* 'Herrenhausen' and purple-leaved *Sedum* 'Ruby Glow'. Plant asters and rudbeckias to combine with plumes of bleached grasses for a crescendo of colour in late summer and autumn, followed by attractive seedheads though the winter.

If you apply a gravel mulch to suppress weeds and hold moisture, maintenance of a prairie planting is minimal, the only arduous job being a rough prune with shears in February before new growth starts to appear.

ABOVE & RIGHT Grasses, which change colour and sway in the breeze, blend with upright flowering perennials in the low-maintenance and drought-tolerant prairie border at Ryton Organic Gardens in Warwickshire, designed by Schoenaich Rees Landscape Architects. The detail (right) includes *Stipa calamagrostis* amid a sea of *Aster amellus* 'Veilchenkönigin' and *Anaphalis triplinervis*.

Steppe and prairie plantings

Perennials from dry continental climates that experience much colder winters come into their own in areas where frosts are prevalent. These steppe and prairie landscapes share with the Mediterranean a relatively open and sparse vegetation. At Lady Farm in Somerset, the dry steppe planting on a slope (see page 100) includes yellow *Coreopsis verticillata* and silvery artemisias widely spaced and informally repeated among rocks and gravel.

In modern styles of gardening, pioneered in continental Europe and North America, plants such as the dramatic foxtail lilies (*Eremurus*), many irises, verbascum, sedum, poppies, cornflowers and many grasses are combined with great effect and, in contrast to the more traditional herbaceous border, need less maintenance as well as surviving periods of low rainfall. Drama comes from strong individuals like *Crambe cordifolia* and *Inula magnifica*, which despite their vigour have deep, questing roots able to tide them through periods of drought. Early summer gives an impressionist picture with bearded irises and oriental poppies to the fore. Later the hazy and more ethereal flowers of grasses contrast with the strong form of sedums and achilleas and the spires of *Salvia nemorosa*.

Dry shade

Even the optimistic gardener finds the dry shade of Victorian shrubberies difficult to deal with. The plants that will survive in such conditions – periwinkle and ivy, *Euphorbia amygdaloides* var. *robbiae* and the peculiar liliaceous shrub *Ruscus aculeatus* (butcher's broom) – are valuable but hardly inspiring. Nonetheless there are many woodland plants well adapted to dry shade, given soils regularly refreshed with leafmould and not too overrun by surface-rooting trees and shrubs. Invariably these plants grow in the cooler and wetter months and include some of the very best and most popular in our gardens. Autumn is an important time as they put out new roots and develop the flowers that will emerge the following spring. A few plants give us colour now, prime among them *Cyclamen hederifolium* which makes a winter carpet of silvered leaves. The winter-flowering *C. coum*, with its perky, short-stemmed flowers and rounded leaves, is

equally easy, and with spring comes *C. repandum*, slower to establish but arguably the loveliest of all.

In the winter and early spring a profusion of woodland perennials flower: snowdrops, hellebores, pulmonarias, anemones, erythroniums, epimediums, tiarella – and all of these to a greater or lesser degree will withstand dry conditions in summer. However, few will prosper in very poor, rooty soil and are worth encouraging with plentiful mulches of good compost and leafmould in the autumn and winter. At Knightshayes Court in Devon a woodland tapestry is woven beneath tall oaks and other trees. More telling in the context of dry gardens is the wide range of such plants that prosper in Frederick Stern's famous chalk garden at Highdown near Worthing. Here the strange, black tubers of *Anemone blanda* have naturalized in sheets under deciduous trees and shrubs and form a blue carpet in early spring. In our garden, Copton Ash, one of the most drought-tolerant of all is *Hacquetia epipactis*, a small relative of astrantia from alpine woodlands. This has fresh apple-green 'flowers' (in reality bracts surrounding tiny yellow florets) in earliest spring and succeeds on the north side of a Leylandii hedge. Like many early-flowering plants, it remains attractive for many weeks as temperatures are low and pollinators sparse. The strong, deep roots of hellebores allow them to resist very dry spells. Other useful plants include *Ophiopogon planiscapus* 'Nigrescens', geraniums in variety, *Brunnera macrophylla* and the soft shield fern, *Polystichum setiferum*.

Living with drought

The most successful and lasting gardens eventually appear to become part of their surrounding landscape, as if they had always been there. The skill of the gardener is to tune in to the climate in their own backyard, enjoying the successes and accepting failures. Those of us who have to live with drought may be more fortunate than most. We have some of the richest flora in the world to tempt us, and our gardens are likely to be more exciting and fascinating as a result. The gardens I have described and many others open under the National Gardens Scheme show how thoughtful gardeners respond to dry conditions. The result in every case is interesting and unique.

OPPOSITE At Copton Ash, Kent, *Cistus ladanifer*, *Helichrysum italicum* and *Hypericum olympicum* 'Citrinum' thrive in the summer drought which intensifies their aroma and quality of flowering.

Hot, dry border

The border is 6–9m/20–30ft long and 3m/10ft deep. The planting is dominated by the hybrid strawberry tree (2), noted for its peeling, red-brown bark and glossy, evergreen leaves. The Mount Etna broom (*Genista aetnensis*) or *Eucalyptus pauciflora* subsp. *niphophila* would give an entirely different feel.

The tree is underplanted with a carpet of veronica and with small bulbs which will flower before the foreground perennials come into growth. Colours are generally yellows, blues and violet against silver-grey foliage, with some strong architectural plants, several of which (agave and aeonium) will need overwintering frost-free. Self-seeding plants (verbascum, omphalodes, eryngium) will bring informality and change from year to year. The foreground can be extended with small, carpeting alpines and dwarf bulbs into a gravelled or stone path. The background may be a boundary hedge or wall, or the planting continued around the tree to form an island bed.

1 *Rosa fedtschenkoana*
2 *Arbutus x andrachnoides*
3 *Verbascum olympicum*
4 *Stipa calamagrostis*
5 *Eryngium giganteum*
6 *Allium cristophii*
7 *Verbena rigida*
8 *Gaura lindheimeri*
9 *Sedum* 'Bertram Anderson'
10 *Yucca glauca*
11 *Origanum* 'Rosenkuppel'
12 *Papaver triniifolium*
13 *Omphalodes linifolia*
14 *Stachys byzantina* 'Cotton Boll'
15 *Veronica peduncularis* 'Georgia Blue'
16 *Arum creticum*
17 *Agapanthus* 'Blue Moon'
18 *Veronica prostrata*
19 *Linum narbonense*
20 *Helianthemum* 'Wisley Primrose'
21 *Euphorbia myrsinites*
22 *Allium flavum*
23 *Lupinus arboreus*
24 *Aeonium arboreum* 'Zwartkop'
25 *Helichrysum italicum*
26 *Cistus ladanifer*
27 *Hypericum olympicum* 'Citrinum'
28 *Thymus serpyllum*
29 *Agave americana* 'Mediopicta'
30 *Lavandula lanata* 'Richard Gray'

265

Withstanding drought

Plants for dry gardens

Dry gardens provide particularly interesting possibilities for gardeners to express more open and sculptural styles of planting. These can be merged into the natural landscape using plants of dry meadows or simply segregated by formal boundaries. I have already mentioned a wide variety of suitable drought-tolerant plants but there follows an idiosyncratic list of personal favourites.

Trees & shrubs

Arbutus. The hybrid strawberry tree, × *andrachnoides*, has great character with warm cinnamon bark and dark evergreen foliage, brought to life by the sprays of white pitcher-shaped flowers in winter. 'Marina' is a recent introduction with pink flowers. Though ericaceous they will tolerate poor alkaline soils and revel in full sun. Their ultimate height is 10m/33ft.

Artemisia. Many of the artemisias are quintessential dry-garden plants. 'Powis Castle' (60-90cm/2-3ft) with its lacy silver foliage remains one of the best; in mild gardens try its parent *arborescens* which grows to 1.8m/6ft or more and has platinum-white foliage.

Ceanothus. Incredible shrubs when given their head and some such as *arboreus* can grow into sizeable trees. I particularly like the smaller, semi-deciduous forms like 'Gloire de Versailles' and the deep blue 'Henri Desfossé', which are among the hardiest. These benefit from hard pruning in spring, which will maintain them to 1.5–2.1m/5–7ft.

Ceratostigma. *C. willmottianum* is one of the finest of autumn shrubs and one of the very few with flowers of true gentian-blue. It has good autumn leaf colour too. It can be cut back hard in spring and treated like a herbaceous perennial.

Helianthemum. Familiar and excellent small (up to 30cm/1ft) shrubs for the hottest gardens. Good varieties include *H.* 'Wisley Primrose' and 'Henfield Brilliant' (vivid orange-red), 'Ben Mohr' (pure orange) and 'St John's College Yellow'; 'Wisley Pink' is the loveliest of all but has a rather lax habit. They are best when regularly trimmed after flowering. Try planting carpets of different colours together, interplanted with small bulbs and grasses and other small, bushy plants.

Helichrysum. The humble curry plant, *H. italicum*, is a valuable silver foil in the dry garden. If you prefer no scent, try *H. ambiguum* which is among the whitest of all foliage plants. Annual trimming will keep them tidy.

Lavandula. So well known as hardly to require comment. Nonetheless, there are many outstanding new varieties, including the silver-grey hybrids of *L. lanata*, 'Richard Gray' and 'Sawyers', and *L. stoechas*

'Willow Vale'. The more tender, cut-leaved species like *pinnata* and *canariensis* make fascinating container specimens.

Lyonothamnus floribundus subsp. *aspleniifolius.* I was first given this Californian tree by Architectural Plants and it is a reasonably hardy and very different woody plant to grow in a warm sheltered spot. Lovely for its deeply cut, fern-like, evergreen leaves and warm, reddish, shreddy bark, it has a narrow, upright habit and is relatively fast-growing to 7.5m/25ft or more. I have it underplanted with penstemons.

Phlomis. A genus which receives less praise than it deserves and revels in hot, dry weather. Most have soft, felted leaves from silver-grey to a unique golden-fawn, all with the typical whorls of hooded flowers, mostly yellow but pinkish-purple in *P. italica* and *purpurea*. *P. lanata* is a particularly good shrub with neat, rounded leaves rather atypical of the genus and growing to only 60cm/2ft.

Yucca. The yuccas bring an important element of form and punctuation. In large gardens the bold species *Y. gloriosa* and *recurvifolia* can form huge clumps. Quite different is *Y. glauca* which has narrow, needle-like leaves and slowly forms tidy, symmetrical rosettes to 60cm/2ft. *Y. whipplei* is the most stunning of all with ferocious, rapier-like, blue leaves and spectacular flowerheads to 4.5m/15ft in height. This is a plant for the patient and brave gardener as it may take ten years or more to flower. It requires a particularly hot and gravelly spot. Superb in Dr Smart's garden, Marwood Hill, in Devon. A number of related plants are well worth trying in mild gardens: *Hesperaloe* has striking, red flowers, *Dasylirion* and *Nolina* species make grassy fountains and, most spectacular of all, *Beschorneria yuccoides* carries huge, arching sprays of greenish-red.

Perennials

Acanthus. The species *A. spinosus* and *A. mollis* are statuesque and imposing plants but too large for many gardens. A number of dwarfer species can justifiably take their place in smaller gardens: *A. hirsutus* has pale yellow flowers and *A. dioscoridis* pink. These spread by underground rhizomes and have flowering stems of 15–45cm/6–18in.

Agave. These succulent and architectural plants give a unique style and are pre-eminent container specimens. In mild gardens with perfect drainage *A. americana* will succeed, though its variegated forms are more risky. Several smaller species, particularly *parryi* and *utahensis*, are much hardier, to −10°c/14°F or lower. Both grow to about 60cm/2ft.

Aquilegia. The deep roots of aquilegias enable many to tolerate very dry spells and some from the western plains and mountains of the USA are well adapted to drought; *tridentata* and *skinneri* have orange-red flowers and *chrysantha* and *longissima* are a particularly elegant, soft yellow. Though relatively short-lived they will seed around in gritty soils. From 30–60cm/1–2ft.

Arum. Curious and useful, these plants are dormant through the heat of the summer, growing and flowering from winter to spring. *Arum italicum* subsp. *italicum* 'Marmoratum' has silver-marked arrow-like leaves, good in shade, and dramatic, red fruiting heads in autumn. *A. creticum* is the finest of all, with sweetly scented, soft yellow spathes in spring. Height 45–60cm/1½–2ft.

Athamanta. Rarely grown but valuable, small umbellifers (30–45cm/1–1½ft). In the species *turbith* and *cretensis* a fine tracery of thread-like foliage is the perfect foil to delicate heads of white, lacy flowers. The former has grown for over twenty years at the Research Garden of Reading University.

Baptisia. A wonderful genus of American prairie perennials (up to 1.5m/5ft). *B. australis* has loose spikes of violet-blue pea flowers in summer, followed by inflated, black pods. Though vulnerable to damage from slugs when small, established plants are very long-lived and trouble-free. Other rarely seen species such as *leucantha* and *pendula* are worth looking for.

Bupleurum. A unique genus of umbellifers with undivided, usually glaucous leaves, well adapted to the driest of conditions. *B. fruticosum* is an excellent shrub (1.8m/6ft or more, but will tolerate heavy pruning), with good foliage and heads of yellow flowers in summer transforming to warm orange-brown seedheads by late autumn. Most other species are small herbaceous perennials, sometimes with attractive, green bracts enclosing the flowers. For the patient gardener *B. angulosum* (30–45cm/1–1½ft) from the Pyrenees is the best of all, but slow to establish.

Centaurea. The cornflowers come in shades of yellow, purple, pink and blue and vary from small alpine

Bupleurum angulosum

tussocks, like *C. simplicicaulis* (25cm/10in), to tall, stately perennials such as *C. atropurpurea* (to 1.5m/5ft). Many also have attractive, deeply cut leaves in deep green to silver-white. They are archetypal social plants, perfect in meadows and wildish areas. Long in flower, with fascinating buds and seedheads, they deserve more attention from discerning gardeners.

Crocus. An addictive group of bulbs which provide colour from early autumn to spring. My favourites at the moment include *C. speciosus* 'Conqueror', *C. goulimyi* and *C. laevigatus*. The species generally have a more delicate beauty than the Dutch hybrids. Good in open, sunny spots where mice fear to tread.

Diascia. An example of the marvellous flora of South Africa, these are unbeatable for their length and freedom of flowering. Though many new cultivars have been raised, the longest-lived with us have been the species, *vigilis* (soft-pink), *fetcaniensis* (warm pink) and *integerrima* (with narrow, linear leaves). All spread steadily to 90cm/3ft across and 30cm/1ft high.

Digitalis. The foxgloves are more varied than many gardeners realize and include a number of good perennial species, particularly useful in dry, shady places. The slender spires of tiny, brownish flowers of *D. parviflora* stand out well against *Euonymus* 'Emerald Gaiety'. *D. laevigata* has more widely spaced, rather tubby, warm ochre flowers and *grandiflora* soft yellow.

Echinops. I would not be without these dramatic and thoroughly distinctive plants, buzzing with bees in high summer. There are several good named forms with drumstick heads of deep blue, plus the pale grey-white species *sphaerocephalus. E. ruthenicus* is distinguished for its silver-white glazed stems and undersides of the finely cut leaves. Height 1.2–1.8m/4–6ft.

Eryngium. The spiky form of these plants is as worthwhile as the metallic-blue flowerheads. Particularly good are selected forms of *bourgatii* with deeply cut, white-marked leaves and *amethystinum* which flowers later than most (45–60cm /1½–2ft). Our native sea holly (30cm/1ft) is a surprising and dramatic plant for poor gravelly soil with full exposure.

Withstanding drought

Ferula. The giant fennels (to 2.1m/7ft or more in flower) are among the largest and most remarkable of herbaceous perennials. They grow through the cooler months and flower in late spring, disconcertingly dying down in high summer. Give them a rich but well-drained soil in full sun. The plant known as 'Cedric Morris' (a form of *tingitana*) has distinctly cut and varnished leaves.

Gaura lindheimeri. One of the most valuable plants for dry and sunny gardens (1.2m/4ft), with a continuous succession of butterfly-like flowers in white or pink from summer on. Combines brilliantly with *Pennisetum orientale*, backed by a blue juniper, in my own garden. Renew regularly from seed or cuttings.

Geranium. The cranesbills include several drought-tolerant species like *G. tuberosum*, which dies down in summer soon after flowering, *macrorrhizum* and the South African *robustum* and *pulchrum*, both of which are pretty hardy. The alpines *G. argenteum*, *cinereum* and *dalmaticum*, plus hybrids like 'Appleblossom' need gritty, sunny places to prosper. Many other geraniums will tolerate dry periods and give value for little effort.

Gypsophila. Babies' breath, *G. paniculata*, is a spectacular if short-lived perennial for sandy soils in full sun, usually seen in double forms like 'Bristol Fairy' and 'Flamingo'. Its hybrid with *repens*, 'Rosy Veil', is a much more reliable and useful frontal plant for a hot, sunny border or drystone wall, seemingly impervious to drought, and forming a froth of pale pink in July and August.

Helleborus. As well as the *orientalis* hybrids, which are such cherished plants for dryish shade, several other hellebores are remarkably tolerant of drought. The evergreen Corsican species *argutifolius*, along with its hybrid × *sternii*, is best grown in full sun in good well-drained soil. For us the Bosnian *multifidus* subsp. *hercogovinus*, remarkable for its finely cut, palm-like leaves, grows well in a very dry and warm spot beneath a 'Cambridge Gage'. It is herbaceous and has flowering stems 30–45cm/1–1½ft tall.

Iris. An amazingly diverse genus with members suitable for wet and very dry soils. The small, winter-flowering *reticulata* brings colour in the bleakest of weather and thrives in gardens that are sun-baked in summer. Adventurous gardeners might try some of the easier Juno irises which come from the Near East: for

Gaura lindheimeri with *Pennisetum orientale* at Copton Ash, Kent.

example, *magnifica*, *bucharica* and the very beautiful *cycloglossa*, all of which will succeed in gritty raised beds in warm, dry gardens.

Limonium. Sea lavender is rarely seen in gardens but is good in open sandy places with other small perennials. 'Violetta' (45–60cm/1½–2ft in flower), a strong violet-blue selection of *L. platyphyllum*, is worth searching out.

Linum. *L. perenne* seems oddly named since individual plants are short-lived; however, it will seed around prettily in dry, sunny places and combines well with soft yellow *Scabiosa ochroleuca*. Much finer and a good perennial is *L. narbonense* with large, silver-blue, finely veined flowers on stems up to 45cm/1½ft. There are several valuable small bushy species too: *flavum* and *arboreum*, both 30cm/1ft, have yellow flowers and *suffruticosum* subsp. *salsoloides*, 5cm/2in, pearly white.

Papaver. A perfect genus for the dry garden, varying from the enormous chalices of the oriental poppies to tiny alpines like *alboroseum* (20cm/8in). The Turkish *P. spicatum* (syn. *heldreichii*) is distinctive for its velvety-grey entire leaves and softest tangerine flowers opening in succession down the stems (75cm/2½ft). *P. triniifolium* is a biennial poppy with exquisitely cut, silver-blue rosettes and orange flowers.

Salvia. A profusion of half-hardy and tender species in this familiar and diverse genus of sun lovers flowers late on into autumn and winter. The Mexicans *S. microphylla* and *greggii* (and hybrid × *jamensis*) will generally tolerate between −5 and −10°C/23 and 14°F and are astonishing for their length and freedom of flowering. They vary in colour from soft yellow to deep raspberry-pink and grow up to 90cm/3ft or more in mild gardens. Easy from cuttings.

Scabiosa. *S. ochroleuca* (90cm/3ft) is one of the loveliest of perennials and gently self-sows in dryish places; its light yellow flowers are produced continuously from June to October. A related plant, *Knautia macedonica*, produces the same effect in deep reddish-purple. For the connoisseur *Scabiosa graminifolia* (45cm/1½ft) will enchant with lilac-blue flowers over tussocks of grassy, silver leaves.

Sedum. One of those essential genera that lift the garden in the autumn. There are many new varieties, some of which eclipse old favourites like *S.* 'Herbstfreude' (Autumn Joy) and 'Munstead Red'. Look out for 'Matrona' and 'Purple Emperor' (both 60cm/2ft). Smaller varieties such as 'Vera Jameson' and the purple-black-leaved 'Bertram Anderson' are very effective in gritty soils with small bulbs, and myriad tiny carpeting forms will run through cracks and crevices in walls and paving, giving a whole range of leaf colours from white to vivid red.

Stipa. One among many good genera of dryland grasses, *Stipa gigantea*, with long-held heads of gold reaching 1.8m/6ft, excels throughout summer and autumn. For a moment it is eclipsed by the long, silvery, silky awns of *S. pulcherrima*, but these are lost all too quickly in late summer. They are collected together from the dry banks of Austrian vineyards and used like peacock feathers in the hair.

Verbena. These are useful plants for late summer and autumn colour. *V. bonariensis* will seed freely, its open habit merging well with many other plants. *V. rigida* is smaller and has deep violet flowers. The latter and carpeting varieties like 'Sissinghurst Pink' are not very hardy but are easily maintained by cuttings.

Veronica. The larger veronicas generally prefer good, reasonably moist soils. However, several of the small carpeting species are extremely drought-tolerant; *V. prostrata* (30cm/1ft across) in its various forms is excellent ground cover for small bulbs. Roy Lancaster's introduction of *V. peduncularis*, called 'Georgia Blue', is especially vigorous and versatile, flowering early in the year in sun or shade and with bronzed winter foliage.

Zauschneria. Hot-blooded North American relatives of willowherb which come into their own in late summer and autumn. The orange-red 'Dublin' remains one of the best for British gardens. Others worth growing include 'Western Hills' (vigorous and with deep red flowers) and 'Sally Walker'; 'Olbrich Silver' has remarkable silver-white foliage but needs hot summers to encourage good flowering. All are particularly suitable in raised beds and drystone walls, and grow to about 30cm/1ft high and 60cm/2ft across, sometimes more in ideal situations.

Verbena bonariensis self-seeded with tobaccos and *Salvia* 'Raspberry Royale' at Copton Ash, Kent.

LEFT Spiky irises contrast with smooth stones in a sea of gravel in Katia Demetriadi's Mediterranean garden at Heathfield in Surrey. BELOW Ripening fruit on espaliered 'Spartan' apple trees, terracotta house walls, Mississippi rocking chairs and a haze of lavender evoke warmer climes than England offers in Kenneth and Carla Carlisle's garden at Wyken Hall, Suffolk. RIGHT Scent and colour, and a paradise for bees, at The National Thyme Collection. Cultivated by Kevin and Susie White at Hexham Herbs, the south-facing raised bed gives thymes the drainage they need to defy the cold, wet winters in Northumberland.

Drought-tolerant plantings abound in Yellow Book gardens – here is a handful to add to the ones that Tim Ingram extols.

Bedfordshire
High View
Manor Farm, Swineshead
The Manor House, Stevington

Berkshire
The Thatch

**Bristol &
South Gloucestershire**
The Brake

Cambridgeshire
Barton Gardens
Pampisford Gardens
Sawston Gardens
Whittlesford Gardens

Cornwall
Eden Project

Denbighshire & Colwyn
Bryn Celyn
Trosyffordd

Dorset
Arne View
Millmead
Toad Hall
24a Western Avenue

Essex
Glen Chantry
Hyde Hall
Wickham Place Farm
Writtle Gardens

**Gloucestershire
North & Central**
The Dower House

Gwent
Croesllanfro Farm
Tredegar House

Hampshire
Crookley Pool
Flintstones
Ulvik

Hertfordshire
Abbotts House
The Barn
1 Daintrees
Wickham Hall

Isle of Wight
Northcourt Gardens

Kent
Withersdane Hall

**Lancashire, Merseyside
& Greater Manchester**
Boundary House Farm
Weeping Ash

Lincolnshire
2 School House

London
74 Allerton Road
1 Grange Park
80 Old Charlton Road

Norfolk
Baconsthorpe Old Rectory
3 Cromer Rd
Desert World
Magpies
Wretham Lodge

Northamptonshire
Ferns, Sulgrave Gardens
Great Harrowden Lodge

**Northumberland
& Tyne and Wear**
Garden Cottage

Nottinghamshire
Gringley Hall

Shropshire
Oteley
Radnor Cottage
Weston Park

Somerset
Copse Hall
Darkey Pang Tso Gang
The Mount, Wincanton

**Staffordshire
& part of West Midlands**
The Wickets

Suffolk
*28 Kingsway, Mildenhall
    Gardens*
The Old Hall
Pightle Cottage
Washbrook Grange

Surrey
Beverstone
Moleshill House
Odstock
6 Upper Rose Hill

Sussex
Little Dene
*The Old Farmhouse, Lancing
    College*
The Patched Gloves

Warwickshire
4 Arnold Villas

Worcestershire
24 Alexander Avenue

*Withstanding
drought*

CHRISTOPHER
HOLLIDAY

with expert insights by
FERGUS GARRETT
SARAH RAVEN
GRAHAM RICE

13 Making the most of high rainfall

We all love blaming the weather. Gardeners have it down to a fine art and rain is usually the chief culprit. It is either too wet or too dry, never just right. If it is too wet, we lapse into the 'we've had no summer' syndrome, and if it is too dry, we complain about wasting time wrestling with a hosepipe. High rainfall or a naturally damp site does have its advantages. Not only does rain dispense with the need to irrigate, but also it promotes lush growth and, combined with cool weather, prolongs the season. A damp garden looks fresh right through the summer and into autumn.

Much of the north of England suffers from being too wet and overcast. Some areas are wetter than most – Cumbria and North Wales are probably at the top of most people's list, so, if you live on the west side of England or Wales, you may as well get used to having more rain than most other parts of the country. The further north you go will mean it's going to be cooler too, although in gardens on the coast, this is usually offset by mild maritime winters. Altitude plays a part as well. The average temperatures drop 2°C/3.6°F for every 100m/330ft you climb, which means a later (and shorter) growing period. Finally, you can be in an area surrounded with mountains, where rain clouds congregate and give you more rain than you know what to do with.

Gardening in a damp climate leads to various problems – and has a few advantages. The main disadvantage is that if a frost follows heavy rainfall, you are more likely to lose frost-hardy plants – unless you have well-drained soil. (Frost-hardy plants will tolerate temperatures down to −5°C/23°F, maybe more if the drainage is good and the frosts not prolonged.) Another side effect of plentiful rainfall is that slugs and snails will be a menace, and a constant one in frost-free areas. If you like wandering round in the garden at night shrouded in waterproofs and wellies, clutching a pot of salt, gardening in damp conditions could realize the potential you never knew you had!

There are compensations, however, and the chief advantage of a wet summer is that the plants will look fresher for longer, having had more to drink. Instead of the gauzy, spent look that gardens in the south and east tend to have at summer's end, in the moist north-west it is possible to be looking good in August and September. As you get further north, this is helped by the fact that the seasons arrive a bit later too, so that, whereas the midsummer herbaceous riot will be past its best in Essex and Cornwall by the end of July, in the north of England beds and borders will be at their flowering peak.

Of course, as well as the effect of climate and factors such as elevation above sea level, distance from the ocean, the slope of the terrain and exposure to prevailing winds, the way we garden also depends on the soil. Some gardens have the wet climate yet are sufficiently free-draining to permit the growing of plants not normally associated with dampness. Others have unenviable clay as well as heavy rain, which poses all sorts of extremes – too moisture-retentive but likely to split and crack in the odd heat-wave. The plants that we grow in the UK do not like extremes. Yet other gardens have high rainfall and in addition are blessed with natural water on site, so the owners must plant accordingly.

I have learned to live with a damp climate in spite of often flying in the face of it with Mediterranean-style planting. And I want to share with you the ingenuity of other keen gardeners who cope with conditions that most of us would baulk at.

A south-facing site with free-draining soil

The stretch of Cumbria where I live was formerly in Lancashire and is treated to 1,090mm/43in of rain a year. I outwitted the problem of high rainfall by accident. I set out to create a subtropical garden with exotic-looking foliage which would look good for twelve months of the year. This is the sort of gardening which can involve wrapping the plants in winter or risk them dying as frost follows heavy rain. Parcelling up plants like Christmas presents has never appealed to me; besides, on a windy coast it can be a losing battle. Fortunately, my garden in Grange-over-Sands enjoys a mild estuary climate with Gulf Stream influence and overlooks Morecambe Bay. The site is sloping and dished to the sun, facing full south. The soil is stony, on limestone, which is of course porous and means that the plants never become water-logged. This is an important part of my happy accident, considering we can get over twenty-four hours of heavy rain regularly, and especially in winter. For example, the nearby flat golf course is frequently flooded.

The best part of the accident was to stumble on a plant which looks exotic, yet thrives in high rainfall. Phormiums are indicated in plant encyclopaedias as preferring moist but well-drained soil. The problem of survival lies in waterlogged roots becoming frosted and the plants dying. With ample drainage for the roots, and ample movement of air by the coast, these plants flourish in my garden and their large, sword-shaped leaves give

PRECEDING PAGES Raindrops glisten on poppies and cow parsley in the wildflower meadow at The Mill House, Cumbria. The drawing is of Dalham Tower, Cumbria, from the Yellow Book 1993.

RIGHT In October the garden at Charney Well, Cumbria, luxuriates with *Phormium* 'Yellow Wave', *P. tenax* 'Purpureum' and *Yucca gloriosa* 'Variegata'. Phormiums and Mediterranean plantings of

rosemary, santolina, *Artemisia* 'Powis Castle' and cordylines survive the winter wet because of the well-drained sloping site. *Vitis coignetiae* is taking on its crimson autumn hues in the background.

SARAH RAVEN

Autumn colour

Damp-loving perennials and shrubs light up the garden with furnace-coloured leaves in autumn and provide a backdrop to the last flowers of the year – such as pink and magenta asters, sky-blue *Salvia uliginosa* and red hot pokers.

One of my favourite shrubs is *Rhus* × *pulvinata* Autumn Lace Group, which is easy to grow in moist, well-drained soil. It performs the same structural role as cotinus does in drier areas. Rhus bursts into flames in late autumn, each leaf turning a different colour – scarlet, orange, gold, deep red and purple.

Some viburnums too, such as *V. opulus* and *V. sargentii*, take centre stage at this time of year, contributing luscious fruits or brightly coloured leaves. Then there are striped phormiums, the crimson-fingered leaves of *Ricinus communis* 'Carmencita' and, at a lower level, the huge, plate-shaped leaves of *Darmera peltata*, outlined in scarlet, merging into green and crimson towards the heart. All relish damp ground and bring rich rewards in autumn.

Making the most of high rainfall

Many tropical-looking plants enjoy damp, steamy conditions in summer. Here *Ricinus communis* 'Carmencita', *Rhus glabra* 'Laciniata', *Eucalyptus gunnii* and *Phormium* 'Sundowner' jostle for space in the Exotic Garden at Great Dixter, Sussex. 'Rapid growth requires generous water availability,' writes Christopher Lloyd, 'so in August we are constantly having irrigation blitzes.'

exactly the exotic look I am after. Where a concrete path and most of the hard core underneath have been removed, *Phormium cookianum* subsp. *hookeri* 'Tricolor' does exceptionally well, in spite of the stony soil. Every time it rains, more stones appear on the surface. In another area of the garden, on a south-facing slate terrace, I used a pneumatic drill to create planting holes 30 cm/1 ft deep in the hard core and then filled them with well-rotted compost. I planted *Phormium tenax purpureum* cultivars and gave them a mulch of newspaper and slate chippings. In the wet summer of 1998 (1,500mm/59in of rain that year), the rate of growth was astonishing. The combination of a naturally free-draining site and plenty of moisture worked its magic. Now, after three seasons, the plants look twice their age. In the plant world I think we can consider this an advantage.

The benefits of good drainage

Winters tend to be getting wetter and more overcast rather than crisp, frosty and sunny. This invariably leads to frost-tender plants just rotting off rather than being killed by the frost. Those that will withstand frost often cannot cope with excessive all-pervading damp during the long winter months. With good drainage you can grow many plants that would not take kindly to frosts following heavy rains and, depending on the duration of the frost and the degree of drainage, many plants will survive lower temperatures. For instance, I am tentatively trying opuntias (*O. robusta*) outside, submerged in a sea of gravel on a steep rockery. These will be more prone to winter wet than frost.

If you are not blessed with naturally free-draining soil, there are several ways you can adapt it. If the water table is high, you may need to install land drains. For waterlogged soil, try trenches dug 45–60cm/1½–2ft deep, half-fill them with coarse stones and infill with soil and generous shovel-fuls of gravel. Alternatively, you can spread a thick layer of sharp gravel and dig it in, adding a further good handful when you plant. A less backbreaking solution is to build raised beds to create the sharp drainage that Mediterranean-looking plants require.

You can then adapt the planting. Tough yuccas, such as *Yucca gloriosa* 'Variegata', can look at home and healthy if

the conditions are right. I have several cistus, not noted for their longevity in damp climates, that are now over six years old. Lavender, rosemary, santolinas, silvery *Artemisia* 'Powis Castle', *Ballota pseudodictamnus* – all thrive, obviously because they depend on sharply drained soil. I find it best to trim the last three plants back quite hard in spring to stimulate new foliage and then again before the end of August so that they can bulk up before the winter. *Acacia dealbata* thrives almost too well and has to be trimmed back after flowering. The biggest success has been with *Echium pininana*, which, if it survives the first winter, will normally survive the second and flower in its third spring, before dying quietly and hopefully self-seeding. Hardy palm trees such as *Trachycarpus fortunei*, the Chusan palm, benefit from the rain but must be protected from a windy spot. *Trachycarpus wagnerianus* would be more appropriate as its leaves are much tougher. *Chamaerops humilis*, the dwarf European fan palm, also likes moisture and feeding and is a much better bet as a wind-tolerant specimen.

Shallow soil and partial shade at Golf Cottage

Even if you haven't as much sun as you would like but have more than enough drainage, there is still a way around the problem of high rainfall. At Golf Cottage in Colwyn Bay the garden created by flower arranger Keith Smithies and his partner Paul Moffatt is bursting with accent plants and luxuriant foliage, topped up with summer colour from perennials, annuals and unusual half-hardies such as brilliant yellow *Euryops pectinatus* and scarlet *Lobelia tupa*. Since moving to Golf Cottage in September 1996 they have not experienced a harsh winter, so even a plant such as *Agave stricta* remains outside in a pot all winter. Soil and light conditions, as well as degrees of moisture, vary in different areas of the garden and the owners have achieved the right balance by planting the most suitable plants in each.

Golf Cottage is set on a slope, 175m/574ft above sea level and roughly a mile from the sea. A natural water-course starts at the top of the 1-acre site, running down the hillside and into a gully which goes out under the road

at the bottom of the front garden. On one side of the back garden, several mature Scots pines provide shelter and shade, and also drainage. Their intricate roots soak up water, even after heavy downpours, and for this area the owners have created an irrigation system with an old hosepipe. Digging planting holes is difficult in shallow soil over tree roots. Here Keith and Paul imported topsoil and layered it with plenty of farmyard manure to improve soil texture. The imported soil did bring a few nettles with it, but was deemed a worthwhile exercise. Every spring they mulch with organic matter and well-rotted chicken manure to boost growth.

The beds and borders at Golf Cottage are full of choice plants, showing that there are plenty of subjects to grow in partial shade in a region of high rainfall, as long as the drainage is good. A notable success is a tall *Melianthus major*, the statuesque glaucous-leaved perennial. The silver sword-like foliage of *Astelia chathamica*

adds permanent architectural interest along with phormiums such as 'Coral Queen' and 'Jester', a variegated fatsia (*Fatsia japonica* 'Variegata'), griselinia and white abutilon. In an area where native ferns were growing well, Keith has enchanced the planting with the more interesting *Dryopteris affinis* 'Cristata'.

One of the problems of living with high rainfall is the inevitability of a large slug population. As a professional flower arranger, Keith has to have plenty of hostas for cutting throughout the growing season. The very top of the garden was found to be too shady but elsewhere he has succeeded in producing luxuriant clumps of foliage in only four seasons. His favourite 'good doers' include *Hosta* 'Sum and Substance' which is lime green and the variegated 'Frances Williams'. 'True Blue' is not as affected by slugs as some hostas but Keith treats them all with nematodes (a biological control method) before the new foliage emerges and the treatment normally lasts the whole season.

*Making
the most
of high
rainfall*

ABOVE Roughly 100cm/40in of rain falls at Plas Llidiardau, Cardiganshire. When conifers, rhododendrons and azaleas were removed from the north-east-facing bank, the moss *Polystichum setiferum* took over.

In the foreground *Geranium macrorrhizum, G. procurrens, Blechnum penna-marina, Acaena microphylla, Parahebe catarractae* and *Arcostaphllus nevadensis* create a dense tapestry effect.

RIGHT A stream feeds the bog garden at Hazel Mount in Cumbria and in early summer statuesque gunneras and the enormous fleshy leaves of *Lysichiton americanus* contrast with irises, rodgersias and hostas.

Keith's unscathed hostas are enough to make anybody envious, but there is another plant that has eluded his slug battle. He has a weakness for delphiniums and the slugs always get there first. He says it is because he is never quite sure where he has planted them and by the time he realizes where the emerging shoots are appearing, it's too late. Next year, he promises, will be better.

In a 'wild area' of the garden there used to be a profusion of foxgloves which Keith hoped would self-seed. For some reason they never took off. With hindsight he blames himself for mulching rather too generously with the bounty of pine needles they have, which were probably too acid for the foxgloves. Sometimes the simplest of plants can defeat us all. The bluebells are naturalizing well, however, which is a compensation.

Where water collects in the bog garden, the planting matches the conditions, so *Zantedeschia* 'Green Goddess' and rodgersia are effective. The thirsty Chilean giant rhubarb, *Gunnera manicata*, is planted by the pond in normal soil, yet flourishes despite being a bog plant.

We should never underestimate the work that has gone into a garden where the plants look healthy, luxuriant and as if they have always belonged there.

Heavy clay at Merlyn

What do you do when faced with the same rainfall at nearby Abergele but have solid clay and acid conditions? Edmund and Joyce Riding are retired and started the garden at Merlyn in 1987. They have never dug over their 2 acres because of the clay and 60 per cent of the garden is grass and 40 per cent given over to borders. They plant with a mattock. Yet they have tamed the site and should be justly proud of their results, for here are extensive borders displaying generous sweeps of planting. Developed from a field, it is mainly flat with a gentle slope away from the house and is open and light.

Faced with the clay, the Ridings have sensibly worked with it, while capitalizing on the acid soil and plentiful rain. Their solution is simple. Every spring they get thirty bales of straw and strew a thick mulch of the stuff on every square centimetre of border. They also add a dressing of ammonium sulphate, as the straw tends to take some of the nitrogen out of the soil. All grass cuttings and shreddings are also added in the bid to cover the ground and lighten the soil.

Lace-cap hydrangeas, hostas, hellebores, daphnes, cyclamen and cistus all do well in the main borders. Perennials are planted in broad sweeps. Hardy geraniums and nepeta soften the edges of beds and when flowering is over they are strimmed back to promote new growth. It looks rather drastic at first, but pays dividends when fresh foliage begins to appear which revitalizes the garden in late summer. A dose of heavy rain soon kick-starts the plants into action.

They also have a stream running through the garden, which the farmer had tried to dam and divert with stones. The Ridings decided to take advantage of it, killed the grass along its banks and planted taxodium, rodgersias, aruncus, water iris and photinia. In a nearby bog garden they have had success with hemerocallis, filipendula, *Euphorbia griffithii* 'Fireglow' and *Photinia davidiana*. Cornus offer year-round interest and are particularly effective in winter, when green and yellow *C. stolonifera* 'Flaviramea' contrasts with the flaming stems of *C. alba* 'Elegantissima' and *C. a.* 'Sibirica'.

There are some plants which have not done so well, however. Meconopsis are devoured by magpies and crows, and pheasants find the tulip bulbs a special delicacy. Rabbits and moles do the usual damage.

The Ridings have triumphed over the stubborn clay by planting suitable plants for the conditions. This does not sound so very amazing, but how many of us are so self-disciplined? The straw mulch pays dividends for the whole season – and who can quarrel with the no-dig policy when it works?

Fergus Garrett

Wet weather tactics

Digging and planting in wet conditions could ruin your soil structure unless the necessary precautions are taken. Planks and boards laid on the ground help to spread your weight and minimize the damage. Placed on a lawn, on the edge of a border and into the border (avoiding as many plants as possible), these make a firm platform on which to walk and work. Scaffolding planks sawn in half are ideal, but if you cannot find these, thick plywood cut to size will do.

In wet weather we leave soil preparation to the last minute. Freshly dug ground is ready to soak up water like a sponge. And once the soil has become saturated just the mechanical action of plunging a spade into it will do some damage. A garden fork, being less physical, is preferable, especially on clay soils.

Organic matter is essential to the soil's wellbeing and a healthy soil means a more tolerant one. Washed horticultural grit (2–4 mm) is a must in heavy soils such as Dixter's Wadhurst clay. Mix plenty of this in and it'll be there for good, always making future cultivation easier. Add it until your soil is loose and crumbly. On light soils grit will not be necessary, just the organic matter in copious quantities.

Always be tidy and clear up as you go along. It not only looks good but allows you to think more clearly as well. Dragging half the garden round stuck to the bottom of your boot cannot be good for the soul.

And what about the gardener in the rain? It can be terribly uncomfortable, so make sure you are warm and dry. Wear waterproofs that allow you to move freely, good warm waterproof boots, a nice hat (knitted by granny is the best) and warm gloves, including several spare pairs to change into as well as waterproof ones.

LEFT Blue Himalayan poppies, here *Meconopsis grandis*, thrive in the humus-rich, slightly acid, damp soil in the wild garden at Dalemain in Cumbria. Jane Hasell-McCosh divides and replants the poppies every few years to maintain vigour and uses sheep's wool to provide an insulating layer against the winter wet. ABOVE At Great Dixter Fergus Garrett works off planks to avoid compacting the heavy Wadhurst clay soil.

At the water's edge

At Stonyford Cottage in Cuddington, Cheshire, Janet and Anthony Overland and son Andrew have adopted an informal approach too. They run a nursery and their philosophy is to work with the conditions given: a damp site with a large 'Monet-style' pool, sandy soil and areas of shade. Bridges lead to an island in the centre and trees grow around the pool up to the water's edge. At the outset, grit and compost were added to the soil, but now the plants are left to get on with it. This is textbook 'right plant, right place' school of thinking.

Specimen trees, chosen to suit the damp conditions, include *Nyssa sylvatica* (black gum), grown for its orange, yellow and red autumn tints, and *Cornus controversa* 'Variegata', prized for its tiered 'wedding-cake' habit and creamy variegated foliage. *Cercidiphyllum japonicum* (the katsura tree) likes 'deep, fertile, humus-rich moist but well-drained soil, preferably neutral to acid, in sun or dappled shade, sheltered from cold dry winds' – which is not asking much! It is thriving here because it is sheltered and has enough moisture, its foliage fading grandly to russets and pinks and the falling leaves smelling of burnt sugar.

In the damp, shady areas *Matteuccia struthiopteris*, the elegant ostrich fern, is in its element. The snowy woodrush (*Luzula nivea*) works well and silver banner grass (*Miscanthus sacchariflorus*) has reached well over 3m/10ft. *Ligularia stenocephala* rewards with numerous yellow flowerheads on black-green stems in early summer.

Candelabra primulas, rodgersias and astilbes thrive by the water's edge. *Phormium tenax* and *Gunnera manicata*, despite having roots in moisture all year round, have survived 7–14cm/3–5in of ice on the pool. The gunnera is covered with straw in autumn and then with its own leaves, which rot down through the winter and eventually become a mulch. The more manageable but less dramatic *Darmera peltata* (syn. *Peltiphyllum peltatum*) contributes its pale flower clusters in spring. *Angelica archangelica*, grown as a biennial, is useful for adding height. The Overlands have found that *Hydrangea arborescens* 'Annabelle' suits their garden, whereas hydrangeas in general do not. Like bamboos, they enjoy moisture but resent sitting in it. *Fargesia murieliae*, with yellow stems and bright green leaves, thrives here in a boggy place above the moisture line.

Fell-side fantasy

Perched on the lower slopes of Catbells (415m/1,360ft), Brackenburn has everything but its own funicular railway. It is home to three streams, a waterfall, a bog garden, terraced borders, mature acers and conifers, an abundance of slopes, and a spectacular site overlooking Derwent Water. The views are enough to inspire any Lakeland romantic writer. In fact, the novelist Sir Hugh Walpole fell for this lovely spot, describing it as 'This enchanted place, this paradise on Catbells'. He converted the 1905 bungalow into a gentleman's residence and lived here from 1920 to 1941. The garden would have been more heavily wooded in his time. After several years asleep under advancing thickets of bamboo and bracken, the garden was 'lost' until Derek and Christine Ellwood restored and improved it in just over a decade. They are still coping with a legacy of mature conifers planted in the 1920s which are showing signs of age. The intense blue of *Picea pungens* is valued for contrast with other conifers, but the tree is on a descending spiral and will have to be removed eventually.

Christine and Derek are perfectionists and it shows. The Bracken Burn, named after the natural beck which drains off Catbells' bracken-cloaked fell-side, runs through the garden. They have gone to a lot of trouble to make sure that the burn flows with the right kind of fall. They had to make it less of a shallow stream and more of a gushing waterfall cascading into pools. These come in very handy, says Christine, as they can syphon from them during drought periods, which is not so easy from a stream.

Droughts are few and far between in an area which has around 2,290mm/90in of rain per annum, but when you are on a natural water supply, water must never be taken for granted. A recent Ruby Wedding present from the family was an elaborate rain gauge! Derek has to check the gutters for leaves on a weekly basis. Apparently, the force of water from their mountainside holding tank is enough to create a Chatsworth-type fountain soaring well above the two-storey residence. At the top of the Bracken Burn's entry through their garden they have planted mainly herbaceous plants, such as rodgersia and lysichiton, the skunk cabbage. Hart's-tongue ferns (*Asplenium scolopendrium*) abound naturally and the oak and apple fern, royal fern (*Osmunda regalis*) and shuttlecock fern

---

Making the most of high rainfall

RIGHT At Lower Hall in Shropshire the River Worfe dominates the garden. A high water table enables Christopher and Donna Dumbell to grow moisture-loving plants such as candelabra primulas, lysichiton, *Primula florindae*, hostas and *Gunnera manicata*. Delicate-looking *Onoclea sensibilis* contrasts with broad-leaved waterside plants. But winter floods and waterlogging can bring disaster. When the river flooded and then froze in the winter of 1979–80, most of the rhododendrons that were thriving on the light, sandy soil were killed. The Dumbells replaced them with roses, of which *Rosa brunonii* is a particular favourite.

GRAHAM RICE

Contented weeds and flourishing flowers

Returning to our Northamptonshire cottage garden after two summer months away, we both bless and curse the rain. The blossoming bindweed is strangling the wheelbarrow propped against the shed, and has sneakily squeezed through the boards to run up the spade on its hook inside. Hairy bittercress, in alarming candelabra, is topped with slender pods poised to fling their seeds into uncolonized territory; **I remember, too late, that I should have worn sunglasses as protection against the spitting seeds as I pull up the plants.**

But the first step outside the door when home from the airport also reveals the unnerving fragrance of a luxuriant tobacco plant. The elder bushes are weighed down with glistening, black berries: I must alert my wine-making friends to bring their buckets. Although there's a sad carpet of rotting petals under the roses, there are still plenty of **blooms to cut for the reviving house in the morning. When it has been a wet summer while we've been away, the contented weeds are a fair price for the flourishing flowers.**

Across the water in our new Pennsylvania home the horticulture is less intense. Deep winter snow sparks woodland flowers in its rapid melt and there it is again: hairy bittercress, accidentally brought from Europe long since and now spreading rapidly northwards through the state. But here it's the sedges which look to be the problem. Over 160 species are found, and it was instantly clear that they would soon be spreading from the marshy woods into any planting we establish and which the deer, temporarily, ignore. But we also have high bush blueberries and, we hope, slipper orchids.

The rain sustains our plants in our absence, the glistening elderberries and roses dripping with flowers prove the point; but it also creates hard weeding, and an increasing devotion to deep mulch, on our return.

(*Matteuccia struthiopteris*) luxuriate in shady corners.

On the opposite side of the garden, in the shade of mature woodland, there is a sloping bog garden, with a stream running through it. Here, Christine has found that the *Camellia japonica* and *C. × williamsii* cultivars do best, surviving the odd cold winter (usually around −5°C/27°F). Because the garden is in the shadow of Catbells, it is planted to accommodate shady areas. If it does freeze it is unlikely to thaw out during the day, so a prolonged frost could cause a lot of damage. However, because Brackenburn is on a slope, cold air flows away from the garden and diminishes the likelihood of a hard frost – which can grip nearby Keswick but leaves Brackenburn relatively unscathed. This area of the garden is also dedi-

cated to generous plantings of candelabra primula, *Iris sibirica*, astilbe and hostas. For late colour there are various eucryphias and for the autumn a young liquidambar. Having torn out the previous invasive bamboos on their hands and knees, Derek and Christine have planted some non-invasive bamboos. 'Don't ask me what they all are,' exclaimed Christine; 'trying to pronounce their names is bad enough!'

In late August a third pond has the merest trickle dribbling into it. This is the frogs' pond. Frogs are essential here to control some of the inevitable slugs that enjoy the rocks and damp. When Christine noticed that the tadpoles were not developing, she tossed tiny chunks of raw rump steak into the pond. After a piranha-like bubbling, the

ABOVE At Eastgrove Cottage in Worcestershire, the tomato-red flowers of *Crocosmia* 'Lucifer' add sizzle to the midsummer scene.

RIGHT Hostas, ferns and *Persicaria bistorta* 'Superba' thrive in the moist, acid soil of the bog garden at Brackenburn in Cumbria, in spite of little sun on this part of the garden during the winter, when the

ground may be frozen for several days. Perched on the lower slopes of Catbells, the steep site makes the most of a natural stream, waterfalls running off the fellside, and the area's high rainfall.

steak is devoured – and she gets sabre-toothed frogs!

Deer are also a menace. Derek and Christine refuse to be caged in with deer fences up to 4m/13ft high, so they have placed brightly coloured windmills along the present fence and strewn lion dung around. The deer are plucky, though, and are totally undeterred by the manic antics of three Scottish terriers. A dog fence and the dogs themselves help keep the rabbits away.

A cerise-pink *Rhododendron arboreum* takes centre stage in spring when the flowers obliterate the foliage. Lakeland gardens often struggle to be colourful after the flush of rhododendrons and azaleas in spring and early summer but at Brackenburn hydrangeas and late-flowering perennials fill the potential late-summer gap. Christine prefers to see *Hydrangea arborescens* 'Annabelle' grown on top of a wall 'because it is so floppy' and she has enough guaranteed moisture to do this. *H. paniculata* 'Grandiflora' also finds favour with her as it is easy to keep in check. Although Japanese anemones, agapanthus, rudbeckia and *Chelone obliqua* all do well, she finds *Kirengeshoma palmata* to be subject to mildew. 'Damp, dank and not enough drainage,' she explains. Roses also struggle for the same reason – and from lack of heat.

Christine's favourite sorbus is *S.* 'Eastern Promise', which looks at home on the upper slopes of the garden. Interestingly, in drier areas she manages to grow *Ceanothus*

thyrsiflorus var. *repens*, *Phormium tenax*, *Yucca filamentosa*, *Hebe* 'Purple Queen', acanthus, and even a *Callistemon rigidus*. Although the conifers have become a worry, Christine holds out against planting more ('*so 1970s*'), while Derek would prefer more conifers and heathers.

Soil erosion at Lamorran House

Located on the Roseland peninsula in a dream-like setting at St Mawes in Cornwall, with fine views towards St Anthony's Head, Lamorran House enjoys a climate even more favourable than the surrounding mild areas. Severe frosts are almost unheard of, barring the odd freak year, but at 1,000mm/40in annual rainfall is only slightly less than that of south Cumbria.

Lamorran's 4-acre gardens are the inspiration of Robert and Maria-Anntoinetta Dudley-Cooke who have gardened here since the early 1980s. Their keen head gardener, Mark Brent, says the climate could not be bettered but, because the gardens are located on a south-facing slope and are subjected to prolonged spells of heavy rain, they are designed and planted to minimize soil creep – the slow but continuous downward movement of the surface soil. The slope is terraced with retaining walls to hold the topsoil. Even so, when sun and drying winds cause cracks in the earth, these fill with rainwater and carry the soil downhill. As a result, levels of topsoil are deeper on the lower levels.

Close planting helps to anchor the soil and provides a dense protective canopy. The slate/shale subsoil drains rapidly and, to keep drainage as free as possible, plants are angled so that the crowns don't catch the rain. To prevent excess drying out of the soil surface, Mark applies mulches in spring and autumn. Even after heavy rainfall the soil can be worked quickly.

These conditions mean that a love of exotica can be indulged to the full. The 120-strong colony of *Trachycarpus fortunei* and half that number of *Chamaerops humilis* provide an evergreen framework and establish the gardens' 'tropical' atmosphere. Aloes make use of however much water is thrown at them and produce such lush growth that maintenance can become a problem. Other less hardy exotics include agaves, beschorneria, furcraeas and cyatheas, all of which enjoy high rainfall but are less tolerant of winter wet. The agaves are treated with sulphur to prevent the fungal attacks that rot soft tissue.

Cyathea medullaris, the black tree fern, barely stops growing in winter because the temperature rarely drops lower than 6–7°C/43–44°F. It is a good example of a plant tolerating the damp climate in winter up to a point. By January and February cooler temperatures prevent it from growing and it may just sit and sulk (the average minimum low would be 1–2°C/34–35°F at this time.) The plant needs to be fleeced to give protection in colder weather.

As well as planting at an angle so that rainwater does not collect, with *Nolina longifolia*, a member of the Agavaceae from south central Mexico, the Dudley-Cookes have taken the additional precaution of planting the rootball on top of a semi-buried rock to keep it proud of the possibly saturated soil. The swollen, corky trunk can reach 3m/10ft and the pendulous leaves, which are 32mm/1½in at the base, gradually taper to a thread and can be more than 2m/6½ft long at the base and up to 2m/5ft at the tip.

Although the rainfall limits the choice of plants from desert climes, it can be turned to advantage when growing New Zealand plants such as the conifer *Dacrydium cupressinum*, bamboos and *Araliaceae*. And the underplanting at Lamorran is sustained with dwarf azaleas, which appreciate the damp conditions and semi-shade provided by *Trachycarpus fortunei*.

The wet climate compounds the problem of lawns becoming compacted by the feet of garden visitors. Spiking in autumn is a tiring but necessary task.

Bold Romantic style with a Northumbrian twist

You don't find many gardens hidden in old quarries. The one at Bide-a-Wee Cottage, a few miles from Morpeth in Northumberland, is a remarkable feat. The sandstone quarry had soil that was initially very mineral, derived from quarry spoil lacking any humus content. After 'a lot of hard work and vast amounts of humus', some areas have good, friable soil, but in others the soil is more like building rubble than compost, with stones coming to the surface every time it rains. Mark Robson, now in his early

thirties, who started gardening here when he was ten, says mulching with chipped bark is a necessity – and there is a ready source at nearby Kielder Forest.

In Northumberland the summers are cool and short, and the rainfall here is 890mm/35in per annum. As well as the inhospitable growing conditions, wind exposure is a problem, alleviated to some extent by mature sycamore and hawthorn. At the lowest level in the quarry, not unsurprisingly, the conditions are ideal for a pond and bog garden. A natural spring feeds the large pool liner.

Mark, influenced by the 'Bold Romantic' European / North American style of perennial planting pioneered by Wolfgang Oehme and James Van Sweden, likes 'strong structure and massed exuberant planting'. He uses bold groups of grasses and foliage for year-round interest and includes some native species, such as *Deschampsia* and *Molinia*, to echo the surrounding landscape of rough natural grassland. He describes this as a 'Northumbrian twist on the Bold Romantic style'. Other favourite plants for the moist areas include *Inula magnifica* and *I. racemosa* which, with their yellow daisy flowers, illuminate the bog garden. For something more restrained, *Filipendula ulmaria* 'Flore Pleno' and *F. palmata* 'Rubra' add subtle touches of white and red-pink respectively.

The quarry does not heat up quickly as it has 6m/20ft sides. In fact it is a frost pocket in winter. There is no problem in keeping roots cool in the summer. The relative cool and reliable rainfall means that the wet or damp areas are never in danger of drying out.

Living with high rainfall

There are some things you cannot change and water-retentive soil and high rainfall are two of them. If you have to contend with both, it is rarely worth going against the grain. Find the appropriate plants (a few favourites are listed below), invest in adequate waterproofs and enjoy the lush growing conditions.

Although rain is often regarded as a necessary nuisance for humans, plants prefer it and if you choose them carefully and they have the right soil conditions to survive, your garden could easily look better than most – especially late in the season.

Study the foliage contrasts at Bide-a-Wee Cottage in Northumberland. In May, the emerging giant leaves of *Gunnera manicata* are echoed by the round fleshy leaves of *Bergenia cordifolia* in the foreground. Variegated *Phalaris arundinacea* var. *picta* and Solomon's seal (*Polygonatum × hybridum*) make effective foils. All these plants are thriving in the moist soil on the edge of the old quarry.

Damp border in hot colours

Yellows, fiery reds and cooling blues feature in this damp, well-drained border in partial shade (7 x 3m/22 x 10ft). Most of the plants are greedy feeders as well as moisture lovers. They reach their peak in mid-summer and high rainfall will keep the display going to late summer. Feed the cannas, hedychiums and the *Cosmos atrosanguineus* during the growing season and lift them before the first frosts.

1 *Iris sibirica*
2 *Ligularia stenocephala*
3 *Canna* 'Durban'
4 *Hedychium spicatum*
5 *Canna* 'Striata'
6 *Hemerocallis* 'Stafford'
7 *Lobelia cardinalis*
8 *Hedychium gardnerianum*
9 *Canna* 'Black Knight'
10 *Hemerocallis* 'Golden Chimes'
11 *Canna* 'Lucifer'
12 *Hedychium densiflorum*
13 *Kirengeshoma palmata*
14 *Agapanthus* 'Blue Giant' seedlings
15 *Rudbeckia fulgida* var. *sullivantii* 'Goldsturm'
16 *Hosta* 'Gold Standard'
17 *Myosotidium hortensia*
18 *Filipendula ulmaria* 'Aurea'

19 *Schizostylis coccinea* 'Grandiflora'
20 *Gentiana asclepiadea*
21 *Persicaria virginiana* 'Painter's Palette'
22 *Cosmos atrosanguineus*

23 *Hosta sieboldiana* var. *elegans*
24 *Hosta sieboldiana* 'Frances Williams'
25 *Euphorbia polychroma*
26 *Tradescantia* 'Osprey'
27 *Hemerocallis* 'Corky'

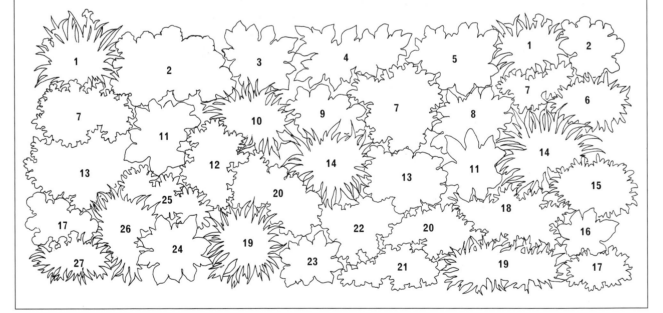

Black-eyed Susan, *Rudbeckia fulgida* var. *sullivantii* 'Goldsturm', is brilliant for lighting up the late-summer border and it has a good, long flowering season into October if it is dead-headed.

Perennials & shrubs for high rainfall

Agapanthus. Valued for its blue flowers in late summer, agapanthus prefers what eludes most gardeners – fertile and moist soil, yet well drained and in full sun. Originally from South Africa, it does appreciate the sun. In a pot, it flowers when younger. In cold areas give a protective mulch. 'Blue Giant' will reach over 90cm/3ft but is normally 60cm/2ft tall. The transparent seedheads can be left in the early part of the winter. *A.* 'Bressingham White' is a good white form.

Canna 'Striata'. This canna has striking variegated leaves of green and yellow with orange flowers up to 1.5m/5ft high. Cannas are thirsty and greedy and need lots of heat to fulfil their potential. In a cool climate dig them up every winter and store in barely moist leafmould in the shed. They need repotting in the spring and plenty of heat to give them a good start before planting in mid-summer. Planted too early and they won't reach their potential in late summer. Provide contrast with the bronze foliage of *C.* 'Black Knight'.

Cardiocrinum giganteum. Not for the faint-hearted or the impatient, this giant lily from China can take seven years or more to flower before dying and leaving offsets. Plant the bulb just below the surface in autumn, in a cool, shady site. It likes plenty of moisture but must not be waterlogged – nor can it be allowed to dry out. Feed well and you will be rewarded with a spire of white trumpet lilies up to 4m/13ft high, and a powerful scent.

Cimicifuga simplex 'Brunette'. Invaluable as an autumn-flowering woodland plant, this prefers moist and fertile soil in partial shade and requires support. 'Brunette' has finely cut, deep purple foliage with purple-tinted off-white flowers on an inflorescence nearly 90cm/3ft high. Originally from northern temperate regions, it is found in moist, shady woodland.

Cosmos atrosanguineus. The intoxicating chocolate-scented cosmos (from Mexico) is a great-value long-flowerer from mid-summer to autumn. It lollops all over the place and needs support or draping over another plant. The chocolate-maroon flowers fit the scent perfectly. The plant favours well-drained but moist soil that is not too rich and in winter is best lifted in cold areas or mulched.

Dierama pulcherrimum. This cormous perennial likes to be in humus-rich well-drained soil with plenty of water and lots of sun in the growing season. Pendulous spikes up to 5ft/1.5m have magenta-pink, dangling, trumpet flowers. Originally from moist mountainous regions of Africa, this one is from Zimbabwe. It looks superb draped elegantly over a pool or pond, as long as its roots are well drained.

Echinacea purpurea 'Robert Bloom'. Mauve-crimson daisies are not thick on the ground and this is good in a well-drained spot in full sun with a good mulch of compost, though it will tolerate a little shade. It reaches about 1.2m/4ft. Originally from central and eastern North America, it grew on prairies or in open woodland. Deadhead to extend flowering interest.

Gentiana asclepiadea. The willow gentian offers a succession of trumpet-shaped, dark blue flowers from mid-summer to autumn. A woodland native, it looks good with ferns and grasses in partial shade and acid soil. Prefers moist but well-drained soil and reaches 60–90cm/2–3ft. It originates from the central and southern mountains of Europe and Turkey.

Hedychium gardnerianum. This Kahili ginger grows to more than 2m/6½ft, given plenty of moisture and a monthly liquid feed. It has fragrant, lemon-yellow flowers with eye-catching brilliant, red stamens. The foliage is lush and luxuriant, so it combines well with cannas for that exotic look. It likes sun or partial shade, sheltered from strong winds. It comes from the moist wooded areas of Asia. In winter it can either be mulched heavily or dug up and kept just moist in the shed.

Hemerocallis 'Corky'. Day-lilies like moist but well-drained fertile soil in full sun, although 'Corky' will

Cardiocrinum giganteum.

PLANTING PLAN

Damp border with a cool theme

Pinks, whites and purples create a cool colour scheme for a damp border in partial shade (9 x 3m/30 x 3ft). The plants need good drainage as they will not survive being waterlogged, especially in winter. A phormium and two elders, *Sambucus nigra* **'Guincho Purple', add touches of purple to enliven the scheme. Foliage plants are valuable – the hydrangea for its felted leaves; the fatsia for its shiny evergreen 'hands', echoed by the rodgersias.**

1 *Fatsia japonica*
2 *Sanguisorba canadensis*
3 *Sambucus nigra* 'Guincho Purple'
4 *Cardiocrinum giganteum*
5 *Phormium tenax* 'Purpureum'
6 *Lysimachia clethroides*
7 *Dierama pulcherrimum*
8 *Filipendula purpurea*
9 *Hydrangea aspera* Villosa Group
10 *Darmera peltata*
11 *Physostegia virginiana* 'Variegata'
12 *Cimicifuga simplex* 'Brunette'
13 *Rodgersia aesculifolia*
14 *Rodgersia sambucifolia*
15 *Monarda* 'Croftway Pink'
16 *Echinacea purpurea* 'White Lustre'
17 *Phlox paniculata* 'Eva Cullum'
18 *Veratrum nigrum*
19 *Echinacea purpurea* 'Robert Bloom'
20 *Phlox maculata* 'Omega'
21 *Schizostyles coccinea* 'Sunrise'
22 *Chelone obliqua*
23 *Astilbe* 'Venus'

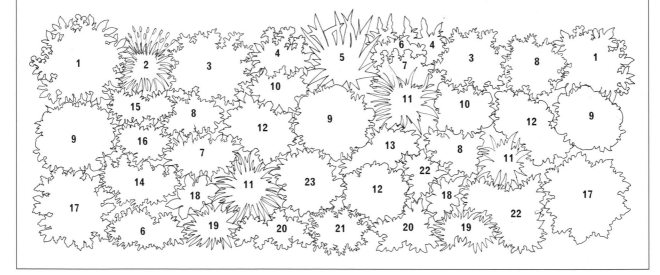

290

Making the most of high rainfall

Sanguisorba canadensis produces bottlebrush-like flowers on tall (1.8m/6ft), sturdy stems from August to October in the cool, damp climate of Cumbria. Divide in spring.

tolerate some shade. Give it a good mulch in spring or autumn. The bright yellow flowers reach about 70cm/28in in mid-summer. Day-lilies originate from China, Korea and Japan. The plants tend to bulk up quickly, so divide them every few years (in autumn).

Hosta 'Gold Standard'. Hostas are slug caviar but coveted by most gardeners nonetheless. Best in partial shade out of drying winds, they must have moist but well-drained conditions and they like a fertile soil. 'Gold Standard' has predominantly gold leaves with a dark green margin and lavender-blue flowers. Hostas originate from China, Korea, Japan and eastern Russia.

Hydrangea aspera Villosa Group. One of the more elegant lace-cap hydrangeas with gorgeously tactile, dark green, velvety leaves. Allow plenty of space as in maturity it can reach up to 4m/13ft. The flowerheads can be more than 15cm/6in across and are blue-purple and lilac-white. Hydrangeas prefer a sheltered spot out of the wind and need plenty of moisture – and well-drained soil. Found in woodland areas of east Asia and the Americas, they appreciate partial shade, plenty of compost and a handful of fertilizer in spring.

Kirengeshoma palmata. As the name suggests, this plant originally came from Korea and Japan. It is a perennial preferring moist, lime-free soil in a sheltered partially shady spot. The palmate leaves are pale green and go well with the pale yellow, nodding flowers emerging in late summer and lasting into early autumn. The stems are about 90cm/3ft high.

Ligularia stenocephala. This plant, which likes to be kept moist without drying out, is best in full sun with shade protection in the middle of the day and shelter from strong winds. The yellow flowers, in early summer, are borne on black-green stems up to 1.5m/5ft tall. It is prone to slug damage when the leaves unfurl.

Myosotidium hortensia. The Chatham Island forget-me-not has blue flowers and glossy leaves that make it an outstanding addition for a moist but well-drained site in partial shade. It appreciates a seaweed mulch and shelter from wind. The leaves reach about 30cm/1ft and the flowers, which appear in early summer, fall below these. Apply a seaweed-based fertilizer monthly.

Phormium tenax 'Purpureum'. Sword-like, bronze-purple, evergreen foliage makes the New Zealand flax a superb accent plant reaching over 2m/6½ft. Plant in full sun in a sheltered location and keep it moist in summer. Tougher than imagined, in well-drained soil

it will tolerate −12°C/10°F and possibly more, if given a winter mulch. Tubular, dull red flowers erupt on stems up to 4m/13ft tall, followed by large seedpods.

Rodgersia aesculifolia. The chestnut-like leaves emerge up to 90cm/3ft high, with fluffy white flowers in large panicles rising above them in mid-summer. Originally from moist woodland and streamsides in the mountains of China and Japan, it prefers moist soil and will stand full sun or partial shade in a sheltered spot. Slugs may damage the leaves in spring.

Sambucus nigra. Elders are tolerant of most conditions but *S. n.* 'Guincho Purple' prefers moist well-drained soil. It colours well in full sun but retains the best

Hydrangea aspera Villosa Group.

colour in dappled shade. The dark green leaves turn blackish-purple and then red in autumn. It can reach up to 5m/16ft but is best pruned hard in late winter to promote new foliage. The creamy white flowers show up well against the dark foliage.

Schizostylis coccinea 'Sunrise'. Invaluable as a long-flowering, late summer and autumn perennial, the Kaffir lily is a sun-lover originally from the streamsides of southern Africa, and prefers moist, well-drained soil. The roots should be kept moist and be planted in a sheltered spot. 'Sunrise' has large salmon-pink flowers up to 60cm/2ft high with strappy leaves. It is best divided frequently as it is vigorous.

Veratrum nigrum. The most perfectly pleated leaves you could hope to find make this plant a talking point and are the reason for growing it. It does not like to dry out, and needs shelter, sun or partial shade. It originates from damp meadows and open woodland in the northern hemisphere. Watch out for slug damage. All parts of the plant are toxic if ingested and the foliage may irritate the skin.

ABOVE Inspired by the exotic Italian Riviera garden at La Mortola, Chusan palm (*Trachycarpus fortunei*), and tender *Cyperus involucratus* complement hard landscaping at Lamorran House in Cornwall. BELOW At Swiss Cottage in Lancashire the 1½-acre site includes a stream with bog garden and a fine collection of acers, sorbus and cornus. RIGHT A bridge straddles a boggy area in Bob Yarwood and Jeny Marriott's 2-acre hillside garden, Dolwen in Flintshire & Wrexham. Damp plantings beside pools and streams include *Salix fargesii* and *S. udensis* 'Sekka'.

Ceredigion/Cardiganshire
Crynfryn
Cwmrhaidadr Garden
  & Nursery
Glangwenffrwd
Henblas
Llanllyr
Nantcellan
Plas Llidiardau
Tynewydd
Winllan

Cheshire & Wirral
73 Hill Top Avenue

Cornwall
Creed House
Heligan
New Marsh Farm
Water Meadow

Cumbria
Beck Head
Chapelside
High Rigg
The Mill House
Palace How
Rannerdale Cottage
Rydal Mount
Scarthwaite
Station House
1 Sycamore Close
Tomarobandy Gardens
Wood Hall

Denbighshire & Colwyn
Golygfa'r Llwelyn
The Old Rectory, Llanfihangel

Devon
Docton Mill & Garden
Fardel Manor
Holywell
Longham
Lukesland
Marden
Southcombe House
Sutton Mead

Dorset
Ivy Cottage

Gloucestershire
The Red House

Gwent
Croesllanfro Farm
Great Campston
Llanover

Gwynedd
Antur Waunfawr
Bryn Gwern
Caerau Uchef
Cefn Bere
Crug Farm
Foxbrush, Felinheli
Goetre Uchaf
Henllys Lodge
Hotel Maes-y-Neuadd
Llys-y-Gwynt
Pentre Bach
Tan Dinas
29-30 Tan-y-Bwlch

Herefordshire
Hergest Croft Gardens

Hundreds of NGS gardens are in areas of high rainfall or have damp areas for moisture-loving plants – here are some to add to those Christopher Holliday has revelled in.

Making the most of high rainfall

SUSANNA LONGLEY
& BRYAN HIRST

with expert insights by
ANTHONY ARCHER-WILLS
CHRIS BAINES

14 Ways with water

The fascination for water is surely universal. It evokes many different moods and stimulates the senses of sight, sound and even touch. You need only imagine the still, gin-clear waters of lakes at Chippenham Park in Cambridgeshire on a sparkling spring morning to feel relaxed and at ease with the world. It is hard to pass a pool or pond without pausing to watch, just for a second or two, the glinting sunlight or the visiting insects or birds. For, whether a water feature has pride of place or is tucked away in a corner, whether it is an air-conditioner or a place setter, it will be a draw for wildlife. Birds will visit; insects, newts, frogs and toads, even small mammals – all will come to drink, feed and make their homes nearby.

Given the power of water and its long history of bringing refreshing pleasure and beauty to the garden, it is not surprising that hundreds of Yellow Book gardens include water features, from tiny bubblers and gurgling wall fountains, classic lily ponds and quiet, naturalistic wildlife pools, to vast expanses of watery delight. The myriad gardens to visit include the grand, sweeping lakes of Blenheim Palace, Oxfordshire, that seem to answer perfectly the surrounding trees and stunning landscape of 'Capability' Brown, and the little tinkling stream at Ivy Cottage in Dorset, which brings the sky down to the earth. At Sutton Place in Surrey, see how Ben Nicholson's marble wall appears to float in the pool. Compare the energy and life evoked by a gushing cascade with the calm induced by the narrow rills at Hestercombe, Somerset, dividing the

garden with slits of blue. Or the mysterious grotto and damp rocks where a river god presides at Stourhead in Wiltshire with the joyful 22m/70ft-high fountain at Stanway Water Garden in Gloucestershire. Then there are unusual contemporary features, such as the three fountains and a stream that flows all the way down the main path at the National Botanic Garden in Wales.

A world of plants

For plant lovers a water feature opens up a fascinating world of plants with environmental constraints very different from those of the herbaceous border. Whatever conditions prevail elsewhere in the garden, the installation of a pond or bog enables gardeners to create lush and exotic effects with leafy hostas and ferns. Only a stone's throw from her dry gravel garden, Beth Chatto has cool pools dressed in lily pads and water hawthorn, overhung by giant gunnera and bordered with skunk cabbages, stately white zantedeschias and scarlet *Lobelia cardinalis*. Among the many atmospheric water gardens in the Yellow Book is the enchanting Trebah in Cornwall, with its waterfalls, rockpools and ravines.

Water's reflective quality brings a further interesting dimension for the plant lover. Using the surface of the water to mirror a fleeting glory – such as Sheffield Park's trees and shrubs in a good autumn or, more reliably, Hampshire's Longstock Park Gardens' collection of candelabra primulas in late spring – doubles the pleasure of a passing moment in the garden. Designing for reflection is rewarding and can make you look at plants differently, both in form and colour; an obviously repeating pattern is often very eye-catching on a bright, still day. For winter drama, sky-piercing clumps of colourful-stemmed willows and dogwoods, for example, are a large-pond owner's favourite. Other woody plants such as acers and bamboos, and herbaceous perennials like iris, daylilies and lilies, always look happy in pond-side situations, and climbing roses can look fantastic mirrored in the surface of the water. Even though the soil beside an artificial pond is probably no different from that elsewhere in the garden, plants thrive in the more humid atmosphere and often brighter light conditions beside the water.

PRECEDING PAGES Jill and Martin Leman's front garden at 1 Malvern Terrace, London, is a haven for plants and wildlife in the inner city, and a sanctuary for humans too. Pots of *Hosta sieboldiana* var. *elegans* and a variegated variety dress the poolside in summer, and water hawthorn (*Aponogeton distachyos*) floats on the water. The drawing is of Llanfair Court, Gwent, from the 1984 Yellow Book.

ABOVE, LEFT The setting of Ivy Cottage, Dorset, and its sloping land is underlined by the meandering natural stream, which provides the house and 1¾-acre garden with a sparkling necklace of reflected light. Anne and Alan Stevens dammed the stream to create the waterfall. Natural boggy areas are ideal for moisture-loving plants, including *Lobelia cardinalis* 'Queen Victoria' and *L.* 'Kompliment Scharlach'.

Moving water

For some people, moving water is essential; a pond is not a pond unless it has a fountain or cascade of some sort. Over the centuries, garden designers and engineers have had a lot of fun with the possibilities of moving water and its power to give a completely different and exciting dimension – as with the stirring and magnificent sight of Chatsworth's famous cascade. And the fun didn't stop in the seventeenth century. Craig Wyncoll and Lionel Stirgiss of Porter's Lodge in Suffolk, have created a water feature that plays classical music! At the other extreme the gentlest tap and trickle of water from a traditional Japanese deer-scare feature inspires more contemplative enjoyment, producing a never-ending rhythm that symbolizes the process of time passing.

Of course, unless you have a natural source, moving water has to be pumped, either with a surface pump, which is powerful and can be noisy and is used only for the largest projects, or a submersible pump, which is sufficiently powerful for most purposes. For a small feature you can fit a low-voltage pump yourself, but a bigger system, perhaps with lighting, will require full mains voltage. Always employ a qualified electrician to install the appropriate protected wiring. It is worth discussing the pump size requirements with a specialist supplier, who will need to know how high you want to raise the water above the pond water level, what shape of fountain spray you want or how wide the lip of your waterfall, the approximate volume of water in your pond, the bore width of the tubing leading to your fountain or cascade fitting and

ABOVE A light-filled lake glimpsed through woodland shadows evokes a sense of fantasy at Vann in Surrey. Tree trunks and giant *Gunnera manicata* frame the view of water nymphs, who have vanished into the undergrowth. The waterside planting of contrasting colours and textures is designed with reflections in mind.

whether or not you have a pond water filter.

Before choosing a fountain or moving-water feature for a small space such as a courtyard garden, remember that the gushing and gurgling may reverberate and be too noisy in an enclosed space, and what you imagined would be a delicate tinkle can sound like a sink emptying.

The role of water

Water has many roles. It can be used as visual focus, drawing the eye from a distance, as does the Frog Fountain at Barnsley House, Gloucestershire, or creating a point of interest as you wander. In Helen Yemm's garden, Ketleys in Sussex, the enclosed pond area is a secluded place for relaxation. Water in John Tordoff's Japanese garden in east London (illustrated on page 34) contributes to the atmosphere of quiet contemplation. The richly planted pond at Malvern Terrace in north London provides a dramatic centrepiece to the small front garden – and it also provides a point of interest for visitors and passers-by.

A rill or narrow channel of water makes an eye-catching slit of reflected sky, drawing the eye along its path through the garden. The channel needs sturdy construction to ensure that the banks remain intact and the feature clean-lined. Rills look effective winding through and around the undulations of a large expanse of lawn, trees and shrubs or making an arrow-straight dart across a long courtyard or down a terraced slope. At Dillingham House in Cambridgeshire, the formal water feature visually links a high-level lawn to the ground-level patio, creating in the

process a spectacular vista as you walk into the garden through the gate opposite the bottom of the rill.

A pond may serve a more practical purpose too. A hot, dry area – such as a sun-baked patio or terrace – cries out for a pond literally to cool the atmosphere and make it welcoming. A regular-shaped and brimful pool with the surface of the water exactly level with the underside of the surrounding paving slabs can be positioned to reflect elements of the house or garden, as well as plenty of sky. On a small, often urban scale, wall fountains and wet-stone features, in which the water bubbles through a pile of pebbles, cool the breeze-free atmosphere and are also safe for children. These features are sold as kits in many garden centres and are ideal for tiny spaces. Some gardeners add shells or glass beads or other waterproof treasures to personalize their feature. Garden centres are also awash with wall-mounted objects, from lions' heads to Neptunes, gargoyles and cherubs, for water to spout from. The construction of shop-bought ones shows how the nozzle, pump, hose and electric wiring are hidden. So that all the water can be caught and recirculated, the bowl beneath needs to be twice the diameter of the height of the fall.

A raised pond brings sitting and pond-watching neatly together. While the ideal height for sitting is 45cm/18in, the pond needs to be deep enough to make close examination interesting – 1m/3ft gives scope for fish and plants. A brick-built, L-shaped, raised pool provides a 'sociable' seating arrangement. It could be designed either as a single unit or as two rectangular ones of different heights fitted together, the change in level at the joining wall creating an attractive cascade. Where the garden is higher than the house, the pond wall at garden level acts as a retaining wall, stepping down to a patio on the same level as the house floor.

Water-garden styles

A formal feature, such as the ponds enclosed by parterres of crisp box hedging at Tythrop Park, Buckinghamshire (illustrated on page 320), or the water lily pool at Tintinhull House in Somerset, is regular in shape and self-consciously man-made, with no pretence at being natural. Because it makes no reference to nature in its

ABOVE Tranquillity and contemplation are the theme of this water garden at Sutton Place in Surrey, which provides the setting for Ben Nicholson's sculpture, known as the Nicholson Wall. Water and sculpture interact to create a single work of art. Look for long enough at the way concave and convex shapes are reversed in the mirror image and you begin to wonder about the nature of surfaces and light.

RIGHT At Sun House in Suffolk the Thompsons' circular pond brings the refreshing influence of water close to the house and reflections of the sky break up the expanse of paving. Planting between the slabs starts with snowdrops and grape hyacinths. Low-growing herbaceous plants, such as *Alchemilla mollis*, hardy geraniums and heleniums, keep the display going into November.

form, a formal pond need not obey other natural 'laws'; for example, it can look fine surrounded by paving or decking – or even edged with metal – whereas a naturalistically shaped one would appear out of place in this setting. Formality lends itself to making reference to the surrounding architecture, drawing together the man-made elements of the garden to create a clear statement of style.

Sometimes the formality is carried through to the planting; a formal feature might be planted with a single species or a repeating pattern of just a few different ones, box or lavender hedging with pots of lilies, for example. While this is a stylish and fashionable approach, for some people it may be a little over-controlled or self-conscious. A popular and more relaxed alternative style is to contrast formal hard landscaping with irregular and very bold planting – as if nature were fighting back at the restraining influence of the feature. Dramatic water or waterside plants, such as gunnera, bamboo, large ferns or iris, play a role in achieving this effect, since their bold shapes will be strong enough to 'do battle' with the relentless flat and even surfaces of the pond and its edgings.

The best ponds look believable in their setting and the outline of a genuinely natural pond, its 'footprint', relates to the shape of the land. An indentation in the shoreline, for instance, might echo unevenness in the surrounding ground. The man-made lake at Garden House Farm in Suffolk is surrounded by undulating banks (created from the pond excavations) that reflect the pond's shape. Elizabeth Seiffer, the current owner and gardener, says that she appreciates the privacy the banks provide as well as the way they keep the focus of the view on the water.

The Japanese garden at Tatton Park, Cheshire, was developed out of a landscape of flooded pits and sandstone rocks, the site strongly influencing the original design. Head gardener Sam Youd, who restored the atmospheric pools and dramatic winding pathways to their former glory, believes that the style, size and location of artificial water features are best dictated by the situation – for example, a cavernous grotto built on a Cambridgeshire fen is unlikely to look appropriate!

Many Yellow Book gardens have a simple wildlife pool tucked away in a quiet corner: a round, pre-formed or butyl-lined pond with a combination of lawn and native waterside plants forming the pond edge – in effect a large, lined puddle. This naturalistic style of artifical water feature is, in some ways, more difficult to create than a formal and obviously unnatural one, and making an attractive, natural-looking pond edge is always tricky.

Even overhanging rocks, prostrate edging plants that drape obligingly or a sloping shoreline incorporating a bog feature tend to reveal the liner at some time of year. If you allow the surrounding ground to provide an edge, the pond's shape will, within or year or two, become distorted under the weight of the water contained by the butyl sheet. Sooner or later the liner will become visible and therefore exposed to ultraviolet light. It will then turn brittle and split. To give a neat and permanent edge and some room for bog and water's-edge plants, it is best to create an artificial shoreline supported underneath by a structural wall.

For the purist a 'natural' pond is planted with native plants to provide food and shelter for native animal species – though many successful wildlife ponds mix native with cultivated plants that are attractive to birds, insects and animals. The ideal position in the garden is remote from buildings or paved areas so that wildlife can visit in shelter and privacy. Often the perfect spot is on the edge of a large country garden with views of fields and countryside beyond the glinting water. At Barnards Farm, Bernard and Sylvia Holmes have created a garden with several ponds and a small lake, and planted trees to add interest to the views of flat Essex countryside. And it is not only a lovely view; like many rural ponds their water is a much-needed haven for local wildlife in an area of intensive agriculture. Sylvia feels that if you have enough water, a good balance between species can be established – and visiting herons can be admired rather than dreaded.

pond garden can look very rural and attractive. Ponds and children can be a joyful combination, but deep water can also be tragic. For older children, water can be the greatest fun. Cyrie Stone of Washbrook Manor in Suffolk says that she never saw her two boys during the summer when they were young – they were too busy building boats and bridges and playing games by her gently flowing stream.

Large features are relatively easier to build and to maintain than small ones, and they make a more dramatic impact. Large ponds can also attract and sustain a proportionately larger and more varied population of wildlife. Even a small pond is better made deeper. At Arley Hall Gardens in Cheshire, of the two small formal ponds, it is the 1m/3ft-deep one that is really easy to look after according to the head gardener. The other is 45cm/18in deep and troubled with excessive algae because the water gets too warm in the summer months.

Location and size

However large or small the garden, a low position in the garden (as it would be in nature) is the most comfortable for an area of water. And an open sunny site, with no overhanging trees, is the easiest to maintain, although there are many beautiful ponds in shady places that bring a welcome splash of sky into the gloom.

If you have young children or regular visits from them, it is wisest to fence your pool to restrict access for free-roaming toddlers – a picket fenced and gated wildlife

Building a water feature

In order to create a permanent and attractive artificial water feature you need a robust, watertight 'receptacle'. This reservoir can be anything water- and weatherproof: pre-formed plastic pond liner, an old galvanized water butt, a concrete tank or a butyl sheet. The best choice in most situations and for most designs is butyl sheeting. It can be made to fit any shape or any depth and, protected from ultraviolet light, a butyl-lined pond will last for

LEFT Fountains of water rhyme with fountains of grasses to cool the atmosphere in this sun-warmed corner at Walnut House in Surrey. This part of Inger and Dirk Laan's garden faces west so the evening sun

lights up evening primroses and the bronze spikelets of *Stipa gigantea*. The water washing over the sides of the large Chinese bowl is circulated through a hole in the bowl's base via a pump in the pond.

ABOVE The formal pools at The Manor House, Bledlow, Buckinghamshire, were created by Lord and Lady Carrington. The garden also includes informal water features fed by fourteen chalk springs.

ANTHONY ARCHER-WILLS

Come let us wallow…

There is indeed nothing quite like wallowing in mud – for hippopotamuses, that is. And you might raise one in your garden if you make a lined pond in a wet hollow without taking special precautions.

We use the term 'hippo-ing' in the trade to describe the sinister, black lump that looks as if a large mammal has taken up residence in the pond and, head down, is feeding out of the baskets that are home to water lilies. If only it was a case of calling the local zoo and having a hippo removed. Unfortunately, it means that water and gases from decomposing matter have collected under the liner and it is no longer anchored to the bottom of the pond: a serious problem that involves lifting sections of the liner and draining off surplus water. It is vital to deal with the hump immediately and before the gases – which are much more difficult to remove than plain old water – accumulate.

It is better by far to avoid the problem in the first place! Situate the pond above the lowest spot in the hollow and use earth from the excavation to raise the hollow slightly. However, if you have no choice but to excavate in a wet hollow, dig a trench from the bottom of the pond to a low-lying ditch or to a sump lined with brick or concrete tubing and linked to an outlet pipe. In the ditch set a perforated land drain, backfilling it with round gravel. Fit a pump to the sump with which to draw excess water from beneath the line should a 'hippo' occur. Also install several perforated air-vent pipes that run from under the pond to the surface to allow gases to escape.

If you take these special precautions during excavation, your pond will be home to frogs and newts rather than humpbacked interlopers.

many years. Lionel Stirgess has created more than ten water features at Craig Wyncoll's Porter's Lodge garden in Suffolk. He finds that concrete water features invariably leak and butyl alone has a tendency to puncture. His most successful formal pond was made using both materials: butyl sheeting laid on a layer of builders' sand, then a concrete base poured over the top of the butyl. Side walls of waterproof concrete blocks were built up and the butyl sheeting pulled up behind them on the outer edge of the pond and then secured by backfilling. He advises not to put fish in a concrete-lined pond for at least a year since they may be poisoned by dissolved chemicals.

When constructing more naturalistic features Lionel Stirgess uses butyl liner alone as concrete blocks do not lend themselves to natural-looking curves. For an artificial shoreline he advises making a slope with a one in three gradient (any steeper and the slope is likely to be unstable; any shallower and the liner tends to show), always keeping the water level topped up so that the butyl is covered. Bog gardens at Porter's Lodge are created by lining an excavated hollow with butyl and piercing the liner a few times in the bottom so that excess water can run away. The hollow is filled with fairly heavy garden soil and planted. In dry weather the bog is watered so that the soil never dries out.

At Beth Chatto's garden in Essex, even though her water features are spring-fed and clay-bottomed, she has had a problem with the edges of her water feature caving in. This was overcome by building small retaining walls using hollow concrete blocks. These were secured by driving angle irons through them and into the soil below. Enriched and improved soil along the water's edge ensured that the blocks quickly disappeared beneath a veil of mosses and other vegetation.

Planting the pond

In containerized ponds, plants are best grown in containers, either permanent brick planting troughs or portable containers, or a combination of the two. Lionel Stirgiss has experimented with incorporating concrete planting troughs within his pond construction, but he finds it just as satisfactory to use portable containers for water plants.

He uses plastic baskets available from garden centres, but anything rot-proof that will let in water and discourage soil from falling out can be used, such as dark brown or black laundry baskets or even old nylon tights. Line baskets and troughs with hessian or geotextile (to keep the soil in) and fill them with clay garden soil (if yours is beautifully light and free-draining, you can buy bags of loam from garden centres or try begging some heavier soil from a friend). Transfer your plant from its nursery container to its new, larger container. Top up the soil and add a layer of 5cm/2in of gravel (again, to deter the soil from floating away).

Water plants

It is useful to group water plants according to the job they do. The deep-water aquatic plants, such as water lilies, with flat leaves that float on the surface and long stems leading to roots growing in soil or containers on the pond floor, shade the water from sunlight thereby inhibiting algal growth and provide hiding places for surface-feeding fish. These plants prefer still water, so plant them away from fountains or cascades.

Floating plants, such as water hyacinth and frogbit, hang in the water with their leaves and flowers sitting on the surface, providing more shade and shelter for pond wildlife. Avoid the carpeting floaters lemna and azolla. They look pretty and harmless enough, but they grow rampantly and will quickly smother your pond and choke other plants.

Oxygenating plants that live under the water's surface are largely grown for their practical benefits, although, if your water is very clear, they can be attractive to look at. The most commonly found is Canadian pond weed (*Elodea canadensis*), but prettier and less rampant are hairgrass (*Eleocharis acicularis*), hornwort (*Ceratophyllum demersum*) and willow moss (*Fontinalis antipyretica*). Some oxygenators, such as frogbit (*Hydrocharis morsus-ranae*), which resembles a miniature water lily, are free-floating plants – so all you do is throw them into the water.

Marginal plants, like flowering rush and bog arum, marsh marigold and water iris, visually soften the edges of the pond and provide shelter for pond animals, birds and

PRECEDING PAGES A sunny area of the 5-acre garden at Elton Hall in Herefordshire is swathed in hot prairie plants and tall clumps of grasses, putting you in the mood to dabble your hands in the raised pond. Roam further into the garden to see more rudbeckias and echinaceas (Anne and James Hepworth hold National Collections of both), among wine and purple-coloured foliage plants.

LEFT The pond in Jenny Woodall's garden at Nyewood House in Sussex is butyl-lined. On the far bank, spires of *Rodgersia pinnata superba* and *Ligularia dentata* 'Desdemona' rise above foliage plants. In the foreground, the plants include hostas, *Primula florindae*, *Hemerocallis* 'Stafford', *Podophyllum hexandrum* and *Lythrum salicaria* 'Robert'.

305

Ways with water

CHRIS BAINES

Watery welcome for wildlife

Some of our most enchanting wildlife depends on ponds, and as so many wet and watery places have been drained or damaged in the countryside, we have lost habitat for frogs and toads, dragonflies and diving beetles, flag iris, ragged robin, water mint and a host of other native plants and animals. Fortunately, garden ponds have come to the rescue, and wetland wildlife is thriving in our cities and suburbs.

The best ponds for wildlife are shallow and unpolluted. Even the tiniest of temporary puddles has a part to play, but if you have room for a pond with a surface area of at least 6–7sq m/65–75 sq ft, the results can be spectacular. There needs to be a point somewhere in the pond where the water is at least 60cm/2ft deep, if frogs are to survive the coldest of icy winter weather. The margins need to be very gently sloping, partly for safety's sake where young children are involved, but also to help more wildlife make use of the water. Birds will bathe in the shallows to keep their feathers clean and so improve their cold-weather insulation. Hedgehogs and squirrels, foxes and other creatures will drink there, and if the smaller animals happen to fall in, a shallow edge will help them to escape.

The plants in a pond provide the platforms for the rest of the natural community. Submerged oxygenators keep the water sweet. Some floating leaves reduce the sunlight penetration and provide egg-laying sites for water snails and damselflies, but too much duckweed, or the dreaded fairy moss (*Azolla*) will cut out the light completely and suppress the growth of submerged oxygenators.

Around the water's edge, it is good to grow a range of different plants. Some, such as yellow flag iris, water plantain and spearwort, prefer to emerge through a few centimetres of water, but many grow best at the boggy margin. Among my favourites are marsh marigold, water forget-me-not, brooklime and lady's smock.

Finally, and perhaps most importantly of all, there is one magical ingredient that is missing from most garden ponds: mud! Many pond creatures spend part of their life submerged, so the mud in the bottom is vital. When you are creating a new pond, a couple of centimetres of sandy subsoil spread over the liner will make all the difference, and as the pond matures it really is important to resist the temptation to 'clean it up'. A muddy bottom, shallow margins, plenty of plants and a clean supply of water should reward you with a garden full of life and a window on the changing seasons.

so on. Plant them individually in water plant baskets and set them at the pond edge so that their soil surface is permanently up to 15cm/6in below water level.

Bog plants for areas of permanently wet soil beside your pond include some of the most attractive, bold and colourful of our herbaceous garden plants, especially in late spring and early summer. Try combinations of primulas, ferns, hostas, bog iris, ligularias and rodgersias for a spectacular water-side picture.

Pond health

The health of a pond is governed by the balance of living organisms – plants and animals, algae and so on – in the water. This balance is affected by the water temperature, the amount of sunlight, oxygen and dissolved mineral salts. A well-balanced pond should have enough oxygen in the water for its water plants and under-water animals to thrive. If oxygen levels get too low, pond water becomes very smelly and unpleasant and unable to sustain its plants and animals – and as plants and animals rot the water becomes even more unhealthy. Oxygenating plants release oxygen into the water; flat-leaved plants shade the water, keeping it cooler and cutting out sunlight thereby discouraging green algae; but too many fish can upset the pond balance – since they use up oxygen and generate waste products. To be sure of maintaining high enough oxygen levels right through the year, consider a moving water feature, such as a fountain or a cascade. This will create a less vulnerable balance, making your pond easier to maintain. Forcing air through water causes it to absorb oxygen which it can then release into the pond water. In the process water is raised from the pond surface via a fountain jet or cascade to add an extra and exciting dimension.

Water and bog plants grow fast. Water plants and animals produce waste material that accumulates at the bottom of the water feature. This sediment encourages algae to grow. It will cloud the water, use up the dissolved oxygen and cause the water to become smelly and unhealthy. Maintenance, especially during the growing season, is therefore important to control the over-vigorous growth of plants and to minimize algal growth.

Year-round maintenance

A water feature adds another dimension to the garden, a focus of interest unlike any other. As in life, though, there's no gain without a certain amount of pain, so do be prepared for some regular maintenance work – though with a little forethought this can be kept to a minimum.

Pond maintenance need not be a particularly fine or time-consuming art. Indeed many garden owners regard pond maintenance as a relaxation rather than a chore: it is not like the careful micro-weeding needed in a rock garden, or the never-ending hoeing in the vegetable plot. A good clean-out twice a year (in spring and autumn) is usually all that is needed to keep a pond in good condition; top up water levels in dry, hot weather and fish for algae and pond weed as required (perhaps a few minutes daily in early summer).

LEFT Look through the window of the shell-encrusted grotto at Kingstone Cottages in Herefordshire and imagine yourself in the world of waterboatmen, frogs and dragonflies.

ABOVE The wooden bridge gives a sense of purpose to Sue and Wol Staines' bog garden at Glen Chantry in Essex, densely planted with *Iris sibirica* 'Butter and Sugar', rodgersias and persicarias.

Aquatic & marginal plants

Alisma plantago. The water plantain is an easy indigenous marginal aquatic which will find its way to water with or without human help. It is a graceful plant with sprays of tiny, white flowers, flushed pink, like gypsophila or crambe, creating a haze for weeks on end and spent flower spikes that look good through winter. Water depth 10–15cm/4–6in.

Angelica archangelica. An easily grown giant for boggy ground, angelica is a self-seeding biennial where happy, which is virtually anywhere moist enough. It rewards with bright green leaves and huge umbels of flowers from May to August.

Aponogeton distachyos. Water hyacinth is a deep-water plant with narrow, lance-shaped leaves, which associate well with water lilies. It has beautiful white flowers in spring and autumn, which are its main growing seasons. Suited to the warmer counties and good in town ponds because it is well behaved, it will reward with a musky scent of hawthorn. Water depth 30–60cm/1–2ft.

Butomus umbellatus. One of the 'must have' aquatic marginals, this is the most beautiful of the flowering rushes. Rosy-pink heads of flower, held not unlike those of an allium, rise on strong, shiny, triangular stems to 90cm/3ft. 'Too much is not enough.' Water depth 10–15cm/2–6in.

Caltha palustris. Jolly marsh marigolds are great for most ponds if you are a lover of bright yellows. They grow just on the waterline and adapt easily to rising and falling water levels.

Canna. Teamed with cyperus and *Thalia dealbata,* tropical-looking cannas are exciting grown in water. Treat them as seasonal bedding and bring them into a greenhouse in winter. Water depth 10–15cm/4–6in.

Cyperus papyrus. The Egyptian paper rush, the papyrus used by the Pharaohs for their parchments, grows to an impressive 2m/6½ft in a warm summer and will add grace to any subtropical water garden. Take it into a frost-free area in winter There are many other cyperus and all are attractive and useful plants. Water depth 10–15cm/4–6in.

Eriophorum angustifolium. Cotton grass is lovely for mass planting in acid, peaty pools. It waves its silky heads through the summer and is especially effective in a naturalistic planting. It does spread where it is happy, but is not a pest. Water depth 0–10cm/0–4in.

Euphorbia palustris. A brilliant explosion of sunshine-yellow bracts in spring, the water-edge spurge is robust and needs siting with equally strong growers, such as gunnera. It keeps the show going right through to autumn when it changes to subtle oranges before dying back in winter. Good in formal or informal waterside settings. Water depth 0–10cm/0–4in.

Filipendula ulmaria. Meadowsweet is one of our prettiest native ditch and waterside plants. Lovely rough foliage is the foil for fluffy, creamy-white flowerheads in summer. Water depth 10–15cm/4–6in.

Gunnera manicata. The granddaddy of all waterside plants and well known to all, this giant needs pampering. With plenty of dung in summer and winter hibernation in a deep mound of straw, he will wake up in spring with an emergence which is almost pornographic. Thereafter, just watch and wonder.

Iris ensata (syn. *kaempferi*). Japanese flag irises offer a colour range from white through to violet, with small standards and large falls. They will tolerate being planted at the water's edge, but prefer drier ground in winter. Their simple beauty is worth savouring. Water depth 0–10cm/0–4in.

Iris laevigata. This Japanese iris thrives in pond margins where its deep blue flowers look ravishing among reeds and lower-growing marginals. Water depth 5–10cm/2–4in.

Iris pseudacorus var. *bastardii.* The most beautiful variant of yellow flag iris, this is a pale creamy yellow. A subtle but arresting sight, reaching 90cm/3ft, it is perfectly happy in wet ground. Water depth 15–20cm/6–8in.

Lysichiton americanus. The aptly named skunk cabbage gives off a peculiar, musty smell which is easily borne as it is such a splendid plant. In boggy places it throws up huge spathes of bright yellow in spring which are followed by whopping great leaves. These carry on through the seasons and are the backbone for many smaller plants. For scale and effect it is without compare. Water depth 0–30cm/0–1ft.

Mentha aquatica. Pretty in flower and with a refreshing scent which cuts the air on sultry days, the water mint is also worth growing to clean the water and keep it in good condition. Water depth 15–30cm/6in–1ft.

Menyanthes trifoliata. Bog bean is a name to conjure with and an unusual plant. It throws long stems over the surface of the water from which rise fleshy leaves and clusters of starry white flowers. These are brief but memorable. Its great asset is that it covers the unsightly edge of the pond in a good mat of foliage. Water depth 10–30cm/4in–1ft.

Myosotis scorpioides (syn. *palustris*). Water forget-me-not is a pretty filler plant which creeps on its rhizomes through other plants at the water's edge. The typical baby-blue forget-me-not flowers thrown up in early summer are so charming that they must be included in any pond. Water depth 0–20cm/0–8in.

Nymphaea. Water lilies are the staple for a pond of any size – from an enormous lake or moat to a tub. The yardstick for choosing is the approximate depth of water in your pool and the colours you like. For a large, natural pond, nothing beats the native white *N. alba*. The truly pygmy varieties, such as 'Pygmaea Helvola' will grow in less than 30cm/1ft of water. The importance of water lilies for shading the water is well known and to see frogs basking between the leaves on a warm day is one of the delights of summer.

Nymphoides peltata (Villarsia). The yellow-flowered water fringe resembles a tiny water lily. It holds its small flowers well above water level. It is a useful plant for shading the surface and is easily managed, with the added bonus of sweetening water and keeping it clean. Water depth 15–60cm/6in–2ft.

Phragmites australis. Norfolk reed is a versatile plant. As a water cleaner it is unsurpassed and is the plant of choice for reedbeds. It was, and still is, used for thatching as it is tough and sloughs off the weather. Fast-growing and fairly invasive, it is a beautiful plant for a large pond or lake. It has silky, purply panicles which dry in winter to form a wonderful silhouette. If it is sensibly managed, there is no reason to fear it. Just buy some waders and enjoy yourself. Water depth 20–30cm/8in–1ft.

Pontaderia cordata. Blue pickerel has intense blue pokers of flower, balanced and complemented by the sword-shaped leaves. It does like hot spots, and if the weather is cool and washed out it may not flower a great deal. For those blessed with the right conditions, it is a fabulous plant with no foibles. Water depth 15–30cm/6in–1ft.

Sagittaria sagittifolia. An aquatic marginal with arrow-shaped leaves and lovely white flowers, this plant has edible tubers which are a magnet for wildfowl who love to snack on them – slightly annoying if you want to enjoy them during the summer. However, it is well worth the risk as they are pretty in every respect. Water depth 15–30cm/6in–1ft.

Stratiotes aloides. The water soldier looks rather like a spider plant or floppy pineapple top floating just below the water's surface in summer and can be seen used to great effect in the sunk garden pond at Great Dixter. In winter it retreats to the bottom of the pond for protection from the cold. This rising and falling is its great gift and the lovely rosettes of foliage with white flowers are a welcome sight.

Thalia dealbata. An aristocratic beauty from the USA, this is a show stopper with its handsome leaves and tall, slender, blue flower spikes. Being frost-tender does put it in the 'bedding' category, along with cyperus and cannas. Deadhead it regularly and cut off spent leaves, and your modest pool will take on the thrill of Hollywood glitz. Water depth 10–30cm/4in–1ft.

Water lilies in the pond at Brook Cottage, Oxfordshire.

Typha laxmannii. One of the best reedmaces for a small to medium-sized pool, this grows to 90cm/3ft and has well-behaved 'bulrush' flower spikes which endure through winter. Easily managed, it is worth having as a foil to plants such as *Iris pseudacorus* and *Butomus umbellatus*. Water depth 20–40cm/8–16in.

Zantedeschia aethiopica 'Crowborough'. Finish off your exotic and glamorous pool with heaps of arum lilies. They look best with other strong-growing exotic plants and a bit at odds with natives. For a 'gasp' factor they are hard to beat and seem so happy in a warm pool that you may never plant them in a bed again. A memory of nights in the gardens of Spain, perhaps. Water depth 10–30cm/4in–1ft.

Here is a sprinkling of the hundreds of NGS gardens with water features to add to the ones that have refreshed Susanna Longley and Bryan Hirst.

ABOVE Water is used as a central feature in the tranquil pebble pool garden at Preen Manor in Shropshire, a garden where water plays an important role in designs by Ann and Philip Trevor-Jones.
RIGHT A zigzag sculpture path leads across the naturalistic pond at Barnards Farm, the garden created on flat Essex farmland by Bernard and Sylvia Holmes.
RIGHT, BELOW Water features can be fun – look out for a watery joke by the terrace in one of the garden rooms designed by Susan Sharkey in her 30 x 15m/ 90 x 45ft garden at 7 The Butts, Brentford.

Bedfordshire
Flaxbourne Farm
Manor Farm
Milton House
Toddington Manor
Tofte Manor

Berkshire
Eton College

Bristol & South Gloucestershire
45 Canynge Road

Buckinghamshire
Tyringham Hall
Weir Lodge

Cambridgeshire
The Elms

Carmarthenshire & Pembrokeshire
Cilgwyn Lodge
Hilton Court Nurseries

Ceredigion / Cardiganshire
Llanllyr
The Mill House
Old Cilgwyn Gardens

Cheshire & Wirral
Cholmondeley Castle
106 Glandon Drive
Tushingham Hall

Cornwall
Trevarno
Water Meadow, Luxulyan

Cumbria
Beck Head
Beckfoot Gardens

Denbighshire & Colwyn
Golygfa'r Llywelyn
Gwysnaey Hall
Plas yn Llan

Derbyshire
Bath House Farm

Devon
Cadhay
Shobrooke Park Gardens

Dorset
Mapperton Gardens
Minterne
The Old Rectory, Litton Cheney

Durham
Low Walworth Hall

Essex
Feeringbury Manor
Olivers
Stamps & Crows

Flintshire & Wrexham
The Cottage Nursing Home
Llangedwyn Hall
Penybryn

Glamorgan
11 Arno Road
Dyffryn Gardens

Gloucestershire North & Central
Paulmead
Snowshill Manor
Warners Court

Gwent
Great Campston
Lilac Cottage
Llanover

Gwynedd
Goetre Uchaf
Gwyndy Bach
Tan Dinas

Hampshire
Lake House
Little Coopers
Lower Mill
Weir House

Herefordshire
Court of Noke
Darkely House
Shobdon Court

Hertfordshire
Jenningsbury
Moat Farm House

Isle of Wight
Northcourt Gardens
The Old Vicarage, Arreton

Kent
Edenbridge House
Mounts Court Farmhouse
Nettlestead Place

Lancashire, Merseyside & Greater Manchester
Clearbeck House
260 Orrell Road

Leicestershire & Rutland
Brooksby Melton College
Long Close

Lincolnshire
Holly House
Little Ponton Hall
Pinefields

London
7 St George's Road

Norfolk
Lawn Farm
Old House

Northamptonshire
Bruyere Court
Old Glebe, Brackley
Turweston Mill

Northumberland
70a The Gables
Loughbrow House

Nottinghamshire
Dumbleside
The White House

Oxfordshire
Epwell Mill
Garsington Manor
Wardington Manor

Powys
Coity Gardens
Ffrwdgrech House
The Walled Garden

Shropshire
Cruckfield House
Harnage Farm
Hodnet Hall Gardens

Somerset
Barford Park
Little Yarford Farmhouse
Rose Cottage

Staffordshire & part of West Midlands
Bleak House
Strawberry Fields
Woodside House

Suffolk
Bucklesham Hall
Heron House

Surrey
Coverwood Lakes
The Old Croft
Titsey Place Gardens
Walnut House

Sussex
Framfield Grange
King John's Lodge
Latchetts

Warwickshire
Avon Cottage
Maxstoke Castle
Woodpeckers

Wiltshire
The Court House
The Grange, Winterbourne
  Dauntsey
Heale Gardens & Plant Centre

Worcestershire
Orchard Bungalow
Upper Court

Yorkshire
Castle Howard
Harewood House
The Old Priory, Everingham

BARBARA ABBS

with expert insights by
ROSEMARY ALEXANDER
ANNA PAVORD
KATHERINE SWIFT

15 Clipping and cutting

Clipping and cutting often seem to be the Cinderellas of gardening activity, akin to housework, a mere tidying process with little scope for creativity. Who would clip and cut when they can propagate, plan planting schemes or strew gravel and decking and call it design? The answer is, of course, thousands of us and many hundreds of the dedicated gardeners whose gardens are open under the National Gardens Scheme.

Lawns and hedges, trimmed trees and crisp parterres may constitute the entire garden, as they often do in France. They can also provide the contrasting element, the green architecture against which the coloured chintz of flower and shrub borders shows to best advantage. Whichever, there must be regular clipping and cutting to make the plants – whether grass, shrub or tree – dense and compact to enhance the effect of architectural solidity. Both the process and the result are eminently satisfying.

A green sward

In the late 1920s when the National Gardens Scheme was born, the perfect green sward was *de rigueur* and involved the gardener in much labour in the search for perfection. In *Everyday in My Garden*, F. Hadfield Farthing gave advice on the cultivation of the ideal lawn. Even though the first electric mower had appeared in 1926, he recommended that, in the first cutting of the spring, scythes or shears should be used instead of a mowing machine. The grass should be rolled frequently with a heavy iron roller. It should be dressed with lime, fine sandy soil and artificial manures, a mixture of one part of sulphate of ammonia, three parts superphosphate of lime and one part steamed bonemeal. Further editions of *Everyday in My Garden* paid no heed to the advances in lawn seed by such firms as Suttons or the invention of the hover mower or, after the Second World War, the development of hormone weedkillers. William Robinson in the 1933 edition of *The English Flower Garden* recommended that lawns be 'dressed once a year with one bushel of salt mixed with fourteen bushels of wood ashes not too much burnt... When you see the wood is consumed spread the ashes abroad and cover them with good soil. Break the charred wood small, mix all well together, do not sift, spread upon the lawn, and roll it in.' This labour-intensive approach to lawns had not changed very much since Victorian times. The effort involved in getting the simplest piece of lawn level, and with an even, green, weed-free sward, was such that few people thought of creating anything more elaborate or dared to deviate from these standards. Certainly the lawn was not meant to be fun.

Today things are blessedly easier. The Suffolk Punch lawnmower range, which came out in 1930, now has cylinder mowers with replaceable cassettes, so the same machine can be used to mow the lawn or scarify it. Cordless lawnmowers are still a bonus for those of us whose pushing days are over but are nervous of long electric cables snaking about the garden. Yet, at a time when it is easier than it ever has been in the past to create perfect lawns, climate change and ecological considerations are making them less fashionable. The perfectly flat, billiard-table effect is no longer the only sort of lawn to have and soft undulations are not only 'permissible' but also desirable. Even stripes like those on the turf at Wembley seem to be losing favour, although the cordless cylinder mower may bring yet another swing in the pendulum of fashion. As well as looking more inviting, grass kept longer helps protect lawns from drying out and turning brown in summer. To avoid using precious water in drought conditions, we are advised to mow more often, say twice a week, with the blades set high, without collecting the mowings. Longer grass catches more dew and the mowings create a mulch.

As well as hotter, drier summers, climatologists are predicting a pronounced increase in winter rainfall in the south of England and a slight increase in the north. There may be a decrease in the number of rainy days but with heavier downpours. Climate change is likely to affect the way the 2,000 sq km/770 sq miles of domestic lawn in Britain are maintained. The increase in rainfall has already resulted in a marked increase in moss in lawns and, like Dr Steven Smith at Moorlands in East Sussex, more of us will need to scarify our grass regularly to remove it. Moorlands is a wetland garden with lawns which slope down to a river and lakes fringed with irises, rheums and primulas at the bottom of the garden. Moss is raked out of the grass in spring and occasionally in season, when the lawns are mown weekly, which is a day's work for one person. When they made the garden, Steven's parents added gravel, sand and wood chips to deal with the soil's tendency to waterlogging, and he has laid drainage pipes, which have to be rodded quite often. Nevertheless, after wet weather, especially in winter, the lower lawns become like bogs.

John King, Rosie Brenan's gardener at Colwood House

PRECEDING PAGES The eighteenth-century parterre at Chevening in Kent creates its striking effect by simple foliage planting inside elaborate swirling shapes. Small orbs of grey, feathery leaved *Santolina chamaecyparissus* are held like beads in an outline of box. The cotton lavender – clipped in spring and again two or three times in summer – is easier to keep in shape than lavender which would make a similar effect. Other plants, such as purple sage, add different colours and textures. The drawing of Raby Castle, County Durham, is from the 1988 Yellow Book.

in West Sussex, has not changed his lawn routines with the changing climate. He looks after Colwood's 'rolling lawns' and the showpiece croquet lawn. 'This is the way I was taught to do it when I was young, and I just keep on,' he says. The croquet lawn is maintained to a finish the Victorians would have appreciated. The soil is alkaline and every month the grass is scarified with an electric lawn rake and fed with Maxicrop iron, the liquid version. Every week it is brushed and mown: up and down one week, across the following week, on one diagonal the week after and on the other diagonal in the fourth week. Regular feeding and scarifying keeps moss at bay. Weeding John does by hand, with a daisy grubber: 'It's very nice, on your knees with the sun shining on your back.'

The other lawns at Colwood get a weekly mowing and John's advice to prevent the build-up of thatch is never to mow the grass in the same direction twice running. Wear and tear is dealt with by overseeding areas in need of renovation, as greenkeepers and groundsmen do, usually

in April, when the soil is slightly warm and still damp. John scarifies and roughs up the soil surface before sowing the seed, which he mixes with John Innes compost. (Alternatively, lawn restorer kits with fertilizer incorporated are available.) After sowing, the area is raked and lightly rolled or trodden. The first cut, after the new grass has germinated and the sward thickened up, is done with care.

Patterns in grass

Strimmers and modern lawnmowers have made intriguing alternatives to flat expanses of lawn so easy. Light and easy to manipulate and adjust, they have made possible spontaneous creativity with grass, allowing gardeners to make informal paths through longer grass, which to my mind are one of the loveliest sights in our summer gardens. Lightweight mowers keep banks smooth, and reveal the curves of dramatic earthworks like the symbolic mounds at Charles Jencks' garden at Portrack in Scotland or the

Evening sun casts shadows across the grass mound in James Fairfax's 2-acre riverside garden at Stanbridge Mill in Dorset. A Flymo and hand shears are used to keep the mound neat, and at the same time leave enough grass to create a texture that emphasizes its shape and contrasts with the smooth lawns and clipped yew hedges that surround it.

KATHERINE SWIFT

The turf maze

I think of the maze as both the oldest and the most modern thing here – as beginning and ending the sequence of gardens at the **Dower House**, which were conceived primarily as a series of small areas that reflect the history of **Morville Hall** and the different people who have lived and gardened here over the centuries.

The maze is situated right in the middle of the garden, and all the other gardens connect through it. The design is based on the ancient unicursal seven-ring maze, which is found all over the world and in every culture, dating back thousands of years. The pattern of it also, for me, recalls in miniature the huge **Iron Age** ring forts which crown the hills all around us

here, and which I find so very exciting. And then at the other end of the time scale it also echoes modern ideas of 'land art' and the new minimalism in gardens.

I started the maze about ten years ago. It is quite simply made out of grass – nothing else. Each strip is the width of the mower, and the difference between the two lengths of grass is just the difference between the top and bottom height adjustment. There is now, after ten years, a sculptural aspect to the maze, caused I think by the passage of many feet along the paths – people love it so! – so that now it looks very three-dimensional, as if constructed from stacked turf. But that was not how it was made at all. **T**his sort of effect couldn't be simpler to achieve: and if you don't get the shape right the first

time, you can just reshape it when the grass grows, and keep on experimenting every time you mow until you get something you like. Any mower will do, but it has to be wide enough to cut a decent path, and it has to have four wheels, not a roller, so that it can ride over the top of the longer grass.

Although in one sense it never changes, in another sense the maze is constantly changing: it is very responsive to the subtle differences in light and weather which pass over the garden in the course of a single day or a single season. It is absolutely magical very early in the morning and in the evening light with the slanting rays of the sun across it, accentuating the lines. And it is especially beautiful in frost or heavy dew. **O**f all the different parts of my **Shropshire** garden, I love this the best.

magnificent eighteenth-century grass amphitheatre at Claremont Landscape Garden in Surrey.

On a much smaller scale is the turf maze at Colwood, a surprisingly romantic/ modern feature in a garden of traditional rolling lawns. The design is based on a mosaic labyrinth at Chartres Cathedral. Rosie Brenan made it by lifting turves from the path area and using them to form the raised banks. She sowed the path area with very fine grass seed and the sides of the banks with ordinary lawn grass. It

looked 'a little lumpy' at first, she says, but the mowing regime soon smoothed out the bumps. Rosie mows the tops of the banks with a 1937 Webb mower, which is about 32cm/13in wide. For the paths, which are broad enough for two people to walk along, a Hayter mower just fits in. The sides of the banks are done with a revolving-head strimmer. When it is freshly cut, 'it looks beautiful', Rosie says, 'just like a cake'. The maintenance may sound laborious, but the mowing is done only three times a year, perhaps four, the final trim in November, just before winter sets in. 'When John King cuts the turf maze',

Rosie comments, 'he uses a strimmer for all of it and he contends it is much quicker'.

Katherine Swift's turf maze at the Dower House, Morville Hall, Shropshire, started as a series of concentric circles made by mowing the grass at the highest and lowest cuts of the lawnmower in a playful, slightly random way. Katherine enjoyed the shaded effect that this produced before realizing that the circles could be connected to create a maze. 'You can play about with grass because it grows so quickly,' she says.

Photographer Andrew Lawson of Gothic House in Oxfordshire was planning changes in his garden and marked out a new layout using the mower. He cut narrow paths in a diagonal criss-cross pattern, leaving longer grass in the centre. He says he made the mistake of leaving the longer grass uncut until early June, when it was 30cm/1ft high and bending over. When he did cut it, the squares were full of unsightly ants' nests and the grass stems were yellow at the base. 'The best way of tackling it is to raise the height of the mower blades and cut the grass regularly but at a higher level,' Andrew says, but admits he learnt how to do that later. He warns that paths cut in the grass for a season seem to cause the earth physically to settle at a lower level, making it difficult to change the pattern.

LEFT The tree in the centre of Katherine Swift's turf maze at the Dower House, Morville Hall in Shropshire, is *Ulmus* 'Regal', a hybrid elm bred to be resistant to Dutch elm disease. The tree marks not only the

centre of the maze but also the centre of the garden, and is for Katherine a symbol of regeneration.

ABOVE The alluring curve of a path through long grass at Chisenbury Priory, Wiltshire, is emphasized by raised strips – higher than the path, lower than the meadow – created with a mower set at its highest.

TOP Geometric shapes cut in the lawn at Gothic House, Oxfordshire, were part of a trial re-design. The lawnmower is a useful design tool and the outcome can be permanent, or temporary, as here.

317

Anna Pavord

Pruning apples and pears

Fruit trees do not die if they are not pruned. Have you ever seen a ghostly pruner in the wild, flitting about with secateurs to get wild blackberries into shape, or to trim up the hawthorn? Gardeners prune fruit trees for their own ends, to enhance fruiting, to keep on top of a tree that is growing in a particular way, as with a cordon or fan, or because they are tidy-minded.

Accept that the diagram in your manual will never look like the tree that confronts you in the garden. Concentrate on principles. Once you understand these, the practice becomes easier to carry out.

You cannot rely on pruning alone to contain the size of a tree. If an apple has been grafted on to M25 rootstock, it will always have the will to do what

destiny dictates: grow into a big, beautiful prize-fighter of a tree. Heavy pruning will lead only to renewed efforts on the part of the tree to fulfil the imperative of its genes. If you want a small tree, choose a cultivar that is inherently puny and check the rootstock on which it has been grafted. If you buy a tree trained as a cordon, espalier or fan, the appropriate rootstock is likely to have been already chosen for you.

Most apples and pears are spur-bearing trees, producing their fruit buds on new shoots which develop from short, woody clusters known as spurs. A few cultivars, such as the apples 'Bramley's Seedling' and 'George Cave' and the pears 'Jargonelle' and 'Joséphine de Malines' are tip bearers, producing their flower buds on the ends of two-year-old shoots. If you are constantly cutting these back, there is little chance of getting any fruit. Tip-bearing culti-

vars should not be the ones you choose to grow as cordons or espaliers.

Before you home in, brandishing a pruning saw, remind yourself why you want to prune. It may be to maintain the tree in a particular form, to increase vigour, to encourage more fruit buds to form, to thin out overcrowded branches (which will, in turn, help to prevent diseases) or to cut out diseased or dead wood.

Just as you need to balance suitable rootstocks with particular styles of tree, so you should regulate your pruning to the vigour of the cultivar. Winter pruning stimulates a tree to make more growth, so the harder you prune, the more growth it produces. This may be at the expense of more useful fruit buds. The more vigorous a tree is, the more lightly it should be pruned. Conversely, if a tree has weak, droopy branches, it can be pruned hard.

Hedge matters

Hand-held cordless hedgecutters have made clipping the tops of serious hedges into castellations or curves more than a fantasy for the home gardener. Even more advanced is the automatic hedgeclipper in use at Het Loo in the Netherlands. The box hedges that make up the intricate parterres are clipped by blades guided by sensors to cut both top and sides.

When trimming a new hedge or restoring an old one, it is important to get the batter at about 20 degrees from the vertical. This receding upward slope allows light to reach the entire hedge surface, especially at the base where die-back and gaps are likely to occur. In areas prone to heavy snowfall, avoid excessively flat-topped hedges, on which snow settles and causes damage. Box, yew and the western hemlock, *Tsuga heterophylla*, need only one clipping, in the second half of the year. Deciduous plants like hawthorn, beech and hornbeam can be cut in late summer, into autumn and even on into winter. Leyland cypress requires two cuts a year, in late May or early June and then in late summer. Privet and *Lonicera nitida* need hard-pruning during the first years and frequent clipping throughout the growing season to maintain density.

Margery Fish planted the lonicera hedges at East Lambrook Manor in Somerset, the cottage-style garden made famous by her books and now owned and restored by Robert and Marianne Williams. Like privet, today *Lonicera nitida* is not widely used as a hedging plant, but with box blight on the increase it is likely to make a comeback. Carefully maintained, a lonicera hedge will stand comparison with any other, but should not be allowed to get too tall. The maximum is 1–1.2m/3–4ft: any higher and it begins to wobble.

At Croft House in Lincolnshire, Peter and Margaret Sandberg grew lonicera hedges by accident. When they bought the house, they thought they would be moving again soon. Fast-growing lonicera was an obvious choice for a hedge. That was thirty-one years ago and well over a hundred trims later: 'a lot of work', say the Sandbergs. For lonicera can grow 10cm/4in in four weeks and needs trimming at least once a month in the summer. The last cut in the autumn has to be timed with care because new growth is frost tender. Any snow has to be knocked off.

Alternate sides of the hedges at Croft House, where visitors frequently mistake *Lonicera nitida* for *Buxus sempervirens* 'Suffruticosa', are cut hard back each year. Peter, who cuts the hedges, uses a petrol-driven hedgecutter to give the hedge a short back and sides, followed by a fine finish with an electric hedgetrimmer. If a lonicera hedge has been neglected, he says, it can, if necessary, be reduced to stumps of about 23cm/9in. Not only that, plants can be cut back, dug up, planted and replanted without any ill effects. Margaret is enthusiastic about their resilience but, she says, 'they are not low-maintenance. But we are not interested in low-maintenance gardening.'

The famous 13m/42ft-high yew hedges at Powis Castle in Welshpool are cut only once a year but their surface area is such that, unfolded and spread on the ground, they would cover 2½ acres. It takes two two-man teams about eight weeks to cut them, 'beginning in August and in a good year, finishing in October', says Peter Hall, the head gardener there. The unusual shape of the yews is due to the fact that they have always been cut from ladders – today carefully secured with guy ropes – so that absolute precision was difficult to achieve. Over the years the bumps and declivities have become more pronounced, adding to their charm.

The garden at Levens Hall in Cumbria was laid out in the seventeenth and early eighteenth centuries, with yew and beech hedges dividing it into sections. Some are 10m/33ft high and have to be trimmed from scaffold towers or a hydraulic lift. Beginning in the middle of August, two men take a total of six weeks to trim all the hedges and topiary. 'It looks quite bonny when we've finished,' says head gardener Chris Crowder. 'We always hope to finish by Christmas but we never do. We should start earlier. Box too could be clipped early but we never have the time.' They start by clipping the beech hedge. No one knows exactly how old it is but it was already famous in the 1800s; one tree came down in 2000 and they are waiting to count the rings. Chris says that cutting the sides of the beech is straightforward, using scaffold towers and electric- or petrol-driven hedgetrimmers. The hedge has grown so wide, however, that it is impossible to reach across the top. There used to be a walkway in the centre of the hedge, supported by poles,

The mature espalier apple against a mellow stone wall at Bourton House Garden, Gloucestershire, is pruned in summer to check growth and to encourage the development of spurs that produce flower buds.

Clipping and cutting

and men could reach the whole surface from there. Today they have to hire a hydraulic lift for a month each year. Strimmers have been used in the past, but recently a strimmer with a hedgeclipper attached has proved to be much lighter.

At Hankham Hall Cottage in East Sussex, Maggie and Simon Buller have screened their drive by creating a free-standing willow fedge, an amazingly quick alternative to a traditional hedge. Maggie emphasizes that to make a successful willow fedge, you need damp ground. She learned how to make this living screen on a course at Ryton Organic Gardens near Coventry. Rows of willow wands are stuck into the ground in the dormant season, at 45cm/18in intervals and at an angle. A further row is 'planted' at the opposite angle, so the willows cross each other diagonally, and they are then woven in and out. Eventually they root and fuse together. The willows grow fast in wet ground and need regular trimming, and Maggie recommends cutting back hard to the original stems, in October, if the fedge needs rejuvenating. It will reward with fresh growth in spring.

Knots and parterres

While knots and parterres seem to have an Elizabethan ring, the concept of outlining beds with evergreens, the centres planted with colourful flowers or gravel, can be applied to very modern gardens as well, where some gardeners use contemporary materials such as crushed glass in place of gravel.

The majority of knots and parterres are made of box.

Anne Jennings of the Museum of Garden History in Lambeth is an expert on box knots and propagates all her own box plants. Small cuttings of box are taken in August or September; twelve to each 7.5cm/3in pot filled with a mixture of 50 per cent peat and 50 per cent perlite and left outside until they root. Anne advises pinching back vertical shoots in the first two or three years to encourage growth from the base. After that new growth should be cut back by about one-third in the middle of May. For low hedges, a simple A-frame made to the height and width of the proposed hedge speeds trimming. It is a great time saver to surround any hedge or shrub that is to be clipped with material that will catch the clippings, particularly if the surroundings are gravel.

At Broughton Castle in Oxfordshire a pretty fleur-de-lis design is filled with roses, while at Chevening in Kent the box outlines grey-leaved foliage plants, such as sage and santolina. At Ham House, Richmond, simple triangles of box are crammed with hummocks of santolina and lavender and punctuated with box cones.

At the Dower House at Morville Hall, Katherine Swift has based the outline of her Elizabethan knot garden on a design in plasterwork at nearby Bentall Hall, using rue (*Ruta graveolens*), wall germander, *Teucrium × lucidrys* and Old English lavender (*Lavandula × intermedia*), plants that would have been available at the time. Her aim is to have nearly all the plants in flower from August onwards until the frost. Then rue and germander, which get shabby in the winter, are cut right down, but she leaves enough lavender (cut back in mid-August to produce neat grey-green mounds by mid-September) to give a sculptural, grey effect over winter. In late winter or early spring Katherine cuts everything really hard back to the wooden frame that surrounds the knot garden. Cutting back in two stages, she believes, helps to prevent die-back. With the first warm weather, the plants start to grow away; if they seem to be getting too tall, they receive another clip to prevent them flopping over later. Lavender cuttings are useful, Katherine says, especially if you are making a new knot or need plants to fill in gaps. She trims the rue into soft, billowing shapes by pinching it out, but advises gardeners who have an allergic reaction to the plant to clip with shears.

ABOVE The figurative *'parterre de broderie'* at Tythrop Park in Buckinghamshire, created in the 1980s, carries the eye out to the landscape, in the tradition of classic French gardens of the seventeenth century. The design, made of dwarf box set against light gravel, is based on playing-card motifs. Here box is king, in contrast to the parterre at Chevening illustrated on page 312, where the box acts as a frame to massed plantings.

RIGHT The gardener cutting immaculate straight lines with hand shears while standing on a plank and wooden trestle has been a familiar sight at Levens Hall in Cumbria for three centuries.

Topiary

Clipped trees have been a feature of gardens since Roman times. As with grass cutting, machinery has made trimming trees and shrubs much less arduous. The box cones that adorn the parterre at Ham House in Richmond are clipped by using a conical frame as a guide. It is easier for beginners to use a planting frame, particularly if they plan to create animals or other elaborate shapes. At Levens Hall in Cumbria the renowned topiary garden contains a hundred different pieces, small and large, in box and yew. No frames are used – the shaping is done by eye. 'We follow the outlines and clip back,' says Chris Crowder. 'Each

piece is an individual and if it goes a bit wonky, it all adds to the effect.'

'The topiary at Levens', continues Chris, 'is a changing scene. From year to year you do not notice any alteration, but from decade to decade or century to century the shapes grow and the details merge. Each generation adds its own and has been doing so for three hundred years. We train new ones and have fun with those. I like one single stem with tiers like a cake stand. The tiers can be balls or spirals. Each year you go to 15cm/6in further and it could end up as anything in time.'

Topiary adds a sense of permanency to a garden, but is

ROSEMARY ALEXANDER

Rescuing a neglected garden

Although this is an age of instant gratification, for the first year after taking over a garden, however neglected it may be, try to live with it before making radical changes. A high hedge, for example, may be giving protection from strong winds. There may be unfamiliar plants which perform well in a particular season which can be retained or planted elsewhere. Paths, lawns and borders may not be where you want them, but they can be altered when you have decided how to adapt the garden to your personality and lifestyle.

An overgrown garden requires caution – early over-enthusiasm in removing trees or cutting down shrubs may well mean revealing something that would have been best left hidden. Try to anticipate the consequences by looking at the surroundings from all angles, including upstairs windows.

In a garden the human eye works rather like a camera on automatic focus. On entering a garden, you subconsciously search for something with a strong outline shape – perhaps an urn or pillar of yew – on which the eye can rest while momentarily refocusing to take in the rest of the scene. Most plants form lumpy shapes and unless there is at least one strong element present the planting will seem restless. Pruning or topiarizing can transform an overgrown plant into a focal point or a strong sculptural form. A mature shrub may be turned into a tree by removing all the lower lateral branches on the main stem. Hidden paths and steps may be revealed in their place.

Overgrown or diseased trees and shrubs can be brought back to vigour by pruning and maintenance. Begin by studying the overall shape and size, and decide how much you want to remove. Most plants respond to being reduced by about one third. Cut out all dead and diseased wood first, and then stand back to see if the plant is still overcrowded. Removing some of the older stems will keep the natural outline shape but allow light and air to circulate.

In spring or late autumn borders can be revamped by laying a large plastic sheet on the adjacent lawn, digging everything out, placing it on the sheet, and then replanting only what you want. If necessary, move herbaceous plants to a temporary holding bed, perhaps in a kitchen garden; at the same time divide large clumps into several smaller ones to save expense when restocking.

Neglected gardens are often free of greenfly, blackspot and other pests because nature has adjusted the ecological balance. Avoid using chemicals that will destroy this fragile balance of bird and insect life.

Thinning out and removing overgrown plants will bring the garden back into proportion with the house and the surroundings. It should also give you space to include your own particular favourites.

by no means permanent. In old age, as at Levens Hall, it is beneficial to cut pieces hard back as, over time, the trunks cannot support the weight. In the case of yew trees this does not reduce their vigour. David Herbert of Ashdene in Nottinghamshire has discovered how brutal you can be with yews. He is locked in a continuous struggle with two magnificent, two-hundred-year-old yew trees. In 1984 they had become so overpoweringly tall, and nothing would grow underneath, that he decided to lop off about 10m/33ft. While performing this brutal cut, slicing horizontally across the trunk, David noticed tiny shoots breaking from the trunk and, remembering a tree he had seen years earlier at an old vicarage in Leicester, he suddenly decided to create spirals round the trees. To keep these shapes, he has to trim the trees every five or six weeks and he uses sheep shears. At first the spirals looked patchy, but the constant and regular clipping has given them a rich density. 'The beauty of it is appreciated after rain. The bark flakes and you can see its colours contrasting with the spiral of greens all the way up. It is immensely hard work – the tree wants to produce great boughs, it has great growth potential and after a fortnight there is new growth. It is a battle of wits between the tree and me. It takes an hour and a half to do the clipping and I have cramp in my hand afterwards, but it is a great therapy.'

David Herbert's words seem perfectly to encompass all that is peculiarly satisfying about both the process and the effect of clipping and cutting in the garden. The battle may never quite be won – very good for the soul – but beautiful subtleties, like rain on bark and shadows on grass, are the reward.

322

Clipping and cutting

Clipped yew columns link the house with the garden and provide vertical accents amid billowing cottage-style planting at Stoneacre in Kent, the National Trust garden that Rosemary Alexander 'rescued' and tended from 1989 to 2000. Existing yews were 'forced into submission', says Rosemary, 'by clearing out leaves and other debris from their centres, then trussing them up with strong yachting twine.'

LEFT A path is mown through a flowering meadow between old apple trees in Bill and June Boardman's Garden in an Orchard, Norfolk. Contemporary sculptures are used throughout the garden. RIGHT In the Ladies' Garden within the moat at Broughton Castle, Oxfordshire, the box-edged beds in the shape of *fleurs de lys* are filled with pale pink old-fashioned roses. RIGHT, BELOW In contrast to crisp hedging, neither the grass nor the hornbeams are too finely manicured in the garden at Upton Wold in Gloucestershire. Ian Bond has allowed the trees in the stilted hornbeam walk to attain a comfortable embonpoint that is perfectly at home in rural surroundings.

Here are a few gardens with lawns and topiary clipped from the Yellow Book to add to the ones Barbara Abbs admires.

Bedfordshire
The Manor House, Stevington

Berkshire
Folly Farm

Bristol & South Gloucestershire
Doynton House
Park Farm

Buckinghamshire
Ascott

Cambridgeshire
Wytchwood

Carmarthenshire & Pembrokeshire
Great Griggs
Scotsborough House

Cheshire & Wirral
Arley Hall & Gardens
The Mount, Whirley

Cornwall
Trewithen

Cumbria
Fell Yeat
Lindeth Fell Country House Hotel

Denbighshire & Colwyn
Plas Nantglyn

Derbyshire
Kedleston Hall
Renishaw Hall

Devon
Bickham House
Kerscott House

Dorset
Manor Orchard
Melplash Court

Essex
The Old Vicarage, Broxted

Flintshire & Wrexham
Chirk Castle
Pen-y-Bryn

Gloucestershire North & Central
Bourton House Garden
Abbotswood

Gwent
The Hawthorns
Penpergwm Lodge
Wyndcliffe Court

Gwynedd
Bryn Eisteddfod
Foxbrush
Talhenbont Hall

Hampshire
Rotherfield Park

Herefordshire
Hampton Court
The Lance Hattat Design Garden

Hertfordshire
Bromley Hall
Mackerye End House

Isle of Wight
Northcourt Gardens
Nunwell House

Kent
Bradbourne House Gardens
Hole Park

Leicestershire
Long Close
Wartnaby Gardens

Lincolnshire
Grimsthorpe Castle
Guanock House

London
37 Alwyne Rd
Fenton House

Norfolk
Lexham Hall
Rainthorpe Hall

Northamptonshire
Canons Ashby House
Easton Neston

Northumberland & Tyne and Wear
Herterton House
Hexham Herbs

Nottinghamshire
Felley Priory
The Manor House, Gonalston

Plant Index

329

Name Index

Acknowledgements

The Publishers would like to thank the following photographers and organizations for permission to reproduce their material. Every care has been taken to trace copyright holders. However, we will be happy to rectify any omissions in future editions.

top = top, c = centre, b = bottom, r = right, l = left
Jan Baldwin 20; Mark Bolton 184–5, 193, 289, 291, 292t; Clive Boursnell 46; Nicola Brown 43, 54, 172, 229, 239, 257; Jonathon Buckley 48, 106–7, 107r, 114, 128, 134, 187, 197, 199, 219, 244, 246t, 251t, 276, 281, 307, 311b, 323; Brian Chapple 169, 283; Val Corbett 36–7, 136t, 160b, 170–1, 174, 234, 271, 272, 279, 280–1, 321; Eric Crichton 31t, 31br, 64, 65, 70, 110b, 150, 315; David Austin Roses Ltd 29b; Melanie Eclare 114, 120–1; Michael Edwards 285; Valerie Finnis 15, 16, 19, 20, 21, 23, 24, 26t, 26b, 29t, 29c; Fox Photos 28cl; Gardener's Sunday 29cr; Fergus Garrett 207; Sir Martin Gilbert 18t, 18b; John Glover 74–5, 138, 153, 160t, 162, 188, 219, 270t, 310; Jerry Harpur iv, 13, 30tl, 30br, 52, 57, 58, 59, 63, 66, 69, 71t, 79, 93b, 99, 154–5, 159, 165, 175, 178, 183, 194, 195, 208–9, 212–3, 217, 248, 270b, 275, 292b, 293, 301, 312, 325t; Marcus Harpur 35, 42, 93t, 124, 141, 200t, 206, 252, 311t, 324; Charles Hawes 156; Caroline Hughes 241; Tim Ingram 265, 267, 268, 269; Nada Jennet 176b; Andrew Lawson ix l, 40–1, 49, 67, 88, 91, 100, 117, 129, 131, 133, 147, 151, 176t, 180, 181, 182, 210, 222b, 224, 228, 230–1, 233, 236, 237, 238, 243, 247, 253, 254, 298, 316, 317t, 317b, 325b; Lord Lichfield 28cr; Marianne Majerus ii, viii l, viii r, 25, 28b, 32, 34, 53t, 53b, 62, 71b, 72, 76, 78, 84–5, 86–7, 92, 101, 102–3, 105, 111tr, 111b, 112, 115, 116, 118, 119, 122–3, 127, 136b, 137b, 137t, 143, 144, 145, 148–9, 166, 177, 200b, 201, 202, 216, 223, 221, 227, 235, 246b, 258–9, 260, 262–3, 294, 297, 300, 302–3, 306, 318; Jackie Newey 108, 278; Clive Nichols x, 81, 110t, 284, 287, 304, 309; Photos Horticultural (Alan Munson) 38, 190, (Michael Warren) 214; Picturesmiths Ltd 47; Vivian Russell 26t, 97; Derek St Romaine ix r, 44–5, 80, 94, 161, 205, 222t, 261, 299; Rosalind Simon 50, 60, 61, 320; Philip Smith 296; Elizabeth Tite 82

Note from the NGS Publications Panel
This book includes only a small proportion of the 3,500 gardens open for the National Gardens Scheme. It is designed to be read in conjunction with *Gardens of England and Wales Open for Charity*, published annually by the NGS, which gives dates and times of opening and full directions for reaching the gardens. The website ngs@ngs.org.uk offers the latest information on garden openings and activities related to the NGS.

While every effort has been made to ensure accuracy in this book, we regret that we cannot be held responsible for errors and cannot guarantee that every garden mentioned will continue to open indefinitely. Please consult the current edition of *Gardens of England and Wales Open for Charity* to check details.

So many people have contributed to *Making Gardens* and helped in its preparation that it would be impossible to thank them all individually. We would like to thank the following:
Her Majesty the Queen
Her Majesty Queen Elizabeth the Queen Mother, Patron of the NGS
Daphne Foulsham, Chairman of Council, the NGS
The main contributors
The people who gave us Expert Insights
The photographers
Jinny Blom for plant text for chapters 10 and 14
Rowland Hilder and Val Biro for permission to reproduce the line drawings that appeared on Yellow Book covers
The garden owners
The NGS County Organizers
Rosie Atkins
Elizabeth Tagge
The staff at NGS Head Office
The staff at Cassell & Co
The designer Ken Wilson